listeners might say, "Now I hear the sound of your voice in my ear when I read to myself."

Ada, Alma Flor.
My Name Is Maria Isabel.
Illus. K. Dyble Thompson.
New York: Simon & Schuster, 1993.

Adoff, Arnold.
Black Is Brown Is Tan.
Illus. Emily Arnold McCully.
New York: HarperCollins, 1973.

Bridges, Ruby.
Through My Eyes.
New York: Scholastic, 1999.

Curtis, Christopher Paul.
Bud, Not Buddy.
New York: Delacorte, 1999.

Gauch, Patricia Lee.
Tanya and the Red Shoes.
Illus. Satomi Ichikawa.
New York: Philomel Books, 2002.

Hickman, Janet.
Ravine.
New York: Greenwillow, 2002.

Howard, Elizabeth Fitzgerald.
Virgie Goes to School with Us Boys.
Illus. E. B. Lewis.
New York: Simon & Schuster, 1999.

Myers, Christopher.
Wings.
New York: Scholastic, 2000.

Naylor, Phyllis Reynolds.
Shiloh.
New York: Simon & Schuster, 1991.

Park, Frances, & Park, Ginger.
The Royal Bee.
Illus. Christopher Z. Zhang.
Honesdale, PA: Boyds Mills, 2000.

Peck, Richard.
A Long Way from Chicago.
New York: Dial, 1998.

Polacco, Patricia.
The Butterfly.
New York: Philomel, 2000.

Rylant, Cynthia.
When I Was Young in the Mountains.
Illus. Diane Goode.
New York: Dutton, 1982.

Sachar, Louis.
Holes.
New York: Farrar, Straus & Giroux, 1998.

Sendak, Maurice.
Where the Wild Things Are.
Illus. Maurice Sendak.
New York: Harper, 1963.

Spinelli, Jerry.
Maniac Magee.
Boston: Little, Brown, 1990.

Staples, Suzanne Fisher.
Shabanu: Daughter of the Wind.
New York: Knopf, 1989.

Strickland, Dorothy, & Strickland, Michael.
Families: Poems Celebrating the African American Experience.
Honesdale, PA: Boyds Mills, 1994.

Tafuri, Nancy.
Mama's Little Bears.
New York: Scholastic, 2002.

Temple, Frances.
Taste of Salt: A Story in Modern Haiti.
New York: Scholastic, 1994.

Wells, Rosemary.
Yoko.
New York: Hyperion, 1998.

EASY BOOKS FOR STRUGGLING READERS

Struggling readers need frequent opportunities to practice. Fluency can be encouraged by allowing them to read easy material. Select inviting books that support readers' abilities. For instance, books with short lines have less dense text and do not intimidate struggling readers the way a full page of text can.

Adler, David.
Cam Jansen and the Mystery of the Dinosaur Bones.
New York: Viking, 1981.

Bang-Campbell, Monika.
Little Rat Sets Sail.
Illus. Molly Garrett.
San Diego, CA: Harcourt, 2002.

Bonsall, Crosby.
Who's Afraid of the Dark?
New York: Harper, 1981.

Byars, Betsy.
Little Horse.
Illus. David McPhail.
New York: Henry Holt, 2001.

Clements, Andrew.
Frindle.
New York: Simon & Schuster, 2000.

Creech, Sharon.
Love That Dog: A Novel.
New York: Harper, 2001.

Danziger, Paula.
Amber Brown Goes Fourth.
New York: Putnam, 2001.

De Paola, Tomie.
26 Fairmount Avenue.
Illus. Tomie De Paola.
New York: Putnam, 2001.

Fine, Anne.
Flour Babies.
New York: Bantam, Doubleday Dell, 1994.

Gantos, Jack.
Practice Makes Perfect for Rotten Ralph.
Illus. Nicole Rubel.
New York: Farrar, Straus Giroux, 2002.

Hesse, Karen.
Out of the Dust, 1997;
Witness, 2001.
New York: Scholastic.

Hoff, Syd.
The Horse in Harry's Room.
New York: Harper, 2002.

Henkes, Kevin.
Chrysanthemum, 1991;
Lilly's Purple Plastic Purse, 1996.
New York: Greenwillow.

Lowry, Lois.
Number the Stars.
Boston: Houghton, 1989.

Porte, Barbara.
Harry Gets an Uncle, 1991;
Harry in Trouble, 1989.
Illus. Yossi Abolafia,
New York: Greenwillow.

Language Arts

LEARNING AND TEACHING

DOROTHY S. STRICKLAND
Rutgers University

LEE GALDA
University of Minnesota

BERNICE E. CULLINAN
New York University

THOMSON
WADSWORTH

Australia ✦ Canada ✦ Mexico ✦ Singapore ✦ Spain ✦ United Kingdom ✦ United States

Education Editor: Dan Alpert
Development Editor: Tangelique Williams
Editorial Assistant: Heather Kazakoff
Technology Project Manager: Barry Connolly
Marketing Manager: Dory Schaeffer
Marketing Assistant: Neena Chandra
Advertising Project Manager: Shemika Britt
Project Manager, Editorial Production: Trudy Brown
Print/Media Buyer: Barbara Britton
Permissions Editor: Elizabeth Zuber
Production Service: Joan Keyes, Dovetail Publishing Services
Text Designer: Kaelin Chappell
Copy Editor: Luana Richards
Cover Designer: Laurie Anderson
Cover Image: © Stanley Martucci/SIS
Compositor: Better Graphics, Inc.
Text and Cover Printer: Transcontinental Printing/Louisville

Printed in Canada
1 2 3 4 5 6 7 07 06 05 04 03

For more information about our products, contact us at:
Thomson Learning Academic Resource Center
1-800-423-0563
For permission to use material from this text, contact us by:
Phone: 1-800-730-2214
Fax: 1-800-730-2215
Web: http://www.thomsonrights.com

Library of Congress Control Number: 2003101512

ISBN 0-534-56746-0

Wadsworth/Thomson Learning
10 Davis Drive
Belmont, CA 94002-3098
USA

Asia
Thomson Learning
5 Shenton Way #01-01
UIC Building
Singapore 068808

Australia/New Zealand
Thomson Learning
102 Dodds Street
Southbank, Victoria 3006
Australia

Canada
Nelson
1120 Birchmount Road
Toronto, Ontario M1K 5G4
Canada

Europe/Middle East/Africa
Thomson Learning
High Holborn House
50/51 Bedford Row
London WC1R 4LR
United Kingdom

Spain/Portugal
Paraninfo
Calle/Magallanes, 25
28015 Madrid, Spain

To Kali Brooke Ream and others like her who are entering the teaching profession.

And to experienced teachers everywhere who continue to be learners.

CONTENTS

CHAPTER 6

Reading: The Emergence of Literacy in the Early Years **197**

CHAPTER 7

Reading: Responding to and Learning from Texts through the Grades **245**

CHAPTER 8

Writing: Launching Children into Writing **281**

PREFACE

WELCOME TO *LANGUAGE ARTS: LEARNING AND TEACHING*

In our work as teachers and as teachers of teachers, we have always been intrigued by language—how we learn it, how we learn from it and with it, and how we learn about it. Language is both personal and social. It is the primary medium for thinking and learning. It allows us to communicate through highly sophisticated processes that are uniquely human. It is the foundation for learning in school.

As educators with many years of experience, we have learned a great deal about how children learn language and how we, as adults, best support that learning. In this book we share what we have learned from research, from classroom teachers, and from our own experiences in classrooms. Our desire to share what we know with each other and with you, our readers, is how this book came about.

Our primary purpose is to improve the quality of instruction in classrooms from kindergarten through middle school. Thus, we focus on what teachers need to know and be able to do to foster oral and written language development in young children and in developing students throughout the grades. We emphasize the interrelatedness and interdependence of all the language arts not only with each other, but also with the content taught across the curriculum. Our love of literature is evident as we cite it as a source of beautiful and interesting language to read, think, and talk about, and to use as models for writing.

By engaging the voices of classroom teachers, we seek to go beyond merely telling about best practice. We show it through rich, active descriptions told by the teachers themselves. In a world of reform and accountability, we balance the need to be cognizant of teacher standards of knowledge and behavior with the need for informed teacher judgment and creativity. Throughout, we stress the need for culturally and linguistically responsive teaching.

A QUICK WALK THROUGH *LANGUAGE ARTS: LEARNING AND TEACHING*

Our book is divided into three major sections. Part One, Contexts for Teaching and Learning the Language Arts, begins with an overarching chapter on contemporary issues and perspectives on language arts learning and teaching. This chapter sets the stage for all that follows by providing readers with insights into various instructional changes and challenges that have occurred since they were young students. This is followed by chapters on organization and management of the language arts program, and the role of literature in language arts learning and teaching. We believe that a well-organized classroom that allows for both structure and flexibility provides an environment where effective learning and teaching can happen. We include literature up front because we feel that quality fiction and nonfiction are major resources for language and literacy development.

Part Two, Language Arts Processes, focuses on key processes of the language arts. We include two chapters each on oral language, reading, and writing. The first chapter in each set provides the background that teachers need in order to understand and promote children's development. This is presented along with implications for instruction and a large number of specific practical activities. The second chapter in each set continues with classroom applications that demonstrate how teachers at various levels of instruction focus on oral language, or reading, or writing as individual curricular elements, and at the same time, integrate each with the others and with content across the curriculum. For example, the first chapter on oral language emphasizes both early and later development of listening and speaking. It includes what is known from research about child development in these areas and what is known about good instruction to support that development. That support is illustrated through concrete examples from the classrooms of teachers and from our experiences. The second chapter on oral language continues with numerous practical ideas that illustrate the dynamics of how teachers best support children's listening and speaking in the classroom. The chapters on reading and writing follow a similar pattern.

Part Three, Links and Supports for Language Arts Learning and Teaching, might be considered the nuts-and-bolts section of the book. The first two chapters deal with supports for written language. Word study, vocabulary development, and spelling are given in-depth treatment in the first chapter of this section. The second chapter focuses mainly on grammar, punctuation, and handwriting support for written composition. In both chapters, readers are provided with examples of effective teaching strategies across all levels of schooling and across a range of diverse learners.

Suggestions for assessment are integrated throughout this book. They appear in each chapter as demonstrations of ongoing assessment appropriately linked directly to instruction in various areas of the language arts. We also thought it important, however, to devote a chapter specifically to assessment as a major component of the language arts program. In Chapter 12, readers are given background knowledge in the key issues related to accountability and assessment as well as key terminology for the types of assessments currently in use.

Chapter 13, the final chapter of this book, is intended to bring the language arts together in ways that mirror their use in the real world. Inquiry is at the heart of this chapter. We write about teachers and students as they raise questions about topics of importance to them and then use the language arts to explore possible answers. Teachers and students at various levels work together to solve problems and further their own learning. As they work, they use all facets of the language arts. They listen, speak, read, write, view, and make use of visual representations. This final chapter represents the culmination of a journey in which various components of the landscape were explored and where the entire landscape can now be viewed as an integrated whole.

SPECIAL FEATURES OF *LANGUAGE ARTS: LEARNING AND TEACHING*

- *A Key Standard with accompanying performance standards* at the beginning of each chapter focuses attention on the critical teaching standards that are the overarching learning goals for the chapter.
- *An abundance of teaching ideas that beginning teachers can easily replicate* are included throughout—for example, ideas for assessment, linguistic and cultural diversity, special needs, use of literature, cross-cultural activities, course management, technology, and home/school connections.
- *Vivid classroom vignettes based on real teaching practice* open each chapter and also appear throughout the book to help make complex concepts and strategies accessible.
- *The teaching of reading receives strong emphasis,* with Chapters 6 and 7 devoted exclusively to reading; there is a focus throughout the text

on methods for incorporating children's literature into the curriculum.

- *Assessment issues and suggestions* as they relate to each area of the language arts are integrated throughout the text and covered in a full chapter.
- *Suggested Activities and Readings* at the end of each chapter offer concrete suggestions for application and reflection on chapter content.
- *The two Language Arts CD-ROMs* include a Tool Bank component with practical materials (forms, checklists, samples, and many other valuable teaching resources) that help teachers implement the strategies discussed in the text. The CD also includes videotaped chapter introductions presented by Dorothy Strickland, related interviews with practicing teachers, and special topics segments featuring Lee Galda and Bernice Cullinan.

Bringing all of this together in one volume has not been an easy task, but it has been worthwhile. There is no other area of the curriculum for which teachers are held more responsible. Fortunately, there is no other area that is more important or rewarding to teach.

ACKNOWLEDGMENTS

Our thanks to all those who made this book possible: Rebecca Brittain for editorial review and participation in the videotaping; Helen Comba for help with the Language Arts Tool Bank; Lisa Green for editorial review; Rebecca Tisdel Rapport for editorial review and Chapter 9; Bevin O'Brien and Margaret Smith for help with the end pages; Joseph Kassick for photography; Kedra Gamble, Barbara Moncada, and Joan Pearlman for participation in the videotaping; James O'Kelly for help with technology suggestions and participating in the videotaping; Ellen Kolba and Sheila Crowell of The Writer's Room for help with supports for written language processes in Chapters 10 and 11; Chauncey Olinger for contributing computer guides to writing instruction; Ginnie Schroder, who shared student-developed rubrics; Stephanie Adams, Kara Ahmed, Mary Belastocki, Joanie Bonick, Margaret Burke, Launa Ellison, Kim Lanza, Karen Lee, Margo McLean, and student teacher Alison Denmark, who generously shared their classrooms with us; and our wonderful editorial team: Joan Keyes, Luana Richards, Tangelique Williams, and Dan Alpert for his extraordinary helpfulness and patience.

DSS
LG
BEC

REVIEWERS

Julie Agard, University of Nebraska, Kearney

Louis Baucom, University of North Carolina—Charlotte

Stan Bochtler, Buena Vista University

Ann M. Courtney, University of Hartford

Paul C. Egeland, Wheaton College

Ann Estrada, Midwestern State University

Deborah Farrer, California University of Pennsylvania

Sharon Ruth Gill, Murray State University

Debbi Hamilton, Columbus State University

Martha Hanlon, Kings College

Rose Heilman-Houser, Slippery Rock University

Mary F. Heller, Kansas State University

Kathryn Henn-Reinke, University of Wisconsin—Oshkosh

Lisa Hutton, CSU—Dominguez Hills

Luther Kirk, Longwood College

Bonnie McKenzie, Ball State University

Anna Mosbo, University of Central Arkansas

Mary E. Robbins, Sam Houston State University

Marie C. Roos, Jackson State University

Adele B. Sanders, University of Northern Colorado

Alexa Sandman, The University of Toledo

Gail Singleton-Taylor, Old Dominion University

Lynne Smith, Northern Kentucky University

Verlie Ward, Walla Walla College

Robert L. Wyatt, East Central University

Myra Zarnowski, Queens College—CUNY

ABOUT THE AUTHORS

Dorothy S. Strickland is the Samuel DeWitt Proctor Professor of Education at Rutgers, the State University of New Jersey. She was formerly the Arthur I. Gates Professor of Education at Teachers College Columbia University. A former classroom teacher, reading consultant, and learning disabilities specialist, she is a past president of both the International Reading Association and the IRA Reading Hall of Fame. She received IRA's Outstanding Teacher Educator of Reading Award. She was a recipient of the National Council of Teachers of English Award as Outstanding Educator in the Language Arts and the NCTE Rewey Belle Inglis Award as Outstanding Woman in the Teaching of English. She has numerous publications in the field of reading/language arts. Her latest publications are: *Preparing Our Teachers: Opportunities for Better Reading Instruction, Beginning Reading and Writing, Administration and Supervision of Reading Programs,* and *Supporting Struggling Readers and Writers: Strategies for Classroom Intervention 3–6.*

After teaching in the elementary and middle schools for a number of years, **Lee Galda** received her Ph.D. in English Education from New York University. After teaching at the University of Georgia for 19 years, she is now a professor in the Department of Curriculum and Instruction at the University of Minnesota. Dr. Galda has received many awards for excellence in university teaching and is also an active volunteer in the public schools. She is a member of the National Reading Conference, the American Library Association, the National Council of Teachers of English, and the International Reading Association and sits on the review boards of many professional journals. Dr. Galda was the Children's Books Department Editor for the *Reading Teacher* from 1989 to 1993, currently reviews trade books for *The Riverbank Review,* and was a member of the 2003 Newbery Award Selection Committee. She co-authored the chapter on children's literature in the third edition of the *Handbook on Research in Reading,* and is the author of numerous articles and book chapters. She is a co-author of *Literature and the Child,* sixth edition, also published by Wadsworth Publishing Company.

Bernice E. Cullinan is Professor Emeritus at New York University, where she has taught for the last 32 years. Her teaching career began in the elementary school grades before she began teaching teachers. A past president of the International Reading Association, she was inducted into the IRA Reading Hall of Fame and was awarded the Arbuthnot Award for Outstanding Teacher of Children's Literature. In 2003 she was chosen as the National Council of Teachers of English Outstanding Educator of the Language Arts (to be awarded in November 2003 at NCTE in San Francisco). Her publications include the *Continuum Encyclopedia of Children's Literature, the Continuum Encyclopedia of Young Adult Literature, Read to Me: Raising Kids Who Love to Read,* and *A Jar of Tiny Stars: Children's Choices of NCTE Award-Winning Poets.*

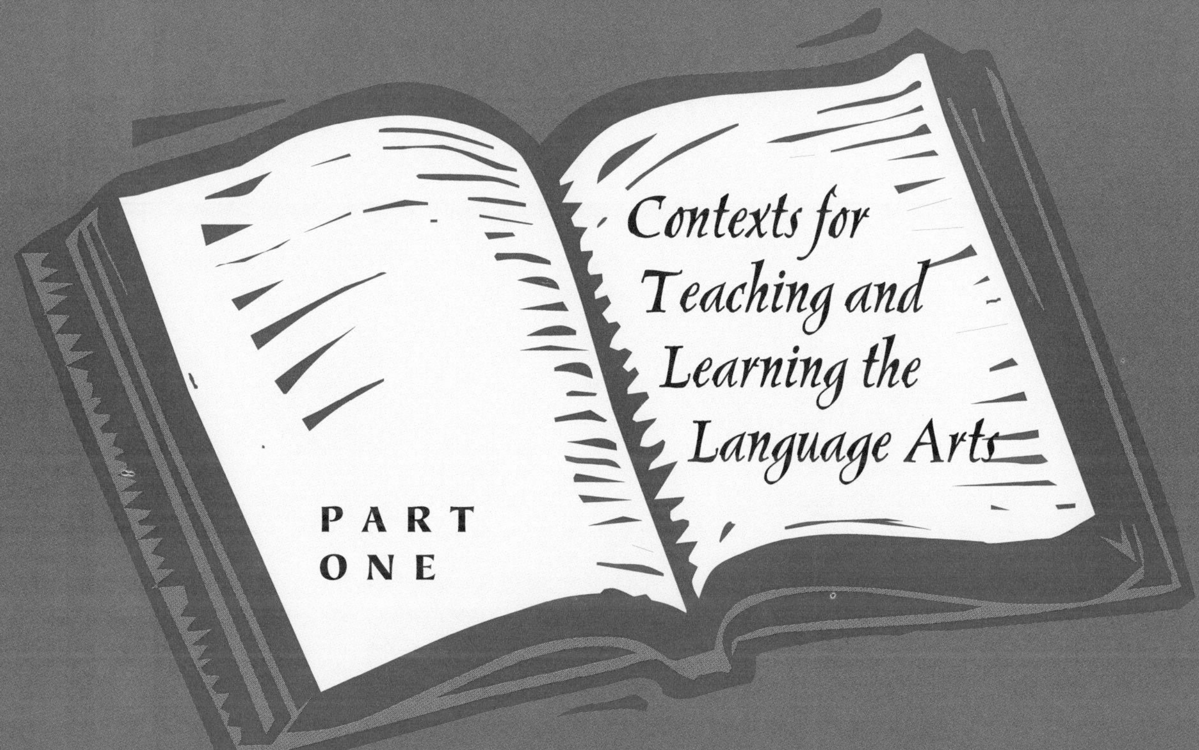
Contexts for
Teaching and
Learning the
Language Arts
PART
ONE

Language Arts: Learning and Teaching

CHAPTER OUTLINE

Key Standard

Effective teachers of language arts/reading are knowledgeable about the major theoretical understandings, research findings, policy issues, and practices that shape contemporary instructional decision making. Such teachers:

- Understand how humans learn and develop, and provide learning opportunities that support a range of individual variation.
- Know the importance of social, cultural, linguistic, and cognitive differences among learners and use this information to guide their instructional decisions.
- Understand how technology influences communication, language, and composition, and make appropriate use of it throughout the curriculum.
- Are familiar with the educational goals and standards of the school district in which they teach and apply that knowledge to their practice.

To get a preview of Chapter 1 and learn about contemporary issues in language arts, visit the Chapter 1 section of the accompanying *Language Arts* CD-ROM.

It is a rainy afternoon in October. Sue Dickson is returning from lunch. She enters her third grade classroom and looks admiringly at its contents. Although the twenty-six children in her class are a bit crowded, they are learning to manage their limited space. Just inside the front door are the students' mailboxes and a listening station. Student-made posters on the walls proclaim "This class loves to read," "Readers write and writers read, that's the way we all succeed," and other sayings related to books. In the far right-hand corner near the sink, the two gerbils, Calvin and Hobbes, sleep peacefully. A nearby chart lists characteristics of gerbils and how to care for them. Several students conducted library research and systematic observations of the gerbils and then shared the information with the class. Other students worked in groups to do similar research on pets of their choice. Each group prepared an informational book to be shared and discussed with the class. These books were placed in the class library for reference. Sue used this activity to do an in-depth comparison of the structures of informational texts and story narratives.

As she considers her plans for the afternoon, Sue reflects on the activities that took place earlier in the day. Throughout the day, she involves her students in a variety of group configurations. Children work as a whole class, in small groups, with partners, or alone depending on the task at hand and their individual preferences. Reading and writing bracket the day with time for reading-writing workshops scheduled in both morning and afternoon.

She glances at the green bathtub filled with pillows in one corner of the room. It is just big enough to hold one child. She must remember to have the children prepare a sign-up sheet to facilitate taking turns. Next to the bathtub is the library corner where a table full of monster books has stimulated a considerable amount of writing, art, and independent reading. She reflects on their discussions about descriptive language and how her students have become increasingly aware of various authors' use of colorful and vivid language to describe their monster characters. Most have begun to apply what they have learned to their own writing and art.

Sue has observed her students' speaking and writing improve in the use of more details and stronger vocabularies, including words such as weird, grotesque, peculiar, and eerie.

Sue approaches her desk, which is completely surrounded by bookshelves and hardly visible. She reaches for the chapter book, Class Clown by Johanna Hurwitz (Morrow, 1987), which she has been reading each day after lunch. This is only one of several read-alouds that occur throughout the day in this classroom. The material varies and includes chapter books, poems, short informational pieces related to a topic under study, and examples of the specific uses of language that she wishes to share. Lately, she has selected examples that use descriptive language and rich details to share during writing workshop.

Today's after-lunch read-aloud is the third chapter book that Sue has read since school began on September 5. When Sue reads, the children are riveted by her expressive voice and gestures. No doubt her excellent modeling has contributed to the developing fluency she has noticed in the students' oral reading. Today, she plans to quit just before the climax of the story. As a follow-up, children will have the option of writing their predictions for the story's ending. Others may continue with work on their pen pal letters or other work they've already begun in their writing notebooks. Before the final reading of the book, Sue will have those students who wrote predictions share them with the others. The predictions will be treated much like any open-ended question in which students must support their responses with information from the story.

Sue glances through the mail she has just retrieved from her mailbox. Among the material is a pamphlet sent from the district office on preparing students for the standardized tests to be given at fourth grade. Third and fourth grade teachers are told to take special note of the test preparation activities. Sue is very aware of the importance of the fourth grade assessment and the need to prepare her students so that they can demonstrate what they know and are able to do. Yet, she is determined not to reduce her curriculum to the content of a single test. She and the other teachers in her school are working hard to achieve a balanced curriculum in which a dynamic and engaging learning environment is also rigorous and grounded in the standards set by the educational community in her district. So far, she feels, it's working.

Joseph Kassick

By varying classroom activities, students are exposed to a great deal of reading and writing.

In Sue Dickson's classroom you see teacher and students busily engaged in a variety of activities, pursuing their interests within the framework of school. You hear a great deal of talk in this classroom, and only some of it is the teacher's. You see lots of reading and writing going on as children are engaged in learning all sorts of things together. Why does Sue structure her class in this way? She bases her instructional decisions on what she knows about how children learn and how best to teach them so that they become literate. How does she do it? She surrounds her students with opportunities for meaningful uses of language, demonstrates and instructs them in literate behaviors and effective strategies, supports their learning, allows them choice in what they do, helps them learn from each other, and believes that all of her students can become fluent and flexible users of the English language. She is knowledgeable, organized, and prepared.

This book is about teaching and learning the English language. It makes use of children's literature as a centerpiece for framing that teaching and learning. Contemporary concerns for instructional reform and accountability provide part of the context for framing the discussion. As human beings we all begin learning language, learning about language, and learning through language (Halliday, 1982; Power & Hubbard, 1996) from the moment we are born and first hear sounds in our environment. We all continue to learn language, learn about language, and learn through language as we live our lives. You are doing this as you read this text: you will learn new vocabulary and information about how our language system works through language—reading and talking, listening and writing—as you simultaneously learn how to teach English language arts. Language is essential to our lives as functioning human beings, and because of this, language teaching and learning is the vital center of all that you will do in the classroom.

Teaching and learning are inextricably related (Vygotsky, 1978) and involve a complex interaction of students and teachers, materials, tasks, and contexts. To talk of teaching is to talk of learning, as teaching does not happen unless learning takes place. Also, as a teacher you will learn from those whom you teach. Effective teachers watch, listen, and consider what is happening in their classroom, learning from what they observe. Many teachers find that this new knowledge results in change and growth—they adjust their plans, alter the curriculum, explore new teaching styles, and pursue new ideas.

Effective teaching is based on a knowledge of how children learn, an understanding of students as developing individuals, and a firm knowledge of the content being taught. As a teacher of English language arts, you will be responsible for helping children develop as fluent and flexible listeners, speakers, readers, writers, and viewers. You will be helping children develop their understanding about how language works, their control over their own language, their repertoire of strategies for language use, and their vision of themselves as language users. Like Sue Dickson, you will have a wonderful opportunity to help children use language that shapes their world.

Changing Views

INSTRUCTIONAL CHANGES

On any visit to Sue's classroom you will see children actively using language. They talk, read, and write together as they engage in the joyful pursuit of literacy. These children do not need to be rewarded with candy, stickers, or pizza when they read or write. They are eager to share what they know as they work together. Sue's classroom is a happy, busy, welcoming place because she likes her students, knows them well, and values the knowledge they bring with them to school. Perhaps most important, Sue's instructional practice demonstrates a deep understanding of how children develop and learn. It reflects a variety of instructional trends that have become major ingredients in today's language arts and reading instruction:

- *Greater emphasis on writing and its relationship to reading.* Attention to **writing** starts early and continues throughout the grades. It is not uncommon to find writing centers in today's pre-kindergarten classrooms, where children are encouraged to draw and write about events that interest them and in response to books and stories shared with them. But, writing is more than just a vehicle for response to literature and events. Today's students are guided to think and talk about what they read as authors or potential authors of their own work. They explore the similarities and differences among various text structures, uses of language, and literary devices.
- *Greater use of trade (library) books combined with the use of textbooks.* **Trade books** are major components of the language arts program. Once considered important as supplementary material, children's literature is now a key component of every aspect of the language arts curriculum. Although many teachers still use textbooks or other commercial programs for literacy instruction and many such programs have improved the quality of their literary offerings, teachers no longer rely on such materials as their sole resource of instruction. Teachers are apt to employ a variety of materials for varied purposes across the curriculum. Children's literature plays an important role among the materials they choose.
- *Increased attention to the importance of student choice both in topics to write about and in materials.* Providing students with some **choices** within the curriculum has been found to increase their engagement in literacy activities (Pressley, Rankin, & Yokoi, 1996). When teachers provide choices, it does not mean that they abrogate their responsibility for decision making. Indeed, there are times when teachers simply assign a task to all students without choices. At other times students are given a virtual free range of choice. Still another very likely instructional scenario gives students a range

Joseph Kassick

These students are learning language through active involvement.

of choices that have been selected by the teacher. For example, students may be asked to write about the same topic, but they may choose the form they prefer—poetry, story, or a letter to a friend. Or, students may choose to read and respond to a book from a preselected list of titles. The title they choose will determine the literature circle group in which they will regularly participate to discuss a book of interest.

- *Increased attention to the integration of the language arts with each other and across the curriculum.* Increasingly, teachers have come to think of the language arts as processes that are instrumental to all learning, rather than as products that are ends in themselves. Thus, it makes sense to help students see the value of reading, writing, and oral language as tools for learning content of interest and importance to them. **Integrating** the language arts with each other and with subject-area content helps make the learning purposeful and more effective.

- *Increased emphasis on the use of ongoing, performance-based assessments that link directly to instruction.* Today's teachers are aware that the day-by-day demonstrations of learning are the best evidence of what students know and are capable of doing. For example, an analysis of a student's writing samples, participation in literature circles, and oral reading provide evidence about his or her accomplishments and needs in written composition, reading comprehension, and reading fluency. **Ongoing, performance-based assessments** help inform instructional decisions in personalized ways that standardized tests do not.

Joseph Kassick

Participation in literature circles provides evidence of what students know and are able to do.

The trends outlined above reflect today's classrooms. They look and feel different from the classrooms that many adults remember from their elementary and middle school years. These classrooms are different because educators know more about teaching and learning than they did in the past. A popular old metaphor for teachers was that of the full pitcher, ready to pour knowledge into the empty heads of students. A more romantic metaphor is that of teacher as gardener. It characterizes the teacher's role as that of providing sun, water, and fertilizer (in the form of materials, time, and a supportive context) and then stepping back and letting the students flower. Neither of these metaphors captures the active, challenging, intellectual exercise that is teaching today.

We prefer the metaphor of the teacher as craftsperson and the student as apprentice (Dorn, French, & Jones, 1998; Graves & Graves, 2003). As masters of the art of language (reading, writing, speaking, and listening), teachers provide their students with examples of effective language use, demonstrations of effective practice, and explanations of complex concepts, and provide the time, materials, and supportive context for students to explore language. Thus, throughout this book, you will find countless suggestions for guiding and supporting children's learning, or **scaffolding,** in every aspect of the language arts. Figure 1.1, Transitions in Language Arts/Reading Instruction, compares some of the changes that have taken place. Scaffolding refers to the process whereby a child's learning occurs in the context of full performance as adults gradually relinquish support (Cazden, 1988). Just as workers very basic skills and strategies, low-level basic skills that merely involve surface-level decoding and the recall of information are hardly enough. Critical thinking and the ability to personalize meanings to individual experience and apply what is read or written in the real world, under many different circumstances and with many different types of texts, may now be termed the "new basics." As Kibby (1993) reports:

> At the turn of the century, high school completion rates were less than 5% and illiteracy was the norm even for second generation Americans; today, high school completion rates range between 75 and 80%, and less than 4% of young adults cannot read. But the era of taking pride in graduating a mass of literate students accompanied by only a sprinkling of critical readers and critical thinkers may have passed; such standards may no longer be sufficient (p. 39).

It is not only what we are required to do with texts that has changed; the texts themselves have changed. Texts are presented to us and generated by us in endless variety: books, magazines, and pamphlets of every conceivable design; letters and memoranda arriving via fax, e-mail, and snail mail; television screens, computer screens, and numerous other electronic screens and displays in our kitchens as well as our offices; and the indecipherable array of documentation for every thing we buy that must be assembled, cared for, or operated. The list goes on and on. Today's learners need skills that help them adapt to constant change. The definition of what it means to be literate has evolved with the increasing demands of all aspects of our lives—personal, social, and economic.

2. *Expectations for student performance have increased.* National, state, and local school-reform efforts have raised expectations for what readers and writers should know and be able to do. Public awareness of the critical need for proficient readers and writers has never been greater. Nor has public criticism of the job the schools are doing. An unprecedented amount of open dissension and debate about the content of literacy instruction has led to state directives and legislative mandates that dictate specific curriculum content.

3. *Expectations for teacher performance have increased.* Current research reviews highlight the need for career-long, high-quality teacher education and professional development to improve literacy instruction, most notably, *Preventing Reading Difficulties in Young Children* (Snow, Burns, & Griffin, 1998) and the *National Reading Panel Report* (2000). In addition, many states and non-governmental agencies have developed standards for teacher performance and/or teacher education and professional development. These are frequently linked to content standards for students. Improving the quality of teachers has emerged as the forefront of educational reform. In addition to

setting standards for students, more and more states and districts are examining those standards to determine what *teachers* should be expected to know and do in order to be effective. Although distinctions are made between the beginning teacher just starting a career and the more seasoned professional, expectations have increased for all teachers. Communities realize that high-quality teacher education and continued professional development are essential to effective teaching and learning.

4. *Accountability for student achievement is at the center of school reform.* Accountability for improving student performance in the language arts takes many forms. Setting and implementing standards for students and teachers represent key elements. However, high-stakes standardized tests are generally the centerpiece of accountability and the barometer by which students, teachers, and school districts are measured. Many states have established performance levels that students must reach on these tests by the end of third or fourth grade. These tests have often had a profound effect on the curriculum and some of the new trends described earlier.

5. *The demographics of the student population have changed.* Compounding the challenges teachers face as they address reform is the growing diversity among the student body. This diversity reflects a changing population that is becoming increasingly rich in its multicultural and multilingual nature. According to the 1990 U.S. census, over 6.3 million children between the ages of 5 and 17 years actually spoke a language other than English at home. Two-thirds of these were Spanish speakers (Garcia, 2000). The number of children in our schools whose home language is not English continues to grow rapidly and presents a challenge for teachers to learn as much as they can about successful strategies for working with them.

6. *Educators strive for a balanced and effective language arts curriculum.* Faced with the challenges described above, today's educators seek to address reform as knowledgeable and capable professionals. Although they understand the need for change, they use their knowledge to effect change in ways that represent what is known about how children learn and how they are best taught. Throughout this text, you will encounter teachers who are working within the context of educational reform. They are professionals who are constantly growing and refining their craft. They use standards to inform their teaching in ways that support their vision of interactive, responsive teaching. They make use of ongoing classroom assessments that allow them to know students as individual learners and to appreciate their individual strengths. They plan instruction to meet children's needs, whether they be bilingual or bidialectal learners; gifted learners; learners who need extra time and attention; or learners traditionally considered average by school standards.

Bernice Cullinan

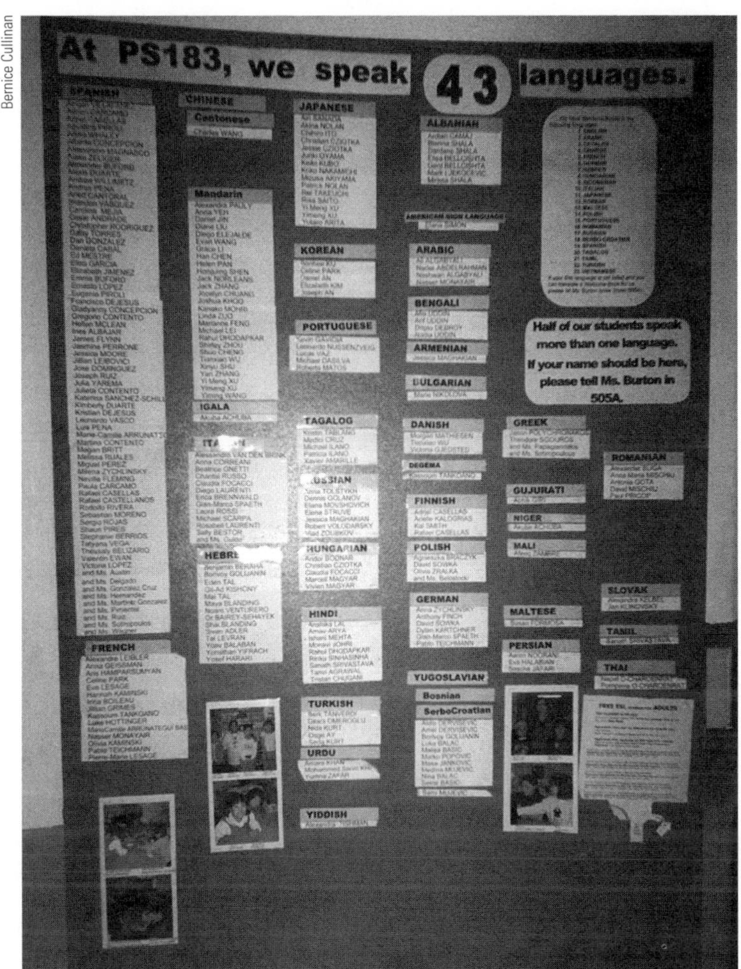

The Welcome bulletin board proudly displays the school's ethnic diversity: In our school people speak 43 different languages.

Sue Dickson, the other teachers described in this book, and thousands of teachers like them all over the world, view language learning as an active, social process, one that has both cognitive and emotional components in which children learn and use strategies and knowledge to pursue meaningful ideas of interest to them. They also know that children learn best in an environment that integrates learning across domains, is supportive, and encourages students to take risks and extend their abilities by trying new things. They are aware of the growing demands for increased achievement in all aspects of language and literacy. They seek balance in their language arts programs, so that they are responsive to the growing demands for rigor and accountability while maintaining a curriculum based on sound principles of teaching and learning.

Learning and Teaching as Processes

AN ACTIVE PROCESS

Dewey (l938), Piaget (1970), and Vygotsky (1962) described active learners as those who are engaged in the learning process, not passively receiving information. Humans learn about language by *using* it (talking, listening, reading, and writing) to learn about their world and to shape that world. More recent developments in the science of learning go beyond these notions of what it means to be an active learner to emphasize the importance of helping people take control of their own learning. Since understanding is viewed as critical to learning, people must learn to recognize when they understand and when they need more information (Bransford, Brown, & Cocking, 2000). For example, the term *active readers* is often associated with good comprehenders. It refers to their tendency to interact mentally with a text. They think with the text as they read—agreeing, disagreeing, questioning, and responding in a variety of ways. Teaching practices that focus on sense-making, self-

TEACHING IDEA

Addressing Diversity

BUILDING A CLASSROOM COMMUNITY

At the beginning of the year, it is worthwhile to spend time having students get to know each other. You can do this in several ways.

1. Ask each child to do a self-portrait and caption the picture with a sentence telling one thing they really like, as in "Elizabeth really likes to read mysteries." Then allow time for class members to see and read everyone's portrait and talk among themselves.
2. Ask your students to interview each other, finding out general information as well as special information, as in "Anna is eight years old and has one baby brother. She went to school in England last year." Have your students present their information to the rest of the class. Then ask each student to try to write down the names of everyone in the class and one thing they know about each person.
3. On the very first day, begin activities that require cooperative group work accompanied by lots of purposeful talk.

Bernice Cullinan

Children learn to use language by dramatizing stories or poems.

assessment, and reflection on what works and what needs improving help foster active learning.

Anne Sherwood, a first grade teacher, creates an environment that encourages active learning. She engages her students in a wide variety of activities that are interesting and fun. Student products that indicate a high level of activity fill her room. Anne's students demonstrate that learning is an active process in which learners construct ideas about language as they engage in language use. Even when learners seem to be passive, as when they are reading, they are active if they are mentally engaged by forming their own questions, making predictions, and deciding what to pay attention to.

Anne is keenly aware that student products only reflect certain levels of activity. She realizes the need to help her students understand the complex processes and structures underlying the instructional activities in which they are engaged. This level of active learning helps them to monitor their own learning and enables them to transfer what they learn to new situations. For example, when Anne's students made maps of their bedrooms, the classroom, and the school neighborhood, they were thrilled with the idea of looking closely at their environments, recreating what they saw through measuring, drawing, creating written signs and symbols, and displaying their work for others to see. Of course, Anne was also proud of the maps they produced. However, her goals extended beyond map making to the development of some fundamental ideas related to measurement and proportion in mathematics and to reading and interpreting graphic representations in the language arts. These understandings were then applied to other graphic texts that her students either created or encountered in their reading.

A SOCIAL PROCESS

Children's learning is greatly influenced by the social context for learning. Vygotsky (1962) argues that learning language is a social phenomenon. From the beginning, children are engaged in communicating with others, a quintessentially social process. It therefore behooves you to create a learning community using strategies like the ones given in the *Teaching Idea: Building a Classroom Community.*

Children speak to be heard, to gain a response from others, to make meaning. Vygotsky further states that the knowledge children construct appears first as an *inter*psychological phenomenon—as something between people—and then later as an *intra*psychological phenomenon—as something individual and internal (Wertsch, 1979). It is through social relationships that children learn new things, which they later internalize. At the same time, children are influencing the environment in which they are learning as others respond to what they say and do. Children learn best by working with others and talking about what they are doing because the roots of language and thought are social. Very often, they can handle more difficult tasks when they work in collaboration with others than they can handle successfully on their own.

Much of children's learning is self-motivated and self-directed. However, other people play major roles as guides in fostering children's learning development (Bransford et al., 2000). They include other children as well as adults (caretakers, parents, teachers, coaches, and so on). But not only do people serve as guides, so too can powerful tools and cultural artifacts, notably television, books, videos, and technological devices of many kinds (Dyson, 1993; Wright & Huston, 1995).

Vygotsky (1962) termed the **zone of proximal development** as the range of tasks that the child can perform with guidance from others but cannot yet perform independently. Vygotsky and Bruner (1986) used the term **scaffolding** to describe the process by which adults guide and support children's learning as they move from their current level of knowledge to a more advanced level. These two important concepts help explain the nature of social interaction surrounding children's learning.

Joseph Kassick

Children develop a sense of community by working together.

Betty Shockley deliberately structures her classroom to encourage social interaction:

> It is early October and children are scattered throughout the room with papers, pencils, books, and markers. Everyone is engaged in writing. There is a hum of talk as students ask neighboring classmates how to spell words. Various children offer spellings and discuss which one is correct, the writer puts down what she considers the best and then goes on. Children are murmuring to themselves, talking with Betty or with the aide or a classroom visitor. Suddenly Ami bursts into song. Other children pick up her song and continue their writing, singing (Galda, Bisplinghoff, Pellegrini, & Stahl, 1995, p. 337).

In Betty's classroom, children work together to learn to read and write. They help each other to figure out words as they read and also to spell words as they write. They share topics and ideas, structures, and strategies. They have choices about working together or alone and most often choose to work with others. Betty demonstrates through her actions and words how important each child is to the life of the classroom, and they come to see themselves and others as knowledgeable, with valuable expertise to share. This community building is a deliberate, planned act. Betty talks a lot about the importance of community:

> Community is just like family and maintaining family and marriage. You always have to work at it. It's never just a given. And so we learn to talk respectfully to each other, and we know that some people can have bad days and we're all human, and we bring our outside life to this inside life too so that we can respect it and look at it and consider it. . . . The community building is just constant, but very aggressive in the beginning and consciously so, to make it very explicit that we are saying this because this is important to us because we live together and we need to know each other. . . . And with as much responsibility in the classroom as these children have, that community base has to be there. You can't say, "Okay, y'all, just go." They've got to learn to share the books and make trade-offs and how to use their time (Galda et al., 1995, p. 337).

The functioning of this community rests on oral sharing of events and emotions, freedom of choice and movement during reading and writing, and the "sea of talk" (Britton, 1970) that surrounds reading and writing. Betty helps children feel that they are valued members of this community, encourages them to listen to and use each others' ideas and expertise, and demonstrates how they can be responsible community members. Being a community allows these students to work toward literacy in ways that each finds useful and satisfying. This "connected teaching" rests on a belief in the "rightness" of the unique perspectives that each student brings to the classroom and the transformation of these perspectives from private to public ideas available for all to absorb (Belenky, Clinchy, Goldberger, & Tarule, 1986). Building an effective classroom community rests on and results in a safe, supportive environment in which students can learn.

Betty makes use of models and demonstrations to move her students' learning forward. For example, in the beginning of the year, she shares personal events from her own life with her students, so that they will have some idea of what is meant by (1) speak in a loud enough voice for your audience to hear and understand what you have to say; (2) look out at your audience when you speak; and (3) stick to the point. She also models supportive questions and comments from the audience. As the year goes by, the amount and kind of coaching changes as her students become more adept in their ability to share their ideas with others and to engage in productive discussions. We will have more to say about the zone of proximal development and scaffolding in Chapter Four under "Language and Thought."

AN EMOTIONAL PROCESS

The way students feel about themselves as learners and about particular learning tasks and situations influences learning (Brown, Bransford, Ferrara,

TEACHING IDEA

Addressing Individual Needs

THINKING ABOUT SUCCESS

During the day, ask your students to think about what they are most proud of doing that day. They can record this on a dated, weekly record form, like the one below. At the end of each day, write brief notes to your students about their positive actions. Then staple the form to the inside of each student's "work home" folder, fill with completed work and send home on Monday (or Friday) for parents to look through, discuss with their child, sign, and send back. You can also include a sheet for notes between you and the parents, writing brief messages about each child each week and inviting the parents to respond.

	Most of the time	***Some of the time***	***Almost never***
1. I think good thoughts about myself.			
2. I practice good manners.			
3. I listen in class.			
4. I work hard to do a good job.			
5. My desk is neat.			
6. My work is done on time.			
7. I share.			

WEEKLY REPORT

E = Excellent S = Satisfactory
G = Good U = Unsatisfactory

Controls talking	
Good attitude	
Courteous to others	
Respects rules	
Follows directions	
Completes assignments	
Work is neat and orderly	
Accepts responsibility	

FIGURE 1.1

Transitions in Language Arts/Reading Instruction

Teachers are moving away from	Teachers are moving toward
Interrogating students after reading	Involving students in student- and teacher-generated discussions
Low-level assignments that merely require students to match, list, circle, etc.	High-level assignments that require students to summarize, categorize, compare and contrast, etc.
Organizing the day around short, subject-matter-based time periods	Organizing the day around large blocks of time designed to integrate subjects
Assigning permanent ability groups as the sole grouping for reading	Using flexible grouping patterns that vary in group constituency and teacher-pupil ratio
Teaching skills and strategies in isolation and in a rigid order	Teaching skills and strategies in contexts that focus on meaningful application and strategic use
Focusing entirely on the "products" of literacy learning	Focusing on the underlying processes involved in literacy learning
Adhering to a narrow instructional frame of reference for all students	Differentiating instruction to account for student variability in language, culture, abilities, and interests

construct a temporary support structure when they repair a building, effective teachers assist students by asking probing questions, modeling and coaching, or giving prompts until students are able to use strategies and skills on their own. In primary classrooms, teachers often track the words as they read aloud predictable big books. They read the book again, and many children "read" along. The teacher's role continues to diminish until children are reading the book independently.

INSTRUCTIONAL CHALLENGES

Although the instructional trends described above are well represented in most schools today, they are also under scrutiny by educators and policy makers seeking to improve student achievement in reading and the other language arts. In the process of educational reform, no other aspect of the school curriculum has received more attention. The challenges are many:

1. *What it means to be literate in our society has changed.* The basics have changed. Although it is still true that becoming literate involves developing some

& Campione, 1983). This has a spiraling effect as students tend to avoid tasks they dislike and situations that make them feel incompetent, thus effectively denying themselves the opportunity for practice when they most need it. Further, it may be that "some learners may not be sufficiently secure to enable them to tolerate mistakes; hence, they may ignore any errors they make or forget about them as quickly as possible. Others may refuse to take the risk of responding incorrectly" (p. 147). In either case, the self-monitoring strategies so important to learning are impossible. Thus, learners' feelings about themselves and their learning situations can have profound implications for subsequent success.

Classrooms that foster children's learning are places that are emotionally safe and supportive. The *Teaching Idea: Thinking about Success* is a good place to start children on their success path. Children's varied individual strengths are accepted and celebrated because all members of the classroom community are collaborators rather than competitors. A safe, supportive atmosphere encourages children to take risks—and learning involves risk taking. In such an environment, children know that their "mistakes" will not be seen as a cause for ridicule but rather as evidence of their effort. Viewed as windows into how a student approaches a learning task, they yield information that may be used to help learners redirect their attempts in more effective ways. Children in such classrooms are much more likely to try new things, to monitor their own learning, and to seek and give help. They are participants in a classroom community in which all children have the emotional and cognitive support of their peers and their teacher as they learn.

In addition to providing a positive, low-risk environment for learning, students thrive emotionally and cognitively when the tasks in which they are involved hold meaning for them and where they can see relationships within and across disciplines. Thus, purposeful activity and integrated learning experiences foster learning that helps students develop language and literacy and use it to make connections across texts, contexts, and content.

Purposeful Activity helps students feel good about what they are doing and promotes learning. Learners succeed when they think they can learn, when they want to learn, and when they see the purpose for learning. Language learning is embedded in a social and cultural context. Children learn language because it has pleasant consequences: expressing the self, enjoying a good story, understanding others, and learning about the world. Learning is easier when the content is of interest and importance to the learner and when the learning tasks make sense.

Simply put, effective classroom practice involves engaging students in tasks in which the purpose is clear to them. The active learners described in this text are engaged in meaningful or authentic learning tasks that require using language to further a meaningful goal such as writing a letter to a pen pal, not in practicing a discrete skill such as adding punctuation to a photocopied letter. Although skills are introduced and applied in context, they are often pulled out as isolated elements for instruction. The use of "real" literature selected by teachers and students to further specific goals, rather than the sole use of textbooks, increases interest and provides a wider array of information and ideas than can be found even in the very best textbook.

Integrated Contexts for instruction promote learning that helps students make connections within the language arts and across disciplines. Learning occurs in a "seamless web" rather than in isolated fragments. Listening, speaking, reading, writing, and viewing are seen as mutually supportive and integrated with each other and across the curriculum in interdisciplinary units of study. Cross-curricular themes allow students to participate in meaningful language and literacy activities as they explore the content through a variety of inquiry-based activities. Students make use of first-hand exploration, such as an interview of someone knowledgeable in a particular area, or a visit to a museum or some other location to collect real specimens. They may read a variety of literature on a topic, visit an author's Web site, and generally make use of electronic media to collect information. The topic or focus may be drawn from children's lives and interests as well as the school district's stated curriculum. Many districts allow for some choice among topics of study by requiring three or four topics at each grade level in science and social studies, leaving time for teacher and student choice as well.

Many teachers structure their entire curriculum around a few big ideas that reach across weeks, months, or even the full school year. Themes such as "changes," "relationships," "journeys," or "interdependence" allow students to think about ideas and issues that are important to them. Themes unify the learning that occurs, helping children make meaningful connections among skills, strategies, and content knowledge.

Karen Bliss, a first grade teacher, created and maintained a single theme across an entire year as she and her students explored the idea of interdependence. This theme involved a study of oceans for the first several months

Bernice Cullinan

Use folded sheets of paper clipped with clothespins over a clothesline to create an adjustable time line.

of the school year. Her students were so interested in what they were doing that their reading, writing, listening, speaking, and viewing activities, as well as much of their social studies and science, were linked to their exploration of the oceans of the world. They learned geography, wrote extensively about oceans and seas and the various continents they border, read extensively from fiction, nonfiction, and poetry, and visited Web sites to get additional information. They painted many beautiful pictures of the oceans and their inhabitants. The children eventually decided to explore rain forests; this interest grew out of their discussion of the ecology of the oceans and their endangered habitats and species.

Some teachers integrate the language arts with one particular content area. For example, Judy Payne teaches language arts/reading and social studies in an integrated curriculum. The independent and whole-class reading and writing that her fifth grade students do relate to the historical period they are studying. This benefits both the language arts and social studies curricula. The trade books the children read make the historical era come alive in a way that a social studies textbook cannot; students are engaged in reading and writing to learn; and they are engaged in pleasurable experiences with books.

Jim Blake and Shelley Rohler, eighth grade teachers in the same school, generally work together each year on one or two themes. They find that the joint planning and sharing of books, videotapes, computer software, and other resources generate creative teaching ideas and make planning easier. The collaboration is extremely well received by their students, who love the idea of working with another class on projects.

All of these teachers make sure that there is a great deal of variety within the theme-based study. Students may pursue a particular aspect of inquiry within a theme. The teachers provide many choices of subtopics to pursue, books to read, and topics to write about. And, it should be pointed out that whereas students are engaged in the study of a particular theme, they also do a variety of other things. For example, they pursue author studies, work on holiday projects, and take advantage of many opportunities for independent reading and writing on topics of their choice. The themes provide unity and coherence to the curriculum. They also provide a meaningful context for teaching strategies for language and literacy and for using multimedia resources meaningfully. Themes create opportunities for purposeful language use as children employ oral and written language strategies to find out about the theme. The oceans theme that Karen Bliss pursued is depicted in Figure 1.2.

In his call for a "deep" curriculum in which students have time to explore ideas and develop strategies for learning meaningful content, Allington (1994) remarks:

> It is difficult for anyone to be thoughtful about topics that are understood only shallowly. In fact, lots of brief lessons on multiple unrelated topics

FIGURE 1.2

Thematic Organization

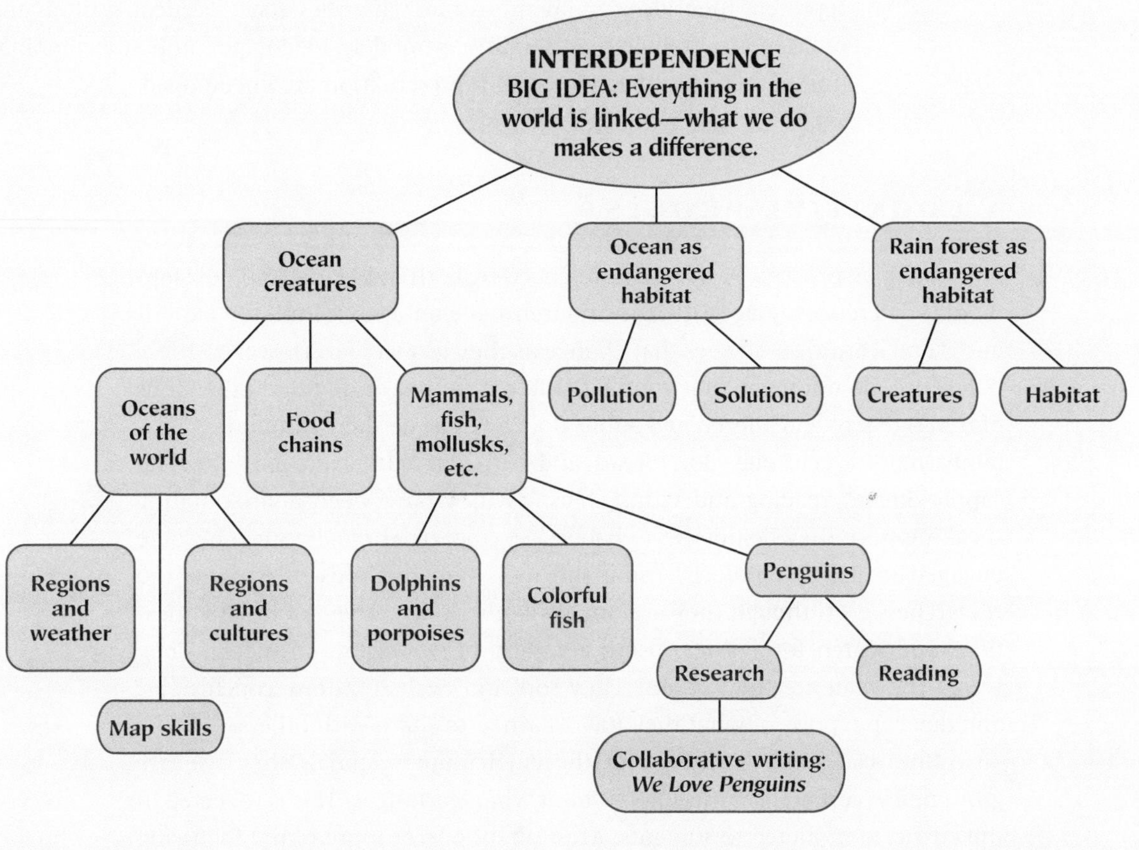

> literally force shallow thinking. If we are to create schools where understanding replaces simple remembering until the test has been taken, our curriculum will necessarily change (p. 26).

It is clear that the teachers described here operate from the following guiding principles for integrating curriculum described by McMahon, Goatley, and McGill-Franzen (1999):

1. *Focus on big ideas for conceptual understanding.* Big ideas enable teachers and students to take time to develop complex understandings, such as the relationships among the content and concepts under study.

2. *Balance process and content.* Integration in this way acknowledges that students use the processes of language arts (listening, speaking, reading, writing, and viewing) along with those of other areas such as science and social studies. They also learn the content associated with these areas.
3. *Attend to multiple means of representing ideas.* Students need multiple ways to represent their ideas and demonstrate what they have learned. Written and oral reports, graphic representations, models, videotapes, and any combination of these or other means of representation are encouraged.

A COGNITIVE PROCESS

As a cognitive process, learning is influenced by both individual and developmental differences (Piaget, 1970). Children have an array of unique experiences and learning strategies that change as they grow older. However, these differences do not mean that younger children cannot or do not do the kinds of things that older children and adults do. They just do them differently. Certainly most 5-year-olds don't read and write as adults do, but they do "approximate" reading and writing, just as they have been approximating speaking since they first began to babble. So, too, older children can become engaged in inquiry projects, using the tools and methods of experienced researchers even though they are not as highly skilled. They formulate questions and search for answers using a variety of strategies and media. They weigh the evidence they collect. They sort and evaluate, draw conclusions, and develop reports of what they have learned to share with others.

Both classroom teachers and the curriculum materials they use are grounded in certain preconceptions about what learning is. This is reflected in the curriculum offered to students. Most often, one or more of the following models of curriculum will be prominent (Wixson, Fisk, Dutro, & McDaniel, 2001):

The **mastery model** is closely associated with competency assessment, discrete instructional objectives, and basic skills. Skills are viewed as discrete, separable entities that can be understood apart from, and independent of, the learner. For example, successful progression through sets of skills, such as a knowledge of the sounds represented by various letters or the ability to punctuate a sentence, is taken as evidence of satisfactory achievement in language arts and reading.

The **cognitive model** emphasizes the relationship between the knowledge that a learner brings to the learning situation and the learning that takes place. For example, the experiences a reader brings to a text influence the reader's ability to comprehend that text. Readers are not viewed as passive receptacles of knowledge from text, but as active participants with perspectives gleaned from personal experiences and previous encounters with text.

Students are expected to draw on their prior knowledge to construct meaning from text and to relate their learning to something in their prior experience.

A **social-constructivist model** views knowledge as collective and contingent upon human beings' interactions with, and shared beliefs about, the world. Language is recognized as a social and cultural construction and, therefore, literacy practices cannot be viewed apart from the social and cultural contexts in which they are learned and practiced. In classrooms where this model influences the curriculum, the cultural and linguistic communities of learners will play a large role in the materials students read, the topics they write about, and the language activities in which they engage.

Throughout this text, you will read about teachers who operate from a combination of cognitive and socio-constructivist models of learning. Learning is not considered to be the accumulation of isolated facts in individual brains, but the active construction of a web of interrelated knowledge (information, concepts, patterns, and strategies) through engagement in a learning situation characterized by the meaningful use of language in social interaction. Meaningful inquiry and problem solving lead to effective generalization and application.

Learning is linking new information to prior knowledge and then organizing that information (Piaget, 1970). Students learn best that information for which they have some *schema,* or knowledge structure. Learning involves making connections between what is already understood and what is encountered. As students learn, they take in new information and alter their understandings to fit the new information, a process Piaget called the "equilibration of cognitive structures" (1977). As learners encounter new information, they integrate it with what they already know, then apply this new knowledge to novel situations (**assimilation**), and restructure schemata to include the new knowledge (**accommodation**), resulting in conceptual change (disequilibration leading to **equilibration**).

For example, a young child may be quite familiar with stories about animals in which the animals are given human emotions and characteristics. This child will know quite a bit about stories (as containing beginnings, middles, endings, and some sort of problem) and about animals (acting as human beings in stories, but not in real life). When this child encounters a book that factually reports on the habits of animals, several things can happen. There will be a recognition of animal names and realistic animal behavior, confirming what the child already knows, and new information about animals to be considered. (Do bunnies live in houses or in burrows?) There will also be recognition of the book itself (something to listen to and look at), as well as new information (not all books tell stories). The child refines and extends concepts about animals and books through this new engagement.

Effective teachers make use of what is known about children's cognitive development. They emphasize what children are likely to be able to do and are capable of knowing, rather than how they differ from an adult model of literacy. As they develop, children use strategies and produce language in forms similar to those of adults, but their experiences and their needs might be quite different (Hiebert, 1991). Effective teachers encourage children to demonstrate what they know about language and to continue developing as language users. Effective teachers know how to introduce appropriate experiences that further children's development. First grade teachers might encourage invented spelling (discussed in Chapter Six) to develop reading and writing ability; seventh grade teachers might implement writing evaluation conferences (discussed in Chapter Twelve) to encourage self-evaluation and reflection. The cognitive levels rubric used by Wixson and her colleagues (2001, p. 75) as a means for evaluating the cognitive level of objectives tied to state standards (Figure 1.3) offers a set of criteria by which teachers can measure the cognitive levels of the learning opportunities they offer students.

FIGURE 1.3

Cognitive Levels Rubric: Depth of Knowledge

Level 1 Level 1 requires students to receive or recite facts and to use simple skills and abilities. Oral reading that does not include analysis of the text as well as basic comprehension of a text is included. Questions require only a shallow understanding of text presented and often consist of verbatim recall from text or simple understanding of a single phrase.

Level 2 Level 2 requires some mental processing; it requires both comprehension and subsequent processing of text or portions of text. Intersentence analysis or inference is required. Some important concepts are covered but not in a complex way. Standards and items at this level may include words such as *summarize, interpret, infer, classify, organize, collect, display, compare,* and *determine whether fact or opinion.* Literal main ideas are stressed.

Level 3 Deep knowledge becomes more focused at level 3. Students are encouraged to go beyond the text; however, they are still required to show understanding of the ideas in the text. Students may be encouraged to explain, generalize, or connect ideas. Standards and items at this level involve reasoning and planning. Students must be able to support their thinking. Questions may involve abstract theme identification or inference across an entire passage. Questions may also involve more superficial connections between texts.

Level 4 Higher-order thinking is central and knowledge is deep at level 4. The standard or the item at this level will probably be an extended activity, with extended time provided. Students take information from at least one passage and are asked to apply this information to a new task. They may also be asked to develop hypotheses and perform complex analyses of the connections among texts.

Strategies for Learning and Teaching

In addition to being active, social, and cognitive, learning is strategic. It is important to make the distinction between learner strategies, those used by the learners themselves, and instructional strategies, those used by teachers to help learners succeed.

LEARNER STRATEGIES

Learner strategies are "specific procedures or ways of executing given skills," such as summarizing or predicting (Jones et al., 1987). Effective learners know a variety of strategies, how to use them, and when they should be used. They are able to monitor their learning, to recognize when they are having difficulties, and to know what steps to take in order to remedy the difficulties. Effective learners know that they can largely control their own learning, persevere in a task until they are satisfied with the results, and attribute success to their own efforts (Jones et al., 1987). They are involved in what they are doing, feel responsible for the success (or failure) of what they are doing, and think about what they are doing (**metacognition**) in order to plan and monitor their use of strategies.

Strategies versus skills

Strategies are distinct from skills (Paris, Wasik, & Turner, 1991). People perform skills the same way every time. For instance, recognizing a word instantly is a skill, reading from left to right is a skill, and knowing the sound of the consonant digraph *wh* is a skill. Traditional skill instruction relies on drill and practice techniques using devices such as flash cards and worksheets to generate the repetition that results in automatic performance.

"Strategies are plans for solving problems encountered in constructing meaning" (Duffy, 1993, p. 232). Unlike skills, these plans cannot be automatized. The uniqueness of each learning situation requires learners to modify the strategies they use to fit the demands of the task. For example, how a writer chooses to describe an event is determined in part by the form used and the intended audience. A personal narrative might be used for younger children, whereas a straightforward report might be used for a more sophisticated audience. Similarly, the way a reader draws conclusions will differ from one text to another because of the clues available and the nature of the text.

Characteristics of good strategic readers

A good strategic reader consciously uses sets of strategies, coordinates those strategies, and shifts strategies when appropriate (Pressley, Goodchild, Fleet, Zajchowski, & Evans, 1989). For example, strategic readers who read new texts will be making predictions, monitoring the accuracy of those predictions, and thinking through the reading until they have understood the text to their own satisfaction. Should they become confused, they might reread to see if they have misread or forgotten something, talk to a friend who has read the same book, or discuss the book with a teacher or a friend. Similarly, when strategic readers encounter an unknown word, they do not rigidly follow a narrow series of memorized steps to figure it out. Operating from a global meaning-making process for achieving a purpose, these readers coordinate and test a variety of strategies available to them in order to figure out the word (Duffy, 1993). Thus, being a strategic reader or writer is about much more than knowing a set of isolated strategies. It is about the effective selection and use of the appropriate strategy or group of strategies to solve the problem at hand.

Perhaps the most critical measure of how well students have internalized a strategy and made it their own is their ability to apply the strategy to new situations. For example, a student may show the ability to *transfer* what is known about making predictions in narrative texts and apply it with appropriate adjustments to informational texts, math word problems, or planning a science experiment. Learning involves transferring appropriate strategies, information, and knowledge of patterns from one situation to another (Brown et al., 1983). In a very real sense, transfer is the essence of what learners do when they learn. They call up familiar knowledge and effective strategies to understand and master new material (Brown et al., 1983). Bransford et al. (2000, pp. 235–236) list several factors that influence people's ability to transfer what they have learned:

- People must achieve a threshold of initial learning that is sufficient to support transfer.
- Spending a lot of time ("time on task") in and of itself is not sufficient to ensure effective learning.
- Learning with understanding is more likely to promote transfer than simply memorizing information from a text or lecture.
- Knowledge that is taught in a variety of contexts is more likely to support flexible transfer than knowledge that is taught with context-specific examples.
- Students develop flexible understanding of when, where, why, and how to use their knowledge to solve new problems if they learn how to extract underlying themes and principles from their learning exercises.

- ✦ Transfer of learning is an active process.
- ✦ All learning involves transfer from previous experiences.
- ✦ Sometimes the knowledge that people bring to a new situation impedes subsequent learning because it guides thinking in wrong directions.

What we know about learner strategies helps to frame some guiding principles for instruction: (1) Teach and review strategies over time in a variety of contexts. (2) Help students to monitor their own learning and understanding. (3) Guide students toward understanding themes and principles underlying a specific strategy rather than simply memorizing a specific set of procedures. (4) Help students build on the strengths they bring to the learning situation and adjust any misconceptions they may have that could interfere with learning.

INSTRUCTIONAL STRATEGIES

The classroom examples and teaching ideas throughout this text present a variety of learner strategies that language arts teachers find useful. These teachers employ effective instructional strategies that involve learners in broad units of instruction designed to foster genuine purposes for learning and create the need to learn strategies so that students will accomplish their goals. They use a variety of instructional strategies in order to do this, including explicit instruction, demonstrations, scaffolded instruction, and cooperative learning among others.

Explicit instruction

Throughout this text you will find examples of teachers explicitly instructing students in literacy activities. Explicit instruction is fully and clearly telling students how to accomplish a task. You may wonder how this fits with what we just said about teaching for transfer. Our discussion of explicit instruction does not mean that we endorse lengthy lectures about how to do something at the expense of actually doing it. Instead, effective teachers know when to offer explicit, lucid explanations and demonstrations that unlock the secrets of literacy (Delpit, 1986) when necessary. For example, about halfway through the year, first grade teachers like Anne Sherwood and Karen Bliss begin to teach word patterns to their students, providing them with linguistic information that helps them read and spell. Judy Payne might teach a reading strategy that helps her fifth grade students read informational texts more effectively. All of these teachers also provide demonstrations and opportunities for guided practice with the goal of encouraging students to become independent learners.

Demonstrations

Demonstrating effective literacy strategies is something that literate people do all the time. Effective teaching involves doing, not just talking about, literate activities. Teachers who listen as they want their students to listen, speak as they want their students to speak, and read and write as they want their students to read and write, provide opportunities for their students to see literacy in action. Demonstrations of the craft of literacy are so powerful that even casual encounters can have far-reaching results. However, deliberate demonstration of a process, often called a "think-aloud," gives students an opportunity to actually get a sense of how literate people think as they perform tasks. Figure 1.4 includes a think-aloud as part of the demonstration component of the scaffolding process.

Teachers can call attention to their own literate practices to help students see how a master craftsperson enacts literacy. Betty regularly brings her own reading and writing to class. She lets her students know that reading and writing play an important role in her life. She does this both casually and formally, as when she invited a guest to participate with her on a "literacy panel." She and her guest answered questions about their literacy practices posed by the students. This text contains many examples of ways to demonstrate the crafts of literacy to your students and ways in which peers demonstrate effective practices to each other.

Scaffolded instruction

As mentioned earlier in this chapter, scaffolding is a procedure for gradually reducing the initially heavy social support of learning and increasing students' independent performance (Roller, Beed, & Forsyth, 1996). Bruner (1983) noted that scaffolding is a natural feature of parents' interactions with their children. Children frequently call on their parents when they need help. Or, parents may determine that a child needs their help. In either case, the assistance given is based on the parent's assessment of what the child can do for him or herself and what help is needed from the parent. For example, when parents teach a child to ride a bicycle, they usually begin by helping the child onto the bike and holding on for quite a while until the child feels comfortable. When the child begins to feel secure, the parent may only hold onto the rear of the bicycle, offering more support only when the bicycle begins to wobble. Gradually, as the child begins to gain confidence, the parent will relinquish support, offering assistance and advice only when needed.

In the classroom, teachers scaffold instruction through a planned series of lessons that involve models, demonstrations, and collaborative practice such as shown in Figure 1.4. They also scaffold instruction by providing "guided practice," often in small, interactive groups or with individuals.

FIGURE 1.4

Scaffolding Instruction: Writing a Friendly Letter

Show Examples (or model)

Read and show examples of friendly letters so that students will have some idea of what they will eventually do. Discuss the content, tone, and parts of the letter. Help students become familiar with how a friendly letter is different from other writing forms, such as stories or informational texts.

Demonstrations

Do a think-aloud at the chalkboard or on chart paper, writing a friendly letter to someone. Throughout the demonstration, say (think aloud) what you are thinking as decisions are made about what will be said, and how it will be said, and as changes and corrections are made:

"Let me see, I think I will start by telling Jodi that I had a good time at her house, and I want to invite her to visit me. I forgot to mention that I have a new puppy. I need to go back and put that in, and I will describe him too."

Think-alouds are demonstrations that make a task transparent for students, as they listen to how a skilled learner goes about a task.

Collaborations

Collaborations may take two forms, collaboration with you and collaborations with peers. Both can be helpful. Following a demonstration, you may want to try writing a group letter in much the same way as the demonstration was done. This time, however, the students will contribute ideas and you will act as scribe and as guide for the process. This may be followed by a joint effort by a pair of students.

Independence

At this point, students have had sufficient experience in low-risk situations to be capable of writing on their own. However, some children may need more guided practice in small groups or as individuals. As children work independently, observe points of difficulty and address them in subsequent lessons.

Teachers provide as much or as little support as the learners need, gradually withdrawing that support as learners become able to function independently. Scaffolded instruction involves observing and assessing children as language users, planning and introducing appropriate activities that will help children build on what they know about language, explicit instruction and demonstration of a successful strategy, and continued interaction among teacher and students as the students incorporate that strategy into their own repertoires. The teacher gradually withdraws from the activity but continues to observe and assess students' demonstrations and intervenes when necessary.

Sue Dickson helps her students work within the form of a friendly letter by presenting and posting the parts of a letter, talking with the class about what a writer might say in a letter or e-mail, and prompting children to respond to the questions that their pen pals or keyboard pals pose. As the children become more familiar and more fluent with the tasks, they will need less and less teacher support for them; they will assume responsibility for themselves.

Figure 1.4 shows one possible series of activities you might use to introduce a particular writing form to your class. The components would be introduced over time. Various content would be used for the models, demonstrations, and collaborative activities. Along the way, students would discuss and evaluate the good features of the letters that were produced and those that could be improved. In their discussions, they would use the language of literacy, such as greeting, closing, and body of the letter.

Cooperative learning

Cooperative learning involves students working together in small groups of generally two to seven members in order to achieve a common goal or task (Johnson & Johnson, 1994). It is based on the idea that people can learn by expressing and exploring ideas and experiences cooperatively. The *National Reading Panel Report* (2000) cited cooperative learning as one of a limited number of comprehension strategies that are effective and most promising for classroom instruction:

> Having peers instruct or interact over the use of reading strategies leads to an increase in the learning of the strategies, promotes intellectual discussion, and increases reading comprehension. This procedure saves on teacher time and gives the students more control over their learning and social interaction with peers (p. 4–45).

Cooperative learning promotes both academic achievement and positive attitudes in the classroom while student motivation, social involvement, and academic interaction among students are enhanced. It is for students of all ages and levels of ability. Working cooperatively not only helps students develop important social skills, it is an excellent way to help them relate appropriately to others with backgrounds different from their own. Students with varied social backgrounds, intellectual skills, and physical capabilities work together to learn subject matter, solve problems, and accomplish tasks. They learn to accept and value individual differences. Cooperative learning means that every member of the group is included, and differences among group members are resolved by the group members. Further, group members work toward solving problems and completing tasks with minimal teacher assistance. The social skills that group membership develops are critical to life within and beyond the classroom.

Effective groups are characterized by the proliferation of points of view about the subject, task, or problem at hand; by the willingness to hear and consider these diverse viewpoints; and by growth in the group members' understanding of the task at hand (Cowie & Rudduck, 1990). When introducing children to cooperative group work, it is important to demonstrate and discuss appropriate group behaviors and to help students recognize key ideas and formulate summaries of those ideas. For example, you will need to consider guidelines for participation, supportiveness, turn-taking, and positive awareness of others' feelings. Clearly state the task or problem that the group will focus on and a time frame for their accomplishment. At the end of the group activity, assess individual learning, but give rewards to the group as a whole.

A good way to initiate cooperative learning activities is to play cooperative games in which a group of children work together against time to accomplish a task or solve a problem. Small-group brainstorming activities or the construction of graphic outlines or webs by a group are excellent, brief tasks to set for children learning to work cooperatively. Paired reading, literature circles, peer writing groups, discussions, and role playing are other examples of activities that call for cooperative learning strategies. These activities are discussed in subsequent chapters.

Through cooperative learning, students practice communication skills of various types. They share ideas, learn to attend to how others think and react to problems, and learn to work with others toward a common goal. This kind of cooperation exists not only within the walls of the classroom, however. A cooperative relationship between home and school is also a vital part of effective language arts learning and teaching.

Making use of technology in the language arts curriculum

One of the most noticeable changes in language learning and teaching has been the influence of technology on the way we gather information and communicate with others. Some have argued that technology has actually changed the way we think about how we think and learn, moving us from response strengthening to knowledge acquisition to knowledge construction (Hooper & Hokason, 2000). Technology has influenced virtually every aspect of our everyday lives. Today's students are active users—not just viewers and listeners. Today's students are apt to take for granted their ability to scan the globe for authentic, meaningful information, engage in chats with other students and professionals living in remote locations, and access important documents without leaving their home. The use of technology fits in well with other kinds of active learning discussed in this chapter. Cooperative group work, project-based instruction, and learning logs are the kinds of activities that encourage students to build their personal knowledge and cognitive abilities. The teaching that emerges necessarily emphasizes the support of students' abilities to frame their own questions, navigate a variety of sources, make decisions about what is relevant and what is not, and learn and think using a wide range of media and information. According to the International Society for Technology in Education (2001), the following areas should be addressed regarding standards for classroom teachers using technology. Teachers should be able to:

- Demonstrate a sound understanding of technology operations and concepts.
- Plan and design effective learning environments and experiences supported by technology.
- Implement curriculum plans that include methods and strategies for applying technology to maximize student learning.
- Apply technology to facilitate a variety of effective assessment and evaluation strategies.
- Use technology to enhance their productivity and professional practice.
- Understand the social, ethical, legal, and human issues surrounding the use of technology in pre-K–12 schools and apply those principles in practice.

Kindergarten teacher and part-time university instructor of technology Jim O'Kelly believes that the computer's capability as a database is an underutilized tool. A database is a set of related data stored in a computer. Although its use is widespread in business and government, it is frequently ignored by teachers. A database can exist in a stand-alone program like *FileMaker Pro*, or it can be part of an integrated program like AppleWorks or Microsoft Works (Norton & Sprague, 2001). A look at the Web sites of major computer manufacturers and sellers (for example, Dell or Gateway) reveals that practically every computer offered for sale comes equipped with one database program or another.

TEACHING IDEA

Literature Link

THE WEEKLY POEM DATABASE

Each week of the school year you could feature a poem, chant, or simple rhyme during opening activities. Use it to talk about rhyme, imagery, unusual vocabulary, to build knowledge of sight words, and so on. The verse must be relatively short (usually no more than eight lines) and, of course, it must be about something that kindergartners can understand. Often, your selections will be humorous, but they can also be simple observations about life or nature. On the last day of the school year, you can provide the children with a compilation of some of the selections in the form of a kindergarten memory book, with a few pages for autographs.

The power of a database to store, search for, and sort information makes it valuable for a number of classroom activities and teacher-support tools. Although many teachers shy away from learning to use a database program because it seems like a long cumbersome process, a half-day inservice session or a couple of evenings with a self-instruction book can make a person expert enough to design databases sophisticated enough for a variety of educational purposes. *The Teaching Idea: The Weekly Poem Database* describes one use that Jim makes of the database in his teaching.

Involving Families and Communities

Effective teachers understand that children have lives outside of school that profoundly influence their literacy learning. Outside the school walls children live in the midst of their families and their cultures, and families and cultures differ among children.

When children's cultures are close matches with the culture of school, there is little conflict between home and school, and the important link between the child's two worlds is easy to forge. However, when a child's home culture differs markedly from the culture of the school, it takes greater effort on the part of the school to establish that link. This effort is well worth it, however, for when teachers and other school personnel take the time to make the community a necessary part of school there is a much greater chance that children will learn. Every family has a wealth of knowledge and skills that help it function; this wealth is a resource that enriches the classroom. Viewing all families as possessing "funds of knowledge" (Moll & Greenberg, 1990) has a profound impact on teachers and their students (Moll & Gonzalez, 1994). Although the issue of school and community policy is not considered in this text, we do stress that family involvement in schools is crucial to successful language learning. You can help children make their school experiences meaningful to their lives outside of school and their outside lives meaningful to their school lives by bringing parents and caregivers into the classroom to share their language and customs; by sending books and writing supplies home with children; by inviting parents to participate in classroom activities such as reading and writing; by sending home explanations and descriptions of what is happening in the classroom and inviting comment; and, above all, by valuing the language and life experiences that children bring from their homes into the classroom (Laklik, Dellinger, & Druggish, 2003). Children with limited language experiences may come from high- or low-income homes. A lack of interaction with parents, who are too busy to spend time with them, and high levels of television viewing can contribute to children's language deprivation, regardless of the socioeconomic status of the family.

In their conclusion to a look at research on families and literacy, Taylor and Strickland (1989) note that "children benefit when we establish literacy in the social and cultural contexts of their everyday lives. . . . We cannot replace family life with classroom experiences, but we *can* recognize the legitimacy of children's social existence and use it as a basis for curriculum and instruction" (p. 275). We would add that children benefit when teachers establish not just literacy, but *all* language learning in the contexts of children's everyday lives. In the remainder of this text we will consider language learning and teaching that focuses on children rather than on curricula and that celebrates the human event that effective learning and teaching can be.

SUMMARY

Like language, teaching and learning are dynamic and creative, changing across time to fill new needs. Learning is an active, social process that involves linking and organizing information, learning patterns and strategies, and transferring appropriate knowledge of content, patterns, and strategies from one situation to another. Learning is linked to development, the way learners feel about themselves, the context for learning, and the content to be learned. Effective teachers plan for authentic learning tasks in which students are actively involved. The classroom context is supportive, and the curriculum is integrated across subject matter. Effective teachers help students learn strategies, patterns, and content—and how to use them. They do this by using a variety of organizational and instructional configurations. Relationships among schools, families, and communities are also important in an effective language arts program, especially if bilingual or bidialectal learners are involved.

ACTIVITIES

1. **Classroom Observation.** Visit a classroom and look for examples of effective teaching practices. Notice the nature of the print environment. Would you consider it print-rich? Do the students appear to be "active"

learners? Share what you learn in class and discuss which practices are exemplary and why.

2. **Learning Journal.** As you read each chapter in this text, monitor your own understanding by keeping a double-entry journal with notes about what you are learning. Draw a line down each page about two-thirds of the way to the right. On the left side of the line, take notes. On the right side, make comments, ask questions, summarize, and make predictions. Think about and note the kind of strategies you are using to organize your knowledge. Another version of the learning journal is a dialogue journal, in which you write notes on the left side and someone else responds to your notes on the right.
3. **For Discussion.** Effective teaching is a great deal of work and requires a remarkable amount of preparation. It also requires a knowledgeable teacher. Talk about the kinds of things you think you will need to know to be an effective teacher. Make a list and keep it, adding to it as you progress through your training and checking off items as you think you've learned them.

FURTHER READING

Allington, R. L., & Walmsley, S. A. (1995). *No quick fix: Rethinking literacy programs in American elementary schools.* New York: Teachers College Press.

Banks, J. A., & McGee-Banks, C. A. (2001). *Multicultural education: Issues and perspectives.* New York: Wiley.

Edwards, P., Pleasants, H., & Franklin, S. (2000). *Path to follow: Learning to listen to parents.* Portsmouth, NH: Heinemann.

Garcia, G. E. (2000). Research on bilingual children's reading development and instruction. In M. Kamil, P. Mosenthal, P. D. Pearson, & R. Barr (Eds.), *Handbook on reading research, 3,* Mahwah, NJ: Erlbaum.

Kibby, M. W. (1993). What reading teachers should know about reading proficiency in the US. *Journal of Reading, 37,* 28–39.

Norton, P., & Sprague, D. (2001). *Technology for teachers.* Boston: Allyn & Bacon.

Pressley, M. (1998). *Elementary reading instruction that works: Why balanced literacy instruction makes more sense than whole language or phonics and skills.* New York: Guilford Press.

Teachers of English to Speakers of Other Languages (TESOL). (1997). *English as a second language (ESL) standards for pre-K–12 students.* Alexandria, VA: Author.

REFERENCES

Allen, J. (2000). *Yellow brick roads: Shared and guided paths to independent reading 4–12*. Portland, ME: Stenhouse.

Allington, R. L. (1994). The schools we have. The schools we need. *The Reading Teacher, 48,* 14–29.

———. (2001). *What really matters for struggling readers: Designing research-based programs*. New York: Addison Wesley Longman.

Belenky, M. F., Clinchy, B. McV., Goldberger, N. R., & Tarule, J. M. (1986). *Women's ways of knowing: The development of self, voice, and mind.* New York: Scholastic.

Bransford, J. D., Brown, A. L., & Cocking, R. R. (Eds.) (2000). *How people learn: Brain, mind, experience, and school.* Washington, D.C.: National Academy Press.

Britton, J. (1970). Language and learning. London: Penguin.

Brown, A., Bransford, J., Ferrara, R., & Campione, J. (1983). In J. Flavell and E. Markman (Eds.), *Handbook of psychology, 3,* 77–166. New York: Wiley.

Bruner, J. (1983). *Child's talk: Learning to use language.* New York: Norton.

———. (1986). *Actual minds, possible worlds.* Cambridge, MA. Harvard University Press.

Cazden, C. (1988). *Classroom discourse.* New York: Teachers College Press.

Cowie, H., & Ruddick, J. (1990). Learning from one another: The challenge. In H. C. Foot, M. J. Morgan, and R. H. Shute (Eds.), *Children helping children* (pp. 235–255). London: Wiley.

Delpit, L. M. (1986). Skills and other dilemmas of a progressive black educator. *Harvard Educational Review, 56,* 379–385.

Dewey, J. (1938). *Experience in education.* New York: Collier.

Dorn, L., French, C., & Jones, T. (1998). *Apprenticeship in literacy.* York, ME: Stenhouse.

Duffy, G. G. (1993). Rethinking strategy instruction: Four teachers' development and their low achievers. *The Elementary School Journal, 93,* 231–247.

Dyson, A. H. (1993). *Social worlds of children's learning to write in an urban school.* New York: Teachers College Press.

Galda, L., Bisplinghoff, B. S., Pellegrini, A. D., & Stahl, S. (1995). Sharing lives: Reading, writing, talking, and living in a first-grade classroom. *Language Arts, 72,* 334–339.

Garcia, G. E. (2000). Research on bilingual children's reading development and instruction. In M. Kamil, P. Mosenthal, P. D. Pearson, & R. Barr (Eds.), *Handbook on reading research, 3,* 813–834. Mahwah, NJ: Erlbaum.

Graves, M., & Graves, B. (2003). *Scaffolding reading experiences: Designs for student success.* Norwood, MA: Gordon.

Halliday, M. A. K. (1982). Three aspects of children's language development: Learning language, learning through language, and learning about language. In Y. Goodman, M. Huassle, & D. S. Strickland (Eds.), *Oral and written language development research: Impact on the schools* (pp. 7–19). Urbana, IL: National Council of Teachers of English.

Hiebert, E. H. (1991). Research directions: Literacy contexts and literacy processes. *Language Arts, 68,* 134–139.

Hooper, S., & Hokason, B. (2000). The changing face of knowledge. *Social Education, 64,* 28–31.

International Society for Technology in Education (2001). *ISTE National Educational Technology Standards (NETS) and Performance Indicators for Teachers.* http://cnets.iste.org/index3.html

Johnson, R. T., & Johnson, D. W. (1994). An overview of cooperative learning. In J. Thousand, R. Villa, & A. Nevin (Eds.), *Creativity and collaborative learning* (pp. 32–45). Baltimore, MD: Brookes.

Jones, F. F., Palincsar, A. S, Ogle, D. S., & Carr, E. G. (Eds.) (1987). *Strategic teaching and learning: Cognitive instruction in the content areas.* Alexandria, VA: Association of Supervision and Curriculum Development.

Kibby, M. W. (1993). What reading teachers should know about reading proficiency in the U.S. *Journal of Reading, 37,* 28–29.

Laklik, L. D., Dellinger, L., & Druggish, R. (2003). Fostering collaboration between home and school through curriculum development: Perspectives of three Appalachian children. In A. I. Willis, G. E. Garcia, R. Barrera, & V. Harris (Eds.), *Multicultural issues in literacy research and practice* (pp. 69–100). Mahwah, NJ: Erlbaum.

McMahon, S., Goatley, G., McGill-Franzen, A. (Spring, 1999). *Integrating curriculum in elementary classrooms to promote higher student achievement.* Albany, NY: English Update.

Moll, L. C. & Gonzalez, N. (1994). Lessons from research with language-minority children. *Journal of Reading Behavior, 26,* 439–456.

Moll, L. C., & Greenberg, J. (1990). Creating zones of possibilities: Combining social contexts for instruction. In L. C. Moll (Ed.), *Vygotsky and education* (pp. 319–348). Cambridge, England: Cambridge University Press.

National Reading Panel Report (2000). *Teaching children to read.* Washington, D.C.: National Institute of Child Health and Human Development.

Norton, P., & Sprague, D. (2001). *Technology for teachers.* Boston: Allyn & Bacon.

Paris, S., Wasik, B., & Turner, J. (1991). The development of strategic readers. In R. Barr, M. Kamil, P. Mosenthal, & P. D. Pearson (Eds.), *Handbook of reading research, 2,* 609–640. New York: Longman.

Piaget, J. (1970). Piaget's theory. In P. Mussen (Ed.), *Carmichael's manual of child psychology, 1,* 703–732. New York: Wiley.

______. (1977). *The development of thought: Equilibration of cognitive structures.* Trans. A. Rosin. New York: Viking.

Power, M. P., & Hubbard, R. S. (1996). *Language development: A reader for teachers.* Englewood Cliffs, NJ: Prentice-Hall.

Pressley, M., Goodchild, F., Fleet, J., Zajchowski, R., & Evans, E. D. (1989). The challenges of classroom strategy instruction. *Elementary School Journal, 89,* 301–342.

Pressley, M., Rankin, J., & Yokoi, L. (1996). A survey of instructional practices of primary teachers nominated as effective in promoting literacy. *Elementary School Journal, 96*(4), 363–383.

Roller, C. M., Beed, P. L., & Forsyth, S. (1996). Direct instruction occurs in context. In C. M. Roller, *Variability not disability: Struggling readers in a workshop classroom* (pp. 69–83). Newark, DE: International Reading Association.

Smith, M. C. (2002). Primary-grade educators and adult literacy: Some strategies for assisting low-literate parents. *The Reading Teacher, 56,* 157–165.

Snow, C. E., Burns, S., & Griffin, P. (Eds.) (1998). *Preventing reading difficulties in young children.* Washington, DC: National Academy Press.

Strickland, D. S., & Snow, C. (2002). *Preparing our teachers: Opportunities for better reading instruction.* Washington, DC: National Academy Press.

Taylor, D., & Strickland, D. S. (1989). Learning from families: Implications for educators and policy. In J. B. Allen & J. M. Mason (Eds.), *Risk makers, risk takers, risk breakers* (pp. 251–280). Portsmouth, NH: Heinemann.

Vygotsky, L. S. (1962). *Thought and language.* Cambridge, MA: MIT Press.

______. (1978). *Mind in society* (M. Cole, Ed.). Cambridge, MA: Harvard University Press.

Wertsch, J. (1979). From social interaction to higher psychological processes: A clarification and application of Vygotsky's theory. *Human Development, 22,* 1–22.

Willis, A. I., Garcia, G. E., Barrera, R., & Harris, V. J. (Eds.) (2003). *Multicultural issues in literacy research and practice.* Mahwah, NJ: Erlbaum.

Wixson, K. K., Fisk, M. C., Dutro, E., McDaniel, J. (2001). *The alignment of state standards and assessments in elementary reading.* Ann Arbor, MI: The Center for the Improvement of Early Reading Achievement (CIERA).

Wright, J. C., & Huston, A. C. (1995). Effects of educational TV viewing of lower income preschoolers on academic skills, school readiness, and school adjustment one to three years later: A report to Children's Television Workshop. Lawrence, KS: University of Kansas.

Organizing and Managing the Language Arts Program

CHAPTER OUTLINE

Key Standard

Effective teachers of language arts/reading provide students with opportunities to learn in a literate and supportive environment that addresses individual needs and backgrounds. Such teachers:

- Use a variety of instructional formats, including whole-class and small-group instruction, and personalized one-on-one instruction, and make use of focused, direct instruction along with indirect opportunities for independent learning and application.
- Use a variety of methods and teaching strategies to accommodate to learner differences, such as linguistic and cultural differences, differences in abilities and background experiences, and differences in interests and motivation.
- Use a combination of materials, including textbooks, trade books, and instructional and informational technologies, to stimulate interest and promote growth in the language arts.
- Coordinate school and community resources, such as school-wide intervention programs, allied professionals, and parents, in order to plan and support instruction.

To get a preview of Chapter 2 and learn about organization and management of the language arts program, visit the Chapter 2 section of the accompanying *Language Arts* CD-ROM.

Marilyn Barnett has been teaching first grade for seven years. Throughout her career, she has been characterized as a "natural" teacher, born to teach first grade. To be sure, she has always enjoyed working with young children. Her excellent reputation was cemented during the early years of her teaching, and it has persisted and grown even stronger over the years. However, Marilyn is a very different teacher today compared to three years ago and especially compared to her first four years. Marilyn, like many teachers, has undergone a change in her thinking about the ways in which children learn and the ways schools can best support that learning. This change in attitude has had a profound influence on the instructional environment in her classroom.

Outstanding fourth grade teacher Janet Longello says she was not born a great teacher and would not describe herself in those terms even though others do. She considers herself a learner, however. Even as a new teacher, she was receptive to new ideas, although she tried them out very cautiously. Concerned with the district mandates to cover the material in the reading program in a specific order and within a specific time frame, Janet felt like a rebel when she skipped a few questions in the teacher's manual or altered the sequence in any way.

Kim Mancino and Bill Kimble are both seventh grade teachers. They teach in different schools in the same district. Both struggle with the same issues: not enough time; adjusting materials to student needs; dealing with students whose interests are frequently focused on matters other than school; and addressing standards and high-stakes assessments in ways that are instructionally defensible and engaging. Although the issues they confront are similar, Kim and Bill find themselves in situations that are vastly different in terms of how they may be addressed.

Addressing Organization and Management Issues across Grade Levels

THE PRIMARY YEARS

Perhaps one of the best ways to characterize Marilyn Barnett's teaching during her early years is to say that it was very textbook-bound. In addition to basal reading texts and skill-focused workbooks, Marilyn relied extensively on textbooks for mathematics, handwriting, social studies, and science. Her plan book reflected a heavy reliance on these materials as the basis for what took place each day. Each area of the curriculum would be listed under a separate time slot with the corresponding textbook title and page numbers to be covered. Instruction tended to be fragmented and unrelated.

Marilyn's transition to a more integrated language arts program came largely out of a desire to use her instructional time more wisely. By deliberately integrating some aspects of language arts instruction into one large block of time, she saves time. More important, her students see how certain skills taught in reading are relevant to spelling and writing as well. This also allows more time for independent writing and independent reading. Textbooks remain important in her classroom, but they are used along with trade books

Bernice Cullinan

Teachers conduct literature discussion groups.

and various other media as one of many resources available to her students. Her planning has changed dramatically. She holds reading as well as writing conferences. Recognizing how important literature is for models of good writing, she moved her read-aloud period to her class's prime time. Read-aloud selections are often based on topics under study in science and social studies. This serves as a significant step in breaking down the subject matter barriers as well.

Shown in Figure 2.1, Marilyn's language arts block has both structure and flexibility. Whole-class time, "on the rug," focuses largely on systematic instruction in reading comprehension, word study skills and strategies, and the conventions of language such as grammar and punctuation. An activity period follows that includes guided reading in small groups and attention to special needs. In addition to the language arts block, Marilyn sets aside time—at least three days each week—for writing workshop, independent reading, and reading aloud.

THE INTERMEDIATE YEARS

Like many teachers in the intermediate grades, Janet Longello was uncertain about her role in teaching reading and writing. Certainly, intermediate-grade students are not the same as primary-grade children. They differ in many ways: age, interests, competencies, sophistication, independence, social concerns, reliance on peers, cognitive reach, and willingness to cooperate. Most intermediate-grade students know the basics of reading and writing, but they rarely read for the sake of showing off a newfound skill. Nor will they write solely for the sake of writing. There must be something inherently interesting in what they read to attract them to reading; they must have a goal in writing beyond demonstrating their skill at writing. At the same time, these students are confronted with challenging texts that require them to deal with new information and difficult concepts and to apply what they have read in a variety of different ways. Writing requires attention to more precise and sometimes subtle uses of language and the development of control over different forms.

With the help of some excellent professional development, Janet's confidence grew. Gradually, during her second year of teaching, she moved toward a more enriched reading program. She would look at the theme of the next unit in the reading program and then pick out trade books on that theme or books by the same author. Janet recalls: "I would use the library books along with the reading program materials. I read them aloud, made them available for independent reading in the classroom, and even sent them along for independent reading at home. To my surprise, both my principal and the reading specialist really liked what I was doing."

FIGURE 2.1

Typical Language Arts Block: Primary Grades

Time	Format	Types of Activities	Instructional Notes
30 minutes	Whole-class (primarily)	*Reading/Writing Aloud:* Teacher models; students observe and respond. *Shared and Interactive Reading & Writing:* Teacher leads; students participate to the extent they can.	Addresses district standards and performance objectives in systematic manner. May involve core literacy program materials, trade books, and content-area materials.
	Direct instruction	*Skills/Strategies Development: Word Study; Written Language Conventions; Handwriting Support* Teacher engages students systematically with support.	Ends with assignment of follow-up activity. These may include: rereading, writing, art, library research, or a follow-up on a specific strategy or skill. May be differentiated to accommodate to different needs.

Approx. 5 minutes — **Planning Time**
Discuss *Who, What, Where, When* for workshop activities.

Time	Format	Types of Activities	Instructional Notes
60 minutes	Small group and one-to-one Direct and indirect instruction	*Teacher-Assisted Acitivities:* Guided reading Direct instruction for special needs Individual conferences	Plan to meet several small groups each day. Allot no more than one-third Activity Time for each small group. Use remaining time for individual conferences and for circulating among students as they work independently. Students experiencing difficulty should meet for small-group or personalized instruction at least three times per week.
	Individuals, pairs, or small groups	*Independent Activities:* Follow-up assignments to whole-class instruction above; Independent reading/writing; Center-based activities; Projects; Computer activities	Establish routines for independent activities. Include short- and long-term tasks.

Janet's language arts block is very similar to Marilyn's, although the time allotments for whole-class instruction and activity time are longer. Both guided reading and literature circles may take place during small-group instruction. Guided reading may involve the use of content-area materials, particularly with those children who need assistance in reading social studies and science texts. In addition to the language arts block, both Marilyn and Janet schedule writing workshops several days each week. They use the framework shown in Figure 2.2.

At the beginning of the year, both Marilyn and Janet begin establishing rules and routines for the writing workshop. Some of the key features they stress include providing a predictable schedule of days and times when writing workshop will be held; establishing a predictable sequence of activities; and establishing the placement, use, and care of writing materials.

Writing workshop is not the only time that writing occurs in these classrooms. Children write during the language arts block and as a part of content-area instruction. Topics and strategies introduced throughout the day are supported and reinforced during writing workshop. Most important perhaps, the structure of the writing workshop makes sense to students. It is purposeful. They know what to expect from their teacher and what is expected of them.

FIGURE 2.2

Writing Workshop Framework

I. Focus Lesson

Generally whole-class instruction. Instruction is focused on a particular aspect of the writing process, such as prewriting, drafting, revision, editing, and publishing; a specific writing strategy, such as audience; elaboration; or specific skills, such as writing conventions, punctuation, and grammar. Time allotments will vary and may be as little as 5 or 10 minutes for early grades to 20 or more minutes for older children.

II. Independent Writing

Students work independently as individuals or they may occasionally collaborate. The teacher circulates among students, conducting conferences with them. Most often topics are self-selected, though at times students may work on similar forms or on topics related to science and social studies themes. Special attention is given to application of the topic discussed during the Focus Lesson.

III. Share Time

Students return to a whole-class setting. Students may volunteer or be selected to share a work in progress, a particular part of a piece that relates to the focus lesson, or a final product.

Bernice Cullinan

Writing workshops are central to language development.

THE MIDDLE SCHOOL YEARS

Teachers in grades 6 through 8 face a unique population, distinct curriculum concerns, and varied school organizational patterns as they plan integrated language arts and literature-based programs. At these grade levels, curriculum planners attempt to provide students with high-quality instruction from subject-matter experts; they establish departmentalized programs in which students receive instruction from a different teacher for each academic subject. They seem to stress subject-area content more than the learning process as they divide the school day into blocks of time in which students move to a new teacher every period, perhaps six or seven times a day. Students must switch their attention to focus on discrete subjects every 40 or 50 minutes. In a traditional program, a typical student schedule may contain math, science, social studies, English, art, music, and physical education. This arrangement creates a situation that causes early adolescents to feel that no teacher or other adult in the school really knows or cares about them, or is available to help them with problems. Their engagement with learning is likely to diminish as they are drawn to interests outside school to seek attention and rewards.

Several years ago, the teachers in Kim Mancino's school opted to work toward a team approach to instruction with block scheduling. The school day had been organized into traditional subject-dominated segments. Kim and her colleagues created a new pattern. Figure 2.3 depicts the plan in which they combined social studies and English.

FIGURE 2.3

Sample Plan: Combined English and Social Studies

Activity	*Group*	*Time Suggestions**
Focus lesson	Whole class	20–25 minutes
Project work and writing in learning logs	Small groups and Individuals	30–45 minutes
Response groups	Small groups	10–15 minutes
Sharing	Whole class	10–15 minutes

*Times will vary.

Kim and her social studies colleague Pat Conley work together to plan language arts and social studies activities around a single unifying theme. For example, when they focus on the American Revolution in social studies, students are grouped roughly by reading ability levels to form literature circles around four historical novels set during the Revolutionary period. One group reads *The Witch of Blackbird Pond* by Elizabeth George Speare, another reads *Johnny Tremain* by Esther Forbes. One group reads *My Brother Sam Is Dead* by James Lincoln Collier and Christopher Collier and another reads *April Morning* by Howard Fast. The students read and respond in literature-response logs either to prompts given by Kim or on their own. They meet regularly in small groups to discuss their reading. Later they write their own historical fiction pieces in which they work hard to meet high standards for accuracy and period authenticity. Pat uses the social studies textbook and a variety of other materials and activities to stress the relevant content of the period.

Kim and her colleagues are delighted with the team teaching arrangement and the extended time frame for language arts in their school. The teachers in Bill Kimble's school, however, opted to maintain the existing program in which students meet for language arts instruction for 45-minute periods daily. Moreover, teachers are urged to focus on test preparation as a major part of their program. This caused Bill to seek some creative ways to build a sense of continuity and coherence to his program. Figure 2.4 outlines the planning sequence he uses. He started by thinking in terms of the entire year. Bill's district is divided into four marking periods of 8–9 weeks each. Bill decided to think thematically about each marking period. He divided each

Joseph Kassick

Students meet regularly to discuss their reading.

into two segments. One focuses on literature and reading comprehension, and the other focuses on written composition. Two weeks of each marking period are devoted to test-taking strategies. For example, Literature/Reading Themes might include studying a memoir or biography. The complementary Writing Theme might involve writing personal narratives, memoirs, or biographies. Students are encouraged to read as writers, responding in logs and discussing the writer's craft. They are also encouraged to write as readers, considering their audience and using writing strategies they have observed and discussed. Bill gives special attention to the comprehension strategies and language conventions listed in the district's standards and performance objectives for seventh grade, simply infusing them into the curriculum where he feels they are most effectively taught. The weeks set aside to address test-taking are devoted to such things as writing to a prompt and answering open-ended questions, as well as other strategies that might be helpful to his students. Bill likes the idea of deliberately spreading this throughout the year and relating it as much as possible to the current work under study. He is concerned that many of his colleagues spend most of the year on test-taking. Others devote as much as 6 weeks prior to the districtwide, standardized test to test-taking strategies.

Each of the teachers described here has worked diligently to address the most important aspects of an effective language arts program—the need for careful planning, strong organization, and consistent classroom management.

FIGURE 2.4

Yearly Plan for Reading/ Language Arts

Departmentalized Middle School Programs
40- to 50-minute periods

I. Divide year into four 8- to 9-week marking periods

II. Plan thematically for each marking period

Weeks 1–3 *Literature/Reading Theme*
Examples: Memoir, adventure novel, historical fiction, nonfiction

Week 4 *Focus on Test-Taking Strategies*
Examples: Responding to open-ended questions; comprehension-monitoring strategies for reading long passages; writing to a prompt; attending to rubrics

Weeks 5–7 *Writing Theme*
Examples: Personal narrative, story or poetry writing, historical fiction, report writing

Week 8 *Focus on Test-Taking Strategies*

III. Select literature for reading focus. Map a plan for introducing strategies for literature study, writing, and test-taking. Plan for a variety of types of assignments: literature response logs; strategy applications for reading and writing; mini writing assignments; long-term writing assignments; group and individual projects.

They realize that poor classroom management can undermine the best of intentions and best attempts at good teaching. When teachers plan various aspects of a supportive instructional environment, they consider a number of things: (1) planning for the emotional, intellectual, and physical aspects of learning in the classroom; (2) selecting and organizing content; (3) selecting and managing materials; (4) managing time; (5) accommodating learner variability; (6) linking instruction and assessment; and (7) coordinating school resources. Although teachers need to think about these elements both separately and as a whole, the learners should be presented with an instructional environment that suggests a unified whole. Specific suggestions for each of these considerations will be offered throughout this book. A brief introduction to each follows.

Establishing a Supportive Classroom Environment

THE SOCIAL AND EMOTIONAL ENVIRONMENT

Organizing for language arts instruction involves many complex tasks. Scheduling time and activities, planning lessons, and grouping students for more personalized instruction are only part of the challenge, however. All of these things should take place in an atmosphere where students feel a sense of community and where they feel free to ask for help and take risks. A classroom that is socially and emotionally supportive has a generally friendly atmosphere. It is a safe and caring place for *all* learners, regardless of their cultural or linguistic backgrounds or their abilities. Students know that learning involves both making mistakes and experiencing success. Strategies that foster a safe emotional climate include establishing classroom rules; being aware of verbal and nonverbal behaviors, such as allowing enough "wait time" for students to respond to questions; organizing diverse small-group instruction; setting up the physical environment so that students can work in small groups and pairs comfortably without disturbing others; planning for student-to-student as well as teacher-to-student interactions (Moye, 1999).

THE INTELLECTUAL ENVIRONMENT

According to Costa (1999):

> The core of our curriculum must focus on such processes as thinking, learning to learn, knowledge production, metacognition, transference of knowledge, decision making, creativity, group problem solving, and knowing how to behave when correct answers are not readily apparent (p. 239).

Costa suggests that the intellectual processes involved as learning takes place *are* the content of the curriculum.

> Curriculum is like a cemetery. It is etched in stone, visited only on special occasions, filled with dead subjects, aligned in straight rows, and is a monument to the past. Furthermore, we keep putting more in and take nothing out! (p. 238).

In an age when the sheer amount of information available on any subject is overwhelming, the ability to frame important questions, use resources efficiently, and think critically with the information available is arguably more important than the ability to accumulate and store factual information to memory. We believe that teachers who teach for thinking throughout the day not only will improve students' competency in the specific areas under study but will also help them become self-reliant, independent thinkers in everything they attempt.

Consider two teachers who take their students on a field trip to the museum. Both teachers engage the children in planning for the trip. However, the first teacher spends most of that time in a discussion of the logistical arrangements regarding time, fees, and travel. Obviously, the second teacher must attend to those things as well. But, time is also spent discussing some of the things that the students are likely to see and do. Museum brochures are used to help frame an anticipatory set for students before they depart. During the trip, the first teacher simply allows students to wander from exhibit to exhibit, touching displays and pressing buttons to hear recorded messages. Teacher number two allows some free exploration as well. However, certain preselected exhibits become the focus of guided viewing and discussion. Through these discussions, the teacher serves as mediator for children's thinking about the displays, helping children focus on particular elements of the display, interpret what they see, and relate it to what they already know. The particular displays or content selected for this kind of attention is far less important than the attention given to developing the underlying thinking processes in which the children engage.

THE PHYSICAL ENVIRONMENT

An enriched physical environment includes opportunities to interact with materials that are intellectually stimulating and provocative, along with opportunities to be quiet and reflective. Depending on the instructional level, such classrooms allow students to work with science and math equipment, art supplies, writing tools for composing, computers and other technologies, and a variety of types of reading materials. Physical groupings of desks and tables encourage both whole-class and small-group work. A quiet, but well-situated place for teacher-pupil conferences offers a bit of solitude with visual access to the remaining students. Signs of projects in progress are obvious to visitors, as are the displays of completed student work. In the upper grades, some of these activities may take place with a specialist in a separate area. However, it is important that the classroom teacher be aware of the nature of the specialized work and encourage displays and discussion regarding that work in the regular classroom.

Providing a Balanced Language Arts Program

Listening, Speaking (Talking), Reading, and Writing have long been considered the key elements of the language arts program. In recent years, an increased awareness of the use and importance of Visual Literacy has led to the inclusion of viewing and visually representing as part of the language arts curriculum (Standards for the English Language Arts, 1996).

Listening is the primary source of language. It is an integral part of all language activities. More time is spent on listening than any other language activity. Through active listening, students gain understanding and appreciation of language and develop their abilities to communicate. Effective listeners are not only capable of restating what they hear, they can also interpret it, respond to it, and evaluate it. Listening instruction involves students in opportunities to listen to language used for a variety of purposes and to use strategies that enable them to monitor their listening comprehension abilities. Expanded discussions of listening can be found in Chapters Four and Five.

Speaking, both formally and informally, is critical to learning the language arts and to learning through the language arts. Talk is used to respond to literature and explore topics of interest and importance to students. It is the key mode of classroom discourse. Students need opportunities to talk for a variety of purposes and in a variety of contexts. These might include class discussions, informal sharing of information, as well as formal presentations, such as reports or panel discussions. Expanded discussions about speaking and talk in the classroom can be found in Chapters Four and Five.

Reading is a complex process in which readers connect with the ideas of others and construct meaning with written text. Readers use a variety of strategies in order to decode and comprehend print. These include the use of sound-symbol relationships, word meanings, and sentence structure. Readers relate their prior knowledge and experiences to what they read, and these influence their understanding. Effective reading instruction involves the use of a variety of experiences with all types of literature with purposeful connections to the other language arts to promote reading comprehension and critical and aesthetic response. Expanded discussions about learning to read and reading instruction can be found in Chapters Six and Seven.

Writing, like reading, is also a complex process. It is used both for personal expression and to communicate with others. Proficient writers understand the recursive nature of various aspects of the writing process: prewriting, drafting, revising, editing, and publishing. They use what they know to make their writing effective. They are capable of writing in a variety of forms and for varied audiences. Effective writing instruction involves students in reading and responding to the writing of others for content and for craft. Effective instruction also involves strategies for clarity, organization, the use of figurative language, as well as attention to appropriate conventions of spelling, grammar, and punctuation. Further information about the writing process can be found in Chapters Eight and Nine.

Viewing is an important part of students' language arts experience. Effective viewing involves the ability to comprehend and respond to visual messages of both print and nonprint media. Daily language and literacy experiences in today's classrooms involve both traditional print media such as graphs, charts, diagrams, illustrations, and photographs as well as electronic media such as CD-ROMS and the Internet. Many of these will be used in combination with each other and with the other language arts. Today's students need to demonstrate ability to gain and use information from a variety of media. Effective instruction in viewing involves students in using and responding critically to visual information in films, presentations, observations, and other visual media and making use of that information for personal use or to report to others through speaking, writing, or visual representations. Suggestions for including viewing as an integral component in learning and teaching the language arts are made throughout this text. For example, spe-

Joseph Kassick

Having access to a variety of media enriches a learner's understanding.

cific suggestions for the use of technology are included in many chapters. Strategies for using nonprint media in conjunction with reading and writing are included in Chapters Six through Nine.

Visually representing is highly related to viewing and to the other language arts. Students use a variety of media to express their ideas and share information, including effective visual representations in combination with talk and writing. Charts, graphs, diagrams, and pictorial means may be used to convey information. Electronic media may be used in conjunction with traditional representations. When creating visual representations, many of the elements of good written composition, such as purpose, audience, and clarity, must be attended to. Students often create visual representations as group projects for sharing research or projects of various types. Throughout this book, we give examples that show how visual representations can be used by students and teachers for learning and teaching. Figure 2.5 offers an example of how visual representation might be included in a social studies unit of study. Creating maps and diagrams helps students depict a particular period and establish a sense of time and place.

Obviously, no aspect of the language arts stands alone either in learning or in teaching. Listening, speaking, reading, writing, viewing, and visually representing are interrelated and interdependent. That is, what students learn through listening they use for speaking, reading, writing, viewing, and representing and so on. Good teaching capitalizes on this. Although teachers may focus on one aspect of the language arts at a time, they deliberately plan for the integration of all the language arts in supportive ways. Effective teachers also know that the language arts are processes and that they require

FIGURE 2.5

Maps and Diagrams as Visual Representation

Maps and diagrams are key means of communicating through visual representation. These may be part of a response to literature, where students draw a map of the location of the story as they visualize it in their minds. This is a great group project. Various groups can work from the same book or story and then compare their conceptualizations. Include the creation of maps and diagrams in thematic study as well. Diagrams that show various plants, animals, or objects related to science and social studies themes allow children to think through how they might represent the ideas so that others can grasp what they are attempting to depict and learn from it.

content and literature experiences that are pertinent and engaging, so that students will apply what they know and extend it to new understandings.

KEY EXPERIENCES FOR LANGUAGE ARTS LEARNING AND TEACHING

During the kindergarten-primary years, a number of language- and literacy-related experiences are standard daily fare in most classrooms. These include

FIGURE 2.6

Framework for Language and Literacy Experiences: Teacher-Directed Activities

Reading/Writing Aloud involves activities in which the teacher models reading and writing processes; students observe, listen, and respond.

Materials Primarily literature (trade or library books); chart paper, chalkboards, or whiteboards

Purposes

- ✦ To stretch students' experiential and literary backgrounds, expand vocabulary, and develop concepts
- ✦ To expose students to varied literary forms: fiction, nonfiction, poetry
- ✦ To enlist varied forms of response, including discussion, drawing/writing, drama, art, and music/movement
- ✦ To expose children to various genres, literary devices, and the crafts of writing and illustrating
- ✦ To expose children to various purposes for reading and writing

Shared and Interactive Reading/Writing involves child participation in acts of reading and writing led by the teacher.

Materials Enlarged texts, such as big books, literature trade books, and content materials (books and charts) for reading; white boards, chart paper, and chalkboards for writing

Purposes

- ✦ To demonstrate/support concepts about print
- ✦ To support comprehension and interpretation
- ✦ To emphasize textual features
- ✦ To provide opportunities for children to apply what they know about reading, writing, phonics, and spelling

reading aloud and **writing aloud;** assisted reading and writing, which may include **shared** and **interactive reading** and **writing; guided reading; word study; independent reading** and **writing;** and **sharing.** Figure 2.6 describes these activities, their purposes, and the materials teachers generally use. It is important to note that all of these activities involve literature in some way and that all relate to interesting content under study.

As students move up through the grades, many of these activities continue, although some may take different forms. For example, teachers

Word Study involves activities that call children's attention to the sounds within words (phonemic awareness); letter and word recognition; and sound-letter relationships.

Materials Name cards, letters, charts, enlarged texts, listening activities for phonemic awareness

Purposes

- ✦ To develop sight vocabulary through environmental print
- ✦ To develop sight vocabulary through the use of students' names
- ✦ To promote phonemic awareness
- ✦ To foster understanding of the alphabetic principle, phonics, and structural analysis

Guided Reading involves small-group instruction with materials geared to learners' reading levels. It usually starts at the kindergarten level with children who demonstrate they are ready.

Materials Primarily core-program materials or sets of leveled trade books

Purposes

- ✦ To monitor specific strategies/skills in a highly focused manner
- ✦ To provide instruction as close as possible to students' instructional levels, gradually increasing difficulty

Independent Reading and Writing

Materials Primarily fiction and nonfiction trade books and leveled books for reading, writing utensils, paper for composing

Purposes

- ✦ To provide time for child to re-enact/practice book experiences and writing experiences
- ✦ To allow children to self-select materials and topics, assume control, and gain independence

Sharing

Materials May involve materials used during Independent Reading and Writing. Students may read aloud selected portions or all of what they have read or written, then entertain questions and comments from the group.

Purposes

- ✦ To provide time for children to recall and share information of common interest to the group
- ✦ To promote oral expression

continue to read aloud to students regardless of the grade level they teach. Informal sharing in literature circles starts early and continues throughout the grades, although teachers typically structure the experience differently with older children. Other types of sharing may become more formal in the upper grades, as students report on projects and incorporate visual representations with their oral and written reports. Word study, independent reading and writing, and sharing also continue throughout the grades. During the intermediate- and middle-grade years, however, word study is likely to focus on common spelling errors or on analyzing the origins of our language. Writing aloud also continues throughout the grades as teachers demonstrate various aspects or forms of writing as they "think aloud" the mental processes going on in their heads as they write.

Managing Time

Issues related to time and time management are among the concerns most often raised by teachers, whether they are experienced or new to the field. Surely, the song "So Little Time and So Much to Do" was written for teachers. At the beginning of this chapter, we shared the ways some teachers at various levels addressed issues of time management in order to provide their students with a variety of language and literacy experiences. Figure 2.6 further outlines what the variety of experiences might include. Reflecting on the ways the teachers described earlier go about their planning reveals a mix of components organized into a unified whole. Not only do they connect the amount of time they have to the various experiences they need to provide, they offer a variety of instructional grouping patterns in order to provide more tailored instruction for every child. Organizing in this way is often called flexible grouping and involves a number of considerations:

- *Teacher/child ratio.* There should be a balance of whole-class, small-group, and individual instruction.
- *Group constituency.* Children should have opportunities to work in both homogeneous groups, where students are working with others at levels similar to their own, as in guided reading, and in heterogeneous groups, where ability levels differ.
- *Special needs.* Students who are experiencing difficulty in the same area may be grouped for extra assistance. The same might be true for those who are advanced and who would benefit from a particular focus that the others are not quite ready for.
- *Teacher guidance.* There should be a balance of direct and indirect instruction. Both require a planned and predetermined structure put in place by the teacher, and both are important.

- *Duration.* Flexible grouping is dynamic. Guided reading groups tend to be longer term than others, though students move in and out of guided reading groups as the need arises. Other groups, such as literature-response groups, may be relatively short term but keep the same membership throughout.

One of the most critical aspects of flexible grouping is the need for every child to be on task virtually all of the time. In order for this to occur, we stress the need for careful planning of both the direct instruction activities offered as well as students' independent activities. At the primary-grade level, teachers often make use of centers as a part of the independent activities in which students engage while they work with small groups. Students may rotate through the centers in a manner scheduled by the teacher. Or, they may simply opt for the center they would like to visit on a given day. In either case, it is important to have a system in place so that students have a clear sense of what they are expected to do at the center and the "rules of behavior" by which they are expected to abide. Independent work should never become "down time," where students engage in inconsequential activities. Independent work involves teacher planning and structure. The result should be a productive time for applying and extending skills and strategies. Figure 2.7 lists some literacy learning centers that can be easily set up and managed for use in the elementary grades. Other activities that teachers frequently offer as possibilities for independent work include assigned follow-up activities to whole-class instruction; independent reading; independent writing; library research; and independent work on theme-based activities in science and social studies.

Joseph Kassick

Providing teacher guidance is an important consideration in managing time.

ity; and encourage teachers to build on diversity rather than attempt to eradicate it.

Student variability not only extends across groups, it is found within groups and even within individuals. Six-year-old Jonelle is not interested in reading on her own, but she loves to paint and draw. Often her drawings will contain words and brief sentences that serve as captions for her work. Jonelle participates fully in the shared reading experiences of her first grade class, but her enthusiasm for writing far surpasses her interest in reading. Jonelle's literacy development is progressing nicely, but it is complex and uneven.

For the past six months, Suresh, a seventh-grader, seems almost fixated on motorcycles. His uncle owns a motorcycle, and Suresh has had an opportunity to ride on it. He reads his uncle's magazines on the topic and visits the Internet to learn about various models. He has also taken out every book he can find in the library dealing with motorcycles. His teacher has insisted that he read in other genres and about other topics, even though she knows that Suresh's independent reading far surpasses his assigned reading in complexity and challenge.

So far, the suggestions offered in this chapter refer primarily to variability in students' abilities, interests, and motivation. Planning a program that offers varied opportunities to learn within a predictable structure is key to meeting these kinds of diverse needs. Still, other kinds of variability may be more challenging to teachers who are truly interested in dealing with diversity. For example, planning and organizing a language arts program that honors cultural and linguistic differences may pose unfamiliar problems to teachers who are not prepared.

The students in Jane Hamburg's second grade class range from those who are just emerging as readers and writers to those who are as adept at literacy as many fourth- and fifth-graders. During her 10-year teaching career, Jane has been challenged by students with severe hearing loss, learning disabilities, and various other physical and emotional problems. She has also worked with students who were extraordinarily capable in particular areas, such as literacy, math, or music. In addition to the variability in their talents and intellectual abilities, Jane's students are diverse in their interests, their cultural and economic backgrounds, and their approach to literacy learning. Jane's encounters with diversity go well beyond her classroom. Over the past 10 years she has observed the school population in her small Midwestern town change radically. Her town, once primarily composed of families with Northern European backgrounds, has experienced an influx of immigrants from Southeast Asia and South America. Most of the newcomers have come to work in low-level jobs in industry and farming. Jane is keenly aware that these children and their families are struggling to survive in a new country with marginal economic support and seemingly endless adjustments to make in language and customs.

Fortunately, Jane and her colleagues have taken a welcoming and enlightened view of these newcomers. Starting with the obvious premise that teachers have always dealt with differences of one sort or another, these kindergarten and primary-grade teachers used ideas such as the ones that follow to build on diversity and foster a sense of community and sharing. The ideas center on making home-school connections, valuing and building on cultural and linguistic diversity, and meeting special needs. Chapter Four contains a variety of suggestions for dealing with cultural and linguistic diversity. Foremost among them is the need to organize the language arts program in order to build bridges between home and school. Following are some of the ways teachers and administrators have capitalized on cultural and linguistic diversity in programmatic ways in both the classroom and throughout the school.

In some districts, educators have reorganized the structure of the school and the nature of how the home and school connect. One such example is the family room. In some schools, a family room has been established as a place where parents who have free time during the day may congregate while their children are in class. Here, parents are encouraged to socialize with one another, browse through materials that might be of interest, participate in English as a Second Language (ESL) classes, and learn about or participate in school and community activities related to the education, recreation, and health of their families. In Jane Hamburg's school, a sewing machine was donated and placed in the family room for parents to use if they wished.

A popular activity in one school's family room is the coupon exchange (Strickland, 1991). Here parents look through the available supermarket coupons, taking those they can use and leaving for others those they cannot. The family room often serves as a means of helping parents of different backgrounds feel comfortable with each other and with the school. Newcomers to a community may use this as a first step toward visiting in the classrooms as observers or helpers.

Not only is the family room important in helping parents become familiar with the school and community, it also provides an excellent means for school faculties to learn about families and their needs and expectations of the school. Throughout the year, the teachers in Jane Hamburg's school take turns covering each other's classrooms for brief periods in order to visit with parents in the family room. These very informal 15-minute coffee sessions help establish a sense of friendliness and respect between parents and teachers. Jane and her colleagues are well aware that acculturation works both ways. They have much to learn from these parents, who, they continue to discover, have numerous talents and interests that can be useful instructionally. Most important, the parents hold expert knowledge about their own children. The exchange of knowledge and ideas between parent and teacher has become a key resource for providing the best learning opportunities possible.

Managing Materials in the Language Arts Classroom

A print-rich classroom is a key component of a strong language arts program. Studies of the home and school environments of young children confirm the need to provide children with environments that are rich in books and other materials to read and talk about (Snow, Burns, & Griffin, 1998). We believe that this same need continues throughout the grades. All children deserve access to a variety of materials that will spark their interests and stimulate reading, writing, and further study. In self-contained classrooms, a print-rich environment will consist of the following:

1. *Functional environmental print throughout the classroom.* This includes charts that help track schedules, routines, and jobs; messages generated by the teacher and students; and print such as directions and reminders associated with activity areas. Lists and labels are an important part of functional print if they are ones that the teacher and students use in the course of their work.

2. *A variety of reading materials and stimuli for reading.* This includes a well-stocked library of books, rotated according to themes under study and student interests.

3. *A variety of stimuli to encourage student writing.* This includes a writing center equipped with paper and utensils for writing, blank books, an easily visible alphabet chart, and a word wall nearby with lists of frequently used words.

4. *Displays of student work.* These should be easily accessible to students for independent browsing and reading on their own. Much of the functional print mentioned above might also be generated by students.

Stocking and managing library resources is a key element of what classroom teachers do. In the best of all possible worlds, there would be three sources of library materials for which teachers would have some responsibility or access: the classroom library, the school library, and the public library. (The *Teaching Idea: Making Use of Technology* gives you some ideas on how to manage these all-important resources effectively.) In addition, we would hope that every child would have a personal collection of reading materials at home. Most teachers have considerable control over the books ordered as trade or library books for classroom use. Most teachers also consult to some

Bernice Cullinan

Books are an indispensable part of a classroom.

extent with library media specialists so that books are ordered for the school library that coincide with themes they intend to teach.

For young children, teachers need to continually add to their supply of picture books for reading aloud, concept books (alphabet, numbers, and so on), and nursery rhyme books. Some of these will be enlarged texts (big books); others will be regular-sized picture books. At all levels, informational books, story books, folktales, poetry, series books, and multiple books by the same author or on the same topic should be available. Of course, many "little books" should be available to beginning readers. These are often leveled so that teachers can more easily match books to students. Even at the first grade level, however, some children are ready to move into simple chapter books and novels. These should be available to them along with a wide range of other materials such as magazines and reference materials. Books should be attractively arranged and housed in areas that make them easily accessible to students. Many teachers like to place the library center near the writing center, so that reference materials and other reading resources are readily available. The computers may also be located in this cluster of centers. Throughout this book we discuss the use of these materials in the curriculum. One key to effective management of materials is to put a system in place that

TEACHING IDEA

Making Use of Technology

PERSONAL CHILDREN'S LITERATURE DATABASE

One way to enrich your literature program is to set up a personalized children's literature database. Each time you preview a book for your students, take a minute and add information about the book to your database. An initial investment of time in designing this database will save large amounts of time in the future when you plan literature activities, and will usually result in a better experience for your students.

The Title, Author, and Illustrator fields are obvious to include. The Library field helps pinpoint the source of the book. Is the book from your personal collection, or did you get it from the public library? The Genre field is useful when looking for books written from a particular literary style.

The Category fields provide additional information about the book. For the book *Tikki-Tikki-Tembo* by Arlene Mosel, for example, Categories 1, 2, and 3 might contain *siblings, China,* and *senior citizens,* respectively. Remember that a database can be revised and enhanced without losing information. One possible revision to this database is a field to record the date at which a particular book was most recently read aloud to your class: Did you read *Tikki-Tikki-Tembo* to the class this year?

is easily understood by students and for which they share the responsibility for the wise use and management of the materials with their classroom community of learners.

Organizing for Thematic Instruction

Teaching through themes is an excellent way to capture children's excitement and enthusiasm for learning while helping them develop the necessary strategies for becoming independent learners. Both content and literary themes support children's language and literacy development, but they do it in different ways. Teaching through content themes provides strong contextual support for second-language learners. Allen (1986) contrasted the ways young, second-language learners used language as they responded to literature with those used as they worked together on a science project. The literary theme supported narration and discussion. It drew out large cohesive blocks of language as children retold stories, created their own written or oral narratives, or discussed books. The science exploration provided opportunities for children to describe precisely, and to record and share observations. It developed vocabulary in very concrete and precise ways. Teachers need to be aware of the benefits of both literary and content themes and to provide a balance of both. Creating opportunities to talk is not sufficient. The linguistic demands and opportunities of the learning tasks must be considered.

A model well suited to organizing language and literacy activities around themes is described in Figure 2.8. Its curriculum framework can be used by teachers in the kindergarten and primary grades to plan and carry out a unit of study that centers on a content theme of interest to young children. The framework helps teachers integrate the topic under study with listening, speaking, reading, and writing. Each day is planned so that children are engaged in inquiry activities that require oral language and problem solving, shared reading and writing, independent reading and writing, read-alouds and response to literature, and sharing. All or most of these would be related in some way to the topic being studied.

Figure 2.9 shows a web depicting how Lisa Harrosh Horst, a teacher of young children, developed the theme "Weather Watch," using this curriculum framework. Note how Lisa plans for both **content objectives**—what she wants children to know as a result of the unit of study—and **process objectives**—what she wants children to be better able to do as a result of the unit of study. With modest adjustments, this plan can be used by teachers who work with kindergarten or primary-grade children. The overall quality and complexity of the children's responses will vary, of course, but this is as much a function of their interests and abilities as it is of their age and grade level. By its very nature, a plan such as this one allows for variability within the group. The activities are designed to allow all children to participate at the level most appropriate to them. Figure 2.10 offers a suggestion about how to involve the home in thematic study.

Integrating social studies and language arts in the intermediate grades presents some special challenges. Although teachers who teach in self-contained classrooms have few constraints on combining subject-area studies, those who teach language arts in departmentalized programs need to work collaboratively to develop an integrated plan. Social studies and language arts are a natural place to begin. Students become better readers as they read about social studies issues in a variety of fiction and informational trade books as well as textbooks. They become better writers as they write about social studies issues and content. Teaching teams that include language arts teachers, social studies teachers, and library media specialists plan exciting

FIGURE 2.8

A Model for Organizing Theme-Based Language and Literacy Activities for Young Children

Element	Activities	Purpose/Intent
Inquiry	First-hand experiences Discussion Problem solving	Exploring concrete phenomena. Thinking, talking, and manipulating materials to learn what things mean, how they work, and why things are the way they are.
Sharing	Oral presentation Audience response	Having opportunities to practice making their personal ideas and experiences understood by others through oral language.
Reading aloud and response	Litening and responding to literature Participation during reading	Listening to and responding to literature through discussion, art, dramatics, and story retelling.
Shared reading and writing	Chart development Text analysis Group reading/rereading	Assisting adults in composing text (language charts), reading it (group-assisted reading), and analyzing it for patterns (letters, words, other textual features).
Independent writing	Drawing/writing Personal conferences	Having access to writing materials and opportunities to express ideas through drawing and writing as a communicative process.
Independent reading	Self-selection Reading and reading-like behavior	Having access to storybooks and informational books and opportunities to approximate reading and reading-like behaviors such as browsing through books, page turning, discussing pictures, and participating in oral recall of text that has been read aloud.

and valuable programs. The following scenario of an integrated day suggests ways to use an expanded time period.

Susan Jacobs, a sixth grade teacher in a departmentalized program, works with her colleague, Mark Jackson, in a combined language arts and social studies block lasting 110 minutes daily. For each theme, Mark and Susan begin by sharing their goals for student outcomes. Mark focuses primarily on the content knowledge he wants students to learn as a result of the

FIGURE 2.9

Theme Web: "Weather Watch"

Inquiry Activities:

- Observe and describe daily weather; pick one label to post.
- Make rain containers; set out to measure rainfall.
- Blind walk; discuss how the weather felt and sounded.
- Take walk on windy day; bring streamers/kites.
- Center: sorting photos of, or actual clothing items for, appropriate weather.

Shared Reading and Writing:

- List words that describe how a particular day looks, feels, and sounds.
- Chart each child's measured collection of rainfall for a day.
- Chart daily weather (1 of 4 choices) and tally up monthly.
- Poem—"So Long as There's Weather," Tamara Kitt

Sharing:

- Personal drawings/writings about weather.
- Experiences in different kinds of weather.
- Favorite weather poem/story.
- Feelings/moods related to weather.
- Favorite article of clothing for a specific kind of weather.

WEATHER WATCH
A theme aimed at helping children to become more aware of the daily weather.

Independent Writing:

- Group/class book with a weather description as the setting/starter.
- Rainfall logs/weather journals.
- Draw/write stories about weather.
- Read *Many Luscious Lollipops* by Ruth Heller. Share and discuss the role of descriptive language in writing.

Read Aloud and Response:

- *Frederick* by L. Lionni. After reading the book, children draw/write about what they'd bring to the cave to help get through winter. Dramatize.
- *Bringing the Rain to Kapiti Plain* by V. Aardema. Discuss drought/why we need water to survive.
- *Hurricane Watch* by F. Branley. Discuss wind damages; move like wind to music or taped sounds of wind/storms.

Independent Reading:

- *Cloudy with a Chance of Meatballs.* B. Barrett
- *Gilberto and the Wind.* M. H. Ets
- *Snowy Day.* E. J. Keats
- *Toad Is the Uncle of Heaven.* J. M. Lee
- *Rain.* P. Spier
- *Brave Irene.* W. Steig
- *Hide and Seek Fog.* A. Tresselt
- *Rainbow* Crow. N. Van Laan

FIGURE 2.10

Connecting Home and School through Thematic Instruction

Involve the home in your theme-based instruction by alerting parents of your plans at the time you introduce the unit under study. Keeping parents informed in this way can lessen their desire for work sheets as a means of informing them of what children are doing in school and also as a means of involving children in "homework." Use the following format:

> Dear Parents,
> Our class has just begun the study of [topic name]. We will learn [goals/purposes]. Our activities will include [list a few, such as trips, experiments, other activities].
>
> Here are some suggestions for exploring these ideas at home: [list a few general, easy-to-do activities and books to share]. There are many other books on this topic that you can obtain from the library. Please encourage your child to share with us what you do together. We are eager to learn and share as much as we can about [topic name], both at home and at school.
>
> Thank you,

unit. Susan's focus, on the other hand, is on process. She shares the language arts strategies she plans to teach or strengthen through the content under study.

On most days, Mark begins with a class discussion of some aspect of the topic under study. This is often followed by a strategy lesson related to reading, research strategies, writing, or study skills. The strategy lessons are conducted by Susan and always make use of examples from the content under study. A brief planning period follows during which students assess where they are in various projects and research activities, and assignments may be given or adjusted. An extensive period of immersion in reading, writing, listening, and speaking activities follows, during which both teachers meet with small groups and individuals to guide their work. Approximately 15–20 minutes are provided at the end of the session for sharing. Figure 2.11 outlines the schedule they follow.

For example, during a study of the American Revolution similar to that of teachers Kim Mancino and Pat Conley earlier in this chapter, Mark and Susan work with the library media specialist to assemble a collection of

FIGURE 2.7

Literacy Learning Centers in the Classroom

Literacy learning centers (LLCs) include any centers that involve literacy in some way. For example:

- **Reading:** Wide assortment of reading materials (some theme related) and class books
- **Publishing:** Writing materials, blank books, alphabet charts, dictionaries, thesauruses, and other writing tools
- **Listening:** Taped books with print versions, head sets and tape player
- **Theme-based** (or Inquiry): Books, activities, and task cards related to themes under study
- **Computer:** Easy games and word processing opportunities
- **Work With Words** (3W): Devoted exclusively to letter and word study activities, such as matching, sorting, creating word banks, word family games
- **Math:** Concrete materials for manipulation, opportunities to read and write as children count, compare, and solve problems

Some Things to Remember about Incorporating LLCs in Your Classroom

- Introduce each center separately over a period of time.
- Model the use of the center.
- Effective centers include clear, easy-to-follow directions for use, choice, multilevel activities, an easy "check-up" system where appropriate.

Accommodating Learner Variability

Teachers constantly deal with a multitude of student variables. Even teachers in settings where children are grouped homogeneously are well aware that although their students may appear to be similar in some ways, they are a diverse group nevertheless. Grouping methods based on a single criterion, such as the scores on a standardized test, fail to account for a range of factors that cause students to vary from one another. Students who test similarly on a reading test, for example, may vary widely in their interests, motivation, and background knowledge. For that reason, many schools prefer to group students heterogeneously. By grouping heterogeneously, schools avert a system of tracking students at an early age, which frequently relegates less able students to a low-level school career; avoid the delusion of homogene-

FIGURE 2.11

Integrated Social Studies/Language Arts Workshop

Activity	Grouping	Approximate Time
Content instruction and strategy lessons	Whole class	30 minutes
Status reports and planning	Whole class or small group	15 minutes
Project work	Small groups or individuals	45 minutes
Sharing time	Whole class	20 minutes

historical fiction, informational books, poetry, films, CD-ROMs, videos, and reference books into the classroom for a 6-week loan. Fiction and nonfiction tape recordings of great American orators as well as material read aloud by Susan and Mark are used to impart content and to focus on listening comprehension strategies.

After an overview of the historical period and a great deal of background information obtained from books, CDs, videos, and films, the students are encouraged to form collaborative learning groups in order to focus on a particular event or person. The groups explore their topic through computer information networks and library research. They read widely, interview knowledgeable people, write letters to request information, view films, listen to recorded reenactments of speeches, and take field trips.

The students who choose James Madison, for example, read Jean Fritz's book, *The Great Little Madison*. They also read from several encyclopedias, textbooks, and other biographies about Madison. They make notes as they read and compile a time line to visually represent the time frame covered by Madison's life. They choose an innovative way to present their findings to the total group; they role-play three scenes from Madison's life. Using a combination of Readers' Theatre and role playing, the group depicts one scene from Madison's early life when he was a small, pale, sickly boy; another scene features his appearance at the Continental Congress where it becomes clear he is not a great orator; and the third shows him calling on Dolley Payne, who later becomes his wife. Students taking the various roles sometimes read their scripts and sometimes memorize the characters' words. Simple props and bits of costumes enhance their presentation. The girl who plays Dolley Madison wears a lace scarf, a wide-brimmed hat, and white gloves. She tries to portray Dolley Madison as Jean Fritz characterizes her—"born to shop."

Throughout the unit, Susan and Mark meet to plan and assess the learning that is taking place. Obviously, Mark's primary concern is whether or not students are gaining content knowledge. Susan focuses on the language arts processes students use to gain and share that knowledge. However, they both observe and make suggestions regarding both content and process. The two feel confident that they are providing a rich, supportive environment for their students. The longer time frame allows more time for students to read, write, think, and reflect in class. Although homework assignments are given, they are grateful for the extended time that integrated instruction provides for guided instruction in the classroom. This is particularly true for those students who rarely complete homework assignments or do them satisfactorily. Susan and Mark say that several principles guide the way they work. First, it is important to become very familiar with each other's goals, so that both team members can help follow through with small groups and individuals. Second, by modeling new strategies for students, they not only help the students but they also help their teammate to understand what is expected. Third, informal, ongoing evaluation helps them work together to adjust their plans according to student needs and take advantage of unanticipated learning opportunities.

SUMMARY

Many factors under the control of the language arts teacher affect children's learning. Effective teachers understand the importance of establishing a vital and supportive community of learners in a comfortable and welcoming physical setting to make children feel at home at school. They forge strong ties with parents, knowing that these connections are key to the intellectual and emotional growth of children. They form strong ties with their colleagues, knowing that shared planning and collaboration will result in more integration of the language arts across the curriculum and throughout the year.

The classrooms described in this chapter are characterized by the creation of a dynamic, interactive atmosphere with a view toward helping children become highly motivated, independent learners. The teachers capitalize on diversity, using many different strategies to ensure that all their students are reaching their potential. They give children a voice in how the classroom is organized, in what they will be studying, and in setting the rules that govern the interactions of all members of the learning community.

ACTIVITIES

1. **Visit two or three elementary classrooms.** How is each classroom organized? What is the physical environment like in each? Map the physical space of the classroom you think has the best setup for encouraging and accommodating children's learning.
2. **After spending time in each classroom, determine which has the most emotionally supportive environment.** How does the teacher foster positive interactions with and between children? Write down examples of what the teacher says to the class or individual children that you feel are encouraging or supportive as well as any examples of children positively supporting each other.
3. **Interview three teachers of early primary-grade students to see if they have found innovative ways to move toward a more integrated day while addressing the time requirements imposed by many state boards of education.** Find out whether or not the state in which they teach has specific time requirements for various subjects at their grade levels. Ask how this influences the way they schedule. If they are attempting to integrate the language arts and teach thematically, how do they account for the time requirements?

FURTHER READING

Peterson, R. (1992). *Life in a crowded place: Making a learning community.* Portsmouth, NH: Heinemann.

Graves, D. H. (1999). *Bring life into learning: Create a lasting literacy.* Portsmouth, NH: Heinemann.

Morrow, L. M. (2002). *Organizing and managing the language arts block: A professional development guide.* New York: Guilford.

REFERENCES

Allen, V. (1986). Developing contexts to support second language acquisition. *Language Arts, 63,* 61–66.

Costa, A. L. (1999). Mediative environments: Creating conditions for intellectual growth. In B. Z. Presseisen (Ed.), *Teaching for intelligence* (pp. 229–243). Arlington Heights, IL: SkyLight Publishers.

Kamil, M. L., Manning, J. B., Walberg, H. (2002). *Successful reading instruction.* Greenwich, CT: Information Age Publishing.

Morrow, L. M. (2002). *The literacy center, 2nd ed.* Portland, ME: Stenhouse.

Moye, V. H. (1999). Conditions that support transfer for change. In B. Z. Presseisen (Ed.), *Teaching for intelligence* (pp. 171–178). Arlington Heights, IL: SkyLight Publishers.

Risko, V. J., & Bromley, K. (2001). Collaboration for diverse learners: Viewpoints and practices. Newark, DE: International Reading Association.

Snow, C., Burns, M. S., & Griffin, P. (Eds.) (1998). *Preventing reading difficulties in young children.* Washington, D.C.: National Academy Press.

Standards for the English language arts. (1996). Urbana, IL: National Council of Teachers of English and the International Reading Association.

Strickland, D. (1991). Making connections: Home and school. *Teachers networking: The whole language newsletter, 10*(4), 8–11.

CHILDREN'S LITERATURE REFERENCES

Collier, J. L., & Collier, C. (1974). *My brother Sam is dead.* New York: Macmillan.

Fast, H. (1961). *April morning.* New York: Crown.

Forbes, E. (1969). *Johnny Tremain.* New York: Dell.

Fritz, J. (1989). *The great little Madison.* New York: Putnam.

Speare, E. G. (1958). *The witch of Blackbird Pond.* Boston: Houghton.

The Role of Literature in Language Arts Learning and Teaching

CHAPTER OUTLINE

Key Standard

Effective teachers use a variety of literature throughout the curriculum to encourage students to appreciate the written word, inspire them to use interesting language in their own writing, and motivate them to love literature. Such teachers:

- Use literature to create learner-centered classrooms that motivate students to read, write, speak, listen, and develop a life-long interest in reading and books.
- Are knowledgeable about books and other literature for children and the ways to foster appreciation for the written word.
- Employ strategies that increase the motivation of learners to read widely and independently for information, pleasure, and personal growth.
- Provide opportunities for creative and personal response to literature.
- Provide experiences with a wide variety of literature throughout the curriculum.

To get a preview of Chapter 3 and learn about using literature in the classroom, visit the Chapter 3 section of the accompanying *Language Arts* CD-ROM.

It's September, and Judy's fifth grade students are beginning their language arts/social studies curriculum by reading Michael Dorris's Morning Girl *as a class. Judy reads the first few chapters aloud, talking with them about how the point of view alternates between Morning Girl and her brother, Star Boy. The class is also reading and comparing biographies of Christopher Columbus, and contrasting the attitude toward European exploration contained in their history text and in books such as Betsy & Guilio Maestro's* The Discovery of the Americas *and Jane Yolen's* Encounter. *All of this reading relates to the overarching theme for the year—that one's perspective influences the way history is created and passed on.*

Just down the hall, Karen's first grade class is beginning their year-long study of the earth's ecosystems. The overarching theme for their language arts/social studies/science integrated unit is interdependence. They are busy learning to read and write during guided reading time and writing workshop, but they spend quite a bit of time reading and researching their science topics and poring over maps of the world.

In yet another classroom, Terry's third grade students are "reading up a storm." Terry reads aloud several times every day, has a large classroom library for children to browse in, and gives them about 20 minutes each morning for quiet, independent reading. This time will lengthen as the year progresses. She also works with guided reading groups, conducts writing workshops, and teaches all of the other curriculum areas for which she is responsible.

All three of these teachers are literature-based teachers of the English language arts. They use children's literature to create motivating, student-centered classrooms. They know a lot about children's literature and about teaching language arts and other curricular areas. They offer their students interesting books to read, important questions to ponder, and time in which to do both. Yet each structures her curriculum a bit differently, capitalizing on the requirements of the particular grade level she teaches, the interests and abilities of her students, and her own strengths and interests. These three teachers meet the standard for effective teachers by using literature as a key component of their curriculum—they just do so in different ways.

Language arts and literature go together naturally. **Children's literature,** often called trade books or library books, contains the stories, poems, and information that motivate children to read for the pure joy and exhilaration of it. Children's literature, written for the pleasure and enlightenment of children, offers students ideas to ponder and discuss and models with which to experiment in their own writing. Good books offer readers the opportunity to experience new worlds, ideas, and emotions as well as to validate their own experiences, ideas, and emotions. Literature is an essential part of learning to read and write, being motivated to learn, and becoming literate, critical thinkers (Neuman, Celano, Greco, & Shue, 2001).

The Benefits of a Literature-Based Language Arts Curriculum

The pleasure that readers get from being captivated by a good book may be obvious, but they also gain many other benefits. These benefits are listed in Figure 3.1.

Teachers who have implemented a literature-based program in their schools report some of these benefits; others have been documented by a variety of studies of reading and writing achievement.

Literature enriches children's oral and written language facility. Literary language is much richer in syntax and vocabulary than spoken language or the simplified language found in controlled vocabulary texts. Further, reading literature increases vocabulary tremendously. Children in grades 3–12, for example, learn the meanings of about 3,000 new words a year. Although some of these words are taught in school, direct instruction can account for only a modest proportion. Beyond third grade, children acquire the majority of the new words they learn while reading.

FIGURE 3.1

Benefits of a Literature-Based Curriculum

- Increased fluency in reading
- Better reading comprehension
- Increased vocabulary
- More experience with more and better literature
- Enhanced depth and breadth of response
- Development of literary understanding
- Development of the concept of story
- Development of the concept of author
- Oral language enhancement
- Increased fluency in writing
- Increased options for writing
- Increased motivation to read

In books, children discover words or a turn of phrase they may never hear spoken. As they read, children add the words of literature to their storehouse of language possibilities from which they draw as they speak and write. Because quality literature contains wonderful writing, children who read literature are exposed to a variety of exemplary writing styles. Readers become sensitive to styles as they read, and their own writing reflects this.

Literature contains a wide variety of structures for telling stories, expressing emotions poetically, and presenting information. Sampling a wide variety of quality literature gives young readers a basic understanding of story structures, poetic forms, and informational structures that enables them to approach new texts with an organizational scheme. Having well-formed expectations about the structure of what they are reading helps children comprehend what they read and effectively organize what they write. Once a certain level of fluency in writing is attained, it is the number and quality of books that students read that influences their subsequent development as writers.

Literature enhances reading fluency, providing practice in reading, which, in turn, leads to fluency. The National Assessment of Educational Progress has shown repeatedly that students who read most, read best. People get better at doing what they practice. Avid readers read continuously and are usually good readers. Intriguing books help struggling readers enter this cycle.

Literature is written with a certain style and grace so that words fall trippingly from the tongue. Many books for very young children use "predictable" language that a young reader can master because the next words to appear sound natural or rhyme. Readers can predict the next sentence

Teachers organize books in ways that help students understand the categories.

because the writer has established a pattern to follow. These patterns, and those that appear in books for more skilled readers, are based on meaning and form rather than on artificial notions of what is difficult or easy for children to read, or on some skill that children need to acquire.

Because literature is based on meaning and form, it facilitates reading for meaning, or comprehension. Literature contains real stories in which something happens that makes sense. Literature contains real information about important and interesting topics. Even the stories, verses, songs, and informational books that are written for very young readers have a point to them that readers grasp. It is easy to talk about something that makes sense, and it is easy to grasp meaning if there is meaning to grasp. Children are meaning makers (Wells, 1986) who actively strive for understanding. When they have in their hands books that make sense, they work hard to understand those books.

Literature motivates readers. It builds a lifelong love of reading because readers catch its magic, ensnared by their basic desire for story and information. Children's books contain the full range of emotions, presenting information and concepts about the full range of human history and knowledge. Literature captures life.

Wide reading of literature brings more than merely experience with language; it also adds to a child's storehouse of information about the world. Independent reading is a major way for children to build background knowledge, knowledge that is necessary for reading comprehension. More knowledge leads to better comprehension. Books provide "windows" on other worlds and experiences that readers could not have directly; such experience becomes virtual experience—as if it had really happened. Virtual experiences add to a reader's knowledge of the world, and this increase in knowledge, in turn, increases a child's possibilities for responding to the world.

Developing a literature-based language arts curriculum can happen in many ways; Judy, Karen, and Terry approached it from very different angles. Teachers have many choices and options within some important cornerstones such as a rich and varied collection of children's books, opportunity for student choice, time for reading, and time for social interactions around books. An essential component, however, is demonstrating your personal enthusiasm for books. What you say about and do with books profoundly influences how your students feel about books. The way you respond to books—with laughter or tears—and the eagerness you demonstrate when it is time for reading signals your love of reading. Imparting that enthusiasm is the first step in creating the magic of reading. Knowledge about books as well as about the social and cognitive development of students helps you build on that enthusiasm and plan an effective literature-based language arts program.

Building a Literature Collection

The books teachers select for their classrooms have an enormous effect on students' developing a love of literature, their view of the world, and their reading and writing skills. Teachers need a core of permanent books in their classroom collection, books that they and their students use as touchstones, returning to them again and again because of their high quality and appeal. Books need to be rotated on a regular basis, drawing from school and public library collections. The selections depend on the current needs and interests in the classroom.

Thousands of children's books are available. How do you choose from among them? How do you know what new books to buy from among the over 4,000 new titles published each year? Many teachers start by asking their school or public librarian for help. Librarians are trained in the selection and use of quality literature; they can help make wise choices as teachers develop a classroom library. There are also excellent resource books such as Galda and Cullinan's *Literature and the Child (5th edition).* The goal is to bring books to children so that they can easily select new ones, as they need them. The more surrounded children are by books, the more likely they will read them. Children in classrooms with literature collections read and look at books much

Joseph Kassick

Children are much more likely to read and look at books if the classroom has a literature collection.

more often than children in classrooms without such collections. Well-designed classroom library corners significantly increase the number of children who choose to participate in literature activities during free-choice periods (Morrow & Weinstein, 1982, 1986).

In many schools, the school librarian picks out 50–100 books appropriate for a grade level and lends them to a class for 6 weeks. Some teachers go to the public library to borrow as many books as allowed. Others spend money allocated for supplies, donated by parent groups, or obtained from other sources on books for their classrooms. Paperback book clubs are a valuable source for classroom books, especially if teachers want sets of ten or more of the same title. Many book clubs have a bonus system so that teachers can obtain extra books for the classroom with each group purchase. Some schools have a birthday book plan in which the child who has a birthday donates a book to the school or classroom library. Sometimes teachers pick up good books at used book sales at the public library, garage sales, or flea markets. Quantity is important but so is quality. Students deserve the best books that you can find.

One of the most important determinants in selecting books for a classroom library is the age of the students. Students in kindergarten, first, and second grade need picture books, easy-to-read books, folk and fairy tales, simple informational books, poetry, and some transitional chapter books for the fluent readers. Third and fourth grade students need more of these transitional chapter books that help fledgling readers move from easy reading into full-length novels, as well as picture books, nonfiction, poetry, and more substantial novels. Fifth, sixth, seventh, and eighth grade students need realistic and historical novels, fantasy and science fiction, mythology, short stories, poetry, biographies, and nonfiction on the subjects covered in the curriculum. Teachers also need to make sure that their selections address the wide range of reading levels that they no doubt have in their classrooms. A classroom library is a microcosm of a school library; it should contain the essence of what students need for individual reading and subject area study.

When choosing books for the classroom, teachers select books that they like themselves. Because they are reading and sharing the books with students, their feelings about the books become readily apparent. Teachers often choose authors whose works they know; if an author has written one or two books they like, chances are they will like others by that author. Teachers also select books that are proven favorites of children. In addition, teachers consider curriculum areas that they need to address during the year and select books that expand a curriculum concept. For example, you might think about your writing program. Are there especially good examples of writing or books about the craft of writing that you want your students to note? There are many excellent books that call attention to language and explore the writer's craft. We talk more about this in Chapter Eight.

Teachers also select books that contribute to an understanding of literature itself. A classroom collection usually contains books by those authors and illustrators they want their students to know. If they highlight several books by the same author or illustrator, students soon recognize their works.

Students begin to recognize different **genres,** or types of books, when they are exposed to them. For this reason, teachers select books of several different genres for their classroom collection. Students in all grades can recognize differences and similarities across genres when teachers provide different types of books and call attention to their form. Having different genres available provides the foundation for genre study in the classroom. Genres are defined in Figure 3.2.

Teachers also need to look for books that are written in the first language of their bilingual students. Fortunately for speakers of Spanish, a growing number of books have been translated into Spanish and are readily available to teachers and students. Arte Publico Press, at the University of Houston in Houston, Texas, publishes Spanish-language titles, as do many of the major children's book publishers. Fewer resources are available in other languages. Children's Book Press in San Francisco does publish bilingual books in several languages, and some of the Canadian presses, such as Tundra Books, also publish bilingual literature, as do the larger children's book publishers on occasion. Resources for finding books are listed in Figure 3.3.

Children need the opportunity to read books written in their first language. This exposure allows them to bring their knowledge of that language to the act of reading—an advantage that English-speaking children have

FIGURE 3.2

Genres in Children's Literature

- Poetry—Condensed, carefully selected language that explores anything in a fresh way.
- Folklore—Narratives and songs that began in tales told by oral cultures and were eventually written down.
- Fantasy—Stories about people, places, or events that could not really exist or could not really happen.
- Science Fiction—Stories that hypothesize about scientific possibilities and the impact they might have on life.
- Contemporary Realistic Fiction—Narratives that could really happen that are set in contemporary times.
- Historical Fiction—Narratives that are set in the past and recreate the life and time of a historical period.
- Biography—Stories about the lives or portions of the lives of real people.
- Nonfiction—Books that present information about a wide variety of topics.

every day. Finding books written in their first language also affirms the value of that language and thus of the children who speak that language. Teachers often supplement their collection of books in other languages with texts produced by students and their families, as described in the *Teaching Idea: Connecting with Families through Homemade Books.*

Literature-based teachers are sure to include books that celebrate the multicultural heritage of North America. Although teachers may want to spend time focusing on the cultures that enrich their classrooms, or time studying one or two particular cultures, they also include books that represent varied cultures in different ways as well. For example, if they are exploring families, they make sure that families from many cultures are represented in the books they select. In this way teachers acknowledge the cultural diversity in gender, ethnic origin, customs, and abilities that is a fact of life in America, whether or not it is present in their particular classroom.

SELECTING CHILDREN'S BOOKS

Teachers can get the information they need to make wise selections in many ways. Each year the community of literary critics selects the books they consider the best among the ones published. The most prestigious awards, the Newbery and the Caldecott, are selected by a committee of the Association for Library Services to Children, a division of the American Library Association. These books are worthy of consideration. A list of all previous winners is

FIGURE 3.3

Selection Aids

Reference Books and Bibliographies

A to zoo: Subject access to children's picture books (4th ed.) (1993). New York: Bowker.

Adventuring with books: Grades pre-K–6 (12th ed.) (1999). Urbana, IL: National Council of Teachers of English.

Best books for children: Preschool through the middle grades (5th ed.) (1994). New York: Bowker.

Bilingual books in Spanish/English for children. D. C. Dale (1985). Englewood, CO: Libraries Unlimited.

Books in Spanish for children and young adults: An annotated guide. I. Schon (Ed.) (1993). Metuchen, NJ: Scarecrow Press.

Children's books: Awards and prizes (1996). New York: The Children's Book Council.

Children's books in print (Annual). New York: Bowker.

Index to poetry for children and young people: 1988–1992. I. Blackburn, Comp. (1994). New York: Wilson.

Index to fairy tales, 1978–1986: Including folklore, legends and myths in collections. N. Ireland & J. Sprug (1989). Metuchen, NJ: Scarecrow Press.

Kaleidoscope: A multicultural booklist for grades K–8 (3rd ed.) J. Yokota (Ed.). Urbana, IL: National Council of Teachers of English.

Library services for Hispanic children: A guide for public and school librarians. A. A. Allen (Ed.) (1987). Phoenix, AZ: Oryx Press.

Your reading: A booklist for junior high and middle school students. B. G. Samuels & G. K. Beers (1996). Urbana, IL: National Council of Teachers of English.

Subject guide to children's books in print (Annual). New York: Bowker.

Periodicals

Bookbird: A Journal of International Children's Literature

Book Links: Connecting Books, Libraries, and Classrooms

Booklist

Bulletin of the Center for Children's Books

The Horn Book Magazine

The Horn Book Guide

Journal of Youth Services in Libraries

Language Arts

The New Advocate

The Reading Teacher

Riverbank Review: Of Books for Young Readers

School Library Journal

available at any library. The Caldecott Award is presented to the illustrator of the most distinguished picture book published in the United States during the previous year; the Newbery Award is presented to the author for the text of the most distinguished contribution to literature for children published in the

TEACHING IDEA

Home/School Connections

CONNECTING WITH FAMILIES THROUGH HOMEMADE BOOKS

Ask students to ask their families to tell them special stories. These may be stories about the students themselves when they were younger, stories about relatives such as grandparents, or stories that are especially meaningful to the family's cultural group. Students can retell these stories in class for a wonderful oral language experience, or you can invite family members to come in and tell their stories. Students can also write their stories down, either through dictation with help from family members or teachers, or on their own.

If students come from a home in which English is the second language, encourage them to write their stories in their first language as well as in English. They can get help from their family members and from teachers. These stories can then become part of a classroom library and, if they are written in a language other than English, resources for reading for English-language learners.

United States in the year preceding the award. These and other awards, such as the Coretta Scott King Award, the Prinz Award, and the Siebert Award, are included in the books listed in Figure 3.3. Often, teachers look for other books by the illustrators and authors who have won these coveted awards; they are a good place to start in building a collection.

The books chosen as outstanding by adults, however, are not necessarily the same ones that children choose. Many states have children vote on their favorite books, and the International Reading Association and Children's Book Council conduct an annual field test in which hundreds of new books are rated by children across the nation. The Children's Choices list, annotated and published in the October issue of *The Reading Teacher,* and the Young Adults' Choices list, published in the fall in *The Journal of Reading,* are sources of information about recently published books that children like—ones that you will also want in your classroom. This information is available through the International Reading Association (www.reading.org). Collected annotations of both of these lists can be found in publications such as *Kids' Favorite Books, More Kids' Favorite Books, Celebrating Children's Choices: 25 Years of Children's Favorite Books,* and *Teens' Favorite Books: Young Adults' Choices 1987–1992,* all published by the International Reading Association. Books that children like, as well as those designated outstanding by adults, belong in a classroom library.

Another promising source of classroom-tested outstanding books lies in Teachers' Choices, also sponsored by the International Reading Association.

Seven regional teams of teachers in the United States try out 300–500 new books annually and rate them for their literary quality and usefulness in the curriculum. Their selections are published in *The Reading Teacher.* Collections of annotated bibliographies can be found in *Teachers' Favorite Books for Kids: Teachers' Choices 1989–1993,* published by the International Reading Association. Given the nearly 4,000 books published each year, having teachers' recommendations is a great advantage.

Materials that can help in selecting books about particular subjects can also be found in the reference or children's room of the local public library. Selection aids are listed in Figure 3.3.

The best way to stay abreast of new books is to read periodicals, such as *The Horn Book, School Library Journal, Bulletin of the Center for Children's Books, Booklist, The Reading Teacher, Language Arts, The New Advocate,* and *Riverbank Review.* Each journal contains reviews of newly published books and articles by knowledgeable writers. In 1989, *The Horn Book Guide* was established; produced twice a year, it contains reviews and quality ratings of all trade books published during each year. In 1990, *Booklinks: Connecting Books, Libraries, and Classrooms* was founded; it is published every two months, and contains articles with themed bibliographies devoted to helping teachers integrate chil-

Bernice Cullinan

The principal shares a book she loves with three teachers.

dren's trade books into classroom learning. Lists of recommended books and books grouped by subjects are also available on the Internet. Teachers interested in children's literature also go to Web sites of individual authors, and to those of professional organizations such as the American Library Association (ALA), and within that Library Services to Children (ALSC) and Young Adults (YALSA), the International Reading Association (IRA), the National Council of Teachers of English (NCTE), and others.

EVALUATING CHILDREN'S BOOKS

In addition to relying on reviews and library reference sources, you need to rely on your own sense of what is good as you select books. You can apply some general criteria when deciding what books to bring into a classroom. Specific criteria differ somewhat according to genre, but here we present general criteria for evaluating stories, picture books, and nonfiction.

Evaluating stories

What makes a good story? In fantasy, authors create a complete world that must ring true within the constraints established, whereas in realistic fiction, the events must be believable within the real world. In historical fiction, the events and episodes must be credible within the context of the historical period described. Science fiction hinges upon the extrapolation of known scientific facts and theories. Generally, stories are memorable because of the way authors manipulate the literary elements of character, plot, setting, theme, point of view, and style.

Characterization is the way in which an author develops a character in a story through description, conversation, thoughts, and actions. Characters become memorable largely because of what a reader learns about them and their motives. A good author makes us care about what happens to a character. Main characters should be multidimensional and should change in some way as a result of the events they experience in the story.

The **plot** is the cumulation of events that happen in a story. It usually involves a conflict such as self against self, self against other, self against society, or self against nature. The action must be logical and credible within the framework of the story. The book must have a clearly defined and satisfying ending, although not necessarily a happy one. Children want to know for sure when their stories end and how things will be for the characters afterward.

Setting is the time and place in which a story occurs. The setting influences the behavior, clothing, beliefs, values, and thoughts of the characters. It also influences what can happen in a story. In an historical setting, the characters and events must remain historically authentic. In fantasy, the setting is often a clearly defined world the author creates.

Themes are underlying ideas that permeate a story and hold it together. Episodes are significant because they develop the theme; it is what makes a story memorable. Good-versus-evil themes often appear in folklore and in fantasy. Themes such as "be true to yourself" or "growing up requires risks" may appear in realistic stories. Themes considering the effect of technology on human life often appear in science fiction. The effect of a particular time and place on a person's life is often a theme in historical fiction. Themes in biography may underscore the direction of a life's work.

Point of view is the perspective from which a story is told. It may be first person, third person, an omniscient narrator, or any combination of these. Many young readers enjoy a first-person point of view when they are reading books about characters that remind them of themselves.

Style is the manner in which a story is told; it is realized in the words selected and the rhythm of the discourse. Good writers use natural-sounding dialogue to reveal character, select strong words to move action forward, and create a mood appropriate to the story with precisely selected words.

Evaluating picture books

What makes a good picture book? In addition to the qualities of style, characterization, plot, theme, setting, and point of view discussed above, or the qualities of good nonfiction, discussed below, picture books, because of their unique blending of visual and verbal art, have specific criteria of their own. So many beautiful books are available that it is difficult to make choices and, at first, the shades of difference are not apparent. Here are some general guidelines for considering qualities found in distinguished picture books.

A true picture book is a **unique combination of text and illustration;** neither can stand alone; neither is as rich alone as they are together. Nonreading children who hear a picture book read aloud once or twice can "reread" it just from the illustrations. Some picture books are wordless.

The **imaginative quality of the art** in illustrations distinguishes picture books and adds a dimension to the text that encourages youngsters to use their imaginations. For example, the small mouse that scampers across the room in Margaret Wise Brown's *Goodnight Moon,* or the antics of the dog in Peggy Rathman's *Officer Buckle and Gloria* are not mentioned in the text. Children spot the imaginative play in the illustrations and delight in it each time the book is read.

Are the pictures an integral part of the text? Is the action in the text reflected by action in the pictures? Ideally, **illustrations reflect, extend, and enrich the text,** help create the mood, and show character delineation and development. Pictures should be accurate and consistent with the text. The accuracy of the illustrations in nonfiction picture books is as important as it is in fiction. A book meant to convey information should convey accurate information in the illustrations as well as in the text. The illustrations should help readers build concepts and understand content.

The artistic merit of a picture book is important because the first art, and often the only true art, many children see is the art in their books. Distinguished picture books contain **original, well-balanced compositions with harmonious use of line, shape, and texture.** Pages flow from one to another and draw the viewer's eye along. The style of the art matches the meaning and message of the book. Style can be characterized in many ways, such as representational or realistic, surrealistic, expressionistic, impressionistic, folk art or naive art, cartoon art, or photography.

The medium the artist uses becomes an item of interest as children explore many picture books. They will begin to recognize watercolor, chalk, crayon, woodcut, collage, or pen and ink. Some teachers encourage students to use the same medium as they produce their own illustrations to understand how artists work.

It is important to remember that many picture books are meant to be read aloud *to* children long before they can be read *by* children. Picture books that contain **interesting words used in interesting ways** enrich children's language storehouse. The language as it is read aloud should fall felicitously on the ear; it will have an inner rhythm and a natural beat.

Evaluating nonfiction

What makes good nonfiction books? **Style** in nonfiction is as important as it is in fiction. The way an author arranges words, gives examples, and states clearly and logically the information to be presented adds to the clarity and quality of a text. Ideally, information should be presented in such a manner that young readers are **building concepts** as they read, rather than merely collecting an array of facts. **Illustrations should amplify and clarify the text,** visually reinforcing the information that the author presents.

Many different considerations enter into planning a literature-rich environment, starting with the materials teachers choose for their collections. The classroom library is central, containing the primary resources needed to immerse students in literature. You should look for quality material, books of recognized authors and illustrators, excellent examples of different genres, and books that enrich the curriculum areas you teach. Furthermore, you can change the books in the classroom library as your students' interests change.

ORGANIZING THE CLASSROOM LIBRARY

Of course, space to house a classroom library is important, as well as room to store materials in an easily accessible place, to display student products, and for students to move from individual to group to whole-class activities. The physical design of a classroom affects the choices children make among activities (Morrow & Weinstein, 1982, 1986). Teachers design their room to accommodate the activities they want to encourage there, as shown in Figure 3.4.

Teachers who want to encourage reading make their classroom library a focal spot in the room, immediately apparent and inviting to anyone who enters the classroom. A sense of privacy or separation from the rest of the room can be achieved by using bookcases, shelves, a piano, or folding screens to partition off the sides. The size of the library corner will depend upon the size of the room and whether it is used for group stories, meeting time, or just for small groups of students to visit. Well-designed library corners have two

FIGURE 3.4

Design for a Classroom Library

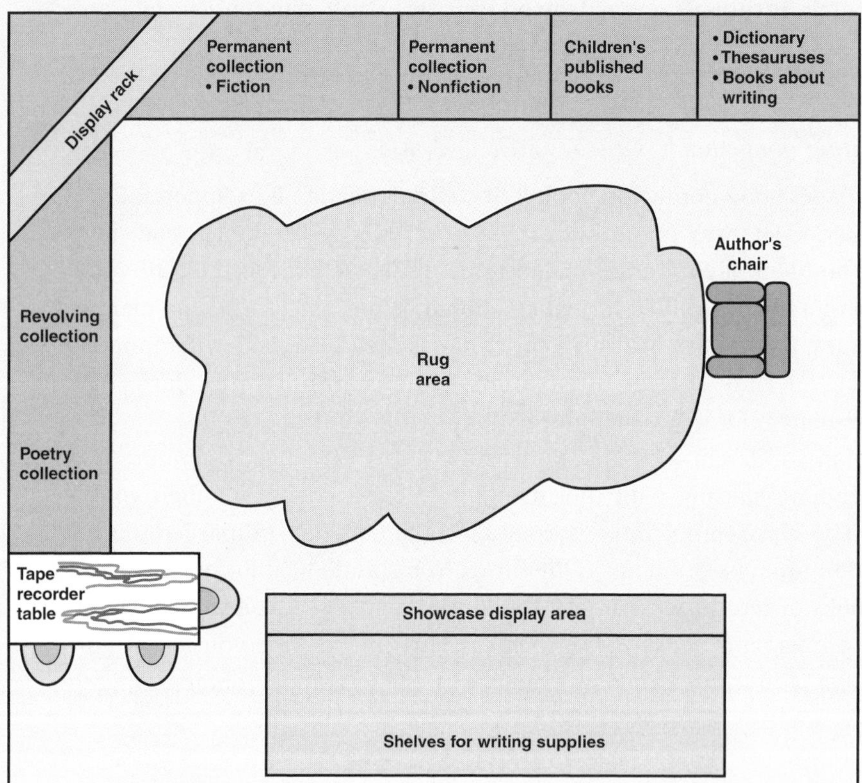

This design allows students to use the classroom library for browsing, talking about books, reading together, formal sharing, and other activities, while also providing a quiet corner away from the desks and tables of the rest of the classroom.

kinds of bookshelves. The first kind houses the bulk of the books, which are shelved with the spines facing out. The other is open-faced, allowing the covers of the books to be seen (Morrow, 1992). Bookshelves of either type need to be easily accessible to students.

Books in a classroom library need to be categorized, but the categories may or may not reflect the traditional ones in the school library. The criterion for categorization is what makes sense to the students. If they are studying communities around the world, they might categorize the books by region of the world or type of community, such as rural, isolated, primitive, or urban, by geographical features such as rivers or harbors, or other factors. In primary-grade classrooms, teachers and students might decide to categorize their library by easy-to-read, picture books, magazines, child-made books, and concept books. In third or fourth grade, students might categorize them as chapter books, mystery stories, poetry, biographies, science, or social studies. In sixth grade, the categories might be science fiction, fantasy, historical fiction, and realistic stories. Teachers can categorize a classroom library based on their and their students' needs.

A rug, pillows, beanbag chairs, rocking chairs, or other comfortable spaces for children to read enhance a library corner. Some teachers have tables, chairs, and writing materials within easy reach. Tape recorders and books on tape are also valuable additions to a library corner, as is a computer where children can use the Internet to read reviews and check booklists or to chat with students in other locations about the books they are reading. Large or small, a library corner is an important part of the classroom!

Structuring a Language Arts Program

Knowledgeable teachers understand that the social, collaborative nature of learning goes beyond the relationship between adult and child, teacher and student, and includes peers. Children reading together and talking about what they have read is an important part of the collaborative process. Hepler (1982) describes a year in a combined fifth and sixth grade classroom in which reading literature is social—the children use the classroom community to "pick their way to literacy." Comments such as "Everyone in the class read it, so I figured I ought to, too," or "I usually read what Tammy reads" show the effect of belonging to a community of readers (Hepler & Hickman, 1982, p. 279).

In this classroom, book discussions occur daily, as does **sustained silent reading,** a designated period of time in which children read from books and other print materials they select. The children support each other in their selections of books and in their evaluations as a community of readers. Talk helps children negotiate meanings. Talk in literature-rich classrooms is made easier by having others who share the same context—that is, hearing the same books read aloud, participating in the shared book discussions, and collaborating on response activities with their peers. Clusters, pairs, and small groups share comments about books that are based on mutual understanding from having read the same books.

Students like to talk with each other about the books they are reading and the stories they are writing. Children strongly influence each other's responses to literature. They also turn to each other for information, for recommendation, and for encouragement or affirmation. Spontaneous book talk generates interest and promotes a positive attitude toward reading. In fact, students become a community of readers *because* they share their responses to books. We discuss this further in Chapters Five and Seven.

The collaborative nature of successful classrooms reflects the importance of the community in which children learn. When teachers value the contributions of individual children, seeing in each of them strengths that they can contribute to the classroom community, children value themselves and each other. Competition is not a part of these environments; collaboration is. Children can practice their literacy strategies and skills in an environment that is safe and supportive, one in which they feel free to take the risks necessary for learning. Such an environment allows children to learn from themselves and from each other, as well as from their teachers.

From talking about reading, children learn the social conventions of reading. They find reading to be a source of pleasure and are eager to engage in it when they share their thoughts and feelings with their peers. Although this kind of talk does occur with books being read aloud to the whole class and books read during independent reading, shared reading, especially in small groups, provides a wonderful opportunity for talking about books.

Children also benefit when they are allowed some measure of choice in the material that they read. Being able to select their own reading material at least some of the time helps motivate them to read. It's always more fun to read what we have selected ourselves than what someone else tells us to read!

Teachers who guide children to become readers provide their students with varied opportunities to read a wide variety of literature. Many teachers combine a literature-based approach with the basal reading series that their system has adopted. Others build their entire program on trade books. Some teachers structure their programs entirely around children's own selections; others select some of the material that children read. What they choose reflects their values, talents, resources, and the particular needs of their students.

Not only do students benefit from social interaction around books and the opportunity to make choices about their reading material, they also benefit when they are able to spend significant amounts of time reading in a variety of ways. Whether students listen to their teachers read aloud, read with partners, in small groups, or alone, they can have valuable experiences with books.

Once you determine what your students need to know for their personal growth and to meet curriculum demands, you can plan lessons to create a balanced language arts program. If you want students to develop their prediction skills in reading, for instance, you might do read-and-think-aloud demonstrations. If you need to focus on end-rhyme to help children develop phonemic awareness, select books that contain end rhymes to read aloud. Perhaps students are studying various expository structures in writing. You would then select books for shared reading that contain a variety of structures and discuss them. Whatever you need to teach, books can help. The remainder of this text is devoted to showing how. Here, we begin by considering various structures for reading books with children: reading aloud, guided reading, shared reading, and independent reading. All have their place in a balanced literacy program, and all deserve the commitment of regularly scheduled chunks of time.

READING ALOUD

For some children, hearing the teacher read aloud may be the only time they ever hear what reading is supposed to sound like. Forty years ago Durkin (1966) found that reading to children was an important factor for those who learned to read before school entrance. She looked carefully at 49 children (out of 5,000) who entered school reading at grade 1.5 or above. She found that neither intelligence nor social class distinguished the readers from the nonreaders. Instead, she found that (1) somebody read to them, (2) someone answered their questions, and (3) the children liked to write or make marks on paper. In fact, she called them "paper-and-pencil kids."

Since then, a number of other researchers have shown the positive impact of reading aloud, but none more convincingly than Wells (1986). Wells began his research with 132 children shortly after their first birthday. Small microphones attached to the children's clothing automatically switched on at various intervals during the day, thus allowing tape recordings of what was happening at those times. Wells kept track of what he called "literacy events," any conversation or activity in which the child's attention was called to print. These included reading to children, writing messages, or noticing print in the environment.

Before school entrance, one child, Jonathan, had been engaged in more than 6,000 book and story experiences. Rosie, at the other end of the continuum, was not read to once before she started going to school. On school entrance assessments, Jonathan ranked at the top while Rosie ranked at the bottom. Sadly, but predictably, at the end of the elementary school years Jonathan still ranked at the top and Rosie still ranked at the bottom in achievement. Six years of schooling could not erase the effects of the crucial preschool experiences with literacy. Wells found a clear connection between the early experience of listening to stories and later educational achievement. Children who had been read to were better able to narrate an event, describe a scene, and follow instructions. More importantly, the children could understand their teachers' use of language.

The authors of *Becoming a Nation of Readers* (Anderson et al., 1985) summarized their stance on reading aloud after a thorough synthesis of the research: "The single most important activity for building the knowledge required for eventual success in reading is reading aloud to children" (p. 23). They go on to note that "there is no substitute for a teacher who reads children good stories. It whets the appetite of children for reading and provides a model of skillful oral reading. It is a practice that should continue throughout the grades" (p. 51).

Selecting books for reading aloud

Selecting books for reading aloud requires some different considerations from selecting books that students will read on their own. Wise teachers select books for reading aloud that expose students to literature of a higher quality and reading level than they could read alone. Books to be read aloud should be stylistically excellent, with pleasing words arranged in pleasing patterns. Teachers often preview books by reading aloud to themselves, discarding those that sound awkward. Folklore, originating in the oral tradition and containing language that plays with sound, is a wonderful choice for reading aloud, as is poetry. Storybooks with intense, gripping plots also are excellent read-aloud fare; young listeners sit on the edge of their seats waiting to find out what happens. Books with vivid characters and natural dialogue are also good for reading aloud. Other considerations for selecting books for reading aloud include the curriculum and the needs and experiences of students. Teachers also select books that reflect the theme they are exploring; books that will enrich students' understanding of themselves and others; books that fit into their literature, reading, science, social studies, mathematics, art, composition, or music curriculum. The *Teaching Idea: Using Read-Alouds to Support the Curriculum* presents ways of using reading aloud to enrich various parts of the curriculum.

Scheduling and conducting read-aloud sessions

How do teachers find time in an already overcrowded day to read aloud? They must cover all the curriculum areas, and children must leave the room

TEACHING IDEA

Assessing the Learning Environment

USING READ-ALOUDS TO SUPPORT THE CURRICULUM

- Select books to read aloud that connect with the topics in the social studies, science, or math curriculum. There are many wonderful nonfiction books that focus on a wide variety of subjects. Use the *Subject Guide to Children's Books in Print* or *The Horn Book Guide* listed in Figure 3.3 to find them.
- Find poetry that expands on curriculum concepts. Use the *Subject Guide to Poetry* or the *Subject Guide to Children's Books in Print* to find it.
- Find fiction that connects to the curriculum, using the *Subject Guide to Children's Books in Print.*
- Check the journals of professional organizations for lists of children's books that they have found notable. Look at the "Notable" books of the National Science Teachers Association, the National Council of Social Studies, the International Reading Association, and the National Council of Teachers of English. These lists are available from the Children's Book Council (www.cbc.org).
- Schedule a read-aloud time at the beginning or end of the time for math, science, or social studies.
- Read aloud from books that are good examples of whatever technique, structure, or genre is being studied in composition.

to work with special-area teachers and attend schoolwide assemblies. Some teachers read aloud the first thing in the morning; one who chose this time noticed that no one was ever late for school. Many teachers read aloud several times during the day. They can read at the end of the day and/or after lunch, or for 15 minutes in the morning and 10 minutes in the afternoon. If they are reading poetry, it takes only a few minutes to read and think about a poem at any time of the day. There is no one best schedule; the important thing is to build reading aloud into a regular pattern of each day and to seize opportunities for reading aloud that occur spontaneously throughout the day.

Interaction patterns during storybook reading vary greatly (Evans, 2002; Galda & Beach, 2001; Spiegel, 1998). The way teachers read books aloud affects students' understanding of how to listen and how to respond to books. The way teachers present books to their students makes the difference between effective and ineffective story-reading situations. Teachers' goals, their students' abilities, and the book they are reading influence the manner in which they present stories. Teachers with similar goals, and the same trade book, can have very different ways of orchestrating the interactions of children around a reading-aloud session; these differences can affect the quality of students' understanding.

There is no "formula" for reading aloud, although the material itself will dictate certain requirements. In general, effective teachers read aloud with enthusiasm and clarity. They use a natural conversational voice for dialogue, pace their reading, and reflect the meaning with their voice. They try not to use a singsong pace for poetry, but rather demonstrate how the sound underscores the sense. Figure 3.5 presents guidelines for successful read-aloud experiences.

When teachers read a picture book aloud, they encourage readers' expectations by talking about the title, cover illustrations, endpapers, title page, author, and dust jacket information. They ask for predictions of what the story will be about. For novels, informational books, and poetry, teachers often discuss the title, cover illustration, dust jacket material, author, section headings, or other clues to understanding what the book will be about.

When teachers read a longer text, they often rely on a synopsis or an overarching framework to aid comprehension. The synopsis for a story includes the basic plot line and the major theme. The synopsis for an informational text includes the major topic, subtopics, and major points of the text. Readers comprehend better when the unifying element or the organizational pattern of a text is known. For example, students who read series books may

FIGURE 3.5

Guidelines for Successful Oral Reading

- Read aloud every day.
- Mix old favorites with a variety of new books.
- Select on the basis of (1) children's interests and abilities, (2) what is going on in the classroom (events, topics of study), and (3) size of the group.
- Become familiar with the story. Practice reading it.
- Make sure everyone can see you (and the illustrations if that is important) and that you can see everyone.
- Introduce the story briefly.
- Read clearly and dramatically, using voice and body to portray characters and convey mood.
- If you are showing illustrations, hold the book so that students can see the illustrations as you read.
- Know the story well enough that you can look at students frequently. This helps maintain order. Most of all, it allows you to share your own responses with students.

have higher comprehension than when reading nonseries books because they (1) know the characters and setting, (2) have a basic understanding of the probable plot line, and (3) have a framework for predicting what will most likely happen (Feitelson, Kita, & Goldstein, 1986; Guthrie & Wigfield, 2000).

Teachers often prepare questions for discussion at various points within the book, perhaps at the end of what is read in one day. Graves and Graves (1994) make the point that there are three parts to any reading event—before reading, during reading, and after reading. Discussion questions or activities can occur at any or all of these times and will vary widely according to the text being read, the students' interests and abilities, and teachers' goals. We consider some of the ways to explore books later in this chapter and throughout the remainder of the text. We consider posing good questions and conducting effective discussions in Chapter Five.

Teachers help students connect with the books they read by the social interactions they allow during oral reading, and the questions and comments they make or encourage students to make. Effective teachers help students connect their life experiences to the books they read, using these experiences to understand what they are reading. Also, the virtual experiences that reading provides can help students understand themselves and others as well as the events that occur in their lives. Finally, teachers help students connect books with other books, building their understanding of the world of literature. The *Teaching Idea: Making Connections between Students and Books* offers ideas for encouraging students to connect to the books they read or hear read.

Make reading aloud an important part of your balanced reading program by doing so every day and selecting books appropriate to the age level you are teaching. Read them ahead of time so that you know what to stress and clarify, and how to read with appropriate intonation, speed, and clarity. Be sure to clarify points children do not understand during the reading. You can also make the book available to your students after reading, through discussion or other response options. Most important of all, make reading aloud an enjoyable experience for yourself and for your students.

GUIDED READING

Guided reading is one part of a balanced literacy program; it is a time when teachers call small groups together for specific instruction. Teachers keep close records of how well students are reading and identify specific skills or strategies that students need to improve. In guided reading, teachers group children who need instruction in similar strategies. They use multiple copies of the same book or basal selection and guide the students as they read through the text, focusing on the skill or strategy being learned. These groups are temporary, rather than stable, and are based on specific needs at specific times. They

TEACHING IDEA

Home/School Connections

MAKING CONNECTIONS BETWEEN STUDENTS AND BOOKS

Select stories, poems, and works of nonfiction that treat a topic or theme that you know is important in the lives of your students. Read these books and poems orally or as shared reading. Follow with open discussions in which you ask questions that encourage children to talk about themselves and their lives as they relate to the book. Provide opportunities for other response activities that do the same.

As you come to know your students, you can connect their lives and literature explicitly by saying things like, "This reminds me of the story Sam told about his dog," and "Your brother's adventure reminds me of the book we read last week." You can also help students connect life and literature when you discuss books in terms of the choices authors make and link those choices to the student authors in your classroom, saying something like, "Karla Kuskin wrote this whole poem about seeing a man with a mustache. This reminds me of Amiko saying that she wanted to write about all the women in red hats that she saw on her way to school this morning."

are especially important as children are learning decoding and comprehension skills and strategies, and are effective ways of assessing and teaching to individual student needs. In Chapter Six we discuss some skills that teachers stress as children are learning to read. In Chapter Seven we discuss teaching comprehension strategies.

INDEPENDENT READING

Children also need time each day for independent reading. All too often, students spend up to 70 percent of the time allocated for reading instruction on worksheets, filling in blanks, or circling answers. In the course of a school year, children bring home an average of 1,000 worksheets and skill sheets completed during reading time. Unfortunately, time devoted to worksheets is unrelated to year-to-year gains in reading proficiency. On the other hand, the amount of independent, silent reading that children do in school is significantly related to gains in reading achievement (Anderson et al., 1985; Galda & Cullinan, 2003).

Even though students should always have the option to read when they finish their other work, they also need a regularly scheduled time to explore books on their own. Just as teachers signal the importance of reading by reading aloud on a regular basis, they also demonstrate the importance of independent reading by scheduling time for it each day. Even 15 minutes is valuable and provides a welcome quiet time for many students. It gives children time to practice the skills and strategies they are being taught, providing an opportunity for them to get hooked on a book, which might translate into reading in their free time outside of school! The *Teaching Idea: Guidelines for Successful Independent Reading* is a good place to start.

Children need choices about what they read. Just as each of us has individual interests, so too do children. Whatever their reading interests, they should be able to make choices that satisfy their tastes. Independent reading is a time for them to do that.

SHARED READING

Shared reading occurs when a whole class or small group reads the same selection or different books that are closely related in some way. Shared reading is sometimes under the guidance of a teacher and is sometimes accomplished by independent groups of children. Books for shared reading may be selected by the teacher, negotiated between teacher and students, or selected by the students. This selection may mean sharing a big book, poems, chants, songs, students' published books, picture storybooks, chapter storybooks, or nonfiction books. A book becomes more accessible to students when it is read as a group because the group discussion clears up any misconceptions and

TEACHING IDEA

Addressing Individual Needs

GUIDELINES FOR SUCCESSFUL INDEPENDENT READING

- ✦ Begin with a relatively brief amount of time. Children unused to Sustained Silent Reading (SSR) might be able to concentrate for only 5–10 minutes initially.
- ✦ Have SSR every day at a regularly scheduled time.
- ✦ Be clear about the rules: Everyone is to be reading a trade book (or magazine or newspaper if you so choose); no one is to be talking or doing other work. Everyone, including you, must have something to read when SSR begins, unless you schedule time for browsing at the beginning of SSR.
- ✦ Discuss how students must respect each other's right to read. Remind them that they will have time to talk later. You might want to plan to end your SSR period with a brief sharing time.
- ✦ Decide in advance how you will handle disruptions. Is there enough room to allow children to spread out? What are the options for those who have no reading material?

enriches partial understandings. The safety net of numbers in shared reading means that no children are left on their own.

Whole-class shared reading

Each student needs a copy of the selection used for shared reading, or at least needs to be able to see the print. For big books, all children must be able to see the enlarged print. Some texts are read aloud by the teacher. Some texts, such as predictable, rhythmic ones, are appropriately read in unison; in this way less able readers are not embarrassed by not knowing a word—the group carries them along. Longer books are read individually and then discussed in groups, read orally by the teacher with students reading along silently, or a combination of these ways.

If teachers are doing the reading, they can read aloud the entire book or the first few chapters with students following along in their own copies of the text. Kathy Harwood begins her shared reading sessions with low-achieving sixth grade students by reading aloud from a book that she knows will interest her students. After reading and discussing several books, she reads aloud from books for which she has class sets so that each student can follow along. Her students feel like successful readers, thinking of themselves as having read the book she is reading aloud because they can follow along in their own copies. This feeling of success is very motivating; readers who feel successful are more willing to read than are those who feel unsuccessful.

Another effective practice is to open each reading session with a read-aloud followed by a **student read-along** in which one or more students read in unison with the teacher. Teachers can vary the pattern by reading the narrative and asking students to read the dialogue for a particular character. Many use **echoic reading** (teacher reads, students echo). Sometimes teachers simply pause so that students can join in, demonstrating to students that their knowledge of language is a dependable source of help. Another effective strategy is to reread sections or entire picture books, inviting students to join in on parts they know.

Teachers are often able to provide tape-recorded readings of a text, some commercially produced and others homemade. Students can listen to the recordings while following along with an individual copy of the text. When reading longer books, teachers sometimes read aloud until students are far enough into the book to be fully versed on character and plot, then have them read the remaining chapters alone. At other times they might only introduce the book and students then read it independently. For students who need extra support, the *Teaching Idea: Paired Reading* is an effective structure.

Small-group shared reading

Another option for shared reading is to have students read in small groups, often called **book clubs, literature circles,** or **literature study groups.** These groups are either assigned by the teacher or formed by students, based

TEACHING IDEA

Addressing Individual Needs

PAIRED READING

Some students are more fluent readers than others. Some need help in order to read fluently. If this is the case in your classroom, try pairing up a fluent reader with a struggling reader. Have the fluent reader read aloud with the students positioned so that they can both see the text. The good reader does most, if not all, of the reading, profiting from the oral practice. The struggling reader profits from hearing a fluent reader. Often, readers who struggle to decode can comprehend quite well when listening. This means that even struggling readers can engage in conversations about texts that they might not be able to read on their own. In a collaborative classroom atmosphere, there is no stigma attached to being the listener and not the reader. The listener might be the best at dramatizing a story or creating an artistic response. This practice is quite effective with English-language learners as well.

on mutual interests. Teachers might set the purpose for the group, establishing in advance the goal toward which the group is working, or the group itself may decide what to accomplish. Sometimes the group is small, three to four students, a size that demands the full and thoughtful participation of all. At other times, the group may be as large as six to eight students, allowing for a wide variety of insights and ideas. A group might read one book in common, or the participants might read different books that link in some way to a common focus of theme, topic, or author.

Small literature groups highlight the social nature of reading and responding. They provide structured opportunities for students to talk through the ideas and problems they encounter as they read, to present their ideas to others, and to consider the ideas of others. Successful groups result in students being more competent, critical readers (Eeds & Wells, 1989). Building on the collective meaning the group has created, students can develop a greater understanding of the books they read, of themselves, and of their world. We discuss this further in Chapters Five and Seven.

How teachers structure shared reading experiences depends on students' abilities and teachers' goals. What is important is that students share a common reading experience. This allows them to help each other make sense of their reading, to share ideas and feelings, and to build a community of readers.

LITERARY STUDY

Literature motivates students to read, is a wonderful resource for practicing specific strategies and skills as they develop their reading abilities, and is also an object of study itself. Shared reading and reading aloud offer wonderful opportunities for studying literature and how it works. Teachers want their students to experience the pleasure of a good book, to understand how good books work, and to appreciate the artistry behind them. Such experiences not only make them better, more critical readers, but also help them develop their writing ability, as we discuss in Chapter Nine. Here we consider how to use literature to study the art of writing, how to conduct an author study, and how to explore themes with children's books. We explore other types of literary study in Chapters Seven and Nine.

Studying the art of writing

Studying the art of writing involves working with literary elements such as setting, plot, characterization, theme, point of view, style, structure, and mood. It involves looking carefully at different genres and discovering the "rules" that operate in specific genres. Any well-written book can be the focus of this type of inquiry, whether story, poem, or nonfiction.

Studying character development is one example. Many times readers are captivated by a book because of the characters, and they get to know carefully developed characters so well they often feel as if the characters are real people. Many students enjoy responding to their reading by writing letters to characters, doing character collages, writing character name poems, or role-playing characters as they interact with other characters or as they are interviewed by others in the classroom. In order to do any of these things well, students have to consider carefully who the character is, what the character is like, what the character thinks and feels, and how the character might respond in any given situation. This is a perfect time to explore *how* authors (and illustrators) develop their characters.

Authors create characters by letting readers know how they look, what they think and say, and how they act, as well as how other characters feel about and act toward them. Authors sometimes directly describe characters and other times allow other characters to indirectly describe them through their thoughts or conversations. Authors might directly reveal a character's thoughts, perhaps by using a first-person point of view, and other times might force the reader to infer those thoughts through the actions the character takes. Asking students to specify how they know a character has a particular trait forces them to delve into the text to see how the author made it work.

In the same way, studying plot structures allows students to see how different types of stories are organized and how this affects the overall tale. Do stories begin with a problem, move toward a climax, and end with a resolution, all in temporal order? Are there flashbacks that allow the author to convey important background information? Are there parallel plots that allow readers to view events from two different perspectives? Is the pattern a circular one, in which characters leave on a quest or journey and return to the same place, changed? Considering plot structure helps readers understand that there are many ways to tell a story. For more details, see the *Teaching Ideas: Studying Character and Setting in Historical Fiction* and *Compare/Contrast Media Interpretations of the Same Story.*

Readers might consider the artistry of a piece of nonfiction. How does the author organize the information to build concepts? How does the structure of the text support a reader's ability to gain information? How does the author's style engage the reader? How does the author distinguish between fact and opinion? What kinds of decisions did the author make about what information to include and what to omit? How did this affect the integrity and accuracy of the text? These kinds of questions push students to view the nonfiction writer's craft as the selection of some among many possibilities for presenting information.

TEACHING IDEA

Literature Link

STUDYING CHARACTER AND SETTING IN HISTORICAL FICTION

Characters in well-written historical fiction are influenced by the time and place in which they live. They are necessarily different from characters in contemporary fiction, as they need to fit into the social norms of the time. As you and your students read historical fiction over time, ask them to consider specific character attributes such as:

- Respect for elders (what characters say and do)
- Language (choice of words and use of slang)
- Responsibilities (chores, jobs)
- Ways to have fun
- The role of school
- Friendships

Students can keep a record of their descriptions of each main character and, once two or three books have been read, can compare the characters to each other and to themselves and/or characters in contemporary realistic fiction. Use Venn diagrams to compare two characters, or construct a chart to note similarities and differences. Then have students compare the settings in each book, and link the differences in characters to the social fabric of the time in which the books are set. If, for instance, a character in a novel set on the prairie when it was first being settled by Europeans longs to go to school, but a character in a contemporary novel resists going, students can discuss how the difference relates to each character's attributes and how much might be a factor of the differences in the availability of school and the difficulty of social communication.

Conversations such as these help students understand the influence of both time and place on an individual's character, both fictional and actual.

TEACHING IDEA

Literature Link

COMPARE/CONTRAST MEDIA INTERPRETATIONS OF THE SAME STORY

Have students compare the print and television, film, or video version of the same story. If possible, have them read the print version first. Have them compare and contrast versions and share with the class. They might consider such things as:

- The differences between the visual representation of the characters in the television or video production versus their prior conceptions based on the print version.
- How the two plots were similar or different.
- How the mood and tone of the story differed in the various versions.

Studying the art of writing can be accomplished through discussion, projects, and writing. It can be part of other response activities such as dramatic reenactment, which requires, for example, a good grasp of plot. It can be an integral part of a writing program, as in the genre studies discussed in Chapter Eight, or of literature-discussion groups. It is one aspect of becoming a critical, responsive reader.

Studying an author

Author studies are no doubt one of the most popular ways of studying literature. Author studies motivate students to read widely for information, pleasure, and personal growth. They are also wonderful for helping students grow in their own writing ability. Students who make personal connections between authors and their works identify characteristics of any author's writing style or an illustrator's artistic style. Author studies help students develop a sense that literature is created by individuals.

Teachers choose authors to study based on their students' interests, reading abilities, and writing needs, and their own curricular goals. The focal author needs to have a sizable body of work; it's even better if that work spans different genres, topics, or themes. Living authors often have Web sites or respond to student inquiry, so teachers often make that part of their selection criteria. If students are just beginning to develop vocabulary and reading strategies, the authors they study will be different than if they are already confident readers. Teachers typically select authors whose strengths center on various literary aspects that they are studying. Perhaps they want to expose students to different genres or to concentrate on a specialty such as fantasy or

Bernice Cullinan

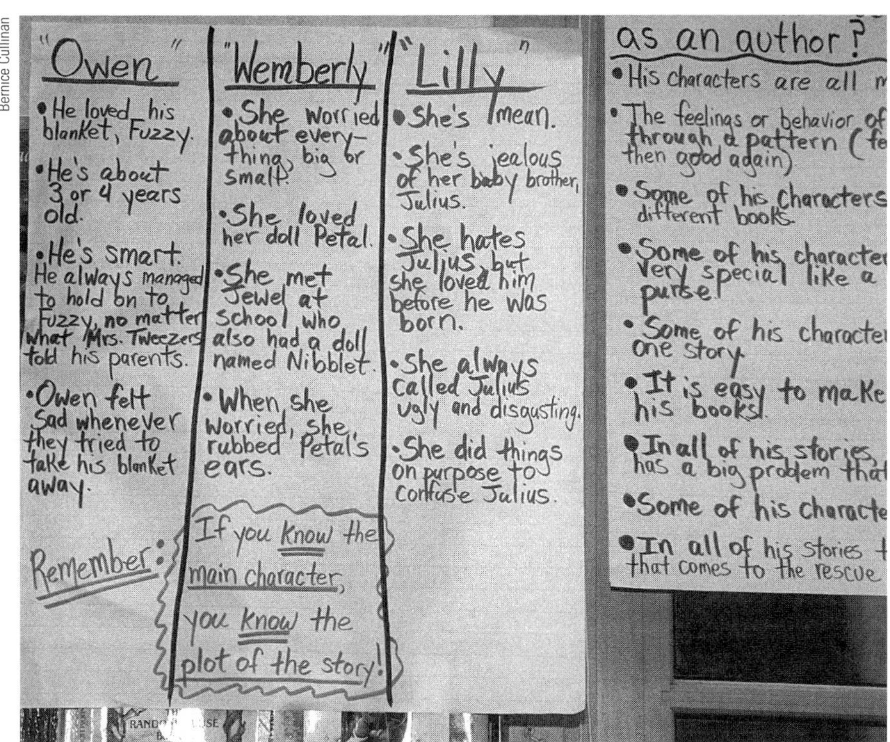

Books by Kevin Henkes are popular with readers; students often choose him for an author study.

mystery. Teachers also connect author studies with other disciplines; the author becomes an expert to be consulted in science or social studies.

Effective teachers encourage students to connect to an author's work in a number of ways. They might have students create an annotated list of the author's books that grows as they read new titles, and ask students to generate questions about the author's life and the author's writing as they read. Does the author write about things that she has experienced? How does she do her research? Where did she get her ideas? Why did she choose a particular point of view? How does she know when she's finished?

Teachers usually help students find biographical information about the focal author. Many fine autobiographies by some of the most popular authors for children are written for child readers. There are a number of library resources, such as *Something about the Author,* interviews with and articles about authors in journals such as those listed in Figure 3.3, and a wealth of information in authors' personal Web sites.

Students can organize their observations about the author's books into lists or diagrams of similarities and differences. They can summarize what they know about the author's life as it relates to her books. They can also organize information about the author's writing process that they have learned through their research.

Effective teachers begin with a brief lesson (perhaps 10 minutes) focused on whatever they want to stress, from the author's skill in creating setting to connections between the author's real life and her writing. Following the minilesson, they allow students time to investigate the focus by reading, writing, talking, and listening, in small groups or as a whole class. The process concludes with a whole-class meeting. They then facilitate sharing discoveries that can be documented as lists, webs, Venn diagrams, letters, and other written documents. Once an author study is completed, the knowledge that students have gained becomes part of the way they read other books and create their own written products. The *Teaching Idea: Tips for Successful Author Studies* lists ideas for planning and for instructional activities.

Patricia Polacco: An author to study

One of our most beloved living authors, Patricia Polacco, is an ideal subject for an author study. Patricia was born in Lansing, Michigan, to parents of Russian and Ukrainian descent on one side and Irish on the other. After her parents divorced, she spent the school year in Oakland, California, with her mother, and summers on her grandparents' farm in Michigan with her father. The farm was a magical place for her, the very spot where a meteorite fell into the front yard, later inspiring her book, *Meteor*. In California, she lived in a diverse neighborhood and became best friends with a young African-American neighbor boy. She later told part of that story in *Chicken Sunday*.

Patricia did not learn to read until she was 14 years old. Today, she is the author and illustrator of over 30 children's books. When she was 14, one of her teachers realized that she had a learning disability called dyslexia and helped her to overcome it. Polacco translated this experience into one of her books, *Thank You, Mr. Falker*. In fact, many of her books are inspired by family, friends, acquaintances, and heroes like her teacher. In *Mr. Lincoln's Way*, a school principal helps a bully change his ways by discovering the child has an interest in birds. *Aunt Chip and the Great Triple Creek Dam Affair* was inspired by two educators: Polacco's mother and Charlotte Huck, a nationally known professor of children's literature and author of several books for children. Aunt Chip satirizes a community that watches television so much that everyone forgets how to read—except, of course, Aunt Chip, the town librarian.

Polacco's family loved storytelling. She often listened to her elders telling stories about their homeland and the family's past. These stories have found their way into her writing. *The Keeping Quilt* is about the quilt her grandmother brought with her when she emigrated to America from Russia. Family members used the quilt as a tablecloth, a wedding canopy, and a baby blanket. *Pink and Say* is a story her grandfather told her about two young soldiers, one of whom was Patricia's relative, who became friends during the Civil War.

Polacco is an excellent author to study—and not only because the connections between her own life and the stories she writes are both apparent

TEACHING IDEA

Assessing the Learning Environment

TIPS FOR SUCCESSFUL AUTHOR STUDIES

Teacher Noel O'Brien, Manhasset Public Schools, advises that in preparation to conduct an author study, one should:

- Collect all the books the author has written.
- Place the books in a basket with two copies for paired reading and multiple copies of some for guided reading or small/large group shared reading.
- Locate audio and video resources.
- Locate World Wide Web information.
- Gather material from the author's publisher.
- Gather ideas for student writing projects and bulletin boards.

Renee Pomerantz and Phoebe Chang of New York University suggest the following activities for author studies:

- Read aloud as many of the author's books as possible.
- Have students take a survey of their favorites among all of the author's books and create a graph showing the group's choices.
- Write reviews of the books.
- Ask small groups to prepare Readers' Theatre scripts for selected books.
- Create a K-W-L chart about the author (What We Know, What We Want to Know, What We Learned).
- Establish literature-discussion groups around selected titles.
- Discuss the author's writing style. Gather examples and develop categories.
- Conduct writing lessons in which you model the author's style and ask students to do the same in their own writing.

and authentic. She also writes and speaks about these connections, and students can read her own words in her autobiography, *Firetalking,* and on her Web site (patriciapolacco.com). She has a distinctive style in both her writing and her art; a Polacco book is easily identified, even though she writes in different genres, including fantasy, historical fiction, and contemporary realistic fiction.

Exploring themes

Another way to approach literary study is through theme cycles. Many teachers enjoy organizing their language arts curriculum around themes; some are even able to create thematic units that cross curriculum areas. Children's books—stories, poems, nonfiction, references, and related media—allow teachers to help students explore ideas in depth and learn numerous ways to approach a particular theme. Often basal materials or school curriculum are organized thematically. If so, alert teachers can build on the themes in the materials they are required to use, broadening them through the selection and use of quality children's material.

Once a theme is identified, resources are gathered. If the theme is a "big question," one that will be explored across time and from many angles, then a lot of material is necessary. Sometimes teachers gather single copies of several books that explore the same theme, have their students read these books, and then explore the theme across books. Or a teacher might select a central book to read aloud or use for whole-class shared reading, and then offer students a collection of individual books that are thematically related that they can choose among for their independent or small-group reading. Or, there might be one whole-class book, sets of books for small groups that are either the same within a single group or varied (called text sets), and then more individual copies of books for independent reading.

This sounds like a lot of work, and it is, but thematic instruction offers students the opportunity to hone their critical thinking skills, develop their own ideas and values, learn about themselves and others, and understand the interrelationships in the web of literature. Thematic instruction allows students to build knowledge from many sources and gives them yet another reason to read. It allows students to make connections across the language arts, and to connect the language arts with other curriculum areas. In thematic study, students read and write as they learn about issues, ideas, and concepts in many disciplines. They come to realize that the skills they learn in one particular part of the curriculum, such as reading, are essential to learning in another, such as science. They also come to understand that the ideas and issues they grapple with in school really do relate to their own lives. Judy, the fifth grade teacher described at the beginning of this chapter, uses themes to organize her social studies/language arts curriculum, and Karen combines social studies, science, and language arts through thematic instruction as well.

Thematic instruction must be carefully planned. Valencia and Lipson (1998) suggest a three-part framework for creating effective thematic instruction: focus, coherence, and instruction. Focus has to do with selecting and developing the theme itself. Valencia and Lipson distinguish between topics and limited concepts and true themes—"big ideas" or "enduring questions" that have relevance for students in both their school and home lives. Statements such as "Living in a diverse society requires respect, cooperation, and negotiation" are big ideas. "Friendship" is a topic, and statements such as "Friends must learn to get along" are limited concepts (p. 103). Good themes, Valencia and Lipson argue, focus on significant, worthwhile ideas, "represent rich, complex ideas that require deep understanding and flexible use of knowledge," and have "relevance and importance beyond the immediate situation," and are thus useful in other parts of students' lives (p. 101).

Coherence, their second criterion, has to do with the content selected to explore the theme and the connections across various types of content. If the content is not coherent, and if students do not see the connections across the various materials and activities, thematic study will fail. The activities that teachers design to help students explore a theme ought to help them make connections across different materials and activities.

Instruction, the third component of Valencia and Lipson's model, relates to both language arts and the content of the theme, whether it be curricular or literary. Teachers need to be clear about what aspects of the English language arts their students are developing when everyone is caught up in the ideas and energy that thematic instruction generates.

For example, one popular and relevant theme in literature and in classrooms has to do with maturation—growth and change. One of many possible "big idea" statements might be: Culture and life experience influence how we change as we mature. Questions to explore might include the following: How does culture influence expectations for children and adolescents? What kinds of conflicts are set up when culture and life experience collide? Students can endeavor to answer these questions by reading novels, memoirs, and biographies, interviewing community members, and creating descriptions of childhood and adolescence as constructed by various cultures. These efforts might culminate in the creation of personal memoirs that capture a particularly difficult moment in the childhood of the writer. Language arts learning outcomes would include reading across genres, interviewing, synthesizing, and writing in a particular genre.

SUMMARY

Children's literature is the foundation for a rich and effective language arts program. Children's literature motivates readers, provides them with invaluable language experience, and offers them opportunities to learn about themselves and the world. Effective teachers create classroom libraries that support their whole curriculum. They make use of reading aloud, independent reading, guided reading, and shared reading to explore the many books that are available today. Not only do they use children's literature to help children learn to read, write, and learn content across the curriculum, they also study the books themselves. As children explore literature by studying the author's craft, studying a particular author, or exploring themes, they continue to have powerful language experiences that help them develop as readers, writers, and critical thinkers.

ACTIVITIES

1. **Select a picture book to read aloud to the whole class or a small group.** Practice reading aloud and then tape-record yourself as you do the actual reading. What did you do well? What do you need to improve upon?
2. **Select a strongly patterned text written for preschool or primary-grade readers.** Use the pattern to create your own story or poem and share this with the class. Discuss the learning possibilities inherent in both texts.
3. **Describe the library in a classroom that you visit regularly.** Describe the predominant authors, genres and subjects of books, and physical accessibility to students. Then describe what you would do with this collection to improve it.
4. **Select a theme and create a text set (collection of different books) around that theme.** Aim for six to ten books in your set.
5. **Select an author to study.** Find biographical information, read and summarize the author's books, and briefly describe five things you would like students to learn about this author.
6. **With a partner, select two or three novels that have won the Newbery in recent years and two or three novels that are extremely popular but not critically acclaimed.** Try to match the books in some way, such as genre or content. Compare the books in terms of style, character development, plot structure, format, and design. Why do you think one is more popular than the other? What are the differences that make a difference in popularity and in critical acclaim?

FURTHER READING

Fountas, I. C., & Pinnell, G. S. (1996). *Guided reading: Good first teaching for all children.* Portsmouth, NH: Heinemann.

Galda, L., & Cullinan, B. E. (2002). *Literature and the child* (5th ed.). Belmont, CA: Wadsworth.

Galda, L., Rayburn, S., & Stanzi, L. C. (2000). *Looking through the faraway end: Creating a literature-based reading curriculum with second graders.* Newark, DE: International Reading Association.

Graves, M. F., Watts-Taffe, S. M., & Graves, B. B. (1999). *Essentials of elementary reading* (2nd ed.). Boston: Allyn & Bacon.

Raphael, T. E., & Au, K. H. (Eds.) (1998). *Literature-based instruction: Reshaping the curriculum.* Norwood, MA: Gordon.

REFERENCES

Anderson, R. C., Hiebert, E. H., Scott, J. A., & Wilkinson, I.A.G. (1985). *Becoming a nation of readers: The report of the Commission on Reading.* Washington, D.C.: U.S. Department of Education, National Institute of Education.

Durkin, D. (1966). *Children who read early: Two longitudinal studies.* New York: Teachers College Press.

Eeds, M., & Wells, D. (1989). Grand conversations: An exploration of meaning construction in literature study groups. *Research in the teaching of English, 23,* 4–29.

Evans, K. S. (2002). Fifth-grade students' perceptions of how they experience literature discussion groups. *Reading Research Quarterly, 37,* 46–69.

Feitelson, D., Kita, B., & Goldstein, Z. (1986). Effects of listening to series stories on first graders' comprehension and use of language. *Research in the Teaching of English, 20,* 339–356.

Galda, L., & Beach, R. (2001). Response to literature as a cultural activity. *Reading Research Quarterly, 36,* 64–73.

Galda, L., & Cullinan, B. (2003). Literature for literacy: What research says about the benefits of using trade books in the classroom. In J. Flood, D. Lapp, J. R. Squire, & J. Jensen (Eds.), *Handbook of research on teaching the English language arts,* 2nd ed. (pp. 813–834). Mahwah, NJ: Erlbaum.

Graves, M. F., & Graves, B. B. (1994). *Scaffolding reading experiences: Designs for student success.* Norwood, NJ: Gordon.

Guthrie, J. T., & Wigfield, A. (2000). Engagement and motivation in reading. In M. L. Kamil, P. B. Mosenthal, P. D. Pearson, & R. Barr (Eds.), *Handbook of reading research, 3,* 403–422, Mahwah, NJ: Erlbaum.

Hepler, S. (1982). Patterns of response to literature: A one-year study of a fifth- and sixth-grade classroom. Doctoral dissertation. The Ohio State University.

Hepler, S., & Hickman, J. (1982). "The book was okay. I love you"—social aspects of response to literature. *Theory into Practice, 21,* 278–283.

Morrow, L. M. (1992). *Literacy development in the early years: Helping children read and write* (2nd ed.). Boston: Allyn & Bacon.

Morrow, L. M., & Weinstein, C. S. (1982). Increasing children's use of literature through program and physical design changes. *Elementary School Journal, 83,* 131–137.

______. (1986). Encouraging voluntary reading: The impact of a literature program on children's use of library centers. *Reading Research Quarterly, 21,* 330–346.

Neuman, S. B., Celano, D. C., Greco, Albert, N., & Shue, P. (2001). *Access for all: Closing the book gap for children in early education.* Newark, DE: International Reading Association.

Valencia, L. S., & Lipson, M. Y. (1998). Thematic instruction: A quest for challenging ideas and meaningful learning. In T. E. Raphael & K. H. Au (Eds.), *Literature-based instruction: Reshaping the Curriculum.* Norwood, NJ: Gordon.

Wells, G. (1986). *The meaning makers: Children learning language and using language to learn.* Portsmouth, NH: Heinemann.

CHILDREN'S LITERATURE REFERENCES

Brown, M. J. (1947). *Goodnight moon.* Illus. Clement Hurd. New York: HarperCollins.

Dorris, M. (1999). *Morning girl.* New York: Hyperion.

Maestro, B. C. (1992). *The discovery of the Americas.* Illus. G. Maestro. New York: Mulberry Books.

Polacco, P. (1988). *The keeping quilt.* New York: Simon & Schuster.

______. (1992). *Chicken Sunday.* New York: Philomel.

______. (1994). *Firetalking.* Katanoh, NY: Owens.

______. (1994). *Pink and Say.* New York: Philomel.

______. (1996). *Aunt Chip and the great Triple Creek Dam affair.* New York: Philomel.

______. (1998). *Thank you, Mr. Falker.* New York: Philomel.

______. (2000). *Mr. Lincoln's way.* New York: Philomel.

Rathman, P. (1995). *Officer Buckle and Gloria.* New York: Putnam.

Yolen, J. (1992). *Encounter.* Illus. David Shannon. San Diego: Harcourt, Brace, Jovanovich.

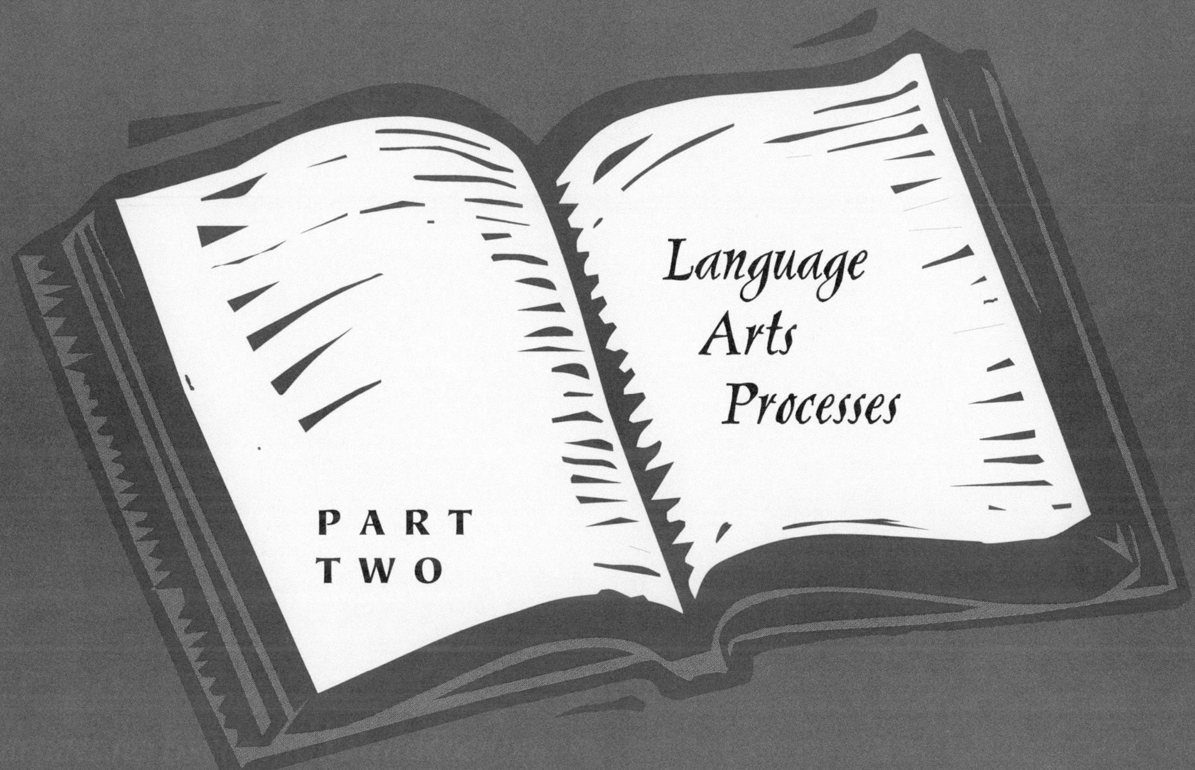

Language
Arts
Processes
PART
TWO

Oral Language: Early and Later Development

CHAPTER OUTLINE

An infant lies on the changing table as her grandmother changes her diaper. Grandma talks to the baby about her pretty blanket, the nice bath she has taken, and what a beautiful child she is. Now and then grandma pauses in her commentary and the child coos back. They seem to take turns and the conversation continues.

An 18-month-old child grabs a book from his toy box. It is a familiar book that has been read to him many times. Although he is holding the book upside down, he "reads" the pictures as he places his whole hand on one page at a time and names the object he sees. Most often, his utterances can only be understood by other family members. "Bottle! Baby! Bib!" The child finishes half the book and waits for the approval he knows will be forthcoming. Satisfied with what he has accomplished, he moves on to other amusements with the same brief but intense attention given the book.

A 5-year-old helps his father plant tomatoes in the backyard. He helps dig the holes for the tomato seedlings and for the sticks the tomatoes will climb. He watches and listens as Dad reads the directions for the fertilizer aloud. Words such as fertilizer, trowel, spade, soil, *and* drainage *are used throughout the process. Now the planting is done. In the days ahead, the two will water, watch, and wait together.*

A family sits at the dinner table. The members consist of Mom, Dad, three children ranging from ages 8 to 13, and a cousin, age 16, who lives with them. As is the custom of this family, each member briefly shares something special about the day. Sometimes the sharing centers on funny incidents. Sometimes it leads to a broader discussion of activities and plans for the future. Most often, it is simply a way of "catching up" with one another.

Key Standard

Teachers of language arts/reading are knowledgeable about children's language development; its importance to personal, social, and cognitive development; and its application to the curriculum. Such teachers:

- Are knowledgeable about how children learn and develop language and understand its role in learning.
- Understand the interrelationships among language and thought processes.
- Understand and respect language variation and the function of the home language in the development of children and take these into account in their instructional planning.
- Use their knowledge of effective communication to foster active inquiry, collaboration, and supportive interaction in the classroom.

1 To get a preview of Chapter 4 and learn about oral language development, visit the Chapter 4 section of the accompanying *Language Arts* CD-ROM.

Bernice Cullinan

Parents build a lasting foundation of language by reading to children from birth.

The scenes described above are ordinary and unremarkable. Yet, they are powerful descriptions of the ways in which language development is supported from birth through childhood. These are merely a sampling of the typical opportunities offered children in many families regardless of their ethnicity, income, geographical location, or first language. They reflect the most basic language experiences children require in their daily lives. It is not surprising that parents and educators relate to these descriptions and concur that they are positive and important. In fact, oral language learning seems so natural that it is often taken for granted.

Fortunately, there is no need to rely solely on our personal knowledge or impressions of what is important. Research, involving systematic studies of young children in many cultures, has provided us with scientific information about how language begins and the factors that influence its development. In this chapter we discuss how children develop as oral language users, stressing what a teacher needs to know about oral language development at home in order to help children continue to develop their communicative ability in school. We consider how oral language begins at home and the factors that affect its development, the characteristics of children's continuing language development during the elementary and middle school years, and the special challenges that language diversity offers to learners and teachers.

Dorothy Strickland

Hannah expresses her joy in books.

Speaking and Listening: Separate Areas of Learning and Teaching

Listening and speaking have traditionally been treated as separate areas of the language arts curriculum. Unfortunately, both in the research and in classroom application, listening has been the neglected side of the pair. When one considers the amount of time students spend listening in school, it is puzzling that listening is virtually ignored in comparison to speaking. Today, many teachers combine instruction in listening and speaking in contexts where students engage in presenting and responding through oral communication. Listening is also combined with strategies for reading, because students use similar strategies for comprehending texts whether they are oral or written. Indeed, a review of the research on listening reveals that some researchers have concern about studies that treat listening as a separate, isolated skill that is completely different from other language abilities (Pinnell & Jaggar, 2003). Throughout this text, we have integrated listening with other areas. However, we felt it important to devote some attention specifically to listening in this chapter. Following is an overview of the teaching of listening as a specific area of the language arts.

Listening: A Special Focus

Although most research on children's language development has focused on speech, the development of listening is also important. Listening provides the foundation from which other communication processes develop. Studies of children with physical disabilities, such as hearing disorders, underscore the interdependence among the various language processes with listening at the base (Lundsteen, 1976). As language is expanded and developed, listening remains the primary mode for acquiring linguistic knowledge and skill.

Listening, like the other aspects of the language arts, is central across the curriculum and across the school day. Children listen for their name to be called, listen to directions, and listen to morning announcements. They listen to stories, to presentations, and to music. They also listen to each other as they work cooperatively or share their writing (see the *Teaching Idea: Listen Closely*). Listening ability is linked to reading comprehension. Listening serves many purposes: performing a ritual, being informed, imagining, feeling (aesthetic listening), and critical listening (Lundsteen, 1990, pp. 216–217).

Rather than passive reception, listening is an active process that involves "receiving, focusing, attending, discriminating, assigning meaning, monitoring, remembering, and responding to auditory messages" (Lundsteen, 1990, p. 216). When people listen, they receive the message the speaker is uttering, decide to attend to that message and ignore extraneous sounds, focus on what they have discriminated (discerned) to be the important components of that message, build meaning, monitor the meaning being created and their

TEACHING IDEA

Assessing the Learning Environment

LISTEN CLOSELY

When children share their writing with a group of peers, have the writer read the piece aloud. A listener then volunteers to retell the piece. After the retelling and a brief discussion of the accuracy of the retelling, the group goes on to discuss the writer's work. This procedure encourages children to listen carefully to their peers.

responses to that meaning, and then respond to the utterance. When children talk to each other, they do all these things in a natural, social way. When children listen in the more formal context of school, they often need to be helped to listen effectively.

Studies focused on listening development and the teaching of listening reveal that individual differences in listening ability can be found in children even as they enter school (Pearson & Fielding, 1982). These include differences in hearing acuity, discrimination, and comprehension. As in other areas of learning, these differences tend to persist, causing the range of ability to become wider as children advance through the grades. Because in elementary school children spend a great proportion of their day listening to others, the ability to be an effective listener is important in the classroom, as well as in the workplace and at home, where parents can be encouraged to talk and listen to their children (see the *Teaching Idea: Involving Parents*) to reinforce school activities.

What can we as teachers do to help children listen effectively? Primarily, we can make them aware of successful strategies for listening (like those noted in the *Teaching Ideas: News Conferences* and *Critical Listening*) as they engage in meaningful activities. We can help them direct their attention to listening and encourage them to listen for a particular purpose. We can help children learn to label or categorize information as they listen by constructing organizers, such as semantic maps. We can make them aware of word signals, such as "first" and "next." We can encourage them to ask clarifying questions as they listen. We can help them learn to paraphrase what they are hearing, using that paraphrase as a comprehension-monitoring strategy (Lundsteen, 1990, pp. 222–223). Most importantly, we can encourage children to moni-

TEACHING IDEA

Home/School Connections

INVOLVING PARENTS

Help parents become aware that, as important as the school is in developing oral language, there is no substitute for the one-to-one language interactions that take place at home. Use a home/school newsletter or parent conferences to remind parents of the importance of helping children build confidence in their abilities to think and express themselves verbally. Book reading, television shows, and movies offer opportunities to discuss what the child likes and dislikes.

Stress the importance of allowing children to talk about their feelings, why they liked one character rather than another, or what might have disturbed them. As adults, we need to listen attentively even to the very youngest children and to respect their opinions.

TEACHING IDEA

From the Research

NEWS CONFERENCES

Shoop proposes a technique that she says is equally successful in building listening, reading, or a combination of listening and reading comprehension. A narrative text is selected to be read aloud, silently, or both. The teacher interrupts at several points to call a spontaneous news conference in which the students play investigative reporters at the scene of one of the story events. Their questioning of each other promotes interpretive and critical responses. Adapted from: "Inquest: A listening and reading comprehension strategy," by M. Shoop, *The Reading Teacher* (March 1986), 670–674.

tor their own listening, to recognize the strategies they use, and to revise these strategies when they are not effective. We can do this by engaging students in meaningful activities that require them to listen actively, and asking them to assess themselves as listeners. Teachers and children can express themselves through the ancient art of storytelling, providing unlimited opportunities for creating and listening to old and new stories. Many ideas for finding stories are included in the *Teaching Idea: Learning about Storytelling through the World Wide Web*.

Good listening goes well beyond merely paying attention; it involves understanding the spoken message. Teachers who foster good listening habits

TEACHING IDEA

Assessing the Learning Environment

CRITICAL LISTENING

Listening carefully and thoughtfully in order to respond to what is heard requires attentive listening and analysis of what is heard. Read aloud or tell a brief story that includes a problem of some sort (a lost child; a child who is tempted to visit someone on the way home from school, although the child has been told to go straight home; an issue of current interest in the news). Have students listen in order to discuss alternative solutions to the problem. Remind them that their suggestions must be based on the facts presented. Be sure to list their solutions on the chalkboard so that the other children can see them when they are discussed as a whole class or in small groups. Have them reach a consensus on the best alternatives.

TEACHING IDEA

Making Use of Technology

LEARNING ABOUT STORYTELLING THROUGH THE WORLD WIDE WEB

Anthropologists have labeled human beings at times as the *Problem Solvers* or the *Toolmakers,* but the most appropriate label—if there is one—is probably the *Storytellers,* for no other species comes to mind that organizes and expresses experiences in narrative form. Yet this essential form of communication is neglected or overlooked in many language arts classrooms. (Some researchers believe that storytelling was the *first* instructional technique and that it is still the most effective!) Often, stories that were once part of the oral tradition for countless generations are now only experienced with retellings mediated by picture storybooks or videos. As valuable as those experiences are, it is a special event when a storyteller, an audience, and a good story meet.

At least four requirements are necessary for teachers to enhance the storytelling experiences by and for their students:

1. Membership in a community of experienced storytellers
2. Understanding of the cognitive, social, and emotional values of storytelling
3. Access to high-quality stories
4. Guidance in developing storytelling skills

Advocates of this ancient and basic form of communication have embraced a modern form of communication, the World Wide Web (WWW), to satisfy these four requirements. The WWW abounds in sites devoted to the art of storytelling. Stories from nearly every ethnic background, covering nearly the entire range of the human experience, can be found on the WWW. Teachers who are interested in incorporating storytelling into their language arts programs, or who wish to enhance their skills at developing young storytellers, will find two Web sites of particular value. Story Arts Online (http://www.storyarts.com) provides lesson plans, an idea exchange service, and articles about storytelling. The National Storytelling Network (http://www.storynet.org) provides links to story archives, storytellers who visit classrooms, newsletters, storytelling events and activities, tips for telling stories well, and nearly every imaginable topic related to storytelling.

tend to be good listeners themselves. They consider what children have to say is important, and they show it. Such teachers help children set purposes for listening as a natural part of each day's activities. Standards for listening can be set with the group, referred to, and reviewed periodically after a discussion or planning period. Compliments for good listening can be given. Seating arrangements and other physical conditions also can support good listening habits. A teacher who plans for good listening experiences will have students who see the value of being a good listener.

Oral Language Development During the Early Years

All humans begin learning language, learning about language, and learning through language from the moment of birth. Sitting on your mother's lap, you listened to a story, pointing at pictures and crooning baby words. Your mother listened to you, smiled at you, and told you what the name of the pictured object was. You uttered another baby word, and she smiled again. What were you learning? You were learning labels for objects, even though you were not yet able to pronounce those labels. You were also learning about those objects as you learned their labels. You were learning that talking to another person is something nice to do and how to take turns talking, and you were learning how to handle a book.

As Britton (1983) notes, reading and writing float "on a sea of talk," and as human beings we are afloat in this sea of talk from the moment we are born. We are born with the potential to communicate through language, and we do so quite rapidly, mastering most of the conventions of oral language before age 5 or 6. We develop our **linguistic competence,** or knowledge of sounds, meanings, and syntax, and our **communicative competence,** or knowledge of the social and linguistic rules that govern different situations. This development is not the result of formal instruction, or the accomplished imitation of adult language, but rather the creative construction of a system of rules for language use. Children, immersed in this sea of talk, actively construct their own rule-governed, meaningful language. What an accomplishment! Moreover, this amazing accomplishment provides the foundation for language and literacy learning throughout life. Indeed, numerous studies indicate that the quality and amount of these kinds of rich language-learning experiences during the years up through kindergarten have a profound effect on how well children succeed or the extent to which they struggle in their later schooling (Snow, Tabors, & Dickinson, 2001).

THE CONTEXT

Systematic observations of children in many cultures developing their oral language have helped researchers understand how language begins and the factors that affect its development. These observations offer a sound basis on which to build programs for continuing development during the school years. Keep in mind the family scenes described at the beginning of this chapter as we discuss five qualities that usually surround oral language development at home.

1. *The atmosphere surrounding oral language development is warm and rewarding.* Parents and older siblings are delighted with every sound, every utterance—and they show it. Children are encouraged to experiment with their language use, and their language miscues, or "mistakes," are material for family stories or special nicknames for years to come. Long before they begin to master their language system, children are listened to as if they make sense and responded to as such, without regard to "correctness." For example, when 10-month-old Anna wants a cookie, she shrieks "Dah-do!" and her mother heads for the cookie tin, rewarding Anna with the desired response. In the safe, supportive environment of home, young language users are rewarded for their approximations rather than scolded for their mistakes.
2. *Language development occurs in a social, child-centered context.* Adults and older siblings accept the child on his or her terms. They talk *with,* rather than *at,* the child and seem to sense the child's need to be an active participant, demanding feedback and shared control. Adults who interact with the child and give help when needed are informally demonstrating language. Adults adjust their language and their actions in response to what the child needs, responding to what the child means, rather than to a preconceived notion of how that meaning ought to be put into words, or encoded.
3. *The context for language and conceptual development is always meaningful.* The natural curiosity of young children drives them to interact with people, places, and things in their environment. They want to know about everything, to touch, taste, and experience it all. As children go about their explorations, adults frequently use language to help them make connections and distinctions. Thus, children are surrounded by multiple examples of language being used in meaningful ways for a variety of purposes.
4. *Children are presented with the entire language system at once.* Adults do not attempt to break down language so that children learn one sound or one sentence pattern at a time. Neither a skills array nor an elaborate management system is used to help guide parents and children through the process. Neither standard nor "correct" forms are required.
5. *Children are learning not only the linguistic aspects of language (phonology, syntax, and semantics) but also how to use language (pragmatics) in a wide variety of situations.* Language users in every child's environment constantly offer examples of how to "do" language: how to request information, how to talk on the telephone, how to talk to friends, how to take turns talking, how to do any number of things with language. As children learn the linguistic "rules"

of their home language, they also are learning the communicative "rules" of how to use this language.

The basic human drive to communicate and a rich language environment seem to be the main factors that propel the process of language learning at home. Let's look more closely at how oral language develops during the early years at home under the conditions just described.

SOME DESCRIPTIONS OF ORAL LANGUAGE DEVELOPMENT

Child language development can be viewed as an ongoing process in which children expand and refine their knowledge of the language system of their home culture. The work of numerous researchers has helped to illuminate our understanding of the language development of the very young child (Bloom, 1970; Brown, 1973; Dickinson & Tabors, 2001; Hart & Risely, 1995; McNeill, 1970; Templin, 1987). Although children vary widely in when and what they learn about language, at least seven general points are important to consider as you plan language experiences for the children in your classroom.

1. *From infancy, children use language intentionally.* That is, they use language to perform some kind of function. The linguist M. A. K. Halliday, after observing his young son, concluded that early language serves one of two basic functions: the **"mathetic,"** or learning function, and the **"pragmatic,"** or doing function (1975). Children go on to differentiate these two basic functions as they develop their language.
2. *Children's early intentional speech consists primarily of one-word utterances that represent an entire thought or sentence.* The meanings constructed rely heavily on context and nonverbal clues. For example, "up" might stand for "Pick me up" or "I want to go up the stairs." Sometimes called **"holophrasic"** or **"telegraphic"** (Brown & Bellugi, 1964), these utterances carry meaning in the same way that an adult sentence carries meaning.
3. *Two-word utterances combine key words to represent an entire sentence.* (Typical examples are "See baby" and "See Mommy.") Context and nonverbal clues continue to help speaker and listener construct meaning. A pivot word such as "see" might be used with many other words. Additionally, the same two-word utterance might mean entirely different things (Bloom, 1970). For example, "Anna doll" might mean "This is Anna's doll" or "Anna wants to play dolls." Utterances such as these are demonstrations of the child's

developing syntactic and semantic systems as the child applies basic semantic and syntactic rules even though the utterances are "incomplete" according to adult rules.

4. *Utterances expand beyond two words.* The word order of adult speech is often present, as in "Going Nana's house" for "I am going to Nana's house." Where adult word order is not present, as in question formation, it gradually develops.
5. *By 3 years of age, telegraphic speech has been replaced by more developed utterances.* Most children have acquired a sufficiently large vocabulary and adequate use of syntax to allow them to be less dependent on their immediate context for communicating.
6. *Experimentation with language increases as children develop the ability to generalize and find patterns and order in language.* Structural awareness becomes evident as children make errors by overgeneralizing. For example, a child who is figuring out how the past tense works in the English language might say things such as "I putted it on the table."
7. *Upon entering kindergarten, most children know a great deal about language.* They have a vocabulary of several thousand words, and they have internalized the phonology and linguistic structures of their home language. They can understand and give varied messages. They know that language is functional, and they use it for a variety of functions, including sharing ideas and facilitating their own purposes.

Language development is a continuous process. Learners vary greatly in rate of development and are typified by an uneven pattern of rapid accomplishment interspersed with periods of self-directed practice. How, what, and when children learn about language varies widely and is influenced by the environment in which they live. Variations in language development are the norm, but the end result is the same. Children become proficient users of their home language by the time they enter school.

ORAL LANGUAGE-LEARNING STRATEGIES

Young children use a variety of language-learning strategies as they develop their language abilities. The use of nonlinguistic cues, questioning, imitation, and the application of operating principles are among the many strategies children utilize as they develop proficiency with language.

Nonlinguistic cues

Children use nonlinguistic cues to help them understand the meanings of language. Children associate the word "cookie" with the food handed to them or the words "Sit down!" with the act of sitting as someone physically places

Bernice Cullinan

Students develop oral language competence by talking with others.

them on a chair. They observe how others express meanings and listen for salient features in the language that interest them. Children often use what they observe to see how others will respond: "See, I sitting down."

Questioning

Young children ask a great many questions to get the information they need to build vocabularies and to make associations among the many objects and actions around them. "What's that?" and "Why?" are major components of their speech. They ask questions about language use, such as "Why you say that, Mommy?" They also ask direct questions about word meaning, such as "What 'few' mean, Mommy?" Sometimes these questions are quite sophisticated.

Four-year-old Adam discussed with his mother the two meanings of the word "hard," talking until he understood the distinction between difficult and solid. This use of language, which Halliday (1975) called the "heuristic" function, serves not only to learn about the world but also to learn about language itself.

Imitation

Imitation is another language-learning strategy of children. However, researchers in child language development stress that this is not a mere echoing of random linguistic events, but a purposeful, selective imitation of words and structures that children are in the process of learning. According to Lindfors:

> If imitation were a mindless, automatic, echo behavior, we would expect a randomness in what children repeat. However, recent imitation studies have identified a clear nonrandom pattern in what it is that children do and do not imitate; that is, there is selection on the part of the child (1987, p. 187).

Children do not simply echo what they hear, they select from the sea of talk that exists in their environment, and they practice those forms that are of interest to them at the moment. It might be a formal greeting, or forming the past tense, or a particularly interesting phrase from a book, but it is a deliberate choice on the part of the child. Delighted with the sentence "I trust it is not a rat!" from Beatrix Potter's *The Tale of Mr. Jeremy Fisher*, 4-year-old Adam used that construction over and over again, substituting various nouns for the word "rat."

General operating principles

Perhaps the most significant aspect of children's language-learning strategies is their use of general operating principles to figure out how language works. Many classic studies of first language acquisition, including Slobin's (1973) study of children speaking more than forty different languages, confirm that children are active noticers and users of language patterns. When children create such forms as "putted," they are demonstrating the use of an operating principle in which they generalize that if the meaning of "past" is intended, then it should be indicated clearly through the use of structures they have learned to use in similar cases. When children apply their self-constructed language "rules" that are appropriate in one situation, such as being at the playground with their friends, to another, such as being at the doctor's office with mom, they are using what they know to operate in the world, and refining that knowledge as they receive feedback from those around them: "No, honey, we don't shout at the doctor's office."

Children view language as "rule-governed," and they process the many examples of language used for a variety of purposes that surround them to figure out for themselves just what the "rules" are. What these rules are varies, of course, according to the customs of the home, but all children learn to operate by these rules before they enter school.

WRITTEN LANGUAGE-LEARNING STRATEGIES

Parents and teachers of young children notice that children use the same strategies employed to develop oral language as they attempt to construct meanings from the print in their environment. Very young children are quick to use pictures and other nonlinguistic cues to identify the picture books they wish to have read over and over again. They frequently ask "What's that?" as they move through a favorite text, asking not only about the objects pictured but about the letters, words, and punctuation marks as well. Board books (small, easy-to-handle books with thick pages) are perfect for toddlers, because they encourage the naming of clearly identified ordinary objects. Frequently, adult and child use these books to play a naming game as each one asks and answers the question, "What's that?"

Imitation of the adult's reading, or "pretend reading," is common among young children, as they attempt to reenact the story reading on their own. Obviously, the more informal experiences young children have with books, the greater their opportunities to learn and apply operating principles related to book handling and linguistic awareness.

Kindergarten teachers often use charts and white boards to record children's thoughts so that they can see their spoken words in print. The *Teaching Idea: Field Trips, Talking, and Writing* is an example of an effective combination of talking and writing with young children. Chapter Six explores the concurrent development of young children's oral and written language in greater depth.

Bernice Cullinan

Readers demonstrate their oral language competence when they dramatize a story or a poem.

TEACHING IDEA

Assessing the Learning Environment

FIELD TRIPS, TALKING, AND WRITING

Sally Perkins integrates talk with written language around firsthand experiences she plans for her kindergarten children. Before visiting the local firehouse, she led several discussions about what her class might expect to see or do. Each prediction was written on a chart entitled "The Firehouse: What We Think We'll See and Do." The predictions were based on books read aloud and the children's background knowledge.

During the trip, the children were encouraged to recall what they had discussed in order to ask questions about what they were experiencing. Upon their return, the children talked about the many things they had seen and done. Later they turned to their chart to confirm or disconfirm their predictions, checking off all they had seen that was expected and adding new items that were not listed. The talk and the writing combined to focus and document their ideas. Each time they returned to the chart, relevant vocabulary and concepts were reexamined and reinforced.

EARLY LANGUAGE DEVELOPMENT IN SCHOOL SETTINGS

Just as parents help children at home develop their language, kindergarten and prekindergarten teachers help foster language development by planning opportunities for children to talk about relevant experiences in the classroom. Erica, a pre-kindergarten teacher, allows time for children to share what they did at various centers each day. This kind of sharing gives children an opportunity to recount through oral language an actual experience that has meaning for themselves and for the listeners involved. Erica encourages the children to use language that is as precise as possible so that the listeners can get a full sense of what is being conveyed. She sometimes uses questions, such as "What more can you tell us about the clothes you wore for dress-up today?" or "Where did you decide to travel in your bus?"or "What did you see along the way?" to encourage children to elaborate.

Erica also encourages children to ask questions of each other. Right from the beginning of the year, she demonstrates the kinds of questions she expects the children to use. By focusing on familiar things that children have actually experienced, Erica facilitates language use among all children, regardless of their home language or developmental status. Informal classroom share sessions also serve as a kind of rehearsal for what children might talk about when parents ask them what they did in school that day.

Oral Language Development During the Elementary School Years and Beyond

Children continue to grow in language competence throughout the elementary school years. Their increasing language ability reflects a growing understanding of the world around them, as well as a growing understanding of the language surrounding them. As the range and depth of their experiences increase, new concepts are formed and expressed through language. As a result, their vocabulary increases, and they learn to represent increasingly complex ideas with increasingly complex syntactic constructions and increasingly precise lexical choices. Using language, they learn about their language itself, developing conscious understandings about how their language works. This metalinguistic awareness, rooted in the beginnings of language, flowers during the elementary school years. As their experiences increase, they also develop their communicative competence, as they learn to use language effectively in an ever-wider variety of situations for an ever-wider variety of purposes.

Many researchers have examined the continuing evolution of language during the elementary school years (Bormouth, Carr, Manning, & Pearson, 1970; Carroll, 1970; Chomsky, 1972; Pellegrini, Galda, & Rubin, 1984; and Strickland, 1962). Their research has confirmed that semantic, syntactic, and pragmatic development continues during the school years.

SYNTACTIC AND SEMANTIC DEVELOPMENT

Chomsky (1972) found several sentence structures that kindergarten children misinterpreted consistently. Misinterpretations concerned meanings of "easy to see" and "hard to see." A doll, whose eyes closed when lying down, was laid on a table. The children were asked, "Is the doll hard to see or easy to see?" Later, the doll was placed out of sight and the children were asked the same question. Children under $5\frac{1}{2}$ said that the doll was hard to see in both instances. Beyond that age some children began to interpret the question correctly. By age 9 all children did. In another study, Carroll (1970) examined children's comprehension of words with multiple grammatical functions—for example, words that can be verbs or adjectives, such as *best, secure,* and *warm.*

He asked 1,500 children in grades 3, 6, and 9 to write sentences illustrating 240 such words. He concluded that learning to understand grammatically ambiguous words is an ongoing process, far from complete even by grade 9.

Research in child language development is of vital importance to classroom teachers, because it relates directly to the cognitive and linguistic demands of the typical classroom. It reminds us that children's language development continues throughout the school-age years. The need to probe and explore children's understandings and interpretations of language and language use is a necessary part of good classroom practice.

Loban (1963) conducted one of the most comprehensive studies of language development in schoolchildren. He followed children from kindergarten through grade 12, beginning with 338 kindergarteners, 30 of whom were rated exceptionally high in language development and 24 rated exceptionally low. Tracking these children over 12 years revealed that all of them increased the number of words spoken each year and increased their effectiveness in speaking. There was a dramatic difference in the amount of increase within each group, however. The high language-development group not only maintained its superiority, but also increased in complexity of sentence structure and added vocabulary until it was about double that of the low language-development group. The high group used a greater number of less common words and was more fluent in language use than the low group or the remaining subjects. The high group continuously used a greater variety of sentence structures and was distinguished by greater effectiveness in the use of language.

What does this mean for teachers of elementary school children? One implication of Loban's study is that once children are considered by teachers to be less fluent than their peers, they are likely to perform in an increasingly less capable manner when compared with their peers. Remember, these children came to school as perfectly competent users of their home language, but, according to school standards, were regarded as less competent than others. In school, with the accompanying insistence on norms and grade-level comparisons, the variety inherent in oral language development in the early years was ignored. Those children whose language competence did not fit as well with school-defined standards of competence were at a distinct disadvantage. We examine this problem more fully later in this chapter.

Teaching practices may be one reason that the students in the group labeled "low" lost ground to their peers. Research suggests that children who speak school-like language, and who speak fluently, get the most opportunities to talk, whereas those less ready with words and assurance are sometimes ignored. Unfortunately, those whose home language differs from the language expected in school are also often corrected when they do speak, thus ensuring that soon they will never orally volunteer anything. Further, these children are often given increased amounts of workbook drill when they need increased amounts of time to use oral language for a variety of purposes in a safe situation. Loban suggests that teachers encourage speech to express ideas, attitudes, and values of concern to the students. Rather than drill on usage, teachers should work with students to achieve coherence and organization in their speech.

PRAGMATIC DEVELOPMENT

A study by Pellegrini, Galda, and Rubin (1984) focused on how children continue to develop in their ability to use language. They asked first, third, and fifth grade children to retell a story to someone who had not heard it and to persuade someone to take them to a circus. The first grade children had difficulty with these tasks, with only a few of them able to do what was asked of them easily and efficiently. By the third grade, the children could handle the tasks easily. Their communicative competence had developed to such a degree that they could understand and encode what their listeners needed to know.

Whereas other researchers studied children's developing ability to understand and use various grammatical structures, Halliday (1975) analyzed children's speech in terms of the function to which they put it. Arguing that children's language is functional from infancy, that it serves a distinct purpose, Halliday identified a developmental pattern that begins with the instrumental, or the "I want" function. In the order in which they evolve, the seven functions are

Instrumental	"I want . . ."
Regulatory	"Do as I tell you . . ."
Interactional	"Me and you . . ."
Personal	"I am . . ."
Heuristic	"Tell me why . . ."
Imaginative	"Let's pretend . . ."
Informative	"I've got something to tell you . . ."

By the time children reach school age, they are using language to perform all of these functions. As a result, their language use is rich and varied. When they get to school, their ability to use language for a variety of functions needs to be encouraged and built upon. Unfortunately, in many classrooms children are asked only to use the informative function. Note that the informative use of language is usually the last to develop in children. Children use it least, and they are least likely to understand its use by others. Effective teachers are aware of the danger of the overuse of telling as a means of teaching. They are also aware of the debilitating effects of restricting

TEACHING IDEA

Assessing the Learning Environment

OPPORTUNITIES FOR TALKING AND LISTENING IN THE CLASSROOM

Activities such as:

Acting out stories
Audio and video taping
Choral speaking
Conferences with peers/teachers about writing or reading
Dialogues
Discussion of mathematics and content area topics
Interviewing
Making announcements
Oral reading
Panel discussions
Puppetry
Radio and TV shows
Reader-response groups
Readers' Theatre
Reporting
Role playing
Sharing time
Storytelling
Story retelling

Activities Involving:

Hands-on experience
Brainstorming
Planning
Problem solving
Collaborative learning
Participation during read-alouds
Song and singing games
A range of listening experiences

children's talk to the informative function. Instead, they plan oral language activities that encourage children to build upon their already established language competence. Classroom practice that is effective in developing children's oral language builds upon meaningful events that require varied uses of language for real purposes. The *Teaching Ideas: Opportunities for Talking and Listening in the Classroom* and *Using Pictures to Foster Viewing and Speaking* list many activities that help develop children's language abilities.

BUILDING ON CHILDREN'S LANGUAGE COMPETENCE

Reciprocal teaching, discussed in Chapter One, exemplifies the type of activity that teachers need to encourage. Reciprocal teaching involves students in summarizing, question generating, clarifying, and predicting as they read or observe phenomena. Children use oral language to communicate

TEACHING IDEA

Assessing the Learning Environment

USING PICTURES TO FOSTER VIEWING AND SPEAKING

Start a collection of photographs or scenic pictures, some with people in them. Have children discuss the pictures:

- Where do you think this takes place?
- Does it remind you of any thing or any place you know about?
- Pretend you are talking to someone on the telephone who cannot see the picture and describe it to them.
- Make up a story to go with the picture. If there are people in the picture, include them in the story.
- Share your story with the group.

about what they are experiencing through print or through firsthand experience. The talk involved is complex and multidimensional and comes from the mouths of the students rather than the teacher.

Cooperative learning is another activity that promotes oral language development. Cooperative learning strategies (Johnson, Johnson, Roy, & Holubec, 1984; Meloth, 1991) offer valuable opportunities to promote students' oral language as they work together to achieve common purposes. When children cooperate to solve problems or complete a project, like the fifth-graders working in cooperative science groups in the *Teaching Idea: Guidelines for Small-Group Work,* they must use language in many ways. They brainstorm, plan, explain, clarify, question, respond, and make use of oral language in numerous ways to help them understand and be understood by others.

Group discussion is a fundamental way to get children involved in talk. Throughout the day, countless opportunities arise for group discussion at every grade level. Often the talk centers on topics under study. Sometimes group discussion is a vital part of a routine, such as the "author's chair," discussed in Chapter Eight. At other times, something of interest may occur spontaneously to command the group's attention. Group planning and sharing, like that involved in the *Teaching Idea: Role Playing,* offer still other opportunities for talk in the classroom. However, attaining a high level of participation and quality content is not something that happens automatically. Teaching strategies that promote good discussions are explored in Chapter Five.

TEACHING IDEA

Addressing Individual Needs

GUIDELINES FOR SMALL-GROUP WORK

The following guidelines were devised by one fifth grade class, which formed cooperative learning groups to pursue various aspects of a science unit.

1. Discuss your topic and decide what information you want to learn.
2. Develop a list of questions. Have one person be the scribe and write them down.
3. Think of all the places you might get the information you need: magazines, books, newspapers, people.
4. Interview one or two people related to your topic. You may divide into pairs:
   - Brainstorm questions for the interview.
   - Decide how you will take notes.
   - Review your notes and share with your small group.
   - Revise, if needed, and report to the whole class.

Note all the opportunities for oral language use in this experience.

Certain student behaviors also promote good discussions, and ground rules for discussion, like those in Figure 4.1, need to be established early in the year and given attention through demonstrations and gentle reminders whenever the need arises. Rather than simply furnishing children with a list of appropriate behaviors, it is generally better to elicit their ideas on what helps make their discussions work, both before and after you have group discussions. Such things as taking turns, sticking to the point, and being attentive while others are talking will probably need to be discussed and then posted. When children have input into establishing rules, they are more likely to understand their need and to self-monitor their behavior in order to keep the discussion running smoothly. Establishing good models of group discussion through whole-class activities helps children work independently of the teacher in small groups. Further, this kind of planning also provides another meaningful opportunity for talk.

Oral interpretation and **response to literature,** discussed more fully in Chapter Seven, are important ways to link oral language and reading. Oral interpretation may take the form of dramatics, Readers' Theatre, or oral reading. At times, oral interpretation may accompany visual representation. **Oral response** may simply be peer or group discussions. When children use speech to extend their understanding of literature, they strengthen their

TEACHING IDEA

Literature Link

ROLE PLAYING

Role playing allows students to use oral language to interpret the feelings and actions of characters in a story. Choose scenes from a story in which there is dialogue. Select two children to role-play the parts. Let them know that although they must follow the story line, they should use their own language. Allow different pairs of children to role-play the same scene and discuss the different interpretations. Scenes that reflect everyday life are generally easier for younger children, because the words used are more like their natural language. For example, the dialogue between parent and child in *Bread and Jam for Frances* (Hoban, 1986) is easy for even young children to role-play, because it is well within their realm of experience.

Historical events and real-life problems also make good material for role playing. Participation in live drama can help children to understand better how it must feel to be in a particular situation, and it gives them the opportunity to use oral language in new ways.

abilities to speak fluently and easily. They learn to use oral language as a means of communicating ideas and as a way of learning.

DEVELOPING VOCABULARY

Opportunities for talk in the classroom range from one-to-one peer or student-teacher conversations to formal oral presentations. In the remaining chapters in this text, even those that focus primarily on reading and writing, we present numerous ways to use oral language to learn, to develop oral

FIGURE 4.1

How to Talk Together

1. Listen to what the speaker is saying.
2. Look at the person talking.
3. Talk about the topic.
4. Don't interrupt.
5. Respond to what the speaker is saying.
6. Give everyone a chance to say something.

language through speaking, and to help children to learn about language. These strategies are embedded within reading and writing because oral language is a natural partner of reading and writing.

Most children come to school with speaking vocabularies of several thousand words and continue to develop their vocabulary throughout their years in school. All of us have and use several vocabularies. For example, we all have a **"listening vocabulary"** that consists of words understood in context when heard. We may not be able to define all of these words precisely, and we may never say some of them, but we understand what the words mean when they are used. Our **"speaking vocabulary"** consists of words we use in our oral communications with others. Our **"reading vocabulary"** consists of words we can read and understand but not necessarily define or use, and our **"writing vocabulary"** is built of words we use in written discourse. These vocabularies overlap to a large extent, but some words appear in only one or two of them. Many of the words in these vocabularies are firmly established and used frequently and with ease; some are less frequently but still confidently used; others are used infrequently and somewhat tentatively.

As children encounter new experiences and learn to read and write, their oral vocabulary increases tremendously. Indeed, as they live their lives, their vocabularies grow and change constantly as new experiences and new needs add words to their personal lexicons. Many of the words individuals know come from what they read. As we discuss in Chapter Four, wide reading increases vocabulary. Children also learn new vocabulary as they learn new information. Studying animal families adds words such as *mare, foal, filly,* and *colt;* studying space adds words such as *planet, eclipse,* and *orbit.* Much vocabulary learning is informal and comes about as the result of language experiences with the world. In the classrooms described in this text, opportunities for learning vocabulary abound.

Children learn best that which they want to know, so using classroom events and the specific needs of individual children to help them develop vocabulary is of great importance. Vocabulary instruction can be embedded in discussions of books. Many times authors use interesting words to describe places, actions, characters, and events. Talking about these words is a natural way both to learn new vocabulary and to increase appreciation of the author's craft. Vocabulary is built when studying topics in science, mathematics, social science, art, music, and physical education as children learn new words in order to read, write, and talk about what they are learning. Teachers often take advantage of children's interests to teach them some of the "tricks of the trade." For example, when a second grade class suddenly noticed that many occupations ended in "er"—teacher, writer, carpenter—their teacher suggested that they explore other words that ended in "er" and talk about what that "er" might do and mean. Learning about "er" led to learning about other

TEACHING IDEA

Addressing Individual Needs

VOCABULARY BUILDING

Primary-grade children enjoy playing with compound words. Print a compound word on a rectangular piece of paper, leaving a slight space in the middle. Then cut the rectangle apart, cutting each word slightly differently. Working together, children can join the pieces of the word puzzles to make compound words:

snow/man   bed\room

Upper-grade children might enjoy exploring word families. Working in groups, have them brainstorm a list of nouns they are familiar with and then try to think of words that are related to each one. For example, *art* might be followed by *artist, artistic, artisan*. After they have some ideas on paper, have them use dictionaries with etymological information to explore their word families. What they learn can be put on a poster and displayed for others to read. Other areas to explore are the history of individual words (such as *sandwich, bread, lady, frankfurter*) and affixes and how they work.

affixes, and the second-graders learned much about vocabulary. Vocabulary instruction is also a natural part of language study. Variety in lexical choices, idiomatic expressions, compound words (see the *Teaching Idea: Vocabulary Building*), and newly coined words are some topics that lend themselves to vocabulary building. Throughout this text we give examples of children learning new vocabulary by using it.

LEARNING ABOUT LANGUAGE

Learning about language involves coming to understand the nature and function of language itself (Halliday, 1982). Knowledge about language evolves almost unconsciously, as children use words such as *say, call,* and *mean* in increasingly more sophisticated ways as they begin to understand that language can be talked about just like anything else. As children acquire and develop language, they become increasingly adept in its use and in their ability to use the terms that describe its use. Terms such as *word, sentence, noun,* and *synonym* are part of the metalanguage, or language used to describe and talk about language.

Children's ability to think and talk "about" language is called **metalinguistic awareness.** The ability to reflect upon and describe language and language processes is related positively to success in formal schooling and literacy. More about the development of metalinguistic awareness is found in Chapter Six.

DEVELOPING FLUENCY

Children come to school knowing a great deal about how language works. Once in school, they can continue to build on this implicit knowledge as they add to their understandings about language and increase their fluent and flexible use of language. Halliday (1982) cautions that as we come to strengthen and extend the child's language development through education we must take care to extend what children have already started to build as a picture of what language is for and what it can do—a picture built through meaningful interaction with others. Too often what serves as language instruction in school bears little resemblance to what the child already knows and feels confident about. Schools tend to impose an artificial discontinuity on the language-learning experience to the extent that children never realize that what the teacher is talking about is merely an extension of what they already know (1982, p. 19). Unfortunately, some children enter school and come to believe that they know nothing about language and that they must now learn grammar. Their implicit knowledge of the grammar of their home language is ignored, and instead they are forced to demonstrate an explicit knowledge of an arbitrary system of "rules" that do not always work!

In recent years, innumerable studies of the efficacy of teaching grammar as a separate subject have led to the same conclusion: grammar drill may teach children enough to pass a weekly test, but most of them rarely use what they "learn" in those drills in their own speaking or writing. However, this does not mean that grammatical concerns should be ignored. Weaver (1979) distinguishes between the formal teaching of grammar and developing students' intuitive sense of grammar through informal instruction. Formal teaching is not especially useful. Much more effective are teachers who use their own knowledge of grammar to help students grow in their understanding and use of language. Wise teachers talk about language with children, using and defining metalinguistic terms such as *noun, verb, adjective, word, sentence,* or *letter.*

Children are already using verbs, adjectives, and sentences in their speech and in their early attempts at reading and writing, but are often unaware of the conventional metalinguistic terms. Knowledge of these terms is helpful to children in the early development of literacy. Further, as discussed in other chapters, in order to talk about the books they read and the pieces they write, students need terminology. It is not a question of not teaching the parts of speech, but of teaching them as children engage in meaningful uses of language.

Children process the oral language that surrounds them as they construct hypotheses about how oral language works. Children also construct operating principles about how written language works. Their innate curiosity about language can be nourished by teachers who know how to recognize children's language hypotheses and how to help them embrace more sophisticated concepts of language through manipulating language.

One of the powerful things about English is its flexibility—how it gives speakers many ways to say the same thing. How we choose to say something depends on the situation we are in and the effect we want to create. This is often referred to as **"register."** There is no single correct way of saying something, but rather a variety of constructions, whether we are writing or speaking. Hillocks (1986) suggests that a fitting goal for writers is **facility:** knowing how to use a variety of syntactic structures, being able to select possible structures, and being able to select the most effective structures. This is a fitting goal for instruction in oral language as well: to help students become as fluent and flexible as possible by helping them learn how to adjust their language to the demands of the topic, audience, and context. A student who can do this is an effective language user.

Teachers can encourage students to learn how language works in a variety of ways. Talking about language in relation to reading and writing is a natural and necessary part of a school day. As children use oral and written language for their own purposes and in their own ways, they will need and want to talk about that language—working with their peers and their teacher to say what they want to say, write what they want to write, and comprehend what they want to read (see the *Teaching Idea: Talking about Language with Children*).

TEACHING IDEA

Assessing the Learner

TALKING ABOUT LANGUAGE WITH CHILDREN

After hearing her second-graders talking about words that show what characters do, Sherry introduced the label "verb" and talked briefly about different types of verbs. Her students had already noticed one of the functions verbs perform. She introduced the formal label and added to their knowledge about function. Jorge noticed that his sixth-graders were attempting to revise some of their writing by moving chunks of words—usually clauses—and he decided to introduce the notion of clauses and some of their functions. His timing was perfect. His students needed to be able to talk about what they were trying to do.

An approach such as this takes the useful and generally used vocabulary of traditional grammar and introduces it to students in the context of their own reading and writing, providing them with an efficient means for examining and discussing language use. These teachers know a great deal about grammar. They use this knowledge to help their students develop as speakers and writers.

In a very real sense, the rest of this book is about teaching children "grammar"—where learning grammar means learning to discuss explicitly one's implicit knowledge of how language works and the concurrent development of that implicit knowledge through the meaningful use of language in a variety of contexts.

ORAL LANGUAGE ASSESSMENT

Teachers can use periodic tape recordings and other anecdotal records like those described in Chapter Twelve to assess student progress in oral language development. Many teachers record interviews with children in the beginning, middle, and end of the year, asking them questions about their interests, families, favorite foods, responses to books, or any other topics that will generate good oral language samples. Checklists can be constructed to consider any number of pertinent oral language development areas, including vocabulary, sentence complexity, sentence construction, pronunciation, enthusiasm for sharing oral information or other areas of interest or concern. Just as students' writing portfolios kept over a year can help teachers chart writing development, oral language samples can reveal children's progress in oral communication.

Language Variation across Families and Communities

The social, cultural, and economic context in which children learn language has a profound effect on the way they communicate. All children grow up in some form of family setting. Most families live in communities where they experience mutual compatibility and acceptance. Like previous generations before them, many have emigrated from other countries or other parts of the United States to seek a better life. For a variety of economic and social reasons, these families tend to remain within their new communities, helping to maintain existing similarities in culture and language. In inner-city and rural settings particularly, the speech of these communities frequently differs substantially from that of Standard English, the language of instruction in the schools. As a result, many children enter school speaking a dialect of English quite different from "school English" or a language other than English.

Language differences between home and school have received considerable attention as a possible cause of school failure. The low achievement of poor black and Hispanic children, in particular, has often been associated with their dialect or language. Terms such as "culturally deprived" and "language deficient" have frequently been inappropriately applied to these children. During the 1960s, linguists looked closely at language diversity as a cause of school failure. Focusing primarily on issues of black dialects, these studies revealed important principles about language diversity that remain helpful to teachers and curriculum developers today. The principles were summarized by Cullinan (1974): All language varieties are equally valid; all language varieties can accommodate all levels of thought; and any variety of Standard English is not intrinsically better than any nonstandard dialect (p. 7). Similarly, recent research in the language development of children for whom English is a second language supports the belief that the learner's home language should be valued and accepted as part of second-language acquisition and learning (Commins, 1989; Walters & Gunderson, 1985; Wolfram, Adger, & Christian, 1999).

The form language takes certainly is important, both economically and politically. Those who speak a Standard English dialect are more likely to be viewed as competent and intelligent. Those who speak in nonstandard forms are more likely to be viewed as less competent and less intelligent. The fact that this is simply not true seems to have had little effect on public perception. Nonstandard speakers are as competent, intelligent, and energetic as are standard speakers. Nonstandard usage does not negatively affect learning unless the atmosphere in the learning environment is one in which nonstandard speakers are silenced. Perhaps more than ever before, today's teachers are likely to encounter bilingual and bidialectal learners. For this reason, it is important to have some basic understanding of language diversity and its role in learning.

LANGUAGE DIVERSITY IN THE CLASSROOM

Every speaker has an individual dialect, or "idiolect," but some speak in a more "standard" fashion than others. Language diversity is present in all classrooms to a degree, but in some classrooms it is a central issue. Many children come to school speaking nonstandard dialects, and increasing numbers of children come to school speaking, or seeking to learn, English as a second language. Keeping in mind the goals of fluency and flexibility, successful teachers build on students' fluency in their home language, their communicative competence in their home culture, and their individual interests and needs. They do this by creating a safe, supportive, meaningful environment in which students can practice evolving language skills as they use oral language for purposeful and enjoyable ends.

Teachers often silence nonstandard speakers by correcting all nonstandard utterances. Rather than promoting standard speech, such correcting results in students who, rather than run the risk of being humiliated, simply do not talk. Correction also alienates students, because the implied message is that they, their language, and their home cultures are not appropriate for school. The result is angry, withdrawn children who do not want to learn Standard English and who therefore do not. Rather than correction, repetition in standard form followed by a question related to the meaning of the utterance is a better response. For example, if a student says, "My papa, he goed to the store," you might reply, "Your papa went to the store? Why did he go to the store?" This kind of response acknowledges what has been said as an important message, provides a standard model, and encourages the speaker to say more.

Teachers can inadvertently silence nonstandard speakers by ignoring the connection between their home language and their cultural identity. How students talk reflects who they are, and how they talk is realized in both form and style. Differences in form, discussed below, are easily recognized. Differences in style and their relation to the home culture are less easily recognized and adapted to in the classroom. For example, in some cultures it is impolite for children to speak directly to adults or to look adults directly in the eye. Not knowing this, teachers may think that such children are rude or uninterested in what is going on in the classroom when they do not volunteer information or look at the teacher. Not knowing about language style in nonmainstream cultures can lead to erroneous decisions. In a study of sharing time, Michaels (1981) found that black children, especially girls, had a very different narrative style from mainstream children. Not recognizing the narrative pattern that is common in the children's home cultures, teachers judged the nonmainstream narratives as deficient. A more productive response recognizes the pattern, explicitly discusses it as a way of telling a story, and then discusses the classic setting-problem-event-conclusion pattern as another way of telling a story. After all, as noted in Chapter Three, there are many ways to structure a plot.

Delpit (1990) notes that teachers miss great opportunities when they ignore the oral strengths of their nonmainstream children. "The verbal adroitness, the cogent and quick wit, the brilliant use of metaphorical language, the facility in rhythm and rhyme," present in many black students' oral language, or the "sophisticated knowledge about storytelling" of many Native American children can enrich lives in the classroom. "Classroom learning should be structured so that not only are these children able to acquire the verbal patterns they lack, but that they are also able to strengthen their proficiencies, and to share this with classmates and teachers" (p. 256).

Accepting and building on children's home language and allowing them diverse opportunities for talk (such as the situations listed in the *Teaching Idea:*

TEACHING IDEA

Home/School Connections

TALKING ABOUT LEXICAL CHOICES

Make a list of items commonly called by different names in different parts of the country. Have students interview people to find out what other names they may have used for those items. You might make a chart with a picture of each item at the top. Then simply list the words as children bring them in.

pancake	bag	soda	sofa
flapjack	poke	soda pop	davenport
griddle cake	sack	coke	couch

Talking about Language with Children on page 141), opportunities that include both informal and formal language, can be accompanied by actually studying language diversity. Children can collect variations in lexical choices (such as the possibilities given in the *Teaching Idea: Talking about Lexical Choices*), explore dialect in children's literature, and discuss different ways of using language for everyday functions, such as greetings. Children can listen to adults and older children, television, and the radio, and collect interesting language samples. As they learn about talk through these activities, they "talk to learn" with each other, with people outside of school, and with their teachers. Teachers cannot force children to alter their language, and trying to do so only creates problems in school. Rather, teachers can "provide students with the exposure to an alternate form, and allow them the opportunity to practice that form in contexts which are nonthreatening, have a real purpose, and are intrinsically enjoyable. If they have access to alternative forms, it will be their decision later in life to choose which to use. We can only provide them with the knowledge base and hope they will make appropriate choices" (Delpit, 1990, p. 253).

The bilingual learner

Language-minority students who possess varying degrees of ability to speak, read, and write in English as well as in their home language are said to be bilingual. Some of these students, those who may be termed English Language Learners (ELL) or Limited English Proficient (LEP), understand and speak little or no English. Many are foreign born; others live in homes where English is seldom spoken. Programs for language-minority students range from those that focus strictly on the target language, English as a Second

Language (ESL), to those that attempt to produce students who are fluent in both their home language and English—bilingual education.

Many times, a combination of programs is offered bilingual learners (Peregoy & Boyle, 2001). Cohen (1980) defines bilingual education as the provision of dominant-language academic and developmental reading instruction to LEP children along with a comprehensive ESL program until such time as they are able to transfer acquired skills into English (p. 5). Children in such programs, generally termed transitional bilingual education, are expected to make a continuous transfer of skills from their first language to the second language with eventual placement in an English-oriented academic setting.

Some bilingual programs are two-way. These classes include English-speaking students as well as native speakers of other languages. Sometimes called bilingual immersion programs, their goal is to help all students become fluent in two languages. Obviously, those who enter school having had some formal instruction in reading and writing in their native language or who have opportunities for two-way bilingual education have a better chance of becoming "balanced bilinguals," competent in both English and their home language.

The type of program offered bilingual learners will depend largely upon the goals the school considers important. If transition to English is valued

John Kassick

Teachers and students need bilingual books at home and at school.

most, an ESL program in which students are pulled out for extra instruction in English will probably be emphasized and little or no use made of the child's native language. We do not endorse this kind of program. If preservation and expansion of the child's native language and cultural identity is highly valued, instruction that makes use of the child's native language will prevail. Often, several varieties of these approaches can be found within a school or district, even when a particular approach has been officially designated.

Because there are currently more than 2.5 million school-age children for whom English is not their first language, the debate about school policy has created strong feelings and often divisive situations. A great deal of research has examined the issues surrounding bilingual education policy. In the past many educators felt that speaking, reading, and writing a language other than English would interfere with developing proficiency in English. We now know that there is no significant interference by the native language in the development of the second language (McLaughlin, 1987), and that first- and second-language development are very similar processes (Hudelson, 1990). Further, the rate of acquisition of the second language is related to the proficiency level in the native language. The two share and build upon a common base (Hakuta & Garcia, 1989). In addition, recent research indicates that there are at least two different dimensions of language proficiency in bilingual children—the use of contextualized language in face-to-face communication (such as conversations on the playground) and the use of decontextualized language more common to school contexts. It seems that fluent bilingual children can alter their language with ease in order to take advantage of the social communicative situation (Hakuta & Garcia, 1989). Often, fluent bilingual children speak a combination of English and their native language, relying on what they know about language to communicate their message. This mixing of the two languages and the use of language strategies acquired in the first language actually help in the development of English as a second language.

Placed in the context of what we now know about children's language development, it would seem that programs for bilingual learners should be **bilingual-bicultural** in nature. Bilingual-bicultural programs support children's concept acquisition and development in their native language as well as in English and make use of the culture and contributions of the minority language to support the curriculum as well as the learner's self-concept. These programs enlist the native-language community, consciously building connections between school and home that result in tremendously successful school experiences for bilingual learners. This approach means that teachers need to learn as much as they can about their students' linguistic and cultural backgrounds.

Native speakers of Spanish comprise the largest group of bilingual learners in the United States, and Figures 4.2 and 4.3 list some of the differences between English and Spanish. Similar information can be obtained or

FIGURE 4.2

Some Differences between the English and Spanish Sound Systems

English Form	Spanish Equivalent	For the Spanish-English Pronunciation of: ____ the Child May Say ____ or To the English Speaker ____ Sounds Like ____	
\i\	\ē\	bit	beet
		pit	peat
\a\	\e\	bat	bet
\a\	\ä\	hat	hot
\ə\	\e\ or \a\	but	bet
\ə\	\ȯ\	fun	fawn
		shut	shot
\a\	\e\	late	let
		mate	met
\u̇\	\ü\	full	fool
\b\	\p\	bar	par
		cab	cap
\b\ (between vowels)	\v\	babies	bavies
\v\	\b\	vote	boat
\sh\	\ch\	shoe	chew
\g\	\k\	goat	coat
		dug	duck
\j\	\ch\ or	jump	chump
	\y\		yump
\m\ (final)	\n\	comb	cone
		dime	dine
\th\ (voiceless)	\s\, \t\, or \f\	thank	sank
		path	pass
\th\ (voiced)	\d\	this	dis
		though	dough
\w\	\gw\	way	guay
\z\	\s\	zoo	sue
		buzz	bus
\zh\	\ch\	measure	meachure
	\sh\		meashure

Source: An adaptation by Robert Ruddell in *Reading-Language Instruction: Innovation Practices*, pp. 273–274. © 1974 by Prentice-Hall, Inc.

FIGURE 4.3

Some Differences between English and Spanish Syntactic Systems

	Examples	
Category	***English Speaker***	***Spanish-English Speaker***
A. Use of verb forms		
1. Subject-predicate agreement	The cars run.	The cars runs.
	The car runs.	The car run.
2. Tense	Joe said that he was ready.	Joe said that he is ready.
	I needed help yesterday.	I need help yesterday.
3. Use of "be"	I am five years old.	I have five years.
	Joe isn't here.	Joe is no here.
4. Negative	He didn't go home.	He no go home, or He didn't went home.
	Don't come.	No come.
B. Use of noun and determiner forms		
1. Plural form	The two cars are big.	The two car are big.
2. Omission of determiner with noun in certain contexts	He is a farmer.	He is farmer.
C. Use of pronoun forms		
1. Omission in question	Is he a farmer?	Is farmer?
2. Omission in statement	It is ready.	It is ready.
D. Use of adjectives		
1. Order	The red cap is pretty.	The cap red is pretty.
2. Ending	The red caps are fine.	The caps red are fine.
3. Comparison	It is bigger.	Is more big.
	It's bigger.	
	It is the biggest.	Is most big.
	It's the biggest.	

Source: An adaptation by Robert Ruddell in *Reading-Language Instruction: Innovation Practices*, pp. 273–274. © 1974 by Prentice-Hall, Inc.

developed for any language. Knowing the common points of difference between English and another language used in the classroom helps you understand why children respond as they do and what "rules" they are operating under. This enables you to respond appropriately to the language your students are using. For example, knowing that a mispronunciation is rooted in a specific language difference rather than in poor comprehension or the lack of ability to apply phonics rules makes a considerable difference in how you respond to a student's reading.

Hudelson (1990, p. 271) summarizes the implications for classroom practice:

> As with native speakers, the focus for second language learners should be on using English to do something (a focus on content rather than on the language itself) rather than drilling language forms (Allen, 1986; Krahnke & Christison, 1983; Rigg & Enright, 1986). Even as second language learners are learning to speak English, they need to speak about meaningful content. As among native speakers, interactive group work where learners work together will benefit both content and language learning. In group work ESL learners may work effectively both with other second language learners and with native speakers (Long & Porter, 1985). As with native speakers, there will be significant individual differences in rates of learning and willingness to use the language (Lindfors, 1987). As in native language settings, the teacher's role is to facilitate both content and language exploration and experimentation, to focus on learners' understandings and misunderstandings, to respond to what the learners are trying to do (Rigg & Enright, 1986).

The implications for teaching that recent research in bilingual education presents are as follows:

1. Facility with the native language is to be encouraged through acceptance of the use of that language and the presence of as many materials written in the native language as possible.
2. Language instruction in the native language should accompany language instruction in English.
3. The environment should be print-filled, with ample opportunities provided for language-minority students to interact with print and each other and with students reading and writing in English.
4. Teaching that stresses processes rather than products is most effective, with the focus on the content being worked with rather than solely on the language itself.
5. Bilingual teachers need to be trained in English as well as in other languages to help students figure out how English is both similar to and different from their native language.
6. Enlisting help from the native community is essential for a truly effective bilingual-bicultural program.

The bidialectal learner

In addition to the growing numbers of children who come to school speaking a language other than English, a growing number of schools must deal with the range of dialects spoken among their students. Cullinan (1974) defines a **dialect** as "a distinctive variety of a language spoken by members of a homogeneous speech community" (p. 197). Dialects can be differentiated according to the four aspects of our language system: phonology (the speech sounds blended to produce words), syntax (grammar rules), semantics (word meanings), and pragmatics (language choices made in different social contexts). Thus, speakers of the same dialect sound alike (I drove my "cah" to work), use similar words to express meanings (We sat on the "davenport" to watch television), use similar sentence patterns (Bill he live in Chicago), and have similar social-use rules (group interaction patterns or nonlinguistic cues, such as gestures). The dialect individuals speak reflects the region of the country they come from and their social and economic background. Dialects spoken by lower-status groups generally are less well accepted than those of higher-status groups. As mentioned earlier, a great deal is known about the dialect called Black English because it has been studied extensively as a possible cause of school failure among black children. Once thought to be a haphazard and substandard language system, Black English, like any other dialect of English, is now recognized to be a systematic and highly predictable form of language. The *Teaching Idea: Peer Tutoring among English-Speaking and Limited English-Speaking Students* provides English Language Learners, as well as those

TEACHING IDEA

Addressing Individual Needs

PEER TUTORING AMONG ENGLISH-SPEAKING AND LIMITED ENGLISH-SPEAKING STUDENTS

Teachers are well aware of the ability of children to help one another even when an adult has failed to do so. Children often find unique and inventive ways to communicate about a topic or learn the rules for a new game. Children's ability to communicate well with one another can be put to use by pairing an English-speaking child with a limited English-speaking child in order to provide special assistance on some aspect of the curriculum. This can also serve as a buddy approach to help the LES child through a period of adjustment. The English-speaking child should be a fluent speaker, a friendly person, and at about the same developmental level as the English language learner. Although schoolwork is the main business these children will be engaged in, opportunities for informal talk are invaluable. As soon as LES children begin to feel somewhat confident, it is a good idea to have them teach some skill or aspects of their language to the others.

children developing Standard English skills, with the opportunity to practice with more fluent children.

Variation obviously exists among speakers within a dialect as well as between speakers of different dialects, and not all blacks speak Black English. According to Shuy (1980), dialect variation is more of a continuum than a polarity, and speakers of one dialect may differ from those of another in such minute matters as the frequency of occurrence of a particular language feature (p. 4). Dialect variations appear to be linked to socioeconomic status (SES). In a study done in Texas comparing black and white, middle and lower SES 4- and 5-year-olds on oral language comprehension, middle SES blacks and whites were more similar to each other in their performance than they were to their lower SES counterparts (Jones, 1973). This data indicates that socioeconomic conditions may play a major role in oral language development.

When the language of the school differs greatly from that of the child, educational achievement often suffers. It is not surprising that the research points to teacher rejection of the learner's language, culture, and experiential background, and not the learner's language itself, as a major cause of the bidialectal learner's poor school achievement (Goodman & Buck, 1973; Simons & Johnson, 1974; Smith, 1975; Cunningham, 1977). As with bilingual learners, teachers who know how oral language is acquired and who have an understanding of their students' dialects will be better prepared to support their language development. Opportunities for talk in meaningful and varied contexts, building on home-language strengths, and encouraging language flexibility will help bidialectal learners develop their facility with language.

Register: a language variation

An aspect of language variation that seems to exist in all language communities is called register. The term *register* indicates language varieties that are set apart from others by the social circumstances of their use. Registers vary according to what people are talking (or writing) about, the interpersonal relations that exist between the speaker and the audience, and the mode in which they are communicating (Halliday, 1978). If a social situation changes, the register a speaker uses may change in its phonology, syntax, and vocabulary, or lexicon, and may be accompanied by nonverbal changes such as differences in gestures and facial expressions (DeStefano, 1978). For example, teachers alter their style and tone of speech when they talk to students at school, chat with families at home, or converse with friends at a dinner party. All of us engage in "register switching" so that our language is more suited to the circumstances in which we find ourselves.

Tacit rules constrain both speakers and listeners (or writers and readers) so that each knows what is and is not appropriate. The minister in an inner-city church will use one register in the pulpit on Sunday morning and another at the church picnic that afternoon. On each occasion he may speak black dialect; however, in one instance his speech will be more formal than in the other. When teachers ask children to speak one way on the playground and another in the classroom, they are generally referring to register rather than dialect. Even very young children acquire a repertoire of registers they learn to use, appropriate to their needs and the situational context. Teachers who offer children various roles and responsibilities within the classroom help develop children's abilities to assume various registers. Calling roll, reading or giving directions aloud, acting as a peer tutor, delivering messages orally, taking charge of a game, giving a report, and leading a discussion group are just a few of the opportunities for register switching that can be offered within the classroom context. Other activities such as choral reading, puppetry, drama, group discussions, reciprocal teaching, and summarizing the events of the day also provide opportunities for talk in a variety of registers.

It is important for teachers to remember that all children, whether or not they speak Standard English, have simply acquired the language to which they have been exposed. The developmental considerations already outlined in this chapter also apply to those children reared in homes where a non-standard dialect or a language other than that of the school is spoken. Teachers must be careful not to make judgments about these children, either positive or negative, based on their language alone. Individual children are influenced by a variety of physiological, intellectual, and social factors, and no gross judgments about language or intellectual competence can be made solely on the basis of their language divergence from Standard English. However, it is important that teachers distinguish between a child whose speech is immature or who lacks language competence and one who is a mature, competent speaker whose language differs in some way from Standard English. In order to do this, teachers must accept the language children bring to school, develop their own knowledge of that language, and build upon it as a basis for further language development, while providing frequent demonstrations of Standard English used for a variety of purposes in a variety of contexts.

The following principles related to language diversity are helpful in guiding instructional decisions in the classroom:

1. *Virtually all children come to school with a viable system of communication—their language.* Although it may be different from what the school expects, it is not necessarily deficient.
2. *All children come to school with a store of experiences and a cultural background.* Again, these may be different, but no cultural background is "deficient."
3. *Competence is not tied to a particular language or dialect.* Users of any language or dialect differ in their language competence, which is more likely to be affected by the quality of speech at home, general intelligence, and the range of background experiences than the dialect spoken.

4. *Teachers need to know something about the language of the children they teach, no matter what language it is.* Knowing the source of divergence when children make "errors" in speech or reading will help the teacher know what, if any, corrective measures should be taken.
5. *The language and cultural experiences children bring to school are worthy and useful as sources for reading, writing, and discussing.*
6. *Although competence in Standard English is a worthy goal for all children, it must not mean a rejection or replacement of one language and culture for another.* Rather, it should be viewed as language expansion and enrichment of the students' home language to include Standard English so that they are given the opportunity and choice to communicate with a broader speech community.

Dillon and Searle (1981) suggest that the environment of most schools is not conducive to language development. In contrasting children's language use at home and at school, they discovered that the school language of the students they studied was restricted whereas the home language was elaborated. Researchers agree that if schools are to foster children's oral language development, all children need opportunities to use their language resources and to build on them. Teachers must plan opportunities throughout the day for students to engage in meaningful and purposeful opportunities to talk and listen. This text offers many ideas about opportunities for talk as children engage in the business of learning. By giving some thought to the talk that occurs in the classroom, planning for it, and monitoring its progress in conjunction with other activities, teachers give status to one of our most important life skills.

SUMMARY

Even though children have acquired most of the basic structures of English by the time they enter school, their language development continues throughout the elementary school years. Research on young children's language suggests that teachers need to be aware of the conditions under which this remarkable accomplishment occurs and provide experiences that are open-ended and flexible enough to accommodate a range of language backgrounds and competencies. Experiences with language used for authentic purposes in a variety of contexts are much more beneficial for schoolchildren than are grammar drills and worksheets. Listening needs attention, both as a separate language art and as one part of an integrated program.

Children who are proficient in oral language tend to be higher achievers on measures of vocabulary and other aspects of language and literacy development. Once children are considered less fluent, they are likely to perform in an increasingly less capable manner when compared with more able children. The difference could be the result of teaching practices.

Teachers need to be aware of the nature of the language diversity among their students, respect it, and use it to build on and expand students' language repertoires. The teaching of Standard English should not involve a rejection of the students' home language and culture. Rather, it should be viewed as an opportunity for students to extend their language choices in order to communicate with a broader speech community, and to bring their language facility to enrich that community.

Although a very large proportion of the school day is spent listening, very little instructional time is devoted to supporting children's listening development. More attention needs to be given to the development of listening abilities at all levels. Teachers can support children's ability to use oral language by deliberately planning for it as an essential part of the language arts curriculum.

ACTIVITIES

1. **Observe and tape record the spontaneous language interaction between a young child (2–5 years old) and an adult for 5 or 10 minutes.** Transcribe the tape using this format:

    Child (extending spoon): More ice cream!

    Mother: Oh, you like chocolate ice cream, huh?

    Child (hesitates a bit): Chocolate.

    Mother: Yes, that's chocolate ice cream.

    Describe the participants and the context of the interaction. Analyze the transcript for evidence of the ways in which adults expand and reinforce the language of young children.
2. **Interview an adult or older child who entered school as a non–English speaker, although English was the language of instruction.** Determine the age at which the interviewee entered school and how much schooling the person had in his or her first language. Ask the person to recall those things that were most helpful and least helpful both in and out of the English-speaking school. In what ways, if any, was the person able to make use of the home language? What would the person do differently if he or she were a teacher of students like him- or herself?

3. **Find a copy of the video *American Tongues* (1987, Center for New American Media, New York) and watch it with some peers.** Many people have very strong feelings about language diversity. After watching the video, talk about how you felt about what you saw and heard on the film. Try to identify your own biases about language so that you can be aware of these and work to keep them from interfering with your relationships with your students.

FURTHER READING

Dwyer, J. (1991). *A sea of talk.* Portsmouth, NH: Heinemann.

Power, B. M., & Hubbard, R. S. (1996). *Language development: A reader for teachers.* Englewood Cliffs, NJ: Merrill.

Hynds, S., & Rubin, D. (1990). *Perspectives on talk and learning.* Urbana, IL: National Council of Teachers of English.

Wolfram, W., & Schilling-Estes, N. (1998). *American English: Dialects and variation.* Oxford, England: Basil Blackwell.

REFERENCES

Allen, V. (1986). Developing contexts to support second language acquisition. *Language Arts, 63,* 61–67.

Barton, B. (2000). *Telling stories your way: Storytelling and reading aloud in the classroom.* Portland, ME: Stenhouse.

Beck, I. L., & McKeown, M. G. (2001). Text talk: Capturing the benefits of read-aloud experiences for young children. *Reading Teacher, 55,* 10–20.

Bloom, L. (1970). *Language development: Form and function in emerging grammars.* Cambridge, MA: MIT Press.

Booth, D., & Barton, B. (2000). *Story works: How teachers can use shared stories in the new curriculum.* Portland, ME: Stenhouse.

Bormouth, J. R., Carr, J., Manning, J., & Pearson, D. (1970). Children's comprehension of between- and within- sentence syntactic structures. *Journal of Educational Psychology, 61,* 349–357.

Britton, J. (1970). *Language and learning.* London: Allen Lane.

Britton, J. (1983). Writing and the story world. In B. Kroll & G. Wells (Eds.), *Explorations in the development of writing* (pp. 51–63). New York: Wiley.

Brown, R. (1973). *A first language: The early stages.* Cambridge: Harvard University Press.

Brown, R., & Bellugi, U. (1964). Three processes in the child's acquisition of syntax. *Harvard Educational Review, 34,* 133–151.

Bruner, J. (1983). *Child's talk: Learning to use language.* New York: Holt, Rinehart & Winston.

Carroll, J. (1970). *Comprehension by 3rd, 6th, and 7th graders of words having multiple grammatical functions. Final report.* Princeton, NJ: Educational Testing Service.

Chomsky, C. (1972). Stages in development and reading exposure. *Harvard Educational Review, 42,* 1–33.

Cohen, B. (1980). Issues related to transferring reading skills from Spanish to English. *Bilingual Education Paper Series.* New York: Research & Development, Inc.

Commins, N. L. (1989). Language and affect: Bilingual students at home and school. *Language Arts, 66,* 29–43.

Cullinan, B. (Ed.) (1974). *Black dialects and reading.* Urbana, IL: ERIC Clearinghouse and National Council of Teachers of English.

Cunningham, P. M. (1977). Teacher's correction responses to black-dialect miscues which are non–meaning-changing. *Reading Research Quarterly, 12*(4), 637–653.

Delpit, L. D. (1990). Language diversity and learning. In S. Hynds & D. L. Rubin (Eds.), *Perspectives on talk and learning.* Urbana, IL: National Council of Teachers of English.

DeStefano, J. (1978). *Language: The learner and the school.* New York: Wiley.

Dickinson, D. K., & Tabors, P. O. (Eds.) (2001). *Beginning literacy with language.* Baltimore, MD: Brookes.

Dillon, D., & Searle, D. (1981). The role of language in one first-grade classroom. *Research in the Teaching of English, 15,* 311–328.

Goodman, K. S., & Buck, C. (1973). Dialect barriers to reading comprehension revisited. *The Reading Teacher, 27,* 6–12.

Hakuta, K., & Garcia, E. E. (1989). Bilingualism and education. *American Psychologist, 44,* 374–379.

Halliday, M. A. K. (1975). *Explorations in the functions of language.* London: Arnold.

______. (1978). *Language as a social semiotic: The social interpretation of language and meaning.* London: Arnold.

______. (1982). Three aspects of children's language development: Learning language, learning through language, and learning about language. In Y. Goodman, M. Haussle, & D. S. Strickland (Eds.), *Oral and written language development research: Impact on the schools* (pp. 7–19). Urbana, IL: National Council of Teachers of English.

Hart, B., & Risley, T. R. (1995). *Meaningful differences in the everyday experience of young American children.* Baltimore: Brookes.

Hillocks, G. (1986). *Research on written composition: New directions for teaching.* New York: National Conference on Research.

Hudelson, S. (1990). Bilingual/ESL learners talking in the English classroom. In S. Hynds & D. L. Rubin (Eds.), *Perspectives on talk and learning* (pp. 264–275). Urbana, IL: National Council of Teachers of English.

Johnson, D. W., Johnson, R., Roy, P., & Holubec, E. (1984). *Circles of learning: Cooperation in the classroom.* Alexandria, VA: Association for Supervision & Curriculum Development.

Jones, B. J. (1973). A study of oral language comprehension of black and white middle and lower class, pre-school children using standard English and Black dialect in Houston, Texas, 1972. Ed.D. dissertation, University of Houston.

Klima, E. S., & Belugi-Klima, U. (1966). Syntactic regularities in the speech of children. In J. Lyons & R. Wales (Eds.), *Psycholinguistic papers* (pp. 145–146). Edinburgh: Edinburgh University Press.

Krahnke, K., & Christison, M. (1983). Recent language research and some language teaching principles. *TESOL Quarterly, 17,* 625–649.

Lindfors, J. W. (1987). *Children's language and learning.* Upper Saddle River, NJ: Prentice-Hall.

Loban, W. (1963). *Language development: Kindergarten through grade 12.* Urbana, IL: National Council of Teachers of English.

Long, M., & Porter, P. (1985). Group work, interlanguage talk, and second language acquisition. *TESOL Quarterly, 19,* 207–228.

Lundsteen, S. (1976). *Children learn to communicate.* Englewood Cliffs, NJ: Prentice-Hall.

______. (1990). Learning to listen and learning to read. In S. Hynds & D. L. Rubin (Eds.), *Perspectives on talk and learning* (pp. 213–225). Urbana, IL: National Council of Teachers of English.

McLaughlin, B. (1987). *Theories of second language learning.* London: Arnold.

McNeill, D. (1970). *The acquisition of language: The study of development psycholinguistics.* New York: Harper & Row.

Meloth, M. S. (1991). Enhancing literacy through cooperative learning. In E. H. Hiebert (Ed.), *Literacy for a diverse society* (pp. 172–183). New York: Teachers College Press.

Michaels, S. (1981). Sharing time: Children's narrative styles and differential access to literacy. *Language in Society, 10,* 49–76.

Pearson, P. D., & Fielding, L. (1982). Research update: Listening comprehension. *Language Arts, 59,* 617–629.

Pellegrini, A. D., Galda, L., & Rubin, D. L. (1984). Context in text: The development of oral and written language in two genres. *Child Development, 55,* 1549–1555.

Peregoy, S. F., & Boyle, W. F. (2001). *Reading, writing, and learning in ESL: A resource book for K–12 teachers.* New York: Longman.

Pinnell, G. S. & Jaggar, A. (2003). Oral language: Speaking and listening in elementary classrooms. In J. Flood, D. Lapp, J. R. Squire, & J. Jensen (Eds.), *Handbook of research on teaching the English language arts,* 2nd ed. (pp. 881–914). Mahwah, NJ: Erlbaum.

Rigg, P., & Enright, D. S. (Eds.) (1986). *Children and ESL: Integrating perspectives.* Washington, D.C.: Teachers of English to Speakers of Other Languages.

Shuy, R. (1980). Vernacular black English: Setting the issues in time. In M. F. Whiteman (Ed.), *Reactions to Ann Arbor: Vernacular black English and education.* Arlington, VA: Center for Applied Linguistics.

Simons, H. P., & Johnson, K. R. (1974). Black English syntax and reading interference. *Research in the Teaching of English, 8,* 339–358.

Slobin, D. I. (1973). Cognitive prerequisites for the development of grammar. In C. A. Ferguson & D. I. Slobin (Eds.), *Studies of child language development* (pp. 145–153). New York: Holt, Rinehart & Winston.

Smith, N. B. (1975). Cultural dialects: Current problems and solutions. *The Reading Teacher, 29,* 137–141.

Snow, C. E., Tabors, P. O., & Dickinson, D. K. (2001). Language development in the preschool years. In D. K. Dickinson & P. O. Tabors (Eds.), *Beginning literacy with language* (pp. 1–26). Baltimore, MD: Brookes.

Strickland, D. S., & Feeley, J. (2003). Research on language learners: Development in the elementary school years. In J. Flood, D. Lapp, J. R. Squire, & J. Jensen (Eds.), *Handbook of research on teaching the English language arts,* 2nd ed. (pp. 339–356). Mahwah, NJ: Erlbaum.

Strickland, R. (1962). The language of elementary school children: Its relationship to the language of reading textbooks and the quality of reading of selected children. *Bulletin of the School of Education, 28*(4). Bloomington, IN: Indiana University Press.

Templin, M. (1987). *Certain language skills in children: Their development and interrelationships.* Minneapolis: University of Minnesota Press.

Walters, K., & Gunderson, L. (1985). Effects of parent volunteers reading first language (L1) books to ESL students. *The Reading Teacher, 39,* 66–69.

Weaver, C. (1979). *Grammar for teachers: Perspectives and definitions.* Urbana, IL: National Council of Teachers of English.

Wolfram, W., Adger, C. T., & Christian, D. (1999). *Dialects in schools and communities.* Mahwah, NJ: Erlbaum.

CHILDREN'S LITERATURE REFERENCES

Hoban, R. (1986). *Bread and jam for Frances.* Illus. Lillian Hoban. New York: HarperCollins.

Oral Language: Supporting Relationships among Talk, Listening, Reading, Writing, and Viewing in the Classroom

CHAPTER OUTLINE

Key Standard

Teachers of language arts/reading provide opportunities for students to develop competence in the use of oral language as a means to communicate about content of interest and importance to them and as a tool for learning in conjunction with reading, writing, and viewing. Such teachers:

- Help students understand the many roles and functions of language.
- Provide opportunities for students to collaborate and participate in a variety of activities linked to reading, writing, viewing, and problem solving, such as choral reading, plays, recitation, reading aloud, and giving and following directions.
- Provide opportunities for students to learn to assess their developing skills as effective speakers and listeners in varied situations and for varied purposes and audiences.

To get a preview of Chapter 5 learn about supporting the relationship between oral language and the other language arts, visit the Chapter 5 section of the accompanying *Language Arts* CD-ROM.

Just after winter break, Lisa Stanzi sits with her second grade reading group, watching a video of the previous day's conversation about a book they have been reading. The group has been discussing literature since the previous August, but the winter break seems to have blunted their conversational skills, so Lisa decides to review the rules of discussion that evolved over the first few months of school.

Lisa begins: "Today, we're going to step back and reflect . . . When I went back and listened to our discussion, it was hard to hear all the conversation . . . We are not [doing] this to pick on anyone. We should respect each other. The purpose of doing this is to reflect on ourselves and the tone of our voices. We should also think about 'What did I add to the discussion?' or 'Am I really saying something interesting?' Also, let's focus on the positive. What do we do well? What can we improve and how can we improve it?" With that, Lisa passes out paper and asks students to write down things they see that are good and things that could be improved.

The students sit, attentive, and watch the video, with only a few occasional giggles. When they finish, they begin to talk. One child notes that they ought to "know what we want to say before we say it." Lisa agrees, elaborating with the comment that "We need to be rehearsed. Not only are you giving your response, but what relevant things can you bring to the group? What's going to provide and promote discussion?" The students go on to discuss turn-taking (they often all talk at once), looking at whoever is talking, and being better listeners. Then, Lisa poses a question about ways to participate in the discussion: "Who is an active listener? Are you really participating in the discussion? Why am I not saying anything? Why do people choose not to say anything?" The students end their conversation by considering these ideas.

Lisa continues to talk with her students about their conversational skills, and in February, she shows another video clip to focus their ideas. Once again she asks them to think about what they are doing that is working, and what is hindering discussions. This is followed by the creation of a chart that serves as a reminder to her students of the behaviors that they have designated as important to good discussions. Almost daily, for the rest of the winter, Lisa asks her students to assess their discussions, paying special attention to their own behaviors (Galda, Rayburn, & Stanzi, 2000).

Lisa chooses to focus on helping her students monitor themselves as they engage in discussions about books. Her students already know that they enjoy talking about the books they read, and watching themselves on video becomes an opportunity for Lisa to help her students see how they are behaving, to bring their working knowledge of successful conversations to reflect on their behavior, and to formulate guidelines for future discussions. Their discussions become avenues for exploring their growing understanding of the books they are reading and for realizing their potential as readers. As one student put it, "In our class we read differently. We think about what we read." Thus, Lisa helps her students develop their skills as members of a discussion group at the same time that she helps them use oral language to become thoughtful readers.

Talk is central to learning and personal development. Vygotsky (1978) argues that we learn through talk. Talk is the medium through which social interaction occurs and learning is socially constructed through talk. Children learn about and through talk during their infancy and preschool years and come to school quite proficient at communicating through oral language. But what happens once children get to school? Sometimes the most frequently taught lesson is how to sit still and be quiet (Pinnell & Jaggar, 2003).

Studies of talk in the classroom indicate that little attention is given to fostering oral language in schools. Cazden (1988), Mehan (1979), and Dillon and Searle (1981) indicate that most of the talk belongs to the teacher, and that even discussions are often dominated by the teacher. School discussions usually consist of a pattern: teacher initiation, student response, and teacher evaluation (IRE). That is, the teacher asks a question, a student responds, and the teacher either accepts or does not accept that response, and then goes on to pose another question. "The classroom-speech event in which this IRE pattern is most obvious is the teacher-led lesson, or recitation, in which the teacher controls both the development of a topic (and what counts as relevant to it) and who gets a turn to talk" (Cazden, 1988, p. 50). Talk of this kind, although sometimes appropriate, is only one kind of talk that is important in classrooms. Indeed, in classrooms where teachers work to help their students gain competence in the use of oral language in school, this kind of talk occurs very infrequently.

In standards-based classrooms like Lisa's, students use oral language to communicate with one another and with the teacher as they talk about issues and ideas that are important to them, using talk to help them understand how they and others think, and to shape and present their ideas. Talk allows children to try out tentative ideas with each other, exchange information, plan, and even have fun. When Allington, Johnston, and Day (2002) studied exemplary fourth grade teachers, they found that "the single most striking

The physical arrangement of this classroom promotes the social interaction that is so important to learning.

feature in these classrooms is the nature of talk; frequent, pervasive, respectful, supportive and productive talk was the norm consistently demonstrated by teachers in their interactions with students" (p. 463).

In this chapter we look at how to structure activities that require oral language to support learning, how to enhance children's reading and responding to books as they develop their oral proficiency, and how to structure oral language opportunities to support writing instruction.

Oral Language in the Classroom

We can talk about oral language in many ways, in part because language varies according to what we are talking about, with whom we are talking, and why we are talking, as well as in other ways. The topic of talk is an important dimension of any oral language event. When children come to school they must learn, often for the first time, how to talk about "school" subjects—reading, writing, books, mathematics, social studies, science, and so on. Learning what topics are appropriate and inappropriate, and learning the specific language that we use in particular subjects—terms such as *genre, style, point of view,* and *summarize*—are enhanced when children are given multiple opportunities both to talk and to listen to others talk about many types of content.

Those with whom we are talking, or our audience, varies also. We can talk to ourselves when we are performing a difficult task, have a conversation with another person, or engage in a group discussion with a small number of other people. We can interview another person, or address a large group of people, as when we present formal reports. These oral language events have different audiences and thus require different skills and different amounts of interaction (Rubin, 1990).

Both content and audience affect the style of our oral language. Language in personal conversation is loosely structured and contains many references to "I," "we," and "you." Speakers are less concerned with structure than with expressing their feelings, beliefs, and interests, with expressing who they are. Speech in more formal situations is like writing, more carefully constructed to convey particular meaning to an audience (Rubin, 1990). As children develop as oral language users, they become more able to use the explicit, or decontextualized, language to convey their ideas that success in school demands.

Oral language also serves varied functions. In Chapter Four, we discussed Halliday's (1975) functions of the oral language of young children. He argued that even very young children use language for the particular purposes of requesting, regulating others' behavior, interacting with others, presenting themselves, asking why, pretending, and informing. Here we consider function in the more global perspective proposed by Rubin (1990). He suggests that we consider two basic functions of talk, the communalizing and the epistemic. The **communalizing** function is social: talk defines relationships between participants. The **epistemic** function involves the speaker's creation of knowledge (Rubin, 1990, p. 8). The communalizing function varies along a continuum that ranges from intimate to articulate; the epistemic function varies from reproducing to transforming knowledge. Figure 5.1 demonstrates how these functions interact and how different classroom situations necessitate different functions.

Most children in schools spend most of their time listening. When they do talk, the task usually requires articulate talk that reproduces knowledge, often in the form of a recitation in response to teacher questioning. Although this may sometimes be a useful form of talk, the other kinds of talk presented in Figure 5.1 are necessary as well for continued communicative, cognitive, and social growth. Children need opportunities to speak both informally (intimate) and formally (articulate), and to use talk to explore and discover as well as to reproduce knowledge.

FIGURE 5.1

Varieties of Classroom Talk

		Communalizing Functions	
		Intimate	**Articulate**
Epistemic Functions	**Reproducing**	teasing some language play	announcements, drama
	Transforming	peer discussion	class debates, group presentations

Source: From Don Rubin (1990). Introduction: Ways of talking about talking and learning. In S. Hynds and D. Rubin (Eds.), *Perspectives on Talk and Learning* (p. 11). Copyright 1990 by the National Council of Teachers of English. Reprinted with permission.

Talk that explores ideas can have a profound effect on learning. Recitation reproduces knowledge; exploratory talk creates and transforms knowledge. **Recitation** asks students to find the correct answers and present them orally. It is like a pop quiz and a "guess-what-I'm-thinking" game combined. Only when students figure out what teachers want them to say is the game, and the recitation, over. With exploratory talk, people play a different kind of game. Exploratory talk might be labeled an "I wonder" game. "I wonder why," "I wonder how," "I wonder if," "I wonder when," and "I wonder whether" are all paths into exploratory discussions. This type of talk depends on students and teachers actively exploring ideas, understandings, and possibilities. It happens when you talk with your students as fellow scientists or fellow readers and writers—that is, as fellow members of a learning community.

Exploratory talk helps children find out about their world. Talk is a means of constructing knowledge; through talk children find out about the world as they question, hypothesize, argue, explain, and play with language. You don't need to teach children how to use exploratory talk—they have been doing so since they first learned to talk—but you do need to invite children to use this kind of talk in the classroom (Lindfors, 1990). If the purpose of school is to educate, then school needs to be a place in which children use talk to explore and to learn, and not only to reproduce. Standards-based classrooms do just that; they invite exploratory talk.

If you value exploratory talk and engage in it yourself, then your students will trust you enough to do so themselves. Exploratory talk is social and needs a collaborative atmosphere in which to flourish; collaborative atmospheres are not possible without the opportunity to engage in talking with peers. The structures that you put into place in your classroom will also signal to your students that you want them to use oral language to learn. Open discussions, small-group work, collaborative projects, paired reading, writing workshop, and literature-discussion groups create the kind of social atmosphere that promotes exploratory talk.

Like reading and writing, oral communicative growth means developing fluency and effectiveness. Children need to be able to speak articulately and with proper volume in order to be understood by others. They need to be able to vary rhythm and stress to enhance meaning. They need to be able to ask questions, give answers, speculate, negotiate, follow directions, give directions, and organize and present information. They do all of these things outside of school and need to continue to develop these skills in school. They need to learn how to take turns in whole-class discussions, as well as in small-group work. They need to learn to adapt their talk to different audiences (friends, parents, teachers, others), different purposes (exploratory, reporting, self-presenting, playing), different settings (home, school, playground, church), different genres of discourse (group discussions, conversations, recitations, presentations), and different subjects (literature, molecules, soccer, street crime, food) (Rubin, 1990).

First we consider discussion, one particular type of classroom talk that has profound effects both on what and how children learn and on the social atmosphere in the classroom. Then we briefly touch on oral presentations by students, including drama and choral speaking. Next, we look at particular strategies that engage children in talk around literacy: small-group discussions about books, and collaborative groups during writing workshop. Finally, we consider conferences as an integral part of language arts instruction.

Discussion

Having discussions does not involve only the teacher asking questions. Indeed, often the best discussions contain very few teacher questions. Dillon (1984) has argued that most discussions are not discussions at all but merely "recitations" masquerading as discussions. These recitations are characterized by an overabundance of the IRE pattern, with teacher-student-teacher turn-taking and the teacher asking known-information questions that require low-level recall of information. In contrast, he says, true discussions have the following characteristics:

1. The matter is open for discussion.
2. The discussants are open-minded.

Lee Galda

When students talk together about their work, they build on each others' ideas and knowledge. Several heads are, indeed, better than one.

3. The discussion is open to all arguments.
4. The discussion is open to any person.
5. The time limit is open.
6. The learning outcomes are open, not predictable.
7. The purposes and practices of the discussion are out in the open, not covert.
8. The discussion is open-ended, not required to come to a single conclusion. (p. 52)

Dillon goes on to say that teachers who want to conduct genuine discussions should ask only genuine questions, questions to which they really want to know the answers. He suggests that teachers state their own opinions (as opinions and not facts), describe how they are feeling, and ask students to elaborate, to ask their own questions, and to ask questions of and respond to other students. He also suggests that "deliberate, appreciative silence" (p. 55) can also be most effective.

Hynds (1992) suggests considering classroom discourse between teachers and students along three dimensions: turn-taking patterns, how teachers signal positive or negative evaluations of student responses, and whether questions are truly information seeking or seeking already known information.

TURN-TAKING PATTERNS

The kinds of turn-taking that occur during the school day can tell you a great deal about the social interaction patterns present in any classroom. For example, in teacher-dominated classrooms, discussions usually occur in the IRE pattern, as in this segment of a discussion of E. B. White's (1952) *Charlotte's Web.*

> **Teacher:** Who remembers what Fern said when she saw her father with the ax? Solana?
>
> **Solana:** She said, "Where are you going with that ax?"
>
> **Teacher:** Right. Exactly. And then what did Fern do?
>
> **Dimitri:** She grabbed his arm.
>
> **Teacher:** Good, Dimitri. What did she want her dad to do?

Notice that after each student turn the teacher talks. The teacher is controlling the discussion, and there is virtually no interaction among students. This style tells the students that the teacher knows the most, that the students need to attend to what the teacher wants them to know and say, and that the teacher's agenda is controlling the discussion. Teacher-talk in discussions of this kind usually consists of questions that have "right answers." This is not a discussion that invites students to explore their thinking through talk or to transform their understandings about a book, a concept in science, or an idea about art.

Contrast this discussion with the following, in which the pattern, and the potential, is quite different:

> **Teacher:** How did Wilbur feel after he was moved to the barn?
>
> **Mandy:** Well, he was feeling sort a sad.
>
> **Patrice:** Yeah. Cause he was lonely. He didn't like being down there in that pig place.
>
> **Joseph:** But Fern kept on coming to visit him!
>
> **Teacher:** Right. Why do you think he was lonely even though Fern kept coming to visit him? What about what Joseph said?

Notice that in this discussion the students talk more than the teacher and that they also talk to each other. This approach tells the students that what they know is valuable, that they need to attend to the opinions and statements of their peers (and themselves), and that although the discussion may be controlled by the teacher's agenda, there is room in that agenda for student interest and opinion.

POSITIVE AND NEGATIVE EVALUATIONS

Another dimension of classroom discussions that is important to consider is the signals teachers give students about the worth of their contributions to the discussions. Listen to the very different signals that this teacher gives to his students even when he is asking questions that have no one right answer:

> **Teacher:** Why do you think Charlotte wanted to help Wilbur?
>
> **Jeff:** Well, she might have felt sorry for him when he was crying and all.
>
> **Amanda:** Yeah, he was pretty sad, and I felt sorry for him. And he was little, and I guess, cute, for a pig, and he was feeling bad.
>
> **Teacher:** Interesting. He was sad and little and cute and even Amanda felt sorry for him! Was there anything about Charlotte that might have made her ready to help someone?
>
> **Alan:** She was nice.
>
> **Teacher:** Any other ideas?
>
> **Maurice:** And she was going to be a mother.
>
> **Teacher:** That's interesting. What do you mean?

This teacher responded with a positive evaluation to Amanda and to Maurice. He ignored Jeff's response, although he could have commented on it when he responded to Amanda. He negatively evaluated Alan's response by asking for other ideas without acknowledging what Alan had said. His responses tell his students how they ought to be responding during this discussion, what kinds of comments (interesting ones) he wants to hear, and, perhaps, how he feels about the students in the class. These implicit evaluations can also tell students how they ought to be reading.

INFORMATION-SEEKING QUESTIONS

Hynds (1992) also discusses the difference between questions that are genuine questions and questions that are "tests." **Genuine questions** ask for information that is not known to the questioner. "What time is it?" or "Is it possible for you to fix my car by tomorrow?" and "How much does this cost?" can all be genuine questions if the questioner does not know the answers.

Most questions that are asked outside of school are genuine questions. Unfortunately, most questions asked in classrooms are not of the genuine kind, but only masquerade as questions. For example, both teacher and students have read *Charlotte's Web* and during a class discussion the teacher asks: "What were the words that Charlotte wove in her webs?" The students know that the teacher knows the answer to this question (unless she really has forgotten, which is another story), and they know that what the teacher is really asking is "Who can remember what words . . ." They know that the teacher is checking their recall of the story. If, on the other hand, the teacher says,

"What did you think of the way Wilbur treated Charlotte when he first met her?" he is asking a real question, seeking students' opinions of, and responses to, the characters they have read about, asking them to explore their ideas orally.

Another way to look at questions is to consider the types of processes in which they ask students to engage. That is, are questions asking for literal recall? Are they asking students to predict, make inferences, or hypothesize? Are they asking students to evaluate? Or, to return to Figure 5.1, are questions asking students to reproduce knowledge or to transform knowledge? Examine the preceding examples again. What kinds of questions did the teachers leading the discussions ask? What kinds of answers did they get? Some general guidelines for asking good questions are listed in Figure 5.2.

IMPLICATIONS FOR CONDUCTING DISCUSSIONS

Following the guidelines given in Figure 5.2 does not mean that you should never ask known-information questions, nor *not* evaluate student responses,

FIGURE 5.2

Guidelines for Good Discussions

1. Don't ask too many questions, and ask questions that are brief and clear. Spend more time allowing children to talk than you spend talking.
2. Wait at least 15 seconds after you have asked a question before you ask another. If your questions require thoughtful answers, you must give your students time to think!
3. Listen to what the children are saying and ask questions that encourage them to amplify what they are saying. Sometimes simply repeating their words with a rising intonation is enough.
4. Ask questions that require children to infer, predict, hypothesize, and evaluate as well as questions that ask them to recall, define, and compare or contrast.
5. Ask questions that cause disequilibrium, that force children to question their own ideas and assumptions, that help them become aware of their logic.
6. Open-ended questions, such as inferring, predicting, and evaluating, allow for a variety of answers. By definition, an open-ended question has no one right answer. When asking these kinds of questions, accept a variety of answers and encourage several children to respond.
7. Give children the opportunity to ask their own questions—of you and of each other. Before they come to school, children learn a great deal about their world by asking questions. Allow them to continue to learn in this manner.

nor always let students talk to each other. It *does* mean that you need to be aware of the discourse patterns present in your classroom and of the implications for the kind of classroom atmosphere you are trying to create. Although recall of facts or ideas is sometimes needed to set the stage for further discussion, this can be framed as what it is, as in "Who can tell Becky what she missed yesterday when she was sick?" Asking for a quick recitation of information is fine; pretending that such a request is a question sends students the wrong signal.

Genuine discussion promotes the use of exploratory language, as in the following excerpt from a discussion.

> **Teacher:** I just can't decide if Templeton saved Charlotte's egg sac because he really liked Wilbur or because he wanted first dibs on Wilbur's food. What do you think?
>
> **Patrice:** I think he did it because he liked Wilbur now. He had been with him a long time and Wilbur was a nice guy, and he even treated Templeton right, and so he liked him.
>
> **Teacher:** Wilbur treated Templeton nicely so Templeton liked him?
>
> **Patrice:** Yeah. And he liked his food, too, sure, but he liked that old pig.
>
> **Amanda:** But he was such a pig.
>
> **Solana:** Who was? Wilbur?
>
> (Laughter.)
>
> **Amanda:** Yeah, but Templeton, too. He was greedy, you know? All through the book he was greedy. He always wanted things to eat, and things to collect, and things that other people, I mean animals, had, and . . .
>
> **Maurice:** Yeah, and he was mean to all those other animals, and he always laughed at Wilbur, and he wasn't a nice friend!
>
> **Solana:** He wouldn't have changed that much, changed from a nasty person into a nice person. Not Templeton.
>
> **Alan:** But sometimes people do change. Like my brother changed a lot after we moved here. People can change.
>
> **Teacher:** People can change. That's a good point, Alan. That doesn't mean that people will change, or that Templeton did change, but people can. What do you think about what Alan said?

Notice that the students spend more time talking with each other than they spend answering the teacher's questions. The teacher's questions are all real questions; none of them asks students to recall facts, to reproduce knowledge. The teacher also encourages students to talk to each other rather than to him, to respond to each other's ideas; the students themselves explore their own responses and react to the responses of others.

Although students enter school quite skilled as conversationalists, they need to learn how to discuss school subjects in the classroom, using the rules of both interaction and appropriate content. Most students need help learning how to discuss. One way that they learn is to watch you demonstrate the kinds of questions, behaviors, and ideas that you feel are appropriate. Children take their cues from the teacher. Early in the year in Lisa Stanzi's classroom, one boy admonished the group to "Just jump right in!" during a discussion, mirroring exactly what Lisa had been saying (Galda, Rayburn, & Stanzi, 2000, p. 12). As you listen to students with interest and respect, you encourage them to do likewise. As you encourage students to ask each other questions and respond to each other's statements, you are reminding students that they can think for themselves. As you talk less and listen more, you are showing students that they really can fend for themselves, turning to you as a resource when they need you. In this way, you help them become independent learners and contributing members of a classroom community.

After you have a number of discussions in which you demonstrate productive behavior, ask students, either as a whole class or in small groups, to generate a set of guidelines for behavior that make good discussions possible. These guidelines might include ideas that you had not thought of! One seventh grade class focused on the rules for social interaction that generated good discussions:

1. Asking real questions.
2. Listening carefully to each other.
3. Acknowledging what someone has just said.
4. Allowing different or unusual ideas without laughing.
5. Being honest about your opinions.
6. Sticking to one subject.
7. Talking to each other and not just the teacher.

A first grade class focused on basic concerns:

1. Talk clearly.
2. Take turns.
3. Listen to each other.
4. Do not laugh.

Notice that both groups noted the importance of engaging with peers in a kind, supportive manner, much as Lisa Stanzi's students did in the opening vignette.

Because children's oral language is greatly affected by the presence of adults (Barnes, Barnes, & Clarke, 1984), they also need to learn to hold discussions without their teacher as a member of the group. If you have developed a collaborative atmosphere in your classroom, demonstrated productive ways of talking together, and established some guidelines for discussion, then students are usually ready to work without your direct participation. O'Flahavan (1995) and Almasi, O'Flahavan, & Poonam (2001) have described what roles teachers might take as participants in peer discussions as they help their students learn to become independent. Although their work centers on discussions about literature, it is applicable to discussion in general. The *Teaching Idea: Teacher's Role in Discussion Groups* summarizes their findings.

Teachers assume two roles as supportive participants in peer-led discussions: they **coach** and they **scaffold.** In a 30-minute discussion period, for example, a teacher might open with some coaching about behaviors for effective interaction or ideas for thinking and talking about the focal text. During the body of the discussion the teacher would then scaffold, listening intently to what students are saying and helping them to elaborate and extend their ideas, and putting their ideas into perspective. Teachers also scaffold as they monitor group processes. When the discussion is finished, teachers revert to the coaching role, helping students assess their practices, or perhaps teaching students something about the content being discussed (O'Flahavan, 1995). By

TEACHING IDEA

From the Research

TEACHER'S ROLE IN DISCUSSION GROUPS

Almasi, O'Flahavan, and Poonam closely examined six peer discussion groups to determine what makes groups more or less proficient. They concluded that focus on the topic, or book, is an important component of proficiency. Those groups whose conversation was coherent, or centered around sustained topics, were most proficient. Interestingly, the proficient discussion groups spent less time talking about group processes than did the less proficient groups. Results indicate that groups need to master group processes and then focus on sustained topics in order to be successful.

Source: Almasi, J., O'Flahavan, J., & Poonam, A. (2001). A comparative analysis of student and teacher development in more and less proficient discussions of literature. *Reading Research Quarterly, 36*(2), 96–120.

coaching before and after discussion rather than during, teachers leave the work of discussion to the students, allowing their ideas to determine what direction the discussion takes while supporting their growing skill by eliciting ideas and helping the group run smoothly.

How do teachers decide what to ask, and what to say, during a discussion? First, they determine goals for the discussion and then develop appropriate questions. Is the goal to ensure that students have a working knowledge of, for example, the solar system? If so, then some "reproduction" that involves literal recall might be appropriate. Is the purpose of the discussion to explore individual responses to a book that students have all read? If so, then the discussion must be a genuine discussion in which the students talk to each other and the teacher participates as a fellow reader, offering opinions and asking real questions, and as a teacher, encouraging students to elaborate and to respond to each other. Is the purpose to promote the use of comprehension strategies, such as those presented in the *Teaching Idea: Linking Reading Comprehension and Discussion?* If so, the shape of the conversation will reflect this goal.

Teachers who promote true discussions, or conversations, in their classrooms provide their students with opportunities to construct knowledge in a

TEACHING IDEA

Literature Link

LINKING READING COMPREHENSION AND DISCUSSION

Raphael (1986) developed a way of thinking about questions about text that helps students develop their reading-comprehension skills. It can also help you think about questions that promote lively discussions. Raphael's system describes three types of questions: Right There, Think and Search, and On My Own. Right There questions have their answers "right there"—in the text. These questions help students learn to find explicitly stated information in a text, but they are not very effective at getting a good discussion started. However, questions that ask students to Think and Search for information that is not explicitly stated, and that ask students to connect their own experience to the text—On My Own questions—promote excellent discussions. Think and Search questions send students back to texts for information that they then piece together, making inferences, to come up with a plausible answer. On My Own questions require students to bring their personal knowledge and experience to bear as they construct answers. Both types of questions require active speculation and connection—fodder for interesting discussions with others who have been grappling with the same questions.

supportive social setting, much like that which Vygotsky (1978) described in his discussion of the social interactions between adults and children that lead to children's independent functioning, or the **zone of proximal development.** Conversations also support English language learners as they develop skill in English as a second language. Tharp and Gallimore (1988) introduced the notion of **instructional conversations** as a way of supporting ELL students' learning. The principles of instructional conversations are similar to those discussed here, with an additional focus on the language that students use to express themselves. (See the *Teaching Idea: Promoting Complex Language in Discussions with ELL Students.*) Teachers restate what children are saying, summarizing and using elaborated language as they encourage children to expand, restate, and support their arguments (Williams, 2001).

In peer-led discussions, the "social drama" (Lewis, 1997) of the group also needs to be taken into account. What children say and how they say it is influenced by their social context. Power relations within groups can grant some members a stronger voice than others might have, can set boundaries that exclude some members, and can create alliances that strengthen the power of certain members. As you listen to groups as they discuss topics and books, pay attention to these social issues and talk through them with your class. If problems persist, many teachers advocate disbanding dysfunctional groups immediately. If the group isn't functioning at a social-interaction level, it will not be proficient at exploring topics or books through discussion.

TEACHING IDEA

Addressing Diversity

PROMOTING COMPLEX LANGUAGE IN DISCUSSIONS WITH ELL STUDENTS

As you engage in a conversation or discussion with your English Language Learners, be sure to listen to the ways in which they express themselves and provide them with opportunities to stretch their English language skills. Just as caregivers do with young children who are learning to talk, restate in Standard English what students are saying, asking them to elaborate on or restate their idea. When you do this, you are providing students with a model of fluent English and asking them to say more, thus encouraging their use of English. It's important to remember that your restatement of their language is not a correction, merely a restatement that provides students with a good model. Also, allow students to use their native language to express their ideas if they need to, and encourage them to work together to translate their ideas into English. Your stance of support and interest will give them the confidence to risk mistakes and to practice their developing language skills.

Oral Presentations, Drama, Choral Reading, Storytelling

Discussion involves exploratory talk that ranges from the intimate to the articulate, whereas oral presentations require articulate talk that is more organized than that required in discussion. Offering students the opportunity to participate in oral presentations allows them to practice a more formal register, giving them additional practice in communicating their ideas to others. Oral presentations can be difficult, however, for extremely shy children. Group presentations, use of props such as charts, flannel boards, and pictures, use of technology such as PowerPoint®, video clips, or other resources such as those presented in the *Teaching Idea: Using Technology to Support Oral Presentations* all help support those students who find it difficult to stand alone in front of their classmates. Sharing a piece of writing or talking about a well-loved book allows for the use of props (the writing and the book) and gives

TEACHING IDEA

Making Use of Technology

USING TECHNOLOGY TO SUPPORT ORAL PRESENTATIONS

Technology can be a useful tool in helping students gather, organize, and use information. It also plays a significant role in oral presentations. Encourage and help your students to go beyond traditional texts and tools and make use of multimedia approaches for their oral presentations. They can use

- Word processing to collect and organize notes, write summaries, prepare written reports and handouts to accompany oral presentations.
- Computer programs to create posters and charts for displays to accompany oral presentations.
- PowerPoint® technology to share information through slide shows, including graphics, sound, animation, and video.
- Digital and video cameras to record information and enhance charts and PowerPoint® presentations.

students practice in formally presenting their own ideas. Group presentations also uphold the collaborative atmosphere that frames much of what occurs in the classroom. Groups of children can do oral presentations about any subject covered in the curriculum. Such presentations give students practice in using the vocabulary associated with specific disciplines. Although discipline-related discussions can do this as well, oral presentations, with their more formal register, demand a more precise use of language.

Oral presentations are often jointly planned, and the talk that goes on as students work together to create their presentation involves them in learning the language of a particular content area. They also learn to use language to plan. This differs from discussion, thus giving them yet another experience of using oral language for a variety of functions in the classroom setting.

Students who work together to create a dramatic reenactment of a scene from a piece of literature, or a choral reading of a poem or prose passage, must also use language to plan. Simultaneously, they talk about the content and use content-specific language. Planning a dramatic reenactment requires discussions of characters, setting, plot sequence, and perhaps of mood, tone, and character motivations. Planning a choral reading requires discussion of meaning and its relation to sound, tempo and stress, and pitch and volume, as presented in the *Teaching Idea: Using Choral Speaking to Explore Poetry*. Choral reading, often performed with poetry, also works nicely with well-written prose that contains rich dialogue. Finally, the oral presentation, dramatic rendition, or choral reading that results gives students practice in the formal use of language because it requires them to reproduce what they have read or heard. These paired or group activities build on the community spirit that you have established in the classroom and provide situations for practicing oral lan-

Bernice Cullinan

Sharing writing and drawing helps young students become comfortable speaking in front of their peers.

TEACHING IDEA

Literature Link

USING CHORAL SPEAKING TO EXPLORE POETRY

Put some of your favorite poems on an overhead projector or computer, and as a class explore how different ways of reading the same poem can create different effects and affect the meaning of the poem. After demonstrating tempo (fast/slow), stress (emphasis), and tone (somber/lighthearted), you can experiment with ways of grouping voices (unison, choruses, single voices paired with other single or blended voices, cumulative voices). When your students have a solid grasp of the possibilities that are open to them, have them work in small groups to identify a poem they wish to prepare and present to the class. As they prepare, they will need to set guidelines for rules of interaction and discuss the poem itself, as well as the procedures for choral reading.

guage that require the use of articulate language but in a low-risk situation. These opportunities are good for both native speakers and English language learners. McCauley and McCauley (1992) describe how choral reading offers ELL students supportive contexts for developing their English language skill through repeated practice in a supportive environment.

You can develop oral language experiences such as these with many different kinds of literature. Poetry, of course, is plentiful, and you can even find collections of poems for two or more voices that are very engaging for upper elementary and middle school students. Paul Fleischman's *I Am Phoenix: Poems for Two Voices* (1986), *Joyful Noise: Poems for Two Voices* (1988), and *Out Loud* (2001) are wonderful collections that can start upper-grade students on an exploration of poetry through choral speaking. Folklore, equally abundant in school libraries, is an excellent source for dramatic reenactments or choral reading for students of all ages. Picture storybooks that contain patterned and repetitive dialogue are excellent resources for preschool and primary-grade teachers who want to facilitate their students' language development. Fergusun and Young (1996) describe how teachers can use these types of stories to help ELL students learn the vocabulary, syntax, and rhythm of story dialogues by inviting students to join in reading the dialogue and then improvise on the dialogue, creating new conversations using the patterns of the text. This imaginative exercise is another low-risk way to help ELL and other students learn the language of story and the structure of English. Young children will transfer these experiences to their dramatic play, providing yet another venue for practicing this more formal use of language.

Storytelling is yet another way for children to use oral language differently from their everyday usage. If you read and tell a lot of stories yourself, then your students will want to learn to tell some on their own. Storytelling is fun for children, and it gives them practice in using the literate language of carefully crafted stories. Primary-grade students tell stories during sharing time, and these stories are usually based on their experiences outside of the classroom. They can also learn some of their favorite stories in the books they read. To become an effective storyteller, students need to learn the plot sequence and any important phrases or dialogue in the story they wish to tell.

Folklore is a good place to start. If, for example, students wanted to learn to tell the story of *The Three Billy Goats Gruff,* they would need to remember that the goats cross the river to get to a new meadow, a troll lives under the bridge, the small billy goat crosses first, the middle billy goat crosses second, and the big billy goat crosses last. All three are confronted by the troll, with the first two being allowed to cross and the big billy goat overcoming the troll. In the end they are all across the river, safe. Phrases they need to remember are "Trip trap, trip trap. Who's that walking over my bridge?" and "Oh, don't eat me. My big brother is coming along next, and he'll make a better meal for you." It can be that simple. As children develop their skills as storytellers, they increase the amount of literate language that they remember and incorporate into their personal renditions of favorite stories. They also learn to use inflection, pacing, and body language to increase the drama of the stories they tell. In Betty Shockley's classroom her first-graders enthusiastically embraced the opportunity to tell stories. It became a collaborative effort, with class members prompting the teller when needed.

TEACHING IDEA

Literature Link

COMBINING VIEWING AND VISUAL REPRESENTATION

After reading a story, have students act out various scenes. The scenes may be predetermined by you or derived through student suggestions. Divide the class into small groups. Assign a scene to each group. Give the following suggestions and have students go off into "quiet" areas to plan their sketch. Each group should (1) decide who will play which parts, adding additional parts if they wish; (2) discuss the general movement of the characters; (3) do a quick run-through. Each group then presents their skit to the class. Those who view the skits may offer positive comment and constructive critique.

You can structure many situations that provide students with opportunities to use oral language to learn language, to learn about language, and to learn through language (Halliday, 1982). We now turn back to discussions, specifically small-group discussions about literature, to consider how students learn about reading and literature through successful small-group discussions. The discussions can take the form of planning for a response to literature that involves both presenting and viewing student dramatizations. (See the *Teaching Idea: Combining Viewing and Visual Representation.*)

Small-Group Literature Discussions

Ways of conducting and promoting small-group discussions of literature have been described by many teachers and researchers, most notably the "grand conversations" described by Peterson and Eeds (1990), the literature circles promoted by Short and Pierce (1990), and the Book Clubs that are central to McMahon, Raphael, Goatley, and Pardo's (1997) Book Club approach. These and other approaches to literature study and literature-based reading instruction are described more fully in Chapter Seven. Here we focus on the content of the oral discussion and how it relates to students' learning about literature and about how they can think and talk about literature.

Many researchers who study discussion come to the same conclusion: Children need to know how to conduct themselves in discussion groups, as we discussed above, and their enthusiasm for the activity is crucial. They need to have had an engaging experience with the book they have read, and to want to talk about it. No matter how good the questions are that teachers frame, if students don't want to talk about them, they aren't useful for promoting engaged conversations about books (Commeyras, 1994). Although framing questions and conversational prompts is important, we also have to let students find their own way to a text, to make their own kind of sense, even when we worry that they might not make it (Roller & Beed, 1994).

Small-group discussions of literature help students explore ideas and issues in literature as they work with members of their group to develop meaning. In this exploratory talk, teachers serve not as the ultimate authority, but as fellow readers who are also facilitators and guides. They help students articulate their own interpretations and perceptions as they learn about literature and how it works, and about how to talk about literature so that they can conduct discussions without their teacher being present. Almasi (1996) suggests that conversations about books have cognitive, social, and affective benefits. In terms of cognitive benefits, students learn about how to interpret literature, and they also develop higher-level thinking skills. Their growing competence during social interactions is a social benefit, and the affective benefit may be that they begin to enjoy reading because they enjoy talking with their peers about books.

Small-group discussions of literature generally center around making connections between literature and life experiences, and between texts; learning about literary elements and genres; and understanding the role of the author. The focus of the discussion is either suggested by the teacher or evolves directly from the students' ideas.

CONVERSATIONS THAT MAKE CONNECTIONS

Many teachers ask their students to make **intertextual connections** between the text they are reading and other texts they have read or experiences they have had. These types of conversations are almost always related to the themes or topics that are being studied. Forged through oral discussion, such connections help students build upon prior knowledge to generate new ideas—in other words, to learn. The discussions often seem to drift "off topic" as students bring their very individual ideas to the discussion. However, what may seem to be a digression can actually be a profound discussion for the children. Newkirk's (1992) description of how one classroom of children talked about books and the sensitive way in which their teacher responded is a model for listening to children. He demonstrates what happens when teachers accept children's experiences as significant and allow them to use these experiences to think about what they have read.

Lisa Stanzi has learned to listen to what her students are saying and search for those connections that are not always apparent to her. Many times she has wondered about the seemingly disconnected comments that some of her students make, but she soon realized that some, but not all, are part of a

Joseph Cassick

Literature groups can meet with or without a teacher to discuss books.

pattern of making connections with idiosyncratic life experiences to develop interpretations and construct meaning. This takes enormous concentration as she listens to what her students say about the books they read, tape-records their conversations, and keeps a journal about what happens each day—but she has learned about how her students make sense of texts and thus how to help them grow as reflective, responsive readers.

If your goal is to help your students engage with texts by making connections to their own lives, you must be prepared to do as Lisa does and listen very carefully to understand how they are making these connections, helping them learn to come back to the text if they go too far afield. Asking questions such as "What in the story caused you to think about that?" or "How does your experience help you to understand the story?" can help students anchor their personal connections in the text under discussion. This is what we want them to do.

Some teachers select books that focus on social issues, and then ask students to consider these issues in light of their own life experiences. Issues such as gender or race discrimination are things that students find in the books they read and in the lives they lead. Discussions that center on issues of social justice are often passionate and can lead to thoughtful refinement of students' values and ideals and perhaps even to behavior that seeks to change their social environment. It is important to realize, however, that these conversations often move substantially away from the book itself. They are not really book discussions but discussions about social issues that arise from a book discussion. Each has value, but they do not serve the same purpose.

If you want to help your students understand the connections among the various books they read, then you may want to ask them about, or suggest your own ideas about, connections to other books. Lisa Stanzi does this with her second-graders early in the fall, setting the stage for intertextual connections across the school year. Lisa works with a basal series that is organized around themes, using the basal as a supplement to the many thematically related children's books that form the main reading material. During the first theme cycle, she often mentions the connections that she makes between texts, beginning with thematic comparisons and branching out into comparisons of character, style, and setting. As she shares her ideas with her students, they begin to spontaneously share their own connections. At the end of the first theme study, for example, she decided to have a conversation about all of the books they had read—a big task for second grade students. She put all of the picture books and the stories from the basal on the floor in the center of the circle of students and asked them to group the books. As the students manipulated the books and talked about why they thought certain books belonged together, they discussed a multitude of connections among the stories. They were learning how to think about books in terms of their relations to other books, and thus how to think about literature as a body of work. This

TEACHING IDEA

Literature Link

VISUAL LITERACY—LEARNING TO READ THE PICTURES

As you work with students and picture books, help them learn to "read" the illustrations as well as the text. Simple techniques such as previewing the text by looking at the illustrations and talking about them promote students' awareness that the message comes from the illustrations as well as from the words. Looking at the illustrations or talking about mood or character helps students realize that the illustrations are designed to make them feel a certain way or help illuminate character. Molly Bang's (1999) *When Sophie Gets Angry, Really, Really Angry* is a perfect book to use to explore the use of color and line to express emotion. *Picture This,* also by Molly Bang, offers a cogent explanation of how artists' choices create different emotions in viewers as well as an interesting activity to explore with students.

As you read picture books, stop and discuss the illustrations, asking students what they see, what's going on in the illustration, and how the illustrations relate to the evolving meaning of the text. Barbara Kiefer's (1995) *The Potential of Picturebooks: From Visual Literacy to Aesthetic Understanding* is an outstanding resource for teachers who want to explore this aspect of the curriculum.

learning also encompasses learning how to "read" the illustrations in picture books to better understand the book, as described in the *Teaching Idea: Visual Literacy—Learning to Read the Pictures.*

Shortly after this, Lisa introduces a brief novel by author Patricia MacLachlan that will serve as the lead-in to a protracted author study, another context that encourages students to make connections among books as they discuss them.

CONVERSATIONS THAT FOCUS ON HOW TEXTS WORK

Not all discussions about books focus on making connections. Talking about books provides a wonderful opportunity for students to learn about how literature works and how to create meaning as they read. Books about children's literature, such as Galda and Cullinan's *Literature and the Child, 5th Edition* (2002), offer ways of thinking and talking about children's books that can be demonstrated for students. Peterson and Eeds (1990) suggest that teachers who want to help their students discuss literary elements and how they work should begin by reading the book that will be studied and carefully considering its style, plot, character, setting, point of view, mood, and theme. This allows teachers to develop strategies that can help students see how authors create stories and poems. Considering structure, organization, accuracy, and style helps students understand how authors create nonfiction.

To prepare for these discussions, teachers begin by reading and thinking about the books they will discuss in terms of the literary qualities or elements that they contain. They can formulate questions that lead students into a discussion of whatever literary element or device they want them to consider. If you have prepared in this way, you will be alert to teachable moments that will help your students develop their growing understanding about how texts work. We discuss the development of literary understanding further in Chapter Seven.

ORGANIZATION AND ASSESSMENT OF LITERATURE-DISCUSSION GROUPS

As students conduct small-group discussions about books, you can be assessing their performance. You will want to be alert to how the group is working in terms of social interaction, how coherent the conversation is, what kinds of connections students are making, if any, and the depth of their growing understanding of text. Further, you will want to teach your students how to assess their own performance as a member of a discussion group. Ideas for assessment of peer-led discussion groups appear in the *Teaching Idea: Assessing Book Discussions*.

TEACHING IDEA

Assessing the Learning Environment

ASSESSING BOOK DISCUSSIONS

Some behaviors that you might want to look for as you observe students in small peer-led discussion groups are listed below. They are useful starting points for you as you observe students, and also for students as they think about their own behaviors.

- ✦ Takes turns
- ✦ Listens to others
- ✦ Responds appropriately to others' questions and ideas
- ✦ Offers own ideas
- ✦ Supports ideas with examples
- ✦ Stays on topic
- ✦ Is supportive of other group members

You can add other items that are specific to your goals.

Teachers organize small-group discussions in a variety of ways. Some have students meet in small groups all at the same time, moving around the classroom from group to group during the discussion period. This works best with students who have learned how to participate in small-group discussions. Other teachers use small-group discussions as one of a number of activities that all students rotate through on a regular basis. While other groups of students are engaged in, for example, painting or dramatic play or a mathematics activity, a peer discussion group meets under the supervision of the teacher. This works well with younger students who are learning how to engage in small-group discussion and need a great deal of teacher support. No organization will work well, however, unless a collaborative atmosphere has been established in your classroom.

Sometimes teachers assign roles such as observer, summarizer, clarifier, organizer, encourager, and timekeeper (Hill & Hill, 1990) to students in discussion groups. Such cooperative learning structures can encourage students to learn roles and responsibilities that help small groups be proficient. Other teachers prefer the less structured framework of "collaboration," offering guidelines for participation rather than roles. The choice depends on the social context of your classroom and your students' abilities and experiences.

Talk that Supports Writing

Writing teachers will tell you just how much talk occurs during writing—a lot! Before they ever get to school, children are already proficient in doing two things with oral language that serve them well as writers: talking to themselves and talking to others.

As they write, children talk to themselves and others about what they're going to write, what they are writing, and what they have written. They may ask for help with spelling, rehearse a sentence before writing it, or utter the words they are writing as they write them. They may comment on the writing process itself, or reread aloud what they have written.

In Betty Shockley's classroom, many of the children compose aloud as they write, either saying the words that they intend to put on paper or spelling aloud. An audible vocalization when spelling means immediate help from neighbors, even if not explicitly asked for:

John: (reading) One time . . .

Jason: (leaning over John's paper) "One" starts with a "o."

Shuntae: How do you spell "Ms. Shockley"?

Kimberly: (jumps up and gets a book, returning with it) Here's how to spell "Shockley." Just go get a book that her name is on and copy it. Her name is on all of the books.

Various opportunities for talk during writing exist in Betty's classroom, ranging from spelling help to collaborating on a writing project. Never told to write silently, these first grade students use talk to support their language learning as they take chances and grow as writers.

Children talk to themselves to guide their writing and to others to seek and get help or to collaborate. They also use talk to get ready to write, exploring ideas to write about with peers or simply saying them aloud to themselves. They also frequently read aloud as they write. Reading aloud offers writers the opportunity for affirmation, recognizing the worth of their own creation. Reading aloud helps writers decide what comes next, or what needs revising. It is also an opportunity for interaction with others who are in a position to listen and respond.

In a look at three different types of peer interaction during writing, McCarthey and McMahon (1992) describe **peer tutoring, cooperative learning,** and **peer collaboration** experiences. They point out that each situation calls for different kinds of talk that serve different purposes. In peer tutoring, a knowledgeable student transmits knowledge to another; this works well when students have expertise that others need. Cooperative learning groups are more fluid and dynamic. Individual students may indeed transmit knowledge, but the group also works together to create and transform knowledge as they talk with one another. Peer collaboration is also fluid and dynamic, with bi-directional transformation of knowledge through conversation. All three types of experiences provide valuable but different uses of oral language to learn. The *Teaching Idea: Co-Authored Composition to Promote Conversation* presents one effective strategy for promoting talk about writing.

Talking with peers and others about a finished written product is another important way in which oral language is involved in writing. This can happen in many situations including informal sharing around the writing table, formal sharing sessions, and conferences.

Listening

As we discussed in Chapter 4, if effective language arts classrooms "float on a sea of talk" (Britton, 1982), then there must be an undercurrent of good listening. As teachers help children learn to talk together, they are also teaching them how to listen.

TEACHING IDEA

From the Research

CO-AUTHORED COMPOSITION TO PROMOTE CONVERSATION

Mark Condon and Jean Anne Clyde (1996) studied the conversations of children who were co-authoring texts for plays, art, and music. They discovered that those partnerships or groups in what Condon and Clyde call "full conversation relationships" were the most powerful, although "partial conversation relationships" also resulted in increased quality of work. They suggest that teachers

- Allow students to choose their partners.
- Discuss the process with students, including how to have a productive conversation.
- Demonstrate the process they want students to emulate.
- Allow students to choose the product that they will create.
- Give students time to work together in the classroom.

Teachers can model careful listening through their responses to what children say by expanding upon their ideas or by asking meaningful questions. Listening to children is also a significant assessment tool. No matter what good prompts or open-ended questions they have developed, teachers who actively listen to children during book discussions follow their lead when what children are discussing reveals their knowledge of, or connections to, the book. These teachers know their students well because they listen to what their students have to say about their interests, about what excites, confounds, or confuses them, and they use this valuable information to plan future lessons. They help students learn to monitor their own listening, to recognize the strategies they use, and to revise these strategies when they are not effective. Such teachers engage students in meaningful activities that require them to listen actively and ask them to assess themselves as listeners. This creates a communicative community with the children in their care.

Using observation checklists based on instructional goals is the best way to assess children's listening ability and progress. Can a young child listen to a story and summarize the plot? Is an older child able to interview an expert and distinguish and remember the most important information shared? Is the class improving in their ability to listen during whole-class discussions? Do individuals respond appropriately to each other during small-group discussions? A wide range of general and critical listening goals that can be used for developing assessment checklists is listed in Figure 5.3. You can also collect

FIGURE 5.3

Listening Goals

General Listening

1. Remembering significant details accurately (with knowledge of specifics)
2. Remembering simple sequences of words or ideas
3. Following oral directions
4. Paraphrasing a spoken message (comprehension by translation)
5. Following a sequence in (a) plot development, (b) character development, (c) speaker's argument
6. Understanding denotative (literal) meanings of words
7. Understanding connotative (implied) meanings of words
8. Understanding meanings of words from spoken context (comprehension by translation and interpretation)
9. Listening for implications of significant details (analysis and interpretation)
10. Listening for implications of main ideas
11. Answering and formulating questions (interactive listening)
12. Identifying main ideas and summarizing (combining and synthesizing the who, what, when, where and why)
13. Understanding relationships among ideas and the organizational pattern well enough to predict what may come next (comprehension by extrapolation)
14. Connecting the spoken material with previous experience and planning action (application)
15. Listening to imagine and to extend for enjoyment and emotional response (affective-toned synthesizing)

Critical Listening

1. Distinguishing fact from fancy, according to criteria
2. Judging validity and adequacy of main ideas, arguments, and hypotheses
3. Distinguishing well-supported statements from opinion and judgment and evaluating them
4. Distinguishing well-supported statements from irrelevant ones and evaluating them
5. Inspecting, comparing, and contrasting ideas and arriving at a conclusion about statements, such as the appropriateness and appeal of one descriptive word over another
6. Evaluating the use of fallacies, such as: (a) self-contradictions, (b) avoiding the question at issue, (c) hasty or false generalization, (d) false analogy, (e) failure to present all choices, (f) appealing to ignorance
7. Recognizing and judging the effects of various devices the speaker may use to influence the listener, such as (a) music, (b) "loaded" words, (c) voice intonation, (d) play on emotional or controversial issues, (e) propaganda, sales pressure—that is, identifying affective loading in communication and evaluating it
8. Detecting and evaluating the bias and prejudice of a speaker or of a point of view
9. Evaluating the qualifications of a speaker
10. Planning to evaluate the ways in which a speaker's ideas might be applied in a new situation

Source: From Lundsteen, S. (1979). *Listening: Its impact on reading and the other language arts* (pp. 59–61). Copyright 1979 by the National Council of Teachers of English. Reprinted with permission.

and analyze listening data to decide on which strategies to present to your students to strengthen their listening abilities. Some children may need more intensive individual or small-group work on listening skills to ensure their development of these crucial skills.

Conferences

Conferring with students is another way of engaging them in a meaningful oral language activity. It not only encourages them to talk and listen in a meaningful context but it also builds a sense of community. Just as in discussions, as you talk with students in conferences, so, too, will students talk with each other. Conferences are different from discussions in that they generally focus on what a particular child is doing rather than an idea that the group wants to consider. Conferences have a more specific focus than do discussions. For example, a conference might focus on a piece of writing that a student is working on, or a student's reading process or comprehension strategies, or a student's process in the science lab.

No matter what you want to teach, conferences are the perfect time to do so. When you confer with students, you know right then what students need to know. They may need to know that it is okay to cross out in their drafts, how to combine two simple sentences, or how changing word order changes emphasis and meaning. They may need to know how to use an index to find information quickly, how to read the word *plague,* or what to call those neat descriptions in the story they are reading. Whatever it is, you can help them, quickly and immediately, and students will most likely learn because they have a need to know.

We discuss reading and writing conferences here, but you can confer with students about almost anything, and they can confer with each other. Students can confer among themselves in individual, partner, small-group, and whole-class situations. Just as in whole-class discussions, as you hold conferences with each student, the students internalize the questions you ask and soon ask the same questions of themselves and of their peers. You can also teach lessons on conferences—how they work, what to expect, how to prepare for them, on how to confer with yourself or with a peer or peers. You can demonstrate conference situations before reading or writing time or during whole-class sharing time. Conferences can take several forms but work best when teachers and students are well organized and prepared, and when students know what to expect from others and what others expect from them.

Joseph Kassick

Children talk to each other in their writing groups; teachers stop by for conferences any time.

TEACHER-STUDENT CONFERENCES

Conferences can be the heart of the teaching that occurs in a classroom. You can confer with a student on a wide variety of topics. What you and a particular student talk about at any given time depends on the student's needs at that particular time. Although the topics will vary widely, how conferences are organized should remain stable.

Scheduling and organizing

The day before a regularly scheduled conference with a student, you should look through that student's work, making brief notes on the strengths and problem areas that you identify. You might want to ask students to leave you a note telling you what they want to discuss the next day. Some teachers find it effective to ask students to write down any questions they might have and bring them to the conference.

You can schedule conferences in different ways: as needed, on a regular basis, or daily. Waiting to confer until a student asks for a conference—"as needed"—is a risky business; you risk losing touch with some students. Those who are floundering may not know how to ask for help; those who are writing a great amount or reading fluently may not think they need help. We suggest that you either hold regularly scheduled conferences supplemented by drop-in conferences or that you drop in on most or all students daily.

Let's suppose that you have decided to schedule regular conferences and see five students each day, all students every 5 or 6 days. If you are working within a 60-minute time period for language arts, for example, you can allot 25 minutes to conferences, giving each student approximately 5 minutes. In reality, some will need less time, some more. You will get better and more efficient at conferring through experience. These 25-minute sessions can be followed by 10 minutes of drop-in conferences and 10–15 minutes of whole-class sharing. A 60-minute schedule will look like this:

10–15 minutes—whole class (introductory activities)

25 minutes—learning activity with scheduled conferences

10 minutes—learning activity with drop-in conferences

10–15 minutes—group sharing

If you have a longer block of time available, then you can see more children each day, see the same number of children for longer periods, or space conferences across the longer time block.

You can physically organize regularly scheduled conferences in different ways. You might prefer to go to students' desks. This practice cuts down on student movement and places you in the midst of the class. But being in the midst of the class lessens the private feeling of a one-on-one conference and requires that you squat down to be at eye level with the student.

You might prefer to have the scheduled students come to you at a designated table other than your desk. Students may do so one at a time, which increases privacy but also increases student traffic and your waiting time, which is time wasted. Or you could assemble the scheduled students at a conference table and squat beside each one in turn. In this approach the students have less privacy, and you are on the periphery of the room. But student traffic is minimized, there is no waiting time between conferences, and you can go back and forth among students, checking to see whether those who were having problems earlier are working easily now.

Atwell (1998) describes how she moves from student to student in a random pattern around the room. Her students know that she will see them during workshop but they do not know precisely when. This suspense helps keep all of her eighth-graders working during the workshop. She is able to see everyone or nearly everyone because on any given day most of her students do not need her help. The conferences take very little time. She prepares for daily conferences by looking at the "plans for the day" records to spot students who might be stuck and by looking through the in-progress folders or reading journals. Systematically reviewing these materials minimizes the time needed to review and allows Atwell time to plan conferences and other instructional activities using the information gained.

Keeping records

A weekly log of daily plans is one record you might want to keep. Your students' permanent and working writing folders are other important records, with their accumulated drafts and published pieces as well as their lists of topics, published pieces, and acquired strategies and skills. The students' reading journals or response logs and a record of the activities they have selected for response are other artifacts that reflect their progress. You will also want to keep conference records, brief annotations of what occurred during the conference. When records are kept across time, you have readily available data for assessment. Further, these records can be used to help plan lessons that respond to students' needs.

Asking questions

Teachers and researchers have identified several types of questions as being useful in conferences, but there is no set format of "best" questions. No matter what type of questions teachers ask, what is said must spring directly from the needs of the child. Effective questions help children focus, help them restate a problem, invite them to expand upon an idea, and point them toward thinking about what they will do next. We discuss specific questions for reading and writing conferences in Chapters Seven and Eight.

STUDENT-STUDENT CONFERENCES

In the kind of classroom we have been describing, students are actively engaged in learning the subject at hand. They are, in many ways, "experts" in the classroom. If teachers allow students to talk to one another about their learning, they tap a valuable resource. Arranging classroom space and time so that there are opportunities for student-to-student conferences signals to students that talking with each other is an effective learning strategy. How they talk with each other reflects how teachers talk with them, because students naturally adapt a teacher's questions for themselves. Teachers can also discuss with their classes effective ways of talking together.

After you have had several teacher/student conferences with each student, you can introduce peer conferences to your students. They probably are already having spontaneous peer conferences as they talk with one another about their learning, but it is productive to generate some "rules" or guidelines for successful peer conferences. Students can be asked to think about and discuss the ways of behaving that make teacher/student conferences work. Then they can generate a list of guidelines for peer conferences that can be discussed and then posted. This can be done with the whole class or in small groups. A fourth grade class came up with the following rules for effective peer conferences about writing:

1. Listen hard when the writer reads.
2. Tell the writer what you heard.
3. Say something nice about the writing.
4. Ask the writer how you can help.
5. Give the writer your best ideas.
6. Tell the writer, "Good luck!"

Student-to-student conferences might be one-on-one, one student asking for help from a small group, or a student asking for help from the whole class. Whole-class sessions typically occur at the end of the language arts period but can occur at any time. The person who shares a piece of writing or a trade book during these sessions is always a volunteer; no student is ever forced to sit in front of the whole class. The class can respond following the guidelines established for peer conferences, can celebrate the accomplishment of a finished piece, can ask questions about the decisions the writer made, can ask questions about the reader's response to the book being presented, or any other useful process.

ASSESSMENT CONFERENCES

Conferences can also be an important part of assessment practices. In an assessment conference, the teacher and the student sit together to discuss the student's performance and progress. Like other conferences, these are structured so that students know what to expect, what their role will be, and what the criteria for evaluation will be. In this type of conference both the teacher and the student evaluate the student's work.

In getting ready for an assessment conference, the teacher and students will need to develop the criteria for assessment together. Sometimes these will be general whole-class goals, such as managing time efficiently, and sometimes these will be individual goals, such as reading books by a variety of authors or publishing more pieces of writing. Of course, these individual goals reflect the values that the class shares as well as the development and interests of individual students. Once these criteria are developed, students need time to think through their progress, examining any relevant documents, such as writing folders and reading logs. You might ask students to evaluate themselves on a standard form in preparation for individual conferences. If you decide to evaluate a particular product as well as general progress, students might be requested to select the work which, in their judgment, best demonstrates their abilities.

When students come to a teacher for an assessment conference, they should bring the work they are going to discuss, any supporting material such as folders, and their self-assessment. The conference might begin with the question, "What have you done in [subject area] that you are most proud of?" Such a question asks students to look at their accomplishments first. Students often think of evaluation as a time to find out what is "wrong" when it is just as much a time to find out what is "right"! After a discussion of the accomplishment that a student is most proud of, the conference moves on to a discussion of what the student most wants to learn next. Discussing students' needs in terms of what they want to accomplish rather than what they have not yet accomplished keeps the conference positive. If the conference includes an evaluation of a particular product, this would happen next, using whatever criteria have been determined in advance.

Assessment conferences are time-consuming, but it is time well spent. They help students focus on their own learning and their own progress. One way to help students feel responsible for, and proud of, their own learning is to give them a responsible role in its assessment.

SUMMARY

Although most teachers focus on reading and writing, oral language is also an important component of the English language arts. Children need opportunities to engage in exploratory talk as they learn new things. During discussions, the turn-taking patterns, teacher evaluations, and kinds of questions asked all project messages about what and who is valued in the classroom. Discussions in which children use exploratory talk, speak more than the teacher, and speak to each other as well as to the teacher are more productive than are discussions that follow the IRE pattern. Questions should be real, information-seeking questions, and should promote thoughtful responses. Open-ended questions call for a variety of responses and promote interaction among the discussants.

Children need time to talk about the reading and writing that they do. Discussion groups allow students to explore books and ideas and enlarge their own understandings. Talk is also important during writing, as children collaborate, consult, and share. Through discussions and other classroom activities, children also learn how to listen effectively to their teachers and to each other.

The conference is another way in which teachers make use of oral language. During conferences, teachers and students talk with each other about the student's work. Assessment conferences provide another arena for talk and help students become aware of their own accomplishments.

ACTIVITIES

1. **Audiotape a class discussion, either in an elementary or middle school or in one of your language arts classes in college.** Then, using what you have learned about effective discussions in this chapter, analyze the discussion. What are the turn-taking patterns? Are the questions that

the teacher asks information-seeking or known-information questions? What sorts of evaluations are present in teacher responses? Is there a pattern of positive and negative evaluations and does this relate to individual students? What is the "wait time" the teacher allows? Are the questions open-ended or closed questions?

2. **Talking with children and giving them time to talk with each other is an important component of the kind of literature-based, child-centered instruction described in this text.** Yet in many classrooms children are required to sit in their seats and speak only when spoken to. Why do you think this happens? How could you go about convincing teachers and administrators that children need to talk? With a partner or partners, develop a list of reasons you might give to a principal to convince him or her of the importance of discussion.
3. **Arrange a visit to a local school.** Watch children on the playground, listening to their oral language. With whom do they talk? What do they talk about? What functions does their talk fulfill? Then watch the same children in the classroom, asking the same questions. Compare the data. What differences do you notice? What kinds of explanations for these differences can you offer? Present your data and tentative explanations to your peers and discuss.
4. **With a partner, read a children's book and brainstorm ideas for discussion with a group of children.** Share the books and the discussion ideas with your peers.
5. **Tape-record a discussion that you have in your language arts class.** Listen to it and talk together about how your class works as a community of learners.
6. **Many people are reluctant to speak up in class.** In a journal entry explore how your school experiences have influenced your behavior as a contributor to class discussions.

FURTHER READING

Evans, K. S. (2001). *Literature discussion groups in the intermediate grades.* Newark, DE: International Reading Association.

Galda, L., Rayburn, S., & Stanzi, L. C. (2000). *Looking through the faraway end: Creating a literature-based reading curriculum with second graders.* Newark, DE: International Reading Association.

Gambrell, L. B., & Almasi, J. F. (Eds.) (1996). *Lively discussions! Fostering engaged reading.* Newark, DE: International Reading Association.

Kiefer, B. (1995). *The potential of picturebooks: From visual literacy to aesthetic understanding.* Upper Saddle River, NJ: Prentice Hall.

REFERENCES

Allington, R., Johnston, P., & Day, J. P. (2002). Exemplary fourth-grade teachers. *Language Arts, 79*(8), 462–466.

Almasi, J. F. (1996). A new view of discussion. In L. B. Gambrell & J. F. Almasi (Eds.), *Lively discussions! Fostering engaged reading* (pp. 2–24). Newark, DE: International Reading Association.

Almasi, J. F., O'Flahavan, J., & Poonam, A. (2001). A comparative analysis of student and teacher development in more and less proficient discussions of literature. *Reading Research Quarterly, 36,* 96–120.

Atwell, N. (1998). *In the middle: New understandings about writing, reading, and learning* (2nd ed.). Portsmouth, NH: Boynton/Cook-Heinemann.

Bang, M. (2000). *Picture this: How pictures work.* New York: Seastar.

Barnes, D., Barnes, D., & Clarke, S. (1984). *Versions of English.* London: Heinemann.

Cazden, C. (1988). *Classroom discourse.* Portsmouth, NH: Heinemann.

Commeyras, M. (1994). Were Janell and Neesie in the same classroom? Children's questions as the first order of reality in storybook discussions. *Language Arts, 71,* 517–522.

Condon, M. F., & Clyde, J. A. (1996). Co-authoring: Composing through conversation. *Language Arts, 73,* 587–596.

Dillon, D., & Searle, D. (1981). The role of language in one first-grade classroom. *Research in the Teaching of English, 15,* 311–328.

Dillon, J. T. (1984). Research on questioning and discussion. *Educational Leadership, 42*(3), 50–56.

Fergusun, P. M., & Young, T. A. (1996). Literature talk: Dialogue improvisation and patterned conversations with second-language learners. *Language Arts, 73,* 597–600.

Galda, L. & Cullinan, B. (2002). *Literature and the child* (5th ed.). Belmont, CA: Wadsworth.

Galda, L., Rayburn, S., & Stanzi, L. C. (2000). *Looking through the faraway end: Creating a literature-based reading curriculum with second graders.* Newark, DE: International Reading Association.

Halliday, M. A. K. (1975). *Explorations in the functions of language.* London: Edward Arnold.

______. (1982). Three aspects of children's language development: Learning language, learning through language, and learning about language. In Y. Goodman, M. Huassle, & D. S. Strickland (Eds.), *Oral and written language development research: Impact on the schools* (pp. 7–19). Urbana, IL: National Council of Teachers of English.

Hill, S., & Hill, T. (1990). *The collaborative classroom: A guide to cooperative learning.* Portsmouth, NH: Heinemann.

Hynds, S. (1992). Challenging questions in the teaching of literature. In J. A. Langer (Ed.), *Literature instruction: A focus on student response* (pp. 78–100). Urbana, IL: National Council of Teachers of English.

Kiefer, B. (1995). *The potential of picture books: From visual literacy to aesthetic understanding.* Upper Saddle River, NJ: Prentice Hall.

Lewis, C. (1997). The social drama of literature discussions in a fifth/sixth grade classroom. *Research in the Teaching of English, 31,* 163–204.

Lindfors, J. (1990). Speaking creatures in the classroom. In S. Hynds & D. L. Rubin (Eds.), *Perspectives on talk and learning* (pp. 21–39). Urbana, IL: National Council of Teachers of English.

Lundsteen, S. (1976). *Children learn to communicate.* Englewood Cliffs, NJ: Prentice Hall.

______. (1990). Learning to listen and learning to read. In S. Hynds & D. L. Rubin (Eds.), *Perspectives on talk and learning* (pp. 213–255). Urbana, IL: National Council of Teachers of English.

McCarthey, S. J., & McMahon, S. (1992). From convention to invention: Three approaches to peer interactions during writing. In R. Hertz-Lazarowitz & N. Miller (Eds.), *Interaction in cooperative groups: The theoretical anatomy of group learning* (pp. 17–35). New York: Cambridge University Press.

McCauley, J., & McCauley, D. (1992). Using choral reading to promote language learning for ESL students. *The Reading Teacher, 47,* 526–533.

McMahon, S., Raphael, T. E., Goatley, V. J., & Pardo, L. S. (1997). *The book club connection: Literacy learning and classroom talk.* New York: Teachers College.

Mehan, H. (1979). *Learning lessons: Social organization in the classroom.* Cambridge, MA: Harvard University Press.

Newkirk, T. (1992). *Listening in: Children talk about books (and other things).* Portsmouth, NH: Heinemann.

O'Flahavan, J. F. (1995). Teacher role options in peer discussions about literature. *The Reading Teacher, 48,* 354–356.

Pearson, P. D., & Fielding, L. (1982). Research update: Listening comprehension. *Language Arts, 59,* 617–629.

Peterson, R., & Eeds, M. (1990). *Grand conversations: Literature groups in action.* New York: Scholastic.

Pinnell, G. S., & Jaggar, A. (2003). Oral language: Speaking and listening in elementary classrooms. In J. Flood, D. Lapp, J. R. Squire, & J. Jensen (Eds.). *Handbook of research on teaching the English language arts* (2nd ed.) (pp. 881–914), Mahwah, NJ: Erlbaum.

Raphael, T. E. (1986). Teaching question-answer relationships, revisited. *The Reading Teacher, 39,* 516–522.

Roller, C. M., & Beed, P. L. (1994). Sometimes the conversations were grand, and sometimes. *Language Arts, 71,* 509–515.

Rubin, D. L. (1990). Introduction: Ways of talking about talking and learning. In S. Hynds & D. L. Rubin (Eds.), *Perspectives on talk and learning* (pp. 1–17). Urbana, IL: National Council of Teachers of English.

Short, K. G., & Pierce, K. M. (1990). *Talking about books.* Portsmouth, NH: Heinemann.

Tharp, R., & Gallimore, R. (1988). *Rousing minds to life: Teaching, learning, and schooling in social context.* Cambridge, England: Cambridge University Press.

Vygotsky, L. S. (1978). *Mind in society* (M. Cole, Ed.). Cambridge, MA: Harvard University Press.

Williams, J. (2001). Classroom conversations: Opportunities to learn for ESL students in mainstream classrooms. *The Reading Teacher, 54,* 750–757.

CHILDREN'S LITERATURE REFERENCES

Bang, Molly. (1999). *When Sophie gets angry, really, really angry.* New York: Scholastic.

Fleischman, Paul. (1986). *I am phoenix: Poems for two voices.* New York: HarperCollins.

———. (1988). *Joyful noise: Poems for two voices.* New York: HarperCollins.

———. (2001). *Out loud.* New York: HarperCollins.

White, E. B. (1952). *Charlotte's web.* New York: Harper & Row.

Reading: The Emergence of Literacy in the Early Years

CHAPTER OUTLINE

Key Standard

Teachers of language arts are knowledgeable about the nature of young children's literacy development and have the skills to support young learners as emerging and conventional readers and writers. Such teachers:

- Help students develop concepts about print, alphabet recognition, phonemic awareness, sound-letter correspondences, and sight-word vocabularies.
- Are knowledgeable about the various language components of literacy development, including phonemes (sounds of language), morphemes (words and meaningful parts of words), semantics (meaning), syntax (sentence structure; parts of speech), and pragmatics (how language works in social context).
- Understand and implement strategies that support the interrelated development of word recognition, reading fluency, and comprehension.

To get a preview of Chapter 6 learn about emergent literacy, visit the Chapter 6 section of the accompanying *Language Arts* CD-ROM.

A mom and her two children sit in a fast-food restaurant. Mom is busy feeding the younger child, who sits in a stroller. The older child, a nearly 4-year-old, munches her hot dog and surveys her surroundings. She notices a garbage receptacle and calls out to her mom as she points to the words on it: "Look, Mom, it says 'trash can.'" Her mother looks up and says, "No, dear, it says 'Thank you.'" Looking puzzled, the child assumes her mother did not look in the right place. "No, mommy," she tries again, "It says 'trash can.'" Mom replies once more as she wipes the baby's face. "No, it says, 'Thank You.'" At this point, an onlooker, who has been watching this scene, intervenes and explains to the mom why she thinks the child is confused. Mom laughs in recognition of what has occurred. She then explains to the child why the words "Thank You" are on the trash can.

Long before formal instruction, young children notice the print in their environment and try to make sense of it. Although the child in the vignette is not yet a reader in the formal sense, she demonstrates knowledge of several important concepts about print and literacy. She knows that certain kinds of markings on objects represent words that can be said (or read) aloud. She distinguishes these kinds of markings from others that may simply be decorative. She also knows that the words on objects usually stand for the things on which they appear. Thus, of course she is confused when the words turn out to be "Thank You."

Whether at home or in pre-kindergarten classrooms, young children are eager to explore the world around them. Books of all types, as well as environmental print, are an important part of their world. Effective teachers skillfully bring books and children together in ways that not only help them learn to read but also make them want to read.

"Read it again, Miss Burke," a small voice calls from the circle. The gentle plea is followed by a small chorus of "yeahs." Miss Burke closes *Whose Mouse Are You?* (Robert Kraus) and replies, "I know that it's one of your favorites, and we will read it again tomorrow. But today I have a new book to share with you. It's a book of poems, and I've selected some that I think you'll really enjoy." For the next several minutes the children sit enraptured by rhythm and rhyme. Each poem is read at least two times, with some children attempting to join in even on the second reading.

Read-aloud time is scheduled at least twice a day in this pre-kindergarten classroom, once in the morning and again in late afternoon. On these occasions everyone is invited to join the group, although rarely does everyone participate. The only rule set down by Jenny Burke is that those who don't join the group must do something very, very quietly. Of course, she has learned that very often the child off in a corner doing a puzzle, drawing, or writing with the materials that are always available, is just as attentive as everyone in the circle. The morning read-aloud time is always followed by a period in which children are allowed to select books and read them independently in groups or as individuals. It is not surprising that most of the books selected are those that have been previously read to the class as a whole. Children set out to find a book, a pillow, and perhaps one or two friends to share a story. It is a noisy time. Arguments can be heard over the identity of a particular letter in a favorite alphabet book. The children sometimes seek corroborating evidence in some other part of the room on a chart or in another book in order to make their case. A reader may be heard to ask, "And what do you think will happen next?" as he reenacts the teacher's reading aloud of a familiar story.

The reading and writing that these 4-year-olds engage in is, of course, simply their own approximations of the adult models they have seen in books, on charts, and on display in the massive amount of environmental print all around them. Nevertheless, they are genuinely engaged in the

Lee Galda

Four- and five-year-olds are able to recognize their names.

processes. The room is filled with print—name charts and reminder notices, notes posted on the refrigerator in the family living area, signs and symbols in the block area, posters and charts on the walls, and an abundance of books placed so that they are easy for 4-year-olds to reach and enjoy.

As Jenny walks among the children during independent reading, she surveys the classroom and observes how different it looks today from a year ago. It was nearly that long ago that she attended a workshop on "emergent literacy," a term she had never heard before. She remembers the notice that accompanied the workshop title: "The presenter will discuss ways to engage very young children in developmentally appropriate reading and writing activities." That workshop, with its accompanying handouts and bibliography, set Jenny on a path of exploration that ultimately involved the director of the Hillside Avenue Daycare Center and all the other teachers and caregivers with whom Jenny works.

For nearly 6 months now, the staff at the center has been participating in a series of informal staff development sessions inspired by Jenny. Every other week, they read and discuss articles on young children's language and literacy development and explore how they might use the information in their classrooms. Everyone has gradually made small but significant changes. Even the caregivers for infants have secured lists of cloth and board books to purchase, something they had not really given much attention to before. Now they are planning a campaign to get senior citizens into the center to expand their newly created lap-reading program. This program will offer babies and toddlers more opportunities for one-to-one interaction with adults during the day. It is all very exciting.

The ideas shared by Jenny Burke and her colleagues at Hillside are similar to those we discuss in this chapter: What does the current research suggest about young children's literacy development? What do young children need to learn about written language? How do they go about learning it? How can teachers and other caregivers support children's natural interest in reading and writing in ways that are developmentally appropriate? What are the implications for school policy?

Current Perspectives on Early Literacy

Early childhood educators have long operated on the premise that children's language and literacy development is interwoven and continuous from infancy. Children come to school with a remarkable knowledge of oral language, but they have acquired considerable awareness and knowledge about written language as well. The 3-year-old who gleefully recognizes the fast-food logo in a magazine or newspaper, even though she is far away from the restaurant itself, is letting us know she is paying attention to print and that it has already become important in her life. For the young child growing up in a print-filled culture, the need to communicate is not restricted to oral language. From a very early age, children are immersed in written language and its importance and function in our society. Thus, the emergence of literacy starts early and develops concurrently with oral language. The term **emergent literacy** refers to the reading and writing concepts and behaviors of young children that precede and develop into conventional literacy. Many engaging activities, such as the library recommended in the *Teaching Idea: Book and Toy Lending Library,* encourage young children's early literacy development.

AN EMERGENT LITERACY PERSPECTIVE

Current investigations into the way young children learn to read and write build on the thinking of educators such as Dewey and Dewey (1915/1962), who cautioned: "[To] find out how education takes place most successfully, let us go to the experiences of children where learning is a necessity" (p. 2). The Deweys contrasted the functional, meaning-driven learning that children engage in before they enter school with "the practices of the schools where it is largely an adornment, a superfluity and even an unwelcome imposition" (p. 2). The perspectives of the Deweys and more recent researchers, particularly Clay (collected in Clay, 1982), provide the foundation for new ways of studying and thinking about early literacy. Teale and Sulzby (1989) list the

TEACHING IDEA

Home/School Connection

BOOK AND TOY LENDING LIBRARY

Select twenty to thirty books and toys, such as puzzles and simple manipulatives, for parents to check out for one week at a time. Articles may be placed in plastic bags for protection. Parents can take turns monitoring a simple check-out system. Offering examples of the kinds of books and toys most appropriate for the age group helps parents make good gift-giving decisions. Most important, this availability of materials encourages them to read and play with their children.

unique dimensions of this research: (1) the age range studied has been extended to include children 14 months and younger; (2) literacy is no longer regarded as simply a cognitive skill but as a complex activity with social, linguistic, and psychological aspects; (3) because literacy learning is multidimensional and tied to the child's natural surroundings, it is studied in both home and school environments; and (4) literacy learning is studied from the child's point of view. Results of these studies provide important understandings about the nature of children's literacy learning and the kind of educational environment that best supports it. The following six points are important to consider:

1. *Literacy learning begins early in life and is ongoing.* It is evidenced when children begin to distinguish between their favorite books and records and demonstrate their recognition of environmental print. These demonstrations of print awareness go well beyond mere imitation, as children are involved in the construction of their own knowledge through experimentation and exploration. The print that surrounds children is meaningful to them, and they work hard to figure out how it works. As children search for patterns and make connections, they bring what they know to each new situation and apply their own childlike logic to make sense of it.
2. *Literacy develops concurrently with oral language.* Fluency in oral language is no longer seen as a precursor to literacy, but as a goal to be accomplished with and through literacy as each language process informs and supports all the others. Harste, Woodward, and Burke (1984) suggest that children operate from a "linguistic data pool" into which they feed what they learn from each language encounter and draw what they need in subsequent language encounters. Parents and teachers constantly hear children making connections between something they have heard or seen and something being

read: "It's like the 'M' in my name," or "It looks like the duck in the park. Where does it say 'duck'?" Thus, oral language encounters provide data for written language encounters, and vice versa.

3. *Learning to read and write are both social and cognitive endeavors.* Children are active participants in the process. Children are not interested merely in learning about literacy; they want to engage in it. A strong desire to communicate stimulates their experimentation with letters, words, signs, and symbols. As children experiment, they not only learn literacy, they learn through it and about it. No one is absolutely sure how Marina, a child in Eileen Bernstein's group of 3-year-olds, came to discover "t's" and "l's." Eileen reports that one morning, Marina marched into the room, took crayons and paper from the shelf, and proceeded to write with an intensity that she never had before. As she wrote, she softly sang "Happy Birthday" to herself. The result was page after page of "t's" and "l's," birthday cards, like the one in Figure 6.1, which she triumphantly distributed to the children.

4. *Learning to read and write is a developmental process.* Extensive observations of children reveal some general developmental patterns in the ways they

FIGURE 6.1

Marina's Birthday Card

acquire literacy. It is important to note, however, that these very general patterns reveal themselves in very different ways among individual children. Christina's mother contends that she cannot remember when her daughter was unable to talk. At age 2, she was already what some call a paper-and-pencil kid. Her younger brother Scott, on the other hand, took his time about talking and seldom seemed to notice the print around him. Although equally as interested in listening to stories as his sister, Scott preferred exploring, playing with trucks, and climbing things rather than drawing and writing. For Scott, the awareness of environmental print and the connections he apparently had been making all along seemed to burst forth daily shortly after he turned 5. It was then, his mother reports, that his daily questions and discoveries about print seemed to appear all at once.

5. *Storybook reading, particularly family storybook reading, has a special role in young children's literacy development.* In their accounts of parents sharing books with children, Taylor and Strickland (1986) observed that the talk surrounding the words and pictures in books inevitably turns to questions about print. Sometimes this happens when children are quite young. When Sarah was in kindergarten, she would often find a particular word or phrase enticing and would ask her mother, "Show where does it say that?" Matthew, who was then 3, would watch this process and also want to see the words that interested Sarah. Then, when telling himself a story, he would point to the print in the book he was "reading." In this way, many children begin to recognize that it is the squiggles on the page that tell the reader what to say. The concept that print carries meaning begins to emerge.
6. *Literacy learning is deeply rooted in the cultural milieu and in the family communication patterns.* Although it is safe to say that children growing up in our print-rich society are exposed to an abundance of print, the nature, quality, and amount of those experiences will differ from one family to another and from one community to another. Whether the print be books of worship, how-to manuals, television guides, the classics, or grocery lists, you can be certain that numerous uses of print are demonstrated daily for young children. Long before formal instruction begins, young children are trying to make sense of their experiences with print. The awareness and understanding they gain, largely through their everyday experiences, are significant and valuable.

CONTRASTING PERSPECTIVES ON EARLY LITERACY

Researchers refer to the foregoing ideas as an **emergent-literacy perspective** and make a point of distinguishing it from a **readiness** point of view. It is an important distinction to make. Whereas emergent literacy emphasizes children's ongoing development of skill in reading and writing, a readiness approach suggests that children are not "ready" to read and write until they are approximately 6 years old. The period before formal instruction in reading and writing is viewed as a time for getting children ready for "real" literacy experiences through systematic instruction in a variety of discrete prereading and prewriting skills. Direct instruction on letter identification, letter-sound relationships, and a variety of visual-perceptual tasks frequently dominate the readiness curriculum (Strickland & Morrow, 1989). An emergent-literacy curriculum, on the other hand, focuses on meaningful encounters with print and talking about print, encounters such as those which children have been having all their lives. Adults play major but differing roles in both approaches. Adults who work from an emergent-literacy perspective focus on providing an environment that ensures that certain literacy experiences will occur. They encourage children's exploration and experimentation with print, intervening only to help them confirm their understandings and move from one level of understanding to another. Adults in a readiness program are more likely to act as transmitters of information about reading and writing, such as letter names and letter-sound relationships. Classrooms operating from an emergent-literacy base provide children with easy access to reading and writing materials, incentives to draw/write stories and messages, time to read and reread favorite books, and time to share their literacy experiences with others.

In today's classrooms, clear distinctions between the two perspectives are less obvious. Effective teachers lean toward a **balanced approach,** steeped in the philosophy of emergent literacy with specifically focused, guided instruction in areas thought to be critical to success in beginning reading. Within a rich language and literacy environment, such teachers plan both focused lessons and informal experiences to develop children's concepts about print, letter recognition, listening comprehension, phonemic awareness, and other types of phonological awareness.

What Young Children Need to Learn about Written Language

To become skilled readers and writers, children need to be knowledgeable in at least four general areas of written language: its functions, its conventions and units, its alphabetic/symbolic principles, and its structural principles. These understandings about language are generally called **metalinguistic**

awareness. Even very young children develop notions of the purposes and processes of literacy acts and structural properties of either their own speech or the written language system (Johns, 1986, p. 42).

FUNCTIONS OF WRITTEN LANGUAGE

Children who see the functional relevance of print are more likely to be motivated to explore its use for their own purposes. Studies of first-graders' perceptions of reading (Johns & Johns, 1971) revealed that most children were not able to verbalize an intelligent perception of the reading process nor any logical, meaningful purpose for learning to read. Most reported, "I think it's a good thing to do," or "It's words and you sound them out if you don't know them" (Denny & Weintraub, 1966).

In a more recent study, Weiss and Hagen (1988) examined kindergartners' awareness of the functions of print. Interviewed individually, each child was shown actual reading materials in groups of three and asked to identify one. If the item was correctly identified, the child was then asked to tell why people read that particular material. Children in this study showed a high awareness of the functions of print and had a good sense of why people read. Of the 110 children interviewed, all but one recognized and knew the purpose for reading storybooks. Other items of high recognition were the newspaper (96 percent) and the telephone book (96 percent). The calendar, magazine, directions, TV schedule, and shopping list all ranked about 80 percent.

Joseph Kassick

Children take great pleasure in writing and drawing. They like to read what they have written to any willing listener.

When asked why people read, children's responses included: "So people can learn how to read," "Because they are fun," and "To get smart."

The two reading materials least recognized by the children were a letter and a menu. Still, the letter was identified by 73 percent of the children. Explanations for why letters are read included, "To see what another person is doing," "Because they want to know what was in the mail," and "Because they got it from someone special." The researchers speculated that the lack of recognition of the menu was due to young children's more likely acquaintance with fast-food restaurants where menus are displayed on the wall.

The difference between the results of the Weiss and Hagen study and those of earlier related studies may be due to the emergent-literacy perspective of these researchers. Perhaps, by framing the study in a manner that revealed what children had learned through their personal and everyday experiences with print, these researchers facilitated children's ability to demonstrate what they knew. The need to account for children's own intentions and their natural search for meaning may be aptly applied to all investigations of their learning. Meaning is central to instruction as well. Johns (1986) advised teachers to make an effort to help students understand the role that meaning plays in reading. Teachers should not assume that the usual methods and strategies used in teaching reading provide a basis for understanding the reading process. According to Johns, most research on learning supports the proposition that it helps the child to learn if he knows the reason for a learning situation and sees a purpose in a task. Inasmuch as reading is not nonsense learning, but a complex learning and mental process, it may be important to identify it as such and to help beginners establish purposes for wanting to learn to read (p. 447).

Whether or not children become lifelong readers is often determined when they are very young. In their research with first grade children, Cunningham and Stanovich (1998) report that "students who get off to a fast start in reading are more likely to read more over the years, and furthermore, this very act of reading can help children compensate for modest levels of cognitive ability by building their vocabulary and general knowledge" (p. 14).

Likewise, a pattern of school failure can begin very early and persist throughout a child's school career. Children's lack of success diminishes their motivation to read, and they read much less than their peers. Anderson, Wilson, and Fielding (1988) found that the independent reading done outside of the classroom reported by fifth-graders varied dramatically, from students reading up to an hour or more a day on average (or 4,000,000 words or more a year!) to students reading less than a minute a day on average or not at all (or reading no words outside of the classroom during the entire year!). The amount of time spent reading is highly correlated with achievement in learning to read (Cunningham & Stanovich, 1998). The upward or downward spiral that begins as children do or don't learn to read (and do or don't learn to enjoy reading) in the primary grades is quite evident by the amount of time they spend reading on their own in later grades and subsequently, how well they do in school.

Children's development of phonemic awareness (individual word sounds) and decoding skills varies widely in the early primary grades. Their instructional experiences also vary. All children learning to read benefit from the kinds of word activities featured in Chapter Ten. All children learning to read also need a wide variety of authentic literacy experiences with real books. Although repetitive drilling of low-level skills disassociated with real reading is often a common teaching practice with those children who learn to decode more slowly than their peers and who struggle with word recognition for a variety of reasons, children do not benefit greatly from such activities. They receive far greater benefit from spending more instructional time participating in higher-level activities that require them to think about real texts. Strickland (2002) cautions, "Skills should not be taught to them in a manner suggesting they can only learn by accumulating disparate pieces of information" (p. 79). Learning to use a combination of tools and strategies such as phonics, word meanings and context, and pictorial clues is most helpful for deciphering unknown words during real reading experiences.

All children need to feel successful as readers and have positive reading experiences, no matter what their achievement levels. All children can become avid readers. Children at the lowest reading levels need many interesting books at their instructional level to give them realistic challenges, authentic reading experiences, and the same sense of accomplishment as their peers who are reading at higher levels. All children's reading improves with consistent practice. And extensive reading makes everyone smarter (Cunningham & Stanovich, 1998)!

Like reading, writing development can begin long before school, and experience experimenting with writing in or out of school benefits children's literacy development. Children demonstrate an awareness of the functions of print in their early writing. From an early age, children who are allowed to experiment with paper and pen write for a variety of reasons. They write their name for the joy of writing it, make signs for their doors, lists for Christmas, write letters to relatives, label pictures, and write stories, poems, and informative pieces. Their writing may not always look like what they mean it to be, but they definitely mean it to be something. Further, they may use one form, like letters, for varied purposes. Figures 6.2, 6.3, and 6.4 show three examples of a preschool child's writing. The first is a letter to an absent Granny, and the intention was to say hello through print, something that Anna had seen her mother and father do quite often. The second, a letter to Mom, was drawn and dictated by the same child. The intention here was quite different; it was to apologize for being uncooperative that morning. Anna had not seen her parents writing to apologize, but she used her own

FIGURE 6.2

Anna's Letter to Granny

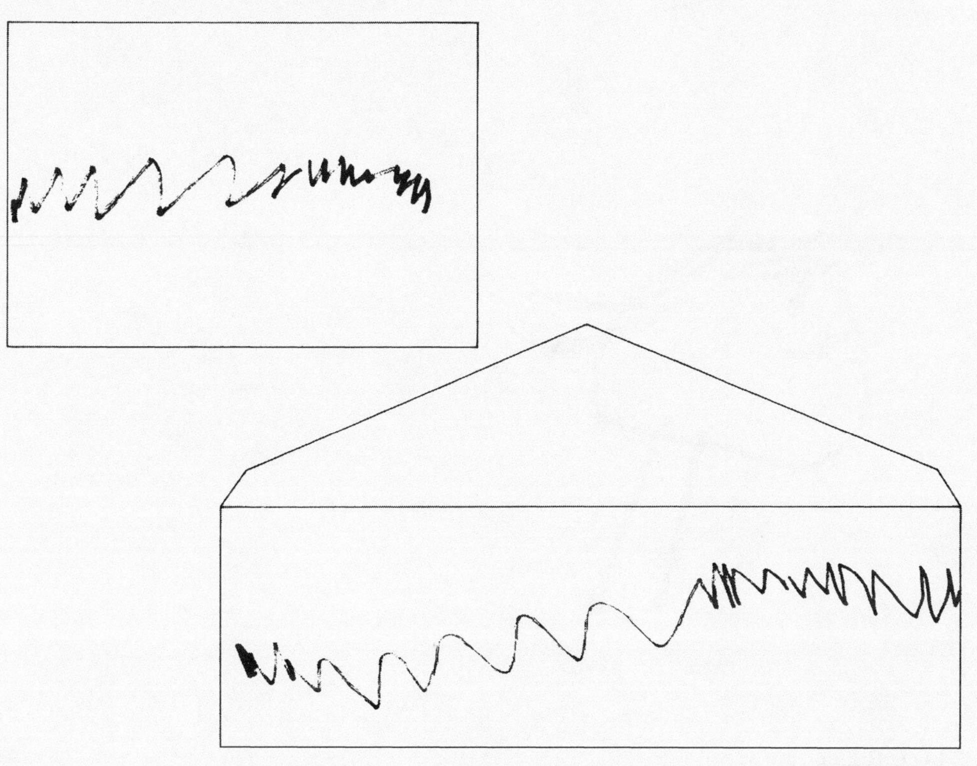

writing to do so. The third example, a list, was not surprising, because she had watched her mother make lists many times, although August was a bit early for writing to Santa! As children develop and encounter more examples of writing being used for a variety of purposes, their own writing repertoire expands. By the time they reach kindergarten, they are writing for a wide variety of reasons, in a wide variety of forms (Newkirk, 1985). Some possibilities for exploring literacy during everyday activities with young children are highlighted in the *Teaching Idea: Demonstrations of Literacy*.

CONVENTIONS AND UNITS OF WRITTEN LANGUAGE

As children become literate, they must acquire knowledge about numerous technical aspects of print. These are the arbitrary conventions that govern

FIGURE 6.3

Anna's Letter to Mom

Mommy,

Sorry we had a hard time this morning!

FIGURE 6.4

Anna's Christmas List

TEACHING IDEA

Addressing Individual Needs

DEMONSTRATIONS OF LITERACY

Make use of ordinary, everyday activities in the classroom to demonstrate the uses of literacy. Preparing a list of items to purchase for a recipe, so that children can watch as the list is generated, helps them feel a part of the process. Later, after the purchases are made, children can help check off each item on the list.

When appropriate, take the opportunity to write a brief note to a parent in front of the child as you read it aloud. Not only is the child "in" on the content of the message, but he or she is made to feel a part of the process.

written language. For example, in English people read and write from left to right and top to bottom. Words in print are separated by blank spaces, something of no consequence in learning to speak. Punctuation functions to mark units of language and to guide the processing of information. The meanings and use of metalinguistic terms such as *word, letter,* and *sound* must be learned as well. As literate adults, these technical aspects of reading and writing have become such an intuitive part of the way we interact with print that we do not think of them as being learned. For children, however, these understandings develop gradually as part of numerous encounters with print. When 5-year-old Tommy dictated, "I like to go swimming," to go with the picture he drew, he was pleased to see the words as his teacher wrote them down and read them aloud. Later, when trying to read them himself, he became confused when he tried to match the writing with the words he had said. Somehow, the sound of "ing" at the end of swimming was always left over. He could hear six syllables, and expected to see six words.

Several researchers have investigated children's understanding of a "word" as a unit of language. In one of the best known of these studies, Papandropoulou and Sinclair (1974), using a list of commonly known words, identified four levels in the development of word consciousness. They asked children of ages $4\frac{1}{2}$ to approximately 11 the question, "Is that a word?" and "What is a word, really?" Most children under 5 years of age were classified as level I, which was characterized by the inability to differentiate between a word and its referent. A typical response was, "Children are words," or "It can be a cupboard or a chair or a book" (p. 244). As children moved through levels II, III, and IV, their concept of a word matured. At level II (5–7 years), children often expressed their understanding of words in terms of how they functioned as labels for things. At level III (6–8 years) words took on the features of elements that made up wholes but did not yet have individual meanings, "A word is a bit of a story."

Children at level IV were able to perceive words as autonomous elements having meanings of their own with definite semantic and grammatical relationships. These children might respond, "Letters form words," or "A word is something that means something." Not surprisingly, researchers studying children's understanding of units of language stress the importance of exposure to print. According to Templeton and Spivey (1980), although children who are more aware of the internal structure of words are generally those with higher levels of cognitive functioning, the ability to think metalinguistically seems to be enhanced by mere exposure to the written language itself.

Reading with big books, in which children can see the print as the teacher reads aloud while tracking the words, is one effective way to help children understand what a word is. As one first grade teacher put it, "I've never found a better way to help kids understand words and spaces and sentences. When they see the print as you read out loud it's like magic. All of a sudden they begin to get it."

Of course, working with children's names is an excellent way to develop the concept of a word. Figures 6.5 and 6.6 give some ideas on how to teach a variety of concepts about print through the use of children's names.

FIGURE 6.5

Developmentally Appropriate Literacy Instruction in Pre-kindergarten and Kindergarten: Concepts about Print

Word Recognition: Name Games

1. Prepare a set of duplicate name cards with identical stickies or simple drawings for each child. During circle time, distribute one set of cards so that each child has his or her name card. Hold up one card at a time from your set and ask, "Whose name is this?" Children match their card with the card you are holding.
2. After children get the idea of how the game is played, remove or fold back the part of the name card with the sticky or identifying picture. Then have them match using the print only.
3. Hang a strip of Velcro at children's eye level in a prominent place. Prepare name cards with Velcro on the back. Place name cards in a large shallow box top or on a shelf near the Velcro strip. When children come in each morning, they are asked to find their name and stick it to the Velcro strip. During circle time, read the names together to see who is in and who is out. This can also be adapted for use with a Helper's Chart.

FIGURE 6.6

Developmentally Appropriate Literacy Instruction in Pre-kindergarten and Kindergarten: Letter Recognition

1. *Guess the Name.* Once children are somewhat familiar with their names, hold up a name card showing only the first letter. Ask questions such as, "I wonder whose name this could be? It starts with the letter 'C.' Jason, could this be your name? Charles, could this be your name? Who else's name could this be? Pat? Carla?" Reveal more letters and continue in the same way.
2. *Name Puzzle.* Write each child's name in manuscript print on a business-size envelope. Make a duplicate on a piece of oaktag or stiff paper. Cut the duplicate into individual letters and place inside the envelope. Have children match the letters to their name on the outside of the envelope. Be sure to model this for the group during circle time before children are asked to do this on their own.
3. *Letter Detectives.* Display one, two, or three names or name cards at a time. Show a letter card. Ask, "Can you find this letter in any of these names?" It is best to start with one name card and work up to three cards once children have the idea. Many children will be able to visually match the letters, whether or not they can identify them in isolation. This is a good beginning.

   Some advanced variations of Letter Detectives involve asking such questions as, "Find the two names that have the same first letter or the same last letter." (Children will need to know positional words.) Or, "Find the name that has the letter 'S' in it." (This would be done without showing the letter.)

ALPHABETIC/SYMBOLIC PRINCIPLES

Drawing is the use of a graphic symbol to represent something in the world, and children do this quite regularly and with very little encouragement needed. Writing is another sort of graphic symbol system, and for many young children writing and drawing are intertwined at an early age. A young child might produce a picture of a cat decorated with large C's, intending the letters to be representations of cats, just as the picture is. Gradually, children distinguish between drawing and writing, coming to understand that when one writes one is encoding not the object itself but the linguistic symbol used to refer to the object. Thus, *cat* comes to be seen as the word *cat* and not the thing itself, although drawing may continue to support writing for quite some time (Dyson, 1982).

Reading and writing require an understanding of how language functions as a symbol system and of the mapping principles between speech and print. This understanding involves learning to recognize letters and words and to match letters and sounds. Because of the lack of one-to-one correspondence between sound and spelling in English, these rules must seem somewhat arbitrary to the young learner. Nevertheless, considerable research evidence supports the notion that once children understand that words contain distinguishable phonemes and that letters symbolize these phonemes in words, they are capable of more effective word-recognition strategies (National Reading Panel Report, 2000; Juell, Griffith, & Gough, 1986; Ehri & Wilce, 1985).

Awareness of words, whether written or oral, seems to come relatively easily to most children. Extensive exposure to print that is meaningful and functional appears to be the key to the development of a sense of the match between the spoken and written correspondences of a word. By contrast, phonemic awareness appears to be less easy to acquire for some children. **Phonemic awareness,** the ability to notice, think about, and work with the individual sounds in spoken words, involves the child's growing sensitivity to phonemes (smaller than syllable speech sounds) that letters represent. Phonemic awareness is only one type of **phonological awareness,** which includes identifying and making oral rhymes and identifying and working with syllables in spoken words (Partnership for Reading, 2001). For example, "cat" has one syllable, but three phonemes. Research indicates that a child's ability to discriminate between phonemes is one of the best predictors of reading success. The major difference between prereaders who do well and those who do poorly on tests of phoneme discrimination lies in their ability to think consciously about the sound structure of words rather than on their ability to hear differences between phonemes (Adams, 1990).

In a review of studies of phonemic awareness, the National Reading Panel (2000) concluded that phonemic awareness does help children learn to read and spell, that it can be taught, and that it is effective under a variety of teaching conditions with a variety of learning (pp. 2–5, 6). The report cautions, however, that teachers need to recognize that acquiring phonemic awareness is a means rather than an end. Teaching children to apply what they know in order to understand and use the alphabetic system is the goal. The report cautioned against undue stress or time spent on phonemic awareness. More is not necessarily better. Children vary in their phonemic awareness. Some children need more instruction than others. Effective teachers vary the amount and intensity of instruction according to need, often working with children in small-group situations.

The National Reading Panel report also suggests that teachers of young children need to realize that like phonics (letter-sound correspondence), phonemic awareness training does not constitute a complete reading program. Many competencies need to be taught in order for children to become successful readers. The report also states that although many phonemic awareness instructional programs were found to be effective, no single program was necessarily effective with all children under all circumstances. A teacher's enthusiasm and feelings of efficacy with a particular program seemed to be a key factor in its success.

TEACHING IDEA

Addressing Individual Needs

STRATEGIES THAT SUPPORT PHONOLOGICAL AWARENESS

Rhyming Activities

- Include nursery rhymes, poems, and storybooks with patterned rhymes in your daily read-aloud selections.
- Read poetry and stories that contain alliteration and word play.
- When reading or chanting a familiar poem or rhyme, pause before a rhyming word and let children fill in the rhyme.
- Encourage and praise children's self-initiated attempts to memorize simple rhymes and songs.
- Provide opportunities for children to match pictures that rhyme. This may be done with the whole class during circle time and independently at centers.

Working with Syllables

Invite children to clap the number of sounds they hear in someone's name: First say the name; then repeat it with the children as they clap with you. Sam gets one clap. Malik gets two. Jennifer gets three, and so on.

Identifying Similarities in Spoken Sounds

Using one-syllable words, model the following in a sing-song manner, stressing the initial sound:
Mom is a word that starts like milk. Can you think of a word that starts like *Mom*?
Continue with other sounds.
Bat is a word that starts like bike. Can you think of a word that starts like *bat*?
In time, some children will be able to distinguish the beginning sound (onset) of the word from the remaining sounds.

Investigations of how children develop their phonemic awareness other than through explicit instruction indicate that nursery rhymes play a large role in this process. That is, 3- and 4-year-old children's early knowledge of nursery rhymes is specifically related to their later development of more abstract phonological knowledge and of emergent reading ability (Maclean, Bryant, & Bradley, 1987). Other strategies that aid in children's phonemic awareness development are presented in the *Teaching Idea: Strategies that Support Phonological Awareness.*

Perhaps the conclusion reached by Perfetti, Beck, and Hughes (1985) best describes the prevailing view. They found that phonemic knowledge and learning to read are mutually supportive. The development of phonemic awareness leads to more successful reading, and engaging in reading activities leads to greater phonemic awareness. They caution against describing the relationship in simple prerequisite terms that suggest that one must necessarily precede the other. Of course, children who write, once they begin to understand the rudiments of the sound-symbol relations in English, are practicing phonics as they struggle to put on paper that which they can say. This step is discussed further in the section on invented spelling later in this chapter.

Teachers of young children should know that phonics instruction builds on children's phonemic awareness. Phonics involves the understanding that in the English language a relatively predictable relationship exists between **phonemes** (the sounds of spoken language) and **graphemes** (the letters and spellings that represent those sounds in written language). Other terms used in the literature referring to phonics include *graphophonemic relationships, letter-sound associations, letter-sound correspondences, sound-symbol correspondences,* and *sound-spellings.* Each of these terms refers to the **alphabetic principle,** which is critical to figuring out the system used by English speakers to read and write words. A review of selected studies of phonics instruction (National Panel Report, 2000) found that phonics instruction taught early (kindergarten and first grade) is highly beneficial. We agree, but hasten to place this instruction in a broader framework of literacy learning and teaching.

First, literacy learning involves the ability to solve problems, think critically and creatively, and communicate effectively. Literacy instruction includes a planned program for the deliberate teaching of word-identification skills and strategies that enable students to write effectively and to read with understanding. Instruction for word identification offers learners a range of organized and relatively systematic strategies to deal with unfamiliar words. Phonics is among the word-identification strategies taught and learned in a comprehensive literacy program. Finally, in every subject area, students apply word-identification strategies, including phonics, in varied situations with increasingly difficult materials (Strickland, 1998, p. 6).

STRUCTURAL PRINCIPLES

Another feature of written language that young children need to learn about is its structure or form. English is written in serial order from left to right and top to bottom. Children need to understand that directionality. They also need to understand the hierarchical order that operates in written language, from how letters form words to how different kinds of texts are structured.

> Information in print is organized in a hierarchy of levels—discourse or text, sentence, phrase, word, letter cluster, letter and sub-letter levels—and the reader has to know which level to attend to at any one moment to be effective. . . . [C]hildren have to learn how to attend to print in serial order

Bernice Cullinan

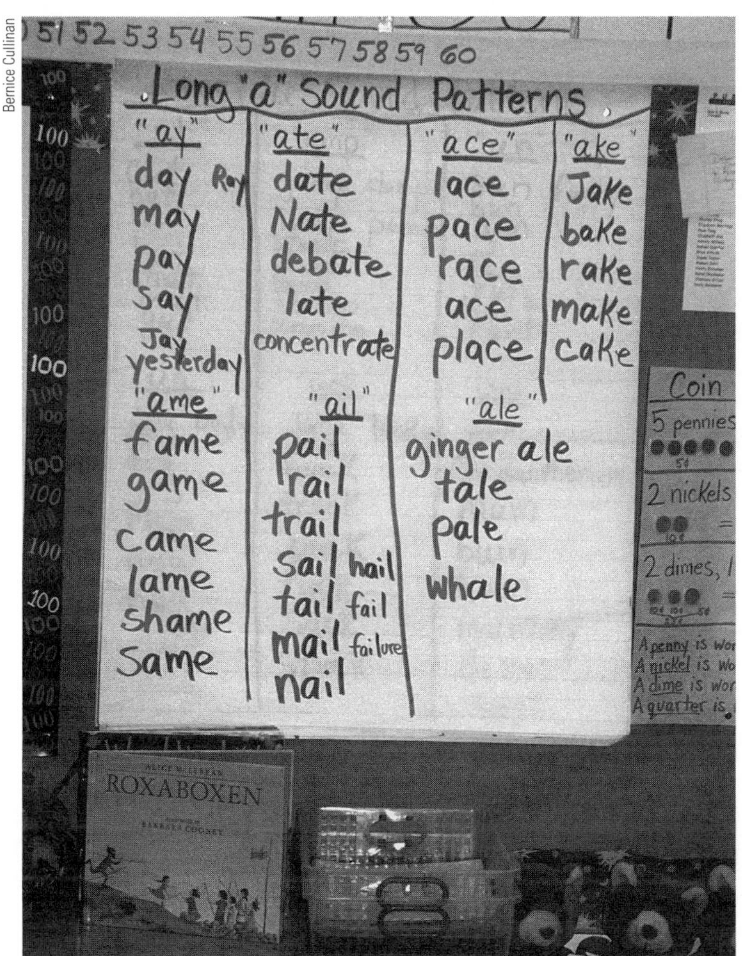

A group of early readers discovered similar sound patterns in words.

> while at the same time deciding which level of the language hierarchy to attend to . . . [even as they] are still constructing their knowledge of the hierarchy and what information can be gained from attending to any or each level (Clay, 1991, p. 113).

The emerging reader/writer is gradually figuring out how spelling, syntactic, and discourse patterns operate in written language. These patterns are learned through contact with various forms of discourse. Applebee (1978) studied the oral narratives of young children and concluded that children even as young as 2 have some sense of story markers such as a formulaic beginning and ending, and the use of the past tense. Three-year-old Adam, requesting a story from his mother, demonstrated his knowledge of story conventions when he demanded, "Tell me a usually story, Mom." "What is a usually story?" queried Mom. "You know," replied Adam, "one that starts 'once upon a time.'"

TEACHING IDEA

Literature Link

BUILDING AWARENESS OF THE STRUCTURE AND FUNCTIONS OF PRINT

Make it a point to share and use a variety of types of texts in classrooms for young children. Storybooks, informational books, concept books such as ABC and number books, simple picture dictionaries, lists, directions, menus, and so on. Model the use of reminders of things to do and notes to others. Help children understand that print is purposeful and functional as well as pleasurable in their lives.

As children become increasingly sensitive to the schematic structure of stories, they use this knowledge to facilitate comprehension and recall. Perhaps one baby sitter's amusing account of a 5-year-old's request (all in one breath) to hear "The Three Pigs—No—The Three Bears—No—The Three Kittens" was evidence of his sudden awareness of an important universal in traditional tales. Of course, story structure is not all that children are learning, because they are also incorporating features of lists, letters, and directions, to name but a few of the other text forms suggested in the *Teaching Idea: Building Awareness of the Structure and Functions of Print* with which they come into contact and experiment.

DIFFERENCES BETWEEN ORAL AND WRITTEN LANGUAGE

Attending to print brings an increased consciousness of how language works. This increased consciousness is one big difference between speaking and reading/writing. Directionality, spacing, and spelling, all important to written language, have no counterparts in oral language. Written and oral language differ in how people say things. For example, when they talk, they can shout, whisper, or smile, but when writing, they must encode that kind of information in language. The writer needs to say, for example, "he said loudly," or "she whispered," because of the decontextualized nature of written language. Gestures and intonation, present in speech, are absent from writing. Instead, punctuation and syntax signal readers what kinds of intonation to infer.

Written language also differs from speech in the type of language or expressions that are likely to be included and in its organization. Speech is much more informal than writing, and even the most articulate speakers are likely to include incomplete sentences, slang, and meaningless vocalizations in their talk. Speakers tend to be highly redundant. Written language is much more concise. Rubin (1980) suggests that these characteristics may be a source of difficulty in learning to read until the child has enough experiences with written language forms to learn the text features that facilitate comprehension. As children come into contact with an increasing number of books, they begin to recognize and understand the specialized language forms that are found in books that are not present in their oral language.

In summary, young children's emerging awareness and understanding of the processes and conventions of written language may be termed **metalinguistic awareness, linguistic awareness, language awareness,** or **print awareness.** All of these terms represent what children need to know in order to read and write. They are in evidence when children demonstrate insights about language as an object and as a process. For example, the youngster in the opening vignette of this chapter demonstrated understandings about print language when she "read" the words *trash can* on the garbage receptacle for the actual words *thank you.* How metalinguistic awareness is demonstrated in children depends upon their interests, experiences, and purpose for using language.

How Young Children Learn about Written Language

Children go about learning written language in much the same way they learn everything else about their world, including oral language. Chapter Two stressed that children play a key role in their own oral language development. They focus on meaning, as they explore and experiment with oral language in an attempt to comprehend the world around them. This is accomplished in a social context in which adults play a significant role, responding to and interacting with children. Although adults seldom attempt to instruct children deliberately in oral language, they help provide conditions that nurture its growth.

Learning literacy and learning oral language share many common elements. Children explore both in order to create meanings and to communicate. As with oral language, literacy learning frequently involves social interaction with others and is largely a by-product of the child's interest in pursuing some nonlinguistic purpose. Three-year-old William pores over the cereal boxes in the supermarket until he finds his favorite. He uses the graphics on the box to "read" what is inside and confidently asks his mom to buy it for him.

Children who live in the print-rich societies of the Western world are surrounded by print, and they are extremely curious about the signs and symbols around them. "That's got my name!" shouts 4-year-old Anna as she and her father approach the A & P Supermarket. At home, Anna wants to know for whom each piece of mail is intended and constantly questions, "Where does it say that?" Anna observes as her parents write notes and letters, create lists of things to buy and things to do, fill out forms, read books, newspapers, magazines, and circulars as well as the labels on jars, boxes, and cans. She frequently asks questions and recreates acts involving literacy as a part of her play. As in most families, reading and writing are such a natural part of the everyday activities of Anna's household that they go unnoticed as distinct events. Indeed, like most children, Anna learns about the functions and conventions of literacy in connection with various aspects of her family life.

Literacy is so embedded in the day-by-day events of families that Leichter (1984) commented, "Locating literacy events in the stream of everyday family activities is a substantial task, especially if one wishes to avoid defining literacy in terms of previously held conceptions" (p. 42). Young children learn about written language in the context of their daily environments. They learn largely through play and a compelling need to know.

CHILD STRATEGIES FOR LITERACY LEARNING

A child's literacy learning is consistently characterized by the qualities of construction and invention. Children seem to be in the process of constantly inventing and reinventing ways to participate with others in the social process of making and sharing meanings (Parker, 1983). Soon to be 4, Nell delighted in the plans for her birthday party. She watched as her grandmother addressed the invitations. She was enormously proud to sign her name (NLL) to each, although she had great difficulty fitting that many letters into such a small space. Her grandmother, well seasoned in such things, stood by with pleasure as she observed once again the sheer joy a child experiences in "discovering" the power and use of literacy. Each year, Nell has been encouraged to sign her birthday invitations. At age 1, she was so impressed with her power to make marks that she made markings on both the invitations and any other paper that happened to be nearby. At age 2 and 3 her writing, although still very much in the form of scribbles, increasingly targeted the space provided, and she had some sense of what her signature implied. Now, almost 4, Nell knows a great deal about written names. She knows that her written name represents her, and she has a very good idea of what it looks like. Moreover, she likes to experiment with writing it. She enjoys drawing pictures and making lines and various letterlike shapes to represent words. Often, her drawing and writing is accompanied by a running monologue. Her speech and writing seem to go together, each acting to support the other. Through active involvement in activities geared to her own level of development, Nell is gradually learning important information about what it is that readers and writers do.

Emerging readers

Teale and Sulzby (1989) offer an account of Jennifer, an emerging reader who, like Nell, enjoys the fruits of a print-rich home. From the time Jennifer was 1 year old, her mother read to her to regularly. At 3 years, 3 months of age, Jennifer was visited by a researcher who asked her to read *Are You My Mother?* (Eastman), a book that had been read to her many times. In an enthusiastic manner, and with a reading intonation, she "read" the entire book, a portion of which follows:

Jennifer	*Text*
Out pop the baby birdie.	Out came the baby bird.
He says, "Where is my mother?"	"Where is my mother?" he said.
[aside to researcher] He's looking for it.	He looked for her.
Looked up; did not see her.	He looked up. He did not see her.
And he looked down; he didn't see it.	He looked down. He did not see her.
So he said he's gonna go look for her.	"I will go and look for her," he said.
Came to a kitten and he said, "Are you my mother?"	He came to a kitten. "Are you my mother?" he said to the kitten.
'N. . . and he didn't say anything.	The kitten just looked and looked.
He just looked and looked.	It did not say a thing.
Then he came to a hen and he said, "Are you my mother?"	The kitten was not his mother, so he went on. Then he came to a hen. "Are you my mother?" he said to the hen.
"No."	"No," said the hen.

It is obvious that Jennifer is well on her way to understanding what readers do, something that is not always obvious to the young child. More often, to the young child, readers appear simply to stare at pages. Occasionally they may say out loud what it is they are reading. The complex cognitive processes that go on in readers' minds are unseen and at best can only be inferred. Newspapers may be used to wrap things in and books may be used to prop things up or press them out. The evidence available to young children is both visible and invisible and sometimes rather variable (Hall, 1987). It is no wonder that 3-year-old Scott challenged his mother when she said she was reading a magazine though her lips were perfectly still, "You're not reading, you're looking."

Scollon and Scollon (1981) report:

> Rachel was trying to get her mother to read to her. Her mother told her to read it herself. Rachel asked, "How can I read?" Her mother said, "With your eyes." She answered, "I can't hold books with my eyes." At another time, Rachel claimed that her baby brother could not read: "Because his hands were too small, but he would be able to when his hands grew. The dog, though, would never be able to read because he had no hands" (p. 62).

All of the children described—Nell, Jennifer, Scott, and Rachel—are in their own way trying to make sense of what print is about. Their notions of reading are varied and developing. As they mature and have more experiences with print, they begin to develop the idea that reading is a distinctly human activity. They become increasingly aware of how print functions and what it is that readers do. They learn this through the evidence provided by the adults around them, particularly through shared storybook reading. They acquire the concepts about reading outlined earlier in this chapter, primarily through adult-child interactions with print. The following are key ideas they learn about reading:

1. In reading, print carries the message. A relationship exists between the words spoken by the reader and the print on the page.
2. Books and print have a certain orientation. Reading is done in a particular order—from front to back; line by line; word by word; top to bottom.
3. Readers make use of letters, words, punctuation, and spaces to determine what is meant and how to say it.
4. The language of books (syntax and vocabulary) sometimes differs from oral language.
5. Readers use print and pictures differently.
6. Readers use particular language to talk about reading and print—page, word, letter, front, back, title, and so on.

What about the child who is not read to from infancy and whose parents are not avid readers themselves? How do these children acquire basic concepts about print? How can schools be expected to cope with young children who are "at risk" by virtue of not having print-rich homes? First, it is safe to assume that all children living in Western societies are routinely exposed to the printed word through billboards, television, and printed materials in the home. Second, we must not prejudge what knowledge children have about print on the basis of their socioeconomic level, or their linguistic or cultural backgrounds. The children described above are all products of "mainstream" families. They are able to demonstrate what they know about print in relatively conventional ways. Just as homes vary in the use they make of print, children will vary in the ways they demonstrate what they know.

Children whose first language is other than that of the school may be more comfortable talking about books and print in their native language. Children who have never been read to may not know many stories but may recognize graphic symbols associated with popular products. By age 4, most children recognize their names and many are able to identify some of the letters in their names. The important point here is that just as children's emerging literacy varies, the ways in which they demonstrate what they know vary. As with oral language, all children learn literacy in basically the same ways, but they can learn only that to which they are exposed.

Schools should avoid making judgments about children's readiness for school entry on the basis of a single measure or limited experience with a child. Young children need plenty of time to demonstrate what they know, and plenty of opportunities to enjoy and make use of print in the classroom. Rather than lament the fact that children have not had the advantages of storybook reading, such experiences should be offered in abundance. All children can benefit from these, regardless of their home orientation. Teachers can use the classroom to broaden children's understanding about reading. At the same time, they can observe children's performances in order to uncover some understanding that might not be revealed through typical assessment procedures.

Emerging writers and spellers

Various researchers have described the evolution of children's writing. Dyson (1982, 1982b) demonstrates how at first children often do not distinguish between drawing and writing, then weave drawing and writing together, and finally use drawing to accompany their writing. Parker (1983) points out the similarities between the development of writing in children and their development of drawing and symbolic play:

> At first, children are unaware of the symbolic meanings of their drawings, and at first their drawing may be invented versions of things which are not generally recognizable and, therefore, not meaningful to others. Gradually, however, as with symbolic play, children construct graphic depictions which become more like real objects. Simultaneously, they discover that their graphic representation is not another actual object, but a symbol of that

> object. Moreover, the ability to engage in this process—this series of successive transformations of reality in drawing—is made possible by speech (p. 45).

Through observation and exploration children acquire important understanding about written language. Through her extensive observations of children, Clay (1975) described several concepts and principles that children discover through experimentation with writing. Evidence of these principles begins to appear in the scribbles that children make long before they are writing conventionally. These principles are as follows:

The recurring principle Children discover that writing consists of the same repeated elements. They feel a sense of accomplishment as they gain control over certain strokes, letters, words, or designs, and they fill an entire page with the same basic mark, as Marina did in Figure 6.1.

The generative principle Children learn that there are rules for arranging and combining the elements used in written language. They use what they know to combine and string letters together in new and inventive ways.

The sign and message concept Children come to understand that writing consists of graphic symbols that carry a message. They learn that spoken messages can be written, but they may not know whether or not what they have written represents what they have said. It is not uncommon for a young child to write letters and letterlike marks on a page only to ask, "What does this say?" Recognizing the potential for print to offer a message is an important step toward literacy.

The flexibility principle As children experiment with language, they discover that letters they know can be varied to produce new letters. An added curve transforms *P* into *B*. They also learn, however, that they must be careful not to produce variations that are unacceptable. They begin to learn something about the boundaries of print conventions. Only certain variations are identifiable as language signs.

The contrastive principle Likenesses and differences between letters, letterlike forms, and words are perceived by children as they explore writing. They comment on the differences in letters such as *B* and *D* and in words spelled with upper- and lowercase letters. Comparing and contrasting written forms comes spontaneously as children act on what they know about written language.

Several researchers have explored children's emerging concepts about the links between meaning and print (Dyson, 1982b, 1984; Ferreiro &

Teberosky, 1982; Sulzby, 1985). What they discovered is that children differ widely in their understanding of the relationships between meaning and graphic forms or symbols. Ferreiro (1986) studied 4- and 5-year-old Argentinian children who demonstrated unique perspectives about how writing represents oral language. Santiago, one of the children Ferreiro studied, had seen his parents write and read his name many times. When asked about his name, "What does it say here?" he pointed to the letter *S* and replied, "This is Santiago's." When asked, "What does it say here?" about the remaining letters, he ran his fingers under them and replied, "Santiago and Daddy has gone to work. Mommy and Daddy." Ferreiro concluded that Santiago considered only the letter *S* as his signature and that the other letters must be about other people. Another child, Javier, said *cat* (*gato*) could be written *AOi,* while *kitten* (*gatito*) could be written *OiA,* and *cats* (*gatos*) could be written *OAiOAiOAi*. Ferreiro suggests that Javier had come to certain conclusions about the relation between writing and what it represents: (1) Written words for similar things should look similar, even though the spoken words for those objects may not sound the same; and (2) when characters refer to more than one object, more characters are needed to represent them (1986, p. 19).

Dyson (1982b) paints the same kind of picture, suggesting that young children operate with undifferentiated concepts, gradually form more distinct concepts, and eventually integrate these concepts into a unified whole. Adults observing young children learning to write should be aware that children's concepts about the links between meaning and form are very complex and change as they gain experience using written language.

Clay (1975) offers a summary list of the concepts about print that young children acquire as they discover how to write. They learn (1) to understand that print talks; (2) to form letters; (3) to build up memories of common words they can construct out of letters; (4) to use these words to write messages; (5) to increase the number and range of sentences used; (6) to become flexible in sentence use; and (7) to discipline the expression of ideas within the spelling and punctuation conventions of English (pp. 11–12).

Invented spelling

The story in Figure 6.7 was written by a 5-year-old who started exploring with paper and pencil during his toddler years. Fortunately for Justin, books, paper, and writing utensils were always available to him along with puzzles, blocks, and tricycles—at home, at the pre-kindergarten program he attended, and in the kindergarten where this response to literature was written. Justin has always been encouraged to write stories and messages on his own and to spell the best he could.

Although it has been common practice to encourage reading during the early years, attention to young children's writing development is a relatively recent occurrence. Typically, children's introduction to writing has been

FIGURE 6.7

Justin's Story

delayed until long after reading instruction was well under way. Observations of preschool children in naturalistic settings where they are encouraged to write on their own reveal that many begin to develop strategies for spelling based largely on their knowledge of the phonological system and their knowledge of letter names (Read 1971, 1975).

Although all children do not invent spelling in the same way, or at the same rate, they do develop in a somewhat similar sequence (Henderson, 1980). Gentry (1982) has outlined five stages that children move through on their way to becoming conventional spellers. Figure 6.8 gives examples of each stage.

FIGURE 6.8

Developmental Spelling

Precommunicative Stage	btBpa	IBALI	LYHAWO	IDMitL
Semiphonetic Stage	MTR	BTM	BD	U
Phonetic Stage	MOSTR	BOTM	BRD	UNITID
Transitional Stage	MONSTUR	BODUM	BRID	YOUNIGHTED
Conventional	MONSTER	BOTTOM	BIRD	UNITED

Source: From R. Gentry (1982). An analysis of the developmental spellings in Gnys at wrk. *The Reading Teacher, 36,* 379.

Stage 1: Precommunicative spelling

Typical of ages 3 to 5, during this stage children string scribbles, letters, and letterlike forms together but they do not associate the marks they make with any specific phonemes. They have not yet discovered how spelling works or the alphabetic principle that letters represent sounds in words. They may write from left to right, right to left, top to bottom, or randomly across the page. Although children may use both upper- and lowercase letters, they show a preference for uppercase.

Stage 2: Semiphonetic spelling

Typical of ages 5 and 6, during this stage children begin to demonstrate a rudimentary understanding of the alphabetic principle that links letters and sounds. Spellings tend to consist of only one or two letters to represent an entire word. Semiphonetic spellers use a letter-name strategy to determine which letters to use in spelling a word. Their spellings represent some sound features in a word and ignore others.

Stage 3: Phonetic spelling

Typical of children 6 years of age, during this stage phonetic spellers continue to make use of letter names as a link to represent sounds, but they also use consonant and vowel sounds in increasingly refined ways. The major achievement at this stage is that children begin to represent all the essential sound features in words they spell.

Stage 4: Transitional spelling

Typical of children 7 and 8 years of age, during this stage transitional spellers stop relying totally on phonological information and begin to use visual clues and morphological information as well. They are more likely to include a vowel in every syllable and attempt to make use of vowel patterns and conventional alternatives for representing sounds, although they may not always use them correctly.

Stage 5: Conventional spelling

By age 8 or 9, most children are capable at this stage of spelling a large number of words conventionally. They have mastered the basic principles of English spelling and are ready for instruction in the basic spelling patterns.

Teachers' knowledge of the development of invented spelling is critical to children's growth as writers. Although invented spelling is not an approach to writing, it is a way to remove obstacles in the path of a young writer. Encouraging invented spelling produces independent, fluent, and powerful writing. It is also efficient instruction. Through the application of rules about the relationship between sound and symbol, children practice and drill themselves at a pace and level of difficulty appropriate to their skills. A beginner may struggle and reread a single sentence dozens of times before finishing it. To write "sun," the beginner may say, "Sun, sssssuuuunnn, sss, ss," and write *S*. Then, "Sunnnn, sunnnn, nnnn, nnnn," and write *N, SN* for sun.

No teacher has the time to motivate, diagnose, and assign the appropriate individualized materials for encoding and decoding that could match the work children do when they write (Sowers, 1982). This fact, however, does not mean all children have to invent the spelling of every word they write. As they read and write and have other encounters with print, they will learn the conventional spelling of hundreds of words. Children need to know that if they know how to spell a word they do not have to reinvent it, they simply have to remember it and write it down. Spelling dictionaries, created by children as they learn new words, help them remember the words they have learned. Word walls, listing frequently written words, are also present in many classrooms so that children have an easily accessible reference when they are writing. Special word walls with content words are often created to accompany science or social studies units.

ADULT SUPPORT FOR YOUNG CHILDREN'S LITERACY LEARNING

Scaffolded instruction, demonstrations, and **direct instruction,** discussed in Chapters One and Two, are three ways that adults assist children in language and literacy development (Cazden, 1983). One example of scaffolding occurs when parents and caregivers engage children in literacy activities, such as sharing simple, predictable books. The adult begins by reading or saying all the words prompted by the text or pictures. Gradually the adult encourages the child to join in and take an increasingly greater role in the reading.

Bernice Cullinan

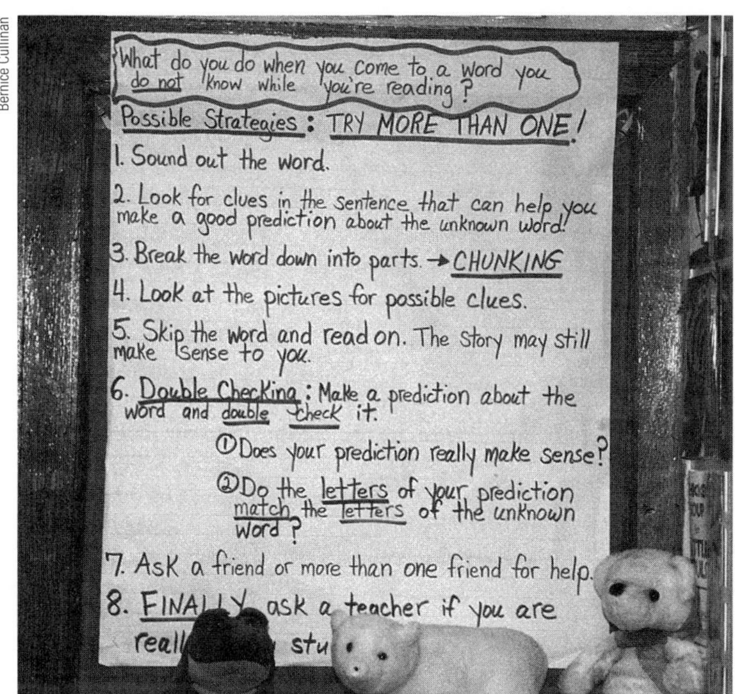

Teachers involve students in creating a chart of strategies to use when they come to a word they do not know when they are reading.

Two-year-old Becky loves to share a particular board book with her mother. Constructed with thick cardboard pages, each page of the book contains the picture of an object familiar to most babies. The routine for sharing the book begins with Becky's mother naming each object as they go along. For example, "Look, see the baby's bottle." By the second or third reading, Becky begins to respond with "bahtee" for bottle. Gradually the routine changes so that Becky's mom no longer does the naming first. Instead she might ask, "Look, what's that?" encouraging Becky to respond with the object's name. This answer might be followed by approving feedback from mom, "Yes, that's the baby's bottle." Eventually, when the spirit moves her, Becky "reads" on her own for brief periods of time. Although the book might be upside down, she turns the pages persistently and names the objects on them.

Parents and other caregivers also provide demonstrations of literacy for young children so that they may acquire their underlying structures. Scaffolds and demonstrations work together as adults interact with children about print in the environment and the storybooks they share. In addition to the written language itself, adults demonstrate their own use of and pleasure in reading and writing. This demonstration may be the most important way that children learn the functions of print in daily life. Cazden (1983) cautions that the texts supplied as demonstrations are "examples to learn from, not samples to copy" (p. 11). The *Teaching Idea: Helping Children Discover What They Already Know about Literacy* shows how one teacher begins the school year by reinforcing his first-graders' literacy abilities while connecting school and their neighborhood.

Direct instruction is a third type of adult assistance in which the adult not only demonstrates literate acts, but directs the child to "say," "tell," or "ask." Often used to develop the social skills or increase the vocabulary of young children, direct instruction may also be employed during book reading and other encounters with print. For example, during otherwise spontaneous interactions, an adult might wish to teach some element found to be unknown to the child. Sentences such as, "That is a motorcycle. Can you say 'motorcycle'?" are typically used.

As pointed out in Chapter One, it is important that children generalize beyond the particular situations in which the scaffold, demonstration, or direct instruction occurs. In life, there is clear evidence that this generalizing happens. In school, however, there is some question about the effectiveness of children's recitations during more cognitive uses of language, particularly during direct instruction (Cazden, 1983, p. 15). Drilling young children on isolated fragments of language, such as decontextualized letters, words, and sound-symbol relationships, is almost always counterproductive. Discussing letters, words, and sound-symbol relations when engaged in a meaningful literacy event is almost always productive. Planning for literacy learning in school must take all forms of adult assistance into account. Most important is the need to encourage children's active involvement and to link literacy to children's natural interests and uses.

TEACHING IDEA

Home/School Connection

HELPING CHILDREN DISCOVER WHAT THEY ALREADY KNOW ABOUT LITERACY

One urban first grade teacher makes a set of slides depicting significant places in the school neighborhood; the barbershop, the supermarket, a nearby church, the school, a gasoline station, and a fast-food restaurant are among them. In each case, he carefully includes the sign telling the name of each establishment.

On the first day of school, the children are shown the slides. They enjoy talking about the familiar places and "reading" the accompanying signs. At the end of the activity, the teacher remarks how pleased he is that they know so much about reading already and, "It is only the first day of school."

Supporting Young Children's Literacy Development in the Classroom

Teachers can do many things to encourage young children to explore and experiment with print. Research in early literacy suggests that schools would do well to model the home environments of children who begin to read and write without formal instruction. Such homes provide children with an abundance of accessible materials for reading and writing. They also provide encouraging, responsive adults, who demonstrate an interest in the child's explorations with print without deliberately setting out to instruct. Classroom environments in which models of reading and writing abound provide children with the encouragement and the materials with which to explore and experiment with print.

CREATING A PRINT-RICH ENVIRONMENT

Parents and caregivers frequently express amazement at how rapidly young children learn to recognize certain fast-food logos and identify the labels on food containers of products that interest them. The classroom also offers many opportunities to capitalize on children's natural interest in print. Teachers may wish to start by labeling key objects and areas in the room. Children's names should be attached to their "cubbies," and each learning center should be identified in writing. Helper charts, recipes, news bulletin boards, calendars, captions for displays, and lists of daily routines and special events are but a few examples of print that may be posted and referred to for information and use by the group.

As discussed in Chapter Three, library and writing centers are places especially devoted to encouraging explorations with literacy. Comfortable chairs, pillows, and carpeting help make a library center cozy and inviting. Plenty of books of general interest, children's original group and individual books, primary dictionaries, and class books should be included. Children enjoy reading these over and over again. Shelving that allows the front covers of books to be displayed fully is preferable. Charts, pictures from class experiences, and displays should be placed low enough for young children to see them with ease.

The writing center is a place where children can dictate stories or write stories on their own. It should be equipped with a table and chairs and a variety of writing supplies. Because young children like to select their own materials for writing, paper of many colors, textures, and sizes, including blank books, should be available. Pencils, felt-tip markers, and crayons have great appeal to young children. A chalkboard, typewriter, or computer can add immensely to interest in the tools available. An alphabet chart and a chart with all the children's names should be available at eye level. Letters of various sizes, colors, and textures, including magnetic letters and alphabet books, should also be available. Depending on space and the age of the children, teachers may wish to combine these centers into a language arts area or place them next to each other so that children can combine their use.

All centers in use in a classroom should make use of literacy in some way. Labeling the spaces where blocks are housed with a diagram and name of the type of block that should be placed there is a functional use of print. Food containers in the housekeeping area and recipes posted for cooking in the area where cooking is done show youngsters that print is an integral part of classroom life. One teacher created an office center in her Head Start classroom. Included were a desk, two chairs, a toy telephone, a poster or two on a nearby wall, plenty of writing materials, paper clips, stickers, and a wide assortment of junk mail. This center soon became a favorite place for dramatic play with "office people" conducting business and a stream of visitors, many of whom had dressed up in the housekeeping area, coming in to take care of business. Interestingly, the business in this inner-city classroom, where many of the children were on public assistance, often reflected the lengthy questioning and filling out of forms that they had seen their parents engage in at various city agencies.

In addition to the products of writing, children need to see writing in production. Teachers should take advantage of every opportunity to model writing in front of their students. On occasion, children should be allowed to watch as adults write notes and letters. The correspondence may be read aloud as it is written and once again after it is completed. Lists, memoranda, and other forms of writing should be demonstrated whenever possible. For instance, environmental print, such as advertisements and logos, provides children with meaningful encounters with written language. They not only begin to recognize graphic symbols and words, they learn how written language works as a communicator of messages. Many kindergarten teachers write a morning message with their children, following the guidelines given in the *Teaching Idea: The Morning Message*.

USING LITERATURE

One of the best ways to share models of writing is to read to children on a regular basis. Chapter Three offers numerous suggestions for reading aloud at all grade levels. At the early childhood level, one particular type or format of literature, known as big books, has become a staple in the literacy curriculum. **Big books,** enlarged versions of children's trade books, allow children to see and react to the printed page as it is being read aloud. The reading is truly shared because children are encouraged to join in on repeated words and phrases. They follow along from left to right as the adult reader tracks the print with a finger or pointer. They soon discover that it is the print and not the pictures that signal the words said by the reader. Placing the big books and the smaller versions that frequently accompany them in the reading center for children to read independently allows children to practice, refine, and extend what they know about reading. Figure 6.9 on pages 234 and 235 details possible activities in big book reading.

Holdaway (1979) contends that the developmental teaching that occurs at home during storybook reading can be transferred to the classroom through the use of big books. This type of teaching contains demonstrations,

TEACHING IDEA

Addressing Individual Needs

THE MORNING MESSAGE

The morning message is an excellent example of the use of scaffolding to guide young children's reading and writing development. Used primarily in kindergarten, children develop increasing independence in understanding and reading written information (Kawakami-Arakaki, Oshiro, & Farran, 1989).

1. On the chalkboard or chart paper, write a brief message to students as they watch. It should be about something that is of interest to the group. The process of writing is demonstrated as you pause to think aloud about what is to be written and to read aloud as the writing proceeds. Afterward, encourage the children to follow along as you read the text aloud, figuring out as much of the text as they can.
2. Discuss the content of the message both for its meaning and for its textual features. Children may relate the text to their personal interests; identify and discuss the meanings of various words; and identify words and letters that are the same, have similar features (for example, same initial letter), or letters that are of particular interest to them, such as those they recognize as being in their names. Writing conventions, such as punctuation and capitalization, may also be discussed.
3. Children may follow by writing messages of their own; these cover the full range of drawing, scribbling, and invented spellings. Encourage them to apply to their independent writing what they have learned through the Morning Message.
4. As the year progresses, children will attempt to take more and more control of the reading and writing of the message. Monitor and modify the tasks to suit the growing abilities of your students.

FIGURE 6.9

Activities to Use with Big Books

What the teacher does before reading:	***What the child does:***	***Objectives:***
1. Stimulates discussion about relevant content and concepts in text.	1. Talks and listens to others talk about relevant content and concepts.	1. To focus listening and speaking on vocabulary and ideas about to be met in print. To activate background knowledge related to text.
2. Reads aloud title and author; uses words "title" and "author" and briefly explains what they mean.	2. Notes what the words on the book cover represent.	2. To build vocabulary and concepts: title, author, authorship.
3. Asks children what they think story might be about, based on title and cover illustration. Or, thinks aloud about what s/he thinks this story might be about.	3. Uses clues from title and cover together with background knowledge to formulate predictions about the story. Or, observes teacher model the above.	3. To use clues from text and background knowledge to make inferences and formulate predictions.
4. Shows pleasure and interest in anticipation of the reading.	4. Observes as teacher models personal interest and eagerness toward the reading.	4. To build positive attitudes toward books and reading.
What the teacher does while reading aloud:		
5. Gives lively reading. Displays interest and delight in language and story line.	5. Observes teacher evoke meaningful language from print.	5. To understand that print carries meaning.
6. Tracks print with hand or pointer.	6. Follows movement of hand or pointer.	6. To match speech to print. Directionality: left to right.
7. Thinks aloud about her/his understanding of certain aspects of the story (self-query, making predictions, drawing conclusions, etc.).	7. Observes as teacher monitors her/his own understandings.	7. To develop an understanding of the reading process as thinking with text.
8. Hesitates at predictable parts in the text. Allows children to fill in possible words or phrases.	8. Fills in likely words for a given slot.	8. To use semantic and syntactic clues to determine what makes sense.
9. At appropriate parts in a story, queries children about what might happen next.	9. Makes predictions about what might happen next in the story.	9. To use story line to predict possible events and outcomes.

What the teacher does after reading:	***What the child does:***	***Objectives:***
10. Guides discussion about key ideas in the text. Helps children relate key concepts.	10. Participates in discussion of important ideas in the text.	10. To reflect on the reading; to apply and personalize key ideas in text.
11. Asks children to recall important or favorite parts. Finds corresponding part of the text (perhaps with help of children) and rereads.	11. Recalls and describes specific events or parts of text.	11. To use print to support and confirm discussion.
12. Guides group rereading of all or specific parts of text for increased fluency with errorless repetition and reinforcement.	12. Joins in the reading in parts s/he feels confident about.	12. To develop fluency and confidence through group reading.
13. Uses "cloze" activities (flaps to cover words) to involve children in meaningful prediction of words. Gives praise for all meaningful (contextually plausible) offerings. Discusses response with children.	13. Fills in possible words for a given slot.	13. To use semantic and syntactic clues to determine what words fit in a slot and why.
What the teacher does after repeated readings:		
14. Focuses children's attention on distinctive features and patterns in the text: repeated words, repeated word beginnings (letters, consonant clusters), punctuation marks, etc. Uses letter names and correct terminology to discuss these features. Extends discussion to developmentally appropriate level.	14. Notes distinctive features and patterns pointed out by teacher and attempts to find others on her/his own.	14. To analyze a known text for distinctive features and patterns. To develop an understanding of the elements of decoding within a meaningful context.
15. Makes books and charts available for independent reading.	15. Selects books and charts for independent reading and reads them at own pace.	15. To increase confidence and understanding of the reading process by practicing it independently.

collaboration, practice, and approximations. The teacher demonstrates reading, and the children collaborate with the teacher to read the text. Then the children practice what they have learned and experiment independently. The children's approximations of the story are accepted and rewarded by the teacher as they read both the large text and the accompanying smaller ones to themselves, each other, and the teacher.

LANGUAGE CHARTS

Language charts, which are usually based on children's own experiences and dictated by them to the teacher, provide an excellent means of helping children develop understandings about written language. Often called language-experience charts, these are especially useful in helping children understand the relationship between oral and written language. As children say what they want to have the teacher write, the teacher scribes for them, writing exactly what they say in conventional spelling. The point is to move from the meaning that the child intends, translate that meaning from oral into written language that mirrors exactly what the child says, and then help the child to read what has just been said.

Both individual and group dictation provide a natural opportunity for the discussion of various textual features. Children notice how print is set down on the page. They match words and letters and find similarities in the beginnings and endings of words. Throughout the discussion, the teacher models the language of literacy using words such as *sentence, word, line, top of page,* and *period.* Figure 6.10 is an example of a group-dictated language chart. The trend toward early independent writing has caused many teachers to limit the use of individual dictation by children in the hope of encouraging them to write on their own. Charts generated by individuals and the group and charts prepared in advance by the teacher, using poems and songs, are still a major part of the early childhood literacy curriculum, however. Language charts play a significant role in the classroom literacy environment. They support children's growing awareness of the relationships between speech and print.

DEVELOPING SKILLS AND FOSTERING CONTINUITY

Despite the fact that most teachers readily embrace the ideas consistent with an emergent-literacy perspective, many voice concern that this approach may neglect the skills children need for success in school. They acknowledge that children do form positive attitudes through storybook reading and independent writing. They also applaud the independence and the competence demonstrated each day as children use literacy for their own purposes. All this

FIGURE 6.10

Language Chart

Field Day
We had Field Day yesterday.
We played outside all day.
We ran races.
Our class won the relay race.
Ms. Cox won the teachers' race.
We liked playing with the water balloons.
Field Day was fun.

may be overshadowed, however, by the perceived need for children to perform in some prescribed manner on a specific set of subskills. For example, reciting the alphabet, identifying letter names, and uttering related sounds when specific letters are displayed is often considered evidence that children have acquired the skills needed to learn to read. Children's abilities to use this information to perform literate acts in conjunction with projects that interest them is considered less important, a by-product of skills acquisition.

Effective teachers of young children view literacy learning as one important part of children's ongoing development. They teach skills and strategies as interconnecting parts of an integrated whole. They are aware that although skills can be learned in isolation, they never function that way, and all too often what is learned in isolation is not transferred to other appropriate contexts. Skills act as underlying components of strategies, as children attempt to construct meaning with language.

The independent writing done by Justin in Figure 6.7 indicates that he knows the sound-symbol relationships associated with the letters *m, g, t, k, d,* and *p,* among others; he knows how to form those letters along with several others as well. He also has a sense of how print looks on a page and knows that there are spaces between words. Most important, however, this youngster has the ability to use text and pictures in an integrated way to tell his own message. Through this piece of writing and many others that he produces on a weekly basis, Justin's teacher and Justin himself are very much aware of his development as a reader and writer. Justin not only knows a great deal about reading and writing, he knows how to use what he knows. Thus, a focus on learner strategies both develops and depends on skill, but a focus only on skills in isolation offers little or no support for strategic learning, the key to independence.

Program continuity

Children who move from a classroom that reflects a learner-centered, emergent-literacy perspective to one devoted to the acquisition of preordered skills may become confused and lose confidence in what they already know. Strickland and Morrow (1989) give the following example:

> Pamela and her mother were quite upset when her first grade teacher sent home a report with a checkmark in the "NO" column after the item "Knows ABC's." The previous spring, Pam's kindergarten teacher had passed along a folder of her writing, which included all but a few of the letters of the alphabet. Pam could read her own writing, and she knew the names of the letters she used. She could identify the letters and the names of the four members of her family. Pam had never learned the alphabetic sequence, however. Since she had no use for the telephone book or the dictionary, there had been no attempt to teach alphabetical order. Unfortunately, her first grade teacher felt Pamela was ill prepared. To her, the ability to recite and identify the letters in alphabetical order was an important prerequisite for success in first grade (p. 83).

Program continuity throughout the early childhood years, from prekindergarten through grade 3, cannot be overly stressed. Children who are allowed to flourish in an environment where they have constant access to print materials to explore and experiment with under the guidance of responsive adults will be frustrated when they are placed in environments where the adults expect to direct every aspect of their learning in small incremental units. Worse yet, as Pamela's experience illustrates, they may be unable to demonstrate what they do know in ways that are satisfactory to those adults. Collaborative decision making about policy and curriculum, both within elementary schools and between those schools and the early childhood centers that feed into them, is essential.

Setting policy for early literacy programs

For a variety of reasons, today's young children are likely to receive some type of literacy instruction in a school setting prior to entering first grade. For example, children of working parents are increasingly enrolled in child-care centers where they receive day-care services from as early as infancy. It is felt by many that these children are more socialized to the school experience and better prepared to handle formal activities at an early age. Also, the apparent effects of television have caused many to feel that most children are ready for more rigorous instruction at an earlier age. Research indicating a positive relationship between academic learning time and pupil achievement has caused some to recommend earlier schooling and a longer school day as a means of promoting excellence through increased time on task. This is particularly true of those children who are deemed "at risk." Moreover, research on the language and literacy development of young children, such as that offered in Chapter Four and in this chapter, indicates that given a supportive, print-rich environment, young children are capable of understanding far more about reading and writing than many parents and educators had previously realized. Finally, longitudinal studies have shown that effective early childhood education has long-term effects on the academic, social, and economic well-being of children.

The trend toward greater emphasis on early childhood education, and on literacy in particular, has raised several policy issues for parents and educators. The issues affect curriculum from pre-kindergarten through the primary grades. Several professional organizations have produced policy guidelines designed to help schools make decisions regarding the education of young children. The National Association for the Education of Young Children has produced several documents on providing developmentally appropriate curricula for young children. That organization has also joined with several others interested in young children to endorse a policy document (shown in Figure 6.11 on pages 240–241), *Literacy Development and Early Childhood,* prepared by the Early Childhood and Literacy Development Committee of theInternational Reading Association. This document represents the conclusions of eminent researchers and teachers, and provides a simple, understandable statement that reflects our current knowledge of how children develop their literacy. As such, this document should provide guidance to curriculum planners. It can also support teachers in their efforts to make schools moreliterate places.

SUMMARY

Children come to school with a remarkable knowledge of oral language, and their awareness of written language also is well under way. Young children's literacy development begins early in life and is ongoing. It develops concurrently with oral language in social contexts. Learning to read and write is a developmental process that is particularly affected by family book reading. Among the concepts about print that young children need to understand are the functions of written language, its conventions and units, and its alphabetic and structural principles.

Young children learn about language by exploring and experimenting with the print in the world around them and by trying out what they know through drawing and writing. They do this not for its own sake, but in the search for the meaning of events and objects that interest them. Adults support children's learning by involving them in literate acts such as book reading

FIGURE 6.11

Literacy Development and Early Childhood (Preschool through Grade 3)

Literacy learning begins in infancy. Children have many experiences with oral and written language before they come to school.

- Children have had many experiences from which they build ideas about the functions and uses of oral and written language.
- Children have a command of language and of processes for learning language.
- Many children can differentiate between drawing and writing.
- Many children are reading environmental print, such as road signs, grocery labels, and fast-food signs.
- Many children associate books with reading.
- Children's knowledge about language and communication is influenced by their social and cultural backgrounds.
- Many children expect that reading and writing will be sense-making activities.

Basic Premises of a Sound Pre-First Grade Reading Program

- Reading and writing at school should permit children to build upon their already existing knowledge of oral and written language.
- Learning should take place in a supportive environment where children can build a positive attitude toward themselves and toward language and literacy.
- For optimal learning, teachers should involve children actively in many meaningful, functional language experiences, including speaking, listening, writing, and reading.
- Teachers of young children should be prepared in ways that acknowledge differences in language and cultural backgrounds, and should emphasize reading as an integral part of the language arts as well as of the total curriculum.

Concerns

- Many pre-first grade children are subjected to rigid formal prereading programs with inappropriate expectations and experiences for their levels of development.
- Little attention is given to individual development or individual learning styles.
- The pressures of accelerated programs do not allow children to be risk takers as they experiment with written language.
- Too much attention is focused upon isolated skill development and abstract parts of the reading process rather than on the integration of talking, writing, and listening with reading.
- Too little attention is given to reading for pleasure; therefore, children do not associate reading with enjoyment.
- Decisions related to reading programs are often based on political and economic considerations rather than on knowledge of how young children learn.
- The pressure to achieve high scores on tests inappropriate for the kindergarten child has led to undesirable changes in the content of programs. Activities that deny curiosity, critical thinking, and creative expression are all too frequent, and can foster negative attitudes toward language communica-

- ✦ As a result of declining enrollment and reduction in staff, individuals with little or no knowledge of early childhood education are sometimes assigned to teach young children. Such teachers often select inappropriate methods.
- ✦ Teachers who are conducting pre-first grade programs without depending on commercial readers and workbooks sometimes fail to articulate for parents and other members of the public what they are doing and why.

Recommendations

1. Build instruction on what the child already knows about oral language, reading and writing. Focus on meaningful experiences and meaningful language rather than on isolated skill development.
2. Respect the language the child brings to school, and use it as a base for language and literacy activities.
3. Ensure feelings of success for all children, helping them to see themselves as people who enjoy exploring both oral and written language.
4. Provide reading experiences as an integrated part of the communication process, which includes speaking, listening, and writing, as well as art, math, and music.
5. Encourage children's first attempts at writing, without concern for the proper formation of letters or correct conventional spelling.
6. Encourage risk taking in first attempts at reading and writing, and accept what appear to be errors as part of children's natural growth and development.
7. Use reading materials that are familiar or predictable, such as well known stories, as they provide children with a sense of control and confidence in their ability to learn.
8. Present a model for children to emulate. In the classroom, teachers should use language appropriately, listen and respond to children's talk, and engage in their own reading and writing.
9. Take time regularly to read to children from a wide variety of poetry, fiction, and nonfiction.
10. Provide time regularly for children's independent reading and writing.
11. Foster children's affective and cognitive development by providing them with opportunities to communicate what they know, think, and feel.
12. Use developmentally and culturally appropriate procedures for evaluation, ones that are based on the objectives of the program and that consider each child's total development.
13. Make parents aware of the reasons for a broader language program at school and provide them with ideas for activities to carry out at home.
14. Alert parents to the limitations of formal assessments and standardized tests of pre-first-graders' reading and writing skills.
15. Encourage children to be active participants in the learning process rather than passive recipients, by using activities that allow for experimentation with talking, listening, writing and reading.

Source: Prepared by the Early Childhood and Literacy Development Committee of the International Reading Association. International Reading Association, 800 Barksdale Road, PO Box 8139, Newark, Delaware 19714-8139.

and by providing varied models of literacy, intervening with direct instruction when appropriate. Schools support children's learning in much the same way. Print-rich environments in which children are encouraged to use literacy for their own purposes work best.

ACTIVITIES

1. **Individually, ask several children 4 or 5 years of age to write their names or anything else they wish.** Using the information given on emerging writers and spellers in this chapter, analyze their writing to see what they know about how written language works.
2. **To investigate children's understanding of the functions of print, gather several items of print commonly found at home or places visited by young children.** Individually, ask several children 4 or 5 years of age: "What is this?" and "What is it for?" Suggested items include telephone book, dictionary, newspaper, television guide, menu, storybook, letter. Finally, compare your findings with those of Weiss and Hagen, whose research is discussed in this chapter.
3. **All of us have different literacy experiences at home.** Take 5 minutes and list all of the ways you have used reading and writing in the past 24 hours. Share and compare that list with your peers, noting similarities and differences among you. Now take 5 minutes and list all of the things you remember doing with print at home as a child. Again, share and compare.

FURTHER READING

Cochran-Smith, M. (1984). *The making of a reader.* Norwood, NJ: Ablex.

Gentry, J. R. (1987). *Spel is a four-letter word.* Portsmouth, NH: Heinemann.

Strickland, D. S. & Morrow, L. M. (Eds.) (2001). *Beginning reading and writing.* New York: Teachers College Press and Newark, DE: International Reading Association.

REFERENCES

Adams, M. J. (1990). *Beginning to read: Thinking and learning about print.* Urbana, IL: Center for the Study of Reading.

Anderson, R. C., Wilson, P. T., & Fielding, L. G. (1988). Growth in reading and how children spend their time outside of school. *Reading Research Quarterly, 23,* 285–303.

Applebee, A. N. (1978). *The child's concept of story: Ages two to seventeen.* Chicago: University of Chicago Press.

Baghban, M. (1984). *Our daughter learns to read and write: A case study birth to three.* Newark, DE: International Reading Association.

Cazden, C. (1983). Adult assistance to language development: Scaffolds, models, and direct instruction. In R. P. Parker & F. R. Davis (Eds.), *Developing literacy: Young children's use of language* (pp. 3–18). Newark, DE: International Reading Association.

Clay, M. M. (1975). *What did I write?* Auckland, New Zealand: Heinemann.

______. (1982). *Observing young readers.* Exeter, NH: Heinemann.

______. (1991). *Becoming literate: The construction of inner control.* Portsmouth, NH: Heinemann.

Cunningham, A., & Stanovich, K. (1998). What reading does for the mind. *American Educator,* Spring/Summer, 8–15.

Denny, T. P., & Weintraub, S. (1966). First graders' responses to three questions about reading. *Elementary School Journal, 66,* 441–448.

Dewey, J., & Dewey, E. (1915/1962). *Schools of tomorrow.* New York: Dutton.

Dickinson, D. K., & Sprague, K. E. (2001). The nature and impact of early childhood care environments on the language and early literacy development of children from low-income families. In S. B. Neuman & D. K. Dickinson (Eds.), *Handbook of early literacy research* (pp. 263–280). New York: Guilford Press.

Duke, N. K. (2000). For the rich it's richer: Print environments and experiences offered to first-grade students in very low- and very high-SES school districts. *American Educational Research Journal, 37,* 456–457.

Dyson, A. H. (1982). The emergence of visible language: Interrelationships between drawing and early writing. *Visible Language, 16,* 360–381.

______. (1982b). Reading, writing, and language: Young children solving the written language puzzle. *Language Arts, 59,* 829–839.

______. (1984). Learning to write/learning to do school. *Research in the Teaching of English, 18,* 233–264.

Ehri, L., & Wilce, L. (1985). Movement into reading: Is the first stage of printed word learning visual or phonetic? *Reading Research Quarterly, 20,* 163–179.

Ferreiro, E. (1986). The interplay between information and assimilation in beginning literacy. In W. H. Teale & E. Sulzby (Eds.), *Emergent literacy: Writing and reading* (pp. 15–49). Norwood, NJ: Ablex.

Ferreiro, E., & Teberosky, A. (1982). *Literacy before schooling.* Portsmouth, NH: Heinemann.

Gentry, R. (1981). Learning to spell developmentally. *The Reading Teacher, 34,* 378–381.

______. (1982). An analysis of the developmental spellings in Gnys at wrk. *The Reading Teacher, 36,* 192–200.

Hall, N. (1987). *The emergence of literacy.* Portsmouth, NH: Heinemann.

Harste, J., Woodward, V., & Burke, C. (1984). *Language stories and literacy lessons.* Portsmouth, NH: Heinemann.

Holdaway, D. (1979). *The foundations of literacy.* Sidney, Australia: Ashton Scholastic.

Henderson, E. H. (1980). Developmental concepts of word. In E. H. Henderson & J. W. Beers (Eds.), *Developmental and cognitive aspects of learning to spell: A reflection of work knowledge* (pp. 1–14). Newark, DE: International Reading Association.

Jalongo, M. R. (2002). *Early childhood language arts, 2nd ed.* Boston, MA: Allyn & Bacon.

Johns, J. L. (1986). Students' perceptions of reading: Thirty years of inquiry. In D. B. Yaden & S. Templeton (Eds.), *Metalinguistic awareness and beginning literacy* (pp. 31–40). Portsmouth, NH: Heinemann.

Johns, J. L., & Johns, A. L. (1971). How do children in the elementary school view the reading process? *The Michigan Reading Journal, 5,* 44–53.

Juell, C., Griffith, P., & Gough, P. (1986). The acquisition of literacy: A longitudinal study of children in first and second grade. *Journal of Educational Psychology, 78,* 243–255.

Kawakami-Arakaki, A., Oshiro, M., & Farran, D. (1989). Research to practice: Integrating reading and writing in a kindergarten curriculum. In J. Mason (Ed.), *Reading and writing connections.* Boston: Allyn & Bacon.

Leichter, H. J. (1984). Families as environments for literacy. In H. Goelman, A. Oberg, & F. Smith (Eds.), *Awakening to literacy.* Portsmouth, NH: Heinemann.

Maclean, M., Bryant, P., & Bradley, L. (1987). Rhymes, nursery rhymes, and reading in early childhood. *Merrill-Palmer Quarterly, 33,* 255–281.

Mason, J., & Allen, J. B. (1986). A review of emergent literacy with implications for research and practice in reading. In E. Rothkopf (Ed.), *Review of research in education* (pp. 3–47). Washington, D.C.: American Educational Research Association.

National Reading Panel (2000). *Teaching children to read: An evidence-based assessment of the scientific research literature on reading and its implications for reading instruction.* Washington, D.C.: National Institute of Child Health and Human Development.

Newkirk, T. (1985). The hedgehog or the fox: The dilemma of writing development. *Language Arts, 62,* 593–603.

Papandropoulou, I., & Sinclair, H. (1974). What is a word? Experimental study of children's ideas on grammar. *Human Development, 17,* 241–258.

Parker, R. P. (1983). Language development and learning to write. In R. P. Parker & F. A. Davis (Eds.), *Developing literacy: Young children's use of language* (pp. 38–54). Newark, DE: International Reading Association.

Partnership for Reading (2001). *Put reading first.* Washington, D.C.: Author.

Perfetti, C., Beck, I., & Hughes, C. (1985). Reading acquisition and beyond: Decoding includes cognition. *American Journal of Education, 93,* 40–60.

Read, C. (1971). Pre-school children's knowledge of English phonology. *Harvard Educational Review, 41,* 1–34.

______. (1975). *Children's categorization of speech sounds in English (National Council of Teachers of English Research Report No. 17).* Urbana, IL: National Council of Teachers of English.

Rubin, A. (1980). A theoretical taxonomy of the differences between oral and written language. In R. J. Spiro, B. C. Bruce, & W. F. Brewer (Eds.), *Theoretical issues in reading comprehension.* Hillsdale, NJ: Erlbaum.

Scollon, R., & Scollon, B. (1981). *Narrative, literacy, and face in interethnic communication.* Norwood, NJ: Ablex.

Sowers, S. (1982). Six questions teachers ask about invented spelling. In T. Newkirk & N. Atwell (Eds.), *Understanding writing* (pp. 47–54). Boston, MA: Northeast Regional Exchange.

Strickland, D. S. (1998). *Teaching phonics today.* Newark DE: International Reading Association.

______. (2002). The importance of effective early intervention. In A. Farstrup & S. J. Samuels (Eds.). *What research has to say about instruction, 3rd ed.* Newark, DE: International Reading Association.

Strickland, D. S., & Morrow, L. M. (1989). Developing skills: An emergent literacy perspective. *The Reading Teacher, 43,* 82–83.

Sulzby, E. (1985). Kindergartners as readers and writers. In M. Farr (Ed.), *Advances in writing research Vol. I: Children's early writing development* (pp. 127–199). Norwood, NJ: Ablex.

Taylor, D., & Strickland, D. S. (1986). *Family storybook reading.* Portsmouth, NH: Heinemann.

Teale, W., & Sulzby, E. (1989). Emergent literacy: New perspectives on young children's reading and writing. In D. S. Strickland & L. M. Morrow (Eds.), *Emerging literacy: Young children learn to read and write* (pp. 1–15). Newark, DE: International Reading Association.

Templeton, S., & Spivey, E. (1980). The concept of word in young children as a function of level of cognitive development. *Research in the Teaching of English, 14,* 265–278.

Watson, R. (2001). Literacy and oral language: Implications for early literacy acquisition. In S. B. Neuman & D. K. Dickinson (Eds.), *Handbook of early literacy research* (pp. 43–53). New York: Guilford Press.

Weiss, M. J., & Hagen, R. (1988). A key to literacy: Kindergartners' awareness of the functions of print. *The Reading Teacher, 41,* 574–578.

Reading: Responding to and Learning from Texts through the Grades

CHAPTER OUTLINE

Key Standard

Teachers of language arts/reading will provide opportunities for students to gain competence in their abilities to enjoy and learn from a variety of literary and informational texts. Such teachers:

- Help students understand that people read for a variety of purposes.
- Help students develop the skills needed to effectively respond to texts.
- Help students use a variety of strategies for comprehending texts.

To get a preview of Chapter 7 and learn about developing children's competence in reading, visit the Chapter 7 section of the accompanying *Language Arts* CD-ROM.

The March wind still has a bite in it, but it is physically and socially warm in Marianne Marino's sixth grade classroom in Glen Rock, New Jersey, a working-class community about 30 miles from New York City. There, in clusters of five and six, sit thirty students deeply involved in reading books they themselves chose from the school library or from the books stacked on every inch of available space in the room. The classroom library fills every bookshelf and windowsill, spilling over to countertops, chalk ledges, and several plastic file crates. The whole room invites anyone who enters to "Come in and read." Author profiles and children's writing grace the bulletin boards, proclaiming that this room is a literate environment, one in which reading and writing are valued and celebrated.

Marianne immerses children in literature from the first day of school. She lets her students know that books are important to her and that she treasures them. She builds a workshop atmosphere and surrounds students with literature of all types, including historical and realistic fiction, short stories, nonfiction, poetry, and folklore. She labels one bulletin board, "Author's Bulletin Board," and uses it to highlight authors of trade books the children read as well as child authors from the class.

Today Marianne begins reading workshop by reading aloud May Swenson's poem, "The Pregnant Dream," in which Swenson embeds and repeats one phrase. Then Marianne reads aloud from a student author, Diane, who has written a piece influenced by Swenson's poem. Diane's poem begins: It is strange. It is not easy. It is hard to understand at times. It makes you sad, and then it will make you happy. It is full of surprises—some good, some bad. It makes you keep on going—Life! *After hearing an established poet's work and a classmate's work, students discuss how the two poems are alike. Diane talks about how Swenson's poem made her think of repeating a phrase, saying the same words over and over to underscore their meaning.*

When the discussion is over, students turn back to their books (without so much as a nod from Marianne!), settling in for a long read. For the next

30 or 40 minutes only the rustling of paper, scooting of a chair, or occasional shuffling of feet breaks the silence. A sense of busy quietude pervades the room.

Near the end of the period, Marianne says, "Let's take about 5 minutes now to write about what you've been reading." Students take out their response journals and begin to write: "I'm reading Many Waters *by Madeleine L'Engle, and it's about Sandy and Dennis—and they're joined in some way. It's sort of confusing, and I don't understand what's going on right now . . . . Now they have gone to another place and are part of each other but they are still separate—and I think I know what's happening."*

After the children finish writing, they talk with their response group for 7–10 minutes. No one is appointed leader; somebody just begins talking about what he or she is reading and others join in.

Marianne says, "Let's move to our whole-group share," and clusters of children hurry to the area rug. Marianne stays in the background and students lead the entire discussion as they talk about what they were reading.

Marianne's classroom is a fine example of a literature-based program in action. During this particular reading workshop, many things were happening. Marianne read aloud to the whole class, and they discussed as a group the work of a published poet and a student poet, with the student poet commenting on the link between reading and writing. An opportunity for response groups to discuss the books that each member has been reading followed. The culminating activity was another whole-class sharing session in which students discussed their books. During the whole-class workshop time, Marianne acted as a facilitator, sometimes expanding or clarifying the children's ideas and their knowledge about literature. The children took the responsibility for leadership. Marianne "led from behind" as her students explored what it means to be a reader and the power reading releases.

Standards-based teachers work hard to implement a literature-based program in their classrooms. They believe that children learn best to read (and write, think, speak, listen, and so on) in a context that provides time for reading and responding to a variety of books, as well as time and instruction to help students develop both their personal responses and their comprehension strategies. These teachers employ different organizational frameworks such as workshops, literature circles, and Book Clubs. They offer multiple learning experiences such as author studies, genre studies, and thematic studies, and focus on varied response and comprehension strategies. They all, however, have one thing in common: they use literature to structure their reading/language arts activities.

In Chapter Three, we discussed why literature is so basic to studying the English language arts. In Chapter Six, we discussed how young children learn to read. Here we consider how young readers develop their repertoire for responding to the books they read and how they learn comprehension strategies as they develop their reading ability.

Joseph Kassick

Getting "lost in a good book" is great motivation for reading.

Response to Literature

In the past, we assumed that meaning was contained within a text and that the reader's job was to discover the meaning that the author intended. A reader did have to decode and comprehend, but this was a rather passive process in that the reader was receiving meaning rather than creating it. Based on research in schema theory and response theory, we now know that this is not the case. Effective readers actively construct meaning as they interact with text. Schema theory (for example, Anderson, 1977) describes how readers bring unique individual and cultural experience and knowledge to the act of reading with comprehension. This knowledge and experience profoundly influences the meaning that readers create as they read, affecting both comprehension and response.

Effective reading involves bringing meaning *to* a text in order to create meaning *from* it. We call this kind of reading **"transactional,"** because of the reciprocal nature of the interaction between reader and text. Reading is a dynamic process in which an active reader engages with a text in order to create meaning. This creation of meaning requires a great deal of work by the reader. After studying transcripts of tape recordings of proficient readers thinking aloud as they read, Langer (1990) described four basic things that readers do. Readers all begin by approaching the text to be read and trying to "step back" in order to begin to make meaning. Once in the text, readers continue to "move through," creating meaning as they read. Sometimes they "step back" to think about what they already know in terms of the new meaning they are creating as they read. Finally, when reading is completed, some readers "step out" and consider the reading experience and the meaning that they have created.

Transactional theory encourages teachers to consider three dimensions of the act of reading and responding: the reader, the text, and the context. Rosenblatt (1938/1983, 1978, 2003), one of the first theorists to describe the active role readers play in creating meaning, believed that a literary work exists only in the "live circuit" set up between the reader and the text. Readers infuse intellectual and emotional meaning into what they read; the meaning they create is shaped by their background experiences. The result is that because no two people have exactly the same experiences, no two readings will be exactly the same. Even within individuals the meaning of a text can change across different readings. Readers construct new meanings each time they read a book because time and experience make them different people. As a group, however, they can still reach some agreement about the meaning of a text, because of the overlapping nature of experiences and a shared understanding of language. At the same time, each reader contributes his or her unique understanding, a unique construction of meaning. In a classroom that is grounded in collaboration and a belief in the worth of each individual student, this combination of shared meaning and individual significance is a natural part of reading and responding to literature.

As readers, our experiences—the people we know, the places we've been, the activities we have participated in—and our personality—who we are, how we present ourselves to the world—all influence the way in which we respond to books. Age and gender influence response, as do reading ability, past experience with books, and reading preferences. Language, cognitive, and moral development also influence how we are able to make sense as we read.

Response is not a one-way street, however, and the text affects what happens when we as readers read by guiding and constraining the making of meaning. The words authors choose, how they arrange them on the page, and the structure of their writing all influence the development of meaning. Even the format of a book can profoundly influence the way in which we read it. The intentional acts of the author create a unique text, and this uniqueness channels response in certain directions.

Just as individual readers and particular texts greatly influence the act of reading, context—in this case the classroom context—also influences how readers read. In Chapter Five, we discussed the social nature of reading and how peers influence the experience of reading. The opportunity to share responses with peers in some fashion has profound implications for response. The social climate of the classroom does so as well. Classrooms that are collaborative and supportive offer students the opportunity to be honest in their interactions with peers around books. Teachers who value individual responses and ideas and who work with students to develop their ideas allow children to feel comfortable taking the risk of sharing their feelings and ideas. Another aspect of context that influences response is the instructional structures that teachers use to build their curriculum. What students are asked to do with a book is a major factor in how they approach the reading of that book (Marshall, 2000; Spiegel, 1998).

Bernice Cullinan

Students who read the same book enjoy talking about it.

RESPONSE AND READER'S STANCE

The genre of the text and the reader's purpose for reading, or the **stance** from which readers approach texts, also affect the meanings they create as they read. Good readers read for a variety of reasons, altering their purpose according to the context in which they are reading and the text they have in their hands. When they read a piece of nonfiction, the primary purpose is usually to obtain information. Rosenblatt (1938/1983) calls this **"efferent"** reading because the primary goal is to "carry away" some meaning to do something with in the real world. Reading a recipe to prepare food or reading a nonfiction science text to learn about migration patterns is efferent reading.

Although readers who are reading efferently certainly notice, at some level, the quality of the prose, the organization, and the quality of the illustrations, they are reading primarily to come away with information rather than to be swept up in a story. This kind of reading maintains a "point of reference." "Readers establish their sense of the topic . . . and monitor their growing understandings . . . . [T]hey use the content they read to develop more articulated meanings which are built on and elaborated as their understanding of the topic grows" (Langer, 1990, p. 814). Successful learning from academic texts requires skill in reading in this fashion.

In contrast, reading fiction is a different act. Readers generally read fiction for the virtual experience that it affords or, as one fifth grade girl put it, to be "inhaled" by story. Rather than focusing on a point of reference, readers of stories and poems look "toward a horizon of possibilities" (Langer, 1990, p. 814). In this kind of reading, or in Rosenblatt's term **aesthetic reading,** readers make sense of new textual information in terms of the sense of the whole that they are building, but rather than converging on one particular point, they become more divergent, entertaining possibilities, making judgments, and considering alternatives.

When students are asked to read a piece of fiction simply to learn facts, they are learning to read fiction from an ineffective stance. This has important implications for planning a literature-based instructional program. The assignments teachers make, and—as we discussed in Chapter Five—the types of questions they ask about text, all signal their students about how to read. If the assigned activities are well designed, however, they allow students to live a little longer under the spell of a good book.

A child's first response is spontaneous, perhaps a chortle of glee when a board book has tickled her fancy. Children are social, however, and learn from the reactions of others. What adults do as they read lets children know what might be appropriate for them to do. As they grow, children learn what is sanctioned and what is not, both in and out of the classroom. As they learn, children grow as readers and responders, moving from pleasure, to understanding, to conscious appreciation (Early, 1960). Even very young children have rich and diverse responses to what they read.

Lawrence Sipe, a professor at the University of Pennsylvania, spent 7 months in a literature-rich first/second grade classroom, recording the conversations students had following the teacher's reading of picture storybooks. Sipe (2002) discovered that students' spontaneous responses to the books their teacher read aloud included textual analysis, making intertextual connections, making personal connections, engaging with the story so completely that they were "living" it, and using the story as the basis for creative expression. Sipe suggests that the students demonstrated rather impressive abilities in literary criticism. This study increases our understanding of the literary capabilities of young readers.

Developing Possibilities for Response to Literature

Response to literature is the term used to describe what happens in the mind during reading or listening to literature, especially stories and poems. It also refers to comments readers make about literature and the activities they engage in after reading or listening to literature. In the classroom, teachers can see children's responses to literature by noticing the books they choose, the comments they make, the stories they write, and the activities they select. Whereas teachers can only infer thoughts and feelings from what their students say or do, they can learn a great deal by sensitively observing their responses when reading. Effective literature-based teachers develop structures that allow them to do just that.

STRUCTURING OPPORTUNITIES FOR RESPONSE

A curriculum that provides numerous opportunities for students to read and respond to literature, both fiction and nonfiction, develops good, responsive readers. Response-rich instructional programs are those in which teachers value the uniqueness and diversity of what children have to say about a book, and know the importance of peers in shaping reading and responding. These classrooms are safe places for students to learn to be responsive readers.

You can develop a response-rich classroom in many ways. What you do depends upon the values you hold, the choices you make, and the resources at your disposal. Teachers with open access to a wide range of children's books will do different things than will teachers who have limited access to fewer books. Teachers who are required to use a reading textbook, or **basal,** will structure their curriculum to include basal materials as supplements to the literature they use. Many teachers combine a literature-based approach with the basal series that their system has adopted. Others build their entire program on trade books. Some teachers use literature programs based entirely on children's own selections; some pursue programs in which students study the same book through teacher-guided discussions; some use a program in which students select books and engage in follow-up activities; and some use a combination of these approaches. No matter how they structure it, teachers who guide children to become responsive readers provide their students with countless opportunities to read a wide variety of literature and to talk with others about that literature. The *Teaching Idea: Ways to Promote Reading Communities* gives other ideas.

Many teachers use a combination of individual, whole-class, and small-group instruction, structuring these combinations in a variety of ways. The most frequently selected structures in literature-based programs are workshops, literature circles, and Book Clubs.

Reading workshops

Similar to writing workshops, discussed in Chapter Eight, reading workshops involve teachers beginning a session with a brief, whole-class lesson, moving to independent reading time, and then to some kind of sharing activity, either oral or written. Workshops are highly structured, yet allow students the opportunity to pursue their individual reading interests. Of course, a teacher

TEACHING IDEA

Assessing the Learning Environment

WAYS TO PROMOTE READING COMMUNITIES

You can encourage your students to become a community of readers in several ways:

1. Give students a designated time and place to discuss books.
2. Create a book review index.
3. Provide whole-class experiences that can become response options for small groups.
4. Structure some experiences that revolve around small groups reading together.
5. Encourage pairs of children to read together.
6. Encourage student-to-student dialogue journals.

might choose to assign reading during workshop time, but most workshop teachers are passionate about offering students choice in what they read. Students learn to expect to learn something about reading or literature at the beginning of workshop time, to have time to read, and to share their reading in some way. The mix of student choice, independent reading, and time to share with others is valued by workshop teachers. Recent research on middle school readers supports the use of a workshop framework. Ivey and Broaddus (2000) suggest that teachers of middle school readers should focus on independent reading, provide access to a variety of reading materials, and learn about students' reading abilities and interests. These research-based guidelines are all met in a literature-based classroom with a reading workshop structure.

Literature circles

Literature circles involve students in small, collaborative groups reading either the same or closely linked texts, discussing them, and working together on some kind of response activity. Literature circles highlight the social nature of reading and responding (Day, Speigel, McLellan, & Brown, 2002). They provide structured opportunities for students to talk through the ideas and problems they encounter while reading, to present their own ideas, and to consider the ideas of others—all of which results in producing more competent, critical readers. Teachers or students can organize the circles and select the books. Circles often meet without a teacher, but teachers can also participate in the discussions, using them as an opportunity to teach lessons about reading or literature, as discussed in Chapter Five.

Book Club

Book Club is an organizational framework that is structured, based on current theory and research about reading and responding, and has proven effective from second grade through middle school. Created by a collaboration of university researchers and classroom teachers (McMahon, Raphael, Goatley, & Pardo, 1997; Raphael, Kehus, & Damphouse, 2001; Raphael, Pardo & Highfield, 2002), Book Club features four components: reading, writing, small-group discussions (called book clubs), and community share. Book Club time often begins with a short whole-class lesson. These range from lessons on procedures, to those on comprehension strategies, to those on literary structures. Then students spend a significant amount of time reading, either independently, in pairs, or with the help of a tape recorder or the teacher. This reading time might also feature the teacher or a student reading aloud. Books usually are selected by the teacher, with some input from students. The whole class might read one book, or the Book Club groups might read different books that are thematically linked. After reading time, students write in response to what they have read. They use reading logs that often contain prompts and "think sheets" for written and graphic responses. Writing is followed by meeting in their small student-led book clubs to discuss the reading. This sequence of reading-writing-discussion allows students to form some individual ideas and responses to their reading and then to share them with others. Book club discussions are followed by community share time in which the teacher brings up interesting ideas or problems that arose during the discussions. To do this, the teacher must circulate as the students are discussing. The *Teaching Idea: Internet Resources for Literature-Rich Classrooms* lists some Internet resources that you can use to select books for your own Book Clubs.

These three basic structures provide varied opportunities for language use, both oral and written, and can be structured to accommodate thematic, literary, or author studies, or to link to another area of the curriculum, depending on the materials selected.

Teachers, curriculum committees, and developers of developmental reading programs identify literature that represents themes, genres, and

TEACHING IDEA

Making Use of Technology

INTERNET RESOURCES FOR LITERATURE-RICH CLASSROOMS

One of the most difficult, although also the most enjoyable, things that literature-based teachers have to do is find the right books for their students. There are many Internet resources that can help you, among them:

www.carolhurst.com/
www.hbook.com/
www.cbcbooks.org/navigation/teaindex.html
www.reading.org
www.scils.rutgers.edu/special/kay/author.html
www.acs.ucalgary.ca/~dkbrown/index.html
www.ipl.org/
www.ala.org/yalsa/
www.ala.org/alsc/
www.ala.org/BookLinks/
www.csusm.edu/campus_centers/csb/
www.yahooligans.com/School_Bell/Language_Arts/Books/
www.riverbankreview.com/
www.multiculturalchildrenslit.com
www.coe.ohio-state.edu/edtl/llc/cm.html

notable authors, as well as literature that presents reading opportunities that might stretch or strengthen students' reading ability. They select literature that reflects local cultures and universal themes. Exposure to classics, distinguished authors, and outstanding contemporary publications is not left to chance. At other times, students choose what they want to read. Decisions about what to read reflect teachers' values, talents, resources, and the particular needs of their students.

Response-rich structures in action

Individual teachers adapt these basic structures to suit the needs of their students. For example, in Betty's first grade classroom children select freely from the hundreds of books that she has collected and displayed across one long wall, down low so that her students can browse easily. As students read individually and in pairs, Betty moves around the room, stopping to hear individuals read, and noting what they've selected and what strategies they are using as they read. When independent reading is over, she gathers students into a group and reads aloud to them, selecting books with strong patterns, books that are songs, books that lend themselves to dramatic reenactment, or books that contain examples of word patterns, sentence structures, or literary elements that she wants to teach. Often, these books are in the form of "big books," so the students can follow along with the words as she reads. Betty teaches phonics lessons, and comprehension strategy lessons as well, during whole-class time. Students have ample opportunity to respond to what they

Bernice Cullinan

A good collection of books arranged to be accessible to students is a must in any literature-based classroom.

read through their writing, oral language activities (especially drama), song, and discussion. Almost all of her students, many of whom did not even recognize all of the letters of the alphabet at the beginning of the year, are reading at grade level by the end of the year. Betty also sends books home with her students. The *Teaching Idea: Sharing Books, Sharing Ideas* offers tips about sending books home.

In another classroom Lisa, the second grade teacher featured in Chapter Five, works within six thematic units organized around the basal series she is using. The basal, which the students call their "literature book," is just one resource among many, as Lisa has collected many trade books to construct activities that allow students to explore the themes. Students read these books at home or in class, and Lisa reads aloud to the group quite often, beginning with picture books and quickly moving on to chapter books. Each day the students have an opportunity to discuss what they are reading, either telling each other about different books or talking about the book they are reading together.

TEACHING IDEA

Home/School Connection

SHARING BOOKS, SHARING IDEAS

Sharing books with children is an important way for parents to support their children's literacy development. You can help parents become involved by doing the following:

1. Provide parents with tips for reading aloud that they might not have considered. For example, during a parent-teacher visit or in a newsletter sent home, tell parents the following:
   - Pick a quiet and comfortable spot and read on a regular basis.
   - Before they read a new book, study the cover and discuss with their child the title, the author, and what the book might be about.
   - During the reading, point out interesting pictures, interesting words, interesting ideas. Wonder about what might be happening and what might happen next.
2. Send home a journal for students and parents to write in after reading, then write back the following day.
3. Send a book and a packet of post-it notes for children and parents to mark pages that children might want to talk about the next day.
4. Help parents with limited literacy skills by sending books and tapes home, and by providing them with information about adult literacy programs they might want to join.

In a third grade classroom, Terry works with her students in guided reading groups. They also have regular chunks of time for independent reading, and she reads aloud to them several times a day. No one is ever without a book, and no one is ever bored! Marianne Marino, featured at the beginning of this chapter, organizes her instructional time within a workshop framework, with students reading, writing, and talking together. Susan works with her fifth-graders using a Book Club framework in which she begins with a brief lesson, moves to individual reading and writing about what has been read, then to small-group student-led discussions, and ends with a whole-class teacher-led discussion. Rose, who teaches seventh grade, also uses a workshop framework, beginning with a brief lesson, moving into writing or reading independently, and sometimes including peer or teacher conferences. Each of these classrooms operates and looks quite different from the others, but they have several things in common: a knowledgeable teacher who serves as an enthusiastic guide, an environment that encourages social interaction about books, a structure that allows students to make choices about what they will do with books, and both the time and the materials to allow students to read and respond to what they read. Figure 7.1 details the characteristics of successful literature-based programs.

Classrooms with these characteristics are places in which students can learn to feel secure about their own responses, can explore the reasons for their responses, can accept diverse responses from peers, and can learn from those responses (Purves, Rogers, & Soter, 1995).

All of the above holds true for bilingual students, for students who speak a nonstandard dialect, and for those students for whom school might be a difficult and alien place. Books are not meant only for those children who have had experience with books. The very experience of reading, thinking, and talking about books makes some children successful in school right from the beginning. Roser, Hoffman, and Farest (1990) initiated a project in the Brownsville, Texas, school system in which they immersed 2,500 kindergarten, first, and second grade children, 80 percent of whom were Hispanic, in literature. Working with 78 classroom teachers, none of whom taught reading with literature or, indeed, did much reading aloud, they introduced about 750 different children's books, a variety of response activities, including writing, and some literature-based reading strategy lessons into the traditional Brownsville curriculum. At the end of their study, they analyzed California Test of Basic Skills scores and concluded that "a literature-based program can be implemented successfully in schools that serve at-risk students. Further, there is every indication that these students respond to such a program in the same positive ways as any student would—with enthusiasm for books, with willingness to share ideas, and with growth in language and literacy" (p. 559).

Chants, rhymes, books with strong rhythm, predictable language, and regular patterns help nonstandard speakers learn how to read in English.

FIGURE 7.1

Characteristics of Successful Literature-Based Classrooms

A Teacher Who Knows about

- Literature
- Children's cognitive and social development
- The lives of children in and out of the classroom
- The processes of reading, writing, and responding
- Options for effective organization
- Planning reflectively and responsively

An Environment That Is

- Safe and supportive
- Collaborative rather than competitive
- Accepting of a variety of individual strengths
- Balanced between individuals and the social group
- Structured fluidly for necessary change across time
- Based on meaningful and functional goals
- About process rather than product
- About the child rather than the curriculum

Student Choice about

- Books
- Reading options
- Focus of study
- Response options
- Time management

Time for

- Reading aloud each day on a regularly scheduled basis
- Students to read on their own, either individually or in pairs or small groups
- Students to respond to the books they read
- Students to discuss the books they read, either in pairs, in a response group, or during whole-class share
- Conferences between teacher and student or peers

Materials

- Lots of books—100 are not too many to have in your room
- A stable classroom collection added to by regularly rotating books from the school and public libraries as well as from student and teacher collections
- A variety of genres, authors, reading levels, topics, themes
- Materials for responding (art, writing, drama)

Paired reading, literature circles, and Book Clubs are beneficial reading configurations for bilingual students when they are paired with English-speaking readers. Sending books on tape home with bilingual students can involve the whole family in pleasurable experiences reading in English. The *Teaching Idea: Teaching for Diversity* describes a literature-rich program that includes sending books home and is quite effective in linguistically diverse first grade classrooms. Finally, reading materials in the students' home language also help students develop their reading ability.

STRUCTURING ACTIVITIES FOR RESPONSE

Just as teachers can structure a literature-based program in many ways, they also have many response options from which to choose. As teachers move among individual, whole-class, and small-group configurations, they can provide a variety of opportunities for response. These activities may ask for talk about text, dramatic and artistic response, or writing. Written activities have the advantage of providing a meaningful context for writing, linking reading and writing in a natural manner. Oral activities provide real reasons for students to shape their oral language to fit the demands of audience, context, and topic; they require students to recognize and adapt to different registers. Activities that require physical or visual expression, like movement, dance, and art, provide children with the opportunity to communicate without words, using the other symbol systems they have available to them. Figure 7.2 offers

TEACHING IDEA

Addressing Diversity

TEACHING FOR DIVERSITY

Faced with the challenge of more and more English language learners in the classroom, 16 teachers and their 162 first grade students, 105 of whom were English language learners speaking 16 different languages, participated in a study conducted by Koskinen and colleagues (2000) at the University of Maryland. They explored the impact of literature-rich classrooms and a reading-at-home program on the children's reading motivation, fluency, and comprehension. They discovered that book-rich classroom environments increased reading comprehension for these first grade students. Further, rereading books at home helped increase student motivation and parent involvement. English language learners who took books and audiotapes of the books home to reread reported practicing their reading more often than those who did not have the audiotapes. See also Garcia's summary (2000) of research on bilingual children's reading.

FIGURE 7.2

Options for Response Activities

Individual/Group: Written

Response journals
Patterned writing
Readers' Theatre
Letters to authors
Letters to or from characters
Story continuations or changes
Note taking
Report writing
Advertisements
Book review file
Formal comparisons of characters, books, authors, etc.
Timelines
Story maps
Reports of author study
Character collage
Literary report cards
Literary letters, advice columns
Clues and questions
Book awards
News reports
Plot profiles, sequencing
Literary interviews
Venn diagrams

Individual/Group: Visual

Art connected to the medium of the book
Art of choice, including various paints, collage, clay
Murals
Maps
Illustrations of the setting
Visual depiction of theme

Individual/Group: Oral

Drama
Role-playing
Storytelling
Puppetry
Flannel board
Debates
Trials
Retellings
Videos
Interviews with author, character, peer reader
Singing/chanting
Choral reading

options for response activities, and the *Teaching Idea: Critically Viewing a Favorite TV Program* involves students in the use of critical analysis as they view television programs.

Whatever teachers choose to do, good response activities are appropriate to a particular text and offer students the opportunity to explore both the text and their own responses. Effective response activities offer students opportunities to think about their **engagement** with the text by talking or writing about their emotions during reading. Students also need to think about the **connections** they make as they relate life and/or other experiences with books to the texts they read. Response activities that ask students to **describe** aspects of the text like characters or style, and to **interpret** symbols, characters' actions and

TEACHING IDEA

Home/School Connection

CRITICALLY VIEWING A FAVORITE TV PROGRAM

With parental permission, students can be assigned to watch a favorite television program on the same afternoon or evening. Have students critique the program in terms of the following:

- The overall message the show sends to viewers, especially children.
- The portrayal of main characters. How are they alike/different from people you know? Choose one character, describe him or her, and discuss how the show reveals what he or she is like (actions, dialogue, dress, and so on).
- Tell what motivates you to watch the show.
- If you had the opportunity to change the show, what might you change?
- If you chose to do something other than watch this or some other television show, what would it be?

intentions, and themes help students read more thoughtfully. Finally, asking students to **judge** the characters and the quality of the text requires that they step back from their reading and consider it critically (Beach, 1987). The *Teaching Idea: Creating a Character Collage* presents one idea for a response activity that asks students to describe and interpret characters.

The primary reason for response activities is to help students become more deeply involved with literature, to experience enjoyment of it, and to further develop the habit of reflecting upon their literary experience. Extensive analysis and cute projects are often time-wasting. Instead, effective teachers offer activities that allow students to engage thoughtfully with the texts they read.

Talk about text

As we discussed in Chapter Five, asking students to talk about books is one of the primary ways that effective teachers help their students become more skilled, knowledgeable readers. This talk can take the form of whole-class discussions, small-group discussions with the teacher present, or small-group discussions without a teacher present. As described in Chapter Five, effective teachers learn to ask the right questions to guide students as they work together to make sense of texts. Listening to students talk about text is also an important way to assess students' comprehension and literary understanding.

TEACHING IDEA

Literature Link

CREATING A CHARACTER COLLAGE

Character collages help students recognize character traits and understand relationships among characters. To create a collage, students must describe characters and interpret their actions and motivations. Character collages are effectively introduced as a group project although they are also viable options for individual response.

To create a character collage, students must consider the following:

- Who is the main character? [Put that character's name or a visual representation of that character in the center of the paper.]
- What is the character like? [Write descriptive words under the name or surround the image of the character with other images that reflect the character's traits.]
- Who else is important in the story? [Put the names or images of other characters around the center image.]
- How does each character feel about the main character? [Draw an arrow from each character to the main character, and write words or add images that indicate these feelings on the side of the arrow.]
- How does the main character feel about the minor characters? [Draw another arrow from the main character to each of the minor characters and write words or add images that indicate these feelings on the side of the arrow.]

The *Teaching Idea: Questions to Ask during a Book Conference* offers suggestions for questions that you might ask during a book conference, one important opportunity for ongoing assessment.

In Lisa's second grade class, her group of twelve are talking about text even as they work together to understand what they are reading. They are reading Sid Fleischman's *The Whipping Boy* and trying to understand how Prince Brat, one of the main characters, is feeling. In the following conversation they build upon one another's ideas to reach a rather profound understanding of character motivation, theme, and humanity in general.

Lisa: That's interesting, Maria. So you're saying that he's almost thinking it's better to stay where he is than to get his freedom and to have to risk it on the streets or possibly go back to the castle.

Sarah: I think the prince didn't want to go back.

Chris: I think he [the prince] likes him [Jemmy, the other main character].

Brett: I think they're gonna be friends.

TEACHING IDEA

Assessing the Learner

QUESTIONS TO ASK DURING A BOOK CONFERENCE

The following questions initiate discussions that extend and strengthen children's comprehension, and provide natural opportunities for you to assess your students.

1. Tell me about what you are reading.
2. How did you decide to read this?
3. Are there parts that are confusing? What are they?
4. If you could talk with the author, what would you say?
5. Does this remind you of anything else you have read? What? How?
6. Who else would enjoy reading this book?
7. What else have you read by this author? How does this book compare?
8. How do you think [the main character] felt?
9. What would you have done [in discussing the main character's actions]?
10. What do you think will happen next?
11. Remind me of what happened next.
12. Do you think this story could really happen?
13. Does this story remind you of anyone or anything you've experienced?

It's also easy to ask a student to read a passage aloud. This gives you opportunities to assess their fluency.

Cameron: In the inside he likes him, but on the outside he's just mean.

Lisa: Mmmm. What does that mean, Cameron? I understand what you're saying about the inside is different from the outside, but why do you think that is?

Sarah: You can always be good on the inside, but be bad on the outside.

Cameron: Like a good heart, but on the outside there's a bad heart.

Lisa: Why would we only be seeing the outside of him?

Brett: I don't think he likes anyone to know that he likes Jemmy.

Jasmyn: Maybe he just wants people to know that on the outside. Like he likes him on the inside, but he actually doesn't know how to tell everybody he does. (Galda, Rayburn, & Stanzi, 2000, p. 81)

In this conversation the students build on the ideas that others offer, Lisa summarizes and clarifies what she hears them saying, and the result is an enhanced understanding of the hidden complexities of character. As they continue to have conversations of this nature, they add to their individual comprehension of the text as they are reading, and to the possibilities for response.

Extending response through drama and art

Besides book discussions, other oral activities involve drama and choral reading, as discussed in Chapter Five. Visual response activities such as art and movement, along with dramatic renditions, invite students to work closely with a text to translate their reading experience into another form of communication. Some, such as dramatic performances, require close attention to aspects such as plot and character motivation and development as well as style. Others, such as painting or drawing, involve students in depicting an aspect of the text in great detail, or in expressing the overall emotional impact in one glorious product.

Writing about text

Just as with talking about text and responding with drama and art, writing about text asks students to return to the text and consider their experience. Many kinds of writing experiences work well in a response-rich classroom. Some might occur frequently, others are cumulative activities.

Written response activities

Taking notes, creating story maps and timelines, writing genuine letters to authors, and writing formal papers that compare characters or books are some examples of writing in response to what is being read. The standard "book report" format has been replaced by a variety of interesting written options. Teachers who are concerned about developing their students' repertoires for response make sure to detail the many ways in which their students can demonstrate that they have read and understood a book. Even a simple activity, such as a book review file, can have enormous repercussions.

Establishing a book review file is easy. Simply ask students to file a review of each book they have read. If they are the first to review a book, they create the master card with the author and title and other bibliographic information at the top. Many teachers ask students to include a note about where they got the book so that others can find it easily. The students then write a few sentences about the book, focusing on what they enjoyed. This card goes into a file that is accessible to the class. As others read the same book, they add their comments to the card. When students want ideas about what to read next, they can go to the file and read about books their classmates have enjoyed. This kind of written response activity asks for thoughtful, purposeful writing and reading on the part of students and builds on the social nature of reading and responding. It requires skill in summarizing and evaluating. As well as requiring higher-level thinking, reading, and writing skills, writing a few sentences summarizing and evaluating a book is actually much more difficult than skimming a book for the information needed to tell about the setting, plot, and characters as a traditional book report format requires. Rather than relying on one product to assess students' engagement with literature, we suggest that you observe them and keep track of the different responses they engage in by looking for the behaviors described in Figure 7.3.

Other writing activities, such as creating a story map or taking notes, function to help students develop and monitor their comprehension of text. In classrooms that employ Book Clubs, teachers often develop writing prompts that help students practice comprehension strategies and explore teacher-structured, alternative ways of responding. Response journals, a very popular form of writing about text, offer students the opportunity to monitor their comprehension, and also develop their responses.

The response journal

The **response journal** is perhaps the most common form of response visible in classrooms. Response journals are notebooks or folders in which students record their responses to the books they read. Many teachers give each student a spiral notebook or a composition book at the beginning of the year and tell them that a journal is a place to jot down thoughts during and after read-

FIGURE 7.3

Response Activities Teachers Often Observe

Janet Hickman (1980) observed students in an elementary school for four months. She found that the following are a good list of response activities that any classroom teacher might observe:

1. Listening behaviors (body stances, laughter and applause, exclamations, joining in refrains)
2. Seeking contact with books (browsing, showing intense attention, keeping books at hand)
3. Acting on the impulse to share (reading together, sharing discoveries)
4. Oral responses (retelling, storytelling, discussion statements, free comments)
5. Actions and drama (echoing the action, demonstrating meaning, dramatic play, child-initiated drama, teacher-initiated drama)
6. Making things (pictures and related artwork, three-dimensional constructions, miscellaneous products like games and displays)
7. Writing (restating and summarizing, writing about literature, using literary models deliberately, using literary sources unaware)

ing, commenting on what they are noticing, thinking, wondering, or feeling as they read.

Like diaries, journals are written in first person, but they are often shared, rather than private. The idea is to give students an opportunity to reflect upon what they read, and to think about what it means to them. Writing in a journal helps students formulate ideas that they can then share with others. It also is a vehicle through which a teacher can teach and a student can learn.

The content of a response journal is determined by what students are reading and what it causes them to think about. Journals can take several different forms, but their primary purpose is to serve as a record of the initial thoughts and feelings that students have about what they are reading. Just as writing in a journal helps students formulate ideas that they bring to discussions, their discussions also influence how they respond to their reading. Lisa's students, for example, reflected on the "inside/outside" distinction that they discussed the next time they wrote in their response journals. Teachers often provide a format for journal entries like the questions presented in the *Teaching Idea: Questions for Response Journals,* or simply ask their students to write what they want to say about a book.

The amount of structure and support that teachers give students reflects what students are capable of doing on their own. If students record the date, title, and author of each book they finish reading on a tally sheet at the back of the journal, their reading progress is evident to anyone who looks.

TEACHING IDEA

Literature Link

QUESTIONS FOR RESPONSE JOURNALS

Asking questions such as these helps students learn how to respond to the books they read. Once they internalize these and other prompts, they can select freely as they write in their journals.

1. What is most important in this book?
2. What does this book remind me of [life or literary experience]?
3. How does this book make me feel?
4. Why did I choose to read this book?
5. What kept me reading this book?
6. What effect has this book had on me as a reader?
7. What questions would I like to ask the author?

Bernice Cullinan

Keeping an independent reading log allows the student and the teacher to assess progress.

In many literature-based classrooms children routinely write in their response journals at the beginning of each day, or sometime during the language arts block, or at the end of the day, or, perhaps, at home. Some write once or twice a week in connection with the book their literature circle is reading. Students in a Book Club classroom write after reading daily. What goes in the journal depends on the writer and reflects their development and interests. Kindergarten children may do no more than record what they have read and draw a happy face to indicate that they enjoyed it; eighth grade students may write pages about a character or a scene that they found particularly moving. Examples of journals that show how they vary appear in Figures 7.4, 7.5, and 7.6. Notice that the journal entries of the two youngest students also include art.

Response journals can serve a variety of purposes in addition to being a place for children to explore thoughts and ideas. They are instant records of what children are reading. They help children keep track of their choices and help them remember what they have read. They force children to think about what they are reading—it is hard to write if you do not think. They also can serve as the springboard to extended discussions and written responses about the books students are reading.

In some classrooms, journals are private, shared only at the discretion of the writer. In other classrooms, they are dialogues, written as letters to and from other students or the teacher. Teachers who use a reading workshop structure often require dialogue journals from their students. Dialogue journals

FIGURE 7.4

Excerpt from a Primary-Grade Journal

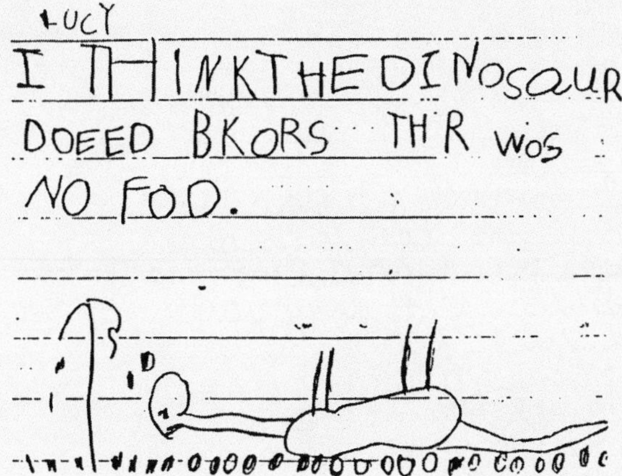

FIGURE 7.5

Excerpt from an Intermediate-Grade Journal

I like Reader workshop
a lot. Tomie chanch my
life becaseI never liket
to read but nowI love reAding
His books and nowIkant
Stop reding.

Maurizio

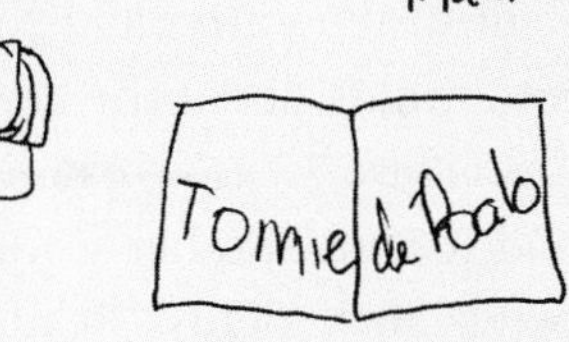

FIGURE 7.6

Excerpt from Sixth-Grader's Response Journal

3/4/86
2-04

I am still reading A
Star for the Latecomer
by Paul and Bonnie
Zindel. It's very sad
I just found out
Brooke's mom has
cancer. This book is
appealing to all readers.
Because it deals with
a problem faced today
by almost every family.
This book gets right to
the point. I wonder how
two authors write a book.
This one is, and so far it
is excellent. I remember
Dark Forces was a Concerned
book. It wasn't that good.
How do authors decide on
there ideas?

with the teacher establish a close reading relationship between teacher and student, give students an audience for the journal, and inform teachers of students' reading strategies, preferences, and concepts. The usual pattern of teacher-student dialogue journals is for the student to write letters to the teacher at specified time intervals—from once a week to daily. The teacher, in turn, reads and responds in writing, in the student's journal. The response should be to the content of the entry, and should end with a question that encourages the student to think about the book being read, or the process of reading and responding. Figure 7.7 is an example of a dialogue journal.

Peers can respond to one another using dialogue journals, effectively establishing bonds between students. Reading and responding to peers' responses establishes a community of readers who know and respect each other's choices, opinions, and feelings. These journals take the same form as teacher-student dialogue journals.

FIGURE 7.7

Dialogue Journal

5-21 I'm at the part when sarah goes to town. I'm afraid that Sarah won't come back. She might get on the train and go back to maine and the Ocean. Why do you think Sarah might leave? Do you think she loves Caleb and Anna? I worried about what she would do, too.	5-22 I was glad when sarah came home. I crid a little like Caleb did. I thought that she might come back becoule she left Sebil behind. Good for you! That's a clue MacLachlan left for us, isn't it! Were you happy at the end? I was! What do you want to read next? Let's talk.

Whatever form a journal takes, it is often the first thing that children do when they stop reading. Sometimes they may record responses as they read along in a text, sometimes when they have finished reading. Sometimes teachers ask students to write on one side of a double page, leaving the facing side blank so that they can go back and reread their response, commenting on their responses after they have completed reading and discussing the book. This type of journal is called a double-entry journal, and teachers use this effective tool to help older students reflect on their own thoughts and recognize how they change as they read and discuss their reading with others.

As you use journals in your classroom, you will develop your own strategies that serve to help your students grow as readers. The journal also helps them grow as writers because it provides a meaningful reason to write. It highlights the use of writing to learn, and the connection between reading, writing, and oral language. Further, writing about what they have read helps students become more discerning, thoughtful, and critical readers as they learn about how they respond and how literature works.

Developing Literary Understanding

Reading, talking, writing, and drawing about books are the ways in which students learn about literature. Teachers structure this learning in many ways. In Chapter Three, we presented ideas about looking closely at an author's works, exploring themes found in literature, and studying the art of writing as examples of ways in which teachers help students learn about literature. Here we add to those ideas by introducing genre study, to which we will return in Chapter Nine.

Why is it important to help students understand how literature works? Learning about literature is like learning about mathematics, or any other curriculum area. Literature is an art form worthy of study. Understanding how literature works allows readers full access into the "family of stories" (Moss & Stott, 1986). This, in turn, makes them more effective readers and writers, able to recognize and appreciate the techniques, structures, and artistic representations they encounter in print. At the same time, learning how literature works helps students become more skilled readers and writers. Knowing how a text works enhances both fluency and comprehension, and knowing options for expressing oneself in print increases one's options as a writer.

GENRE STUDY

Understanding genre distinctions and conventions, for example, helps students to realize the breadth of reading material available to them, to learn to recognize the hallmarks of excellence, and to understand how genre conventions both support and constrain writers. In Chapter Three, Figure 3.2 lists and defines the major content-based genres of children's literature: poetry, folklore, fantasy, science fiction, contemporary realistic fiction, historical fiction, biography, and nonfiction. Within these eight genres, many other distinctions can be made. Mysteries, for example, are a "subgenre" that contain the conventions of a mystery story, but they might be fantasy, science fiction, contemporary, or historical fiction as well. The same is true for other subgenres such as animal stories, romances, sports stories, and adventure stories. Picture books, a genre based on format in which illustrations have an equal or greater importance in the conveying of meaning as does the text, also appear within all of the eight major genres. Thus, you can approach genre study in many different ways, depending on the decisions you make about what your students are interested in, what they already know, and what they need to know.

Lisa, for example, realizes that her students have a fairly good understanding of the distinction between fantasy and realism in fiction by the time they reach her second grade classroom, but they are having difficulty recognizing and applying this distinction. She begins to ask her students to notice what is happening in the stories they read in terms of whether it is real or make-believe. They discuss, for example, how some writers begin their stories in the "real world," slowly drawing a reader into a fantasy world, whereas others just write the whole story in a fantasy world. As they grapple with Chris Van Allsburg's picture books, they will have to understand the fantasy/realism distinction in order to comprehend the story.

Once Lisa is satisfied that her students not only know the differences but can also recognize them in their reading and understand what the authors are doing, she complicates things by introducing the differences between contemporary realistic fiction and realistic historical fiction. Once they understand the present/past distinction they can compare the contemporary and historical realistic novels of Patricia MacLachlan, noting how her writing is similar and different across those two genres. When they begin reading nonfiction, Lisa complicates things even more by introducing books in which authors blur the genres of nonfiction and fantasy. For example, a book that students regard as nonfiction because it gives "facts" about a topic includes a fantasy fiction frame that propels a narrative in which facts are embedded. Joanna Cole's Magic School Bus books are a well-known example of this blurring of genre lines.

As Lisa works with her students around a theme of "Life Long Ago," she helps them build their understanding of the differences between what is "true," what is "real," and what is "pretend," and how different authors manipulate those ideas to get their point across. In order to understand the texts, students have to understand what is fact and what is fiction. They grow to appreciate how an author might embed facts within a narrative structure, and how that narrative structure could be realistic or fantasy. These second grade readers will eventually make quite sophisticated distinctions as they develop their understanding about genre conventions.

Many teachers of young children begin with the simple distinctions that Lisa begins with—contemporary or historical, realistic or fantasy, nonfiction or fiction. Even older students who have not had a rich diet of reading may need to consider these distinctions. Other teachers might explore other genre characteristics with their students, such as the variable characteristics of biography or nonfiction (Harvey, 2002). All biographies share the convention of being a story about the life or part of the life of a person living or dead, but they range along a continuum from being completely based on verifiable fact to containing a great amount of fictional material created by the author. This type of genre study not only helps students clarify their ideas about genre, it also develops their critical reading ability.

One of the many things genre study helps children learn about is style. Students who study folklore, for example, soon come to recognize how the oral language origins of folktales influence the way the tale is told in print.

Song, chants, repetition, and melodic phrases all attest to the spoken nature of the original tale. Students also learn to recognize the elements and motifs common to folklore, such as the beautiful, kind princess; the wicked stepmother; the brave prince; the clever fox; or the magic of three. Once students understand these conventions, they can begin to see how various authors incorporate folkloric elements and style in their own writing in other genres, noting, for example, the similarities and differences between fantasy and folklore.

Many teachers of grades 6–8 help their students notice structures that cross genres. The classic quest tale, for example, can be found across the genres of folklore, fantasy, science fiction, realistic fiction, and historical fiction. Recognizing the classic quest story embedded within different genre conventions gives students the opportunity to consider their reading in a different light.

Studying genre leads students to many different insights about literature, provides them a rich framework from which to construct their own writing, and helps them become more comprehending, critical readers. We discuss genre study as it relates to writing in Chapter Nine.

Balancing the Literacy Program

In many respects, a balanced literacy program is a lot like the folkloric elephant described by blind men who are each touching one particular part. What they "see" depends on what part they are touching. Balanced reading is similarly complicated, containing many aspects that create the kind of balanced instruction students need to develop as avid and responsive readers and thinkers.

In a very real sense, all of the chapters in this text relate in some way to a balanced reading program. The balance we seek consists of activities and instruction in reading, writing, listening, viewing, and speaking, for a wide range of purposes, with a wide range of texts. It includes instruction in word-level reading strategies such as that described in Chapter Six, and in text-level comprehension strategies, described below, as well as learning about literature and how it works. A balanced program offers opportunities for teachers to effectively utilize explicit instruction, teacher and peer coaching, and individual learning. Similarly, balanced instruction consists of whole-class, small-group, and individual learning experiences. Effective teachers pay attention to student motivation as well as achievement, and are careful to make use of the rich resource of children's literature as they plan their instructional program. Balance also involves writing, because reading and writing are inextricably intertwined in an effective literacy classroom. Finally, in a balanced literacy program, students both learn and practice the skills and strategies that they need to be successfully literate (Pressley, 1998).

Elsewhere in this text we discuss other components of a balanced literacy program. Here we focus on an important aspect of reading—comprehension of text. Reading is much more than decoding and fluency, and students continue to learn to read as they encounter new texts, both within and out of school. Even fluent readers need comprehension instruction if they are to become the powerful, critical readers that they are capable of becoming.

DEVELOPING COMPREHENSION

As children learn to decode text and develop increasing fluency, they also need to learn how to understand the texts they are reading. A child may read a text passage with few to no errors, and yet demonstrate little or no comprehension when questioned about the passage. Fortunately, through many studies of good readers, research helps us understand what good readers do in order to comprehend texts (Snow, 2002) and thus helps us identify the strategies that students need to learn. Comprehension involves using prior knowledge to predict, asking questions, creating mental images, clarifying confusions, summarizing during reading, and reflecting on what has been read. Perhaps most important, comprehension involves self-monitoring of understanding while reading (Blanchowicz & Ogle, 2001; Pressley, 1998). Graves, Watts-Taffe, and Graves (1999) structure the essential strategies a little differently, but with the same core components: using prior knowledge, asking and answering questions, making inferences, determining what is important, summarizing, dealing with graphic information, imaging and creating visual representations, and monitoring comprehension. General characteristics of effective strategies are, they note, conscious efforts, flexible, applied only when appropriate, and widely applicable.

How are these strategies best taught? Certainly an important component of effective strategy instruction is an engaging text. Students are motivated to practice comprehension strategies when they want to be able to read and understand something important to them. Some hallmarks of effective instruction have been identified by researchers. Pressley (1998) describes what he calls "transactional strategies instruction," a highly effective way of teaching comprehension strategies: First, teachers explain and model the target strategy. Second, students practice the strategy as they read in "real" rather than artificially constructed texts while the teacher scaffolds. Third, the teacher gradually releases responsibility to the student, withdrawing support as the student gains in skill and confidence. Fourth, steps 1–3 occur over time—months, if not years. Effective comprehension strategies are not learned in a day or even weeks. Fifth, teachers teach their students to monitor their comprehension, to be metacognitive about their comprehension. Sixth, teachers encourage students to read extensively to improve their fluency, increase their background knowledge, and develop the habit of reading (Pressley, 1998). Figure 7.8 suggests a reading-comprehension monitoring strategy for helping students

FIGURE 7.8

Reading-Comprehension Monitoring Strategy

Benefits

- Helps students deal with difficult content-area texts
- Helps students deal with long passages on high-stakes tests

Before Reading

1. Note vocabulary and concepts that you anticipate may be troublesome to your students.
2. Guide students through a quick preview of the chapter or passage, noting headings.
3. Help students predict what the selection might be about. Interject key vocabulary words and concepts into the discussion.

During the Reading

4. Model the process. After introducing the selection, read aloud the first paragraph or two, as students follow along. Reflect on one or two things you learned, or wonder about, from the passage.
5. Guide students to participate in the process with strong support. Have students read the next paragraph or two silently. Ask one student to read aloud. Call on students to summarize what they learned or to tell one new thing they learned from the passage. Discuss what students have shared and then continue with the next paragraph or two.
6. Guide students to participate in the process with less support. Have students read the next paragraph or two silently. Ask one student to read aloud. Have students write their key points on paper or sticky notes. Share and discuss what students have written.
7. Continue with decreasing support. Have students read silently. Eliminate oral reading. Have students write key point independently. Share and discuss what students have written. Students continue reading and writing independently.

After Reading

8. Use the key points gathered throughout the reading and discussion of the selection to review important ideas and things to remember.

Notes

- During discussion, encourage students to use the new vocabulary they have learned from the selection.
- Students may volunteer their contributions individually or they may collaborate in pairs or small groups and then share with the class.
- Key ideas may be recorded on chart paper or a whiteboard and used for the summary discussion.
- After the chapter or passage is introduced, struggling readers may be pulled aside for close support using this strategy, while others work independently.

understand difficult content-area texts or long passages such as those found in the high-stakes tests most students are now required to take.

Using this general description, we can see how instruction in these strategies fits nicely with some of the instructional designs we have presented. For example, Book Club lends itself very well to a balanced literacy program that focuses on comprehension strategies. The opportunity for whole-class instruction before reading allows teachers to explain and demonstrate whatever comprehension strategy students need to learn. Reading time allows students to practice the strategy, and writing allows them to reflect on their understanding. The writing prompts that Book Club teachers often provide students can easily serve as a vehicle for encouraging application of a strategy. For example, a prompt might ask students to think about what they already know about a character and situation and predict what happens next, or a prompt might ask students to note places in the text where they were confused, or to generate questions that they want to answer. Book Club discussions offer students a chance to express their own understandings, evaluating them in light of their classmates' ideas. This is often a time in which students go back into a text to clarify or support arguments. They also help one another resolve difficulties by clearing up misunderstandings. Community sharing can extend these discussions or provide another opportunity for you to touch on comprehension strategies in action.

Having a variety of strategies to teach, knowing that the teaching and learning of these strategies may take years and a lot of practice, and understanding that different texts and situations require different emphases makes strategy instruction seem quite complicated—and it is. But, it is also vital. Graves and colleagues (1999) help simplify our thinking about strategy instruction by pointing out that there are only three times in any reading event in which a teacher can offer instruction: before, during, and after reading. They describe how a "scaffolded reading experience" can be structured.

A prereading experience can consist of activities to motivate and set purposes for reading, activate background knowledge, build text-specific knowledge, teach vocabulary and concepts, relate reading to students' lives, help focus the reading process, and suggest already-known strategies (Graves et al., 1999, p. 140). During reading, activities consist of silent and oral reading, providing cues to students as they are reading when appropriate, modifying the text if necessary. These activities, of course, depend on the students, the texts, and the purpose for reading (pp. 147–149). Postreading activities include many of the activities we present in this text: discussion, drama, writing, artistic responses, and related activities such as field trips (pp. 152–155). Again, these activities easily fit into a Book Club, reading workshop, or literature circle framework, as well as a guided reading framework.

Effective, balanced literacy instruction requires an active, involved teacher who knows the needs of the students, the demands of the curriculum, and the processes and strategies that make a difference. Such a teacher offers students experiences that help them understand that people read for a variety of purposes, helps students develop skill in responding to the texts they read, and helps students develop a variety of strategies for comprehending texts.

SUMMARY

Classrooms that offer students rich reading material, time and choice, and many opportunities for response, both structured and nonstructured, allow students the opportunity to become more engaged, responsive readers. Reading workshops, literature circles, and Book Clubs are three structures that support students' development as responsive readers. Within these structures, students have opportunities to talk about books with others, both peers and teachers, to respond through dramatic and artistic activities, and to write in a variety of ways for a variety of purposes. As students read and respond, effective teachers help them develop their understanding of how literature works. Effective teachers also help students develop and use comprehension strategies that enable them to continue to grow as effective, critical readers.

ACTIVITIES

1. **Write your own reading autobiography.** To help you understand yourself as a reader, ask and answer the following questions:

    - When and how did I learn to read?
    - What kinds of books did I like to read when I was young?
    - What kinds of books do I like to read now?
    - What is the most memorable experience with books that I had as a child?
    - Who were and are my favorite authors?
    - What is it about their books that makes them favorites?
    - When and where do I like to read now?
    - For what purposes do I read now?

2. **There is a heated debate between people who would allow children complete freedom of choice in the books they read and those who would insist that children be exposed to a literary canon of "good" books. In a paper or in class, discuss your position.** What are the implications for practice from both positions?
3. **Spend some time in an intermediate-grade classroom observing the literacy block.** Note what books children have access to, what activities

they engage in, what opportunities for assessment are available. Notice also the opportunities for both literary and reading instruction that occur. Describe what you have seen to a classmate and discuss.

4. **Select a genre that you enjoy and develop a series of discussion questions and other activities that might help young readers develop their understanding of that particular genre.**
5. **Select a book that you enjoy and develop a series of writing prompts that will help students develop their strategies for response, their literary understanding, and their comprehension strategies.**

FURTHER READING

Galda, L., & Cullinan, B. E. (2002). *Literature and the child* (5th ed.). Belmont, CA: Wadsworth.

Garcia, G. E. (2000). Bilingual children's reading. In M. L. Kamil, P. B. Rosenthal, P. D. Pearson, & R. Barr (Eds.), *Handbook of reading research, 3,* 813–824. Mahwah, NJ: Erlbaum.

Graves, M. F., Watts-Taffe, S. M., & Graves, B. B. (1999). *Essentials of elementary reading* (2nd ed.). Needham Heights, MA: Allyn & Bacon.

Hill, B., Johnson, N., & Noe, K. (1995). *Literature circles and response.* Norwood, MA: Christopher-Gordon.

Pressley, M. (1998). *Reading instruction that works: The case for balanced teaching.* New York: Guilford.

Raphael, T. E., & Au, K. H. (Eds.) (1998). *Literature-based instruction: Reshaping the curriculum.* Norwood, MA: Christopher-Gordon.

Raphael, T. E., Kehus, M., & Damphousse, K. (2001). *Book Club for middle school.* Lawrence, MA: Small Planet.

Raphael, T. E., Pardo, L. S., Highfield, K., & McMahon, S. I. (2002). *Book club: A literature-based curriculum.* Lawrence, MA: Small Planet.

REFERENCES

Anderson, R. C. (1977). The notion of schemata and the educational enterprise. In R. C. Anderson, R. J. Spiro, & W. E. Montague (Eds.), *Schooling and the acquisition of knowledge* (pp. 415–431). Mahwah, NJ: Erlbaum.

Beach, R. (1987). Strategic teaching in literature. In B. F. Jones, A. S. Palincsar, D. S. Ogle, & E. G. Carr (Eds.), *Strategic teaching and learning: Cognitive instruction in the content areas.* Alexandria, VA: Association of Supervision and Curriculum Development.

Blanchowicz, C., & Ogle, D. (2001). *Reading comprehension.* New York: Guilford Press.

Day, J., Speigel, D. L., McLellan, J., & Brown, V. (2002). *Moving forward with literature circles.* New York: Scholastic.

Early, M. J. (1960). Stages of growth in literary appreciation. *The English Journal, 49,* 161–167.

Feitelson, D., Kita, B., & Goldstein, Z. (1986). Effect of listening to series stories on first graders' comprehension and use of language. *Research in the Teaching of English, 20,* 339–356.

Galda, L., Rayburn, S., & Stanzi, L. C. (2000). *Looking through the faraway end: Creating a literature-based reading curriculum with second graders.* Newark, DE: International Reading Association.

Graves, M. F., & Graves, B. B. (1994). *Scaffolding reading experiences: Designs for student success.* Norwood, NJ: Gorden.

Graves, M. F., Watts-Taffe, S. M., & Graves, B. B. (1999). *Essentials of elementary reading* (2nd ed.). Boston: Allyn & Bacon.

Harvey, S. (2002). Nonfiction inquiry: Using real reading and writing to explore the world. *Language Arts, 80,* 12–22.

Hepler, S., & Hickman, J. (1982). "The book was okay. I love you"—social aspects of response to literature. *Theory into Practice, 21,* 271–283.

Hickman, J. (1980). Response to literature in a school environment. Paper presented at the Impact of Child Language Development on Curriculum and Instruction, National Council of Teachers of English Annual Meeting.

Ivey, G., & Broaddus, K. (2000). Tailoring the fit: Reading instruction and middle school readers. *The Reading Teacher, 54,* 68–78.

Koskinen, P. S., Blum, I. H., Bisson, S. A., Phillips, S. M., Creamer, T. S., & Baker, T. K. (2000). Book access, shared reading, and audio models: The effects of supporting the literacy learning of linguistically diverse students in school and at home. *Journal of Educational Psychology, 92,* 23–36.

Langer, J. (1990). The process of understanding: Reading for literary and informative purposes. *Research in the Teaching of English, 24,* 229–259.

Marshall, D. (2000). Research on response to literature. In M. L. Kamil, P. B. Mosenthal, P. D. Pearson, & R. Barr (Eds.), *Handbook of reading research, 3,* 381–402. Mahwah, NJ: Erlbaum.

McMahon, S. I., & Raphael, T. E. (with V. J. Goatley & L. S. Pardo). (1997). *The book club connection.* New York: Teachers College.

Morrow, L. M., & Weinstein, C. S. (1982). Increasing children's use of literature through program and physical design changes. *Elementary School Journal, 83,* 131–137.

Moss, A., & Stott, J. C. (1986). *The family of stories: An anthology of children's literature.* New York: Holt.

Pressley, M. (1998). *Reading instruction that works: The case for balanced teaching.* New York: Guilford Press.

Purves, A., Rogers, T., & Soter, A. (1995). *How porcupines make love III: Readers, text, cultures in the response-based literature classroom.* White Plains, NY: Longman.

Raphael, T. E., & Au, K. H. (1998). *Literature-based instruction: Reshaping the curriculum.* Norwood, MA: Gorden.

Raphael, T. E., Kehus, M., & Damphousse, K. (2001). *Book Club for middle school.* Newark, DE: International Reading Association.

Raphael, T. E., Pardo, L. S., & Highfield, K. (2002). *Book Club: A literature-based curriculum* (2nd ed.). Newark, DE: International Reading Association.

Rosenblatt, L. M. (1938). *Literature as exploration.* New York: Appleton Century. (New York: Modern Language Association, 1983 [4th ed.].)

______. (1978). *The reader, the text, the poem: The transactional theory of the literary work.* Carbondale, IL: Southern Illinois University Press.

______. (2003). Literary theory. In J. Flood, D. Lapp, J. R. Squire, & J. Jensen (Eds.), *Handbook of research on teaching the English language arts,* 67–74. Mahwah, NJ: Erlbaum.

Roser, N., Hoffman, J., & Farest, C. L. (1990). Language, literature, and "at-risk" children. *The Reading Teacher, 43,* 554–559.

Sipe, L. R. (2002). The construction of literary understanding by first and second graders in oral response to picture storybook read-alouds. *Reading Research Quarterly, 35,* 252–275.

Snow, C. (2002). *Reading for understanding: Toward an R&D program in reading comprehension.* Report of the Rand Reading Study Group. Arlington, VA: Rand.

Spiegel, D. (1998). Reader response approaches and growth of readers. *Language Arts, 76,* 41–48.

Strickland, D. S., Ganske, K., & Monroe, J. K. (2001). *Supporting struggling readers and writers: Strategies for classroom intervention 3–6.* York, ME: Stenhouse.

Wells, G. (1986). *The meaning makers: Children learning language and using language to learn.* Portsmouth, NH: Heinemann.

CHILDREN'S LITERATURE REFERENCES

Fleischman, S. (1986). *The whipping boy.* New York: Greenwillow.

L'Engle, M. (1986). *Many waters.* New York: Farrar, Straus, Giroux.

Writing: Launching Children into Writing

CHAPTER OUTLINE

I*n Lesley Yeary's kindergarten during writing time, children are scattered throughout the room, busily engaged with language. Today Michael and Matthew are sitting at the computer, carefully word-processing their handwritten Ghostbusters Pop-Up Book. Lesley is circulating around the room, stopping to talk to Ruth, who is writing a book about vegetables. "Are you going to write about just the ones you like?" asks Lesley. "No," answers Ruth, "I'm going to write about some I don't like." Brittany and Maura, writing partners, are working together on a book about Snow White. They're working with folded, stapled pages, Maura on the left-hand side, Brittany on the right.*

Brittany: *How 'bout you make Snow White on one page and then I . . .*

Maura: *You ready? First we have to write the words—you know—like once upon a time there was a princess named Snow White that lived with her stepmother, the queen. You write* once upon a, *okay? [She begins drawing.]*

Brittany: *This is the good queen, the real mother.*

Maura: *I'm making the bad queen. She has rosy cheeks. She has to be a witch. She has a crown.*

Brittany: *She has brown hair. The real queen.*

Maura: *This is the step-queen. I'll make a blue dress.*

Brittany writes on her side of the page:

ONS TUPAN/A TAM/TAR WAS/A PANSS/N AdM/SND Wid

Maura writes:

She IvD/we her STAP/Moth The QueeN/N

Maura: *One day she . . . there was a hunter, a huntsman, he took Snow White into the forest and said, "The queen told me to kill you but I won't, I'll think of something." You write that part, okay?*

Brittany writes on her side of the page:

ONe/DAY/the/WAS/MAE.

Tricia is working on a shapes book. Cut in the shape of a giant crayon, each page contains a color word and a sentence, such as "Purple. Grapes are purple."

Key Standard

Teachers of language arts/reading have the knowledge and ability to help students develop competence in the skills and strategies involved in the writing process. Such teachers:

- Help students understand that composing is a process.
- Help students build competence in various aspects of the writing process to become effective writers.

To get a preview of Chapter 8 and learn about developing children's competence in writing, visit the Chapter 8 section of the accompanying *Language Arts* CD-ROM.

Mary and Jennifer are working on a rainbow story. Written conventionally, it reads: "Animals run from a forest fire. A rainbow comes back and saves them from the fire."

Ralph is working on dinosaur books. He runs back and forth to a poster that has names and pictures of various dinosaurs, with a trip for each letter in names like Stegosaurus: check the poster, run back and write "S," back to check the poster, run back and write "t", and so on. Then he draws a picture of each dinosaur he has listed, one per page.

Meanwhile, Ruth has completed her vegetables book and "reads" it to us: "This is lettuce in a bowl. This is cucumber in a bowl. Here's a red pepper. Here's tomato. Here's the salad dressing. I thought about my salad at my house."

Derek and Daniel are working together to make a train book, modeling their product on a book that Daniel has brought from home.

Michael and Matthew are still busy at the computer, beaming with pride at putting their book into "real" form. All except independent, self-sufficient Ruth are busily working with writing partners, and all are working hard, using each other and everything in the room as resources for their own writing. A happy buzz of busy children fills the air.

This is not an unusual sight in Lesley's classroom. Every day the children—and Lesley—are immersed in language, both oral and written, because they are engaged in meaningful encounters with print. This involvement has not happened by magic, or by accident, but because Lesley has carefully considered how children learn to be literate, both through her professional reading and her careful observation of her students. Over time, Lesley has developed effective ways to organize her classroom for language learning. She has attended conferences, read professional journals, talked with colleagues, and tried various ideas in her classroom. Her literacy curriculum is the result of her growth as a teacher, and is grounded in her meticulous planning, record keeping, and active teaching. Her students understand that

Bee Cullinan

Young children often use a combination of words and pictures when communicating in writing.

writing is a process and occurs over time. They relish their control over topics and forms and enjoy working together to craft their written words.

Teaching composition—helping children learn to communicate through writing—is a messy business. Writing is *not* orderly and linear—it *is* disorderly and recursive. As writers write, they pause, think about what they have said or are going to say, change what has been written, write more, reread and scratch out a word or two, change their minds about what they want to say next. The act of putting words down on paper forces a conscious attention to language that usually is not present in the oral language of informal social interaction, the kind of language use that children are comfortable with and good at.

How does a teacher take a class full of proficient speakers and help them become proficient writers? As discussed earlier, most children make the transition from oral language to print when they enter school. Here we consider how to help them develop as writers and refine their ability to capture their own experiences in print.

A classroom in which children are busily engaged in developing their writing ability looks the same as a classroom in which children are busily engaged in developing their reading ability. In both cases the children are actively pursuing meaningful ends as they practice the skills of reading and writing. In both cases there are lots of books and other materials as well as the time and space in which to use them. In both cases collaboration is fostered by oral interaction among the children. In both cases, too, there is a teacher who is knowledgeable, who is a reader and a writer, and who serves as guide in the process of becoming literate.

A Literature-Rich Environment

A school day that contains frequent and happy encounters with children's literature is part of an atmosphere conducive to the teaching and learning of composition. The opportunity to hear and read quality literature is an important component of a writing classroom. Just as children learn to talk in an atmosphere filled with talk, so too do they learn to write when they are surrounded by others' writing. Other people's written works serve as models. Children internalize a variety of styles, structures, and ideas while reading or being read to. While writing, all children draw on these experiences as readers to inform their own composition. Literature also serves as the occasion for writing, as in response journals, letters to authors, and Reader's Theatre.

The link between the literature children read and the compositions they write is sometimes unconscious and subtle, sometimes conscious and very direct, as they come to "read like writers" (Smith, 1983). The assumption is that by consciously noticing how other authors write, writers increase their own repertoire of options and thus improve their own writing ability. Teachers can bring about this conscious notice of other authors' choices in several ways. As they read to their students, they stop and savor an especially appealing phrase, description, or name. They encourage children to notice structural patterns by inviting them to chime in and read along. They explore different ways to express ideas as they read books that treat similar themes in different ways. They demonstrate "reading like a writer," consciously noting while reading aloud the choices writers make.

One common literature-related activity is writing in response to the books children read. As described in Chapter Seven, this activity not only helps students learn about themselves as readers and about the literature they read, but also helps them realize that they can discover what they know through writing. Practice in thinking through writing, which is essentially what responding in writing is all about, pushes writers to explain, illustrate, and examine their responses as they use writing as a tool for critical thinking about literature. It also provides meaningful practice in writing about experiences, in this case personal experiences with literature.

Many classroom teachers comment on how children naturally and easily incorporate literature into their lives, including their lives as writers. Betty's first grade students weave together the stories they tell, the stories they read, and the stories they retell, using their experiences with books as a scaffold on which to hang their own compositions. Karen's kindergarten students often respond during writing workshop to the books they hear read in read-aloud time, adding bits of their own lives to the pictures and text they create. Judy's fifth grade writers have a rich experience with historical fiction from which to draw in their own writing. Leslie asks her sixth grade students to think about the class books they read as they write, to learn about writing from writers whose books they enjoy. Children transfer characters and events directly from stories to their own writing, reshape stories to include themselves and their own lives, and use literature to make sense of their own life experiences through writing. The influence of literature on children's writing is pervasive and occurs with or without deliberate intervention by teachers.

As you read the following examples, notice words from stories that child readers have tucked inside their heads and used in their own writing. We consider these "borrowings" reflections of literature in children's writing.

> This is a storey a bout me, wen I snees the holl worlld spins a rouwnd wen I sneesthe flours blow awa and wen I snees the gras jumps. And wen I snees the holl room shacs. And wen I snees evereey botey ses Michael you are to louwd.

Notice the parallel construction and a sense of poetry in this piece. The repetition of "Wen I snees" brings a feeling of melody and rhythm to the way a 5-year-old expresses his view of his world.

The student who wrote the next example not only "borrows" a character from literature, he also adopts many of Donald Sobol's techniques, such as the use of clues, a quick and decisive resolution, and an opening for a sequel:

> Detective Brown Strikes again.
> Last evening at the park. A clown was kidnapped. But Detective Brown is determined to find the kidnapper. He has one clue so far. His clue is a note that the clown must have dropped so someone could find him. While Detective Brown kept walking and looking at the ground, he found some peanuts laid one behind the other. So he followed the track of peanuts being a smart Detective and it took him straight to a old, plus odd, looking house. Detective Brown automatically thought it was a trap. Mr. Brown a short, stubby, and a mighty brave guy heard noises coming from the house. Then a clown came running out the front two tall men right behind jumped out, pulled out his gun, and said "Stop"! I'm a detective putting this case away. "Oh", I almost forgot. The police cars drove up and got the kidnappers. From there the kidnappers were on the way to jail. Detective Brown smiled and said Another case solved. But what's ????? tomorrow . . .

It is clear that these writers experience many stories; they absorb the language, structure, and format of the stories they hear and use them in their writing. Because the language of literature differs from the language used in ordinary conversation, the source of this literary language becomes apparent. Many established authors report similar practices in their own writing, talking about trying on different writers' styles as they developed as writers.

This natural absorption of literary language into children's expressive language adds great power to their language repertoire (Lancia, 1997). The results are clear-cut: The writing of children who read quality literature reflects this quality. The writing of children who read controlled-language texts reflects the minimal nature of those texts. What a wonderful argument for a literature-rich classroom environment!

Meaningful Contexts for Language Use

Children learn to talk because talk is functional—it enables them to accomplish what they want to accomplish. A major impetus for learning to read and write is also functional—we learn to be literate because it enables us to do what we want and need to do. Facility with written language increases our ability to create meaning from experience, to communicate meaning, and to represent ourselves to others (Birnbaum, 1980). Studies of preschool children who were interested in, and practiced, reading and writing indicate quite clearly that children focus first on the meaning-making capacity of written language and later on the culturally mandated conventions it employs. Early writers understand the utility of written language; it has a real function for them: to convey meaning. In other words, writing and reading have real functions for children and these functions are meaning-based. Children learn conventions later as they realize that they need them to communicate with others. Children, for example, learn to spell conventionally, form letters correctly, and write legibly so that others can easily read and understand the texts they produce.

Writing can serve a variety of functions that span the entire curriculum, given thoughtful organization and planning. Writing helps readers discover and record their responses to what they read. It can be a powerful tool for both learning and presenting what is learned in science, social studies, and mathematics, as well. And it is only by writing that children learn to be writers. As teachers become familiar with the students in their classroom—with

Bernice Cullinan

Recipes, writing, reading, measuring, cooking, and eating go hand in hand.

their strengths, interests, and needs—they can make decisions about how to introduce meaningful contexts for writing. Amidst the specific nature of each individual student, however, there are some general developmental patterns.

How Children Develop as Writers

In general, young writers grow in their ability to **differentiate,** moving from global wholes to specifics. They grow in their ability to **decenter**—to take a variety of audiences into account. They develop in both the forms of writing that they use and the functions that these forms serve. Experimentation with a variety of forms leads to facility with a variety of forms. This development is not a linear acquisition of discrete strategies, however, but a series of "successive reorganizations" of strategies that have been a part of their writing from the beginning (Harste, Woodward, & Burke, 1984). Children add to their understanding of good writing as they develop, increasing both the number and the sophistication of their concepts about good writing (Calkins, 1986).

Describing general development does not in any way imply that young children are "deficient" in their writing abilities. As Newkirk (1985) argues, if we look closely at what children do with writing rather than look at what they do not do, we can see that even very young children produce—in a different but quite recognizable form—the same types of writing that adults produce.

Children write signs, arguments, excuses, and letters, all extended non-narrative writing, as well as the more familiar stories, lists, and poems. Newkirk argues convincingly that "children can appropriate a variety of written forms in addition to the story; they do so by attending to the demonstrations of written language surrounding them" (p. 598). Thus, assuming that children must begin with narrative may not be accurate. Newkirk goes on to show that, although children may not write for a variety of audiences, they do appropriate forms that address wide audiences:

> [I]t is misleading to claim that children are limited to immediate audiences or to subjects close to their immediate experience. Rather there seems to be a range of appropriation, a set of forms that young writers can use—some to address a known audience, some a more distant audience. Some are used to narrate what is happening, some to frame arguments or convey information. Developmental theories of writing development invariably underestimate this range of possibilities (p. 600).

Anna, the writer whose early approximations of letters and lists appear in Figures 8.1–8.3 (which you saw earlier in Chapter Six), produced the pieces that are reproduced in Figures 8.4–8.6 during her first years in school. Figures 8.7–8.9 are pieces that she wrote at the beginning of middle school. The forms she used at each age remained the same, whereas her control of the form, of the range of variations within it, and choice of content changed as she matured.

Many forms and purposes for writing are available to very young children, and they do not develop as writers in a linear fashion. Several quite diverse studies of writing development have found that there is no one sequence, no fixed path. It is virtually impossible to write a detailed curriculum for writing; writing is too messy, too variable, too subject to influence from the environment. Further, children seem to take what is being taught and abstract from that information their own hypotheses that they then test

FIGURE 8.1

Anna's Letter to Granny

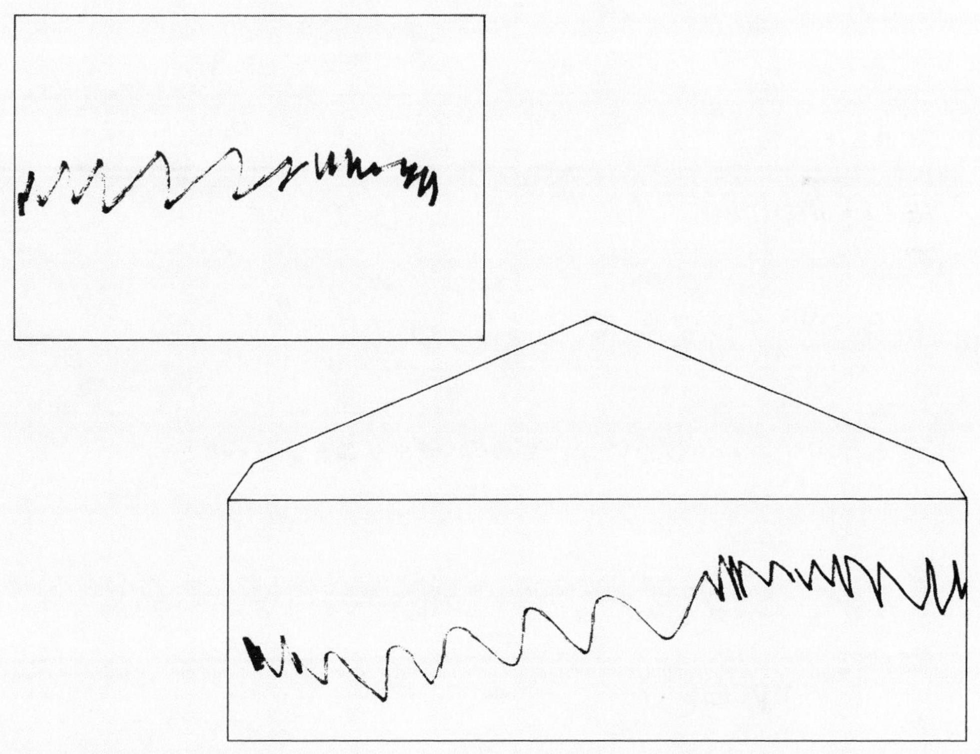

FIGURE 8.2

Anna's Letter to Mom

Mommy,

Sorry we had a hard time this morning!

FIGURE 8.3

Anna's Christmas List

FIGURE 8.2

Anna's Letter to Mom

FIGURE 8.3

Anna's Christmas List

Anna, the writer whose early approximations of letters and lists appear in Figures 8.1–8.3 (which you saw earlier in Chapter Six), produced the pieces that are reproduced in Figures 8.4–8.6 during her first years in school. Figures 8.7–8.9 are pieces that she wrote at the beginning of middle school. The forms she used at each age remained the same, whereas her control of the form, of the range of variations within it, and choice of content changed as she matured.

Many forms and purposes for writing are available to very young children, and they do not develop as writers in a linear fashion. Several quite diverse studies of writing development have found that there is no one sequence, no fixed path. It is virtually impossible to write a detailed curriculum for writing; writing is too messy, too variable, too subject to influence from the environment. Further, children seem to take what is being taught and abstract from that information their own hypotheses that they then test

FIGURE 8.1

Anna's Letter to Granny

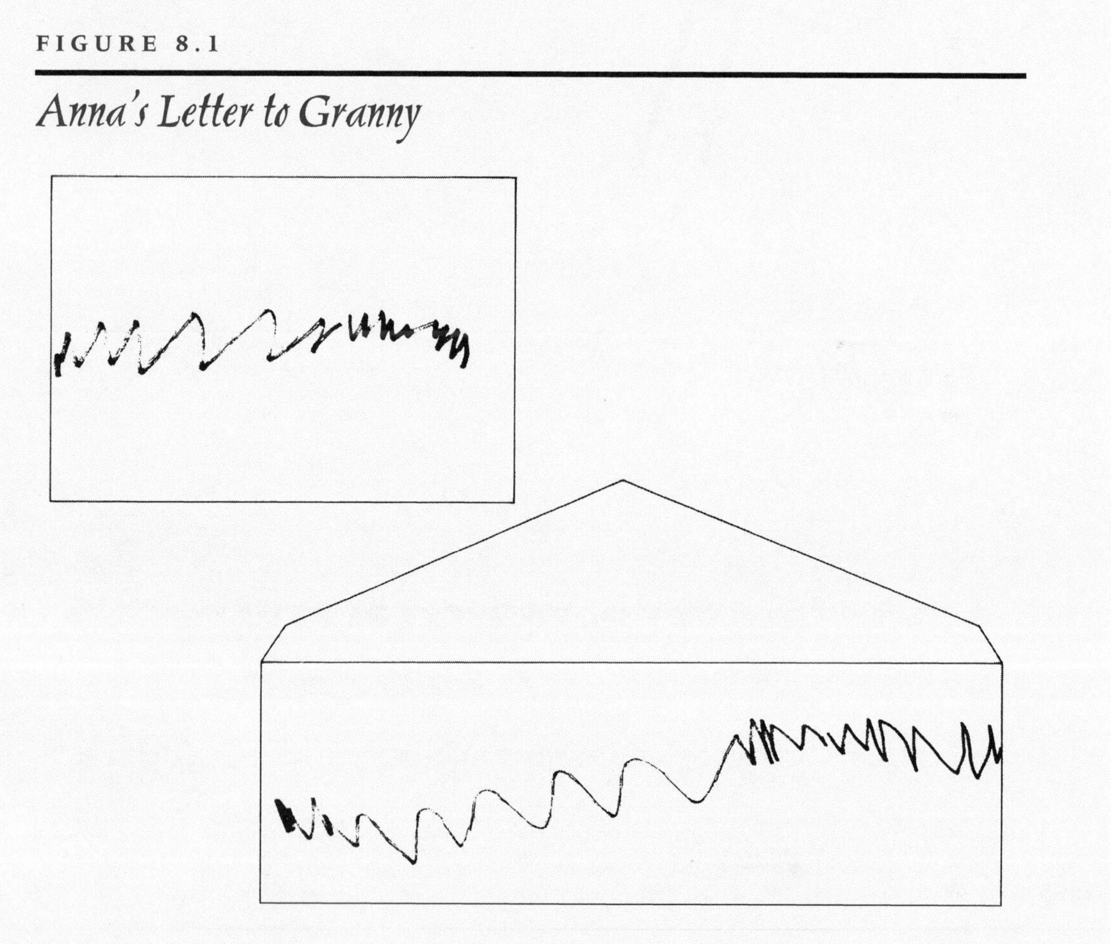

FIGURE 8.4

Anna's Story—Beginning of Elementary School

BY ANNA

Tony AND the Bed

Tony Got out of the Bed.
Tonys mum Got Him oatmeal.
Tony You Better Get Ready For school.
TONY Got Ready For Schol.
THE END!

FIGURE 8.5

Anna's Letter—Beginning of Elementary School

Dear ADAm, I ma at School
I will see you Atd School

HAPPy HalloWEEn

Love Anna

FIGURE 8.6

Anna's List—Beginning of Elementary School

and refine. They, in a sense, are learning more than they are being taught. At the same time, however, a general description of development is valuable for constructing reasonable expectations for student progress.

Several researchers, teachers, and professional writers have described a gradual movement from fluency to clarity to effectiveness (Mayher, Lester, & Pradl, 1983). However, young children are capable of grappling with concerns about clarity and effectiveness, and they do attend to these matters when they write. The following model is descriptive of the writing cycle of all writers; that is, writers begin by getting their words down. As they move through the cycle of drafts and revisions, they work toward clarity and effectiveness. As they develop as writers and work on various pieces, they attend to different issues in order to clarify their work. The skill of the writer, the form, the topic, the audience, and the context make for a complex interaction. Teachers work to develop writers who are fluent; confident of themselves as authors; knowledgeable

FIGURE 8.7

Anna's Story—Beginning of Middle School

Sara woke up oner morning to her little sistir screaming. "Mama, Papa" she yelled. her parents ran upthe stairs and in to her sisters room. "Hush Cara" she could hear her mothe rs gental voice. "Mama is Cara going to be all right?" "Yes, I think so." When Sara's father took the sheets of the bed he found a sharp knife. "Oh, no. Check to see if Cara has any cuts on her." Sara's mom gently checked. when she came to Cara's nightie she saw a hole. Betty, sara's mom lifted Cara's nightie. She scaned the baby's chest when she came to her far left side she saw a deep cut. "Oh Lord Jhon she's been Stabbed." "Sara, SARA Wake up." sara opend her eyes and looked up to her father's eyes. "O father, the dream... How's Cara." Three weeks later Cara was asleep in bed. She roled on a knife and got stabed in her ribs, the knife enterd her heart. She died durring surgery.

about their options as writers (topic, form, stylistic choices); and flexible in their choices. The essential component in this model is fluency—without the ability to put words on paper, writers cannot learn to clarify and precisely shape their written language. Attention to meaning, to getting the words down, comes first. As children grow as writers, they attend to issues of revision (adding or reordering information, word selection) and writing conventions (grammar, spelling, handwriting, and mechanics) as they endeavor to say exactly what they want others to understand.

FIGURE 8.8

Anna's Letter—Beginning of Middle School

Dear Mom and Dad,

My bunkies are really nice. Lize arrived last night. She's nice.

I need a fan, a clock $7.50 for camp ring, Cup-o-soup.

I passed my swiming test. I also almost have my canoeing basic, my art basic and my riding basic. Mary found the D-3 requirements and I am in level four for riding.

Love ya,

Anna

Dear Wafer,

I really miss you, don't claw the couches and eat moms plants, And please try not to get into a fight with the cat next door.

Love ya,

Anna

Language Diversity and Composition Instruction

Children who speak a nonstandard dialect and children who are learning to be bilingual are actively engaged with their linguistic environment, just as are speakers of Standard English. Most linguists today argue that nonstandard

FIGURE 8.9

Anna's List—Beginning of Middle School

95' BIRTHDAY WISH LIST!!!!!!!!!

1.C.D player
2.Cranberries , no need to argue(c.d)
3.duffle bag
4.Indiglo watch (NOT DIGITAL OR CLUNKEY)
5.pierced ears
6.a nice pair of earrings
7.3 lessons a week
8.mini- safe for my diary
9.hootie and the blowfish c.d
10.dressage saddle
11.bryer dressage saddle
12.-13. Woredrobe for a horse(sheet, blanket,bell-boots,show pad etc...

dialect features do not make learning to write more difficult than do standard dialect features. That is, the dialect anyone speaks is never like the formal written prose that is currently the goal of school-sponsored writing. Spelling and grammatical errors in writing occur regularly whether the writer speaks Standard or nonstandard English. Assuming that how a person speaks directly and profoundly affects how that person writes assumes that writing is speech written down—and we know that it is not that simple. Further, to assume that speakers of nonstandard dialect will automatically encode nonstandard features of their everyday conversational code as they write ignores what we know about linguistic variation. Speakers change their language according to what they are talking about, to whom they are talking, and the context in which they are talking, as they engage in register-switching according to the demands of the moment. Writing, for speakers of any dialect, requires different language than does speech. Different types of writing require different uses of language.

Even given this, however, speakers of nonstandard dialects often have a more difficult time becoming literate—as our schools define literacy—than do speakers of more standard dialects. This may be due in part to differences in the rules of use and patterns of discourse structures between a nonstandard speaker's home and school communities. The mismatch between the codes of school and the codes of the home community may be responsible for the misinterpretation of classroom demands and the subsequent lack of success experienced by many nonstandard speakers. Thus, the problem is not a purely linguistic one but a cultural one as well.

The kind of classrooms described in this text can go a long way toward diminishing the clash between home and school cultures. Teachers who operate under the premise that all students are competent language users and who expect their students to succeed are the kind of teachers that all students need to have—regardless of the dialect they speak. Regular and substantial time spent writing about meaningful topics, in forms that are useful to the student-writers, is important to both standard and nonstandard speakers, as is writing for a variety of audiences. Being a part of a writing community, engaging in collaborative activities, and instruction in the processes of writing all contribute to successful experiences in writing. Teaching specific strategies and techniques, mechanics, spelling, and grammar in the context of the students' own compositions is also effective when working with nonstandard speakers. Finally, a rich and varied diet of reading—both professional and student-authored texts—and the use of writing as a tool for learning across a variety of contexts, likewise contribute to success in learning to write, both for standard and nonstandard speakers. In short, the teaching practices we advocate in this text are appropriate for all children, regardless of dialect (Farr & Daniels, 1986). When working with speakers of a nonstandard dialect, the interpretations of, and responses to, language events in the classroom are affected by cultural codes. Effective teachers are sensitive to the part that this may play in their students' classroom lives.

A considerable amount of research indicates that the native language does not interfere significantly in the development of a second language (McLaughlin, 1987). Further, proficiency in the native language is positively related to the rate of acquisition of the second language. That is, the better a speaker, reader, and writer is of, for example, Spanish, the quicker that person will learn English (Hakuta & Garcia, 1989). For example, young Spanish-speaking students learning to write apply the rules they have developed for their Spanish writing to their English writing until they learn the rules for English. Their facility with Spanish helps, rather than interferes, with their development of English literacy. These young writers seem to utilize separate systems, with the system developed for Spanish informing the one developing for English (Edelsky, 1986).

Bilingual students need a great deal of interaction with print in both languages, but do not need to perfect oral English before they learn to write English. Rather, facility in both languages develops simultaneously (Edelsky, 1986). The kinds of teaching strategies presented here—a literature-based, process approach to writing, with plenty of time and support for the practice of writing—work well with bilingual students. However, effective teachers also accurately assess bilingual students' progress and understand and evaluate the language strategies such as spelling, punctuation, and segmentation that they practice both in English and in their native language when possible. Further, it is vitally important to acknowledge and honor the language and culture of bilingual students' home communities.

As we discuss teaching and learning in a writing classroom, we present ways to encourage the development of writing proficiency for all speakers, regardless of dialect or first language.

The Writing Classroom

Writing has many uses in today's classrooms. It supports all areas of the curriculum, helping students learn as well as present their knowledge. Writing can also be the object of study when teachers create contexts in which children focus on their use of written language, often in a writing workshop. The term "workshop," as initially used by Graves (1983), calls to mind an image of cooperation among members of a community of people striving to master a craft—in this case, the craft of writing. The essential images here are those of community and craftsperson.

Community implies cooperation, a working together toward a central goal. In the writing workshop, the goal is the creation and growth of writers. Everyone in the community works together to help each other reach this goal. Students discuss each other's writing with the goal of mutual growth rather than criticism. Teachers work with students as members of the literate community that has been established in the classroom. The context that supports a writing workshop includes (1) a supportive environment in which students and teachers work together to become better writers; (2) constant and self-directed practice of the craft of writing; (3) regular chunks of time devoted to the craft of writing; (4) effective instruction in writing strategies and skills; and (5) regular chunks of time devoted to reading and responding to literature. Effective writing workshop teachers are writers themselves, for only those practicing the craft of writing can respond as writers and be the master craftspeople from whom students can learn. The *Teaching Idea: Teachers as Writers* presents ideas about ways to begin to become a writer.

At first glance, a writing workshop classroom may seem utterly chaotic. Some students will be staring off into space, some reading, some writing furiously, some talking to one or more peers; the teacher could be anywhere—writing or reading but most likely conferring with individual writers. It looks chaotic, but it is not; the writing workshop functions only because each student knows exactly what to do and where and how to do it. Most importantly, all students want to write and know that their writing will be valued. Workshop consists of more than just students writing, however. Teachers also present whole-class lessons, work with small groups, and have students share their work. The writing workshop takes a shape that best fits a particular classroom situation.

ARRANGING THE CLASSROOM

When planning an effective writing workshop, teachers decide how to organize the physical classroom. One of the assumptions underlying a workshop is that writing is a social act, so student desks are arranged in clusters. Corners for conferences are another feature of some writing workshop classrooms. Often these "corners" are merely spaces in front of bookshelves or file cabinets. The point is to give children some semiprivate space in which to talk.

TEACHING IDEA

Assessing the Learning Environment

TEACHERS AS WRITERS

Effective writing teachers become writers themselves, learning to express themselves fluently through the written word by writing often and for many purposes. One way to begin is to keep a journal in which you write about what is happening in your classroom, at home, or in the world. You might want to keep a response journal for your own reading. Whatever you write about, try to do it regularly and talk about it with your students. When your students write, write with them for a few minutes. If you write for classroom publication, just as your students do, they see how important writing is to you. You might try writing and publishing a story for your students as an end-of-the-year present. If you have friends who enjoy reading and writing, you can establish a response group in which you share literature and your own writing. Graves' *Discover Your Own Literacy* (1990) is a good resource for ideas about practicing the craft of writing.

Joseph Kassick

Students who share their writing become good friends and work well together.

Many writing workshops also have a conference table, usually the table where small groups of children work with the teacher in other curricular areas as well. This table is a place where students and teacher work together. Some contain a "Do Not Disturb" table where writers can go and not be interrupted by their peers. If space does not permit a second table, "Do Not Disturb" signs that students place on their desks are also effective. Sometimes writers are "hot" and don't want to stop to help someone else.

A workshop classroom will usually have a designated area where the whole class comes together to share their progress and their products. A reading corner often works well for this. Other teachers simply have sharers move to a spot where they can see and be seen by their classmates, who remain in their places.

GATHERING MATERIALS

Writing workshop classrooms also contain a variety of writing and publishing materials, all of which are easily accessible to the children. These include, but are not limited to: a classroom library; a variety of paper; blank books; various pencils, markers, crayons, paints, and other art supplies; staplers and staples; tape; white-out; scissors; cardboard and other thick paper for binding books; hole punches; heavy thread, yarn, or dental floss for binding books;

large embroidery needles for binding books; dictionaries; thesauruses; books about writing and writers; and, of course, writing folders.

If students are keeping writing notebooks (as discussed in the *Teaching Idea: Writer's Notebooks*) and write in them on a regular basis, then these notebooks can be kept in student desks or "cubbies" or in an easily accessible file or cardboard box. Students need to have access to their notebooks when they want them without having to bother the teacher.

Writing folders are an essential part of a writing classroom. Each student needs to have two folders: one that is a cumulative record of all writing done, and one that is a "working" or "in progress" folder. This latter folder might contain a list of possible topics, a dated record of published pieces, a list of editing skills the writer knows and is responsible for, a personal dictionary of words the writer has learned how to spell, a list of new techniques the writer has tried and mastered, and all the versions of the current piece. Like notebooks, these folders need to be clearly labeled and stored in an easily accessible location.

Using computers

As more students become familiar with computers and more schools are able to put computers into classrooms, teachers are challenged to find ways to use computers effectively to enhance literacy instruction. For example, using a word-processing package to record children's dictated writing has been very effective for many primary-grade teachers. Some primary teachers also encourage students to use the computer as they compose. They have found that when the computer replaces paper and pencil many children write more, revise more willingly and more extensively, and thus work longer on single pieces. The result can be not only longer, more detailed, and generally "better"

TEACHING IDEA

Addressing Individual Needs

WRITER'S NOTEBOOKS

You might find it useful to have your students keep a writer's notebook (Calkins, 1994; Fletcher, 1996) in which they record thoughts, interesting information, things they have seen or heard, anything that intrigues them. These should be fairly small, spiral notebooks that can be carried around easily. Students can use these notebooks as sources of ideas for writing. Of course, they are also writing as they fill the notebooks! This activity encourages students to be keen observers.

pieces, but a realization by the children that they can manipulate text, changing it at will and as often as they like to produce the effect they want (Strickland, Feeley, & Wepner, 1987).

Upper elementary and middle school writers can also experience the joy of using the computer as a tool for writing. Some children are motivated by the opportunity to work on the computer. For some writers, revision becomes easier, faster, less tedious, and thus both more frequent and more complete. However, this revision may be limited to editing concerns such as spelling, mechanics, and syntax rather than encompassing whole-text concerns (Daiute, 1986).

Although clearly not a panacea for problems with composition, the computer equipped with an appropriate word-processing program can be an effective tool for many young writers. Figure 8.10 lists some useful software; new software is reviewed in professional journals such as *The Reading Teacher*. If there are enough computers in a classroom to allow young writers to become comfortable with word processing, and if computers are regarded as one of many tools for composing, then their use can facilitate drafting by eliminating problems with handwriting. With practice and direction from the teacher, some students will find that computers help them revise more easily. It is not, however, the answer to problems inherent in composition, nor does it help all students become more effective writers all of the time. Before the computer can become useful, students must spend time learning how to use it.

One of the instructional decisions teachers make is deciding how much time to devote to learning word processing rather than to actual composing. A good instructional program can help students become efficient keyboard users. As with other instructional decisions, it is the teacher's knowledge, beliefs, instructional practices, and goals, rather than the computer itself, that make the difference. The computer can help good teachers teach writing, just as plenty of paper and pencils, time and space, and administrative support help good teachers teach writing.

The computer does have a function beyond that as a tool for writing. Langer (1986) suggests that the computer can also be a "tool for supporting the active use of language in social situations" (p. 118). As writers interact around the computer, they attempt to solve language and computer problems. This interaction, which requires thinking and talking about these problems, is a perfect example of functional language use. The potential for collaborative learning is the most consistently found benefit of using a computer to compose. For example, first and second grade children who have access to a computer may not use it much for revision, but may work collaboratively, which results in planning talk, self-monitoring talk, and responding to what is composed (Dickinson, 1986). This explicit talk about language, which composing collaboratively on a computer seems to encourage, may in fact be the most important effect of having computers in the classroom.

FIGURE 8.10

Technology for Writing Classrooms

Software

1. *Bank Street Writer III* (Publisher: Scholastic). An easy-to-use word processor program that includes options for teacher-created lessons. The AppleTalk Network version enables classroom electronic mail and collaboration. (Apple, MS-DOS, Macintosh)
2. *The Bilingual Writing Center* (Publisher: Learning Company). An easy-to-use Spanish/English version of The Writing Center. Bilingual spell check and thesaurus, pictures. (Macintosh)
3. *Clifford's Big Book Publisher* (Publisher: Scholastic). Creates big books with Clifford, the big red dog, and other characters. Variety of backgrounds, clip art, and fonts available. (Apple, MS-DOS)
4. *The Children's Writing & Publishing Center* (Publisher: The Learning Company). Creates stories, reports, and newsletters. Variety of theme-related headings, clip art, and fonts available. (Apple, MS-DOS)
5. *Dinosaur Days* (Publisher: Pelican/Queue). Creates dinosaur diaries in seven different sizes with a variety of dinosaur backgrounds, parts, and props available. Provides speech with Echo Board or Cricket Speech Synthesizer. (Apple, MS-DOS, Macintosh)
6. *Make-A-Book* (Publisher: Teacher Support Software). Prints real books in five different sizes. Variety of fonts available. Provides speech with Double-TalkPC, Echo PC, COVOX Speech Thing, or Sound Blaster. (MS-DOS)
7. *Monsters & Make-Believe* (Publisher: Pelican/Queue). Creates monster stories in seven different sizes. Variety of monster backgrounds, parts, and props available. Provides speech with Echo Board or Cricket Speech Synthesizer. Has Spanish version without speech. (Apple, MS-DOS, Macintosh [without speech])
8. *The New Print Shop* (Publisher: Broderbund). Creates signs, posters, banners, cards, and calendars. Variety of graphics and graphic layouts available. (Apple, MS-DOS; original version available for Macintosh, Commodore, and Apple IIGS)
9. *POW! ZAP! Ker-Plunk! The Comic Book Maker!* (Publisher: Pelican/Queue). Creates comic books with classic comic book components: speech bubbles, sound and special effects, props, heroes, and heroines. (Apple, MS-DOS)
10. *Robot Writer* (Publisher: Pelican/Queue). Creates robots and robot reports with robot parts and props. Provides speech with Echo Board or Cricket Speech Synthesizer. (Apple, MS-DOS)
11. *SuperPrint II* (Publisher: Scholastic). Creates posters, calendars, and bulletin board displays in a variety of sizes, up to 6 feet tall. Theme-related graphic packs are available. (Apple, MS-DOS)

Web Sites

1. http://www.poetry4kids.com/index.html Guides students in writing humorous poetry.
2. http://teacher.scholastic.com/writewit/poetry/index/htm Popular poets help students write first drafts.
3. http://www.inspiration.com Site that helps with prewriting idea generation.
4. http://www.filemakerworld.com Helps in recording ideas and manipulating them.
5. http://www.hyperstudio.com Presentation software.

Source: Part of this figure was reprinted by permission of the publisher from Strickland, D. S., Feeley, J. T., & Wepner, S. B. *Using Computers in the Teaching of Reading.* New York: Teachers College Press (Appendix: pp. 191–218.)

THE WORKSHOP IN ACTION

Time is an essential element in a successful writing workshop. Time to write and talk about writing is crucial. Students need to write every day, or at least 4 days a week (Graves, 1994). Some primary teachers are able to devote the whole morning to reading and writing; others can allocate only certain hours. Upper elementary and middle school teachers usually allocate specific blocks of time. Time can be found in a busy week by taking the time formerly reserved for spelling, grammar and usage, punctuation and capitalization, and handwriting, because all these skills can be taught within the context of the writing workshop.

How teachers organize their workshop depends on what best suits their needs. Atwell (1998) begins her eighth grade workshops with a 5- to 10-minute lesson, or a brief, to-the-point lecture. Then she checks with each writer to see what the plans are for the day and records that on a chart. Fifteen minutes into the hour, everyone is at work. The last 10–15 minutes are devoted to "group share," a time in which writers discuss their pieces with the class, receiving helpful feedback. Her workshop time plan looks like this: 9:00–9:15 lesson; 9:15–9:45 workshop; 9:45–10:00 group share.

Other teachers might not begin with a brief lesson each day, perhaps teaching a short lesson at another time. Or they might begin with a read-aloud session followed by discussion and a quick check to see what children are planning to work on that day. Workshops do not always end with a group share. The configurations vary, but are usually a combination of whole-class,

Bernice Cullinan

When students know how to supportively respond to one another, reading and discussing each other's writing builds community and develops writing skills.

small-group, and individual work time, with the bulk of the time devoted to the students' own writing. Teachers can usually find daily opportunities for teaching, writing, and sharing.

David introduces his third grade students to writing workshop with a general description of the procedures they will follow and some ideas for getting started:

> Today we're going to begin writing workshop. What we'll do each day at this time is get out our writing folders, which will be stored in these boxes, and return to our places. At the beginning of each workshop, I'll talk to you briefly about things you're learning to do with your writing. I'll only talk for about 10 minutes. Then I'll ask you what you're planning to do during workshop. After you've told me what you'll be working on, we'll all get to work. When you're writing I want you to write as quickly as you can—don't worry about what your piece looks like for now. We'll have time to fix it up later. I'll be working on my own writing for the first few minutes, then I'll begin to have conferences with you.
>
> I'll talk to one person at a time while the rest of you work. After about a half-hour it will be time for you to put your work in your folders and go over to the rug area where we'll talk about what we've done and some people will share their work. Sharing time will last about 10 minutes.
>
> Now, what I want to talk about today is how to select topics to write about. I'm going to write about taking all three of my dogs—at once—to the vet and what a circus it was with all three dogs trying to get out of the examining room. That happened last weekend, so I think I can remember enough of what happened to write it down. Think about some things that have happened to you lately. I know that some of you have gone on trips, some have had relatives come and visit, while some have learned how to do new things. Take just a minute and think about what you could tell us about in your writing. Then I'll go around the room and you can each tell everyone what you might write.

Later that week, David's students are scattered about the room, busily engaged in composing. Two are seated on the rug together, talking animatedly about the new puppy that one of them just got. One little girl is deep in conversation with David as they read her just-completed piece together. A number of children are sitting at tables, busily working with pencil, crayon, markers, and paper. Along the back wall sit several pairs of children, one in each pair listening while the other one reads a newly completed text. In a corner the aide is talking with a small group about ideas for what to write next.

Workshop might begin with a brief lesson, at least for the first several weeks. Initially, the content of the lessons will probably be **procedural,** focusing on how the workshop will operate. The first lesson might resemble the one David presented to his third grade class. He briefly explains the

Joseph Kassick

Young writers devote intense attention to their task.

procedures the students will follow for future writing workshop sessions. For the next few weeks he will elaborate and repeat his explanations. To get the students started writing, he will demonstrate how he selects his own topic, carefully choosing something that is fairly ordinary, and carefully mentioning how he can remember enough about the event to write about it. He will also give specific instances of things that he knows his students have experienced recently.

Today, after a minute or two, he asks his students to state and briefly explain what they are thinking of writing about. Reminding them that the important thing is to write—that he doesn't want anyone to worry about how their pieces look for now, he makes sure everyone has pencils and knows where to find the sharpener and extra paper. He then releases them to write, calling them back for a whole-class share at the end of the workshop session.

Discussing the procedures students need to follow in order to keep the writing workshop going in a smooth and orderly fashion is a logical beginning. Early lessons include descriptions of the teacher's role, the students' roles, and the teacher's expectations, and then move on to specifics within these general procedures (Atwell, 1998). For example, one of the first lessons might be on how students will function in the classroom. Some teachers quickly present basic "rules" to their students, others develop a list of agreements, or rules, in collaboration with their students. In many classrooms, lists like that reproduced in Figure 8.11 hang in clear view.

FIGURE 8.11

Workshop Rules

1. Write on one side of paper only.
2. No erasing.
3. Keep everything you write in your writing folder.
4. Put the date on everything you write.
5. Be ready to write when workshop begins.
6. When conferring with a peer, talk quietly.

After the first few weeks of school, students need fewer procedural lessons as they learn to function independently. As you observe students, you can decide what procedural lessons are necessary, including those listed in Figure 8.12.

Once the introductory activity is completed, it is writing time. Asking each student "What are your plans for today?" or "What will you be working on today?" provides information that helps teachers know who needs to talk

FIGURE 8.12

Procedural Lesson Topics

1. Location and use of appropriate materials
2. Schedule and expected behavior
3. Options for working with peers
4. Functions of designated special areas such as the "Do Not Disturb" section and the conference table
5. How to sign up for drop-in conferences
6. How to prepare for conferences
7. How conferences work
8. How to conduct peer conferences
9. What to do with a piece that is ready for editing
10. Procedures for whole-class sharing
11. Options for publishing finished piece

TEACHING IDEA

Assessing the Learner

USING STUDENT RECORDS TO ASSESS STUDENT PROGRESS

When students keep a daily record of their work during writing workshop, have them record their plans on a record sheet in their writing folder. You can peruse these records to assess individual student progress. These sheets become an important record to refer to during parent conferences.

You can also keep a record yourself if you ask students to let you know what they are working on. Record their plans on a sheet with names running down the left margin and a space for each day of the week running across the page. As you use these check sheets, you can develop your own shorthand for noting what students are doing. At the end of each week, check each student's progress and note who needs to do what during the next week. This type of record keeping offers you opportunities to assess the whole class as well as individual students, and makes grouping for instruction easy.

with them, who needs extra support, and who is progressing independently. Recording each child's plans on a daily basis gives teachers a record of what each child is doing. It also forces students to think about and articulate where they are in their writing, thus focusing their attention on what they will need to do. Additionally, students often get ideas about what they might write about or what they might do during workshop by hearing what their peers are planning (Atwell, 1998). In other words, stating their plans gets them ready to work and can also be a good tool for assessment, as described in the *Teaching Idea: Using Student Records to Assess Student Progress.*

The first day is the only time all your students will be at the same place in their writing—the beginning. By the end of the first workshop, students are as they will be until the last day of school—at different places in the writing cycle.

The Writing Cycle

Authors who describe their writing process often identify certain phases they go through in their own writing. They talk of getting an idea, thinking and talking about that idea, drafting their pieces, revising them, editing, and publishing. These writers go on to describe how drafting, revising, and rehearsing occur, recur, and occur simultaneously, and how drafts are abandoned sometimes. It seems the only certainty is that a writer begins with an idea and sometimes ends up with a published piece. As we said above, the act of writing is not clear or sequential but rather variable, doubling back on itself as writers work at crafting their words into pieces that satisfy them. Writing cannot be neatly packaged into a 5-day schedule.

Sowers (1985) has described a writing cycle from initial idea to published product. Within that cycle, described below, are underlying processes, such as drafting and revision, that characterize what writers do. Successful writers use strategies that help them find ideas, develop ideas, draft pieces, revise, and edit them. Knowing what some of these strategies are and when to introduce them to students is an important part of teaching writing. Understanding the phases of the writing cycle, some strategies writers use, and ways to help students learn and select from these strategies marks effective teachers of writing.

SELECTING TOPICS

For some writers, deciding what to write about can be the most difficult step of all. For generations teachers have been giving children topics to write about—"What I Did on My Vacation," "My Autobiography," "Pets I Have Loved," "Spring"—behaving as if we believe children are not able to write without being given topics. Indeed, after several months of teacher-provided topics, children do have a difficult time selecting their own! With older children, teachers may have to work hard to convince them that they have things they can write about, but it can be done. If you help your students understand that the stuff of their lives, the "ordinary" things they see and do and feel every day, are topics for writing, they'll have more than enough topics.

You can demonstrate this approach when you compose in front of students. Initially, you need to select ideas for topics with care, making sure that they reflect the small things in life (the crazy trip to the grocery store on Christmas Eve) rather than the big things (a bicycle trip through France). When students understand that authors write about everyday things and see that you write about everyday things, they will feel free to write about the same kinds of things.

Students can also generate topic ideas through their discussions with each other. Knowing that one student has decided to write about the day she learned to roller skate can help another remember the day he learned to row a boat and can make him feel that this might be worth writing about. Talking in small-group or whole-class settings about ideas for writing—either during introductory activities, writing time, or class share—helps students develop their own ideas for topics by listening to the ideas of others and trying out some of their own. Brainstorming ideas can lead to a list, jotted down on a sheet attached to the inside of their writing folders and consulted as the need arises.

Often, students find new topics reading through their writing folders. If they are writing in journals on a regular basis, then reading through their journal entries helps them find topics they would like to revisit and further develop. Another source for topics is the literature that children read and hear. Literature is full of topics rooted in the lives of authors. Also, children are frequently reminded of their own lives as they read. Thus, literature can give rise to ideas about specifics in their own lives that children can write about. One student, temporarily at a loss for an idea to write about, read an old, abandoned draft about her summer in Maine. From this draft she got an idea—to write about the day she and her mother saw a bear when they were picking blueberries. She might also have "found" that same topic by reading McCloskey's *Blueberries for Sal.*

Effective teachers help students realize what they can write about by discovering what students know. Each student has a wealth of knowledge and experiences that are different from anyone else's—every child has something to say. Your job is to help the child realize what it is. Graves (1990) suggests making a list of all students and writing down one or two things that each knows about. You can then use this information to help students find their own topics, perhaps through gentle suggestions and/or questions during individual conferences.

All of these ideas are ways to help students realize that what they live, they can write about. Children learn best when they connect what they are doing in school with their lives. Writing about topics from their own lives makes this connection, legitimizes children as knowledgeable individuals, and helps children learn how to write.

Once students have had some experience in selecting their own topics, they can come up with a list of ideas for effective topic selection. They will have learned to write about small things they know a lot about rather than big things they know less about. After students have witnessed effective topic selection, thought about how to select good topics, tried writing on their own topics, and discussed the process, they can then generate some guidelines and apply them in their own topic-selection process.

As teachers write and talk about their writing, they also demonstrate good strategies for selecting and developing topics. These include demonstrating how to choose between a topic one knows little about and a topic one knows a lot about; what writers might do to learn more about topics they are interested in; and how to narrow a large topic to a more focused one. Further, teachers can demonstrate how writers think and talk about what they are going to say about their selected topics. This is the next phase in Sowers's writing cycle—rehearsing or "percolating."

GENERATING IDEAS

Graves (1983, 1994), Calkins (1994), and many others talk about how writers need to spend time talking and thinking about what they are going to write. This mental work happens during topic selection, as well as before and during drafting. Some call this activity "rehearsal," stressing that writers need to talk and think about what they are going to write before they write it. Mayher, Lester, and Pradl (1983) dubbed this process "percolation," a nice metaphor for the activity that occurs as a piece is being "brewed." Whatever we call it, writers do think, read, talk, observe, and even write to get ready to write. Consciously or unconsciously, writers begin writing long before they sit down to paper and pencil.

This phase in the writing cycle overlaps others as the writer shuttles back and forth and ahead and returns again in an overlapping cycle of idea generation/percolation/drafting and revision. Certain actions, however, at least partially differentiate one part of the cycle from another. Rehearsing, or percolating, involves much thinking, talking, reading, observing, and interviewing/data gathering in a variety of ways to help writers know at least a bit of what they have to say. Some students might go to a conference corner to discuss their ideas. Others go to the library to find more information about their topics. Others sit quietly by themselves, thinking. All of these writers are percolating, getting ready to create a draft about their selected topics. Some will be ready to write almost immediately, some will decide to abandon these topics for now, some will write after an hour or two of preparation. Each writer must follow an individual pattern with each piece—each has different needs.

Teachers help students think about their topics by showing them strategies to use like brainstorming, interviewing, observing and recording, and researching and note taking. These activities and others like them are all aids to developing ideas for writing. No one should ever be required to do any of them all of the time; they are resources to select among. These activities are described in the *Teaching Idea: Helping Students Generate Ideas for Writing*.

Brainstorming, interviewing, observing and recording, library research, and drawing are strategies that students will want to use at one time or another. Sometimes, however, all the "percolation" they need is to think about their ideas, during writing time and at odd moments throughout the day in and out of school. Some young writers even report waking up in the morning with ideas about how to tackle the topic they have selected! All of this "percolation" often leads to the next phase of Sowers's writing cycle, drafting.

PUTTING WORDS ON PAPER

Just because writers start putting words on paper, or drafting, does not mean that the "percolation" has stopped. They do, indeed, keep thinking, talking, and gathering information as they write. How writers actually put words on paper varies, of course, from one writing event to another. Sometimes they are pretty sure about what they want to say, and their words simply flow across the page with minimal rereading and revision. At other times they pause and plan, pause, reread and revise, write and scratch out, and scribble in the margins things they have forgotten to say.

Meaning is what writers pay attention to in drafting. Their primary goal is to get the words down on the page, to transfer to the page that which they want to say. Putting words down on paper is easier for some than for others. Young children who are full of confidence in their own abilities will draft with more ease than will older ones who have learned to be wary of writing in school. Older students may focus so much on getting the surface elements—spelling, punctuation, and usage—correct that they lose the sense of their message. If they focus on form too soon, they won't develop the fluency necessary to evolve as effective writers. Your job is to help students know that successful writers often do not get it right the first time, that early drafts usually are messy and incomplete, and that drafts are only steps toward a finished product, not the finished product itself.

One good way to introduce students to the concept of drafting is to write a first draft in front of the class. Using chart paper or an overhead (so the draft can be saved), you can compose aloud, writing and making thought processes explicit. This should be real composing—not just presenting a text written the night before—so that students can see and hear what happens as someone writes. You can demonstrate some behaviors that help students become less hesitant to draft. You may, for example, skip the first sentence—waiting until another draft to work on the lead—and simply plunge right in. You can show students how to invent a spelling for a word they are unsure of, and how to underline an awkward section rather than stop writing to spend time revising it.

The aim here is to reassure students that it is okay to forge right ahead and write—trying to get it perfect before it is down on paper practically guarantees that writing will be difficult. Teachers convince students of this through their demonstrations as a fellow writer and through the things they talk about in conferences and whole-class meetings.

Discussions with, and demonstrations by, peers also help writers overcome "writer's block." Knowing that a friend has trouble getting words down on paper can make a student feel better about her own struggle to draft. Knowing what a classmate does to overcome difficulty can help another develop a strategy for overcoming writer's block. Many children like to know that their favorite authors have the same kinds of problems. Just as students can read about authors and their ideas for writing, they can also read about authors and their writing processes; how they, too, are sometimes at a loss for words; and what they do to overcome this. Children need to know that authors do not magically produce perfect text, and that becoming an author is hard, but rewarding, work.

TEACHING IDEA

Addressing Individual Needs

HELPING STUDENTS GENERATE IDEAS FOR WRITING

Brainstorming

Brainstorming involves tossing out ideas—*any* idea—as fast as they pop into your head. A good way to introduce this technique is to select a topic that the whole class will have ideas about, such as school lunches, and then have the class call out words/phrases that come to mind as they think about the topic.

Your job is to record their ideas on the board or a piece of chart paper. Once the students have run out of new ideas, review the list they have generated, and demonstrate how to use these ideas to begin writing.

After reading over this list, you might demonstrate how to organize random ideas, provide a specific but tentative statement of a writing plan, and explicitly request alternative ideas from students. Here are some guidelines for successful brainstorming:

1. Try to come up with as many ideas as possible.
2. Don't decide what you will use or discard until you have finished brainstorming.
3. Think of unusual, "far-out" ideas, too.
4. Don't worry about following one line of thought—explore in any direction; "ricocheting" is good.
5. Listen to the ideas of your friends and expand on them.
6. Don't discard any ideas. You might be able to use them later!

Interviewing

Interviewing is practiced in a number of ways. Whole-class interviews of class guests are one way to help children learn to ask good questions in an interview. Another interview situation that might be more commonplace in the classroom occurs when a writer wants to

Sometimes children are reluctant to abandon themselves to a draft because they are concerned with spelling, punctuation, grammar, and handwriting. It is only through repeated demonstrations and discussions that teachers are able to persuade these children to worry about the surface features of their writing later when they are revising and editing.

Revising during drafting

When writers draft, they usually do not do so in a completely forward-moving way. Instead they write recursively, pausing to reread, write more, change a word or two, reread, write more, reread the whole piece, write, change a bit, delete, or add pieces here and there. In short, most accomplished talk with a peer about an idea for writing. In essence, what the peer needs to do is "interview" the writer about the idea. You demonstrate good questioning techniques in individual conferences, in introductory activities, and in group sharing, helping students elaborate on information.

You can also demonstrate how a listener can ask the writer to "tell me about your idea," and how the writer can tell as much as he or she knows about that idea. Then the listener can ask questions of the writer. Listeners might want to ask for more information, or they might want to ask why the writers did or felt something.

Observing and Recording

Children are natural observers; observing the world around them is one of the key ways they learn about their world. Observation is also one important way of getting ready to write. While observing and recording, children will be using writing to get ready to write as they record their observations.

Library Research

Sometimes students are very interested in a topic and want to learn more, either just for the fun of it or as preparation for writing. With the help of the school librarian, teach students how to use the library to conduct research and how to take and organize notes.

Drawing

Another way of getting ready to write, which many young children rely on, is drawing. Drawing and writing are closely connected as part of the young child's developing symbol system. Encouraging students to get ready to write by drawing helps them make use of the communicative strategies with which they are comfortable.

writers revise as they write. They write recursively, doubling back on their words, actually revising what they have written or planning what they will write as they are drafting.

What seems to happen when writers pause in their writing is planning. Children move from sentence-level, or **linguistic,** planning (what to say next) to whole-text, or **rhetorical,** planning (thinking about the theme, structure, or style of the piece) as they develop as writers (Flower & Hayes, 1981). This is not surprising, because children are already good at the type of sentence-level planning necessary to sustain conversation and have had little practice at whole-text planning, which involves consideration of purpose and audience. Children seem to do little spontaneous planning before writing.

Although upper elementary students begin to understand rhetorical planning, they still tend to generate content rather than plans when asked to plan a piece. However, some young children can generate quite sophisticated plans. This suggests that, although whole-text planning may not arise spontaneously in young writers until middle childhood, teachers can help students learn to do this kind of planning through conference questions, group planning, and other teacher-led activities. Through instruction and demonstration teachers can help children to plan first with assistance and later on their own as they grow as writers.

REVISING

Revision, or changing something already written, happens during and after drafting. Sometimes writers revise during drafting as they reread, sometimes after they draft as they work toward a final form for their pieces. It is hard to tell where drafting leaves off and revision begins. Studies have attempted to document the order in which young children revise, only to find that although there may be some general pattern, there is also wide individual variation. Some young children do little or no revision in their writing or in other media such as painting; others continually revise in their art, their building, their dramatic play, and their writing. Revision is more than mere "editing" of the conventions of a piece; it also involves looking at content and style.

Children who write and revise regularly often focus first on spelling, then motor-aesthetics (how the piece looks), then mechanics. They move next to topic and information revisions, and finally to whole-text revisions such as adding, deleting, and reordering material (in that order) (Graves, 1983). However, this does not mean that children do one thing at a time and nothing else. These are merely areas of concentration, what seems to be important to children at particular times in their development as writers. Primary-grade writers often do little spontaneous revision, focusing instead on writing extensively and fluently.

When children have the opportunity to write regularly and often, they gradually master the conventions of written language and at the same time learn to wait until a close-to-final draft to worry about those conventions. Thus, as spelling, handwriting, and mechanics become more automatic, they also become less important to writers who are focusing on meaning and writing frequently and fluently. These writers know they will have ample time to attend to these concerns once they are ready to revise.

Effective teachers help students learn to revise. First, they notice what students are doing on their own. Do they revise at all? What do they focus on? What are they ready to learn next? You might show individual students during conferences how to use carets, margin writing, arrows, cut and paste, or inserts. They will soon show their peers. Or you might do a whole-class demonstration of how to add information to a piece.

Talking about how to add information often is most effective when students are writing about personal experiences. Because they know firsthand what they are writing about, they have the information they need to add in their own heads. They come to know what they need to add (or delete) through questions and discussion with teachers and peers during conferences and whole-class sharing. If computers are available, learning how to move chunks of text in a word-processing program encourages revisions from those who do not want to "copy over." You can address many revision concerns during demonstrations, conferences, or whole-class lessons.

Effective teachers talk about how successful authors create texts that intrigue readers, perhaps discussing the difference between showing and telling, exploring the writing of favorite authors to see how they show their readers where and what happens. Effective teachers also help writers focus on a central point, or theme. Graves (1994) suggests asking students to consider the "main idea" of a piece. Asking them to articulate what a piece is about helps them focus on the important aspects of the piece and can often help them delete extraneous text and add important information.

Effective teachers know what to teach and when to teach it because they understand writing processes and strategies. They understand because they write themselves, and they read about writing. Some excellent resources for developing this understanding are Murray's *Write to Learn* (1990), Zinsser's *On Writing Well* (1990), and Fletcher's (1993, 1998) *What a Writer Needs* and *Craft Lessons*. Knowing what to teach also depends on your observation and assessment of students' strengths and needs. When you see that students are trying to use dialogue in their pieces, then it is time to help them discover how dialogue works by examining the trade books they read and the pieces they write. When you see that students are beginning to search for the right word, then it is time to help them learn to use the thesaurus and consider connotations as they revise, and, of course, as they read. We discuss helping students grow as writers across different genres in Chapter Nine.

Students revise for meaning profitably only if *they* want to revise because *they* are not satisfied with their piece. The desire to revise must come from the writer and the reason to revise must be a real one—one that arises from the needs of the writer and the particular piece. Teachers help by providing time and space for writing, an atmosphere conducive to taking risks and growing in writing ability, a forum for talking about writing, demonstrations of the strategies and options available to writers, and ways for students to publish their writing.

Still, there will be some writers who simply do not want to revise. Sometimes it is best to leave them alone. If they don't want to revise, they probably won't revise effectively when forced, and the overall result will be negative feelings about writing and revising. Sometimes, however, you may need to nudge reluctant revisers into revision by (1) asking students to write on their papers during conferences, (2) making one revision attempt a prerequisite to publishing,

(3) encouraging them to work in pairs with students who are accomplished at revision, or (4) helping them to revise their own pieces in a student-teacher conference. The difficult part is to encourage them firmly, but gently.

EDITING

Editing involves looking closely at a piece of writing, finding errors, and fixing them. In a summation of studies of student errors in their writing, Hull (1989) concludes that "perhaps the most important pedagogical implication of these studies is that students can learn to edit through repeated acts of locating errors and imagining alternatives to them in contrast to learning about errors in the abstract in hopes of somehow inhibiting them" (p. 181). When a writer has decided to publish a particular piece, that piece needs editing. Now is the time to make sure that spelling, usage, punctuation, and capitalization are in correct form. Of course, as writers revise pieces, especially in later drafts, they attend to some editing details, but editing isn't the focus until just before publication.

Editing can take place through individual student editing, editing groups, editing conferences, or teacher editing. When editing is the responsibility of each student, teachers get an accurate picture of each student's editing abilities. However, a valuable opportunity for peer teaching and learning will be lost. Further, this puts teachers in the position of either "correcting" all pieces prior to publication or letting pieces that are not correct be published. Many teachers do publish less than perfect copy. They do so because their primary goal is to publish their students' work. This policy is usually explained to parents and administrators, perhaps in a letter, and is often quite effective in the early grades.

Effective teachers encourage students to work with their peers to edit, either with an "editing partner" or in "editing groups." This format has the advantage of having two or more pairs of eyes looking at a piece just as professional writers have. In the real world, no one gets published without at least one other person reading and editing as well. Working with a partner or partners also increases the sense of cooperation and community, and provides the opportunity for peer teaching and learning.

Yet another alternative is teacher-student editing conferences in which teachers discuss editorial concerns. During these conferences, students focus on what they know needs "fixing up," not what you see. Sometimes teachers ask students to circle words if they are unsure of the spelling, to draw a box around questionable punctuation marks, and so on. The point is to get students to look at their own texts and locate possible errors. Learning to find their own errors is crucial. If students can recognize an error, they can learn the convention. If students cannot find their errors, how can they know to worry about the conventions of written language? You can find them easily—but you do not need the practice. Students do. You can then show individual students how to do what they need to learn to do—a little at a time.

As you discuss grammar, style, mechanics, and spelling with your students, students can determine what "rules" they have mastered and can proofread for before they have an editing conference. Many teachers ask students to maintain an "Editing Responsibilities" sheet in their folders that they add to as they master new skills and check against as they edit their own pieces. This sheet will also contain spelling words and mechanics skills. It serves as an excellent record of each student's growth over time in the areas of grammar and mechanics and is useful during parent-teacher conferences, during evaluations, and in planning small-group and whole-class lessons.

Within the context of editing, effective teachers talk about grammar, mechanics (capitalization and punctuation), and spelling. These conventions of written language make it possible for all of us to communicate with each other in writing. These conventions are important when writers have an audience with whom they want to communicate. They have nothing to do with the quality of ideas, but have a great deal to do with the quality of written communication.

PUBLISHING

Unless they are writing a personal diary or journal, writers usually write for an audience. They write so that their writing can be read, so that they can communicate with others. Publishing student work provides student writers with an audience other than their teacher, an audience that compels them to try their best to "get it right" so that a variety of people will understand them. Teachers and peers are students' most immediate audience, but their audience can be even wider. Publishing is also a wonderful way to involve parents in the writing program, as described in the *Teaching Idea: Involving Parents in the Writing Classroom.*

One of the most obvious outlets for publishing is providing books for the classroom library. Placing students' published books in the classroom library increases the collection, provides writers with ready access to their peers as audience, and imbues them with a sense of authorship. Their books occupy the same shelves as the books of favorite authors. Students' books can span the genres, including stories, poems, and informational pieces. There are several ways to construct books, and basic instructions can be posted close to the necessary supplies. You can also enlist the help of parent volunteers or even set up a before- or after-school book construction plant. Making books is the perfect opportunity for students to learn about the parts of a book: the title page, copyright, dedication, and author pages.

Newspapers offer another outlet for students' writing. They can be typed easily onto dittos, stencils, or computer disks by students, aides, or parent volunteers and run off for each member of the class. Some classes actually develop a market for their papers among other students and sell them to earn money to buy more writing and publishing supplies than the school can provide.

TEACHING IDEA

Home/School Connection

INVOLVING PARENTS IN THE WRITING CLASSROOM

Inviting parents and other members of the community to be a part of the life of the classroom can have far-ranging benefits. A letter sent home at the beginning of the year to explain the writing program and suggest how parents can help can result in both support at home and welcome parent volunteers. Interested parents may want to volunteer for an hour or so a week to come to school and be a part of a writing workshop, working with children as they write. If your classroom has a computer, having a parent volunteer to help students learn to operate the word-processing program can be a great timesaver. Parents can edit spelling dictionaries or final drafts before publication. They are quite useful also at publishing books. Ask parents to make books, type, or track down materials for a writing classroom. Merchants often either provide materials or offer substantial discounts if they know what they are being used for. And parents are an important audience for children's writing. Inviting parents to a "Read-A-Thon" of children's works, making sure that they know they are welcome to drop in and read their children's writing, and allowing students to check out child-authored books to take home, are all ways to involve parents in your writing program.

Publishing a paper is a good opportunity to explore the various parts of a newspaper and how newspapers are produced.

Class magazines can be handled in a number of ways. They can be regularly scheduled or scheduled as needed. They can be genre-specific (poetry, descriptive essays, stories); themed (nature, Christmas, growing up); or eclectic. Whatever best suits the needs of student writers should be the guideline for setting up criteria for a student magazine. No one should have to contribute, and everyone who submits a piece should be included in the magazine. This is not the time for competition. Magazines can be typed and run off on dittos, stencils, or computer disks.

Bulletin boards in the room, in the hall, and in the office provide easy-to-use publishing space. You can turn a bulletin board over to students for their use, or invite students to contribute to themed bulletin boards. An author-of-the-week bulletin board in which a photograph, brief autobiography, and current works of a student author are highlighted is a great way to honor individual writers. However the bulletin board space is used, the materials should be displayed attractively and changed frequently, and students should be allowed to spend time reading what is posted.

Manuals and instructions for how to operate or care for equipment in the classroom are another outlet for publication. Work in science, social studies, and math can also lead to the writing of manuals and instructions as well

FIGURE 8.13

Some Magazines That Publish Children's Work

Boy's Life Magazine, 1325 Walnut Hill Lane, Irving, TX 75038.
Children's Digest, 111 Waterway Blvd., Indianapolis, IN 46202.
Children's Express, 1440 New York Ave., NW, Suite 510, Washington, DC 20005.
Highlights for Children, 802 Church St., Honesdale, PA 18431.
Humpty Dumpty's Magazine, 1100 Waterway Blvd., Indianapolis, IN 46202.
Jack and Jill, 1100 Waterway Blvd., Indianapolis, IN 46202.
Language Arts, National Council of Teachers of English, 1111 W. Kenyon Rd., Urbana, IL 61801.
The Reading Teacher, International Reading Association, 800 Barksdale Rd., P.O. Box 8139, Newark, DE 19714-8139.
Stone Soup, P. O. Box 83, Santa Cruz, CA 95063.

as the more usual reports, which can be published as books and magazine or newspaper articles. Good models for this kind of writing can be found in many of the informational books published for children each year.

A number of magazines accept student writing; several are listed in Figure 8.13. The local newspaper also may have a "kid's page." If not, encourage the editors to incorporate one. Occasionally, children's book publishers run competitions. Whether it is a national journal, a statewide magazine, a hallway bulletin board, a classroom library, or a chance to read over the school intercom, outlets for publication are an important component of a writing workshop. Publication provides positive reinforcement for the effort of writing, adds to the purpose for writing, and provides the wideness and diversity of audience necessary to help students develop their potential as writers. After the effort of drafting and redrafting, thinking, and talking, publication—a chance to share one's best—is richly deserved.

Writing Conferences

What teachers say and do during a writing conference is crucial to the success or failure of the writing workshop. The best organization, room arrangement, and record keeping in the world will not matter if you are not a knowledgeable, responsive listener during conferences. Here are some basic guidelines for conferences.

Regularly schedule conferences so that each student knows when he or she will have an opportunity to work one-on-one with you. Regularly scheduled conferences can be supplemented by drop-in conferences in which you stop by a student place and ask if they need a quick conference.

Students should know what to expect during a conference, what procedures they need to follow, and what materials they should have with them. During the conference the student writer should talk more than you talk; the writer should indicate what help is needed. Your job is to listen hard and respond to what the writer is saying. At the close of a conference a writer should be able to state what he or she plans to do next (Graves, 1983; Murray, 1979).

Effective teachers have identified several types of useful questions, but there is no set format of best questions for a conference. Effective questions spring directly from the needs of the student writer. What you say also depends on where the writer is in the writing cycle, relating to content, style, process, or editing concerns. Many teachers find "following" questions quite effective. In these questions you restate what the student has said, often with just a rising intonation to indicate a question is being asked. This invites students to expand on what they have said. Questions that help students focus are also effective. Keeping records of what is discussed during conferences helps you assess the growth of individual writers as well as plan classroom instruction.

Conferences between peers are also an effective tool in the writing workshop. Model and discuss good conference techniques and behaviors, and then invite students to have conferences with a peer. When carefully regulated, these can be valuable learning experiences, but they do not replace the opportunity for teaching and learning that student-teacher conferences offer.

SUMMARY

A literature-rich classroom in which written language is used for a variety of meaningful purposes helps children become writers. The opportunity to hear and read beautifully crafted language and to write on a regular basis enables children to develop their written language skills. Writing takes time, and children need to be allowed to progress at their own pace. As writers, they will generate their own topics, and get ready to write by doing brainstorming, interviewing, observing, and drawing. During drafting, they will sometimes begin to revise, as they learn to manipulate language so that they can say in writing exactly what they mean. As they produce pieces they want to share with others, they begin to focus on revision and develop their editing skills. They learn how to capitalize, punctuate, spell, and alter their syntax to produce the desired effect. Publishing children's writing is important to the writing process. After working hard on their writing, children need to see their language in print. Student-teacher conferences offer opportunities for one-on-one instruction and assessment.

ACTIVITIES

1. **Select one of your pieces from your writing folder and examine the development of that piece from initial inception through final draft.** What processes did you go through as you worked on that piece? How did you select the topic? How did you focus? What kinds of revision concerns are evident across your drafts? What sorts of editing did you need to do? Using the evolution of this piece as your source for examples, develop a series of demonstrations or minilessons that you think will be useful when you begin teaching.
2. **In small groups, formulate questions that you would like to ask a writing-process teacher.** Then interview such a teacher and write up your questions and the teacher's answers for distribution to other class members.
3. **Divide the class. One half of the class will play the roles of parents (irate, confused, and genuinely interested), the other half will play the role of writing-process teacher.** The "parents" should generate questions about how the classroom works, how the teacher teaches, why there are "mistakes" on their children's written work, etc. The "teachers" should answer these questions collaboratively.
4. **With a peer acting as a student, generate a series of questions that you might ask when having a teacher-student conference regarding an early draft of a piece of your peer's writing.** After you have actually had a conference with your peer, discuss your behavior. Were you listening to what the writer had to say? Did your physical position promote collaboration? Did you always make it clear that you were leaving the decision making up to the writer? What did your questions focus on?

FURTHER READING

Atwell, N. (1998). *In the middle: New understandings about writing, reading, and learning* (2nd ed.). Portsmouth, NH: Boynton/Cook/Heinemann.

Calkins, L. McC. (1994). *The art of teaching writing* (2nd ed.). Portsmouth, NH: Heinemann.

Fletcher, R., & Portalupi, J. (1998). *Craft lessons: Teaching writing K–8.* York, ME: Stenhouse.

Fletcher, R. (1996). *A writer's notebook: Unlocking the writer within you.* New York: Avon.

Graves, D. M. (1983). *Writing: Teachers and children at work* (2nd ed.). Portsmouth, NH: Heinemann.

Graves, D. M. (1994). *A fresh look at writing.* Portsmouth, NH: Heinemann.

Ray, K. W. (1999). *Wondrous words: Writers and writing in the elementary classroom.* Urbana, IL: National Council of Teachers of English.

REFERENCES

Atwell, N. (1998). *In the middle: New understandings about writing, reading, and learning* (2nd ed.). Portsmouth, NH: Heinemann.

Birnbaum, J. (1980). Why should I write? Environmental influences on children's views of writing. *Theory into Practice, 19*(3), 202–210.

Calkins, L. M. (1994). *The art of teaching writing* (2nd ed.). Portsmouth, NH: Heinemann.

Cochran-Smith, M. (1984). *The making of a reader.* Norwood, NJ: Ablex.

Daiute, C. (1986). Physical and cognitive factors in revising: Insights from studies with computers. *Research in the Teaching of English, 20,* 141–159.

Dickinson, D. K. (1986). Cooperation, collaboration, and a computer: Integrating a computer into a first-second grade writing program. *Research in the Teaching of English, 20,* 357–378.

Dyson, A. H. (2002). *The brothers and sisters learn to write.* New York: Teachers College Press.

Edelsky, C. (1986). *Writing in a bilingual program: Habia una vez.* Norwood, NJ: Ablex.

Farr, M., & Daniels, H. (1986). *Language diversity and writing instruction.* New York: ERIC Clearinghouse.

Fearn, L., & Farnan, N. (2001). *Interactions: Teaching writing and the language arts.* Boston: Houghton Mifflin.

Fletcher, R. (1993). *What a writer needs.* Portsmouth, NH: Heinemann.

———. (1996). *A writer's notebook: Unlocking the writer within you.* New York: Avon.

———. (2002). *Poetry matters: Writing a poem from the inside out.* NY: HarperCollins.

Fletcher, R., & Portalupi, J. (1998). *Craft lessons: Teaching writing K–8.* York, ME: Stenhouse.

Flower, L, & Hayes, J. R. (1981). The pregnant pause: An inquiry into the nature of planning. *Research in the Teaching of English, 15,* 229–243.

Graves, D. H. (1989). *Experiment with fiction.* Portsmouth, NH: Heinemann.

———. (1989). *Investigate nonfiction.* Portsmouth, NH: Heinemann.

———. (1990). *Discover your own literacy.* Portsmouth, NH: Heinemann.

———. (1992). *Explore poetry.* Portsmouth, NH: Heinemann.

———. (1994). *A fresh look at writing.* Portsmouth, NH: Heinemann.

Graves, D. M. (1983). *Writing: Teachers and children at work* (2nd ed.). Portsmouth, NH: Heinemann.

Hakuta, K., & Garcia, E. E. (1989). Bilingualism and education. *American Psychologist, 44,* 374–379.

Hansen, J. (2001). *When writers read* (2nd ed.). Portsmouth, NH: Heinemann.

Harste, J. C., Woodward, V., & Burke, C. (1984). *Language stories and literacy lessons.* Portsmouth, NH: Heinemann.

Hull, G. (1989). Evaluation: The conventions of writing. In K. S. Goodman, Y. M. Goodman, & W. J. Hood (Eds.), *The whole language evaluation book* (pp. 77–84). Portsmouth, NH: Heinemann.

Langer, J. (1986). Computers and conversation. *Research in the Teaching of English, 20,* 117–119.

Mayher, J. S., Lester, N., & Pradl, G. (1983). *Learning to write/Writing to learn.* Montclair, NJ: Boynton/Cook-Heinemann.

McLaughlin, B. (1987). *Theories of second-language learning.* London: Arnold.

Murray, D. (1979). The listening eye: Reflections on the writing conference. *College English, 41,* 13–18.

———. (1990). *Write to learn.* New York: Holt.

Newkirk, T. (1985). The hedgehog and the fox: The dilemma of writing development. *Language Arts, 62,* 593–603.

Ray, K. W. (1999). *Wondrous words: Writers and writing in the elementary classroom.* Urbana, IL: National Council of Teachers of English.

Smith, F. (1985). Reading like a writer. *Language Arts, 60,* 558–567.

Sowers, S. (1985). Learning to write in a workshop: A study in grades one through four. In M. F. Whiteman (Ed.), *Advances in writing research: Volume 1, Children's early writing development* (pp. 297–342). Norwood, NJ: Ablex.

Strickland, D. S., Feeley, J. T., & Wepner, S. B. (1987). *Using computers in the teaching of reading.* New York: Teachers College.

Zinsser, W. O. (1990). *On writing well.* New York: HarperCollins.

Writing: Writing across the Genres

CHAPTER OUTLINE

The first and second grade classroom bustles with the energy of many groups working on different reading and language arts activities. One group of four girls sits at a back table reading Bernard Most's fantasy If the Dinosaurs Came Back, *scrutinizing the comic illustrations that portray possible interactions of people and dinosaurs in the modern world. After they finish reading, one girl thinks about whether she could ride on an apatosaurus's back to school without falling off; another wonders how she would care for a pet triceratops in her backyard.*

The paperbacks they are reading are a special school edition of Most's story, which has an appendix with photos of animals living today, such as the armadillo, ostrich, and Komodo dragon, under the question, "What makes these animals look like dinosaurs?" As the girls study each photo, sharing their knowledge of dinosaur characteristics, one looks closely at the crocodile and says excitedly, "I think there was a dinosaur that looked just like a crocodile!" Everyone considers the photo of the crocodile, and Mrs. Rapport replies, "I think you may be right, but I'm not sure. What can we do to find out?" A girl says that Gabe, a boy in the class who really likes to read about dinosaurs, might know whether a dinosaur that looked like a crocodile existed and might even know its name. When Gabe isn't sure, another girl reaches for a dictionary to look up "crocodile" to read whether it says anything about its dinosaur ancestors. The other three girls excitedly choose a variety of dictionaries from those available in the classroom, not willing to wait to see what the first girl will find, and begin to search for the word "crocodile." Although they all discover that crocodiles are reptiles who swim in tropical swamps, no one finds any mention of the relationship of the crocodile to dinosaurs. "We could go to the media center to look for a book with dinosaur pictures," suggests one girl as the next logical step in their continuing search for information.

Key Standard

Teachers of language arts/reading have the knowledge and skills to help students become effective writers of a variety of types of texts for different purposes. Such teachers:

- Provide well-crafted trade books from all genres that can be used as models for student writing.
- Help students recognize the techniques and strategies used by successful writers in all genres.
- Create a supportive, collaborative writing environment.
- Ensure that young writers have ample time to create publishable works.

To get a preview of Chapter 9 and learn about writing across the genres, visit the Chapter 9 section of the accompanying *Language Arts* CD-ROM.

Mrs. Rapport types the word "dinosaur" into the card catalog computer when none of the girls is sure how to spell the word and all agree it's important to spell it correctly. A long list of books appears on the screen, and one girl immediately notices that they all have similar numbers and so are located together on the shelves. After finding the group of books, each girl randomly selects one and sits at a nearby table to search for an illustration of a dinosaur that looks like a crocodile. No one can find anything after looking through a couple of books, so one girl goes back with Mrs. Rapport to the dinosaur books still listed on the computer screen. The teacher reads aloud each title until reaching Dinosaurs That Swim and Flew *by David C. Knight. The child eagerly notes the exact number of the book, and chanting it, returns to the shelves with the teacher where she quickly discovers the book. She tells everyone else to come and look at what she has found: illustrations of dinosaurs that look like crocodiles.*

The girls rush to check out the book and return triumphantly to their classroom, showing the student teacher and Gabe their "crocodile dinosaur." Mrs. Rapport reads aloud the pages that describe the dinosaur mesasaurus, a giant lizard with fearsome teeth that was three times bigger than modern crocodiles. The girls talk about how big crocodiles are and are amazed that mesasaurus could be so much bigger, as big as their classroom. They compare and contrast other aspects of mesasaurus and crocodile, then ask for paper and begin drawing and labeling their dinosaur and writing facts they have learned to share with the rest of the class and their families. The library book is left propped on the chalkboard for free reading and writing time later.

One child's desire to know about a dinosaur has now infected an entire class. A picture book fantasy has compelled children to interview possible dinosaur experts and to use reference books and other nonfiction resources available in the media center in an authentic search for information vital to them. Science and language arts have overlapped naturally. The children are eager to share what they have learned, both orally and in writing and drawing. They have conducted research to answer a compelling question of their own. They have worked cooperatively to find the information they need while their teacher served as a guide, asking questions and giving aid and suggestions when needed.

Teachers like Mrs. Rapport are ready to build on their students' interests and enthusiasms by supporting their eagerness to learn. This leads naturally to reading and writing across a variety of genres, even as students are learning to read and write. These first and second grade students are not polished readers and writers by any means, but they are eager to work on their reading and writing in support of what they want to learn. Their teacher knows that students need to learn to read and write for a variety of purposes, and she seizes the moment, even though the topic may seem like science, to teach language arts.

In a literature-rich writing classroom, students have multiple opportunities to create polished writing from the pieces they create during writing workshop, the information they find doing research in science or social studies, the ideas and experiences they find in the books they read, and the things they wonder about. They may take a fragment of a personal experience and craft it into a polished memoir, as Calkins (1994) describes. Or they might take a "true" story that they have written and fashion a piece of fiction from it. They might, as did the students in Mrs. Rapport's classroom, take ideas that they learn in other content areas and fashion them into reports or poems. Whatever the genres children are working on, their "seed ideas" (Calkins, 1994) are "grown" into polished pieces through the same basic process.

During this process, children decide what they are interested in and use literature to study examples of polished pieces in the target genre. They then work with teachers who instruct them in appropriate strategies and structures and provide the help children need as they work to create a piece that can be shared with others. In this chapter we present how several different teachers work with their students to help them learn to write nonfiction, biography, historical fiction, and poetry. In each case, students have rich literary experiences on which to build, personal enthusiasm for the subject, and a great deal of support from their teachers. The written work that they produce is usually accompanied by an oral experience that adds to their facility with language as well as to their sense of possibilities for communicating their ideas to others. In many ways, writing across genres embodies the heart of excellence in teaching the English language arts.

Literary Experience, Research, and Writing

When adults hear the word "research," they often visualize people dressed in white coats, working in a sterile lab filled with complicated equipment trying to find the cure for cancer. Or perhaps they think of engineers with clipboards, strapping a crash-test dummy behind the wheel of an SUV to propel it down a track into a cement block wall. Whatever is imagined, research means that people have a need to know, to discover, to explore. Children are driven by the same urges, whether they ask, "Why do wolves howl at the moon?" or listen to a teacher read aloud E. B. White's (1945) *Stuart Little* and wonder what a radiator is. They have an innate desire to investigate and record their world.

Research can drive the elementary school curriculum, especially in classrooms where children's questions and interests are paramount. Teachers in these classrooms plan learning experiences and ask questions that stimu-

Joseph Kassick

Effective teachers observe students' research projects in process and help them formulate topics and questions.

late children's curiosity. They provide daily opportunities for careful observation and sharing of what children have examined. Children in such a community of active learners are encouraged to think about the hows and whys of their discoveries, first through oral language, then through writing. They are encouraged to talk and write about what they **K**now, **W**hat they would like to know, and what they have **L**earned (or K-W-L exercises). They discover how to use the many different resources available to them in their schools, homes, and communities to answer questions that arise from their contemplation of the world.

These children are given many opportunities to write about topics that interest them because their teachers understand that the process of reporting discoveries cannot be learned in one attempt.

> Some children have to do two or three formal reports before they sense how to choose a subject and how to formulate effective questions. There is no need to rush to help children succeed. Rather, a tone of discovery, sharing in community, and a sense of wonder about the information is what the teacher seeks to foster in the children. The process of learning how to learn—to formulate questions, read, and find any area of knowledge unique to yourself—eludes a majority of students over a lifetime (Graves, 1989).

The goal of all teachers must be to create learners who love to learn and who possess an intrinsic desire to do so.

Effective teachers in the best literacy classrooms have identified a wide range of specific books in all genres they want to share with children for many instructional and aesthetic purposes. They also believe that children need to make their own reading selections and provide their students ample time for free reading of their choices. These same teachers conduct daily writing workshops where children write freely about topics they have chosen. They also have children write in many different formats and for many different purposes in all areas of the curriculum. They know that they need to teach children directly how to write nonfiction well so that their voices have as much passion as is apparent in their personal narratives about a new baby sister or frisky dog. They know that there are some elementary differences between fiction and nonfiction writing that they want children to be able to identify and then use independently in their own writing. They read poetry frequently for pleasure and to enhance learning across the curriculum, so children experience a wide variety of poetic forms, images, and lyrical words that serve as effective models for writing poems of their own. These teachers believe in the power of first-hand observation and experience in order to give children a wealth of ideas. Children are empowered and excited to write what they know because they have learned so much.

This kind of teaching will look different in every classroom, at different grade levels, and across varied content areas and curricula, but effective teachers understand that the process of developing fluency, control, and effectiveness in writing begins by immersing their students in the powerful examples that can be found in children's literature.

DEVELOPING NONFICTION WRITERS: TRADE BOOKS

Often when children switch from writing personal narratives to writing reports and other types of nonfiction, their writing can seem lifeless and boring, the most dreaded labels known to writers. When reporting on nonfiction topics, children often spend a great deal of time gathering piles of facts but much less time compiling them into long, often disorganized lists. They do not seem to be able to assimilate what they have learned into what they already know. As poets they write words that have great sensory appeal, but their science reports are dull and dry. They write engaging, humorous stories, but when writing about famous people in history, their subjects remain as flat as the page.

In her acceptance speech after winning the Kerlan Award in 2000, Patricia Lauber compared most textbook writing to spinach. "It may be good for you, but you wouldn't choose to read it." The words she writes in her information books paint a picture for the reader and are compelling reading. When thinking about the importance of simplicity and choosing the right words, Lauber contrasts Hendrick van Loon's alliterative line, "ships sailed the seas" with "international commerce expanded." "At times when I'm struggling to express some difficult scientific concept in terms that are both accurate and understandable, I often stop, stare at the offending sentence on the computer screen, and repeat silently, 'Ships sailed the seas.'" Lauber is an adept creator of metaphor and alliteration. Her information writing has elements often associated with fiction: tension, conflict, and intrigue. These are qualities that readers appreciate and that novice writers can emulate.

Children need to read as writers, to study writing of acclaimed nonfiction authors and to apply what they have observed to make their own writing sing. Teachers need to read as writing teachers. They need to discover nonfiction books that not only provide good information but also serve as models for their young writers. They need to focus not merely on what is written but on how it is written, so that they can encourage children to look beyond the educational or entertaining elements of these books to the craft employed by their creators. Like Patricia Lauber, many accomplished authors talk about favorite writers whose work they return to again and again for inspiration. Young writers and their teachers must do the same.

A number of studies of children's writing in the last 20 years have found that exposure to high-quality trade books from many genres—rather than texts characterized by controlled vocabulary, short sentences, and stiff style—inspires children to write more elaborately, naturally, and meaningfully. Not only did children's writing style resemble what they were reading but those who read and discussed trade books from all genres also wrote in a greater variety of forms. They took more risks in their writing and used more complex sentences and richer vocabulary (Dressel, 1990; Eckhoff, 1983; DeFord, 1981).

For weeks Adam, a 7-year-old, has been poring over NASA photographs in *National Geographic* and books about space by Seymour Simon and other well-known children's science writers. Adam has filled his space log with illustrations and interesting facts about our solar system and outer space phenomena like constellations, black holes, and comets. In the process of becoming a space whiz, he read *Say Something* by Mary Stoltz, a book about a boy and his father who, while fishing, discuss the world, its many creatures, and their habitats. Stolz repeats "say something" throughout the book, as she compares grass to a green living room, a tadpole to a brown bead on a string, and snow to a shawl for the north wind's shoulders. Adam quickly recognizes her appealing use of a strong, rhythmic pattern and descriptive, figurative language and decides he can share all he has learned about space by writing a book like *Say Something*. He writes:

> Say something about space.
> Say something about infinity.
> Infinity is space. Space never ends. Space is the hat for God.
> Say something about rings.
> The rings are propellers that go round and around like a windmill.
> Say something about stars.

Stars are the pictures in space.
Say something about comets.
Comets are the floating heads that are in space because they have hair coming out the back.

Adam might not have made his expressive comparisons had he not read *Say Something* and responded so positively to Stolz's similes and metaphors. He might not have used a pattern like her question-answer format to share the observations he garnered from his reading and study of detailed space photos. He might not have arranged his text on the page as poetically if he had not studied Stolz's writing style.

What do young children learn from studying Joy Cowley's *Red-Eyed Tree Frog?* Much more than just what can happen in a typical tree frog's day in a tropical rain forest. They learn that dramatic, close-up photographs really help tell the story by allowing readers to notice much more than they could see even if they were visiting the frog's habitat. They learn that instead of simply listing what frogs eat (and what may want to eat a frog!), an author can ask the question, "What will it eat?" and answer that question through a spirited narrative of frog's encounters with other forest creatures. They learn the importance of using strong, descriptive verbs like *slips, slithers, flicks,* and *JUMP!* to describe action in a story. They learn how an author can conclude with a "Did You Know?" section to share other facts about tree frogs that weren't included in the story. Thus, when they share information about an animal they have studied, they may also choose to write an engaging day-in-the-life narrative.

Robert Burleigh tells of Admiral Byrd's lonely Antarctic survival in *Black Whiteness,* an intriguing title for the true story of one man's adventure in a frozen world where the sun never shines for months at a time during the winter. Older children learn how a nonfiction author can write poetically to describe life on the brink, and the fact that in a place so inhospitable

There is also a terrible beauty:
afternoon skies that shatter "like broken goblets"
as tiny ice crystals fall across the face of the sun;
blood-red horizons, liquid twilights
and pale green beams, called auroras,
that wind in great waves through the towering dark.

Readers of *Black Whiteness* learn how authors create a true sense of place. They learn the meaning and significance of voice when they read excerpts from Byrd's own journal, which eloquently describe not only the Antarctic and what Byrd must do to endure there but also his volatile feelings, ending with his joyous appreciation of "the sheer beauty and miracle of being alive."

They begin to see what they need to do to make the people they are writing about come alive and to make their own writing sound natural and compelling.

How does a writer engage the reader and set the scene immediately in the beginning of a book? Men glide on the moonlit water in a small boat that they anchor in a forbidden portion of the river. They know they should not be there, but they want to collect honey to sell in the market. A hint of tension is felt in the seemingly serene story beginning. Men talk quietly, but Deben doesn't answer. A splash is heard. What has happened? Deben has been killed silently and then slipped from the boat by a huge tiger that no one is aware of until it is too late. The reader is hooked and wants to read Sy Montgomery's book *The Man-Eating Tigers of Sundarbans* to learn more about the relationship of people and tigers in a faraway place.

Montgomery often asks direct questions that help her readers make personal connections to the unusual story she is telling of tigers and people. "Have you ever tried to give your pet cat a bath?" Or she warns the reader, "So if you see a tiger, stand your ground—don't run!" Children writing reports can experiment with directly addressing their audience and with point of view to find the best way to share the information they have gathered. Copying Montgomery's storytelling style helps them energize their own writing.

Teachers have many resources to help them identify high-quality nonfiction books for young readers, including nonfiction book awards that highlight a genre sometimes neglected by other award committees in the past. The Orbis Pictus Award is presented annually by the National Council of Teachers of English to the most outstanding work of nonfiction published during the previous year; a substantial list of honor books is also identified. The American Library Association recently established the Robert F. Sibert Informational Book Award, which is given annually to the author of the most distinguished informational book published during the preceding year. The Boston Globe-Horn Book Award also presents a yearly nonfiction award. Compiling a list of past award and honor books gives writing teachers many high-quality nonfiction books to share with novice writers. Reading high-quality literature and writing well are integrally linked. Figure 9.1 lists some outstanding writers of nonfiction for children.

BECOMING SCIENCE WRITERS: OBSERVATION, RECORDING, AND WRITING

When children read and write across genres, they realize that they can tell what they know in many different ways. Encourage your students to keep writer's notebooks for recording ideas and observations for writing workshop and also introduce them to the use of journals and other types of expository writing in other areas of the curriculum. For example, observation and

FIGURE 9.1

Some Outstanding Nonfiction Authors

Joanna Cole
Elisha Cooper
Pat Cummings
Lois Ehlert
Russell Freedman
Jean Fritz
Gail Gibbons
James Cross Giblin
Diane Hoyt-Goldsmith
Jean Craighead George
Kathleen Krull
Kathryn Lasky
Patricia Lauber
Sandra Markle
Jacqueline Briggs Martin
Patricia and Frederick McKissack
Jim Murphy
Milton Meltzer
Andrea Davis Pinkney
Laurence Pringle
Doreen Rappoport
Joanne Ryder
Seymour Simon
Diane Stanley
Walter Wick

hands-on inquiry activities are among the hallmarks of good science teaching. To enhance learning, encourage students to first discuss and then write about their discoveries in blank books or small notebooks.

On the first day of a new science unit on plants and seeds, children in a first and second grade class are asked simply, "What is a seed?" Their teacher writes every idea presented on an overhead, asking more questions to get children to expand and explain their concepts of "seed." One child poetically says, "Seeds have tiny baby plants inside them that are just waiting to wake up." After children have shared all they know about seeds—and they know quite a bit from past experiences—they are divided into groups, and each is given a tray of small items. Their task is to determine which items are seeds and which are not. "If you plant it, will it grow?" is written on a strip adhered to the tray. Lively discussions begin as children examine items as diverse as sesame seeds, raisins, tiny crackers, sunflower seeds, corn kernels, an avocado pit, and a bean. After dividing the items into two piles—one which they believe is seeds and one which they believe is not—the children discuss and debate their reasons for their designations for each item. They are now eager to learn more about how plants grow.

Each group will be planting bean seeds in a number of different containers. They have heard their teacher read aloud books about seeds by Eric Carle and Marc Brown and watched her model the planting steps listed on sentence strips in a pocket chart. Each group labels a number of different containers after they brainstorm what is important to the growth of seeds. They

Bernice Cullinan

Children illustrate their report writing using colorful markers.

decide they are going to experiment with the amount of light, water, and warmth necessary for optimum growth. One container will sit on the classroom windowsill and be watered regularly; another will be kept on the sill but flooded with water daily; one will sit on the windowsill but never be watered; another will be kept in a box while watered regularly; and the last will be watered regularly while growing inside the refrigerator in the teacher's lounge. Students predict what will happen to the plants. Which will grow best? Will any not grow at all? They talk about the possibilities and write their predictions in their science logs where they have already drawn pictures of their seeds.

Each day children measure and check on the growth and development of their plants and record, by writing and drawing, any changes they observe. They carefully remove and replant small plants to scrutinize root development. As new seed and plant vocabulary words are encountered, they are added to the science word wall to aid them when they write in their logs.

The teacher reads aloud books like Peter Parnall's (1987) *Apple Tree*, and then reads the book aloud again so that children can examine how Parnall describes what he observes. The children agree that his lead gives them a striking image of the apple tree: "It is thick and gnarled. Some branches seem like witch's claws, poking, grasping, twisted like a mass of melted wire." Parnall's illustration of the tree confirms what they have envisioned. The young scientists evaluate the descriptions in their logs to see if they need to add more detail to make their own words say more and show more.

The teacher has taught other minilessons on how to organize information in their science logs and how to label and write captions for their drawings, often using examples from nonfiction books by authors such as Lois Ehlert and Gail Gibbons. They pore thoughtfully over the pages of these books searching for ideas to enliven their own work. Children frequently discuss their findings with each other, sharing exciting discoveries and information. Eventually, what they have observed and recorded in their logs is compared to their earlier predictions.

Besides reading the nonfiction plant books that their teacher has checked out from the public library and made available in the reading corner, these students also enjoy looking at fiction and traditional stories involving plants and seeds. They read and dramatize a traditional version of *Jack and the Beanstalk* (Cauley, 1983) during their language arts class time. They compare the story to Raymond Briggs' *Jim and the Beanstalk* and Sid Fleischman's *McBroom and the Beanstalk,* both fractured fairy tales with great appeal. They talk about whether or not what happens in these versions of the traditional story could happen in real life. Mabel Watts's poem "Maytime Magic" (in Prelutsky, 1983) is written on chart paper and read chorally. Some children decide to use the descriptions they have written in their science logs to write poems about what their seeds and young plants remind them of.

They listen intently to their teacher as she reads aloud from Christina Bjork's (1988) *Linnea's Windowsill Garden* and respond by making personal connections to their own joy at planting seeds and watching them grow. They laugh at the change of luck that causes the piles and piles of popcorn to bury the farm in a new version of Carl Sandburg's (1999) Rootabaga Story *The Huckabuck Family and How They Raised Popcorn in Nebraska and Quit and Came Back.* They learn a great deal about Vietnamese culture from Sherry Garland's (1993) *The Lotus Seed.* The children's days are filled with seeds and books and growth.

Children participating in cross-curricular units of study such as this one on seeds and plants have numerous opportunities to express themselves in many different ways. They draw on their prior experiences to consider what conditions seeds need for optimal growth and to make predictions about what will happen to the seeds when they do not have enough (or have too much) water, warmth, soil, or sunlight. They talk frequently about what they observe with each other and their teacher, who directs their attention to, and scaffolds their learning of, the most important information they discover. They write daily in their logs after examining their plants, and they use their descriptions and new vocabulary words to write creatively as well. They read a wide range of high-quality fiction and nonfiction related to their study, both for information and for pleasure. With the guidance of their teacher and through collaborative small-group work, children solve problems and discuss findings with each other. Each time they discuss what has happened to their plants, they make more sense of what they have learned. Each time they write in their logs, they discover more of what they know. Each time they listen carefully to what classmates have to say, they realize what they want to share.

These students are busy employing the scientific method as they learn to communicate effectively with each other in a variety of ways. They are learning to record their observations in logs, to write in response to reading, to record questions and ideas, to write labels and captions, to write scientific information, to communicate with others, and to write poetry. They are learning to learn from a variety of sources and to compare their sources, as described in the *Teaching Idea: Comparing Sources*.

BUILDING ON INTEREST: RESEARCH, WRITING, AND ORAL PRESENTATIONS

Because academic choice is an important part of the responsive classroom in which she teaches, third and fourth grade children in Margaret Burke's class become experts on one major topic that interests them. During the first goal-setting conference shortly after the year begins, Margaret gets to know the children and their parents, learning as much as she can about who her students are outside of her classroom. Margaret also discusses the project with students and their parents at this time so that children can begin exploring areas of interest. Parents are informed that much of the project work will be done at home and that children will be seeking their guidance when deciding on the best topic for in-depth study. Although they don't begin working on their research officially until the end of March, many children spend the fall and winter reading books and articles about their topics, percolating and rehearsing what they know while interviewing experts, sharing ideas with each other, brainstorming, and searching Web sites for information. Long before spring, the children have many opportunities, both with Margaret and with the media specialist, to learn how to do research, take notes, and how to present what they know to others. They are also exposed to many well-written nonfiction texts, talking about their organization and the writers' craft.

TEACHING IDEA

Assessing the Learning Environment

COMPARING SOURCES

Gather numerous books on various reading levels about a topic of interest. Read the books together and then evaluate them as informational sources by comparing them along appropriate dimensions. For example, you might want to develop a chart in which you list the title, genre, and kind of illustrations, followed by a list of what students learned from each book. They can then compare the information they gained from varied sources, both in amount and in kind. Some books, for example, might not give as many "facts" but instead give students a better "feel" for a particular subject.

The first question Margaret asks at the second goal-setting conference in March is, "Have you been thinking about your topic for your project?" By this time, many children have talked to her about their ideas and possible books on their subjects, but some still need help in narrowing the focus of their research or in making a choice from all their interests. The emphasis is on finding an interesting and enjoyable topic; creating the project should be fun. It will also be their only homework during the next month or so. Children and their parents receive two project contracts, one to be kept by them and one that must be signed by a parent and returned to Margaret for the child's project file at school.

Students identify their topic and ways they will share information about their project with others. All third-graders will write a report at least one page long; fourth-graders must write at least two pages. Students must also use a visual aid (a play, book, map or chart, a series of drawings or cartoons, a model, a videotape, a collection of photos, a collection of objects, a poster, or a cassette tape) for sharing what they know with their classmates. They are asked to check which of the listed possibilities they will create. They also must list the types of resources they plan to use: the school media center; the public library; personal interviews; television, film, videos, or radio; the Internet; books, magazines, or newspapers; or other sources. Students are asked to record important topic questions that they will be researching; what they are going to do in order to answer their questions; and supplies they will need. When they give Margaret their contracts, they have a general idea of how their information will be organized and where they will find what they need to know. Their plan is in place, and their work can begin. Margaret sends home a calendar for students to sign up for a time to share what they have studied and to invite parents to attend when the students are "teaching."

Margaret models how to narrow a topic on the overhead projector, beginning with the general topic *snakes*. After discussion with her students, she finally decides to narrow the topic and learn all she can about *rattlesnakes*. She fills out a contract and thinks aloud about how she will share what she knows with everyone in the class. She teaches a minilesson on brainstorming questions, similar to those described in the *Teaching Idea: Activities to Generate Ideas for Writing,* that will guide her research and reporting on rattlesnakes. She arranges the questions in the order she thinks is best for teaching about rattlesnakes. With the children's participation, she creates a list of what she is going to do, the resources she will use, including interviewing a zookeeper if possible, and the supplies she will need to present her project.

The children have about a month to complete their research, write reports, create some sort of visual aid, and prepare a 10- to 20-minute oral presentation for the class. During this time, students are encouraged to rehearse what they are learning with each other and at home so that they

TEACHING IDEA

Addressing Individual Needs

ACTIVITIES TO GENERATE IDEAS FOR WRITING

One primary-grade teacher and her students were interested in studying animals. Their experiences provided them with information about animals, and also a wealth of ideas for their own writing. They:

- ✦ Read many trade books—fiction, nonfiction, and poetry—about animals.
- ✦ Searched for information on the Internet.
- ✦ Took a field trip to the zoo.
- ✦ Created a mural in which they placed animals in their native habitats.
- ✦ Categorized animals.
- ✦ Created a web of the five types of vertebrates.

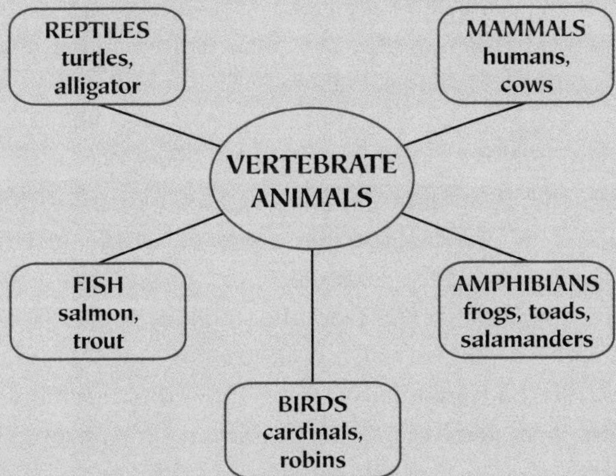

- ✦ Conducted a survey using student-generated questions about favorite animals.
- ✦ Tabulated and reported survey results.

really get to know their subject well and are sure that what they find is most interesting to everyone. They ask each other questions that can lead to further research. Frequent discussions result in written reports that echo the same voice as the one the child uses when informally sharing his or her research. Students also learn what others need to know in order to visualize what they are trying to teach.

For 3 weeks, two children present their projects each day. The audience listens intently, knowing they will share remarks about what they have learned after their classmate's presentation has ended. Margaret asks probing questions to help her students expand their presentations or share information they may have forgotten. After they present their projects, the children assess themselves, writing a paragraph or two evaluating their experience, what they liked best and what they might have done differently. They also assess each presentation, commenting positively about what they enjoyed most, what they learned, and any other questions they might still have. Margaret writes an evaluation for each child, emphasizing their successes as teachers of the other students in their class.

By the end of the year, students have learned to choose a topic and find and collect information about that topic. They have learned to write interesting reports and to create visual aids that enhance their oral presentations. They have learned to create an oral presentation that will engage their classmates. They have also learned to narrow topics, brainstorm ideas, and plan effectively by creating a list of what they need to do and the resources they need. They have also had a great deal of practice in active listening as they respond to one another's "rehearsals" as they craft their written and oral presentations and listen critically to final presentations.

Bringing home to school: Learning what you already know

When La, a third-grader, and her father meet with Margaret at their first goal-setting conference of the year, they talk to her about La's Hmong dance lessons and her other interests. After the conference, La thinks of many possible project ideas, but determines that she won't be studying an animal like many of her classmates. She has decided to learn more about Hmong musical instruments since her father and grandfather know how to play many of them. She can interview them for expert information and can record her grandfather while he plays.

La writes her report and creates a poster with photos, and on the day of her presentation, has her father visit the class with his unusual instruments. After her brief introduction and before he plays each instrument, La's father passes them around for students' inspection. Students make predictions about how each will be played and how each will sound and are surprised at how right or wrong they are. They talk about how one instrument sounds like bagpipes, another like an accordion. La tells stories of the importance of music to the Hmong people; of how music is played for 24 hours straight during funerals; and of how young men play music outside favored young women's windows, signifying their interest in them.

Margaret has pulled down the world map to show students where Laos is located in relation to China, India, and Japan, and how far away it is from

Minnesota, where La's family now lives. She asks La whether one song her father has played is music for dancing, only to discover it's a funeral piece. Margaret wonders what music is played during La's dance lessons. La shows her classmates one of the dances she has learned, and when encouraged by Margaret, kneels and performs another where she sways gently while delicately moving her hands. Soon Margaret is next to her, asking La if she would teach the other students how to move their hands as she is doing. All the boys and girls in the class are soon watching La intently, her fingertips barely touching, her arms undulating to the music.

La has one more thing to share, something that Margaret turns into a guessing game. She holds up an elaborately embroidered piece of fabric with two long tails attached to the top edge. Students are asked if they have any ideas about what the cloth is used for. Some suggest a wall hanging, a dress, a head wrap. La smiles shyly and tells students that it is a Hmong baby carrier, one her mother uses with her baby brother, whom all the children know well since he is often the subject of her writing and sharing. Margaret helps her tie a doll to the back of another girl in the class, and the children are amazed by the ingenuity. Earlier in the year while on a field trip to the Minneapolis Institute of Arts, Margaret had seen a baby carrier displayed, and not knowing what it was, turned to La for an explanation. La knew just what the beautiful cloth was and agreed to bring her mother's in for her report.

Children in Margaret's culturally diverse class are encouraged to share what they know about themselves and to explore the world so that they know much more when they leave her class. Margaret's students think of themselves as accomplished readers and writers. They are a community of seekers and learners, invited into a room that is filled with bins of books on every subject, intriguing objects, art and science materials, writing tools of every description, and nooks and crannies for reading and play rehearsals. They have a mentor who knows them well and genuinely connects home and school in a supportive network. They can transform their personal knowledge through writing and oral sharing into public knowledge, just as published writers of nonfiction trade books transform their own interests and knowledge into information that they share with children.

RESEARCHING, WRITING, AND REPORTING

Students in Launa Ellison's fifth and sixth grade class spend a great deal of time conducting in-depth research on three self-selected topics of interest during the year. They produce well-documented reports based on information gathered from at least three sources, and teach everyone else in the class what they have learned in an oral presentation accompanied by a "Make or Do" project, a visual aid to enhance sharing such as a model, display, or a play.

Learning to learn from sources: Taking notes

Novice report writers often try to copy everything they read when they search for information to put into a report. When they do this, the information goes in through the eye and out through the hand, never stopping to lodge in the brain. To help students overcome this tendency, Launa models the process of note taking with different nonfiction text examples. Although she requires students to have at least fifty note cards when writing their reports, compelling them to write from an abundance of information, Launa emphasizes that the most important aspect of note taking is to cover the important points, not necessarily to collect an exact number of facts. In a series of minilessons, students hear how Launa determines which is an important fact and which is not. Then they see how she paraphrases each fact, writing it on a note card (or on one page of a small tablet or on a small piece of notebook paper that has been folded and cut into fourths). She allows them to read a passage on the overhead, then covers the text and asks students to write the most important points of the passage. Launa's students learn to think critically about their subjects and the information they read.

They are not reading simply to look for answers to questions asked before they even begin their research, they are also discovering and evaluating new ideas. Her students practice note taking with similar texts and participate in class discussions of why the facts they have chosen are important. They learn how to organize and categorize facts, deciding on headings that describe each cluster. They practice writing sentences that describe the topics, using the clusters of facts to create paragraphs with supporting information for each topic sentence. With practice, students learn to actively construct categories and concepts that make sense to them. Their understanding and ability to organize information help them write better reports.

Learning to learn from sources: Developing style

From studying opening paragraphs by authors like Diane Stanley and Russell Freedman, students learn to write appealing leads that state the purpose and main ideas of their topic in a way that will get readers interested in the story they will tell. They begin to understand the important functions of a provocative title, descriptive subtitles, a clear table of contents, and a bibliography through study and discussion of books by writers such as Kathleen Krull, James Cross Giblin, or Milton Meltzer. They contemplate how to write conclusions that really do sum up the most important aspects of the topic they are studying. They consider what they really want readers to learn and remember.

As described in Chapter Seven, Launa's students have read and critically responded to a number of high-quality children's nonfiction trade books, noticing the liveliness of the writing in contrast to the terse writing found in encyclopedias and dry history texts. They study how biographers select, organize, and present information, describing their subjects so well that readers feel they know the person by the end of the book. They know how to write engaging nonfiction before they decide on an interesting topic, and they understand the importance of using multiple resources in order to expand and corroborate their ideas. They have considered the writer's craft and are ready to write commendable nonfiction of their own. They know exactly what Launa expects from them because she gives them the handout reproduced in the *Teaching Idea: Directions for Report Writing*. She also asks them to report on their progress midway through the process on the form reproduced in the *Teaching Idea: Progress Report Update*.

To help students select a person for their biography projects, Launa brings in piles of biographies from the public library. Students spend a few days browsing through the books, identifying people who intrigue them. During this time, each student must find three famous people as possible subjects for further research, listing name, gender, race, why the person is famous, and why the student may want to learn more about each person for each of the three. After thinking about the possibilities and talking with Launa and other students, the students select the person they want to get to know.

Writing a biography

Ethan had heard about C. J. Walker a number of times but wasn't sure why she was so important and what she had accomplished to be so well thought of by some of the adults he knew. He decided she would be an interesting person to research for his biography. He found one library book about her life, and three Web sites using the Internet search engine Google, one of several available to young researchers. Others are listed in Figure 9.2. He also found a number of photos of her, her company, and her products searching Google's Images. He began reading and writing facts on separate note cards, needing at least fifty or more to have enough information to cover Walker's life. While taking notes, he thought about whether or not students in his class would understand the information he was gathering and find it interesting. Most of the time, he paraphrased the information he found, but occasionally he wrote down a direct quote that he thought would be meaningful in his final report.

After Ethan read and took notes on all his sources, he organized his note cards into separate piles. He discovered three major categories: Walker's childhood and early life, how she became famous, and what happened to her after she achieved her fame. His seven-page report included photos he found on the Internet, including a reproduction of Walker's image on a U.S. postage stamp. After finishing his biography of C. J. Walker, the first African-American businesswoman to become a millionaire, Ethan was surprised to discover that his mother uses many of her beauty products and that the logo

TEACHING IDEA

Assessing the Learner

DIRECTIONS FOR REPORT WRITING

When Launa's students begin work on their first report of the year, they are given a handout that reviews and outlines the steps for creating quality reports. The research and writing process is carefully delineated in the following directions.

1. Choose a manageable topic that really interests you.
2. Find three or more sources. Make a source card for each, including the author (last name, then first name), title, date published, publisher, and city for books you use. Source cards for Web sites should include the site title and Web address.
3. Take notes on 3×5 cards or in a small tablet. Write only one concept on each card and use your own words. (This requires you to evaluate ideas and rephrase them rather than simply copying them.) Notes should be short, only one or two sentences long. Some ideas may be so important that you want to quote them directly. Be sure to copy those ideas exactly as they are stated in the text, and put quotation marks around them. Put your name in the right-hand corner of each card, and the source number and page number where you found the fact in the left-hand corner.
4. When you have fifty or more cards and feel sure you have covered the topic, sort the cards into piles of similar content.
5. Sort each pile to put the cards in the order you think is best for writing about them.
6. Write a topic sentence for each pile on a different colored card. Put it on top and bind the pile with a rubberband.
7. Put all of the piles into the logical order you want to present them in your report. Number the piles.

has not been changed over the years since her death. He was able to bring in these products to show his classmates.

Susan B. Anthony was suggested when students were trying to think of important leaders for a student newspaper article they were writing. Linnea, another fifth grade student in Launa's class, and the other students involved in the search for the ideal leader didn't really know anything about her, so she decided to research Anthony's life. Like Ethan, Linnea used Google and Google Images and found an Internet Web site with a great deal of information about Susan B. Anthony and the house where she lived, which is now a museum. She also found two Anthony biographies and a history book about women's voting rights that had more facts about her involvement in the early women's rights movement.

8. Write an introductory paragraph for the whole report. The first sentence should state the topic, but not give information about it. The following sentences should tell what will be covered in the report in the order that the information will be covered. The paragraph should make your reader want to learn more about the subject.
9. Decide what pictures, maps, or other visuals you want to include in your report and create them or have them copied. If you photocopy, you must cite your source.
10. Now begin writing. Put your introductory paragraph on the first page. Then start a new page for each pile. At the top of the page, make the topic sentence the first sentence of the paragraph. Double-check to be sure that all the information that follows in the paragraph relates to the topic sentence. Put your illustrations in as you write so they fit appropriately with the words describing them.
11. Revise the information in the paragraph to be sure it is clear and holds the reader's attention. Check each paragraph to be sure you have followed all the conventions for good writing, proofreading for spelling, punctuation, and grammar, so that your report is easy to read.
12. Write your conclusion or summary on a separate page. Restate what you have learned and how you feel about your topic.
13. Put your source cards in alphabetical order by the author's last name to make your bibliography. List all the bibliographic information you have on each card. The bibliography is the last page of your report.
14. Number the pages of your report, then create a table of contents with the titles of each part of the report on the left side of the page and the page numbers on the right.
15. Make an interesting cover that is relevant to your report information. Include the title of your report, your name, and a visual. Use some color to add interest.

Launa Ellison, fifth/sixth grade teacher,
Minneapolis Public Schools

Linnea produced more than fifty note cards and carefully put the number for each resource in the upper right-hand corner of each card to keep track of the source of each fact she recorded. When sorting her cards, Linnea found that she had three major content areas. Part One had subheadings on Anthony's early life, her teaching, and her involvement in the temperance movement. Part Two included information about her role in the women's rights movement, with subheadings on Elizabeth Cady Stanton, the New York Married Women's Act, women's voting rights, and the Civil War. Part Three focused on both Anthony's and Stanton's deaths and summarized their contributions and accomplishments.

Launa's students are a diverse group, coming from a variety of cultures and communities. Several of her students are English language learners. But

TEACHING IDEA

Assessing the Learner

PROGRESS REPORT UPDATE

During the research time allotted for their biographies, Launa checks on student progress by having them provide information about their note taking and organization. Students check off the following steps as they are completed:

So far I have ____ different sources. I have _____ note cards.

___1. My cards are sorted into piles of like topics.

___2. I have used a strip of paper and given each pile a word label.

___3. I have studied the piles and put them into the best order for writing my biography.

___4. I have numbered the piles in order.

___5. I have put the cards in each pile in the order I want to use them.

___6. I have evaluated the piles and at least half of the note cards are about why the person is famous. Yes No (circle one)

___7. If YES, go on. If NO, you need to get more note cards quickly.

___8. On the strip of paper on top of each pile, write a topic sentence that will let the reader know what you will be writing about in this section.

___9. You are ready to begin typing your first draft. Use Times #14 and double space. Write your topic sentence at the top of the page. Then look at your cards, in order, and make up sentences in your own words. If you copy anything, even just a few words, you must use quotation marks and list the source and the page of your quote. Remember to start each new topic at the top of a new page.

all of her students succeeded at their research projects. Why? Because Launa's students choose their own topics, they find research to be an enjoyable task. They have time to explore their topics and a variety of materials to help them. They have first-hand knowledge of how to investigate a person's life, and know that if they get lucky, they may just find diaries, letters, real conversations, speeches, or other primary source material that will give them a direct connection to the person they want to know. They rehearse their information writing regularly with Launa and their peers and revise and edit collaboratively. They have regular conferences with Launa during writing workshop to seek her help and advice on specific concerns they have about their writing.

Biographer Diane Stanley states in her Author's Note for *Bard of Avon: The Story of William Shakespeare,* "Like detectives, historians gather all the

FIGURE 9.2

Internet Search Engines for Student Researchers

- Ask Jeeves for Kids! http://www.ajkids.com
  You can type in any question on this kid-safe search engine.
- KidBibs http://www.kidbibs.com
  A good resource for writing with lots of book ideas.
- KidsClick! Web Search http://www.sunsite.berkeley.edu/KidsClick!
  A team of librarians has selected 5,000 Web sites in fifteen categories.
- Northern Light http://www.northernlight.com
  Information from many different sources including newspapers.
- Yahooligans! http://www.yahooligans.com
  A Web guide with sites organized into six different categories with downloadable pictures, sounds, and video clips.
- Information Please: Kids' Almanac http://kids.infoplease.com/
  Information about history, sports, science, the world, and other topics with links to other useful sites.

known facts together until a pattern begins to appear. And when that pattern reveals the life of one of the most exceptional writers of all time, what an exciting discovery that is!" Young writers revel in the same thrill of discovery. Another noted biographer's tips are presented in the *Teaching Idea: Kathleen Krull's Ten Tips for Writing Biographies*.

Launa's students are able to synthesize a great deal of information from many different nonfiction sources, including books, articles, and Web sites, and to evaluate, prioritize, and organize facts to present a life story of someone of interest to them. When writing their reports, they think about their audience and select information they feel will be appealing to listeners who know little about the person. Ethan's and Linnea's enthusiasm for the people they studied is conveyed by their engaging writing. They have learned how to breathe life into a pile of facts, to present a life in a way that would allow classmates to enjoy their discoveries. With the help of posters and other visual aids, they are able to tell other students about the accomplishments of C. J. Walker and Susan B. Anthony without having to read word-for-word from their reports because these are now people they know well. They can talk about them and their accomplishments just as readily as they can about those of friends or relatives.

Launa also builds in opportunities for assessment. One such opportunity involves students assessing one another's work with a rubric similar to that presented in the *Teaching Idea: Assessment of Report Writing*.

TEACHING IDEA

Literature Link

KATHLEEN KRULL'S TEN TIPS FOR WRITING BIOGRAPHIES (ABRIDGED)

1. Are you nosy? Pick a person you'd love to know better. The more passion you have for your subject, the more energy you'll spend and the better your biography will be.
2. Make a list of nosy questions and actually interview a favorite relative, neighbor, friend, or even teacher. Try not to be afraid or shy. Take notes and listen carefully.
3. Or pick someone, dead or alive, you don't know personally—your favorite genius in the creative arts (that includes rock stars), an athletic hero, a history maker. In *The Lives of . . .* I prefer dead people. Information about them can be easier to obtain, and they can't complain when you mention their underwear, etc. Notables on commemorative stamps have to be at least 10 years dead, and I think the U.S. Postal Service has a point in waiting until someone can be viewed in perspective.
4. Unleash your best detective skills on encyclopedias, newspapers and magazines, biographies at the library, and Internet searches. You can't just lift chunks from the Net and drop them into your bio, any more than you can do this with encyclopedias or other sources. You have to process this information, interpret it, put your own spin on it.
5. Look for juicy details to make your information come alive. What did they wear? What did they do in the middle of the night? How weird was their family life? What did they crave?
6. After you've soaked up all your information, don't use it all. Being selective is the magic key. Use only the most savory, cream-of-the-crop stuff, plus the facts that move your narrative along. Look for the arc, or shape, of a person's life. Every life story has a beginning, middle, and end. Aim for the most dramatic part and tell what led up to it. What traits enabled them to overcome what obstacles?

Turning Fact into Fiction: Writing Historical Fiction

History is literally his story or her story, stories of real people who participated in real events—stories that when vividly told link children living now to children who lived long ago and whisper truths that speak directly to them. When writing historical fiction, many elements, including dialogue, setting, point of view, and the interaction of real people and fictional characters, must be considered in order to tell a good story that has just the right balance between fact and fiction.

7. Try tweaking your story by taking a point of view other than the standard third-person omniscient. You can use bystanders, or the neighbors as in *The Lives of . . .*, or you could take the "warts and all" approach of a critic, divulging faults as well as redeeming qualities. Or, how would they tell their own story? How would one of their children? How would one of their teachers? How would a space alien?
8. Pick a number of words you want to end up with—say 500 or 1,000. Revision—the constant reworking that professional writers must do to get publishable prose—is a tricky concept to grasp. Manipulating your material until you get your 500 words will give you a taste. Immersed in the process of elimination, you find yourself coaxing out what really matters. Lots of interesting stuff gets dropped while I try to find the essence of a person. This is delicate, almost like being on a tightrope. Here is where you can polish your biography into a small gem.
9. I'm always trying to use combinations of words and ways of telling the story that are unique to me. Some other clues to pithy writing include:
   - Think simple, clear, vivid, concise, and rethink clichés.
   - Stick to facts—interpret but don't make up facts or dialogue.
   - A sense of compassion helps—some lives are more tragic than comic.
   - Humor really helps—look for little ironies.
10. Above all, have fun! After all, when you're gossiping, it's hard not to.

Source: Krull, K. (1999). Writing biographies for inquiring minds. *Book Links, 8*(5), 21–23.

In her book *Talent Is Not Enough,* author Mollie Hunter writes that

> an author should be so steeped in the historical period of the book that you could walk undetected in the past. You'd wake up in the morning and know the kind of covers you'd have over you, know the kind of bed you'd been sleeping in, the amenities of getting dressed, even to the change you'd have in your pockets . . . . This, for the historical novelist, must be the end-purpose of research: to be able to think and feel in terms of a period so that the people within it are real and three-dimensional, close enough to hear the sound of their voices, to feel their body-warmth, to see the expression in their eyes. All the rest one learns—dates of events, types of weapons, location of incidents, political background—all the logistics of history, as it were, are no more than fixed points of reference for the structure of a book (p. 43).

TEACHING IDEA

Assessing the Learner

ASSESSMENT OF REPORT WRITING

The following rubric is used by Launa Ellison to assess students' achievements in nine areas she has designated as important when writing a good research report. The highest possible total is 45 points.

Report Name ______________________ Created by ______________________

Evaluator's Name ______________________ Date ____________ Total Points ________

Points	5 4	3 2	1	0
Cover				
_____	Has title, author, color, neat relevant picture, interesting	Missing something, or is messy.	Has only title and author.	Missing
Table of Contents				
_____	Correct pages, using . . . to numbers, uses capital letters on first word, and spelling is correct.	Some mistakes in numbers, page setup, punctuation or spelling.	Is sloppy or misnumbered.	Missing
Introduction				
_____	Page is clearly titled, on separate page, tells what you will write about in correct order, interesting.	Has 1st sentence correct and mentions topics in the right order but is boring.	Is too short and does not mention topics in right order.	Missing
Topic Sentences				
_____	Tells what the topic is. Each on a new page. Sentences are interesting.	Topic sentences are all about the same, uninteresting.	Topic sentences short with some mistakes.	Missing
Spelling & Punctuation				
_____	No mistakes.	Less than ten errors in report.	Has 10–20 errors.	Over 20
Quality				
_____	Topic is rich with interesting descriptions in student's own words, flows easily from idea to idea.	The information is good but does not flow well, sometimes sounds like it is copied from books.	The information does not cover important areas of the topic.	
Illustrations				
_____	5 or more relevant graphics integrated neatly, with source notes.	Has less than 5 pictures, they do not have relevance, missing sources.	Few pictures, which aren't neat or noted.	Missing
Conclusion				
_____	It is clear what you have learned.	Sentences have little meaning.		Missing
Bibliography				
_____	Three or more sources, alphabetized Last name, first. *Title*. City: Publisher, date.	Less than three sources, problems with correct form for bibliography		Missing

Bernice Cullinan

A writer's group responds to a classmate's writing.

In the best historical fiction, historical fact is seamlessly woven into the fiction to create an authentic and appealing story. Readers learn about the past as they are mesmerized by action-packed sagas of interesting people dealing with significant problems. If authors have been diligent in their research, what they write is true. Accomplished writers of high-quality historical fiction spend a great deal of time studying an era before they begin writing their novels. They look for important historic details that breathe life into the characters and their story. Although the goal is to create a suspenseful, dramatic narrative, the writer of historical fiction has the additional burden of ensuring accuracy and authenticity. The fact that the people in the novel lived long ago becomes irrelevant when students are caught up in a good story that also seems to apply to what they know of the world. Good writers make tales of the past as inviting as contemporary fiction for young readers.

How can teachers help older students write historical fiction? In order to create believable characters, students need to consider dialogue, action, and description. The best way to discover how people spoke during the period of time in which students are interested is to read a good novel from the same period and location. While reading, students should note any idioms and other unusual speech patterns the author has employed to bring the characters to life, either in a journal or on note cards. Do some characters speak differently from others? When written by skilled authors, dialogue gives readers a sense of how people spoke during the time when the story takes place while still being understandable.

After reading the novel, students can role-play the dialogue of favorite characters, considering not only the words and phrases used but also the tone of voice and emotional state of the character. While reading, students should note historical details such as the type of clothing characters wear, food they eat, and places where they live. How characters respond to the conflict in the story depends on what motivates them, what they believe, how they feel. What does the author do to share that kind of information with the reader? In addition to reading historical fiction, students can research the time period and people living then by using informational resources such as biographies, nonfiction history trade books, movies about the period, and information they find on the Internet. Before they become overwhelmed with the amount of information they have gleaned from their research, students should begin sorting it, searching for and clustering key ideas. Young writers won't be as steeped in history as authors like Mollie Hunter, but they can gather enough facts to write accurate tales of their own.

Students are now ready to choose and develop characters and write their stories. Once they have decided on a main character, they need to think of the event that will show who this character is and what he or she stands for. Questions such as the following help students focus on the decisions they must make as an author:

- What does the writer want to say about the time period and the events that take place?
- What information is most vital to the story they want to tell? Listing important incidents helps them organize.
- From which point of view should the story be told? Who is the best character to tell the story?
- How will the story begin?
- How will the story end?
- How will it be structured?
- Can the story be told by the main character in a letter or journal entry?
- Should it be told as a narrative?

Students should begin free writing, introducing the characters, time and place, and the problems they face. All the details should be put in the first draft. When revising, students can decide if the story is clear and well told; if all the details are important in the telling; if some material needs to be expanded; and if the story is well organized. After the final revisions are made, students need to edit their work for spelling, punctuation, grammar, and usage, asking themselves questions such as, "Did I follow standard conventions?" and "Is my story easy to read?" If so, the story is ready for publication.

ONE YOUNG WRITER'S STORY: "GETTYSBURG GHOST"

Students come to write historical fiction from many directions. They might learn about someone through reading a biography and decide to turn that person into a character in historical fiction. They might learn about an event in history through reading historical nonfiction and recreate that event as historical fiction. Or they might have family stories that they can spin into more elaborated tales. Other students might be inspired by trips they have taken to historically significant places.

For as long as he can remember, 10-year-old Aaron has heard his grandfather tell stories of the Civil War, its battles, and of Abraham Lincoln and other influential people of the time. He has visited Gettysburg, Pennsylvania, and spent the day touring the battlefield, listening to a historian describe what happened at each significant site. He has looked across the terrain from Little Round Top and Cemetery Ridge, imagined the desperation of Picket's Charge, probed bullet holes that pocked homes in town and studied the cannons that blazed in all directions. He has solemnly walked the rows of soldiers' graves in the cemetery, pausing for the longest time next to those of young men from his home state of Minnesota. He has read Lincoln's *Gettysburg Address* and understands the power of his words. He was fascinated by all the everyday items found on the Gettysburg battlefield that once belonged to the men who fought and died there. He bought a gold button from the uniform of a Union corporal at a nearby antique store specializing in Civil War paraphernalia.

When Mike Erdman, his fourth grade teacher, introduces a unit on historical fiction and tells students they can read about whatever time period interests them, Aaron knows just what to ask for when the book mobile comes to school later that day. He can hardly wait to begin reading Patricia Lee Gauch's *Thunder at Gettysburg,* the historical fiction book the librarian helped him find. He relives the battle through the experiences of Tillie, the young girl from Gettysburg who was caught in a farmhouse in the middle of the fighting, a real eyewitness to the battlefield carnage. Tillie feverishly cared for countless men torn apart by bullets and cannon, her hands blistered from toting hundreds of buckets of water. Aaron pays close attention to Gauch's use of dialogue and the details that give such a dynamic sense of a place that he has visited. He studies Stephen Gammell's atmospheric and dramatic pencil drawings of the soldiers, Tillie, and the setting of this horrific battle. Aaron also reads other nonfiction resources, including historical trade books about the battle by authors Jim Murphy and Milton Meltzer. And he is still most impressed by the fact that boys not much older than he is, from towns near where he lives, fought and died at Gettysburg.

When given the opportunity to write historical fiction about the Battle of Gettysburg, Aaron knows the story he wants to tell. In "Gettysburg Ghost," a combination of the research he has done and his love of ghost stories, his main character, a young Minnesotan named Samantha whose brother is fighting for the Union in the Civil War, has recurring nightmares about a terrible battle in a place called Gettysburg. In her worst dream, she finds herself at a farmhouse on July 3, 1863. The small house is packed with wounded men crying out for help.

When in her confusion she is mistreated by an older woman, who thinks Samantha has spilled precious water and screeches,

> "You addled, stupid . . ." A man says, "Leave her be." The woman replies, "I'll finish with you later, turtle." She turns up her nose and walks away like an arrogant peacock. I turned around to see who had saved me and, to my horror, I saw my brother, Ben! So this wasn't a dream! He really had been hurt by a cannon! I hugged my brother, but he wouldn't talk. All he did was take a gold button from his coat and pin it on my nightshirt.

Samantha is so happy to awaken in her own bed and discover that what had happened was just another bad dream; that the cold water she thought was dousing her was just Ben's dog Lincoln licking her face; that Ben was probably fine. Her mother rushes into her room because she has heard her crying out in her sleep. Aaron ends the story with their shocking discovery, a good example of the tension he has created between dreams and reality throughout the story:

> "Samantha, where did you find that?" asked my mom, pointing down at my night shirt. I looked down, and there was the gold button.

As in other books he has read, Aaron ends his story ambiguously. Is Samantha's dream actually reality? How can she have been transported to Gettysburg and yet be sleeping in her own bed? Is her brother dying in a farmhouse hundreds of miles from his sister and his Minnesota home? All are questions for his readers to ponder. As a thoughtful and avid reader, Aaron has learned a great deal about how to craft an interesting story. His beginning engages the reader immediately.

> I woke with a start. Every bone in my body ached. Slowly it all came back to me. Last night, me and mama were carrying the water buckets into our cabin on Black Lake, when we just happened to stumble upon the most cantankerous animal in the world, the porcupine. No sooner had we seen him than he had flipped his little spiky rear at us and had given us a dose of his own special medicine.

Samantha is a spunky character the reader wants to get to know. Aaron gives her a strong voice that hints of a life lived long ago, when people said things like "me and mama" and used words like "cantankerous." We soon learn that her troubled sleep is partially due to her wounds from the porcupine, an animal Aaron has seen on the Minnesota Trail at the zoo.

The setting in the Gettysburg farmhouse is similar to the one described by Gauch, with Aaron's main character, Samantha, first finding herself in the same house that sheltered Gauch's Tillie during the battle. Samantha hears a cannon explode.

> I awakened to a farm in the daytime. Bullets whizzed through the air next to it. I heard cannon blasts and the cries of hurt men. I looked through a hole made by a bullet spray. Men in gray suits were leaping a stone fence. Confederates! Cak! Cak! Cak! Three men fell. GaBOOM! Bodies went flying. I was in the middle of a full-fledged battle!

Many of Samantha's experiences mirror those of Tillie.

Aaron follows his story with an epilogue where he shares some of the information about the battle, such as the number of men killed on either side, he has learned during his research. He knows that this type of information cannot be naturally included in his narrative but that his readers may want to know some of these other facts about the battle. He is very proud of his published story, which features his illustrations of guns and cannons on the front cover and Ben's dog Lincoln on the back. He dedicates his story "To Mr. E, who told me to take my time." Aaron is able to take his time because his teacher gives him all the time he needs to read and remember, to write, rehearse, and revise. It is time very well spent.

Writing Poetry

Words are the tools of all writers, but they are the poet's playground. Poets revel in words, the way they sound and how they mean what they mean. They make lists of words on napkins while waiting in a restaurant for their entree to be served. They hear and record the music in everyday speech. There are thousands of words in the English language, and the poet wants to own them all. Whereas novelists may think in chapters and writers of short stories in paragraphs, poets think in a much more concentrated manner. They condense the meaning and feelings that a novelist may need many pages to express into a handful of verses or a even a single image. Like scientists, poets deal in observation and revelation. They spend a lifetime, not looking for the

In a collaborative classroom, students are willing to share their thoughts and feelings in poetry about themselves.

cure for cancer or a new strain of hardy wheat to feed the world's hungry, but seeking through their words to understand what it is to be human, to suffer, to rejoice, and to endure. Poets invite us to look at ourselves and all that may seem so familiar and mundane with new eyes. They give us insights that make the ordinary extraordinary. No wonder children are naturally drawn to poetry with its rhythm and word play that reveals such truth.

Just as children exposed to many different types of narrative and exposition write using a variety of forms, children who read, hear, and discuss a wide variety of poetry also experiment with a variety of poetic forms. They appreciate figurative language and create their own metaphors and similes; suddenly everything reminds them of something else because they are learning to look at the world as poets do. They play with words and learn to enjoy revision, searching for the very best words and experimenting with placing them in just the right order on the page to convey their own truths. White space becomes eloquent and line breaks significant. As young poets, children learn to notice life in greater detail, using all their senses to create poetic images with great sensory appeal. Poetry becomes a favored means of expression for many children who somehow know a poem is the best way to represent the intensity of their feelings. They have seen how poets write about their real lives in ways that are relevant to them. They long to unearth the poetic details that can bring their own realities to life.

When asked to give young poets advice about writing poetry, nearly all poets emphasize the importance of reading widely, hearing the work of many poets and looking for favorite poems for their own collection. In 1977, David McCord won the first National Council of Teachers of English Award for

Excellence in Poetry for Children in recognition of his aggregate body of work for children ages, 3–13. During the next 5 years, poets Aileen Fisher, Karla Kuskin, Myra Cohn Livingston, Eve Merriam, and John Ciardi also received the award. Since that time, the award has been granted only every 3 years to poets Lilian Moore, Arnold Adoff, Valerie Worth, Barbara Juster Esbensen, Eloise Greenfield, and X. J. Kennedy. Bernice Cullinan's *A Jar of Tiny Stars* is a collection of children's favorite poems from the first ten poets to win the award and is an outstanding reference for those children and teachers who are looking for a place to begin their search for favorite poems and poets.

Effective poetry teachers share poems with children every day, sometimes during reading, or to welcome children in the morning, during writing workshop or in science class. They read children's poetry by contemporary poets to find those whose work fascinates them and will spark their children's interest as well. A favorite anthology or two, like Jack Prelutsky's *The Random House Book of Poetry,* are always nearby, as are many poetry-teaching references like the ones listed in *Further Reading* at the end of this chapter. The reading corner is filled with poetry books about children and their families and friends like Richard Margolis's *Secrets of a Small Brother,* Janet Wong's *A Suitcase of Seaweed and Other Poems,* Eloise Greenfield's *Nathaniel Talking,* and Nikki Grimes's *Meet Danitra Brown*. If the class is going camping, they read aloud poems from Kristine O'Connell George's book *Toasting Marshmallows,* and they write poems about their experiences when they return. Children in these classes learn to make poetic comparisons by enjoying the similes and metaphors in Valerie Worth's *All the Small Poems,* where a patch of growing asparagus looks like snakes. They learn the meaning of personification when the desert in Diane Siebert's *Mojave* proclaims:

I am the desert.
  I am free.
    Come walk the sweeping face of me.

Children learn the joys of sound through the onomatopoeia (using words that imitate sounds), alliteration (repeating the same letter at the beginning of successive words), and consonance and assonance (internal and end rhymes made by repeating consonant and vowel sounds) in such books as Arnold Adoff's *Street Music: City Poems*. They recognize the power of repeating rhythmic sounds in poems like David McCord's "The Pickety Fence." Poetry taken in healthy daily doses fortifies children's expressive capacity.

When asked what poetry is, children most often use the word "rhyme" in their definitions. They love the sound of rhyming words and feel that rhyme is essential in writing good poetry. It is fun to experiment with making meaning while using words that rhyme, but it is also quite challenging. Young poets often end up saying almost anything, regardless of meaning, for the sake of rhyming.

Introducing free verse to children puts the emphasis on what they want to say; it frees them to concentrate their efforts on the meaning of what they are writing. Free verse is not merely prose written haphazardly on the page and made to somehow look like poetry. Those poets who use the form select their words and images carefully and pay particular attention to the placement of text on the page. They create internal rhymes and use strong rhythms, just not necessarily in set patterns. Teachers familiar with poets such as Arnold Adoff and Gary Soto, who write child-pleasing free verse, can share this form with their child poets as an alternative to the rhyming poetry that is wonderful to listen to but much more difficult to write. Many different forms of free-verse poetry, like those listed in the *Teaching Idea: Experimenting with Poetry,* have great child appeal.

Poets find their ideas everywhere, as children can discover by reading Karla Kuskin's *Near the Window Tree,* where each poem is preceded by a short description of how she thought of the idea. Children who learn to read like poets and who learn to observe the world like poets soon have many ideas of their own. Many poets, though certainly not all, keep some sort of writer's notebook, like those described in Chapter Eight, filled with observations, dreams, word lists, brainstorming, funny thoughts, snippets of conversation, favorite lines from books they are reading, and anything else that strikes their fancy. A notebook is a place to hold onto thoughts and words, because every writer knows that good ideas can easily escape. You can model this by keeping a notebook of your own, sharing what you write there as regularly as you share polished pieces you have written. Does a product name sound really funny or seem peculiar? Why is soap named Dial or Ivory or laundry soap named Tide? Write these notions in your notebook. Did you have the nightmare again about not being in class until it was time to take the final? Into the notebook! Much of what writers put in their notebooks never finds its way into a poem, but the occasional gem will turn up.

To write poetry is to experiment with words and ideas. Once children have ideas, they need to be encouraged to make long lists of good words, anything that comes to mind about their topic, and then to choose the best of the words on their lists, the ones that sound just right together. Children suddenly enjoy using tools like the thesaurus to add words to their lists. They create phrases and lines and write them on cards or strips of paper that can be physically manipulated to find just the right order, line breaks, and form for what they want to say. And finally, they write rough drafts of their poems and read them aloud to themselves, to their friends, to their teacher. They change the placement of the lines so that each ends where there is a natural pause. They sometimes leave more white space, skipping lines for effect, or even decide to have one-word lines for more dramatic impact and a better beat. They remove dull lines, or they elaborate to add detail. They put their poem

TEACHING IDEA

Literature Link

EXPERIMENTING WITH POETRY

- A **concrete poem** creates a picture of its subject with words. Have children read books like *A Poke in the I,* Paul Janeczko's collection of concrete poems, and create picture poems of their own.
- Bring in piles of *National Geographic* or other sources of descriptive prose. Have children cut out interesting words and phrases. Play with these to create a **found poem**.
- Children love to do **acrostic poems** using their names. Have them write their names (first and last if they can manage both) down one side of the paper, then use each letter to begin a word or line that describes them.
- **List poems** are usually free verse made up of short phrases or one-word lines that describe something, tell how to do something, or name things. Have children brainstorm possible topics, make lists of anything that seems to be related to that topic, and then choose the best ideas for their poem.
- Have children pretend to put on a **mask**, to turn themselves into someone or something else for a while, and write about what they are thinking or feeling.
- **Odes** are celebratory poems written to honor someone or something that is highly prized. It is a good form for special occasions such as birthdays, Mother's or Father's Day, etc.
- Children laugh out loud at **limericks** in books like J. Patrick Lewis's *A Hippopotamusn't: And Other Animal Verses*. They easily discover the pattern and enjoy writing their own.
- **Epitaphs** (poems in praise of someone who has died), **clerihews** (light verse about someone famous), **dialogue poems** (conversations with two or more voices), and other interesting forms are also fun to experiment with. Look for examples of many different forms in Avis Harley's books *Fly with Poetry* and *Leap into Poetry*.

away for a while, and then read it again. These young poets revise and revise (some accomplished poets do this over a hundred times over a period of months!) until the poem is just right and ready to be published. And then they revise once more!

When the children in Mike Erdman's third and fourth grade class walk to the river, they always carry their notebooks and pencils with them, along with a bag or backpack for any interesting finds: old bird's nests, plants, rocks, leaves, bugs, and branches. Everyone is on the lookout for anything interesting or unusual, and so they often stop, observe, write, and sketch. When they arrive back at their classroom after meandering along the riverbank for an hour or so, they have a great deal to talk about and write about, many questions that need to be answered, and sketches that will become more elaborate works of art.

Mike shares poetry every day. On a river walk day he might read Byrd Baylor's *Everybody Needs a Rock,* and the children will come back with a treasure trove of rocks. They describe their favorites using as many sensory words as they can. They each study their rocks and write what their favorite reminds them of. They decide why they selected this particular rock over all the rest. Then Mike reads "Stone" by Charles Simic, where the poet declares, "I am happy to be a stone." The children look at their rocks differently after hearing the poem. They keep them handy on their tables or in their cubbies all year long.

Joanne Ryder is one of Mike's favorite poets and soon becomes a favorite of his student naturalists. Her book *Inside Turtle's Shell* is the inspiration for a class anthology of animal poems called *A Howl in the Moonlight.* Everyone, including Mike, works for days polishing their poems, getting them just right, so that they can be published. Everyone, including Mike, illustrates their poems about timber wolves or bears, garter snakes or muskrats, or other Minnesota animals. They also write about and draw domesticated animals like dogs, cats, and horses. And, of course, some write poems about the turtles that they see by the river.

Aaron uses what he has learned about poetry from reading Ryder's poems and those of many other poets to write his own animal poems. He

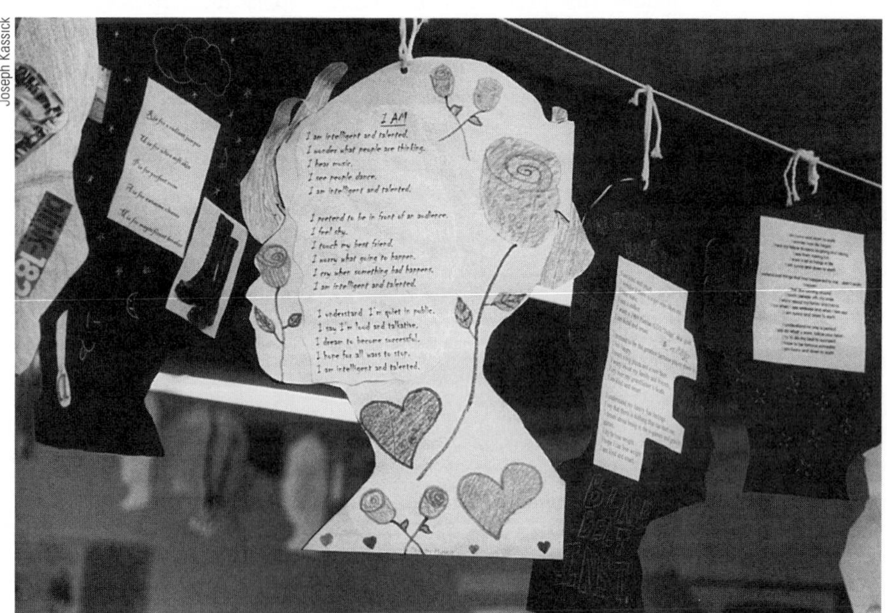

Joseph Kassick

Students artfully display their poetry.

compares a bat to a fighter plane, and his cat acts just like a naughty, though much loved, child. Both poems have repeated lines and sounds. Although the first is written in free verse, Aaron has successfully experimented with patterned rhyme in the second poem. Aaron writes about a bat:

Bat flying around,
skinny bat,
skinny bat
Mother nature's own
little fighter plane.
Bat picks up
Another aircraft
on his built-in
sonar.
This aircraft is smaller,
slower, unknowing.
Fast bat, fast bat
Eat those gnats!
  SPLAAAAAAT
MMMMMMMMMMMMMMM
  FAT
  BAT.

And he writes about a cat:

Small cat
Silly little guy.
Sweeter than a
piece of cherry pie.
Cries for his mom.
Cries for his dad.
Poor little cat
must be awfully sad.
Gets into trouble.
Gets chased by a dog.
Then he goes to play near
The Muckermann's bog.
Gets slimy and
dirty, then he walks
on the rug.
First he gets punished,
but then gets a
hug. Happy little cat,

pretty and
clean
Doesn't care
about that dog who was
terribly mean.
Plays all day and
into the night.
Then he yawns a
little yawn and purrs good night.

As an effective poetry teacher, Mike Erdman gives children many opportunities for observing their world and for reading how other poets record similar observations. He knows that writing good poetry takes a great deal of practice and enough time for ideas to ferment. He keeps a writer's notebook and writes with the children, telling them how he finds ideas and chooses words that are just right. He is playful with language and encourages children's language play. His students learn about many different types of poetry, from rhymed verse to free verse, from narrative poetry to odes and limericks. Children read poetry, their own and that of published poets, aloud and sometimes memorize favorites to share with another class or the principal. Children's words and ideas are celebrated in Mike's class.

SUMMARY

Young writers can experiment with writing in many genres. In this chapter we discussed recording and writing as scientists, preparing research papers, writing historical fiction, and writing poetry. Whatever the genre, effective teachers surround students with well-written trade books that offer excellent examples of well-crafted writing. Teachers help students recognize the strategies and techniques that successful published writers use effectively and encourage young writers to borrow from these examples, trying them on for size.

Effective teachers demonstrate how to work through the writing process, whether showing students how writers take notes to generate and organize ideas for nonfiction writing, how to brainstorm sensory words and images for poetic writing, or how to make decisions about what is necessary to a story and what is not during revision. Effective teachers understand that student writers draw their inspiration from many sources, and that time to think, talk, explore, and write is crucial to the development of an effective piece, whatever the genre.

ACTIVITIES

1. **Decide on a genre in which you want to become "expert."** Collect several (5–10) trade books that exemplify excellence in that genre that you could share with children. Then find and read professional material about teaching the genre, perhaps beginning with some of the suggestions for further reading in this chapter.
2. **After you have become "expert" in your chosen genre, find a peer who has studied a different genre and teach each other what you know.**
3. **Using the knowledge you have gained through genre study, develop a series of demonstration lessons that you would use to help students learn how to write in the genre.** Consider using the trade books you have found, and also plan lessons in which you will demonstrate a writing technique.
4. **Develop a poetry collection that contains many examples of poetry in a wide variety of forms.** Organize the collection so that it becomes a useful resource for teaching poetry writing.
5. **Examine the curriculum for your school or area.** Look for opportunities to integrate reading and writing into the study of science, social studies, mathematics, art, music, or health. Then begin to gather resources and ideas that will support reading and writing in the other content areas.

FURTHER READING

Buss, K., & Karnowski, L. (2000). *Reading and writing literary genres.* Newark, DE: International Reading Association.

Fletcher, R. (2002). *Poetry matters: Writing a poem from the inside out.* New York: HarperCollins.

Graves, D. H. (1989). *Explore fiction.* Portsmouth, NH: Heinemann.

______. (1989). *Investigate nonfiction.* Portsmouth, NH: Heinemann.

______. (1992). *Explore poetry.* Portsmouth, NH: Heinemann.

Heard, G. (1989). *For the good of the earth and sun: Teaching poetry.* Portsmouth, NH: Heinemann.

Hopkins, L. B. (1998). *Pass the poetry, please!* New York: HarperCollins.

Janeczko, P. B. (1999). *How to write poetry.* New York: Scholastic.

______. (2002). *Seeing the blue between: Advice and inspiration for young poets.* Cambridge, MA: Candlewick.

Livingston, M. C. (1991). *Poem-making: Ways to begin writing poetry.* New York: HarperCollins.

Portalupi, J., & Fletcher, R. (2001). *Nonfiction craft lessons: Teaching information writing K–8*. Portland, ME: Stenhouse.

Zarnowski, M., Kerper, R. M., & Jensen, J. M. (Eds.). (2001). *The best in children's nonfiction: Reading, writing, and teaching Orbis Pictus Award books.* Urbana, IL: National Council of Teachers of English.

REFERENCES

Calkins, L. M. (1994). *The art of teaching.* Portsmouth, NH: Heinemann.

DeFord, D. (1981). Literacy: Reading, writing and other essentials. *Language Arts, 58,* 652–658.

Dressel, J. H. (1990). The effects of listening to and discussing different qualities of children's literature on the narrative writing of fifth graders. *Research in the Teaching of English, 24,* 397–414.

Eckhoff, B. (1983). How reading affects children's writing. *Language Arts, 60,* 607–616.

Graves, D. H. (1989). Investigate nonfiction. Portsmouth, NH: Heinemann.

Hunter, M. (1990). *Talent is not enough.* New York: Harper Trophy.

Stead, T. (2002). *Is that a fact? Teaching nonfiction writing K–3.* Portland, ME: Stenhouse.

CHILDREN'S LITERATURE REFERENCES

Adoff, A. (1995). *Street music: City poems.* Illus. K. Barbour. New York: Harper.

Baylor, B. (1985). *Everybody needs a rock.* Illus. P. Parnall. New York: Simon & Schuster.

Bjork, C. (1988). *Linnea's windowsill garden.* Illus. L. Anderson. New York: R & S Books.

Briggs, R. (1970). *Jim and the beanstalk.* New York: Coward-McCann.

Brown, M. (1981). *Your first garden book.* New York: Little, Brown.

Brown, M. W. (1947). *Goodnight moon.* Illus. C. Hurd. New York: HarperCollins.

Burleigh, R. (1998). *Black whiteness: Admiral Byrd alone in the Antarctic.* Illus. Walter Lyon Krudop. New York: Simon & Schuster.

Carle, E. (1991). *The tiny seed.* New York: Simon & Schuster.

Cauley, L. B. (1983). *Jack and the beanstalk.* New York: Putnam's.

Cowley, J. (1999). *Red-eyed tree frog.* Photographs by N. Bishop. New York: Scholastic Press.

Cullinan, B. (Ed.). (1996). *A jar of tiny stars: Poems by NCTE award-winning poets.* Honesdale, PA: Boyds Mills/Wordsong.

Fleischman, S. (1978). *McBroom and the beanstalk.* Illus. W. Lorraine. Boston: Little Brown.

Garland, S. (1993). *The Lotus Seed.* San Diego: Harcourt.

Gauch, P. L. (1975). *Thunder at Gettysburg.* Illus. S. Gammell. New York: Putnam.

George, K. O'C. (2001). *Toasting marshmallows: Camping poems.* Illus. K. Kiesler. Boston: Houghton Mifflin.

Greenfield, E. (1988). *Nathaniel talking.* Illus. J. S. Gilchrist. New York: Black Butterfly Children's Books.

Grimes, N. (1994). *Meet Danitra Brown.* Illus. F. Cooper. New York: Lothrop.

Harley, A. (1999). *Fly with poetry.* Honesdale, PA: Boyds Mills.

———. (2001). *Leap into poetry.* Honesdale, PA: Boyds Mills.

Janeczko, P. (2001). *A Poke in the I: A collection of concrete poems.* Illus. C. Raschka. New York: Candlewick Press.

Knight, D. (1985). *Dinosaurs that swam and flew.* Illus. L. J. Ames. Englewood Cliffs, NJ: Prentice-Hall.

Kuskin, K. (1975). *Near the window tree.* Illus. K. Kuskin. New York: Harper & Row.

Lewis, J. P. (1990). *A hippopotamusn't: And other animal verses.* Illus. V. Chess. New York: Dial Books for Young Readers.

Margolis, R. (1984). *Secrets of a small brother.* Illus. D. Carrick. New York: Simon & Schuster.

McCord, D. (1999). *Every time I climb a tree.* Illus. M. Simont. Boston: Little, Brown.

Montgomery, S. (2001). *The man-eating tigers of Sundarbans.* Photographs by E. Briggs. Boston: Houghton Mifflin.

Most, B. (1996). *If the dinosaurs came back.* Little Big Book Plus. Boston: Houghton Mifflin.

Parnall, P. (1987). *Apple tree.* New York: Macmillan.

Prelutsky, J. (Ed.). (1983). *The Random House book of poetry.* Illus. A. Lobel. New York: Random House.

Ryder, J. (1985). *Inside turtle's shell and other poems of the field.* Illus. S. Bonners. New York: Macmillan.

Sandburg, C. (1999). *The Huckabuck family and how they raised popcorn in Nebraska and quit and came back.* Illus. D. Small. New York: Farrar, Straus, Giroux.

Siebert, D. (1988). *Mojave.* Illus. W. Minor. New York: Crowell.

Simic, C. (1999). *Selected early poems.* New York: Braziller.

Stanley, D., & Vennema, P. (1992). *Bard of Avon: The story of William Shakespeare.* Illus. D. Stanley. New York: Morrow Junior Books.

Stolz, M. (1993). *Say something.* Illus. A. Koshkin. New York: HarperCollins.

White, E. B. (1945). *Stuart Little.* Illus. G. Williams. New York: Harper.

Wong, J. (1996). *A suitcase of seaweed and other poems.* New York: Simon & Schuster.

Worth, V. (1987). *All the small poems.* Illus. N. Babbitt. New York: Farrar, Straus & Giroux.

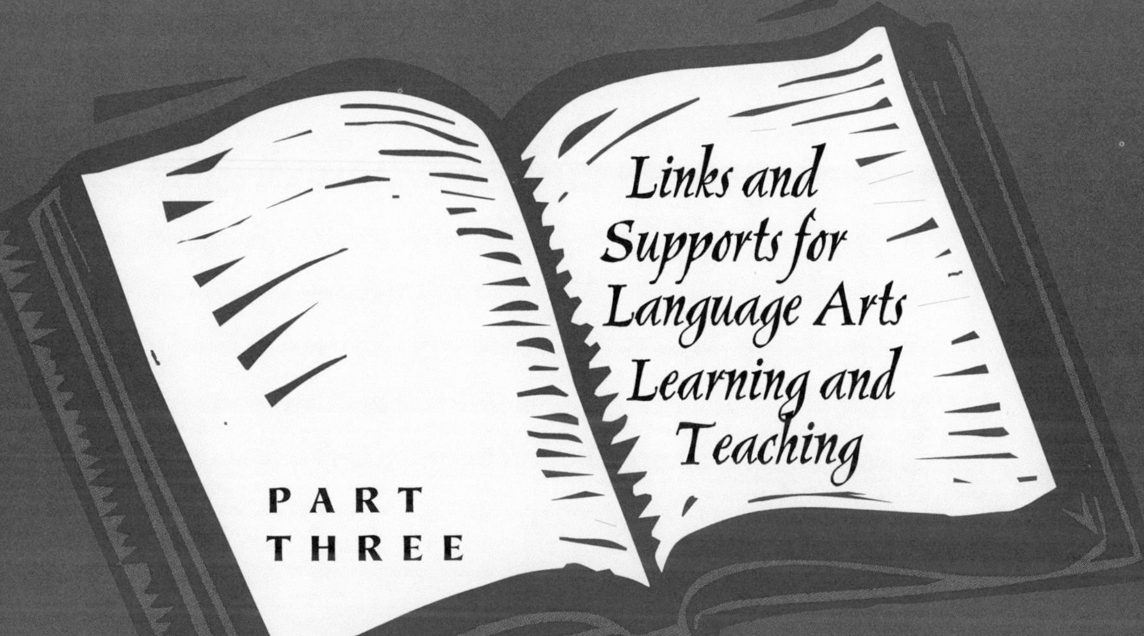
Links and
Supports for
Language Arts
Learning and
Teaching
PART
THREE

Word Study, Vocabulary, and Spelling Supports for Literacy

CHAPTER OUTLINE

Key Standard

Teachers of language arts help students acquire and apply enriched vocabularies and knowledge about English language structures in order to read and spell with competence. Such teachers:

- Understand how the written language system works and how to apply that knowledge to ensure a sound program of word study for children.
- Understand the importance of vocabulary development in students' overall language development and reading comprehension.
- Understand basic principles related to spelling development and its relationship to reading.
- Understand that conventional spelling is a writing tool.
- Implement a balance of both direct and contextual approaches to word study, vocabulary, and spelling instruction.

To get a preview of Chapter 10 and learn about word study and spelling, visit the Chapter 10 section of the accompanying *Language Arts* CD-ROM.

Every other Monday morning, third grade teacher Laura Wade comes to school with a few extra hangers and some slightly used file folders from the doctor's office where her mother-in-law works. As she enters the classroom, the children who are there for Early Care Breakfast circle around her asking to help. Ms. Wade chooses Loretta to get her the step stool and accepts a balancing hand as she begins to take down the hangers. Draped over each hanger is a file folder with the same word printed boldly in red, blue, or green on the front and the back. She plucks the folders from the pegs and strings that make her room a spider web of learning. Then she puts them on her desk, and Loretta asks, "Do you want me to put these in the spelling library, Ms. Wade?"

"In a minute, Loretta. After the rest of the class gets here."

When the bell rings and the rest of the class fills the room, Laura gives them a chance to settle down, then holds up the first file folder.

"All right, class, begin."

They say the red word on the first folder, giving each letter sound clearly and distinctly and making a distinct pause after each of the syllables.

"Ward robe."

Then they spell the word rhythmically, pausing between syllables.

"Now, let's write this word in the air. . ."

The class waits.

"In cursive!"

They all smile and the fun begins as still chubby hands swirl their way through W and R and D and B. As usual, some children get carried away with looping the W. They giggle and start all over. The space is filled with letters.

Ms. Wade has just used sight, sound, and movement to imprint this word physically in the minds, eyes, and hands of her class.

She takes the lesson a step further.

"Say the small words that are in this large word."

"Robe." "Ward."

"What is a wardrobe?"

Loretta waves her hand furiously; she's been waiting for this moment. "A wardrobe is a place where you keep clothes."

Ms. Wade nods a smile. Then asks, "Why don't we call it a WARD CLOTHES?"

Hector practically leaps out of his chair with the answer. "Because it's an old word, and robe used to mean all kinds of clothes."

Ms. Wade doesn't pursue the rest of the word history. In her seventh grade class she would show her students that WARD *at one time meant* GUARD. *She likes them to become familiar with the historical changes of words in English as a preparation for reading literature from the nineteenth and twentieth centuries. But her third-graders just need to apply what they have been learning.*

She has them enter WARDROBE *in the spelling section of their notebooks and gets ready to start on the next word. But first, she asks one more question.*

"Why is this an important word for you now?"

The children pause, not sure of what she wants.

"It's really an easy answer." Then all the lights go on at once.

"It's part of the title. The Lion, the Witch, and the Wardrobe."

"And what's the writer's rule about words in a title?"

"Never, never *misspell them."*

The lesson continues as each of the words in the folders is worked on. Finally, she asks Loretta to put the folders in the spelling library. Tomorrow a group will alphabetize them, then copy them into the Class Spelling dictionary on the computer.

Laura Wade takes another look at her lesson plan. She has met her goals of mixing modalities—using speech, sight, hearing, and movement—and she has used a critical thinking question for each of the words. When the class is over, she drapes each of the hangers with blank folders, ready for the next spelling/reading/vocabulary lesson.

Word Study

LEARNING TO READ WORDS

Children need to explore words and how they are formed. They need to learn how to make use of this information in order to read, write, and spell. For many children, some of the most fundamental understandings about words are learned even before kindergarten as they learn to recognize their names. Name recognition helps establish fundamental understandings about words, such as:

- My name has meaning. It stands for me.
- My name is a word.
- Words are formed with letters.
- The letters in a word must progress in a certain direction.
- When the letters are changed they are no longer my name.
- Other people have names that may have some of the same letters as mine.
- Other words may have some of the same letters as my name.
- Other words may sound the same at the beginning or end as my name.

As children begin to broaden their repertoire of words, they learn that:

- Groups of words express ideas and make messages.
- The meaning of a word may change depending on how it is used with other words.
- Similar word parts are used over and over again.
- Knowledge about word parts can be used to read and spell.

As children proceed through the grades, they continue to build on their knowledge of words. They increase what they know about the patterns within words and the ways to learn words. Effective language arts teachers like Laura Wade provide a broad range of opportunities for children to learn about words and how they work in our language system. Laura puts into practice what cognitive and developmental scientists have demonstrated and what good teachers have always known. First, there is no one way for every child to learn. Second, most children learn best when they learn the same

Patterned language with repetition of words helps beginning readers and writers.

thing in different ways. Utilizing different modalities allows teachers to reach all children more easily and to teach each child thoroughly.

GUIDELINES FOR WORD STUDY

Learning to read and write involves coming to know the power of written language. Teachers help children develop an understanding of the reading and writing processes and how they are used to communicate. Fundamental to these understandings is the ability to recognize and write words.

Effective teachers help students build a network of understandings about language. Children apply what they know in order to problem-solve when faced with challenges in their reading and writing. For example, a child who knows that the letters *sh* usually represent the sound heard at the beginning of *ship* will try that sound when encountering the word *shower* for the first time. The ability to segment the word *shower* into sounds (phonemes) can help the child, who is beginning to develop sound-letter correspondences, to spell it. Knowledge that the prefix *un* usually means the same as *not* can help a child uncover the meaning of *unwise,* even though it may be the first time he has actually read that word. Fostering students' understanding of the language system requires a context in which words are discussed and explored in a variety of ways. Teachers and students need to talk about words, how they are constructed, and their origins. In addition to regularly scheduled direct instruction on the nature of our language system, students should be encouraged to do their own exploring and make their own discoveries as independent readers and writers. These discoveries become the focus of class discussion and further exploration. Classrooms that promote effective word study are those in which:

- *Children hear written language so they can learn its structure and take in new information and ideas.* Stories, informational texts, directions, and lists are read aloud and discussed. Children soon learn that each form has its own discourse structure. Figure 10.1 offers a list of books that stimulate word play and discussions about language.
- *Children are helped to become aware of the sounds of language, to enjoy those sounds, and to use this knowledge as a tool in becoming literate.* Language play that centers on rhymes and word families is fun and calls attention to the sounds in the language. Books for young children often feature repeated refrains with rhyme and provide children with an opportunity to join in on the read-aloud experience.
- *Children have many experiences working with written symbols so they can learn how to look at letters and use this information to read and write.* Shared writing, in which children observe teachers and parents writing as they say the letters and words aloud, helps develop a sense of how written language works.

FIGURE 10.1

Good Books for Language and Word Play

- *Go Hang a Salami! I'm a Lasagna Hog! And Other Palindromes* by J. Agee (Farrar, Strauss & Giroux)
- *A Snake Is Totally Tail* by J. Barrett (Atheneum)
- *A Gaggle of Geese: The Collective Names of the Animal Kingdom* by P. Browne (Atheneum)
- *Yours Till the Banana Splits: 201 Autograph Rhymes* by J. Cole and S. Clamenson (Morrow)
- *Jamberry* by B. Degen (Harper & Row)
- *Miss Alaineus: A Vocabulary Disaster* by D. Frasier (Harcourt Brace)
- *A Chartreuse Leotard in a Magenta Limousine: And Other Words Named After People and Places* by L. Graham-Barber (Hyperion)
- *The King Who Rained* by F. Gwynne (Dutton)
- *A Chocolate Moose for Dinner* by F. Gwynne (Dutton)
- *The Sixteen Hand Horse* by F. Gwynne (Prentice-Hall)
- *Up, Up and Away: A Book about Adverbs* by R. Heller (Scholastic)
- *Kites Sail High: A Book about Verbs* by R. Heller (Scholastic)
- *A Cache of Jewels and Other Collective Nouns* by R. Heller (Grossett & Dunlap)
- *C. Is for Curious: An ABC of Feelings* by W. Hubbard (Chronicle Books)
- *Cat, What Is That?* by T. Johnston (HarperCollins)
- *Eat Your Words: A Fascinating Look at the Language of Food* by C. F. Jones (Delacorte)
- *Taxi: A Book of City Words* by B. Maestro and G. Maestro (Clarion)
- *There's an Ant in Anthony* by B. Most (Morrow)
- *Zin! Zin! Zin! A Violin* by L. Moss (Simon & Schuster)
- *Baloney, Henry P.* by J. Scieszka (Viking Penguin)
- *Tyrannosaurus Wrecks: A Book of Dinosaur Riddles* by N. Sterne (Crowell)
- *Eight Ate: A Feast of Homonym Riddles* by M. Terban (Clarion)
- *In a Pickle and Other Funny Idioms* by M. Terban (Clarion)
- *Too Hot to Hoot: Funny Palindrome Riddles* by M. Terban (Clarion)
- *Guppies in Tuxedos: Funny Eponyms* by M. Terban (Clarion)
- *Funny You Should Ask: How to Make Up Jokes and Riddles with Wordplay* by M. Terban (Clarion)
- *Time to Rhyme: A Rhyming Dictionary* by M. Terban (Wordsong)
- *The Z Was Zapped* by C. Van Allsburg (Houghton Mifflin)
- *Runaway Opposites* by R. Wilbur (Harcourt)
- *As: A Surfeit of Similes* by N. Juster (Morrow)

- *Children learn the conventions of print and how books work so they can use this knowledge as readers and writers.* As literacy emerges during the earliest years, children learn basic concepts about print and book handling, such as directionality and how to hold a book and turn its pages. Later, they learn about periods, question marks, and capital letters and how punctuation brings clarity to what is read and written. Older children deal with increasingly complex text both in content and format. Informational texts, for example, present special challenges involving the use of headings, graphs, charts, and glossaries. At each stage, effective teachers deliberately teach the print conventions and give children many opportunities to apply them under a variety of circumstances.

- *Children read and write continuous text on a daily basis, so they can use and expand their knowledge about letters, sounds, words, and language.* Numerous opportunities for application of what is learned are critical to deep understanding. Most of what children learn through word study should be internalized so that the knowledge becomes second nature to the learner. Writers are thus free to think about expression and readers to concentrate on understanding.

STRATEGIES FOR WORD STUDY

Learning to recognize letters

Word study usually starts when children begin to notice words in the environment and, of course, their names. Name game activities, discussed in Chapter Six, stimulate a barrage of questions about letters and words. This is a good time to do some serious work on the alphabet. Here are some tips from two kindergarten teachers, Jennifer Fontura and Meg Doolan. Their students learn to recognize the letters of the alphabet in ways that are enjoyable and meaningful:

Bernice Cullinan

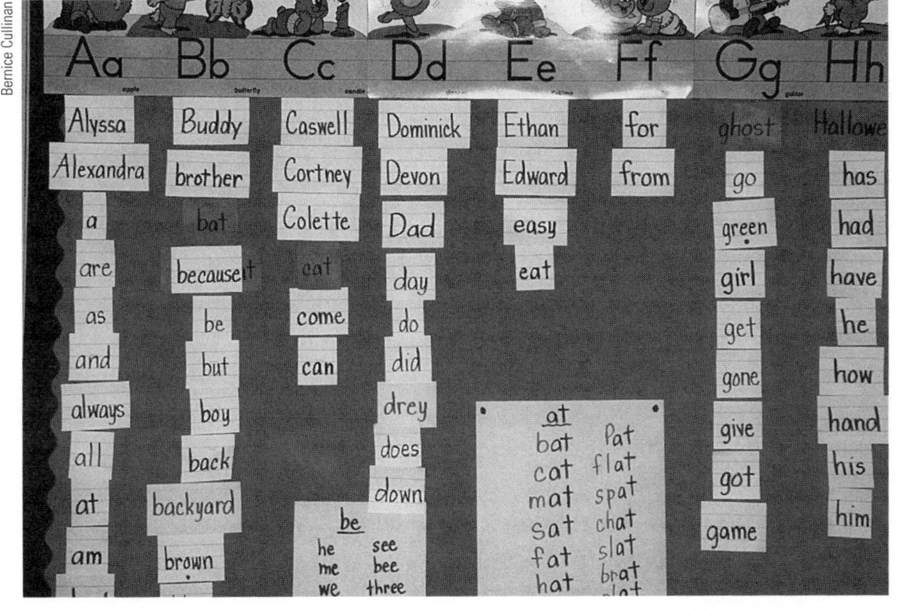

One strategy for teaching students the alphabet is to focus on letters that have special meaning to them, such as their names.

- *Focus on letters that have special meaning for children,* such as the letters in their own names.
- *Teach the alphabet song.* This is fun for children and gives them something to rely on when they attempt to use dictionaries or locate particular letters on alphabet charts.
- *Encourage children to experiment with letter forms,* using clay, play dough, or finger paint. Allow them to practice writing letters on the chalkboard or on small, individual whiteboards.
- *Make simple picture dictionaries available* for children's use.
- *Make a class alphabet book* and individual books as class activities.

Making and sorting words

Many teachers make heavy use of strategies for **making words** and **sorting words.** Making words is an activity in which children are individually given some letters in alphabetic order, as few as four or five for young children or eight or ten for older children, that they use to make words. During a 15-minute activity, children may make as many as twelve to fifteen words, beginning with two-letter words and continuing with longer words until the final word is made. The final word always includes all the letters that children have that day (Cunningham & Cunningham, 1992). Older students can be given letters from a secret word, such as *biology* or *revolution,* taken from a science or social studies unit. They can work independently or in small groups to make as many words as they can from the letters they have been given. If no one figures out the secret word that uses all the letters, you can provide clues until someone comes up with the word.

From the word *spring,* younger children make *in, pin, pig, rig, rip, rips, nips, spin, snip, pins, sing, ring, rings,* and finally *spring*. The teacher guides them through the process, pronouncing each word clearly and emphasizing the sounds so that students can use what they know about phonics in order to spell. Children listen intently to the sounds in words in order to make them and then try to remember and select the letters that can represent those sounds. Brief, frequent lessons of this type build the awareness of sound/symbol correspondences that children need for reading and spelling.

Making-words activities often end with a word sort. Here, children sort words according to specific features. In the list of words made from *spring,* children might sort all those that end like the word *plays (pins, nips, rings)*. Two words may be selected from the group, such as *pig* and *spin*. Other words, such as *big, thin, fig,* and *win* may be offered for children to sort and place in the right group with either *pig* or *spin*. Teachers and students seem to like making words and sorting. Both make use of fairly simple instructional formats and lend themselves to an enormous number of possible opportunities for word study.

Sorting words according to meaning and structure

Words may be sorted according to a variety of features. Most often, the following categories are used: initial letters, letter clusters and blends, vowel/consonant patterns, syllables, parts of speech, plurals, common roots, word families, and words related to a topic. **Closed sorting** requires children to sort according to a given category or group of categories. **Open sorting** involves giving children a group of words and having them decide on the categories. Students may use a game format, in which they group words or picture cards in categories of their choice and have others guess the category.

The following words were offered to second-graders as a center-based, independent activity:

couch, ham, engine, cheese, wheel, chair, catsup, table, tire

Children were allowed to work in pairs if they wished. After deciding on categories and completing the activity, they were asked to create a set of words for others to group.

Analyzing words needed to learn from texts

Teachers of older children know that an awareness of language structures is an important element in acquiring mature reading and writing skills. They also employ strategies—such as noticing word patterns, root words, and morphemes (meaning patterns)—that involve the direct teaching of word analysis.

After fourth grade, many young readers experience some difficulty in moving from the narrative mode so prevalent in early schooling to the expository mode of informational text. Even fluent readers experience difficulty, often because they have not been made conscious of their own word-unlocking skills. Good teachers use different strategies to help students become aware of the skills they already possess in order to apply them consciously to newer and more difficult reading tasks.

Todd Cobb, an experienced fifth grade language arts teacher, begins his class on Wednesday by writing this word on the board:

restarted

He then asks his class to examine the word and break it into parts.

"You mean syllables, Mr. Cobb?"

He accepts this answer as a beginning and nods. "OK. Come up to the board and show us what you mean."

Darryl, caught in the middle of a growth spurt, lurches from his desk and bounces, all arms and legs, toward the board. He takes the chalk Mr. Cobb gives him and puts slashes between the word's sections:

re/start/ed

The class looks at the word with a "So?" in their eyes. Mr. Cobb writes another word on the board.

recombined

"How about this one?" and holds out the chalk for the next hand.

When she is chosen, Latesha separates the syllables the way they sound to her.

re/com/bined

"What do these words have in common?" he asks.

Another voice is heard from. "Well, they both have *re* to begin with, and they both end in *ed,*" Gupta points out.

"What words do you have if you take away those two elements?"

His students know the answer (*start* and *combine*). They also easily identify both base words as verbs.

Mr. Cobb then makes the task harder. "What do we call the word part *re* and the word part *ed*? And what does each of the word parts do?"

The answers are longer in coming, but after some discussion students agree on calling *re* a prefix and saying that a prefix usually changes the meaning of a word. They have a more difficult time with *ed.*

Sarah says it's an ending; Li Ann disagrees. She wants to call it a suffix, but Karl doesn't like that term. Lucia then adds that it changes the tense of the verb but not the meaning. At this point Mr. Cobb steps in. "This kind of ending is called a suffix, which is a type of *affix.* It tells you something more about the verb—in this case, its tense. An affix can also tell something about nouns. If I add an *s* to *dog,* what do I learn?"

The class choruses "That it's a plural!"

Now the class is involved; now they are ready to learn more about the structural analysis of words in English because they have discovered the rules themselves. In the process they will develop the analytical skills they need to make them advanced readers of informational texts.

This is a class of fluent readers, most of whom arrived in kindergarten reading the basic sentences in picture books. By second and third grade they were confident readers, and now they usually skim through the stories in their readers as soon as they get a new one. As good readers, they find all the clues to new words in the movements of plot and the expectations of genre. Even the technobabble of science fiction is easily, if not always accurately, deciphered.

But soon the language of instruction changes. As the highly contextualized story books and narratives give way to informational prose, students see less and less of selections that tell the story of *How Sammy the Seal Learned to Swim.* Instead, they read an explanation of how the bullet-shaped body of the seal is an adaptation for swimming and for temperature control. The familiar boundaries of story genre, with characters, setting, plot, causality, and other relationships are built in. Now the reader must make the connections; the reader must understand organizational patterns of comparison and contrast, thesis statements, persuasive techniques, and, above all, definition.

Words, too, become more elaborate. Again, the fluent reader quickly makes a judgment about what the word is by looking at it as a whole, often just the first few letters. Then comes the "guesstimate," which gets trickier as the reader confronts new content. Making guesstimates less chancy is an important part of the language arts instruction in the upper elementary years. Techniques that are unconscious need to be made conscious so that fluent readers can forge ahead and less fluent readers can keep up. Knowing and naming, or in other words defining the structures of words, opens the doors to the worlds of science, social studies, math, and all the other special subjects that are taught outside the world of story.

Learning about words through language history and linguistic diversity

The knowledge that English is a living and growing language is an important element in achieving literacy. Students can then bring their own language backgrounds and their own interests to the topic of language history.

Principal June Nomura remembers her first day in an American school. She was 12 and scared, overwhelmed by the sounds of a language she had read but seldom heard, and certainly not shouted. Of course, in Japan she had seen American television, but it was always dubbed in her own language. Commercials offered more clues because the words on the packages and tags were usually in both Japanese script and English script. The words she knew best were the food words: her home town had a pizza restaurant and her supermarket had corn flakes. When she was very little, before she could read in Japanese, she even thought that corn flakes and cola drinks were Japanese foods.

Now she is a principal in a junior high school, and her favorite task is about to begin—orientation for foreign students. She remembers her own first day and does exactly what her teacher did. First she pulls down the world map; then she takes the pointer and taps the beige shape that is the United States. She says, "America." Next she picks up the list of names and begins to read. As she says each name, she gestures for the student to stand up.

"Yukiko Yamashita. You are from Japan." She points to Japan. Then she points to the United States. "Now you are in America. Welcome to America."

When all the students are standing, she opens her arms wide as if to embrace them all and says: "Welcome to America."

Throughout the year, she meets with these students regularly. As their English improves, she tells them how America was built by people from many different countries who spoke many different languages. Then she tells them that American English has changed because of these people.

First she turns to Greta, from the Netherlands.

"Without Greta's home language, we would not have a word for *cookie,* or *boss.* And the pioneers would not have known what to call their *wagons.* Thank you, Greta, for your language."

Then June hands out copies of a list of American English words borrowed from other languages. Each year her list is different, depending on which languages are represented in the school or in the class. Today's list reads:

Borrowed Words

Arabic	algebra, sugar, zero
Aztec	avocado, chocolate, tomato
Chinese	silk, tea, tycoon
French	garage, language, plateau
German	kindergarten, noodle, zinc
Hindi/Urdu	bandanna, pajamas, shampoo
Italian	corridor, lava, studio
Japanese	honcho, samurai, sushi
Native American/Canadian	moccasin, raccoon, toboggan
Pacific Islands	bamboo, taboo, tattoo
Spanish	arroyo, lasso, tornado

As the students read the list, she walks around the classroom to answer questions about reading or pronunciation. She sees a raised hand and goes to Teresa.

"Where did avocados, chocolate, and tomatoes come from?"

"By the way you are asking that question, Teresa, I think you already know the answer," the principal smiles.

"From Mexico?"

"And the rest of Central America. The rest of the world did not know these foods until the fifteenth century."

The class catches on. "So sugar comes from the Middle East?" "And algebra?" "Did the Germans invent kindergarten?"

Suddenly word study turns into a social studies class.

Then Massimo raises his hand. "Where's the pizza?"

Now the class is just where she wants it. "Thank you, Massimo, for asking that question. Our next class assignment is to make a long list of food words from other languages."

Vocabulary Development

IMPORTANCE OF BUILDING RICH VOCABULARIES

A student's vocabulary plays a critical role in every aspect of literacy learning. Words are the keys to constructing meaning with texts. A rich vocabulary boosts a student's oral and written expression, reading comprehension, and viewing comprehension. Some might think that learning vocabulary is simply about learning words. This is true only to a limited extent. Many words stand for concepts. They not only help us name things, they also help us think and talk about ideas. Words help us develop conceptual frames to which we can link new ideas to think and talk about. Yet, as Johnson (2001) put it, "Words seem like such ordinary things, and most of us take them for granted" (p. 1).

Although vocabulary can be directly taught, much of what children learn about words and their meaning is a result of their natural exposure to language. They learn many more new words from their reading than they do through conversation or through watching television. Hayes and Ahrens (1988) analyzed written language from varied genres, spoken language from television shows of various types, and adult speech in different contexts, ranking the frequency of the words used in the three categories. They found that children's trade books contained many more unusual, not as frequently used words than most adult speech or prime-time television shows. Children learn more new vocabulary words through reading and discussing high-quality trade books than through any other language activity.

Reading volume, especially the amount of time children spend reading independently, "is still a very powerful predictor of vocabulary and knowledge differences between children, even when performance is statistically equated for reading comprehension and general ability" (Cunningham & Stanovich, 1998, p. 11). Children who read more in and out of school develop much larger vocabularies than those who don't. With larger vocabularies, children's ability to acquire knowledge becomes a much easier task. The more knowledge children acquire and the more fluent readers they become, the more new vocabulary words they add to their lexicon. The range of differences between children who read and those who don't magnifies as they move through the grades.

Vocabulary learning is both complex and fascinating. Words have multiple meanings and many meanings have multiple words to represent them:

> Mother watered the *plant* so that it wouldn't die.
>
> Dad was tired from working at the automobile *plant* all day.
>
> *Plant* the key under the mat, where no one will see it.

We use words such as *gifted, bright, smart, apt,* and *adept* to describe children who are outstanding students. All of these convey the same idea. Many words are derived from other words, for example, *health, healthy, healthiest, healthful, unhealthy*. The derivative words share a common meaning, yet they differ in meaning because of their affixes.

McArthur (1996, pp. 1026–1027) identified eight different kinds of words, three of which are relevant for vocabulary instruction:

> ***Lexical words:*** These words have describable meanings. They are usually nouns (*cabin, Ruston, breeze*), verbs (*hiked, imagine, standing*), or modifiers (*strong, never, happily*).
>
> ***Grammatical words:*** These are the structure words that serve to link lexical words. Included are conjunctions (*and, because, in case*), determiners (*all, this, many*), interjections (*aha, oops, wow*), particles (*to see, look up*), and pronouns (*they, that, she*).
>
> ***Onomastic words:*** These words are the names of particular persons, places, and things not usually listed in dictionaries but important and often intriguing to children (for example, Chase Howard, Superior Grille, the Hair Port).

Two additional descriptions of words that are important to teachers are obvious from previous discussions of word learning in this book. **Phonolog-**

Bernice Cullinan

Effective teachers employ a variety of creative ways to expose their students to new vocabulary.

ical words are the spoken forms of words. **Orthographic words** are the written form.

Vocabulary development is a lifetime undertaking. As teachers we play a critical role in enriching and extending children's vocabularies. Effective teachers combine direct instruction of vocabulary and strategies for learning vocabulary with numerous opportunities for exposure and use of new vocabulary. They know that most words are not learned by looking them up in a dictionary. They are learned in the context of experiences with listening, speaking, reading, writing, and viewing. Through such use, the complexities and nuances of word meanings are developed. The *Teaching Idea: Creating a Word Bank of Vocabulary Items for Responding to Literature,* is a functional way to focus on key vocabulary and concepts from books read aloud. This process can be adapted to virtually any grade level.

Strategies for vocabulary building

Like all good teaching, vocabulary instruction should be grounded in how children learn. Bromley (2002, p. 9) offers four underlying assumptions to guide successful word learning:

- *It is personal.* Successful word learning is different for each individual. Learners vary in terms of how they learn and what they know, greatly influencing what they learn.
- *It is active.* Successful word learning requires students to manipulate information by thinking, talking, or writing to make knowledge their own.
- *It is flexible.* Successful word learning may occur easily, without much effort on your part or the student's, or it may require intense, direct instruction.
- *It is strategic.* Successful word learning happens when learners use a variety of strategies, depending on the new word and the situation. Conscious use of a strategy, process, or way of learning new words helps students become independent.

Vocabulary can be practiced through analysis and memorization, but discovering and sharing high-level words and technical terms that students already know creates excitement about word study.

Jack Sanchez is a coach—he coaches the town softball team, and he coaches soccer after school. He thinks like a coach, and he acts like a coach. When a new crop of kids comes to school, he first wants to know what they do well. He uses an in-class writing assignment to determine their knowledge of specialized vocabulary. He tells them that they will be writing about something they know how to do well—a sport, an interest, a task, a hobby.

Jack models the approach by closing his eyes and visualizing himself playing baseball. He tells the students that he is seeing a specific game in which he hit a game-winning double. Then he starts telling what he is seeing,

TEACHING IDEA

Literature Link

CREATING A WORD BANK OF VOCABULARY ITEMS FOR RESPONDING TO LITERATURE

Elementary school students need extra support when they move from the spoken word to the written word. Students who understand everything from plot to character motivation still have difficulty in translating their insights into words on paper. Creating a word bank of specific words from the literature that is read aloud gives all students the opportunity to put their thoughts into words. The blank sheet of paper is less forbidding when they have already chosen some of the words that they will use.

Tell students that they are going to help create a word bank for everyone to use for responding to the book you will be reading. Create a sheet with these headings and print them on acetate for the overhead projector.

WORD BANK
Title
Author
Publishing Information
People Places Things

Using the acetate copy, project the WORD BANK on a screen and ask a student to volunteer information for the first three lines. Students can write the information either on the board or on the acetate. When everyone has agreed that both the information and the spellings are correct and complete, begin the day's reading.

After you finish reading, ask students to think about which people, places, and things are important so far. List these on the acetate or on the board, then ask students to choose the ones they think should stay. Keep the ones everyone agrees on and cross out the rest.

Before the next read-aloud session, show the list they have chosen as a way to get back into the story. Once again, at the end of the session, add names to each list and then ask for a vote. Note that each time you do this, students are naturally focusing on the importance of each element on the list.

When the read-aloud is complete, review the list one more time, then hand out individual WORD BANK sheets for students to copy the final list. Of course, students can add other names to the list. They can also use the words to summarize the plot, to describe the action of the story, or to give details of character and setting. Remind them to check the spelling of each word they use from the word bank when they complete their journal entries or draft responses to the reading.

When you have read at least three books, review the word bank for words that have been used more than once. Words like *plot, character, motivation, setting, short story, novel,* and *poem* will most likely be repeated. Students can use these words to build a literary dictionary for the class.

taking his listeners along with him. They see the situation he faced, where the opposing players were standing, how he figured out where he wanted to hit the ball, and what pitch he actually hit. When he is finished, he opens his eyes and asks the class to tell if there was anything they didn't understand.

Usually at least one student asks a question about technical language, which Jack first explains, then writes on the board. Today, the question is about the phrase "high and inside." Jack explains the term by showing where the ball was in relation to his body and adds that he will add the explanation to his essay.

Then he talks the students through their own visualizations. He tells them to close their eyes, imagine they are doing something they like and are good at, and see themselves doing the activity. He also tells them to use the technical words they associate with what they are doing. As they visualize, Jack notices which students are smiling or nodding their heads. Then he asks one of those students to volunteer their response by keeping their eyes closed and telling what they are seeing. He makes notes of the technical words the student uses and the clarity with which they explain their craft or sport.

Today, he discovers that Lara is learning Plains Indian drumming and singing from her Lakota grandfather. Her technical terms include the words *vocables* (syllables used for singing) and *honor beat* (the final beat at the end of a passage). Alex is learning to identify dinosaur fossils from his uncle Todd and uses the terms *sedimentary rock* and *Cretaceous era*. Once Jack finishes writing their words and definitions on the board, hands of other students eager to share what they know go up across the room. By the end of the week, Jack has discovered cartoonists, gymnasts, basketball and hockey fans, budding filmmakers, junior carpenters, and a whole range of other specialists. Dwayne, for example, silent from the first day, finally described his weekend job with his stepfather, cutting and laying carpeting.

For each craft and each interest, there are special words. All the words first go on the board, where they are defined and their spellings noted. Later they are added to the classroom computer to create the special vocabulary used by Mr. Sanchez and his knowledgeable fifth-graders. As Jack explains to a visitor, "Everyone is an expert in something. Imagine what we'd learn about acquiring language if we could ask a baby."

Word banks in the content area

As teachers read, talk about, and investigate a topic of interest or unit of study, they can record key words relevant to the topic on a chart or word wall. The class then discusses each word before adding it to the list, noting any special features it may have that will help them remember its meaning and spelling. This word bank becomes a valuable resource for discussion and for writing reports. Words that go beyond the topic and are developmentally appropriate for spelling are added to the class spelling list. For example, when

Bernice Cullinan

Students learn to read and spell words related to their unit of study.

studying how things grow in third grade, children would be held accountable for spelling the word *plant,* but not for *photosynthesis*. A fourth grade class generated the following words during an ecology unit:

Eco-Jive

recycle	herbicide	pollute
ecology	pesticide	pollution
environment	insecticide	pollutant
exhaust	ozone	natural

This is only a limited selection of the words generated during a 6-week unit of study during which students used a variety of resource media for information and generated their own multimedia reports. Discussions centered on vocabulary strengthened their conceptual knowledge and their understandings about words. Talk about affixes, roots, and word meanings came about as needed. The relevance to their reading and writing was obvious to all.

Learning about prefixes, roots, and suffixes

Children can begin to learn about some of the most common prefixes, suffixes, and roots (or base words) in the primary grades. Prefixes are letter groups that come before a root word to give it a new meaning. The prefixes *re, un,* and *in* appear most frequently in English. Less common prefixes should be taught in the later grades or discussed whenever they come up in discussion during a read-aloud time or when students are reading or viewing. For example, the prefix *anti* (against; opposite) is commonly used in content-area materials. Middle-grade children are likely to read or hear the words *antifreeze, antisocial,* or *antibiotic* at home and at school. Exploring the meaning of *anti* not only helps unlock the meaning of these words, it helps students learn a basic principle about how words work. Figures 10.2, 10.3, and 10.4 list common prefixes, roots, and suffixes taught in elementary and middle school.

Connecting vocabulary study to everyday life

Experienced teachers know that the more engaged students are, the more they will begin to teach themselves. They will discern patterns, discover rules, and share what they have learned with enthusiasm. Turning vocabulary study into a process of discovery can be achieved by understanding what you want your students to achieve in a lesson and then allowing them different ways of achieving it. For example, you might decide to construct a lesson or a series of lessons around the concept that the English language, like most languages, changes over time and that one of the ways it changes is by borrowing words from other languages.

FIGURE 10.2

Common Prefixes Taught in Elementary and Middle School

Prefix	***Definition***	***Example***
over-	too much	overflow
re-	again	review, revoke
un-	not	unhappy, untrue
un-	reverse	untie, unpack
in-	into	insight
in-	not	inert
ex-	out	exit, extinguish
de-	away, from	deflect, detour
com-	together, with	commune, communicate
dis-	opposite	dishonest, dismiss
pre-	before	prevent, predict
sub-	under	subway, submarine

FIGURE 10.3

Common Roots Taught in Elementary and Middle School

Root	Definition	Example
graph	writing	autograph, autobiography
gram	thing written	telegram, monogram
spect	look	inspect, spectacle
port	carry	portable, important
dict	say	diction, dictionary
rupt	break	interrupt, rupture
scrib	write	inscribe, describe
cred	believe	credit, discredit
vid	see	video, evidence
aud	hear	audience, auditorium

FIGURE 10.4

Common Suffixes Taught in Elementary and Middle School

Suffix	Definition	Example
-ly	in the manner of	lightly, slowly
-er	more	higher, stronger
-able/-ible	able to	believable, visible
-est	most	hardest, greatest
-less	without	fearless, hopeless
-ness	quality or act	kindness, softness
-arium	a place for	aquarium, terrarium
-ling	small	duckling, gosling

You might begin by writing these words on the board:

pizza	*Italian*
salsa	*Spanish*
crepes	*French*
potato	*Native American (Taino)*
bagel	*Yiddish*

With a large number of students who speak or listen to other languages, you might add or substitute other Americanized food words for the ones in the list above. Then you can ask students where they can find these words in everyday life. Some students may suggest the dictionary, but most will mention a restaurant, a fast-food place, or a supermarket. Then you can divide the group into teams according to the languages you have listed. The students' mission is to find as many food-related words as possible that have come into English from other languages. Their resources are menus from fast-food or family restaurants, the school cafeteria, TV and radio commercials, and interviews with people they know. They may also look at cookbooks and check out the different foods in their local supermarkets.

The goal for all teams is to compile a minidictionary of food words, showing which language the food comes from and giving a short description and the source of the information. You can hand out index cards on which the researchers write each word, its origin and meaning, and its source. Students should have at least one full week to gather their information and complete the project.

Example:

Food Word: bagel

Language: Yiddish

Description: A round bread with a hole in it made from flour and cooked by boiling and baking.

Source: The Bagelry, Mr. Sol Kolba

Spelling

Spelling is important to written communication in that conventional spelling is necessary for readability, and facility with spelling removes a potential barrier to reading fluency. Luckily, a significant amount of research has examined the teaching of spelling, and we do know how children develop as spellers, how they best learn to spell, and how spelling best fits into the writing cycle. Good spellers know how to find their spelling errors, know how to use dictionaries and other spelling resources, and can remember the correct spelling for many words, calling on their knowledge of high-frequency words, word patterns, and alternative spellings (like *ph/f*).

When given access to pencil and paper, young children will "write." Once these emergent writers make letterlike forms, they begin to invent spellings for the words they want to write, as we noted in Chapter Six. This continues in the primary grades when children are encouraged at school to make their "best guess" at how to spell words rather than to stop and seek help or look up words as they try to put meaning on paper. Invented spelling reveals the linguistic principles under which a student is operating. These spellings are deliberate and systematic, and represent an increasing sophistication. Inventing spelling does not negatively affect either reading development or the development of conventional spelling. What it does do is allow children to operate on their hypotheses about how standard written English works and to write unencumbered by worry about correct spelling. It also allows them to use in their writing the exact words that they want to use, like *scwed* (squid) and *youkalites* (eucalyptus), rather than limit themselves to words that they can spell, such as *fish* and *tree*. As they learn to read and come in contact with more and more print that is conventionally spelled, children begin to abandon their early strategies and to explore more conventional strategies, such as within-word patterns. At the same time, most children are being directly exposed to within-word patterns, such as those in Figure 10.5, in the spelling instruction they receive in school.

The initial and necessary step in learning to spell is developing the concept of "word." Adults often forget that what is perfectly clear to them is often a mystery to young children. Experience with literature, language experience, and the opportunity to try to put their own meanings on paper all help children come to know what a word is. Once this knowledge is firm, they can then begin to learn the common patterns associated with spelling these words (Henderson, 1990).

According to brain scientists, we have at least two kinds of memory: procedural and semantic. **Procedural memory** allows someone to get on a bike and ride around the park with only a wobble or two even after 10 years of not riding. Procedural memory is also in place when a woman turns left at the corner and then realizes she is going to buy bread because she always turns left when she goes to the bakery. Procedural memory stores the way individuals do things. It creates habit.

Semantic memory, on the other hand, stores words, definitions, concepts, and behaviors that people have at some time put into words. Difficulties arise when someone is asked to put into words something stored only in procedural memory. Most people know a good cook who is always willing to share recipes with friends, but friends are always disappointed with the results they get. The good cook is not purposely forgetting something. If the friend watched him, she would see that he makes changes as he goes along, depending on taste and smell. Experts can't always give details that show what they know how to do. The same is true of good readers and spellers.

Many children begin reading at an early age, and the process of reading is something they never have to think about, something they never have to put into words. Spelling is also a part of these children's unconscious knowledge. Armed with this insight and an understanding of procedural and semantic

FIGURE 10.5

Selected English Spelling Patterns

Vowels

single consonant (short)—*hat, fed, big, pot, bug*
blend (short)—*fast, tell, pill, rock, luck*
r-controlled—*car, germ, girl, work, burn*
long vowel-consonant-e—*take, bite, bone, cute*
ee—*feet*
ea—*clean*
e—*he*
gh—*high*
y syllable *I*—*my*
oa—*boat*
o, ow—*no, snow*
ew—*chew*
un—*tune*
ui—*suit*
oo—*noon, book*
oi, oy, ow, ou—*boil, boy, how, out*
ld, nd—*wild, find*
ld, lt, ll, st—*cold, colt, poll, host*

Consonants

blends (*bl, br, cl, cr, dr, fl, fr, gl, pr, qu, sc, sk, sl, sm, sn, sp, squ, st, sw, tr, tw*)
final *k* (*ck, c, k, ke*)
digraphs (*gh, ch, sh, ph, wh, th*)
homophones (*heir* and *air*)
compound words (*snowman*)

Source: From Edmund Henderson, *Teaching Spelling* (2nd. ed.), 1990, Houghton Mifflin. (A more detailed list of common English spelling patterns, marked for grade level, appears in that text on pages 221–236.)

memory, you can help children make conscious what they know. You can begin by working with children to analyze the patterns of constantly misspelled words, looking for double consonants, the schwa, plurals, homonyms, or blends, and teaching one pattern at a time. Students can make a chart of common words they misspell that follow this particular pattern, describing in writing their difficulty with the pattern. They can write sentences using words with the pattern. When writing on their own, they can review their drafts to see if they contain any words with the problem pattern. Students will soon see mistakes with the pattern and correct them as they write, just as they often naturally revise content. Eventually, knowledge that has been stored only in procedural memory is also stored in semantic memory.

English spelling patterns will gradually appear in the writing of bilingual students as well, as they are given the opportunity to read and write in both their first language and English. Just as in the teaching of mechanics, teachers who know the bilingual student's first language can help facilitate the development of conventional English spelling patterns operating in the two languages (Edelsky, 1986).

SPELLING DEVELOPMENT

Children's spelling ability is developmental, with all children moving through the following stages, though not at the same pace.

Emergent spelling

In Chapter Six, we discussed the emergence of spelling. When children become aware of letters and their ability to form letterlike forms on paper, they begin to experiment with letter formation. By learning to recognize their names and other environmental print, they learn that words are made up of letters. At this stage, they may use a series of random letters, and even numbers, to make words (*lbZt* to spell *boat*).

Semiphonetic stage (letter name spelling)

With the benefit of some exposure to games and activities that promote phonemic awareness and phonics, children soon learn that certain letters and sounds often go together. At this stage, they may use one to three letters, virtually all consonants, to spell entire words (*b* or *bT* for *boat*).

Phonetic stage

Gradually, vowels are added along with more consonant sounds (*bot* for *boat*). As children's awareness of how words sound and work increases, more vowels are added. Formal spelling instruction is appropriate at this stage. Children have some knowledge to work with, and they can begin to see the patterns in words and build on that knowledge as they move closer and closer to conventional spelling.

Toward conventional spelling

Children continue to refine their understanding of the alphabetic principle and to learn more complex consonant patterns. They learn about long vowel spelling patterns (*home, cane*), other less common vowel patterns, and *r*-controlled vowels (*fern, fir, fur*). Some common spelling generalizations often taught during this stage of development are listed in Figure 10.6. Children also build on what they know about syllables, affixes, and roots, and they learn to use what they know about words with related meanings to figure out the

FIGURE 10.6

Frequently Taught Spelling Generalizations

Capitals

1. Proper nouns begin with capital letters.
   Linda, Sampson, United States, Atlantic Ocean

Plurals

2. Plurals of most nouns are formed by adding an *s*.
   cat, cats; desk, desks; book, books
3. Plurals of nouns ending in *ch, s, sh,* or *x* are usually formed by adding an *es*.
   bunch, bunches; dress, dresses; brush, brushes; box, boxes
4. Plurals of some nouns are formed by changing their singular form.
   child, children; man, men; woman, women; goose, geese; mouse, mice
5. When a noun ends in a *y* that is preceded by a consonant, the plural is formed by changing the *y* to an *i* and adding an *es*.
   baby, babies; fly, flies; party, parties

Possessive Forms

5. Possessives of most singular nouns are formed by adding an apostrophe followed by an *s*.
   boy, boy's; dog, dog's
6. Possessives of most plural nouns are formed by adding an apostrophe.
   players, players'; ladies, ladies'
7. Possessives of some plural nouns are formed by adding an apostrophe followed by an *s*.
   men, men's; children, children's

Vowels

8. When an *r* follows a vowel, the sound of the vowel is neither long nor short but is *r-controlled,* meaning that the *r* influences the sound of the vowel that precedes it.
   sir, tar, fur
9. An *o* at the end of a word usually represents the long /o/ sound.
   tobacco, tomato

Suffixes

10. A word that ends in a *silent e* usually keeps the *e* when a suffix beginning with a consonant is added.
    grace, graceful; nine, ninety; taste, tasteful
11. A word that ends in a *silent e* usually drops the *e* when a suffix beginning with a vowel is added.
    make, making
12. A word that ends in a single consonant preceded by a vowel usually doubles the final letter when a suffix beginning with a vowel is added.
    tag, tagged; stop, stopped, stopping; fat, fatter
13. A word ending in a *y* that follows a consonant usually changes the *y* to *i* before a suffix is added, unless that suffix begins with *i*.
    party, parties; empty, emptiness

spelling of unknown words. Many of the words they use in their own writing are spelled correctly, even those with irregular spelling patterns.

THE SPELLING PROGRAM

Spelling development depends on a well-conceived program of instruction. As children move through the grades, certain essentials must be in place to implement an effective spelling program. On a daily basis, students need numerous and varied experiences with the following:

Reading. Learning to spell involves the ability to form visual images of how words look. By repeatedly seeing words in print in the books they are reading, children learn word patterns that they apply to their spelling.

Writing. All types of writing provide practice with spelling. Students apply what they know from word study activities to solve spelling challenges.

Word work. Some high-frequency words (for example, *are, were, was* in the primary grades) simply need to be taught directly and reinforced through constant exposure. **Word walls,** where words are listed alphabetically for easy reference, serve students well when they are writing. Words related to content units may receive similar treatment through the word banks discussed earlier in this chapter. **Making words** and **sorting words,** also discussed earlier in this chapter, help students see the similarities in words and learn about spelling generalizations. That knowledge is used to spell as well as to read. Work with **prefixes, suffixes,** and **root words** helps students develop the skills needed to solve spelling problems. The *Teaching Idea: Using the Writer's Craft Approach to Study Prefixes and Suffixes* offers several suggestions.

Teachers who want their students to learn to spell high-frequency words, or words that reflect a particular spelling pattern, often ask them to study ten to fourteen spelling words per week (depending on the grade level), then ask them to choose two or three additional words with which they are having problems, and two or three more words that they'd like to spell to use in their own writing (Graves, 1994). When children are studying these words, a cognitive monitoring technique is an effective strategy for them to use. They should look at the correctly spelled word, close their eyes and visualize that word, write the word without looking at the model, and then check their word against the model. Younger children can say the word and spell it softly to themselves (Snowball & Bolton, 1999). The process should be repeated two or three times or until the child knows how the word is spelled without having to refer to the model. The visual recreation of target words is a powerful tool for learning to spell. Careful attention to sound, quite helpful and neces-

TEACHING IDEA

Literature Link

USING THE WRITER'S CRAFT APPROACH TO STUDY PREFIXES AND SUFFIXES

Everyone has a favorite author. For some children, it's the unknown writer of their favorite big book or read-aloud book. For others, it is the author of a series of adventure or fantasy tales, particularly one who publishes at least a book a year. Many cartoonists or comic book artists also have a large and devoted following. The wise teacher makes use of the reader's fascination and loyalty to an author to teach language arts.

At the beginning of the year and regularly throughout the year, take a survey of students' favorite authors. Some names and titles may be on the list all year; others will be added; a few will be deleted. Make sure that your small library of "extra" books includes as many of the popular authors as possible. (*Reminder:* Over the years, popular authors often stay on the lists, so an initial investment or PTA grant will reap yearly rewards.)

Tell students that they will study their favorite authors, not just to learn about plot, characterization, and theme, but also to learn how to put words together and how to increase their own vocabularies. Good authors make good teachers.

Begin a language arts lesson by telling students that they are going to hunt prefixes and suffixes. Allow them to choose a book from among their list of favorites and assign each reader the task of finding at least one word for each of the following prefixes and suffixes:

Prefixes	***Suffixes***
anti-	*-est*
bi-	*-hood*
intro-	*-ism*
micro-	*-less*
mis-	*-like*
pro-	*-ology*
re-	*-or*
super-	*-tion*

Students reading the same book may work in pairs or small groups. On the board, show the headings you want students to use:

TITLE AUTHOR PUBLISHING INFORMATION

WORD (print word; give page number; underline the prefix or suffix; define the word; tell what the prefix/suffix means in that word)

Tell students that the goal is to find at least one word for each prefix and suffix. If they have difficulty finding a word in one of the author's books, they can read another book by that author or switch authors.

Allow the students class time as well as homework time to complete the task. When the work is finished, have students read aloud the words they have found and post the results on the class bulletin board or on the class computer. For a follow-up activity, have students work in pairs to compose sentences for ten of the class words. Discuss the effect the prefix or suffix has on the base or root word.

sary for invented spelling, becomes less helpful as students develop conventional spelling. Asking students who are developing conventional spelling to think about how words look rather than how they sound helps them retrieve the visual patterns they have learned.

When children are learning to spell words that they use in their reading and writing across the curriculum, it is usually a waste of time to test those words. The true motivation for learning to spell is not a weekly test but facility in written communication. However, should it ever be necessary to test, the test-study-test sequence with self-correction of mistakes is the most effective way to test spelling. Children study only those words that were misspelled on the first test early in the week, practice them during the week, and test again at the end of the week.

Sara Angeletti teaches children in the elementary grades to spell using their own reading and writing. She asks students to notice high-frequency words or to find particular word patterns in the books they are reading and write these words on a class list. Then all students write each word on their personal list. The class selects the words from the list that they want to learn (those that would be most useful to them in their writing), and each student writes these words in his or her individual spelling dictionary. Sara then gives a spelling "test" in which she calls out the words. Her students look the words up in their spelling dictionaries, making sure that they have the correct spelling in the dictionary entries. Parents have become involved in her spelling program too, by volunteering to edit the children's spelling dictionaries. They note errors in spelling, but leave it up to the individual students to correct those errors.

Dictionary use. Editing is a natural time to help children learn how to use a dictionary. As they check their spelling and word choices during editing, it is natural that they will need to use an age-appropriate dictionary. Lessons that help children learn dictionary skills should be embedded in a real task—editing their own work—rather than being exercises that are divorced from any meaningful context. You may want to talk about or demonstrate how a dictionary works, followed by some individual lessons during editing conferences.

Several copies of different dictionaries should be readily available for children. Different dictionaries provide a range of complexity for students and will encourage children to compare the books and use them appropriately. One dictionary may have many words in it and be best for a quick check. Another might be more fun to browse through because of its colorful illustrations. When teachers talk to children about dictionaries as an invaluable writer's tool as well as a source of interesting information, children are eager to use them.

Individual dictionaries that students construct from their own spelling words also provide practice in dictionary skills. Primary-grade students will be able to practice simple alphabetizing by putting words in a dictionary organized by letters, with one or two pages devoted to each letter. As students are ready, they can learn to alphabetize by the first two letters, then three, and so on.

Starting with very simple dictionaries in the primary grades, children learn to use dictionaries as a resource for spelling. Children need to practice how to locate unfamiliar words they are looking for in the dictionary. They should be taught to use what they know about spelling to predict how the word might be spelled.

- They might think of words they know that are similar to the word they want to spell (*telephone—telegraph*);
- Use what they know about the sounds in the word;
- Use what they know about the root and affixes the word contains;
- Use the dictionary to check for correct spelling (double letters; endings such as *ible* or *able*).

Proofreading. Proofreading is used to locate misspelled words and other mechanical errors in writing drafts. Even at the beginning stages of writing, children can be taught to look back at their writing in order to check for spelling errors. Wilde (1996) suggests that students be taught to proofread as they engage in the writing process. Proofreading is introduced at the editing stage, where students are taught specific strategies for finding and correcting misspelled words.

In the primary grades, teachers model editing and proofreading as they demonstrate the writing process for students and as they make corrections

Bernice Cullinan

To facilitate correct spelling, ask children to select words they would like to look up and add to a personal dictionary.

during shared writing activities. Students are also asked to return to their own independent writing in order to check their spelling. The point here is to get students in the habit of looking back over their work. First for revision: "What do I want to change or add?" Second, to look for errors in mechanics: "Did I use capital letters where needed? Do my sentences end with periods?" Finally, they are taught to ask: "Are the words spelled correctly? What can I do to correct misspelled words?" Even if children move only a bit closer to the conventional spelling of a word they attempt to correct, they are being given opportunities to practice the spelling strategies they know.

As students progress through the grades, they are increasingly held responsible for their spelling errors. They are taught strategies for proofreading, such as circling and then writing unknown words two or three different ways and choosing the one that looks "right," and keeping records of frequently misspelled words. Teachers use what they learn about students' misspelled words and their attempts to correct their spelling errors as the basis for further instruction.

Spelling instruction in the primary grades

Throughout their discussion of word study for young learners, Bear, Invernizzi, Templeton, and Johnston (1996) offer several suggestions to help learners as they move through various stages of word learning and spelling:

- Encourage children to experiment with and manipulate words through word study activities.
- Encourage writing from the earliest stages.
- Allow children to develop their own sensitivity and reasoning ability about why words are spelled a particular way.
- Keep standards for spelling appropriate to the developmental level of the child.
- Monitor students' word study and spelling abilities so that they can be helped to make a smooth transition from one stage to another.

Independent use of strategies such as those described earlier in this chapter should also be encouraged, for example:

1. Check to see if you recognize any smaller words that may help you remember the spelling.
2. Check to see if you notice any spelling patterns or root words that may be helpful.
3. Check for anything that might be special about the word (double letters, silent letters, and so on).

4. Think of ways you might be able to change the word by changing a letter or group of letters, by adding a prefix or suffix, by making it plural, and so on.

The emphasis in kindergarten and early primary grades should be on invented, not corrected, spelling. Clarke (1988) found that young children who wrote regularly using invented spelling were superior to those in more traditional programs on measures of word decoding and phonics knowledge. Children who spend time writing naturally practice their spelling strategies and become better spellers.

Spelling instruction beyond the early grades

Older students need to produce a great deal of writing in order to perfect writing conventions such as spelling. Spelling longer unknown words in their own writing gives them the opportunity to practice the strategies introduced in this chapter. Through the years, students' knowledge of the English orthographic system increases, and they become increasingly better spellers. The Directed Spelling Thinking Activity (Zutell, 1996) brings together language-based literacy instruction and word study. Once again, many of the activities discussed earlier are included in this strategy, which consists of six steps:

1. *A pretest for prediction and discussion.* The teacher initiates student predictions by giving the group a brief spelling test on words that represent a specific pattern or feature. Students share their attempts at spelling the words and discuss their spelling strategies.
2. *Assisted word sorting.* The teacher guides the students through a group word-sorting activity much like the ones discussed earlier in this chapter.
3. *Word hunting.* Students scan through familiar books and other written materials to generate words for individual and class word banks containing words with the feature under study.
4. *Cooperative and individual word sorting.* Students work in pairs, and then individually, to sort a combination of teacher-supplied words and their own examples. Each set of words is collected into a deck that is used as the basis for reading and sorting activities.
5. *Practice activities.* Once students and teachers agree on the sets of words on which they will focus, a variety of practice activities, such as the one described earlier in this chapter in which students use a practice sheet to *Look, Say,* and *Write* words, can be created.
6. *Measuring and recording student success.* At the end of each lesson cycle, an individualized spelling review is recommended. This can be peer administered and checked. Students and teacher use this and the generation of personal lists of new words to be learned as the basis of monitoring growth.

STRATEGIES THAT SUPPORT SPELLING DEVELOPMENT

Time must be set aside for instruction targeted to teach children strategies for spelling unknown words. The strategies taught will vary according to grade level and to the competency of the learners. Regardless of the grade level, students will benefit from discussions of what they already know about the patterns in the language and their knowledge of how the language works. The *Teaching Idea: Helping Students Become Aware of the Spelling Rules They Already Know* describes an approach that can be adapted to any grade level.

Selecting words for spelling instruction

Throughout the grades, students constantly add to the list of words they know how to spell. Common sources of spelling words include: the **high-frequency words** in written language; words generated according to **common linguistic features,** such as a particular spelling pattern (*ight, ack*) or inflectional ending (*ed, ing*); **spelling generalizations;** or words selected from **content units** currently under study. Often, teachers may also include **personalized lists** of words generated cooperatively with students according to the words they frequently misspell in their writing.

High-frequency words appear so often in written language that they should be learned as early as possible both for reading and for spelling. Figure 10.7 is compiled from many lists of such words that are available. Teachers should add relevant words that come up in the course of instruction. High-frequency words are introduced in the early primary grades first for reading and then for spelling.

Working with high-frequency words

- Words may be introduced in the order that seems best for the learners at hand and made available on a word wall for children to refer to as needed. Introduce and post only a few at a time, preferably as they arise during the course of reading and writing.
- Use the words as a part of focus lessons during writing workshop. Establish these as words they constantly need for both their reading and writing and that they are expected to read and spell correctly.
- Students who need to may create personal dictionaries of these words. Or, on a book mark, they may list the ones they have most difficulty remembering.

Integrating spelling with writing

As much as possible, effective teaching links spelling with writing. Although it is best to encourage students to make their "best guess" about spelling during drafting, when editing it is important to ask students who have attained a

TEACHING IDEA

Addressing Individual Needs

HELPING STUDENTS BECOME AWARE OF THE SPELLING RULES THEY ALREADY KNOW

September is the month when teachers and students learn about each other. Teachers review work that they hope students have learned; students expect to take a new diagnostic every other day that measures how well or how inadequately they perform certain tasks. Often, by the end of the month, teachers are disappointed and students are discouraged. The following activity can help you frame the year's work in a positive way.

Tell students that they are going to discover some of the things they do well. Then, using a state-approved spelling list for a grade level one or two years below your students' current one, dictate twenty spelling words. Make sure to pick a variety of words that contain common patterns, including plurals and doubled consonants.

When you have finished, use the overhead projector to show the list to the class. Use index cards or paper to mask all the words except the one you are reading. As you read the word, point out the spelling issue each contains. For example, for the word *circus,* you might say:

> This word begins with an *s* sound that is spelled *ci.* Then it has a *k* sound that is spelled *cu.* It also has the neutral vowel we call a schwa spelled with a *u.* Finally, it uses the letter *s* to spell the final *s* sound. If you spelled this word correctly, you know four spelling rules. Put a check mark next to the word and add the numeral 4.

For a word like *planning,* you might say:

> This word can be tricky. It uses the suffix *ing* to change the verb *plan* into a noun. Because *plan* is a single syllable containing a short *a* sound followed by a consonant, we double the final consonant when we add a suffix beginning with a vowel. If you spelled this word correctly, you know three spelling rules. Put a check mark next to the word and add the numeral 3.

Continue showing and analyzing the words. Answer any questions that students might have, then ask how many students scored 20 on the test. Most of the class will be able to raise their hands.

Finish the activity by handing out another sheet of spelling words for homework. These words should be at the same grade level and contain the same rules. After the next test, use words that demonstrate other rules. Finally, move up to the current grade level.

Remember: Success alone is neither a motivator nor a teacher. Analysis of success and thoughtful practice make the winning combination.

FIGURE 10.7

High-Frequency Words for Reading and Spelling

a	about	after	all	am
an	and	are	as	at
but	by	came	can	come
could	day	did	do	down
ever	for	from	get	go
going	got	had	has	have
he	her	here	him	his
I	if	in	into	is
it	just	like	little	look
made	make	many	may	me
more	most	must	my	no
not	now	of	often	on
only	or	other	our	out
said	saw	see	she	so
some	that	the	their	them
then	there	they	this	those
to	two	up	very	was
where	which	who	why	will
with	would	you	your	yours

reasonable level of conventional spelling skill to look carefully at their work, to circle words they are unsure of, and to use the dictionary or ask for help. The *Teaching Idea: Teaching Spelling as an Editing Skill* explores this approach further.

Learning to see misspellings is an important part of becoming a good speller. Graves (1994) suggests that looking at drafts on a computer screen may help students locate spelling errors that are harder to find in often messy handwritten drafts. During editing conferences, you can call on students' knowledge of words and word patterns, the sight-word vocabulary of each student writer, and the patterns that underlie our spelling system to help students use what they know. Words identified as problematic during editing conferences can be added to a list or a dictionary of words that the writer is responsible for knowing.

As students read, as they find and correct their own spelling errors during editing, and as teachers instruct individual students informally during conferences and formally through whole-class discussions of spelling patterns,

TEACHING IDEA

Addressing Individual Needs

TEACHING SPELLING AS AN EDITING SKILL

You can help your students learn to recognize spelling errors by providing them with some structured practice in doing that. Begin by working with a high-frequency word list, grouping a few of the words in groups of three and four, with all but one word in each group spelled correctly. The students' task is to find the incorrect word and write it correctly. After children are proficient at doing this, have students spend time looking at their writing, circling the misspellings that they see, and then correcting them. Teach your students to use friends, the class dictionary that they are compiling, books, the glossary in their spelling books, and standard dictionaries (usually consulted by pairs of children for added support) as resources for conventional spellings. They then enter the word, spelled correctly, in their personal dictionary. If you do this biweekly at the beginning of the year, initially it will take a lot of class time, but as students become more proficient, it will become less time-consuming, and eventually students will do it as a matter of course as they edit their own writing.

If you have to give a spelling grade, you can divide the number of errors remaining after editing for spelling by the number of words written. Practices like this one, developed by Sara Angeletti, more accurately reflect the kind of spelling behaviors that writers use than do traditional practices such as studying lists of words and taking a test every Friday. It also teaches students both spelling and editing skills.

students gradually internalize the conventional spellings of thousands of words, and their drafts progressively become freer of error. Students learn best that which they need to know and continue to use. Thinking of conventional spelling as a tool that writers need, rather than as an end in itself, results in both good writers and good spellers. Although correct spelling should never be emphasized to the point that it interferes with the expression of ideas, writers need to know that correct spelling is one way that we make our message clear to the reader. The *Teaching Idea: Correcting Spelling in the Context of Writing* offers another suggestion for integrating writing and spelling.

Monitoring and assessing spelling development

Weekly spelling tests have long been a traditional way to assess older students' performance in spelling. Yet, teachers and students are aware that many students score well on weekly tests and often misspell the very same words in their writing. This is a primary reason that many teachers have moved toward a strategy approach to spelling that goes beyond the spelling of a particular set

Spelling and writing improve when both are made public in classroom displays, and when students read their writing aloud.

TEACHING IDEA

Addressing Individual Needs

CORRECTING SPELLING IN THE CONTEXT OF WRITING

Transforming your class into a writer's workshop gives both you and your students wide-ranging opportunities to grow as writers. An atmosphere of openness and sharing, with expectations that ideas will be transformed into words, webs, and ultimately drafts, provides even novice writers with the sense that they are not alone, and that the blank sheet of paper or the blank screen will not stay empty for long.

At the beginning of the year, hand out writing folders to each student, preferably a folder with two pockets. If your classroom is equipped with computers, you will also assign a disk or a file to each student. An important part of the writing file, whether on the computer or in the folder, is the Individual Spelling Guide. On it, students record the words that they have difficulty spelling—either words they have identified themselves as difficult or ones that keep recurring when you and they review their work at the end of a workshop day or during a workshop conference.

Yes, spelling is important, even during drafting, even during webbing. Although the writing process is described in steps—topic selection, drafting, revising, editing, publishing—it is in fact a recursive process. Each step of the process, except for the publishing, can happen more than once and in more than one place. Beginning writers may need the relief of not having to "worry about spelling," but as their confidence and experience grow, they will benefit from building spelling skills along with writing skills.

of words and seeks to improve a student's overall ability to spell independently. Of course, both instruction and assessment should convey this broader approach. Gill and Scharer (1996) offer a rubric that goes well beyond the usual spelling test as a measure of spelling development. (See the *Teaching Idea: Spelling Assessment Matrix.*) Teaching to the rubric helps ensure that students will have the benefit of a spelling program that is integrated across the language arts. The rubric replaces the single letter grade formerly given on students' report cards. Parents respond favorably to it and agree that it is more informative than a single letter grade (p. 94).

Communicating with parents about the spelling program

Most parents have been taught spelling in ways that are far different from the way their children are being taught. They remember spelling drills and tests and very little linking of spelling instruction with written composition. Spelling errors in their writing were certainly acknowledged, and they were penalized for them. But, little may have been done to help them proofread or concentrate on their own specific spelling errors. Workshops for parents,

Each writing workshop can include a self-check period. For example, students might be encouraged to read what they have written as they complete a page. During this pause, they get a chance to see where their ideas have taken them and where they think they might want to go next. In addition to underlining or highlighting words or sentences they like, have them circle or put a question mark over any words they are not sure of. Note that this approach does not mean that students should pause every time they are unsure of a word, rather that they should continue the idea-gathering process until they pause to review. Depending on the age and experience of the writers, they will edit or change anything they see as obviously wrong. Novice writers can simply put the draft or brainstorming sheet in the folder until the next time.

In the early weeks of school, spend time making the rounds during each workshop day. You will get a sense of which students are struggling with ideas as well as with mechanics, which students appear to be struggling with the physical act of writing, and which students write so fast that they cannot force themselves to stop until the period is over. You will also learn what spelling patterns the entire class has difficulty with. This knowledge will help you construct minilessons that benefit everyone. At the end of the minilesson, direct students to write the rule and an example in their Individual Spelling Guide.

Once you have gathered a general sense of class progress, review each folder and schedule individual conferences. Although the conference will focus primarily on ideas, organization, and content, do leave time to review with the student those spelling words and their patterns that seem to give him trouble. When they make their revisions after the conference, they can add the new words/patterns to their Individual Spelling Guide.

Because you are asking students to focus and to be aware of their own problem areas, over time they will become better spellers—except of course on e-mail, but that's a problem for another day!

TEACHING IDEA

Assessing the Learner

SPELLING ASSESSMENT MATRIX

The following rubric was developed by teachers to show students' classroom participation in spelling activities and their spelling development:

Primary Grades	***Always*** A	***Sometimes*** B	C	***Never*** D	E
Participates in group instructional activities					
Identifies relationships among and between words					
Demonstrates expanding knowledge of grapho-phonetic relationships when uncertain of correct spelling in written discourse					
Correctly spells high-frequency words in purposeful writing activities					
Participates in self-editing and peer editing					
Uses available resources to use conventional spelling					

Upper Grades	***Always*** A	***Sometimes*** B	C	***Never*** D	E
Participates in group instructional activities					
Identifies relationships among and between words					
Demonstrates expanding knowledge of grapho-phonetic relationships when uncertain of correct spelling in written discourse					
Correctly spells high-frequency words in purposeful writing activities					
Participates in self-editing and peer editing					
Uses available resources to use conventional spelling					
Spells conventionally in final drafts					

Source: From Gill, C. H., & Scharer, P. (1996). "Why do they get it on Friday and misspell it on Monday?" Teachers inquiring about their students as spellers. *Language Arts, 73*, 89–96.

in which the spelling program is outlined and where parents are ensured that spelling is an important part of the language arts program, help ease any discomfort parents may have about a spelling program that appears very different from what they know and value. The following points should be emphasized:

1. Correct spelling is important!
2. Spelling is developmental. In the primary grades, sound-symbol relationships, high-frequency words, and common spelling generalizations are emphasized through daily instruction. Children are encouraged to problem-solve unknown words, applying what they know about spelling and moving forward. Though initially most spellings in children's writing may be "invented," children bring increasing accuracy to their spelling as they make use of what they have learned.
3. Beyond the primary grades, students should use "invented" spelling *only* with uncommon words, new vocabulary words, and words they would not be expected to know how to spell at their grade level. Any "invented" spellings should be circled on writing drafts and corrected during the final editing process after content and organization have received their attention.
4. Spelling lessons are taught during the Language Arts block. Spelling lists may include words from the district's word study program and the content areas, as well as personal words that individual students misspell in their writing or ones they want to use in their writing.
5. Students keep track of spelling lessons taught as well as words they have mastered and words they still need to work on.
6. Students use a variety of strategies to spell unknown words: word walls, dictionaries, word booklets, spell checkers, personal lists, textbooks, and so on.
7. Students should only seek help from parents, teachers, and peers *after* they have edited their own work and have diligently attempted to find and correct misspellings themselves.
8. Parents may assist with editing by circling misspelled words. Students should first attempt to correct the spelling on their own. At times, it is fine to simply provide a correct spelling—for example, when time constraints are severe or the task is overwhelming for a student. Even then, avoid giving all the correct spellings. Allow students to learn to use the resources they have so that they can develop independence.
9. Final editing should always be done for any piece of writing that is to be turned in or shared with others.

SUMMARY

During their elementary school years, children learn thousands of new words, both in and out of the classroom, through reading, writing, viewing, and discussion. The more linguistically rich experiences children have and the more they read, the larger their vocabularies. The larger their vocabularies, the better children are able to comprehend what they read and the more sophisticated their oral and written expression becomes. Word play and word study increase their understanding of the English language system as well as their interest in words themselves.

When teachers provide children with frequent opportunities to write, they expand their knowledge of the power of words. Older children become adept communicators who have an increasing sense of audience as they write for many purposes. They want their writing to be clearly understood by readers, and so they become good spellers. Ultimately, children are meaning-makers who learn to use language to say and write what they need to express to others.

ACTIVITIES

1. **Borrow a social studies or science content-area textbook and teacher's manual from an upper-elementary-grade teacher.** Examine the ways that vocabulary instruction is handled. Do the strategies appear to be consistent with what you have read about and discussed? What new strategies did you learn about? What concerns you about the way vocabulary and concept development is handled? Share what you learn with others.
2. **Interview teachers at both the primary- and intermediate-grade levels of instruction.** Ask how they go about teaching spelling. Do they use a commercial spelling program, a locally developed program, or a combination of these? How do they evaluate spelling? Find out what they consider to be working and what they are concerned about. Compare what you learn with others.
3. **With others in your group, collect several commercial spelling programs.** Discuss their similarities and differences. Based on what you have read in this book, what (if anything) would you add or delete from these programs to create your own spelling program for a particular grade level?
4. **Collect a writing sample from a student or a folder of writing samples.** Work with a partner to analyze the spelling errors and make suggestions for instruction.

FURTHER READING

Bromley, K. (2002). *Stretching students' vocabulary.* New York: Scholastic.

Cunningham, P. M. (2000). *Phonics they use: Words for reading and writing.* New York: Addison Wesley Longman.

Ganske, K. (2000). *Word journeys: Assessment-guided phonics, spelling, and vocabulary instruction.* New York: Guilford.

Gentry, J. R. (1993). *Teaching kids to spell.* Portsmouth, NH: Heinemann.

Pinnell, G. S. & Fountas, I. C. (1998). *Word matters: Teaching phonics and spelling in the reading/writing classroom.* Portsmouth, NH: Heinemann.

Strickland, D. S. (1998). *Teaching phonics today.* Newark, DE: International Reading Association.

REFERENCES

Bear, D. R., Invernizzi, M., Templeton, S., & Johnson, F. (1996). *Words their way.* Englewood Cliffs, NJ: Merrill/Prentice-Hall.

Bolton, F. (1999). *Spelling K–8.* New York: Scholastic.

Bromley, K. (2002). *Stretching students' vocabulary.* New York: Scholastic.

Buss, K., & Karnowski, L. (2002). *Reading and writing nonfiction genres.* Newark, DE: International Reading Association.

Clarke, L. K. (1988). Invented versus traditional spelling in first graders' writings: Effects on learning to spell and read. *Research in the Teaching of English, 22,* 281–309.

Cunningham, P. M., & Cunningham, J. W. (1992). Making words: Enhancing the invented spelling-decoding connection. *The Reading Teacher, 46,* 106–113.

Cunningham, A., & Stanovich, K. (1998). What reading does for the mind. *American Educator,* Spring/Summer, 8–15.

Edelsky, C. (1986). *Writing in a bilingual program: Habia una vez.* Norwood, NJ: Ablex.

Fresh, M. J., & Wheaton, A. (2002). *Teaching and assessing spelling: A practical approach that strikes the balance between whole-group and individualized instruction.* New York: Scholastic.

Gill, C. H., & Scharer, P. L. (1996). "Why do they get it on Friday and misspell it on Monday?" Teachers inquiring about their students as spellers. *Language Arts, 73,* 89–96.

Graves, D. (1994). *A fresh look at writing.* Portsmouth, NH: Heinemann.

Hayes, D. P., & Ahrens, M. (1988). Vocabulary simplification for children: A special case of 'motherese'! *Journal of Child Language, 15,* 395–410.

Henderson, E. H. (1990). *Teaching Spelling* (2nd ed.). Boston: Houghton Mifflin.

Johnson, D. (2001). *Vocabulary in the elementary and middle school.* Boston: Allyn & Bacon.

McArthur, T. (Ed.) (1996). *The concise Oxford companion to the English language.* Oxford, UK: Oxford University.

Nagy, W. E., & Scott, J. A. (2000). Vocabulary processes. In M. L. Kamil, P. B. Mosenthal, P. D. Pearson, & R. Barr (Eds.), *Handbook of reading research, 3,* 269–284. Mahwah, NJ: Erlbaum.

Snowball, D., & Bolton, F. (1999). *Spelling K–8: Planning and teaching.* York, ME: Stenhouse.

Wilde, S. (1996). *You kan red this!* Portsmouth, NH: Heinemann.

Zutell, J. (1996). The Directed Spelling Thinking Activity (DSTA): Providing an effective balance in word study instruction. *The Reading Teacher, 50,* 98–108.

Written Language Conventions: Grammar, Punctuation, and Handwriting

CHAPTER OUTLINE

Key Standard

Teachers of language arts help students acquire and apply the grammatical and mechanical conventions of language in their writing. Such teachers:

- Help students understand and use the structures and conventions of language to convey meaning.
- Assist students in editing their writing for syntax, spelling, grammar, usage, and punctuation.
- Understand basic principles related to handwriting development and instruction.
- Set appropriate expectations for grammatical and mechanical conventions and for handwriting appropriate to the developmental levels of students.

To get a preview of Chapter 11 and learn about grammar, punctuation, and handwriting, visit the Chapter 11 section of the accompanying *Language Arts* CD-ROM.

Lorraine Baker asks her eighth-graders to incorporate some sentence-level changes every time they revise their writing. She begins preparing students for this task at the very beginning of the year by selecting several sentences each week from the students' own writing and putting them on the board for a minilesson. She looks for sentences that are complex and asks students to analyze them to see how they are constructed. Recording students' responses on the board, she creates models that students can then use in their own writing.

For instance, this week she has the following sentence on the board: D.J.'s brother Kevin is an excellent golfer who has won several tournaments. *She begins by commenting on how smoothly the writer has combined a number of ideas instead of stating them all in separate sentences. She reinforces this point by asking students what some of the individual ideas are. Their responses include* D.J. has a brother; His name is Kevin; Kevin is an excellent golfer; He has won several tournaments.

Then Ms. Baker directs her students' attention to the way the writer has combined these ideas, using this discussion to introduce or reinforce the names of the parts of speech and their function in the sentence. "What nouns are in these sentences?" she asks first, circling each noun as it is named. "How does the writer use these nouns in the combined sentence?" she asks next. As she points to each one, she asks, "What does this noun do in the sentence?" She wants her students to see that nouns can have different functions—that Kevin, *for example, functions as the subject of the combined sentence, whereas the phrase* D.J.'s brother *consists of nouns that modify the subject. To prompt them, she asks, "Which words tell us who Kevin is? Which words answer the question Who? or Which one? about Kevin?"*

She contrasts the phrase D.J.'s brother *with the word* excellent *in the predicate of the combined sentence. "What kind of information does this word add?" she asks.*

"It answers the question What kind of golfer?" one of her students responds, remembering an earlier lesson on adjectives.

"What about who has won several tournaments?" *asks another student. "Doesn't that also tell what kind of golfer Kevin is?"*

*"Yes, it does," Ms. Baker replies. "This is another kind of modifier. What the writer has done here is to take a sentence—*He has won several tournaments*—and turn it into a relative clause by changing* he *to* who.*" She writes the new term,* **relative clause**, *on the board before asking, "Do any of you have an example of a relative clause in your own writing?"*

A few hands go up, and Ms. Baker calls on the students to read aloud their sentences containing relative clauses. One student hesitates, then says, "This looks like a relative clause but it doesn't begin with who. *It starts with* that.*"*

"Why don't you read it," suggests Ms. Baker. "Some relative clauses do begin with that *or* which *instead of* who.*"*

"The book that was on the floor looked like mine," the student reads out loud while Ms. Baker writes the sentence on the board. Then she asks the students what they think.

"You could say it was on the floor,*" a student points out. "That's like* He has won several tournaments.*"*

"Yes," Ms. Baker agrees. "This is a relative clause, and it uses that *to replace the word* it.*" She moves on at this point, not wanting to burden the class with too much information. In another session, she'll return to this subject and explain why* that *and* which *are used in relative clauses. And when enough students need to make the distinction in their writing, she'll explain when a relative clause is separated from the rest of the sentence by commas and when it isn't.*

Ms. Baker concludes the lesson by asking students to return to their own writing and, using the sentence on the board as a model, combine ideas expressed in shorter sentences to make at least one longer, more complex sentence. She urges them to try to use a relative clause if they can.

In subsequent weeks, she will introduce some of the other building blocks of sentence combining—for instance, introductory phrases and clauses and subordinate clauses—focusing on how they function in a sentence and how they are punctuated. By the end of the year, her students will have absorbed a great deal of grammar as they work on their writing.

Grammar

Today's teachers tend to use the word *grammar* to mean the analysis and description of language rather than the prescription of correct forms. One reason to teach grammar is to make it easier to talk about some of the rhetorical issues in writing—that is, the choices we make when we construct sentences. If they are going to talk about sentence combining or varying sentence structure and length, students need to be able to identify the parts of speech and describe their function in sentences. Effective teachers use their own knowledge of grammar to help students grow in their understanding and use of language. They talk about language with children, using such metalinguistic terms as *noun, adjective, verb, adverb, sentence, word,* and *letter* as children encounter these things in their own reading and writing. In order to talk about the books they read and the pieces they write, students need to know the terminology.

Over the past 40 years, innumerable studies of the efficacy of teaching grammar as a separate subject have all led to the same conclusion: grammar drill may teach children enough to pass a weekly test, but most of them rarely use what they "learned" in those drills in their own speaking or writing. There is no transfer from drills on "proper" syntactic constructions to real usage, or from drills on parts of speech to the ability to discuss language using metalinguistic terminology. Further, a focus on "correct" grammar can inhibit fluency in both speaking and writing. Finally, advances in linguistics have demonstrated just how limited is the traditional grammar that is taught in schools. The parts of speech, their functions, kinds of sentences, and syntactic constructions that traditional grammar stresses are both inconsistent and inadequate. It is not a question of not teaching the parts of speech, but of teaching them as children are engaged in meaningful uses of language.

The study of traditional school grammar wastes time because it is not useful; it does not truly describe language and how it works. Time spent on traditional grammar teaching and practice takes time away from actual language use. However, that does not mean that grammatical concerns should be ignored. Weaver (1979) distinguishes between the formal teaching of grammar and developing students' intuitive sense of grammar through informal instruction. Teachers can show students how grammatical constructions work and tell them what they are called, quickly and efficiently and without drills, when they have a need to learn generated by their reading and writing. The instructional focus should be on children's developing knowledge of form and function through their immersion in authentic language activities.

GRAMMAR AND USAGE

Grammar is a set of rules for language. It involves the study of the forms and structure of words and their arrangement in phrases and sentences. Whereas grammar refers to the form and order of language, **phonology** refers to its pronunciation and **semantics** refers to its meaning. Grammar is so integral to language that young children learn and use the grammar of the language to which they are exposed without even thinking about its structure. In the primary grades, children write as they speak, with little formal attention to grammatical form. As children mature in their writing, they learn that grammar, punctuation, and spelling are writing conventions. They learn that knowing something about the conventions of grammar helps make their writing more effective and precise.

Systems of grammar

Three types of grammar dominate the field of English language study and influence its instruction. They are traditional, structural, and transformational-generative grammar. Each is described briefly here.

Traditional grammar focuses on the rules of the language and is the type of grammar taught for many generations in the schools. Traditional grammar gave us the parts of speech and their functions: nouns, pronouns, verbs, adverbs, adjectives, conjunctions, prepositions, articles, and interjections. Sentences are classified as simple, compound, complex, and compound/complex. Sentence types are defined as declarative, interrogative, imperative, and exclamatory. Traditional grammar lends itself to highly prescriptive teaching. Teachers often make considerable use of workbooks and worksheets; students may spend much time diagramming and parsing sentences. Unfortunately, overemphasis on abstract study of the forms of language apart from its use in writing can lead to the memorization of rules with little ability to apply them appropriately (Hillocks & Smith, 1991).

Structural grammar is descriptive. It involves the analysis of the structure and features of language, and includes features already discussed in earlier chapters: phonemes, the sounds of the language; morphemes, the smallest units of meaning; as well as the forms, functions, and sentence patterns of a language. Teachers who use structural grammar help children see how words function in language. For example, the use of **slotting,** which refers to the slot or function of a word in a particular sentence, can help children understand how their language works:

> Jack ______ down the street. (English-language speakers will only fill in a verb in that slot.)
>
> Jack wore a _____ hat as he ran down the street. (This sentence will yield an adjective from students.)

Manipulating sentences and discussing how they work can help students gain insight into the structure of their language and gain a sense of their own power in its use.

Transformational-generative grammar involves the relationship between the **surface structure** (form) of language and its **deep structure** (meaning). Based largely on the work of Noam Chomsky (1957), transformational-generative grammar suggests that sentences can have an underlying meaning. As Weaver (1996) explains, "Chomsky suggested that what a grammar really ought to do is account for native speakers' intuitive understanding of language structure" (p. 30). The following example is offered:

> The operation was performed by a new surgeon.
>
> The operation was performed by a new technique.

On the surface, these sentences have the same structure: noun phrase, verb phrase, prepositional phrase. Nevertheless, our intuitive sense suggests that in the first sentence, *a new surgeon* is the deep, or underlying, subject of *performed*, but in the second sentence we know that a new technique cannot perform an operation and that *technique* cannot be the deep subject of *performed* (pp. 30–31).

Teachers who understand transformational-generative grammar are more inclined to discuss the intent of a sentence. They therefore help students recognize that actual intent is easier to determine in oral language than in written language, where the speaker's intonation is not available. A reader, on the other hand, must consider the information that surrounds a sentence in order to determine the writer's intent. The use of sentence combining and sentence expansion techniques as tools for improving writing grew out of research based on transformational-generative grammar. Thus, the two sentences below:

The dog is frisky.
The dog is a beagle. become *The frisky dog is a beagle.*

Children are encouraged to rewrite sentences from their own work or the work of others using adjectives and adverbs to expand sentences and conjunctions to combine sentences.

Usage refers to the conventions of language appropriate to certain situations. Grammar has been called the rationale of a language and usage its etiquette (Newkirk, 1978). As discussed in Chapter Four, students come to school speaking a variety of dialects of English. They simply learn the structure of language they have been exposed to, which often differs from Standard English. Double negatives, rather than single negatives, may be the norm at home. Thus, "I ain't got no pencil," rather than "I don't have a pencil," may sound "right" to some children. Children can learn to expand their language repertoires to include Standard English forms as alternatives to the nonstandard varieties they speak at home. Teachers do this best by not attempting to eliminate or substitute one dialect for another, but by helping students understand the importance and value of using Standard English forms in many situations and by giving them opportunities to use, compare, and contrast language forms in a variety of meaningful ways.

STRATEGIES FOR INSTRUCTION IN GRAMMAR AND USAGE

Both grammar and usage are best taught in brief lessons that focus on a specific skill or strategy. These minilessons are often based on needs that students demonstrate in their writing. Teachers focus on a specific element and then give students plenty of opportunities to find examples of it in literature and in their own writing. As new elements are introduced, those that were formerly taught are constantly revisited, compared, and contrasted with skills and strategies introduced in new lessons. Teachers mix and match a variety of strategies to keep grammar and usage lessons interesting and pertinent to students' lives as readers and writers. They make use of posters that remind students of key elements taught in minilessons. They use books that involve language play such as the ones discussed in Chapter Ten. They collect sentences that are relevant to topics under study, and they guide students in manipulating sentences to see how they do or do not work. They compare and contrast various ways of saying the same thing, discussing which way is most appropriate under certain circumstances.

Expanding sentences can be introduced as a game, even with first- and second-graders. This is a good way to provide students with some models for and practice in adding information to their sentences. It's also a good way to begin accustoming students to naming the parts of speech and identifying the functions they fulfill in their sentences.

Start by writing a minimal sentence like *Dogs run* on the board. Point out that it has two parts: the part that tells *who* or *what* the sentence is about (*dogs*), and the part that tells *what happens* (*run*). With older students, you can add the information that words like *dog* are called **nouns** and words like *run* are called **verbs.** In addition, you can explain that the two sentence parts have names. The *who or what* part of the sentence is called the **subject,** and the *what happens* part is called the **predicate.** These names describe the function of the words in the sentence—what the words do. The parts-of-speech names simply tell us what kinds of words are in the sentence.

Call on students to expand either the subject part of the sentence on the board or the predicate part. You might want to prompt their expansions by asking questions: *What kind of dogs? What size dogs? What color dogs? How do they run? Where do they run? Why do they run?* As students answer, insert their expansions. If you have colored chalk available, use one color for additions to the subject and another color for additions to the predicate.

When you have several additions to each part of the sentence, go back over students' suggestions and name the parts of speech. For instance, if students have added *large* and *spotted* to the word *dogs,* point out that these words are **adjectives:** they describe or add information about a noun. If students have added *fast* to *run,* tell them that it's an **adverb,** a word that adds information like *how* or *where* or *when* to a verb. (With seventh- and eighth-graders, you can identify prepositions and articles as well.) When you have named each part of speech, ask students to suggest additional words that fall into the same category—noun, verb, adjective, or adverb.

Then point out that the sentence still has just two main parts: the subject and the predicate. Draw a line to separate the two parts. Students should see that all the words they have added to the subject are part of the subject, and all the words they have added to the predicate are part of the predicate. (Colored chalk makes this especially apparent.)

Finally, rewrite the expanded sentence on the board and read it out loud, so that students can hear how it sounds. As a follow-up, give students a second sentence—for example, *Cats cry*—and ask them to work individually or in pairs to expand both the subject and the predicate. Encourage them to use the sentence on the board as a model.

The *Teaching Idea: Words in Color* gives one idea for exploring syntax and metalinguistic terms with primary-grade children.

As you read to your students, you might stop and reread a particularly interesting sentence, put that sentence on the board, and talk about the syntax and alternative ways to say the same thing. You might notice sentences in the book that are "incomplete" in a formal sense and talk about why the author may have chosen to use those constructions. Students can learn to talk about alternative ways to frame their written language, experimenting with the syntax until they get it just right for their intended meaning. A simple question like, "What's another way Lisa could say this?" can spur some interesting discussion of syntax. You can also provide students with demonstrations of their own syntactic decision making as you write in front of students and talk to them about why you are writing what you are writing.

By the middle elementary grades, children are quite capable of contrasting formal and informal English forms. They know that oral and written language are often different. Much of this is learned through their need to express themselves through writing. Instead of distinguishing between "right"

TEACHING IDEA

Addressing Individual Needs

WORDS IN COLOR

You can help your primary-grade students explore standard syntax and metalinguistic terms and play with language by physically manipulating cards with words written on them. Give each part of speech a color—the verbs red, nouns blue, adjectives brown, determiners pink, adverbs yellow, and so on. Then draw varied sentence patterns in matching colors on large sheets of paper—for example, a pink line, a brown line, a blue line, a red line, and a period. Placing cards on the appropriate color lines, children can construct sentences such as (pink) *Some* (blue) *cats* (red) *are* (brown) *large.* OR (pink) *The* (brown) *best* (blue) *team* (red) *won.*

Your students will begin to talk about these sentences. When they notice that the patterns they use always have a "red word," you can teach them the conventional name for those red words—verbs. They don't need a lesson in how verbs work; they have already experienced that for themselves.

and "wrong" usage in students' writing, teachers help students more if they make the distinction between edited written English and informal spoken English. A **contrastive analysis** ("We say X in informal spoken English, but in edited written English, we say Y") destigmatizes students' speech—especially if they have different linguistic backgrounds—and provides them with a framework that actually makes it easier to learn how to edit their written work.

Todd Jennings makes it a point never to tell his fifth-graders that sentences like "Shawn and me went to the movies" are wrong and that you should always say, "Shawn and I went to the movies" instead. He uses an approach that he describes as "on the one hand . . . on the other hand . . . ." When he encounters examples of informal spoken English that wouldn't be considered correct in formal written or spoken English, he puts them up in the left-hand column of a special display board in a corner of his room. The examples come from a variety of sources—magazines, books, and newspapers; his own speech and writing; and the speech and writing of his students. He also encourages his students to add examples they've encountered.

Whenever a new example is added to the display board, Todd asks someone to read it out loud. Then the students suggest equivalents in edited written English. On this day, for example, a student adds *I never seen him before* and explains that a character in a story she's reading says this. Todd asks her to describe the way the character talks in general, and another student joins the discussion, noting that the story takes place 50 years ago and the character lives in the country. The students conclude that this sounds like the right way for this character to talk.

Then Todd asks for alternative ways to express the same thought. Students come up with *I've never seen him before* and *I never saw him before.* Both go up in the right-hand column on the display board. Todd sums up the discussion by stating, "You can write *I never seen him before* to show how someone speaks. But if you're not writing dialogue, you need to use edited English and write either *I never saw him before* or *I've never seen him before*."

By the end of the year, the display on this board is many pages thick, and it serves as a dictionary of usage. When students come across a vernacular usage in their reading or writing, they check the display board first, looking for an equivalent expression in edited written English. If they can't find one, they rush eagerly to tell Todd that they have something new for the board.

Todd's students also use the display board as a source of vernacular expressions to use when they create characters and write dialogue for their stories. By giving them the resources for code-switching, Todd has enabled his students not only to appreciate and understand the appropriateness of informal spoken English but also to use edited written English in the contexts where it is appropriate.

The **challenges of pronoun usage** are often a problem for many students both in spoken and written form. The *Teaching Idea: A Minilesson in Pronoun Usage* describes an instructional strategy that can be used to help students avoid a very common mistake.

Punctuation

SUPPORTING THE DEVELOPMENT OF PUNCTUATION AND CAPITALIZATION SKILLS

Capitalization and punctuation are also best taught in the context of their use; students who learn mechanics as they need them in the context of their own writing not only use punctuation correctly, they also learn more forms—and more varied forms—of punctuation than do students who learn mechanics as a separate subject. Writers understand how mechanics work to make meanings more precise and help readers make sense of texts (Calkins, 1980). There are reasons for capitalization and punctuation: to segment words into units, to help identify those units (as in possessive rather than plural), and to give voice to writing. Just as is true of spelling and grammar, mechanics are not ends in themselves but are, rather, tools for effective written communication.

First grade children who learn punctuation within the context of their own writing use periods to segment their writing in a variety of ways: after individual words, after phrases, at the end of lines, at the end of a whole page, and correctly. Actively engaging with print, these young writers form, test, and refine hypotheses about how periods work. The ease of learning various punctuation marks depends on the validity and clarity of the appropriate explanations for use. For example, defining an apostrophe as "belonging" is a meaningful explanation to a child. An abstract definition of a sentence, or "when you want to stop" for a period is not (Cordeiro, Giacobbe, & Cazden, 1983).

Students who write have many more opportunities to punctuate than language arts texts or worksheets provide. Children do many things as they write, and teachers who try to tap their intuitive knowledge of, for example, segmentation, are often more successful in teaching difficult punctuation, such as period use. These results are similar to those reported by Edelsky (1986) for bilingual learners.

Like children who are native speakers of English, bilingual students use their knowledge of how language works as they attempt to punctuate. Bilingual students make use of what they know about their first language as they learn to write in English. Teachers who know something about the rules and mechanics that operate in their students' first languages are able to see how

TEACHING IDEA

Addressing Individual Needs

A MINILESSON IN PRONOUN USAGE

A perennial problem in pronoun usage—both spoken and written—is when to use the subject form (*I, he, she*) and when to use the object form (*me, him, her*). Speakers of English often err by using the subject form when the object form is needed, and vice versa, when a compound subject or a compound object includes a personal pronoun: *Jim and I, her and Toni, him and me*. Because errors occur only in this context, you can teach your students a simple strategy for avoiding a very common mistake in pronoun usage.

Begin by writing these pairs of sentences on the board:

Jim and I got to the bus stop early.
Jim and me got to the bus stop early.

The bus driver waved to Jim and I.
The bus driver waved to Jim and me.

Her and Toni left for school at 7:30.
She and Toni left for school at 7:30.

This letter is for her and Toni.
This letter is for she and Toni.

Toni thanked he and I.
Toni thanked him and me.

He and I answered Toni's letter right away.
Him and me answered Toni's letter right away.

Call on students to read each pair out loud; then discuss which one sounds correct. Keep a tally of how many students voted for each sentence. Then go back through the list and ask students to read each sentence out loud with just the personal pronoun as the subject or object. (In the final two pairs, read each sentence twice—once with each of the personal pronouns in the subject or object place.) Again, ask students which sentences sound correct and keep a tally of how students vote.

Students should find that when they eliminate the noun in the compound subject or object—when just one pronoun is left as the subject or object—it's much easier to hear which sentence sounds correct and which sounds incorrect. Students who can't tell whether *Her and Toni left for school at 7:30* is correct should see right away that *Her left for school at 7:30* is incorrect.

Students might also find it reassuring to know that sometimes they make errors in pronoun usage because they are trying too hard to be correct. We work overtime to make sure that students use *I* in the subject position because sentences like *Me and Toni were late* are so common in the speech of young students. However, students start to think that *me* is always incorrect and *I* is always correct. As a result, they end up using phrases like *between you and I* or *for Alex and she* in an effort to avoid a usage that they mistakenly think is wrong.

If you have students in your class who come from Spanish-speaking families, you can also use this lesson to point out an important difference between the personal pronoun *I* in English and its equivalent (*yo*) in Spanish. Remind students that when we write *I* in English, we always capitalize it. In Spanish, none of the personal pronouns starts with a capital letter. In English, only one does. It's easy to remember which one because it's the only pronoun that is one letter.

Bernice Cullinan

Display students' work to encourage them to write more.

they are applying those rules in English. Over time, with exposure to English print, instruction, and many opportunities for writing for a variety of audiences, bilingual students do learn the conventions of English mechanics (Edelsky, 1986).

Students don't need to have mastered the rules of punctuation and capitalization to begin taking responsibility for correcting mechanics when they write. A great deal of instruction goes on during editing conferences. When you notice that your students are having trouble reading each other's writing because of the lack of end punctuation, you can develop a series of lessons and demonstrations to teach end punctuation and add it to the editing checklist that your students use. During editing conferences, encourage students to read their pieces aloud to listen for the places they needed to punctuate. If you (1) identify the skill that your students are ready to learn, (2) teach lessons that help them use the skill, and (3) follow up those lessons with individual instruction during conferences, your students will learn the mechanics they need to know.

Marsha Phillips has introduced her second grade class to editing as the final step in the writing process, but she doesn't wait until all the revisions are complete to start working on mechanics. While students wait their turn for individual conferences with her, she has them look through what they have written to check punctuation, capitalization, and spelling. She finds this a painless and productive way to reinforce whatever minilesson she has taught that week—and even to introduce new material.

For example, this week—since it is still close to the start of the school year—Ms. Phillips has written on the board the simple rule for marking the beginning and end of a sentence that she presented to the class earlier in the week: *Begin the first word of each sentence with a capital letter. Put a period at the end of the sentence.* Now, as she confers with one student at her desk, the rest of the class is either making the changes they have discussed with her or preparing for their own conferences.

Their preparation focuses first on revision—what they think they might like to add or change—and then on mechanics. As they read their work, students check to see whether they have started and ended their sentences correctly. If they spot errors, they make changes in the first draft. If they're not sure about the correctness of what they have written, they make a check mark in the margin. For instance, Turner has written, "How would you feel if you saw a ghost." He knows he's followed the rule on the board and put a period at the end of the sentence, but when he reads it out loud, it doesn't sound right. He's not sure whether he needs to change what he's written, so he makes a notation in the margin.

When Turner sits down with Ms. Phillips for his conference, they first discuss what details he could add to his description of the haunted house. Then he points out the sentence that he's checked and reads it aloud. Ms. Phillips tells Turner that he's right—this is the end of a sentence—and he's also right in guessing that it needs a different punctuation mark. She asks Turner to read the sentence out loud again and listen carefully to what the end sounds like. Turner hears the rising inflection and gleefully announces, "It's a question." This is the perfect opening for Ms. Phillips to introduce the question mark as another way of marking the end of a sentence.

When the conference with Turner is over, Ms. Phillips asks the class for their attention for a moment. She explains that Turner has written a sentence that needs something different at the end. She reads Turner's sentence out loud and asks the class how this sentence is different from "I'd feel scared if I saw a ghost."

One or two students identify Turner's sentence: "It asks a question . . . It's a question."

"Yes, it's a question," Ms. Phillips confirms, "and it needs a different punctuation mark at the end: a question mark. Who knows how to write a question mark?" A number of hands go up, and she asks all the children to trace a question mark in the air. "Yes," she agrees. "It's written like this." She goes to the board and draws a question mark; then, under her rule for punctuating a sentence, she writes, *If the sentence asks a question, use a question mark (?) at the end instead of a period.*

As the students continue to check the way their sentences are punctuated, some will now find opportunities to use a question mark instead of a period.

Punctuating dialogue can be very challenging for students. The *Teaching Idea: A Minilesson in Punctuating Dialogue* shows how to help students sort out the kinds of punctuation that go with specific circumstances and some simple rules that make it easier to remember what to do.

TEACHING IDEA

Literature Link

A MINILESSON IN PUNCTUATING DIALOGUE

When you are teaching grammar, usage, or mechanics, the most effective way is to provide a minilesson tied to the students' writing. For fourth-, fifth-, or sixth-graders beginning to use dialogue in their stories, for example, learning to punctuate dialogue correctly is an obvious choice.

On the board, write some dialogue from one of the books the class is reading. Remove all the quotation marks and run the lines of dialogue together, without new paragraphs to separate them. Here is an example from Lois Lowry's *Number the Stars* (pp. 46–47 in the Yearling edition):

> Your names? the officer barked. Annemarie Johansen. And this is my sister— Quiet! Let her speak for herself. Your name? He was glaring at Ellen. Ellen swallowed. Lise, she said, and cleared her throat. Lise Johansen.

Call on a student to read the passage out loud. Then ask students to identify who is speaking in each case. There will probably be some confusion about which words go with which speaker. Point out that writers can use punctuation to help their readers understand dialogue more easily.

Ask if anyone knows how to indicate (1) the exact words each person is saying and (2) when the identity of the speaker changes. Have students come up to the board to add quotation marks around the exact words of each speaker. If one student is unsure or makes an error, ask the class to make suggestions. Summarize what students have done by articulating the following rules:

- Quotation marks come in pairs—one at the beginning of the speaker's words and one at the end.
- The second quotation mark in a pair comes **after** the punctuation mark at the end of the character's words, whether that punctuation mark is a comma, a period, a question mark, or an exclamation point.
- A comma is used to separate the character's words from words like *she said.*

Then ask one or more volunteers to show how the writer can indicate when a new character begins to speak. Again, summarize what students have done to the example on the board by stating this rule:

- Each time a different character begins to speak, start a new paragraph.

Finally, ask students to turn to the original passage in the book and see how the author punctuated the dialogue. Here is the original passage from *Number the Stars*:

> "Your names?" the officer barked.
>
> "Annemarie Johansen. And this is my sister—"
>
> "Quiet! Let her speak for herself. Your name?" He was glaring at Ellen. Ellen swallowed.
>
> "Lise," she said, and cleared her throat. "Lise Johansen."

Individual punctuation guides can be very helpful in tailoring instruction to individual needs. The *Teaching Idea: Individual Punctuation Guides* helps students address their own personal challenges with punctuation.

TEACHING IDEA

Addressing Individual Needs

INDIVIDUAL PUNCTUATION GUIDES

Writing gives students a reason to learn how to punctuate. Instruction in punctuation can and should be geared to what students are writing—for example, how long and complex their sentences are or whether they are using dialogue. Because students' needs will vary, even within the same class, you can make minilessons in punctuation meaningful by having students develop individual punctuation guides.

Supply students with spiral notebooks to use for their guides, or hand out individual sheets of paper with appropriate headings on them: HOW TO END A SENTENCE, HOW TO USE COMMAS, HOW TO PUNCTUATE A QUOTATION, WHEN TO USE A SEMICOLON. If you're using individual sheets, give students a way to keep them together in a folder or looseleaf binder. If students have spiral notebooks, they should divide their notebooks into sections, using the headings above and leaving enough pages in each section to add multiple examples. A third alternative, if students have access to computers, is to let them create and update their punctuation guides on the computer.

As you read your students' writing, notice what kinds of punctuation issues are coming up for most of them. Provide a punctuation rule and an example either in a minilesson at the beginning of a writing workshop session or in a conference. For instance, for first-graders you will probably want to emphasize the fact that a period marks the end of a sentence, and a capital letter marks the beginning of the next sentence. Students should enter this rule, in their own words, in their punctuation guides, followed by an example taken from their own writing. When students start combining two sentences to make a compound sentence, explain the use of the comma (along with a conjunction) to mark the place where two independent thoughts are joined to make one. Again, students who are writing compound sentences should add the rule, in their own words, to the punctuation guide and illustrate it with an example from something they have written.

Students' punctuation guides can grow throughout the year, with new rules entered as their writing increases in sophistication and new examples added as they apply each rule in subsequent pieces of writing. In addition, students should use their punctuation guides whenever they write—especially when they are editing their work.

Notice that the punctuation guides will vary considerably. Some will contain only rules about end punctuation and commas in compound sentences, whereas others will include the punctuation of quotations and the use of commas in a series. As their writing increases in fluency and complexity and students need to learn additional rules of punctuation, you may be able to direct them to classmates who have already added the new rules to their punctuation guides. The individual punctuation guide gives students an important tool for peer editing sessions.

ASSESSING SENTENCE STRUCTURE AND MECHANICS

In Jay Gordon's sixth grade classroom, student writers turn frequently to favorite books for models, even when they are editing their work. When Jay teaches grammar and punctuation, he frequently begins by sharing a sentence or two from what he is currently reading, noting how the author has used sentence structure and punctuation to help convey meaning. His goal is to have his students vary sentence length and structure—and punctuate these more complex sentences correctly.

Before they begin to draft their current stories, Jay's students all take favorite books from their classroom library and identify a few sentences that they find especially interesting or exciting. They copy these sentences into their journals, and after each one, they write a brief explanation of what makes it work. Annette, for example, writes, "I like this very long sentence because it's turned around. It begins 'On the other side of the door,' instead of having that part of the sentence at the end. Also, the sentence right after is very short, so you really notice it."

Jay asks a few students to share these journal entries with the class, choosing examples to illustrate a broad range of sentence structures. With the examples on the board, the whole class engages in a discussion of the rhetorical techniques writers use to combine and connect ideas, to create contrast and surprise, to hook readers or keep them in suspense.

As students work on the stories they are currently writing, Jay circles the room, glancing over their shoulders, and reacting with a "Wow" and a brief explanation when he spots sentences that really work. Kenneth, for example, has written, "Doug Dean, a sixth grader in Woodlake Junior High, loved baseball." "That's great," comments Jay. "I like the way you put the information about who Doug is right into the sentence that tells us he loved baseball. That whole phrase," he adds, pointing to the words, "is a modifier, the same way an adjective is." Later on, when Kenneth is ready to edit his story, Jay will tell him that he needs a second comma to set off this modifier.

At another table, Tonya is frowning as she reads what she has written: "The bell rang. Dan came in. He sat right next to Emily. She was surprised." "Mr. Gordon, this sounds boring," she complains.

Jay nods sympathetically. "You have a lot of important information here, but maybe you could say it differently. What don't you like?"

Tonya whispers the sentences to herself. "They all sound alike," she says.

"Why don't you check out the way another writer has handled this problem?" suggests Jay, handing Tonya the copy of the novel she has pulled off the library shelf. "See if you can find a place where this writer has solved a problem like yours by combining sentences."

Tonya starts to page eagerly through the book, reading sentences in an undertone to catch the rhythm of a longer sentence that doesn't sound boring.

PROOFREADING AND EDITING

Proofreading and editing take place toward the end of the writing process. As indicated in previous chapters, students generally start by generating topics to write about. They expand and elaborate on their ideas about the topic as they develop a sense of how they want to draft their piece. Even as the piece is developing, students may move sentences or leave spaces in where they want to return to elaborate on an idea. As they proceed to draft and redraft, more sentences are generated. Some are combined or changed and new ideas may come into play. At some point, when students feel comfortable about having all or most of their ideas in place, they may wish to have a conference with the teacher or with a peer. This first conference should focus primarily on ideas and the revision of text to make it clear to the potential reader.

Although proofreading and editing generally occur after all of the author's ideas are in place and the revision process is complete, it is part of a recursive process and can occur at any time during writing. But, it is at the final stages of writing that grammar, spelling, and punctuation get the writer's careful attention. Here again, peer conferences can play a key role in helping students see where they might need to edit their work.

Bernice Cullinan

Writers check their spelling and punctuation as part of the editing and revising process.

Proofreading and editing marks can be useful tools for even the youngest writers. First-graders learn to take a second look at their work to see what they might do to make their writing and their art better. Teachers can give simple minilessons to the entire group on how to insert a word over a space where it will be added or how to circle words that need to be checked for spelling. In addition, they can give specific help to individual students at the point of need as they attempt to apply what they know as they revisit their writing. Figure 11.1 gives common proofreading marks.

Making use of technology to examine written language conventions is a useful way to help students focus on specific aspects of writing. A computer hooked up to a larger screen allows teachers to scaffold students' ability to revise and edit their own pieces. The *Teaching Idea: Using Technology to Examine Written Language Conventions* shows how that might be done.

FIGURE 11.1

Proofreading Marks Frequently Used for Editing

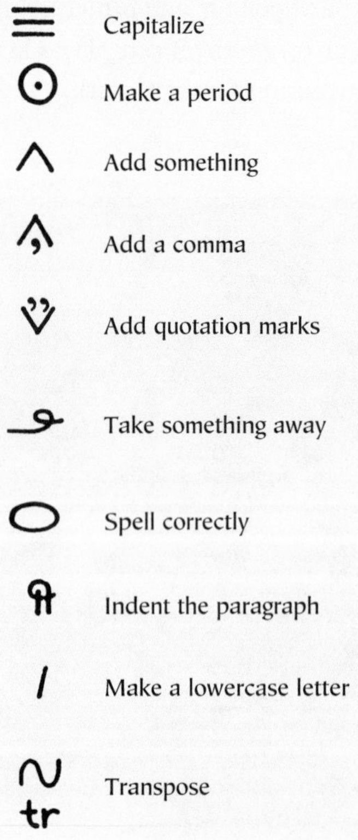

≡	Capitalize
⊙	Make a period
∧	Add something
∧ with comma	Add a comma
∨ with quotation marks	Add quotation marks
delete mark	Take something away
○	Spell correctly
¶	Indent the paragraph
/	Make a lowercase letter
∾ tr	Transpose

Computers can make writing and revising an easier task for students.

TEACHING IDEA

Making Use of Technology

USING TECHNOLOGY TO EXAMINE WRITTEN LANGUAGE CONVENTIONS

From time to time it is useful for young writers to come together to discuss and analyze a piece of writing that is still being developed by its author. The use of a computer, a word-processing program, a projector (or a large TV screen connected to the computer), and a sample of writing still in the "works" can be the source of rich experiences in developing writing skills that would be cumbersome to attempt without such technology. (This piece can be a sample from a volunteer, from your own writing, or one found on the World Wide Web, among many possible sources.)

Let's say that one focus of a writing program has been on the development of a strong topic sentence for a paragraph. Using the projector, display a paragraph and engage the students in a conversation on the problems facing the writer with the displayed piece. Perhaps there is no topic sentence in the paragraph. Maybe it is too broad or too vague. As students focus on possible remedies to the problem, challenge them to revise the piece. The ease of cutting, copying, and pasting with a word-processing program allows you to make multiple versions of the revised paragraph that can easily be viewed, often side by side, by your students and subjected to their discussion and analysis. This approach can be used for all manner of writing issues—for example, the use of descriptive words or imagery, grammar, and mechanics.

In a similar vein, it can be useful to run a piece of work through a word-processor's grammar checker. As the grammar checker alerts writers to possible flaws in a piece of writing, students can discuss whether or not the identified error is truly an error, whether the correction proposed by the grammar checker is useful, and what they could do otherwise.

Assessing Grammar, Usage, and Punctuation

Children apply what they know about the language conventions of grammar and usage as they use language throughout the day. Teachers listen to how students express themselves and observe their writing to assess what children have learned. By engaging students in the writing process, teachers help them apply what has been taught as they guide them in revision and editing. Students need opportunities to try out various writing conventions. In many cases, they may feel that something simply doesn't sound right, but they don't always know what to do about it. Peer conferences and teacher/pupil conferences in which various conventions are discussed and applied can be very useful in helping students apply what they know. Teachers need to keep in mind that making things "sound right" in writing is difficult when it varies from the speech patterns with which students are familiar. This takes time and many experiences before it becomes integrated into the personal language repertoire of the learner. This is particularly true of the learner whose first language is not Standard English. Teacher assessment and student self-assessment should take place on an ongoing basis as well as in periodic review of specific work samples. Teachers often use a simple mechanics checklist like that in Figure 11.2 to help them determine what their students can and cannot do on their own. Then, working from students' needs as writers, and aided by their own knowledge of mechanics, the teachers determine which mechanics their students need to learn.

Correcting run-on sentences and fragments often presents a major problem for many students during editing. The *Teaching Idea: Correcting Sentence Construction in the Context of Writing* shows how you can help students with this very common problem.

Using primary-trait scoring to assess and address specific problems

Primary-trait scoring is a term used to describe the practice of focusing on one or two elements of writing—for example, introductions, transitions, supporting details, or closings—and considering just those features of a given story or essay in the response we make or the score we assign to the piece of writing. Primary-trait scoring simplifies writing assessment and helps students focus on specific skills that may need strengthening.

Teachers also use a form of primary-trait scoring to focus students' attention on individual skills in usage, sentence construction, or mechanics. Tina Small, for instance, alternates between two approaches to student writing in her seventh grade classroom. Sometimes she responds only to content

FIGURE 11.2

Mechanics Checklist

Date	Name	Initial Cap	Prop Nouns	End .	End ?	End !	, In List	Poss.	Dial Punc.

+ = Correct use always
✓ = Mostly correct
− = Confused use

TEACHING IDEA

Addressing Individual Needs

CORRECTING SENTENCE CONSTRUCTION IN THE CONTEXT OF WRITING

In the middle school years, students start to grapple with the construction and punctuation of longer, more complex sentences. You can use their own writing to help them recognize and correct those two perennial problems in sentence construction—run-ons and fragments. Find several examples of each in the students' own papers and either copy them onto acetate for the overhead projector or write them on the chalkboard, in two separate groups headed "Run-ons" and "Fragments." Be careful not to include more than one error per student, and do not identify the student authors. In fact, you can safely reassure students that all of them have made similar errors at some point.

Model the first item in each group for the students, verbalizing your thought process as you go. Students should see that there is usually more than one way to rewrite both run-ons and fragments. Point out the punctuation changes that need to be made—for example, changing a comma to a period and starting a new sentence to correct a run-on or deleting a period and incorporating a fragment into the sentence that precedes it. Work through the rest of the items with the students. Ask them to explain why they are making each correction, and encourage them to find alternate ways to rewrite each item.

Finally, ask students to read through whatever writing assignment they are currently working on, looking for similar problems in sentence construction. They can read aloud to themselves or to each other, listening for the places that sound like the end of a sentence. When they hear a sentence ending, they should check the punctuation and see whether they need to add end punctuation (to correct a run-on) or whether they need to expand the sentence or combine it with another sentence (to correct a fragment).

Conclude the editing session by asking students to formulate, in their own words, a rule for correcting run-ons and another for correcting fragments. Write these rules on the chalkboard and ask students to copy them and keep them for future editing sessions.

and organization in her first reading of an essay, ignoring sentence-level concerns until after the paper has been revised. On other occasions, though, she targets one or two sentence-level skills in a minilesson and then focuses on those skills—in addition to content and organization—when she responds to the students' first drafts.

For her current assignment, Ms. Small has told the class that she will be focusing on two related sentence-level concerns: combining sentences and using the semicolon. During the course of the marking period, she has provided minilessons on sentence construction, showing students how to combine sentences for greater rhetorical effect, as well as how to correct fragments and run-ons. She has recently taught her students how to use a semicolon to join two independent clauses. Using a semicolon, she points out, helps us avoid the mistake of connecting two sentences with a comma only (which results in a run-on). The semicolon also gives us a sophisticated alternative to the use of a comma and a coordinating conjunction like *and* when we combine two sentences to make a compound sentence.

At the end of her minilesson on the use of the semicolon, Ms. Small tells her students that she expects them to use semicolons in the persuasive essays they are about to write. "When I read your first drafts," she explains, "I will be reading to make sure that you state your position clearly and support it convincingly. But I will also be reading to make sure that you have used a semicolon correctly at least once in your essay. I'm not going to worry about spelling, or usage, or capitalization until the second draft. But in this first draft, I want to see semicolons used to connect sentences."

In her written feedback on these first drafts, Ms. Small highlights students' use of semicolons. When appropriate, she also suggests other places where a semicolon would be an effective way to combine two sentences. In students' second drafts, in addition to revisions of content and organization, Ms. Small will expect to see expanded use of the semicolon.

Ms. Small's students are accustomed to this approach. At the beginning of the year, Ms. Small decided on a limited set of sentence-level skills—in punctuation, usage, sentence construction, and spelling and capitalization. She then focuses on them one at a time through minilessons and primary-trait scoring of student writing. In this way, Ms. Small is able to teach and reinforce a valuable set of skills in the context of student writing.

Handwriting

OVERVIEW OF HANDWRITING DEVELOPMENT

Pre-kindergarten and kindergarten children love to experiment with writing tools of all kinds, and they will write on anything that is available to them. Gradually, they associate the making of marks with written communication. Adults help them hold a pencil and crayon; recognize and form some uppercase and lowercase letters, usually beginning with the letters in their names; and write their names and a few other words of interest to them.

Early primary-grade children are experiencing greater confidence and fluency in their letter formation and spelling. Writing is far less laborious than it was during their early years. Adults help them combine their knowledge of the conventions of writing, such as when to use capitals, with their knowledge of letter forms, and use lined paper that requires attention to letter formation in terms of what goes above and below the increasingly smaller spaces between the lines.

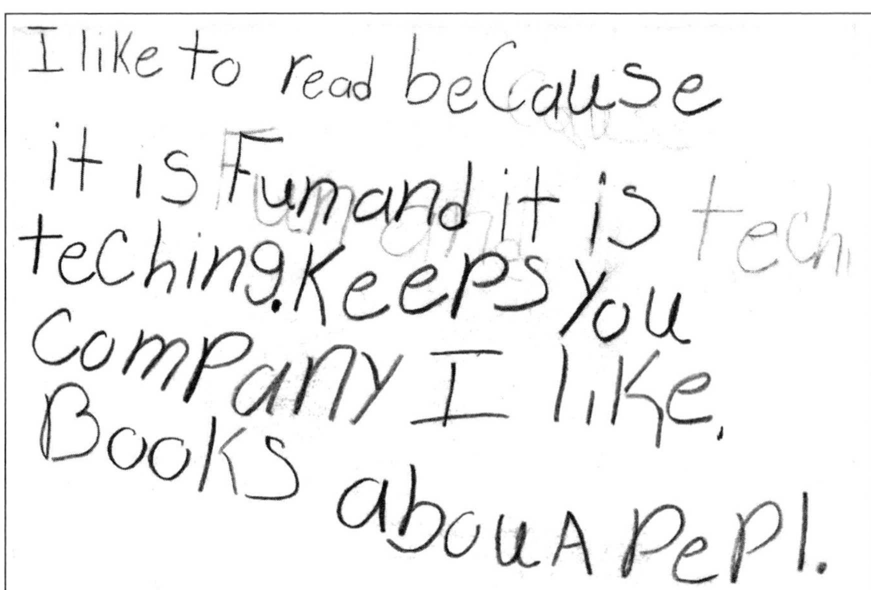

An example of a first-grader's handwriting.

Later primary-grade children are introduced to cursive writing, which they learn to read and write. They learn to form and join letters. At times, many children continue to alternate between manuscript and cursive.

Intermediate- and upper-grade children are fluent with both manuscript and cursive forms. They tend to use cursive writing for reports and special writing projects and develop their own distinctive styles.

STRATEGIES FOR TEACHING HANDWRITING

Like listening, handwriting is less well researched than other areas of the language arts curriculum. For many years, handwriting instruction was influenced more by tradition than by research on what works best for children. In 1986, Koenke reported research findings that seemed to deny much of what was typical practice at the time. For example, in most schools children are taught manuscript in first and second grade and cursive in the third grade, although there is no research evidence to support this approach. Nor does research support the superiority of one handwriting manuscript or method over another.

Many teachers of kindergarten children believe that larger pencils are more appropriate for little hands than smaller ones. Again, Koenke found that children do not write better with the beginning pencils. Even the size of the paper may not be an advantage or interfere with writing until third grade when children are introduced to cursive handwriting and need the support of special paper. Perhaps the real lesson here is that very young children can benefit from a wide selection of writing and drawing tools during the earliest years, as they explore the dimensions of space and materials through their artistic and written expression.

The conventional wisdom that prefers that manuscript be taught before cursive is grounded in the belief that manuscript is easier to read and to write. Certainly, it is more like the print in the beginning reading materials. Only two lowercase letters, *a* and *g*, are apt to be formed differently in typed or handwritten forms. Barbe and Milone (1980) also suggest that manuscript be taught first because young children can copy manuscript strokes more easily than cursive forms. Most children have little difficulty moving from manuscript to cursive in second or third grade. They are highly motivated, and many commonly confused letters, such as *p* and *q* and *b* and *d*, no longer present a problem. Students who are learning to write in cursive may need to begin the transition from manuscript with those seventeen letters that are written much like they are printed and are connected easily. Then students can move on to those letters that have a significantly different formation (*s, r, f, z,* and sometimes *e*) and to those with midpoint connections (*b, o, v,* and *w*). There is some research to suggest that because cursive is continuous writing, it may be easier for some children with physical disabilities (Kaufman & Biren, 1979).

The **D'Nealian handwriting** is an innovative manuscript and cursive handwriting program developed by a classroom teacher, Donald Neal Thurber (1987). D'Nealian uses most of the same basic forms for manuscript that children need for cursive handwriting. As shown in Figure 11.3, in the manuscript form, letters are slanted and formed with continuous stroke. In the cursive form the letters are simplified. Only five letters—*f, r, s, v,* and *z*—are shaped differently in the cursive form. Both forms were designed to increase legibility and fluency and to ease the transition from manuscript to cursive handwriting. Many primary-grade teachers prefer the D'Nealian system. However, research has not yet documented its superiority over more traditional forms. Figure 11.3 shows some common forms of manuscript and cursive handwriting that are taught in today's schools.

By the time children reach the intermediate years, they tend to develop a preference for either manuscript or cursive although many develop their own distinctive combination of the two. Peck, Askov, and Fairchild (1980) found that intermediate-grade children who wrote in manuscript wrote faster and just as legibly as children who wrote in cursive, leading them to suggest that personal preferences should be taken into consideration at these levels. Legibility and speed are important assets for writers as they concentrate on their ideas rather than the formation of letters.

In today's pre-kindergarten and kindergarten classrooms, children are encouraged to experiment with written forms and invented spellings before formal writing instruction. Young children write labels, draw and write stories, and keep journals. As a result, many kindergarten teachers instruct children in the formation of upper- and lowercase letters and teach them to write their names. In addition, teachers follow the lead of individual children and intervene when requested to help with letter formation, emphasizing the

FIGURE 11.3

Commonly Taught Forms of Manuscript and Cursive Handwriting

Manuscript Alphabet

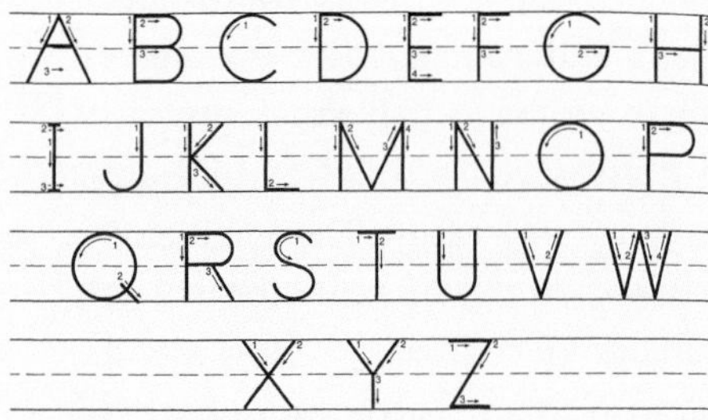

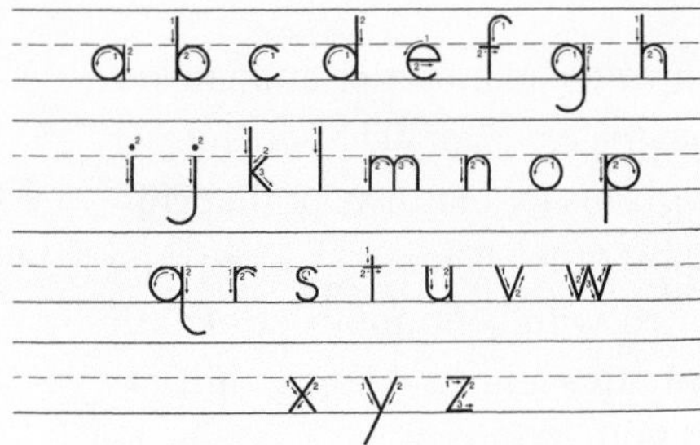

Cursive Alphabet

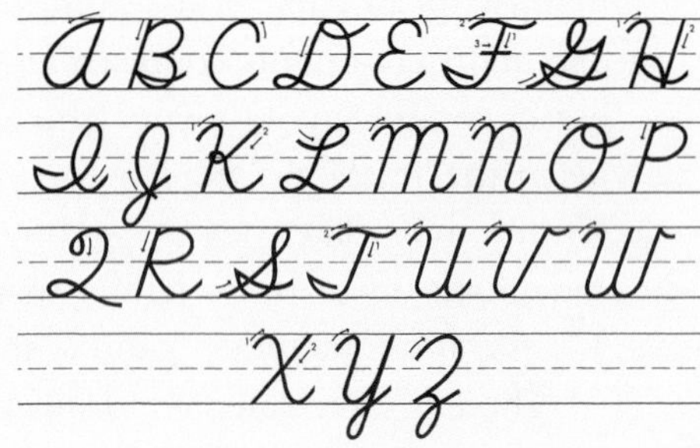

D'Nealian Manuscript Alphabet

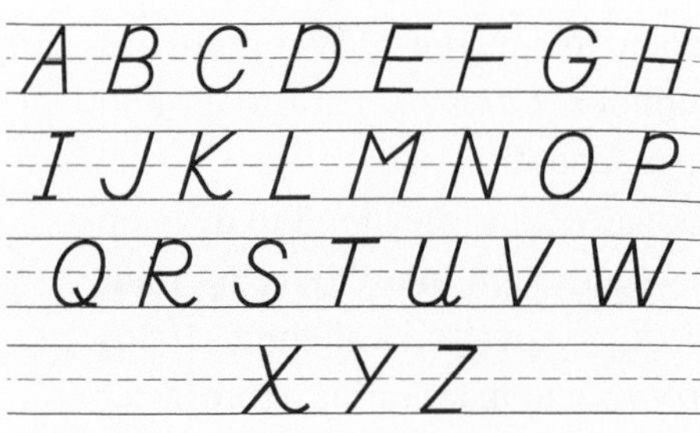

D'Nealian Cursive Alphabet

starting points and the direction of movement used to form each letter and grouping letters that are similar in these respects. By the time they reach first grade, most children already exhibit established habits of letter formation, either through explicit instruction or through experimentation. Thus, although most first grade teachers continue to introduce or review the forms used in their school's handwriting curriculum, they are apt to stress legibility equally as much as specific letter formation.

HELPING STUDENTS WITH SPECIAL NEEDS

Helping left-handed students with handwriting tends to be the most perplexing problem for teachers. Below are a few tips that teachers have found helpful over the years:

1. Provide left-handed students with special small-group and individual attention.
2. Stress correct paper position to help left-handed writers avoid "hooking" their hands and wrists in order to see what they are writing.
3. Encourage left-handed students to hold their pencils slightly farther back than right-handed students. This enables them to see what they are writing.
4. Allow left-handed students to sit to the left of the chalkboard for better visibility.
5. Provide left-handed scissors and other left-handed utensils.
6. Know that letter reversals are common among left-handed children. Special attention paid to frequently confused letters such as *d* and *b* and *p* and *q* helps.

ASSESSING HANDWRITING

The use of computers has caused some to suggest that handwriting is no longer important. Although it is true that both children and adults are increasingly apt to use computers for drafting their ideas and for communicating with others, handwriting remains an important means of written communication. Handwriting is used throughout the day for a variety of purposes. Obviously, it serves both the writer and the prospective reader if the message is clearly stated and legible.

Like grammar, usage, and punctuation, handwriting is best assessed through actual writing in meaningful contexts. The *Teaching Idea: Tracking Handwriting Development in the Primary Grades* offers a simple monitoring system for assessing young children's handwriting development throughout the year. Perhaps most importantly, students can observe their own progress as they see their handwriting change over time.

TEACHING IDEA

Addressing Individual Needs

TRACKING HANDWRITING DEVELOPMENT IN THE PRIMARY GRADES

When your primary-grade children enter the classroom each morning, have them sign in on their individual sign-in sheets (one lined page per child) and stamp their signatures with a date stamp. Ask them to take their time and use their very best handwriting. This is meaningful handwriting practice for the children, and it provides an excellent record of their writing development across the year, and saves time taking roll. It is also a wonderful present to give parents at the end of the year, especially if you teach kindergarten and your students are just mastering the writing of their names.

You might have students (1) view anonymous examples of illegible and legible writing; (2) identify which is easier to read; (3) list their descriptors of the legible sample (for example, letters sit on the line, spacing between words is roughly equal, letters are well formed and proportioned); then (4) individually or in pairs apply their criteria to their own handwriting. Alternatively, various samples of advertising clipped from magazines and newspapers can prompt discussions on whether the handwriting is or is not legible and efficiently produced. Throughout the grades, students need to be made aware that their message can be misunderstood or unreadable if it is not legible. Handwriting is a writing tool. Learning handwriting is like learning to type on the computer in that being a good handwriter or typist makes it just that much easier to compose.

Parents can assist by monitoring homework and encouraging care in work products. Annette Palmer's handwriting policy, shown in Figure 11.4, places responsibility for care in the completion of work products on the student and also reassures parents that handwriting legibility and neatness still matter in today's schools.

SUMMARY

Writing is a composing process in which content and meaning should be the composer's first priority. Nevertheless, grammar, punctuation, and handwriting also play important roles. The mechanics of written language are best

FIGURE 11.4

Handwriting Policy of a Sixth Grade Teacher

1. Although students are encouraged to use the computer for word processing, we still value and expect legibility and quality penmanship.
2. Messy or illegible handwritten work will have to be redone.
3. Even first drafts must be legible enough for someone else to read without too much difficulty.
4. Parents, please review homework assignments and ask your child to redo any homework that you feel is messy or illegible (or has been completed on notebook paper ripped out of a spiral notebook).

Annette Palmer
Grade 6

taught and assessed through class discussion and opportunities to write for a variety of purposes. A combination of focused instruction on specific skills with ongoing review and application in context is key to students' long-term learning. Language play, in which students manipulate specific structures and forms, helps them gain a sense of how their language works as they develop a sense of control and increased confidence over written forms.

ACTIVITIES

1. **With a partner, observe a group of children as they proofread and edit their writing.** How do youngsters demonstrate their understanding of how the language works? Compare and discuss what you think might be appropriate follow-up instruction.
2. **Interview one or two teachers to find out the most troublesome problems in grammar, usage, or punctuation at their grade level.** Find out and share with others at least one tip that these teachers find helpful in addressing the problems.
3. **Collect writing samples from children in the same class.** Note the differences among them. Are there things that you would work on across the entire group? With individuals?

FURTHER READING

Fletcher, R., & Portalupi, J. (2001). *Craft lessons: Teaching writing K–8*. Portland, ME: Stenhouse.

Graves, D. (1994). *A fresh look at writing*. Portsmouth, NH: Heinemann.

Hogemann, J. A. (2003). *Teaching grammar: A reader and workbook*. Boston: Allyn & Bacon.

Strickland, D. S., Ganske, K., & Monroe, J. (2001). *Supporting struggling readers and writers: Strategies for classroom intervention*. Portland, ME: Stenhouse.

Weaver, C. (1996). *Teaching grammar in context*. Portsmouth, NH: Heinemann.

REFERENCES

Barbe, W. B., & Milone, M. N. (1980). *Why manuscript writing should come before cursive writing* (Zaner-Bloser Professional Pamphlet No. 11). Columbus, OH: Zaner-Bloser.

Bloomfield, L. (1933). *Language*. New York: Holt, Rinehart.

Calkins, L. (1980). Punctuate! Punctuate? Punctuate. *Learning Magazine* (February).

Chomsky, N. (1957). *Syntactic structures*. The Hague: Mouton.

Cordeiro, P., Giacobbe, M. E., & Cazden, C. (1993). Apostrophes, quotation marks, and periods: Learning punctuation in the first grade. *Language Arts, 60,* 323–332.

Edelsky, C. (1986). *Writing in a bilingual program: Habia una vez*. Norwood, NJ: Ablex.

Handwriting research and resources: A guide to curriculum planning. (2002). Columbus, OH: Zaner-Bloser.

Hillocks, G., & Smith, M. W. (1991). Grammar and usage. In J. Flood & J. R. Squire (Eds.), *Handbook of Teaching the English Language Arts* (pp. 591–602). New York: Macmillan.

Kaufman, H. S., & Biren, P. L. (1979). Cursive writing: An aid to reading and spelling. *Academic Therapy, 15,* 209–219.

Koenke, K. (1986). Handwriting instruction: What do we know? *Reading Teacher, 40*(2), 218–220.

Newkirk, T. (1978). Grammar instruction and writing: What we don't know. *English Journal, 67,* 46–54.

Peck, M., Askov, E. N., & Fairchild, S. H. (1980). Another decade of research in handwriting, progress and prospect in the 1970s. *Journal of Educational Research, 73,* 283–298.

Portalupi, J., & Fletcher, R. (2001). *Nonfiction craft lessons: Teaching information writing K–8*. Portland, ME: Stenhouse.

Thurber, D. N. (1987). *D'Nealian handwriting (grades K–8)*. Glenview, IL: Scott Foresman.

Weaver, C. (1979). *Grammar for teachers: Perspective and definitions*. Urbana, IL: National Council of Teachers of English.

______. (1996). *Teaching grammar in context*. Portsmouth, NH: Heinemann.

CHILDREN'S LITERATURE REFERENCES

Lowry, L. (1989). *Number the stars*. Boston: Houghton.

Linking Assessment and Instruction

CHAPTER OUTLINE

Key Standard

Teachers of language arts and reading are knowledgeable about a variety of assessment tools and strategies; they skillfully use the results of assessment to make instructional decisions and to encourage student self-assessment. Such teachers:

- Understand and use assessment as a means to determine what their students know and are able to do in meeting national, state, and local standards and what kinds of experiences they must offer students to further their growth and development.
- Are knowledgeable about assessment-related issues and the purposes, characteristics, and limitations of various types of assessments.
- Use the results of assessments to reflect on student learning and to modify their own teaching and instructional practices.
- Maintain accurate and useful records and work samples of student performance and communicate student progress responsibly to parents, appropriate school staff, and to the students themselves.
- Guide students so that they can assess their own work and monitor their own progress.

To get a preview of Chapter 12 and learn about language arts assessment, visit the Chapter 12 section of the accompanying *Language Arts* CD-ROM.

A group of fourth grade teachers in a New York City school agreed to work collaboratively in a staff development project to learn new ways of teaching and assessing reading and writing. Effective strategies for improving reading comprehension were particularly important to these teachers because their students faced the New York State English Language Arts test in early spring. The teachers met once a week during lunchtime and sometimes for the period following lunch. The staff arranged coverage for the "Lunch and Learn" forum, as the entire school faculty was also committed to raising test scores. The teachers chose a study book, Strategies That Work: Teaching Comprehension to Enhance Understanding, *by Harvey and Goudvis (2000) and research by Taylor and colleagues (2001) to guide their work. They agreed to read a chapter each week, try a comprehension strategy with their students, take notes on what happened, and be prepared to share what worked and what didn't at the next focus session. The group brought new teaching ideas into their classrooms while maintaining established practices that worked effectively. Students continued to keep writing notebooks and reading journals responding to what the teacher read aloud in class and to books and poetry they read independently. They continued to make connections to what they read, ask questions, locate important information, infer, predict, visualize, and write, write, write.*

The teachers scaffolded learning by explaining a new strategy, demonstrating how to apply it, and thinking aloud to model the mental processes they used when they read. Later they directed guided practice with a group of students and moved toward independent practice where students could apply the strategy to a new genre or format. The teachers found that listening carefully to students talk and carefully reading what they wrote gave them a clear picture of how well students were learning to use each new strategy.

The group used a variety of informal assessment tools and strategies to document and monitor student progress. They agreed that this kind of ongoing assessment was extremely useful because it helped them know their students better and enabled them to plan instruction that better served individual needs. The quality time spent on reading good literature, writing in a variety of modes, listening to each other, and speaking out about their own learning meant that every student's voice was valued, and everyone, including the teacher, was part of the learning community.

At the end of the year, the teachers—indeed the entire district—celebrated the success of the fourth-graders. Their scores on the statewide tests rose by 30 points, the biggest increase in the entire city. Students were justifiably proud of their accomplishments, and the teachers felt like true professionals. Word about the improved test scores and the teachers' enthusiasm spread. Other teachers formed grade-level groups, selected their own book choices for study-group discussion, and worked together in similar ways. In this school district, teacher learning proved to be contagious. Teachers were heartened to discover that improvement in test scores can occur in an atmosphere where sound learning and teaching practices are also fostered.

Key Issues and Types of Assessment

Assessment is a critical part of every instructional program. It is also a major issue. Pressure groups function as pendulums swinging from one extreme to another, demanding more and more standardized tests at one point and flexible assessment guidelines at another. In the ensuing hullabaloo, it is easy to forget that effective instructional programs balance the two. For a number of instructional and political reasons, standardized tests continue to be used to measure the success and progress (or lack thereof) of districts, schools, and children. However, a more contextualized, authentic assessment of individual students' progress based on observing students as they learn in the classroom, and adjusting instruction accordingly, is the essence of reflective teaching.

Classroom teachers are primarily responsible for the day-by-day assessment and evaluation of student performance, and they use a variety of assessments as they attempt to determine what their students are learning and not learning. Effective teachers infuse assessment into the instructional process and use the results to adjust instruction to meet student needs. A teacher listens intently as his fifth grade students discuss Katherine Paterson's *The Great Gilly Hopkins,* which they have just finished reading aloud. On his clipboard is a checklist of components of literature discussions that help him assess his students' developing sense of how to talk together about literature. He combines this form with his students' response journals, reading record cards, and their evaluations of themselves as readers and members of a discussion group to assess their growth as readers and members of this classroom community.

Down the hall, another teacher confers with her first grade writers. After each conference, she pauses for a minute to check off items and jot down a few notes on the preprinted conference record forms she keeps for each child. She uses these forms, in conjunction with other observation records and the children's writing folders, to document each student's progress in learning to write. Her students' cumulative writing records are filled with these forms and page after page of hastily scrawled sticky labels containing brief, dated anecdotal comments like, "Helped Omar spell his name: OMR."

Across town, the seventh grade language arts teachers are gathered together to watch a videotape of one of them leading a literature discussion. When the tape ends, they discuss what they saw, assessing student strengths and effective teaching strategies. They then consider the implications of the video as they continue to reassess the effectiveness of the systemwide language arts program. All of these teachers are involved in a crucial dimension of good teaching—ongoing observation and assessment. But, other kinds of assessment have a very strong impact on what they do.

Concern over student performance has led to widespread reform efforts that include **standardized tests,** often mandated at the state or federal level and designed to ensure accountability at the school and district levels. These tests sort districts, schools, and sometimes even teachers in terms of how their students perform. Such tests are often called **high-stakes tests,** because they are frequently used to determine the allocation of resources for remedial services and other kinds of interventions. The trend toward greater use of standardized tests and the publication of test results in the local press has had a profound influence on instruction. Understandably, educators are increasingly making attempts to match instruction to what they anticipate the tests will require. This trend has not been without controversy, however. Many educators are concerned that in an effort to do well on standardized tests, schools often narrow the curriculum to the content of the test. Furthermore, they claim that an inordinate amount of time is spent preparing for these tests and that many areas of the curriculum that do not lend themselves to this type of measurement are being ignored. Those who favor standardized tests counter that they are objective measures that effectively encourage schools to live up to their commitment to excellence in education. In their opinion, time spent teaching to the test is a good thing, especially when the material being tested truly represents the basics of what good education should be.

Standardized tests are generally of two types. A **norm-referenced standardized test** is constructed by administering it to large numbers of students in order to develop norms. The norms represent the average scores of a sampling of students selected for testing according to factors such as age, sex, race, grade, or socioeconomic status. Once norms are established, they become the basis for comparing the performance of individuals or groups to the performance of those who are in the norming sample (Vacca, Vacca, & Gove, 2000). **Criterion-referenced standardized tests** are relative newcomers to statewide testing. The rationale for these tests is that the content measured is related to specific instructional objectives. Test performance is measured against a criterion or acceptable score for each objective measured. Based on particular cut-off scores, children may be placed in various categories. For example, some tests categorize students as below basic, basic, proficient, or advanced.

Ironically, at the same time that the use of high-stakes, standardized tests is increasing, a strong effort is afoot within the educational community to encourage teachers to examine children's ability to engage in literacy tasks and document their learning at the classroom level through contextualized measures, often termed **authentic assessments.** These measures, with an eye toward the greater context of children's lives outside of the classroom, are the kinds of assessments you will read most about in this chapter. They are extremely useful to the classroom teacher because they are closely linked to the curriculum. In this way, they resemble criterion-referenced assessments in that they gauge student performance on a task or set of tasks relative to local standards or expectations and within the context of the classroom.

The main purpose of authentic assessment is to provide students and teachers with information useful in promoting growth in literacy (Au, Scheu, Kawakami, & Herman, 1990, p. 575). Authentic assessment involves the administration of a variety of types of informal inventories, tests, and measures, as well as the collection of anectodal notes and work samples. Students

Bernice Cullinan

Fill hallway bulletin boards with self-testing techniques.

and teachers work collaboratively to determine and then act on what is and is not going well. Teachers reflect on student progress to determine the effectiveness of their teaching strategies, curriculum, and materials. It is a constant process in which instruction and assessment are inextricably linked. In this chapter we focus on observing language learners as they engage in various tasks and on the products of their work. We stress the use of portfolios as a framework for thinking about authentic assessment because they offer concrete examples of how you might document and monitor student progress.

Strategies for Classroom Assessment

OBSERVING LANGUAGE LEARNERS

Effective teachers are effective observers. They study what students do every day in various situations to make decisions about instruction. They watch students to learn what they can do and what they have difficulty doing. Such teachers identify potential social, emotional, and cognitive strengths and weaknesses. They observe students in groups to see who takes a leadership role, who invites classmates into discussions, who shares information and resources with others, or who might dominate a group with a personal agenda. However, these teachers also need to know what to look for in each area of the language arts. For example, a reading attitude questionnaire might include questions such as, Do you like to read? Why? Are you a good reader? Why? What do good readers do that makes them good readers? What kinds of books do you like to read? Have you ever read any books more than once? Which ones? Why? What is one of your favorite books? Why is it a favorite? Do you have a favorite author? Why is that author a favorite? Which of the author's books have you read? How do you choose the books that you read? Who else likes to read the same kinds of books that you like? Where and when do you most like to read? Do you see any differences between the ways you read at home and the way you read at school? Students' responses to questions like these help a student do self-evaluation and provide information for teacher-student and student-parent conferences.

Collecting, recording, and using what is observed

Effective teachers employ a variety of strategies to keep their observations as rigorous and bias-free as possible. We all have personal biases based on our experiences growing up. Describing behavior without adding an interpretation at the same time can make our biases less influential. Several descriptive entries can often reveal patterns in student responses or other behaviors.

Systematic observation is also important. The key word here is *systematic,* because systematic observation also eliminates some of the influence of bias. For example, when a teacher regularly writes down the setting, the materials, the task, and the purpose of the task in which students are engaged, she can avoid interpretation and judgmental statements. Observing voluntary independent reading before school starts reveals a different picture than observing a small group of children discussing an assigned reading because the contexts are so different.

Becoming an effective observer involves identifying personal biases. Each of us has a history of what we like and do not like in children, what we may or may not expect from children from certain families, and how we feel about individual children. This knowledge and involvement can be a strength, but it can also be a weakness if it is allowed to interfere with our objective observation of children. One way to identify the role that personal biases play in your observations is to learn to distinguish between observed behaviors and inferences or judgments about those behaviors. Although it is virtually impossible to delete all that is subjective about what we see, we can attempt to distinguish between what is happening and the judgments we make about it.

Four children in the reading corner during independent reading time—four different responses. Sara is reading her book, turning pages regularly as she lies on her stomach on the rug with the book propped up in front of her. David is sitting on top of a pillow, holding his book and looking off into space. Chandra is similarly perched, holding her book and staring out the window. Juan is sitting cross-legged on the rug, systematically looking through several books. These are the behaviors their teacher *observes.* He might *infer* that Sara is engrossed in reading, especially since he knows she loves to read. He might also *infer* that Juan is in the process of selecting a new book to read and is not wasting time, especially since he knows that he has just finished a book. When he looks at Chandra and David, he sees two children doing pretty much the same thing, and yet *infers* that Chandra is thinking about what she has just read while David is daydreaming. The teacher may think he "knows" these things because he knows these children well, and he may or may not be right. It is important to know the difference between objective observations and inferences.

How often you record behavior will vary. Recording observable behavior as it occurs naturally in the classroom is called **event sampling,** in which the teacher records everything that happens during a particular event such as whole-class reading discussion, independent reading, or peer conferences. Recording what a particular child is doing during a given time is a **time sampling** technique. For example, a teacher observing five children during writing workshop, checking to see what each child is doing every 5–10 minutes, is time sampling. *How* you observe your students depends on what you want to know.

Observation takes a variety of forms. The forms of observation and record keeping that we describe here are particularly useful for classroom teachers.

Anecdotal records. Anecdotes are brief notes about an observation of a specific incident, such as, "Sally gets along well with other students; she helped Peter with his story today." Written at the moment of the observation, they are often fresh and lively. Notes can be quickly scribbled on index cards, Post-its, or self-adhesive address labels and then transferred to an organized, individualized filing system without the need to recopy them. Interesting anecdotes, quickly recorded, become a part of a child's literacy record. They enrich other types of literacy profiles. An example of a page of anecdotal information about one fourth grade student appears in Figure 12.1.

FIGURE 12.1

Andrew's Anecdotes

9-12
Andrew is sitting in a corner with his back to the class totally absorbed in his book, Cooper's The Dark Is Rising.

9-18
Andrew has convinced Luis to read the Cooper series. He is lending his own books to L.

10-1
Andrew has been asking the librarian for everything he has on the Arthur legend.

10-4
Andrew brought in a beautiful picture of a sword + shield. He'd done them at home w/color pencil.

10-9
Andrew a bit at a loss now that he's finished Sutcliff books. He wants more K.A.

10-13
Andrew is reading M's Castle and finding it hard going. He is interested, he says, it's just not a story.

Checklists. A checklist is a list of relevant behaviors associated with an area of study. Checklists are easy and quick to use but must be constructed carefully so that all behaviors relevant to the area being assessed are included. The *Teaching Idea: Book Selection Checklist* is appropriate for children in upper elementary and middle school. Checklists can be used to simply check off the presence or absence of target behaviors at a particular observation period, to check off target behaviors over time, and to indicate the frequency or control of a behavior through symbols such as A = Always, F = Frequently, N = Never, C = Control, D = Developing, or N = No evidence, or through the simple use of a plus, check, and minus recording system. They can represent individual students or whole classes, depending on your needs.

TEACHING IDEA

Addressing Individual Needs

BOOK SELECTION CHECKLIST

Name: John S.

Date: Dec. 13

Context: in library with whole class during selection time – sat with Jim A., Gene, Joshua + Ken.

Asks	Checks	Time
peers ✓	cover ✓	0-5 minutes
good friend ✓	jacket info ✓	5-10 minutes
teacher	author info	10-15 minutes ✓
librarian	first few pages ✓	15-20 minutes
other adult	ending	20+ minutes

Books considered:

1
2
3 ✓
4
5 or more

Book finally selected: The White Mountains

Comment: Gene has read all of Christopher's trilogy – He seems to have convinced J. to try them. J. usually likes what G. likes, but this is a new genre for him.

Interviews and **questionnaires** enrich the information teachers obtain from observation. These may be added to reading conference records and reading journals students keep. The *Teaching Idea: Reading Attitude Questionnaire* exemplifies a questionnaire that you can create, administer, and discuss with your students.

Formal observations. Formal observations are the most comprehensive observational records. They are used to document a child's behavior or progress, to support or disconfirm evaluation findings, or to document the impact of the curriculum or the effect of instructional strategies. Formal, systematic observation in which observer bias is kept to a minimum involves systematic procedures for sampling behavior and for determining the reliability of the observations; they have standard recording formats. Creating a good observation schedule involves (1) defining the problem (what do you want to learn from the observation?); (2) describing the setting (giving a context to the target behaviors); (3) labeling and categorizing behavior (clearly defining what is to be observed); and (4) making inferences (valid conclusions supported by careful documentation of observed behavior) (Boehm & Weinberg, 1987, p. 23).

Teachers create formal observation schedules that contain traditional categories already developed by researchers or other teachers or categories unique to their own purposes. Some teachers think a system of predetermined categories could cause them to miss part of the unusual things children do with language. Instead, they prefer to observe children in a variety of language tasks across time using a more open observation system. (See the *Teaching Idea: Open-Ended Observation Schedule.*) After several observations, they make sense of their data by writing a **biographic literacy profile** similar to the one shown in Figure 12.2. They try to see situations from the viewpoint of the students, so they ask themselves the following questions as they observe students (D. Taylor, 1991, p. 9): What is happening? What is really going on? How do children make sense out of the complexities of their everyday lives? How does a child construct and use language? How does a child conceptualize a problem as well as a solution? How does a child become a member of a community of learners? How does a child theorize about how to do something? How does a child lead others in problem-solving situations to arrive at workable solutions?

Writing biographic literacy profiles takes a great deal of time; it is wise to start slowly by writing one or two before tackling several. Teachers who have used them think the time spent is well worthwhile; they learned to see and appreciate students as they never had before. Some felt it changed their ways of teaching, and it gave them a lot of information they could share with parents during conferences.

Many teachers carry a clipboard with sheets of self-adhesive labels to observe students during writing workshop, whole-class share time, library

TEACHING IDEA

Addressing Individual Needs

READING ATTITUDE QUESTIONNAIRE

How Do You Feel About Reading?

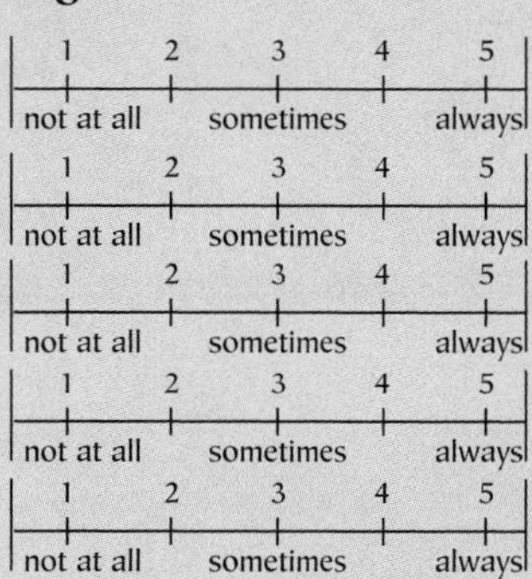

1. Reading is an important part of my life.
2. I read often in my spare time.
3. Reading is my favorite subject in school.
4. I would rather read a book than draw a picture.
5. I like to buy books and have a place to keep them at home.

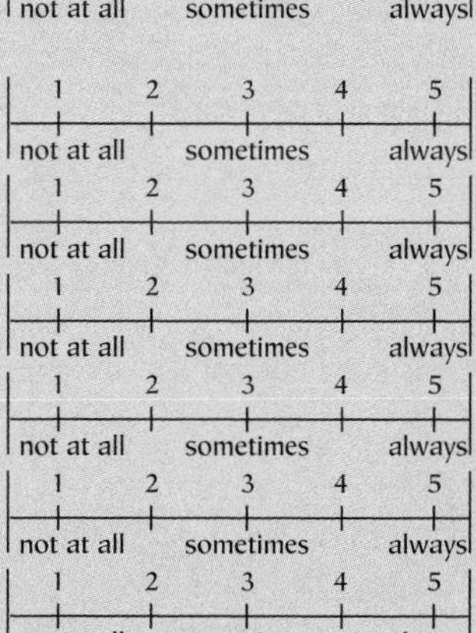

6. When I find the kind of books I like, reading can be fun.
7. I like free reading time in school.
8. I like to find library books to read.
9. Reading school books is a waste of time.
10. I would like to belong to a book club.
11. Reading makes me feel good.

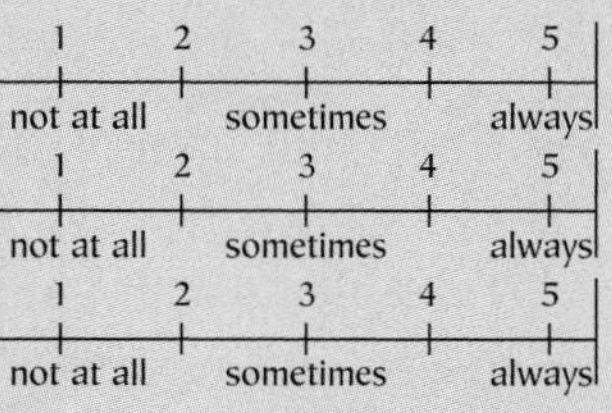

12. I dislike reading because most of the time I am being forced to read.
13. Reading is a fun way of learning.
14. I like to read before I go to bed.

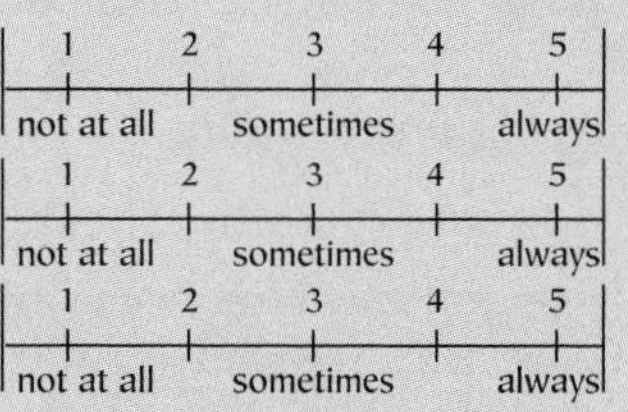

15. I often find extra books or stories to read about something that interests me.
16. I like to look through the books at the library.
17. Reading is boring.
18. I usually read several books during summer vacation.

Source: Reprinted from Tunnell, M. O., Calder, J. E., & Justen, J. E. (1988). A short form reading attitude survey. *Reading Improvement*, 25(2), 150–151.

TEACHING IDEA

Assessing the Learner

OPEN-ENDED OBSERVATION SCHEDULE

My Observations of:

Child: Date:

Partners:

Language event:

Physical setting:

Description: (behavior, conversation, etc.)

visits, or math projects. Like a proud parent, they write down the clever things students say or do. They often combine these observations and student self-assessments with formal observations to prepare for parent conferences or end-of-term reporting. Reflecting on varied types of information helps them make sense of the data they collect.

Using observations to make instructional decisions

Alison Epstein draws implications for instruction in reading, writing, listening, and speaking from ongoing assessment in her kindergarten class in New York City. Alison has a Poetry Center—a simple rack on which she hangs large sheets of paper printed with poems. Each child has a poetry notebook filled with copies of group poems as well as individually written or chosen

FIGURE 12.2

Biographic Literacy Profile

Mike: First Grade

Through October and November, Mike has become more actively involved during shared reading sessions. He can provide phrases or sentences as we approach new texts. He uses a variety of strategies with unknown words: looking for parts of the word that are familiar to him, thinking of what would make sense, thinking of whether a piece is fiction or nonfiction, using knowledge of letter sounds. He turns back pages to reread when he is unsure of himself and does self-correction as he reads, if his attempt doesn't make sense to him. When reading aloud to the group, he is very expressive (at times asking the group, "Don't you like the way I read that part?").

Mike's written vocabulary is expanding at a rapid rate. It is about double that displayed in September. He has also begun to make connections between spellings of word families (me, be, we, fat, sat, rat, cat, man, fan, can). His day book entries continue to follow the pattern of "I liked. . . ." In his journal, he has been much more consistent in the addition of the text that tells his stories. He works on one story right after another, always marking the finish with "The END," then launching into his next topic. He has written some stories that are clearly fiction-adventure stories but has also written some nonfiction pieces (and stated that as he worked on them—that they were true). He works very independently as he writes, only asking for help on occasion. He is quite confident in his ability to figure words out for himself.

poems. Poetry written on charts hangs around the classroom on chalkboards, posters, and illuminated enlarged book pages. Today Alison is using "Hickory Dickory Dock," the well-known nursery rhyme about the mouse that ran up the clock. Alison has printed the verse on large chart paper and now hangs it in the front of the room. Students gather on the carpeted area to read it, recite it, to point to the words, and in general, to enjoy the rhyme. Alison, an effective observer, does not allow the session to pass as just another pleasurable experience; she watches to see who knows how to match the spoken and written words. She insists that children touch the pointer to a word they see that matches the word they say. They know the verse by heart; they confirm the match between words in print and words they say.

Alison does not use the session to check on word matching alone; she observes for several different behaviors. She watches to see who listens carefully, who attends to the child leader with the pointing stick. She listens to which children speak clearly and confidently to say the word as their pointer touches it. She observes who is considerate when another child speaks and who waits a turn to talk.

Alison further extends the teaching and learning through activities. Some children make individual word-pattern flip charts from 3 × 5 cards. They write the base pattern or root segment (for example, *ock*) on the bottom card and attach several cards cut in half as the top part. On each small part of the card, a child writes a beginning sound or blend to create a word when it is matched with the root pattern, such as *d* (dock), *s* (sock), *j* (jock), *bl* (block), *cl* (clock). Alison notes in her journal the children who understand base words and combining blends or single letters to the base. She decides that these students are ready to work with word patterns; she will begin to introduce more basic patterns to them.

Observing speakers and listeners

Just as there are many contexts in which to observe oral language, there are also many ways to describe it. Halliday (1975) has proposed a system, discussed in Chapter Four, that enables teachers to classify language according to function. This system is exhaustive but not mutually exclusive, because one utterance can—and often does—serve more than one function. Another way to categorize children's oral language in terms of the way they use it is with Tough's system (1985), described in Figure 12.3.

You can also develop your own guidelines and categories for observing specific types of oral language activities. Lee and Rubin (1979) present a set of linguistic tasks that apply to students across all age levels, shown in Figure 12.4. Strickland and colleagues (1989) found these tasks to be an excellent interpretive framework to study language functions during literature-response groups; they also work for any form of group discussion because they exemplify behaviors that teachers typically encourage. Assessment matches practice when you use these categories.

It is a good idea to observe your students closely when they make oral presentations. You can also involve students in developing, using, and perfecting an observation checklist. The *Teaching Idea: Student Strategies for Oral*

FIGURE 12.3

Functions of Language

1. **Self-maintaining**
   Strategies
   - Referring to physical and psychological needs and wants
   - Protecting the self and self-interests
   - Justifying behavior or claims
   - Criticizing others
   - Threatening others
2. **Directing**
   Strategies
   - Monitoring own actions
   - Directing the actions of the self
   - Directing the actions of others
   - Collaborating in action with others
3. **Reporting on present and past experiences**
   Strategies
   - Labeling the components of the scene
   - Referring to detail (e.g., size, color, and other attributes)
   - Referring to incidents
   - Referring to the sequence of events
   - Making comparisons
   - Recognizing related aspects
   - Making an analysis using several of the features above
   - Extracting or recognizing the central meaning
   - Reflecting on the meaning of experiences, including own feelings
4. **Toward logical reasoning***
   Strategies
   - Explaining a process
   - Recognizing causal and dependent relationships
   - Recognizing problems and their solutions
   - Justifying judgments and actions
   - Reflecting on events and drawing conclusions
   - Recognizing principles
5. **Predicting***
   Strategies
   - Anticipating and forecasting events
   - Anticipating the detail of events
   - Anticipating a sequence of events
   - Anticipating problems and possible solutions
   - Anticipating and recognizing alternative courses of action
   - Predicting the consequences of actions or events
6. **Projecting***
   Strategies
   - Projecting into the experiences of others
   - Projecting into the feelings of others
   - Projecting into the reactions of others
   - Projecting into situations never experienced
7. **Imagining***
   Strategies
   - Developing an imaginary situation based on real life
   - Developing an imaginary situation based on fantasy
   - Developing an original story

*Strategies which serve *directing*, *reporting*, and *reasoning* may serve these uses also.

Source: Tough, J. (1985). *Listening to children talking: A guide to the appraisal of children's use of language* (pp. 82–84). London: Ward Lock Educational.

FIGURE 12.4

Linguistic Tasks

1. Ordering information when giving directions or explanations so that listeners can follow
2. Taking account of the discrepancy between their own informational position, background, and experience and that of their listeners
3. Shifting their style of speech according to their listeners or their purposes
4. Being aware of their point of view so as to be consistent and change only by intention
5. Analyzing their information in relation to the problem to be solved

Source: From Lee, D. M, & Rubin, J. B. (1979). *Children and language: Reading and writing, talking and listening* (p. 71). Belmont, CA: Wadsworth.

Presentation can help students learn which elements make a good oral presentation, recognize the elements when they see them, and discover the preparation required to develop them.

You will also need to develop other ways to study students' oral language. You can discuss with students possible items or topics to study and ways to collect information as well as ways to assess it. One group of students brainstormed a list of the different kinds of "talk" they use: street talk, lingo, slang, home dialect, "Spanglish," e-mail talk, rap, and hip hop. You may want to study syntax (word order) or syntactic patterns. You can review the literature on language development and examine the curriculum guidelines to determine what forms of syntactic development might occur during a year. You could then develop an observation instrument appropriate for a specific group of students.

Assessing children's listening behaviors can be useful to both teachers and students. Lundsteen (1979) divides her comprehensive list of listening behaviors into general listening and critical listening, as first introduced in Chapter Five and reproduced in Figure 12.5. Select a few target items from this extensive list and construct an observation instrument appropriate for your students.

Bernice Cullinan

A strategy for assessing student performance is observation of individual or paired oral-language performances.

TEACHING IDEA

Addressing Individual Needs

STUDENT STRATEGIES FOR ORAL PRESENTATIONS

1. Time your presentation so that you can accommodate questions and comments from the class.
2. Consider what your audience already knows about your topic, and offer new and interesting information as opposed to widely known information.
3. Use the appropriate level of language for your audience, neither too detailed or complex nor too general or simple.
4. Adequately prepare for your presentation, so that it goes smoothly and remains interesting to the audience.
5. Use visuals where helpful.

FIGURE 12.5

Listening Goals

General Listening

1. Remembering significant details accurately (knowledge of specifics)
2. Remembering simple sequences of words and ideas
3. Following oral directions
4. Paraphrasing a spoken message (comprehension by translation)
5. Following a sequence in (a) plot development, (b) character development, (c) speaker's argument
6. Understanding denotative (literal) meanings of words
7. Understanding connotative meanings of words
8. Understanding meanings of words from spoken context (comprehension by translation and interpretation)
9. Listening for implications of significant details (analysis and interpretation)
10. Listening for implications of main ideas
11. Answering and formulating questions (interactive listening)
12. Identifying main ideas and summarizing (combining and synthesizing the who, what, when, where, and why)
13. Understanding relationships among ideas and the organizational pattern well enough to predict what may come next (comprehension by extrapolation)
14. Connecting the spoken material with previous experience and planning action (application)
15. Listening to imagine and to extend for enjoyment and emotional response (affective-toned synthesizing)

Critical Listening

1. Distinguishing fact from fancy, according to criteria
2. Judging validity and adequacy of main ideas, arguments, and hypotheses
3. Distinguishing well-supported statements from opinion and judgment and evaluating them
4. Distinguishing well-supported statements from irrelevant ones and evaluating them
5. Inspecting, comparing, and contrasting ideas and arriving at a conclusion about statements, such as the appropriateness and appeal of one descriptive word over another
6. Evaluating the use of fallacies, such as: (a) self-contradictions, (b) avoiding the question at issue, (c) hasty or false generalization, (d) false analogy, (e) failure to present all choices, (f) appealing to ignorance
7. Recognizing and judging the effects of various devices the speaker may use to influence the listener, such as (a) music, (b) "loaded" words, (c) voice intonation, (d) play on emotional and controversial issues, (e) propaganda, sales pressure—that is, identifying affective loading in communication and evaluating it
8. Detecting and evaluating the bias and prejudice of a speaker or of a point of view
9. Evaluating the qualifications of a speaker
10. Planning to evaluate the ways in which a speaker's ideas might be applied in a new situation

Source: Lundsteen, W. (1979). *Listening: Its impact on reading and the other language arts* (pp. 59–61). Urbana, IL: National Council of Teachers of English.

General questions help us evaluate students' progress during different types of oral language activities. Each should be observed in the process of ongoing development of a specific child. For example, you might ask:

> Does Emily take an increasing role in group discussion?
>
> Are her contributions useful and pertinent?
>
> Is she a good listener during group discussion?
>
> Does her speech show sensitivity to the needs of others?
>
> Does she participate enthusiastically in a variety of oral language activities?
>
> Is she developing in her ability to present before a group?

Obviously, ongoing classroom observation is the best way to assess children's oral language use. Observation schedules, checklists, note cards, sticky notes, or journals make it possible to record observations quickly and easily. Tape-recording oral language interactions and presentations adds to the pool of data you collect. Returning to primary data—the child's real voice—is the best way to hear progress.

It is a good idea to conclude some oral language activities with a group evaluation of the process. You might ask:

> What did we accomplish during this session?
>
> Did everyone who wanted to speak get a chance to do so?
>
> Did only a few people do most of the talking?
>
> Were we good listeners?
>
> Did we stay on the topic?
>
> If not, was the digression meaningful?
>
> Are we generally satisfied with what occurred?
>
> How can we improve the next time?

Periodic discussions of group behavior in oral language activities help all participants become thoughtful members of a classroom community. It is a natural way for them to discover criteria (rubrics) for high-level communication.

Making sense of data. Once you have collected data about students' oral language use, you are ready to analyze it and make inferences about students and your own teaching. For example, if a teacher observes the use of language functions in a first grade class, he can develop individual profiles of each student. He might want to look at various contexts and determine what functions of language occur most often in each context. He can assess his instructional program by asking:

> Are students using language for a variety of purposes?
>
> Are the purposes linked to the task at hand and the social context?
>
> Is there a range of functions observable across students?
>
> Does the classroom provide situations that promote a variety of functions?
>
> How can I expand opportunities for students to use language in a variety of ways, for different purposes with different people? (Pinnell, 1985, p. 60)

These questions force you to look at your class as a group and to think about your teaching in relation to oral language functions.

If you have collected listening data, you can examine it to see other types of presentational strategies that might strengthen students' listening abilities and to see which students might benefit from small-group work on listening skills. The information you collect helps determine presenters, strategies to teach, and grouping decisions for your next sessions. Grouping students of varying abilities together helps them learn and gives the skilled child an opportunity to be recognized.

As you look at your instruction to identify occasions for oral language use, you may want to expand the contexts to observe and apply the results of assessment to instruction. What your students do today guides your plan for tomorrow.

Observing readers

Reading is a transactional process with reader, test, and context all influencing the act of reading. Reading is not a unitary construct; it has many dimensions. Assessment of readers is also multidimensional. Jane Medina, Reading Specialist in Orange County, California, says,

> I think basing instruction on assessment is much trickier for reading than for any other subject. Planning lessons when your math students bomb a regrouping test is pretty obvious. Redoing the scientific method when your kids' projects are devoid of hypotheses is not too hard to figure out, either. Using reading assessments to inform your practice requires a lot of reflection, though.

Jane Medina continues,

> Of all the assessments I've used over the years, the most useful one I've found is the informal reading inventory. I've used several different informal reading inventories, and although none of them is perfect, they always provide me with lots of information about my students' strengths and weaknesses, which helps in planning my instruction for them. Knowing the approximate grade level helps me form flexible groups. The depth of information I get from the results and from observing the child during testing is invaluable.

I placed the pre-primer level reading selection in front of Eric. While I was writing his name on my copy, he touched the paper once, pushed it a little, and then ignored it. I began to guess that print had little meaning for him. I was right. He could read only two or three words, so I asked him to identify the letters he recognized. He didn't know many. This assessment told me that I needed to start very close to the beginning in planning reading instruction for Eric.

Sinai, on the other hand, confidently grasped his reading selection and glanced over the first paragraph, hoping that I wouldn't consider this cheating. He read quite fluently and looked up and smiled at me when he was done. Although his confidence and fluency were great strengths, I could tell that Sinai had a problem similar to Eric's. Both boys did not understand that print has meaning.

Three things told me that Sinai considered reading a performance rather than a search for meaning. First, Sinai's miscues included many substitutions

Bernice Cullinan

Observe readers outside of school as well during class.

that didn't make sense in the context of the selection. Also, many of the miscues were nonsense words. Second, Sinai's retelling of the story showed me that he was able to tell me several details of the story, but that he had missed the main idea. Third, the follow-up comprehension questions confirmed and refined my understanding of Sinai's reading: he was unable to describe the sequence of events, he was unable to make inferences, and he didn't understand the main character's motivations.

Sinai and Eric both desperately needed to see that getting a message is the reason people read. Since Eric had very little decoding ability, I began by reading aloud children's stories to him and his group, which we would discuss. We then wrote our own versions of the story using the Language Experience Approach. Those stories became the basis for word study and phonics instruction.

Because Sinai was older and had more reading experience and ability than Eric, we began by reading stories at his independent and instructional levels and discussing the contents. What was most beneficial for Sinai was brainstorming the reading strategies he used while reading. I made specific plans to emphasize the strategy of trying to make sense of what the stories are saying, and what to do if they don't make sense. He and his group developed a reading brochure that listed what to do before you read, what to do while you're reading, and ways to respond to what you've read. We named the brochure *How to Survive Reading.* We refer to the brochure whenever we read a new story. Each student has a copy of the brochure to use independently.

Many situations involving reading provide opportunities to observe readers in action. For example, consider response to literature, the variety of ways students use reading, oral reading, discussing reading, how students talk about books they read, the types of books they read, and what they write about what they read. What you observe depends on what you want to know, and that depends on the contexts for reading. For example, kindergarten or first grade teachers might observe how much students use environmental print—labels, signs, charts, written directions—in the classroom. Intermediate-grade teachers might observe how students use books, the Internet, or reference aids, such as tables of contents, indexes, or glossaries, to obtain information. Teachers of pre-school and primary grades will want to use Marie Clay's Concepts of Print Test (1979), observe book-handling skills, response activities, and knowledge of other reading behaviors. Effective teachers observe students reading orally from a variety of texts, listen to oral discussions of books, watch book discussion groups, and notice how students settle down to independent reading. All aspects of the curriculum deserve their attention; their observations inform their teaching.

What to observe. The criteria you use to construct checklists or to inform your observations reflect the reading event and your purpose for observing. For example, a teacher may observe a book discussion group to note which aspects of the text are discussed. The three *Teaching Ideas: Literature Discussion* (for primary, intermediate, and upper grades) contain checklists for whole-class discussions. Teachers discover what students focus on and the topics they discuss in literature circles, noting what they say rather than how they say it.

A teacher might tape-record a reading and discussion session to analyze for types of responses generated. She will look at who participated and the

TEACHING IDEA

Literature Link

LITERATURE DISCUSSION—PRIMARY GRADES

Name: Date/Book:

Group:

- Understands story gist
- Recalls sequence
- Recalls details
- Understands cause and effect
- Understands character type
- Engages with story

Comments:

TEACHING IDEA

Literature Link

LITERATURE DISCUSSION—INTERMEDIATE GRADES

Name: Date/Book:

Group:

- Understands story gist
- Recalls plot sequence
- Considers genre demands
- Considers characters'
  - motivation
  - interaction
  - growth
- Considers theme
- Evaluates categorically
- Evaluates analytically
- Generalizes
- Engages with story

Comments:

TEACHING IDEA

Literature Link

LITERATURE DISCUSSION—UPPER GRADES

Name: Date/Book:

Group:

- Understands story gist
- Understands plot structure
- Considers genre demands
- Considers characters'
  motivation
  interaction
  growth
  development (author's technique)
- Considers theme
- Considers style
  word choice
  sentence structure
- Evaluates categorically
- Evaluates analytically
- Generalizes
- Engages with story

Comments:

types of questions asked, using the same tape recording to examine participation in oral discussion and her own questioning techniques. If she does this early in the school year, it will help her get to know her students and how they respond to literature. Periodically tape-recording a story reading and discussion session can determine stable or changing patterns and help you compare what your students do in groups with what they do independently. Your assessment informs your practice.

A **running record** or **miscue analysis** reveals the strategies students use when they read. By recording students' oral reading by marking their **miscues,** or instances where what a student read deviated from the text (Goodman, 1983), you can discover precisely what strategies the reader is using and what the reader needs to be taught. Figure 12.6 illustrates key elements of the miscue coding system and shows a brief sample of a coded text. As the student reads, note patterns in the word- and sentence-level strategies she is using. After the oral reading is complete, discuss the book with the reader, asking comprehension questions and taking notes to check her understanding of the passage. Using both a narrative and an expository text will result in a fuller picture of which texts are the easiest and most familiar to the student, which strategies are used, and the strategies she needs to learn.

FIGURE 12.6

Miscue Analysis

Once upon [on] a time there were [was] three bears. One was a great big [daddy] bear. One was a middle-sized [H] bear. And one was a small [baby sc] bear. sc

Key:

We	=	repetition of word or phrase
We	=	omission
We [me]	=	substitution of word or phrase
sc	=	self correction
H	=	help from teacher
RR	=	rereads sentence

To get a general picture of how students operate as readers, observe them engaged in reading events in the classroom or library. Teale (1988, p. 176) suggests noting the following about primary-grade readers:

> Do they look at books during free time?
>
> Can they find specific books?
>
> Do they have favorite books, authors, and illustrators?
>
> Can they retell familiar stories?
>
> Can they remember details and predict outcomes?
>
> Do they turn pages while "reading" familiar books?
>
> Do they "read" based on pictures, the "gist" of the book, or the print?
>
> Do they attend to environmental print?
>
> Can they point to words?
>
> Do they know letters and some letter sounds? Which ones?

Here are some things to note about upper-grade readers:

> Do they read during free time?
>
> Do they visit the library during free time?
>
> Do they talk with peers about books?
>
> Do they read during library time?
>
> Do they read until forced to stop?
>
> Do they get involved in books quickly?
>
> Do they read without pause during independent reading?
>
> Do they discard a book if they don't like it?
>
> Do they make predictions about outcomes?
>
> Do they reread if they haven't understood?
>
> Do they reread for pleasure?
>
> Do they recommend books to others?
>
> Do they ask for recommendations from peers? Adults? (p. 176)

Your own enthusiasm for reading goes far in helping your students develop a positive attitude toward reading, but you must first know your students' attitudes toward reading. The *Teaching Idea: Reading Attitude Survey* also helps you do this by asking students to indicate their agreement or disagreement with eighteen statements using a 5-point scale.

TEACHING IDEA

Assessing the Learner

READING ATTITUDE SURVEY

Tell Me about Your Reading

Name: Date:

Do you like to read? Why?

Are you a good reader? Why?

What does a good reader do that makes him or her good?

What kinds of books do you like to read?

Have you ever read any books more than once? Which ones? Why?

What is one of your favorite books? Why is it a favorite?

Do you have a favorite author? Why is that author a favorite?

Which of the author's books have you read?

How do you choose the books that you read?

Who else likes to read the same kinds of books that you like?

Where and when do you most like to read?

Do you see any difference between the way you read at home and the way you read at school?

Some teachers start the school year by sitting down and talking with students about books and reading. They ask about students' reading habits, attitudes, and their favorite books and authors. This information can also be gathered in writing by asking students to complete a brief questionnaire such as the one found in the *Teaching Idea: Self-Assessment of Reading.*

Making sense of the data. Interviews and questionnaires about reading attitudes help teachers find out about students as readers. Combining this information with observations of students reading, responding, and discussing books in the classroom, as well as reading conference records and reading journals, will build an accurate picture of individual strengths as students read over time in a variety of contexts. This information will help you make sound instructional decisions.

Miscue analysis, running records, and tape-recorded oral reading segments help you determine what strategies students are relying on and reveal what they need to learn. Effective teachers observe discussions and take notes during reading conferences. They assess reading response journals, logs, and

TEACHING IDEA

Addressing Individual Differences

SELF-ASSESSMENT OF READING

Name______________________________ Date ________________

Some of my favorite stories, poems, informational books are:

I like fiction, poetry, nonfiction best because:

My favorite author or illustrator is: because:

The best time for me to read is: because:

I have changed as a reader since ________ because now I _______

My reading has improved since the beginning of the year because:

The problems I am still having with reading are:

What I would like to read next is:

records to determine how much students read and what they notice when they read. Try to discover how students feel about reading, the uses they find for it, and the importance it has in their school lives. All of this is necessary information to plan effective instruction.

Observing writers

Effective teachers of writing spend a great deal of time observing students as writers. It is only through careful observation that you can know what kinds of questions to ask and what kinds of responses to make during writing conferences to help develop your students' writing abilities. You can learn a great deal through observing students as they work with others during writing workshop, as they participate in whole-class writing activities, and by looking at what they are producing and the processes they are going through during writing workshop.

Keene and Zimmerman (1997) state that good readers create sensory images in their minds as they read. Good writers make creating those images a much easier task. Rebecca Dotlich, a poet who likes to play with language, creates a number of sensory images about an object without ever actually using the name of the object. As she developed the idea, she produced a book of poems that she calls *Riddles Come Rumbling: Poems to Ponder*. The book works in two directions: it can be used as a means to get readers to infer unstated meaning from text and as a model for creating sensory images to describe an object. Alison Epstein used the strategy in her kindergarten class by having students draw a picture in the center of a page and then write words the picture made them think of around the edges. You might also read aloud the following page and others from Dotlich's book and then ask students to identify the object the poem describes. Later, students can use the poetic form as a model for writing their own riddle poems.

I curl,
I coil,
I sidewalk-slide,
I slip,
I slink,
I garden-glide,
I speak,
In reptile-tongue
(a hissssss)
I try to bite,
You hope
I missssssssss.

What is it? (a snake)

Discover what students know and are trying to do by observing them writing and talking with them about their work. Students involved in activities associated with their writing often provide opportunities for observation. We know that some students tend to be visual learners who are aided in their writing by drawing pictures. Some find drawing a parallel or preliminary necessity to writing. Strickland (1999) found that students who were bogged down in their writing got a burst of writing energy by taking time to draw pictures about their topic, story, or poem. Creating a visual narrative seemed to be effective for these learners. Mentally envisioning and drawing a story character or scene before they wrote helped them write fluently. Artists and poets are frequently visual thinkers; they see pictures in their mind's eye before they put words or brushes or lines on paper.

What to observe. As is true of oral language and reading, what you observe depends upon the students you teach, your classroom practices, and what you want to know. Teachers of beginning writers may want to focus on children's invented spellings, their skill in getting words onto paper, and control over spatial features. They may develop an observation schedule similar to one Teale (1988, p. 174) developed:

Do students draw or write first?

Do they hold pencils/markers/crayons correctly?

Do they use invented spelling? At what level?

Do they segment? How and where?

Can they reread their own writing?

Do they share their writing with others?

Do they listen to and respond to peers' writing?

Blank forms are given in the *Teaching Ideas: Mechanics Checklist* (individual student records) and *Whole-Class Reading/Writing Record*. Regular observations at least twice a month will help you form an accurate picture of what young writers can do (Teale, 1988).

Upper-grade students develop control over the conventions and techniques of written language as they write, share their writing, and discover new ways to make their messages clear. They can use editing sheets or checklists like those found in Chapter Eleven on their own or peers' work. For these students, you can demonstrate how you edit your own work by putting an excerpt of your writing on a transparency and literally marking it with editing marks in front of the students. Samples of the work of real writers (previous students' or famous writers' manuscripts) show that numerous editorial comments and changes are typical, even routine, which is often an important revelation for student writers. Excerpts from E. B. White's *Charlotte's Web*

TEACHING IDEA

Assessing the Learner

WHOLE-CLASS READING/WRITING RECORD

Name	***Date***	***Book/Piece***	***Goal/ Assessment***	***New Goal***

manuscript and Walt Whitman's *O Captain, My Captain* are available at most libraries.

In addition to checklists, upper-grade students can "take dictation" to demonstrate their developing control of conventions. Getting words onto paper from oral dictation is difficult even for experienced writers. You can use excerpts from informational, narrative, and poetic texts. Using the same passage at the beginning, middle, and end of the year, and having children write what they hear, gives you yet another record of how children's skills are developing.

Spelling can be assessed by using checklists or by simply looking at students' edited drafts to determine (1) which words are conventionally spelled; (2) which words the student corrected during editing; and (3) which words are neither conventionally spelled nor corrected. This information will help you prepare the next spelling lesson. Assess student writing in terms of the functions it serves. Students use writing to establish ownership, to form and maintain social relationships, to remember or recall, to describe, to request information or items, to record information, to present information, to tell true and imaginative stories, and to pretend. At any grade level, closely observing students as they write and examining the pieces they produce can systematically reveal their uses for their writing. The information obtained helps you assess not only what students can do but also what the curriculum encourages them to do.

You can also document how students spend their time during writing workshop across a number of days. Are they selecting a topic, percolating ideas, drafting, revising, editing, preparing for publication, or holding conferences? A time-sampling procedure enables you to document the amount of time students spend on each phase of the writing cycle and their revision strategies on an open-ended observation form. Look for answers to these questions:

> To whom do the students go for help?
>
> How frequently do they consult peers? How many peers do they consult?
>
> At what phase in the writing cycle do they ask for help?

Check on revision strategies by asking students to compose without erasing, or to compose using ink. They can use a different colored pencil for revisions. This is not a daily technique for writing workshop—merely a way to check on revision in order to decide when to demonstrate new ways to revise. Examining revised drafts allows you to see what types of revisions students are making, what strategies for revision can be inferred, and how those strategies change over time.

The last week of school, Fran Zimmerman returned writing samples and portfolios (or work folders) the students had kept all year long, including papers from the first week of school. The third-graders were shocked by the immaturity of their own work. "Look at that baby writing I did. That's terrible. I can't believe I wrote like that." Portfolios make self-assessment visible, almost mandatory.

Making sense of the data. Combining the information from systematic observation with information from student folders (records they keep and pieces they write), anecdotal notes or checklist information and summaries from conferences, you can create a thorough view of each student's work. A clear picture of student performance informs your decisions about teaching strategies and curriculum.

A primary-grade teacher may discover that his students are ready for systematic instruction in word families when he sees their invented spelling. An upper-grade teacher may note that her students are not doing much content revision, but rather focusing on surface-level features in the editing process. This signifies a need to spend some instructional time on revision strategies and demonstrate their use. If your students are not writing a lot of pieces, you may conclude that you need to lengthen the amount of time for writing workshop. If the writing your students do for science reports is not as interesting or as carefully crafted as that done during writing workshop, you may want to study the authors' craft in exemplary science books with the students. The data can be used to document and examine the progress of individual students and to look for patterns of strengths and weaknesses in the instructional program.

Observing viewers

Students need help in becoming critical viewers as well as critical listeners and readers. The following are some suggestions to consider as you plan videotape experiences and assess student learning. Select the items most appropriate to the material on the videotape and the age/grade level of your students:

- Recognize the theme or central idea presented.
- Recognize and recall details that help develop the theme or central idea.
- Recognize the organizational structure of the text.
- Paraphrase, retell, or interpret segments of the text.
- Determine purpose (entertain, persuade, inform).
- Make judgments, form opinions, and draw conclusions from the text.
- Analyze use of the elements and conventions (humor, irony, setting, metaphor, etc.) that contribute to meaning.
- Analyse their own response to the text. (New Jersey State Department of Education, 1998, p. 146)

MAKING USE OF PORTFOLIOS

The term **portfolio** refers to a folder of work. Portfolio assessment is an ongoing process of collecting materials for authentic assessment. Teachers and students select work samples to show what students know and are able to do as readers, writers, and language users. The portfolios include free writing, drafts, and published pieces of writing, persuasive letters, poems, stories, journal entries, play scripts, conference notes from problem-solving groups, drawings, lists of books read, written responses to literature, e-mail correspondence, and other writing. Long used in the visual and performing arts, they demonstrate effort, progress, and achievement over a period of time. Artists keep samples of their work; dancers keep photographs of performances. Portfolios can be used in classrooms in all areas of the curriculum; they show evidence of student learning and provide an alternative or extension to formal tests.

Portfolios differ from tests by showing what students can do in real-life situations; tests show what students know about a body of knowledge in controlled situations. Portfolios show effort through many drafts of a completed project; tests show performance in a one-time standardized situation. Teachers and learners evaluate portfolios in a mentoring situation; tests are scored by mechanical means in mass processes. Portfolios reveal performance on a meaningful task; tests assess all students on the same dimensions. Portfolios focus on individual achievement, whereas tests tend to reveal comparisons among learners. Figure 12.7 gives further differences between tests and portfolios.

Types of portfolios

Valencia and Place (1994) and others concur that there are at least four different types of portfolios: showcase, documentation, process, and evaluation portfolios. Composite portfolio systems combine features of more than one type.

Showcase portfolios display students' best or favorite pieces of work; students choose the pieces that go into the portfolio. The showcase portfolio may be a group photograph album, a class-published book, a museum display, or other group presentation. They are available for classroom visitors and for contributors to look at repeatedly.

Documentation portfolios (or working portfolios) show an individual student's progress over a period of time; the dated samples illustrate progress across the year. These are working portfolios; teachers, students, and parents actively refer to them. Documentation portfolios are best kept in expandable files, notebooks, or flexible boxes easily available to students, teachers, and parents.

Process portfolios contain the steps students have followed to complete a given project; they usually contain students' reflections on their learning and

FIGURE 12.7

Differences between Portfolios and Standardized Tests

Portfolios

- Contain a broad view of development and achievement
- Show effort across many drafts of a completed project
- Show progress in first and last parallel assignments
- Represent a range of learning activities
- Make it possible for students to assess their own progress
- Allow students to set their own goals
- Show individual achievement
- Allow for differences among students
- Represent a collaborative approach to assessment

Tests

- Do not measure what is taught
- Assess a limited range of learning activities
- Are scored mechanically; allow teachers no input
- Assess all students on the same dimensions
- Allow outside agencies to control assessment
- Do not involve students in self-assessment
- Stress achievement only
- Separate assessment from teaching and learning

a step-by-step list of actions taken. A process portfolio can serve as a model for a child who wants to learn how to do a certain project.

Evaluation portfolios include examples of students' work used to make summative assessments according to established standards. Representative work samples and evaluations are sent with students to subsequent classrooms or grade levels. Similar to cumulative record folders, evaluation portfolios provide a history; they are usually kept in expandable, accordion-fold cardboard file folders and stored in filing cabinets. Students add work samples to them annually and send them with a letter they write to the teacher for the next year (Valencia & Place, 1994).

Showcase, documentation, process, evaluation, and composite portfolios work well for material used to report to parents. The portfolios contain sufficient material to determine progress in nearly every area of the curriculum. Some teachers work with students to select illustrative work samples from the portfolios to send home with a letter. Teachers frequently make copies of the portfolio samples sent home in case material needed in the future is lost or misplaced. *The Teaching Idea: Letter Sent Home with Portfolio* helps explain this kind of assessment, which may be new to parents, and you can, of course, change it to fit your students and parents.

TEACHING IDEA

Home/School Connection

LETTER SENT HOME WITH PORTFOLIO

Dear Parents:

I invite you to look carefully at your child's work and recognize how much effort goes into preparing portfolios. Portfolios differ from the report cards we used to send home because portfolios contain a true sampling of your child's work. We used to use paper-and-pencil tasks as the main way to evaluate students, but we know that this gave a limited view of what they could do. Now we encourage students to demonstrate their learning in a variety of ways by including actual work samples. The portfolio shows what they know, builds on individual strengths, and encourages independent learning.

We used to exclude students from the assessment and evaluation of their progress, but this did not allow self-assessment. Now we encourage students to take an active role in assessing and evaluating their own progress and setting future learning goals. Students construct meaning from the world around them, and this process involves self-evaluation, independent learning, and a lifelong commitment to learning.

You can see that the portfolio is more than a progress report. it is a representative sampling of your child's recent work, learning interests, and evidence of a commitment to continued learning. Read through it together. Talk about what you see. Celebrate the beauty of a mind at work.

Cordially, ______________

Getting started and maintaining portfolios

Farr and Tone (1994, p. 12) propose two key principles to follow when planning portfolio assessment:

1. Documentation or working portfolios are more immediately useful to teachers and students than showcase, process, or evaluation portfolios. Working portfolios contain drafts, ideas, artifacts, pictures, and numerous records that promote student involvement in analyzing portfolio contents—not just examples of the student's best work.
2. A primary goal of portfolio assessment is to develop students' ability to do self-assessment so they can monitor the effectiveness of their language use and learning throughout their lives. This requires adequate class time for students to work with their portfolios, ongoing student-teacher conferences, and regular formal student-teacher portfolio conferences.

The guidelines given in Figure 12.8 will help you use portfolios effectively.

FIGURE 12.8

Guidelines for Portfolios

1. Remember, portfolios belong to students; they must therefore decide, with the guidance of the teacher, what goes into them and who sees them.
2. Build on established procedures; expand writing folders.
3. Start small; initially use portfolios in one subject area only.
4. Model the use of portfolios by keeping your own portfolio, sharing with students what you keep in it and why you value it.
5. Encourage students to share their portfolios with school board members, parents, peers, and other classes.

Setting up portfolios in the classroom. Nance Wilson's students had not used portfolios previously; they started by putting Post-it notes on their papers and choosing some to keep in a folder. Students simply wrote a comment about a paper on a Post-it note, stuck it onto the paper, and filed the paper and note in a folder. They discussed what they put into their portfolios and why they chose to include it. Gradually, the students together planned what should go into a portfolio; they developed criteria for selecting and a process for collecting materials for their portfolios. To avoid having portfolios become a catchall for papers, they listed objectives or goals they wanted to achieve. They stapled the list to the side of their expandable portfolios. Each time they filed a paper, they checked off the objective that the paper fulfilled. The papers they inserted in the folders were relevant and illustrated a point or fulfilled an objective. The group decided to have regular "Portfolio Days" and "Portfolio Cleaning Days."

What Goes into a portfolio and who decides? A portfolio includes what the teacher and the students choose. The primary source of material is student work samples, including drafts of writing of all sorts from persuasive letters, to poems, to stories. Student journals with records of problem solving in groups make valuable entries. Written literature responses, play scripts, Readers' Theatre scripts, webs, character collages, timelines of book settings or series are all possibilities. Students are a natural source of information for portfolios. Self-evaluations, personal comments, self-reflection on progress in writing, spelling, goal setting, and peer evaluations are appropriate entries. The *Teaching Ideas: Step-by-Step Guide to Setting Up Portfolios* and *Checklist for Starting Portfolios* will help you and your class get going.

TEACHING IDEA

Addressing Individual Needs

STEP-BY-STEP GUIDE TO SETTING UP PORTFOLIOS

First Term

- Introduce the concept of portfolios.
- Show students your portfolio; discuss what you keep in it and why.
- Decide with students what will be included in their portfolios.
- Distribute expanding file folders.
- File baseline samples of key areas (writing, a reading miscue inventory, a math activity, etc.).
- Inform parents about the process.
- Introduce self-assessment procedures.
- Discuss criteria for selected areas of the language arts and reading.
- Hold regularly scheduled conferences to discuss work samples.
- Plan lessons based on portfolio assessment.
- Toward the end of the term:
    - Have students organize their portfolios and complete written evaluative comments about the portfolio samples.
    - Conduct end-of-term conferences.

Second Term

- Continue to develop minilessons based on information from conferences.
- Expand criteria charts for selection of work to be included.
- Conduct midterm goal and portfolio conferences.
- Toward the end of term:
    - Have students organize portfolios.
    - Complete teacher evaluations.
    - Conduct end-of-term evaluations.

Third Term

- Follow the same procedures as in second term.
- Invite parents to write a letter to their child about their portfolio.

Fourth Term

- Have each student evaluate their own and a partner's portfolio samples.
- Replace end-of-term conferences with letters about personal growth (student to teacher, teacher to student).
- Prepare work samples and letter to send on to the next teacher.
- Send portfolios home with students.

Source: Adapted from Rolling Valley School, Fairfax County, Virginia, and Clemmons, J., Laase, L., Cooper, D., Areglado, N., & Dill, M. (1993). *Portfolios in the classroom: A teacher's sourcebook* (pp. 51–60). New York: Scholastic Professional Books.

TEACHING IDEA

Assessing the Learning Environment

CHECKLIST FOR STARTING PORTFOLIOS

1. Choose one subject area and a purpose for keeping a portfolio, for example, written responses to selected trade books.
2. Establish selection criteria for what to put into the portfolio.
3. Create a space and filing system to keep the portfolios, using sturdy milk crates, portable file cases, cardboard cartons, or other large container.
4. Generate criteria for creating a rubric to judge the quality of the entries.
5. Model how to apply the rubric to a piece of work.
6. Have students assess their own work on a regular basis (see the *Teaching Ideas* on pages 480 and 481 in this chapter for examples).

Analyzing portfolios. Portfolios make it possible for both students and teachers to evaluate the process and products of learning continuously. Students can determine what they do well, what they would like to improve, and what they want to achieve by keeping simple records, work samples, writing occasional self-reflection papers, and meeting with teachers in joint assessment conferences. Teachers can determine how well their students are doing by meeting with their students to discuss their interests and how they affect reading and writing (or with other teachers to discuss the strategies and skills that help students learn). Students can examine others' reactions to what they write and reflect on their writing and reading responses. They can compare their evaluations of their work over time and make judgments about their own progress.

Teachers are required to make summative evaluations at grading periods, before parent or student conferences, and in preparation for reports to administrators or officials. They can evaluate the volume of reading and writing, the content it reflects about student interests, and the evidence of their growth as language users. Portfolios contain records of what students know and are able to do.

Rubrics for portfolios. Developing rubrics is a critical step in using portfolios for authentic assessment. **Rubrics** state criteria, standards, and specifications for performance in accomplishing a task. A rubric is a statement of what constitutes quality—a declaration of expectations—a means of self-assessment. Rubrics state the expected performance at each level. An

exemplar is a sample product that shows the level of performance described in the rubric.

Rubrics require teachers to clarify (to themselves, their students, and their parents) what they are trying to teach and what they think students should know and be able to do. For example, the *Teaching Idea: Early Reading/Writing Rubric* developed by Dorothy Strickland for kindergarten identifies specific skills to assess.

Teacher Michelle Carey worked with her third grade students to create the *Teaching Idea: Student-Designed Rubric for Writing*. She and her students also developed a student reflection sheet to accompany it, shown in the *Teaching Idea: Self-Assessment through Reflection.* Portfolio materials developed with students are meaningful to them; they phrase concepts in their own words and so they easily understand them. The *Teaching Idea: Rubric for Sixth Grade Science*

TEACHING IDEA

Assessing the Learner

EARLY READING/WRITING RUBRIC

Level 1	*Level 2*	*Level 3*	*Level 4*
Name Recognition and Writing			
Attempts writing own name	Writes part of name	Writes first name	Writes first and last name
Recognizes first name	Points out friend's name	Identifies classmates' names	Recognizes all classmates' names
Drawing-Writing			
Scribble writes	Writes from left to right about picture	Adds words to pictures drawn	Writes recognizable words
Draws picture	Expresses meaning	Writes and draws message	Conveys meaning through words and pictures
Alphabet Recognition and Writing			
Knows no letters	Recognizes first letter of name	Recognizes first name	Recognizes whole name
Shows little interest in writing letters	Writes random strings of letters	Attempts to write meaningful signs	Writes for a purpose, to convey a message, uses invented spelling

TEACHING IDEA

Assessing the Learner

STUDENT-DESIGNED RUBRIC FOR WRITING

(5) Excellent

- Used lots of descriptive words.
- Makes sense.
- Capitals and punctuation used correctly.
- Neatest handwriting.
- Spelled all words correctly.
- My best work!

(3) Pretty Good

- Used some descriptive words.
- Makes sense most of the time.
- Used some capitals and often punctuated correctly.
- Spelled most words correctly.
- Neat handwriting.
- OK, but not my very best work.

(1) Careless

- Hard to read, does not make sense.
- Sloppy handwriting.
- Did not capitalize or use correct punctuation.
- Rushed work.
- Spelled few words correctly.
- Used few descriptive words.
- I did not work as hard as I could on this piece.

TEACHING IDEA

Assessing the Learner

SELF-ASSESSMENT THROUGH REFLECTION

How Did I Do?

Name________________________________ Date __________________

Does this piece show your best work? Why?

How would you score this piece?

Why did you give yourself that score? Explain.

What do you think is the best part of this piece? Why?

What would you like to do better on your next piece?

TEACHING IDEA

Assessing the Learner

RUBRIC FOR SIXTH GRADE SCIENCE ESSAYS

Level 1	***Level 2***	***Level 3***	***Level 4***
Answers few questions/issues	Answers some questions/issues	Answers almost all questions/issues	Answers all questions/issues
Information is not accurate or complete	Information is somewhat accurate and somewhat complete	Information is mostly accurate and complete	Gives accurate and full information
Language does not reflect learned science vocabulary and is used incorrectly	Language does not reflect learned science vocabulary	Uses some science-specific language	Consistently uses science-specific language
Reasons, details, and examples are few and show little understanding of reading or lab work	Uses some reasons, examples, and details	Uses many reasons, examples, and details from readings and lab work	Consistently uses reasons, examples, and details from readings and lab work
Shows no plan of organization, difficult to understand	Organizational plan shows weaknesses	Has a plan for organization but does not follow through	Follows plan for organization of essay, including an introduction and a conclusion
Mechanical errors interfere with reading and understanding paragraphing	Has some mechanical errors	Very few mechanical errors	Makes few or no mechanical errors (i.e., spelling, punctuation, grammar)
Messiness interferes with reading or understanding	Paper has some crossouts, errors	Paper has few crossouts and typos	Paper is neatly done

Source: This rubric for science essays was developed by Ginnie Schroder with sixth grade students and teachers.

Essays was developed by Ginnie Schroder with sixth grade students and teachers.

Using portfolios for self-assessment

Having students learn to assess their work and monitor their own progress is an important goal of authentic assessment. This helps them take responsibility for their own learning and helps them use self-assessment to enhance their knowledge of content and performance of skills. Authentic assessments, such as those generally included in portfolios, support and encourage student self-assessment. Several researchers (Farr & Tone, 1994; Graves & Sunstein, 1992; and Paris & Ayres, 1994) recommend that students take part in the planning of their portfolios. During a portfolio conference, ask students to show the work that illustrates their usual performance, areas they want to improve, and examples that they think reflect their best work. Guide their evaluations with comments such as, "I see that you are really doing a good job with X but you still seem to be struggling with Y. Let's set a goal for the next marking period." An excellent use of portfolios comes during parent conferences. Dated student work samples reveal visible progress or the lack of it in student work.

Students may keep portfolios of their work, reading-response journals, a list of books they have read, and reading logs to accumulate a wealth of information to document growth. Students see their own progress when they study their journals and portfolios. The materials also help you know what to teach. Students' work gives evidence of what needs to be taught. Some

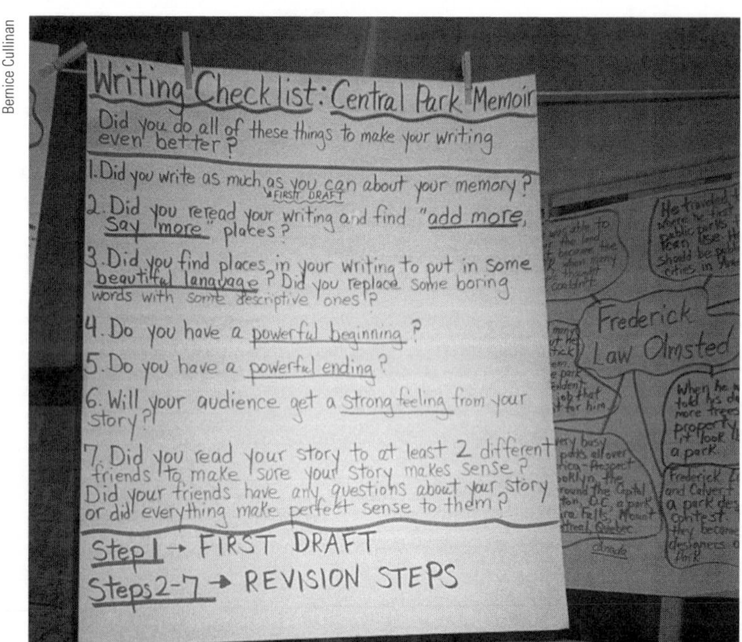

Bernice Cullinan

Encourage a variety of ways for students to assess themselves.

teachers devise a checklist to serve as a student self-assessment form. One approach has students reflect and assess what they have learned in letters to their parents at the end of a grading period. At the end of the year, students then write a letter to next year's teacher. They list goals by making statements such as "I hope to be able to do . . . I want to learn . . ." Figures 12.9 and 12.10 give samples of such letters.

Using portfolios to guide instruction

Teachers combine their knowledge of a subject area with information from observations, portfolios, anecdotal notes, checklists, and conferences to make instructional decisions. The language arts curriculum encompasses a

FIGURE 12.9

Vincent's Letter to Next Year's Teacher

Dear Sixth Grade Teacher,

This year I have accomplished many goals. I also have goals for next year. I shall talk about those later. I will talk about what I like to write and how I see myself as a writer. These are important so that you can know what I like in my stories and see what I can do to make the stories richer.

I like to write poetry because I am able to put a great force in what I write with many backup details to help push the force. I also like to write adventure stories but I did not really write any this year. In my adventure stories I like them to be long but still holding the viewer's grip.

I see myself as a writer who wants to create a total picture of a scene in the reader's mind with one sentence. I also see myself as a writer who wants the viewer to see the writing in a main track but also in different tracks.

Goals that I accomplished were to use description every way I can to make the story more "seeable." Another goal that I accomplished was having a main feeling to my poetry.

I am now able to use quotation marks freely as I choose. Another goal was to make something short abut not meaningless such as a few powerful phrases. It is now easier to combine ideas and make something worth more. I am able to start a poem slowly and the end flows along still with description.

Goals for next year are to see if I can write different types of stories such as a description writing piece. I would also like to see if I can write one piece but then write it in a different style to see the differences and see how flexible my writing is. As I end this I think I have and will improve greatly.

Vincent McGill

comprehensive body of knowledge, skills, and strategies that students need to master. Portfolios help teachers take advantage of multiple assessment strategies that link directly to curriculum materials. The results of norm-referenced and criterion-referenced tests, described earlier in the chapter, may be collected and analyzed as a whole assessment rather than as an isolated assessment. Publishers who create textbooks and other instructional materials for use in the classroom frequently develop both norm-referenced and criterion-referenced tests. Having assessment instruments linked to the instructional materials becomes an incentive for teachers to use both aspects of a publisher's products.

You can devise many alternative ways to assess mastery by identifying the skills expected for the grade level and choosing ways for students to demonstrate mastery within a meaningful context. For example, if you expect your students to make intelligent use of commas at their grade level, rather than give them a test in which they place commas on an artificially constructed manuscript, instead look at their work in their writing folders or portfolios to

FIGURE 12.10

Colleen's Letter to Next Year's Teacher

Dear Sixth Grade Teacher,

In fifth grade, I don't see myself as a very good writer. I feel like I set standards for myself in terms of scores and I can't seem to meet them all.

I did learn minimally this year. I excelled in leads and endings and I also learned a lot of new vocabulary words from book talk and silent reading.

I would like to be better at expository writing. (I know we do a lot in sixth grade.) I would like to learn how to turn notes into writing.

This year I also wanted to work on leads and poetry. This year I learned that poetry does not have to rhyme. You can express your feelings better.

The kinds of writing I like are, fiction/fantasy, and poetry.

I am good at writing leads and at writing endings.

Your new student,

Colleen Cook

see if they use commas when needed. This tests the application of a skill; it incorporates good teaching and authentic assessment.

When you look through students' portfolios and find that few have a sense of their own voice in their writing, you may want to develop a minilesson on capturing voice in words. Collect samples from writers with lively, dignified, intense, and restrained writing voices, use them as models, and talk about what they do. Similarly, you can pull together the students who don't use commas appropriately and have a session on commas. Portfolios are living proof of what students need and what you need to teach.

Student and teacher portfolio conferences

Student-teacher conferences are a key means of supporting student self-assessment. The primary purpose of conferences is to help students understand their strengths and needs. Unlike more formal self-evaluation procedures, conferences allow teachers to follow the lead of students, offering the feedback necessary to prompt as well as guide reflections. The number of conferences held varies widely among teachers; however, most agree that a minimum of one conference per term or marking period is critical. Such conferences are in addition to those held around individual pieces of work, such as in writing workshop. Tierney, Carter, and Desai (1991) identify three types of conferences used in conjunction with portfolios.

1. *Planning conferences* help students pull together their portfolios, including self-evaluative remarks. For example, "I don't know if this is good enough to go in. I did a better job on the story when I did it for the class newspaper. What do you think? Should I keep this draft?"
2. *Sharing conferences* involve having students share their portfolios with classmates. For example, "This is what I've written about bugs and creepy crawlers. I have some information pieces, some pictures, and some jokes about them."
3. *Formative conferences* involve joint assessment of the portfolios by the teacher and each student as they develop goals for the future. For example, "I've learned about descriptive writing, and I think I want to learn about persuasive writing next." "Why don't you think about expository writing, too? That's a natural direction to take after descriptive and persuasive."

Reporting to parents. Portfolios are extremely valuable in reports to parents and administrators. Marianne Marino's sixth grade students share their portfolios with peers at the end of each marking period. This becomes a practice session for sharing them with adults; students prepare their portfolios to share with family members for at-school parent conferences or take-home sharing sessions. The family member responds to the work samples on a special sheet inserted at the back of the portfolio.

STRUCTURED PERFORMANCE ASSESSMENT

Increasing numbers of school districts are attempting to bridge the gap between classroom assessment that informs instructional decisions and more formal assessment that informs systemwide decisions. One form of formal assessment, **structured performance samples,** involves observing children participating in tasks that are part of, or closely resemble, classroom tasks and are systematically assessed to answer predetermined questions (Teale, 1988). Periodic, formal assessments using structured performance samples involve setting an interesting task for students and evaluating their performance on that task. This differs from regular teaching only in that a predetermined task is set and students' performance is formally evaluated. That is, if a class regularly reads and discusses children's books in small groups, you might target specific discussions as time to formally assess both reading and social behaviors. Formal assessments that combine reading and writing might involve giving students a passage to read and a writing task to perform after reading that closely reflects the kinds of reading and writing that occur routinely in your classroom.

These performance assessments can be structured so that they occur across classrooms or school districts, and developed so that they are criterion-referenced (may be scored according to predetermined criteria). They then become measures that accurately reflect student performance as well as "key indicators of accountability and sources of directions for key decisions, such as curriculum development" (Farr, 1992, p. 34).

Performance assessment, anecdotal notes, checklists, and portfolios that contain language artifacts, and student self-assessments are part of an integrated assessment program that reflects the complexity and variability of language learning.

SUMMARY

Teachers who carefully observe and assess their students' reading, writing, speaking, listening, and viewing performances are able to make good instructional decisions and develop appropriate lessons based on their students' needs. Authentic assessment of students' work is critical in ensuring that all students are learning up to their potential. Rubrics, often created with students, clearly state the criteria for judging the quality and level of excellence of student work.

Teachers and students collaboratively assess real work, collected in student portfolios, to identify the strengths of learners and to report on their progress. The information in portfolios is also used to encourage students' self-assessment, ownership, and responsibility for their own growth. Because students and teachers regularly discuss individual progress toward language arts goals based on many work samples, they are able to share their insights with parents and administrators.

Effective assessment fosters reflective thinking on the part of students and teachers. Students set personal goals, while teachers set goals for individuals and for the group. Progress is monitered, outcomes examined, and results are used to rethink the past and plan the future.

ACTIVITIES

1. **Find a classroom where students are keeping portfolios for one or more areas in the language arts.** Meet with two students to talk about the work they have included in their portfolios and why they have selected each piece. Compare and contrast the students' work from early in the school year to the last piece or two in their portfolios.
2. **Start your own writing portfolio.** Keep samples of your work for one semester or more. Record the date on each sample. Use the criteria stated in William Zinsser's book *On Writing Well* (HarperResource, 2001) to assess the quality of your writing.
3. **Conduct a case study of a student.** Record your observations of the student with peers and alone, at work and at play, at school and at home. Make inferences about the child's use of language. Administer an informal reading/writing inventory and a reading/writing attitude survey. Ask the student for work samples in several subject areas. Meet with the student to collaboratively assess progress and growth.
4. **Find a local artist who keeps a portfolio.** Invite the artist to your classroom to show students the contents of the portfolio. Ask the artist to discuss criteria used for selecting the various pieces kept in the portfolio. Discuss with students any parallels between the artist's portfolio and their own.

FURTHER READING

Anderson, C. (2000). *How's it going? A practical guide to conferring with student writers.* Portsmouth, NH: Heinemann.

Bridges, L. (1995). *Assessment: Continuous learning.* York, ME: Stenhouse.

DeFina, A. (1992). *Portfolio assessment: Getting started.* New York: Scholastic.

Farr, R., & Tone, B. (1994). *Portfolio and performance assessment: Helping students evaluate their progress as readers and writers.* Fort Worth, TX: Harcourt Brace.

Gill, K. (1993). *Process and portfolios in writing instruction.* Champaign, IL: National Council of Teachers of English.

Hansen, J. (1998). *When learners evaluate.* Portsmouth, NH: Heinemann.

Roderick, J. A. (Ed.). (1991). *Context-responsive approaches to assessing children's language.* Urbana, IL: National Conference of Research in English.

REFERENCES

Au, K. H., Carroll, J. H., & Scheu, J. A. (1997). *Balanced literacy instruction: A teacher's resource book.* Norwood, MA: Gordon.

Au, K. H., Scheu, J. A., Kawakami, A. J., & Herman, P. A. (1990). Assessment and accountability in a whole literacy curriculum. *The Reading Teacher, 43,* 574–578.

Boehm, A. E., & Weinberg, R. A. (1987). *The classroom observer.* New York: Teachers College Press.

Bouchard, D. with Sutton, W. (2001). *The gift of reading: A guide for educators and parents.* New York: Orca.

Clay, M. (1979). *The early detection of reading difficulties* (3rd ed.). Portsmouth, NH: Heinemann.

______. (1982). *Observing young readers.* Portsmouth, NH: Heinemann.

Clemmons, J., Laase, L., Cooper, D., Areglado, N., & Dill, M. (1993). *Portfolios in the classroom: A teacher's sourcebook.* New York: Scholastic.

Dillon, D. R. (2000). *Kids insight: Reconsidering how to meet the literacy needs of all students.* Newark, DE: International Reading Association.

Dwyer, J. (1989). Assessing Oral Language. In J. Dwyer (Ed.), *A sea of talk* (pp. 94–105). Portsmouth, NH: Heinemann.

Farr, R. (1992). Putting it all together: Solving the reading assessment puzzle. *The Reading Teacher, 46,* 26–37.

Farr, R., & Tone, B. (1994). *Portfolio and performance assessment: Helping students evaluate their progress as readers and writers.* Fort Worth, TX: Harcourt Brace.

Fresch, M. J., & Wheaton, A. (2002). *Teaching and assessing spelling: A practical approach that strikes the balance between whole-group and individualized instruction.* New York: Scholastic.

Galda, L. (2001). *Kids insight: Looking through the faraway end.* Newark, DE: International Reading Association.

Goodman, K. L. (1983). A linguistic study of cues and miscues in reading. In H. Singer & R. B. Ruddell (Eds.), *Theoretical Models and Processes of Reading* (3rd ed.). Newark, DE: International Reading Association.

Graves, D., & Sunstein, B. (1992). *Portfolio portraits.* Portsmouth, NH: Heinemann.

Grimes, N. (1995). You've gotta have heart! In the "Poetry Plus" column by M. Strickland. *Creative Classroom* (Jan./Feb. 1999), 37–39.

Halliday, M. (1975). *Explorations in the functions of language.* London: Arnold.

Harvey, S., & Goudvis, A. (2000). *Strategies that work: Teaching comprehension to enhance understanding.* York, ME: Stenhouse.

Harwayne, S. (1999). *Going public: Priorities and practice at the Manhattan New School.* Portsmouth, NH: Heinemann.

Hickman, J. (1981). A new perspective on response to literature: Research in an elementary school setting. *Research in the Teaching of English, 15,* 343–354.

Keene, E. O., & Zimmerman, S. (1997). *Mosaic of thought: Teaching comprehension in a reader's workshop.* Portsmouth, NH: Heinemann.

Kushner, M. (1999). *Public speaking for dummies.* New York: IDG Books, www.Kushnergroup.com

Lee, D. M., & Rubin, J. B. (1979). *Children and language: Reading and writing, talking and listening.* Belmont, CA: Wadsworth.

Lundsteen, S. (1979). *Listening: Its impact on reading and other language arts.* Urbana, IL: National Council of Teachers of English.

Micklos, J. (2001). Results of NAEP testing. *Reading Today, 18*(6), 13. www.reading.org

Neuman, S., & Celano B. (2001). Access to print in low-income and middle-income communities: An ecological study of four neighborhoods. *Reading Research Quarterly, 36*(1), 8–26.

New Jersey State Department of Education. (1998). *Directory of test specifications and sample items* (p. 19). Trenton, NJ: Self.

Paris, S., & Ayres, L. R. (1994). *Becoming reflective students and teachers with portfolios and authentic assessment.* Washington, D.C.: American Psychological Association.

Pellegrini, A. D., Galda, L., & Rubin, D. L. (1984). Context in text: The development of oral and written language in two genres. *Child Development, 55,* 1549–1555.

Pinnell, G. S. (1985). Ways to look at the functions of children's language. In A. Jaggar & M. T. Smith-Burke (Eds.), *Observing the language learner* (pp. 57–72). Newark, DE: International Reading Association.

Ray, K. W. (1999). *Wondrous words: Writers and writing in the elementary classroom.* Urbana, IL: National Council of Teachers of English.

Strickland, D. S., Dillon, R., Funkhouser, L., Glick, M., & Rogers, C. (1989). Research currents: Classroom dialog during literature response groups. *Language Arts, 66,* 192–200.

Strickland, M. R. (1999). Poetry plus. *Creative Classrooms* (Jan./Feb.), 37–39.

Taberski, S. (1999). *On solid ground.* Portsmouth, NH: Heinemann.

Taylor, B., Peterson, D., Pearson, D., Jaynes, C., Knezek, S., Bender, P., & Sarroub, L. (2001). *School reform in reading in high-poverty schools.* (Paper presented at AERA, Seattle, April, 2001.)

Taylor, D. (1991). From the child's point of view. In J. Roderick (Ed.), *Context-responsive approaches to assessing children's language* (pp. 32–51). Urbana, IL: National Council of Teachers of English/National Conference on Research in English.

Teale, W. (1988). Developmentally appropriate assessment of reading and writing in the early childhood classroom. *The Elementary School Journal, 89*(2), 173–183.

Tierney, R., Carter, M., & Desai, L. E. (1991). *Portfolio assessment in the reading and writing classroom.* Norwood, MA: Gordon.

Tough, J. (1985). *Listening to children talking: A guide to the appraisal of children's use of language.* London: Ward Lock Educational.

Tunnell, M. O., Calder, J. E., & Justen, J. E. (1988). A short form reading attitude survey. *Reading Improvement, 25,* 146–151.

Vacca, J. L., Vacca, R. T., & Gove, M. K. (2000). *Reading and learning to read* (4th ed.). New York: Addison Wesley Longman.

Valencia, S. W., & Place, N. A. (1994). Literacy portfolios for teaching, learning, and accountability: The Bellevue Literacy Assessment Project. In S. W. Valencia, E. H. Hiebert, & P. P. Afflerbach (Eds.), *Authentic reading assessment: Practices and possibilities* (pp. 134–156). Newark, DE: International Reading Association.

Zinsser, W. O. (1990). *On writing well: An informal guide to writing fiction.* New York: Perennial Library.

CHILDREN'S LITERATURE REFERENCES

Dotlich, R. (2001). *Riddles come rumbling: Poems to ponder.* Honesdale, PA: Boyds Mills/Wordsong.

Finchler, J. (2000). *Testing Miss Malarkey.* Illus. Kevin O'Malley. New York: Walker.

Paterson, K. (1978). *The great Gilly Hopkins.* New York: HarperCollins.

Pattou, E. (2001). *Mrs. Spitzer's garden.* Illus. Tricia Tusa. San Diego, CA: Harcourt.

Language Arts Teaching and Learning across the Curriculum

CHAPTER OUTLINE

Inquiry as a Way of Knowing

Planning an Inquiry-based Curriculum
- *Guidelines for Planning*
- *The Guidelines in Action*

Bringing Language and Literacy Together Through Inquiry
- *Talking to Learn*
- *Listening to Learn*
- *Reading to Learn*
- *Writing to Learn*
- *Viewing to Learn*

Teaching as Professional Inquiry and Change
- *Teachers as Learners in the Primary Grades*
- *Teachers as Learners in the Intermediate Grades*
- *Teachers as Learners in the Upper Grades*

Summary

Activities

Further Reading

References

Key Standard

Teachers of language arts and reading are skillful in the ways they integrate instruction within the language arts (listening, speaking, reading, writing, representing, and viewing) and with content-area subjects across the curriculum. Such teachers:

- Are knowledgeable about methods of inquiry.
- Know how to plan for the integration of the language arts through thematic units across the curriculum.
- Use a variety of techniques to build and capitalize on student interest and enthusiasm.
- Build on and extend students' background knowledge.
- Help students generate questions relevant to a unit of study.
- Systematically teach research skills and other tools of inquiry.
- Provide opportunities to use oral language, reading, writing, listening, viewing, and visually representing what they know.
- Help students share what they have learned with others.
- View themselves as lifelong learners, engaging in ongoing professional development activities that involve inquiry and reflection about the learning and teaching in their classrooms.

To get a preview of Chapter 13 and learn about teaching language arts across the curriculum, visit the Chapter 13 section of the accompanying *Language Arts* CD-ROM.

Kali, a beginning teacher, met Terence, who is from Johannesburg, South Africa, when they served as International Camp Counselors. Kali tells her middle-grade students about Terence, a soccer player. Terence's father was a professional soccer player, and his mother was an Olympic swimmer in South Africa. The students are interested in professional athletes and immediately laser in on Terence, soccer, and South Africa. Kali's students decide they want to study South Africa. She agrees because it fits into the curriculum; her students want to know more about the country; and they have access to a knowledgeable resource person. She asks the class to think about what they would like to know and to list questions they want to answer. Their initial list includes:

> *What language do South Africans speak?*
>
> *Is it safe to live in South Africa? What is apartheid?*
>
> *Is there another country right in the middle of South Africa?*
>
> *What animals live there and in what kind of environments?*
>
> *What sports do people play there?*

Kali realizes that she will need to do some serious and careful planning to make this a worthwhile inquiry for her students.

Kali immediately recognizes her students' interest in South Africa as an excellent entry into an area of study that might otherwise seem remote and unappealing. In-depth studies of the continents of Africa and Asia are a part of the social studies curriculum in this middle school. Fortunately for Kali and her students, however, the flexibility in the curriculum allows her to focus their study on South Africa, even if it does not link directly to the content of the social studies curriculum. More important, even as a first-year teacher, Kali realizes that many of the strategies that her students will need to develop their oral and written language skills can be taught through virtually any content of interest and importance to them.

Inquiry as a Way of Knowing

Innovation and change in educational practice have guided teachers as they investigate different methods to teach different types of curricula; they have also helped teachers move from skills to literature-based programs to integrated curricula. In a skills-driven curriculum, students memorize numerous facts and demonstrate their knowledge on standardized tests. Experts or people in power establish criteria to assess acceptable, minimal, and failing performance. In a literature-based curriculum, teachers supplement a basal text with a variety of literature. In some cases, teachers teach only books; the program becomes a course in literary criticism. Unfortunately, a literature-based curriculum sometimes becomes a study of specific books (and thus a study of literature only) rather than a broad-based approach to multiple points of view and multiple ways of learning. Many teachers now use an inquiry approach that weaves subject areas together around a topic in an integrated curriculum with a variety of resources to enhance the study. The chief obstacles to integrated programs are limited access to resources due to lack of knowledge, financial considerations, and an insufficient amount of information available on a topic.

An inquiry approach is neither a strategy nor a method, but is instead a philosophical stance that arises from inquisitiveness, questions, and curiosity. It requires that teachers listen carefully to students who ask What, Why, and How questions. Teachers use student questions and interests to frame the curriculum. This approach also requires teachers to take on many roles. Pataray-Ching and Roberson (2002) suggest that inquiry teachers often assume six roles in their classrooms:

1. Teachers engage in self-inquiry, asking questions of personal and professional inquiry to improve students' learning.
2. Teachers carefully organize the physical environment of the classroom to motivate interest and to support access to resources.
3. Teachers listen and observe students in order to support their interests and push their thinking and further inquiry.
4. Teachers continually pose genuine and thoughtful questions that encourage reflective thinking and clarity on topics under study.
5. Teachers assist students in organizing their inquiry in ways that establish habits of mind and procedures for independent learning.
6. Teachers are co-learners in the classroom—open to learning *by* and *with* students.

Planning an Inquiry-Based Curriculum

GUIDELINES FOR PLANNING

When you plan for inquiry-based instruction, you have many things to think about: the theme or topic; the goals; how you might introduce the topic; the activities with which to engage students; and the various ways to assess the learning. What follows is a framework for planning that we have used with teachers at various grade levels to structure their planning and pursuit of the unit of study. At the same time, the framework allows them enough flexibility to accommodate school and district curriculum goals and the specific needs of their students.

Initial planning

Your initial planning includes everything that needs to be in place before the in-depth study begins. During this stage, you select the theme of the inquiry and establish key goals and objectives.

Selecting the theme. This may be a content theme, which generally links directly to the science or social studies curriculum. Or, it may be a literature-based inquiry, which may be fiction or nonfiction and center on a topic, such as stories about the Civil War. It may also be an in-depth study of an author's work and life. Or, it may center on a particular literary genre, such as biography or historical fiction. Either content-area or literature-based inquiry may emanate from the district curriculum guide as something that you are required to teach and students to learn. Themes may also spring from the naturally occurring events in the news or in the environment or from students' interests. A strong curriculum will include all of these types of themes over the course of the year.

Establishing goals and objectives. Goals and objectives fall into two basic categories. One category links to the content under study, the knowledge that students will gain from the unit of work. The other category involves the language processes, or language arts, to be developed through the unit, including written, oral, and visual language. You need to link the goals and objectives to the district's content standards, making sure that specific areas of the curriculum are addressed as you teach in a way that has unity and meaning for your students. Of course, as students move through the unit, you will find many opportunities for learning that are not established in the initial planning. Think of that as a bonus to the many objectives that must be deliberately planned for in advance.

Introducing the theme

Teachers often complain that students are not interested in the topics they must study. They also complain about students' lack of background knowledge. Both of these problems can be offset with a little thought and planning up front. Of course, you won't always be as lucky as Kali to come across a naturally occurring event that whets students' appetite for learning. In most cases, you must plan for some kind of motivational event. Strategies that we have seen used successfully include a display of artifacts from a particular period, an invited guest speaker who creates interest and evokes questions, or a demonstration or science experiment that arouses curiosity. Try to schedule a field trip to a museum or other point of interest related to a unit of study *before* you launch the unit rather than after, which is more typical. Any of these methods can get students' attention and stimulate discussion. Concepts and terms related to the topic begin to emerge right from the beginning. Both teachers and students are frequently amazed by how much students already know. Inaccurate background knowledge will also emerge, which you can use as a motivational tool for inquiry. Of course, reading aloud and showing videos related to an area may also be used as initial motivators, but in our experience these are best saved for the actual study. True hands-on activities seem to provide the best stimulation and motivation.

Brainstorming activities, in which students share what they think they know about a topic, are very appropriate at this point. Followed by discussion, the brainstorming can lead to a series of questions listing what students decide they want to know about a topic. This can lead to a discussion of the many ways to investigate the answers to their questions. In today's information age, even the very youngest students should know that they have multiple sources of information: books and other print materials, computer databases,

Bernice Cullinan

In this age of technology, students use multiple sources for information including computer databases and the Internet.

interviews with knowledgeable people, and firsthand gathering of actual materials and data. Much of the time students spend in their quest for information will be spent searching for answers. Many of your instructional strategies will be designed to help them learn where to search, how to search, how to select what is appropriate to their questions, how to organize what they learn, and how to share it with others.

Planning ongoing activities

Virtually every instructional strategy described in this book can be applied to an inquiry-based study. As you and your students embark on your investigation, you—and they—will engage in a variety of instructional activities in which they—and you—gain knowledge about the topic under study, improve their abilities to learn through language, and improve their use of language. Examples of ongoing opportunities for teaching and learning include library research strategies; computer search strategies; field-based observations, including note taking; interview strategies, including questioning and note taking; response strategies to literature, videos, and speakers; and writing-process strategies.

Assessment

Both ongoing, formative assessment and summative assessment at the end of the unit are important. Base your assessment activities on the established combination of knowledge and process goals and objectives, and link them to the district's content standards. Opportunities for assessment include project work, either individual or group projects; class participation, both whole class and small group; personalized reading conferences with you on related reading material; reading logs; personalized writing conferences with you on writing assignments; demonstrations of the application of skills and strategies taught through all or selected language arts activities; demonstrations of knowledge gained through all or selected activities; and teacher-made tests.

THE GUIDELINES IN ACTION

Students' initial enthusiasm for South Africa leads Kali to pursue that topic as a potential inquiry-based thematic unit. She reads the school district's curriculum guide, the state standards, and an early draft of this textbook for guidance. The district's content goals are to learn about another country, to become aware of different languages and customs, and to learn about the nature and habitat of animals in South Africa. Its process goals include learning and improving students' abilities in the language arts of listening, speaking, reading, writing, viewing, and visually representing information. Kali carefully includes activities and skills that relate to researching a topic, evaluating information, and organizing information for presentation to others. She makes listening, speaking, reading, writing, viewing, and visually representing knowledge a natural part of the unit.

Motivational stimuli

Kali and her students eagerly anticipate welcoming Terence, who has graciously agreed to be the class's first guest speaker. When Terence arrives, the students bombard him with questions:

Is it safe to live in Johannesburg? "Yes, but the crime rate is high in cities especially at night, often the result of racial differences." What was your school like? "We have school year-round. We have summer when you have winter. It's very warm there, 60°F to 90°F in the summer." What do you call cotton candy? "Candy floss." How does it feel to have another country (Lesotho) right in the middle of your country? "It seems strange at first because the laws change and everything is different, but you get used to it quickly." What position do you play in soccer? "I'm the goal keeper." Is your team good? "Yes, we are semiprofessionals." The questions continue until Terence invites the students out to play soccer.

Brainstorming vocabulary

Kali describes her strategy: "First we brainstorm to create a list of words students think might relate to our topic; it's OK if the list includes some words that do not relate to the topic. Students dictate, and I write the list on the chalkboard or overhead transparency as they explain how the words relate or do not relate to the topic. Later the group decides which words should remain on the list; they copy the list into their journals. This exercise activates their prior knowledge and helps them share knowledge; they learn from each other."

Kali's students learn that South Africa has eleven official languages that have variations in pronunciation of specific words and dialects: South African or World English, Afrikaans, Ndebele, Northern and Southern Sotho, Swati, Tsonga, Tswana, Venda, Xhosa, and Zulu. The language situation was partially affected by apartheid, which separated the different peoples living there and gave particular privileges to those of European origin. Using the dictionary, students find that the word *apartheid,* literally "aparthood" in the South African language Afrikaans, means "a rigid policy of segregation." No wonder there are so many languages!

Ongoing activities

Kali finds very few research resources, but the school media specialist works to provide more. Students search encyclopedias and dictionaries to locate maps and definitions. They discover basic information: South Africa is a country in southern Africa that became a fully democratic republic in 1994; the currency is the rand; and the capital is Pretoria. They discover that the Kingdom of Lesotho is a country in southern Africa bordered on all sides by South Africa. It is like an island inside South Africa and became independent from Britain in 1966.

Kali continues to search public libraries and bookstores to gather books for her classroom library, but unfortunately most of the books are out of date, published before apartheid was voted unconstitutional in 1994. She e-mails friends in South Africa and talks to travel agents familiar with the area. Even the Internet has very little information. The students consider other ways to investigate their topic. Based on their early questions, interests, and the available resources, Kali chooses to concentrate on weather, sports, animals, monetary practices, and government, topics that can be integrated into social studies, science, math, art, and language arts.

Reading, viewing, and visually representing information

Kali and the media specialist search for films, videos, theater, art books, art exhibitions, and books for reading aloud. They find the movie *The Lion King,* native African art books, travel brochures, and African dance videos. They locate revealing trade books about the country and its people: Uzo Unobagha's *Off to the Sweet Shores of Africa and Other Talking Drum Rhymes,* Isaac Olaleye's *The Distant Talking Drum: Poems from Nigeria,* Floyd Cooper's *Mandela: From the Life of the South African Statesman,* Conrad Stein's *Cape Town,* Ken Wilson-Max's *Halala Means Welcome: A Book of Zulu Words,* Michael March's *Guide to South Africa,* and Beverly Naidoo's *Journey to Jo'burg: A South African Story.*

Basis of the thematic unit

Kali explains: "I'm starting with a focus on science and animals because I know how much kids like animals. I want them to search for information from multiple sources and to observe several animals to identify specific characteristics. I also want them to communicate to others the information they learn through travel magazines, films, and books. *National Geographic* and photo essays about animals contain excellent descriptions and illustrations of Africa's animals.

"Next, I introduce the 'Big 5' animals native to Africa—giraffe, rhinoceros, elephant, lion, and zebra. We discuss the ones we have in our area zoos. After introductory activities, student pairs choose an animal to study, describe, and illustrate; their illustration and description is placed in a class book we call 'Purrs and Grrs.' I evaluate their entries based on unit goals for researching and presenting information.

"We need to explore the difference between the currencies of U.S. dollars and S.A. rands. I give students a conversion chart showing that 1 dollar = 8 rands and ask them to convert 4 dollars to rands, and 240 rands to dollars. This leads to a series of lessons on using different number bases. We also estimate how much specific foods cost, purchase supplies, and prepare a South African meal using the closest equivalent products. And we learn to convert Fahrenheit to Celsius, which is how South Africans measure temperature.

"Language arts and literature permeate the entire thematic unit. We locate 'key-pals' through teacher friends in South Africa, and my students correspond with their students. We look at travel videos, search web sites, and read current trade books, fiction, poetry, and nonfiction books as well as magazines.

Students write in their reader-response logs and record facts and ideas for the informational books they are preparing."

Organizing what they have learned

"Students systematically record relevant information in their journals. As a culminating activity, everyone contributes to a class booklet that encompasses our main subjects: animals, foods, currency, weather, government, sports, and any other things we have learned. We discover that we have learned a lot about South Africa and want to visit there some day."

Students gather information

On the left side of a double-page journal, students write a question they ask under "What I Want to Know." On the opposite side of the page they write "What I've Learned So Far." They continue to add to the list of questions they want to ask and record the relevant information learned as they obtain it. Part of the learning is selecting relevant information from what they find.

Students share and demonstrate what they have learned

Student sharing of what they have learned continues for many weeks and shows up in various ways. Students present informational books they have compiled individually and in small groups. Murals of jungle environments appear on classroom walls and in hallways. Habitats created in terrariums nurture small creatures; future environmentalists record conditions conducive to growth. Kali schedules individual and group oral reports daily, and frequently invites guest experts to class. She also holds individual writing and reading conferences, gives teacher-made tests, and observes students' application of the skills and strategies taught. Her ongoing assessment involves students, parents, media specialists, administrators, and peers.

Bringing Language and Literacy Together through Inquiry

TALKING TO LEARN

We humans use language to communicate and to learn about the world in which we live. We learn the linguistic and social rules for using language by participating in its use with others. Teachers can observe children's oral language use by tapping into their ongoing stream of language through careful observation and by taking anecdotal records or tape recordings. Psychologists (Piaget, Weaver, & Inhelder, 1972) and linguists (Chomsky, 1965) have discarded the notion that a child merely imitates or mimics language; instead they developed the concept that a child is a hypothesis tester, a thinker who over time unconsciously formulates the rules of language intuitively. Children are not passive responders who echo whatever they hear; they develop a grammar and actively discover how language works. Children acquire linguistic and communicative competence through interaction with people and objects (Brown, 1973; Wells, 1981). According to Halliday (1975), children express meaning through their earliest communications; they use different cries for hunger, for loneliness, and for pain. Prelinguistic children use nonverbal means to express their biological needs, to regulate the behaviors of others, and to assert their own importance. By the time they utter their first words, children already understand what language is for and how it functions in human interaction.

Teachers develop strategies to facilitate talking in the classroom. They include pair-share or partner reading and talking. All the teacher needs to say is, "Turn to your neighbor and discuss the book you just read." These practices, also called buddy reading or shared reading, encourage kids to talk about the books they read. That's what adults want to do, so why not children?

Book talk

Talk is natural. We all like to talk about the books we read. Notice the way Oprah Winfrey moved books from low sales to the Best Seller List. She simply read the books and talked about them. She invited other people to talk about the books, and sales went even higher. The television book talks correspond to classroom literature circles, book clubs, book-sharing time, and show and tell, some of the few opportunities for students to talk more than teachers. During show and tell, children give a narrative account about a past event or an object brought from home; in Book Clubs they discuss plot, characters, setting, theme, language style, and how a book relates to their personal life (text-to-self) or to the world at large (text-to-life). They discuss how one book reminds them of another one (text-to-text). They learn to read more critically by discussing books with peers.

LISTENING TO LEARN

One of the times students are willing to listen is when teachers are reading aloud. Anderson and colleagues (1985) summarized years of research and stated in *Becoming a Nation of Readers* that the single most important activity for building the knowledge required for eventual success in reading is reading aloud to children (p. 23). The benefits are greatest when the child is an active

Bernice Cullinan

Reading aloud to children is one of the most important activities leading to their success as readers.

participant, engaging in discussions about stories. It is a practice that should continue throughout the grades (pp. 23, 51), as numerous studies have affirmed (Fielding, Wilson & Anderson, 1986; Greany, 1980; Walberg & Tsai, 1984; Trelease, 1990; 2001).

In Melissa Reichelderfer's (2002) third grade classroom in Chambersburg, Pennsylvania, both she and her "Super Readers" read aloud every day. Describing the program in "Bringing Out the 'Super Reader' in Everyone," Reichelderfer explains that Super Readers are students who read aloud to small groups of students every day. The sessions last 15–20 minutes, allowing approximately 15 minutes for reading the book and 5 minutes for discussion. She uses the time to share favorite stories and to model what good reading looks like and sounds like. She says that "good" reading behaviors involve reading with fluency and expression. Reading sounds more like a conversation than a labored, drawn-out process. Super Readers get an opportunity to read favorite stories orally; this encourages them to practice good reading behaviors. Every child in the group has an equal opportunity to practice and become a Super Reader, including struggling, at-risk readers.

Early in the school year Reichelderfer sends home a letter that informs parents about the class's Super Reader literacy event. Students may choose any book, usually one that takes about 15 minutes to read aloud, that they feel comfortable reading. Students prepare by reading and rereading the stories silently and orally. Rereading the stories builds confidence, fluency, and expression. She encourages students to practice reading their books orally at home with their parents as the audience. The support and involvement of the parents is important to the success of the Super Reader program.

The Super Reader program has many benefits: it adds to the balanced literacy program; students share with their peers in a nonthreatening environment; the preparation needed to become a Super Reader involves rereading a book many times, which leads to confidence and fluency; and being a Super Reader makes students more aware of good reading behaviors. Finally, and most importantly, students view themselves as readers. Reichelderfer witnessed tremendous growth in all her students and continues the Super Reader program. Evidence-based practice in teaching low-achieving students appears in a more comprehensive report by Strickland, Ganske, and Monroe (2002).

READING TO LEARN

Many schools use a combination of textbooks and trade books to develop a program of learning to read as well as a program of reading to learn. Teachers' guides and instructors' manuals that accompany textbooks suggest lesson plans, activities, discussion questions, and independent activities; however, problems arise if the textbooks are too difficult for some students, too abstract for others, or too simplistic for a few. Using a variety of trade books provides a wide range of readability, a sharp focus on a particular topic, and a choice for students. It is difficult to teach students to think critically if they read only one textbook and from it arrive at one right answer for a question. Learning to think critically requires children to read a variety of sources, compare accounts, evaluate diverse reports, and take ownership of their own learning. The thousands of excellent trade books that are widely available make it possible to provide alternative sources and excellent models of writing that get students excited about learning.

Using fiction and nonfiction trade books in every area of the curriculum allows students to:

- Choose books on topics that interest them.
- Find books at their independent reading level.
- Explore different kinds of texts.
- Compare reports on the same topic.
- Read focused reports by experts.
- Explore varied perspectives and topics.
- Immerse themselves in a culture.
- Assess the impact of scientific discoveries on humans.

Each content area has specific ways—discipline-related ways to think, talk, and write—to structure its information. For example, science relies heavily on reports of experiments, step-by-step directions, and expository prose. Writers in social studies often use chronological narratives to trace the development of a historical period, country, era, or movement. Biographers shape the factual information about a person in innumerable ways—including narrative, chronology, flashbacks, and anecdotal reports by others—to structure the story of a person's life. Students who read widely from trade books in all curriculum areas learn to deal with a variety of text structures.

Knowledge of different text structures helps students become better readers and better writers. Students who recognize text structures comprehend more rapidly when they read and have options to choose from when crafting their own texts, as can be seen in the writing examples in Chapter Nine.

During the school years, students read more nonfiction books in science, social studies, and math than they read in all categories of fiction combined. Most school and public libraries contain 85 percent nonfiction and 15 percent fiction. State and national tests of reading ability use nonfiction selections almost entirely. During a lifetime, we probably read nonfiction twice as often as we read fiction. However, we seldom teach students how to read nonfiction. The *Teaching Idea: Reading Nonfiction* gives ideas on how to go about teaching students to read nonfiction, and Figures 13.1 and 13.2 list many trade books for teaching language arts across the curriculum.

Using trade books makes it possible to promote critical reading and thinking and to encourage students to pursue individual interests in any discipline or in reading any genre. Poet Paul Janeczko teaches critical reading when he asks students to notice the techniques a poet uses in a poem. For example, discussing William Carlos Williams's poem "The Great Figure," he states, "Notice that the poet uses short lines to give the poem a frantic, staccato feel, like the sound of a siren." Janeczko (2001, p. 54) points out the poem's quick pace and its evocative sound and sight words to call attention to images the poet creates. He asks students to notice a repeated line, onomatopoeia, or alliteration. Sharon Creech reveals a reluctant poetry admirer and poet in *Love That Dog* (2001). The teacher's comments and the student's hesitation become clear; however, the student gradually shows increasing acceptance, even admiration, of poetry and poets.

Teachers help students become aware of the subtleties of writing when, during share time in writers' workshop, they ask: What do you notice about this piece of writing? What did the writer do in this story to make you want to keep on reading? What do you notice in this poem that makes it interesting? Critical reading is careful reading; readers notice—and relish—subtle details.

TEACHING IDEA

Literature Link

READING NONFICTION

- Use trade books to study content areas, and to compare information and text structures.
- Trade books use photo essays, narrative, time lines, and graphic displays.
- Collect numerous trade books about a topic of study; give groups of students two or three books to examine.
- Ask students to look for a table of contents, side headings, index, glossary, and references.
- Ask students to notice the number, placement, captions, and medium used for illustrations and photographs.
- Ask students to skim or scan a page for specific information.
- Ask students to use a K-W-L (tell what they know/what they want to know/what they learned) strategy as they read the books.
- Ask students to compare texts collaboratively and generate a list of alternative ideas the texts present.
- Encourage students to present the information to the whole class and compare what the groups discover.
- Discuss how knowledge of text structure helps students in reading comprehension and provides them with explicit models for informational writing.
- Use think-aloud strategies to model critical thinking for students.

WRITING TO LEARN

Learning through writing has had increasing success in the past two decades. Journals—notebooks or folders in which students write about their thoughts and opinions on any subject, topic, or event in their lives—can be put to excellent use in a variety of ways during inquiry studies. You can introduce journal-writing techniques through lessons, modeling, and demonstrations. Students write about their personal responses and the meaning they gain from action, reflection, talk, and deliberation. Journals often contain drafts and works in progress. Journals are places to develop ideas and record observations, reactions, analyses, and evaluations. Students are actively engaged in their own learning; they clarify what they think and know by putting it into words. Britton (1982) explains that students shape meaning at the point of utterance when they speak; they shape meaning at pencil point when they write. A child expressed this process by stating, "I didn't know what I thought

FIGURE 13.1

Integrating Math, Language, and Literature

Problem Solving

Anno, Mitsumasa. (1983). *Anno's Mysterious Multiplying Jar*. New York: Philomel.

Scieszka, Jon. (1995). *Math Curse*. Illus. Lane Smith. New York: Viking.

Tang, Greg. (2001). *The Grapes of Math: Mind-Stretching Math Riddles*. Illus. Harry Briggs. New York: Scholastic.

Multiplication and Division

Hutchins, Pat. (1986). *The Doorbell Rang*. New York: Greenwillow.

Set Theory

Jenkins, Emily. (2001). *Five Creatures*. Illus. Tomek Bogacki. New York: Farrar Straus Giroux.

Measuring

Hopkinson, Deborah. (2001). *Fannie in the Kitchen: The Whole Story from Soup to Nuts of How Fannie Farmer Invented Recipes with Precise Measurements*. Illus. Nancy Carpenter. New York: Atheneum.

until I saw what I said." When learners write about what they are learning, they discover what they know.

Journals are not private, like a diary; they are meant to be reflected on and shared. Journals, however, should not be subjected to "grading." Students believe, "If I write my most honest, personal opinion and you (the teacher) go over it with a red pencil to correct my spelling and grammar, I won't give you any further evidence of my stupidity." If students know their writing will be corrected, they stop writing freely and are guarded about what they write.

Students share their journal entries with others in pairs, small groups, or with the whole class. They learn from one another's perspectives. They take responsibility for their own thinking and develop respect for another person's point of view. They hear examples of other writing-to-learn strategies from their classmates. It is imperative that you value the diversity in their journals and praise the connections students make among the things they learn. Wooten (2000) describes how students make intertextual links across books and literary experiences. Sharing motivates students to think through

FIGURE 13.2

Books on Science-Related Subjects

Compare the reports on penguins, spiders, wolves, and other creatures.

Atwater, Richard, & Atwater, Florence. (1938). *Mr. Popper's Penguins.* Illus. Robert Lawson. Boston: Little, Brown.

Chester, Jonathan (1995). *Penguins of the Antarctic.* Berkeley, CA: Celestial Arts, distributed by Tricycle Press.

Dewey, Jennifer Owings. (2001). *Antarctic Journal: Four Months at the Bottom of the World.* New York: HarperCollins.

Facklam, Margery. (2001). *Spiders and Their Web Sites.* Illus. Alan Male. Boston: Little, Brown.

Fontanel, Beatrice. (1992). *Penguin: A Funny Bird.* Photos Andre Fatras & Yves Cherel. Watertown, MA: Charlesbridge.

Markle, Sandra. (2001). *Growing Up Wild: Wolves.* New York: Atheneum.

Montgomery, Sy. (2001). *The Man-Eating Tigers of Sundarbans.* Photos by Eleanor Griggs. Boston: Houghton.

Pringle, Laurence. (2001). *A Dragon in the Sky: The Story of a Green Darner Dragonfly*. Illus. Bob Marstall. New York: Scholastic.

Ryder, Joanne. (2001). *Little Panda: The World Welcomes Hua Mei at the San Diego Zoo.* New York: Simon & Schuster.

Sayre, April Pulley (2001). *Dig, Wait, Listen: A Desert Toad's Tale.* Illus. Barbara Bash. New York: Greenwillow.

Sierra, Judy. (2001). *Antarctic Antics: A Book of Penguin Poems.* San Diego, CA: Harcourt.

Zoehfeld, Kathleen W. (2001). *Dinosaur Parents, Dinosaur Young: Uncovering the Mystery of Dinosaur Families.* Illus. Paul Carrick and Bruce Shillinglaw. New York: HarperCollins.

an idea and to value what they believe; hearing other students' connections expands everyone's horizons and the realm of possible areas to explore.

Pat Juell (1985, p. 187) believes that journals help her students:

Become independent and creative thinkers.

Develop new connections.

Clarify ideas.

Appreciate differences of opinion.

Learn that writing is thinking.

You can initiate journal writing in many ways. Ask your students to write:

- In journals as homework
- As they work in class
- For 10 minutes at the beginning or end of classroom period

VIEWING TO LEARN

Viewing plays a key role in developing media literacy. Films and videotapes are staples of the elementary curriculum. Students of all ages experience a variety of media in their everyday lives. These include print in the form of books and magazines, plus television, advertisements, audio and video tapes, computer software, and video games, to name just a few. In school, students benefit from the use of these materials when they support the curriculum. The well-planned use of media offers students an opportunity to see how various media function as learning resources. They also learn to critique the use of the media under discussion and the value of the specific material offered via a particular type of media.

Students should therefore be encouraged to use a variety of media when they prepare reports. Most will make use of books, computer databases, and videotapes when available. A group discussion of the usefulness of each medium and how the information from each was combined will expand students' abilities to use a variety of media resources more effectively.

Teachers often use a variety of media to strengthen material already introduced through firsthand experiences and secondary (print) experiences. Sometimes viewing is used to stimulate interest in a topic that teachers wish to pursue. Other times interest arises spontaneously as children are exposed to topics and stories through visual media. Visual media can be approached in the same way as any other type of text:

Before viewing: Introduce the film or video. Briefly discuss any important ideas, key concepts, and material that might present difficulty for the group. For some types of films, and depending on the purpose for viewing, a prompt can be given for children to think about. Do not overdo the introduction, however. Keep in mind that children need opportunities to problem-solve and to reach their own understandings and conclusions.

During the viewing: If the film is a narrative, *never* interrupt. Let children enjoy the story as you would a book read aloud. Reflections and discussion can come later. If the viewing involves a content-area piece, it is appropriate to pause at times and even to review a section for specific focus and discussion.

After the viewing: Post-discussion depends on the nature of what was viewed and the purpose for viewing it. As with read-alouds, sometimes the best way to begin a discussion is simply to ask students to express what they think or how they feel about what they saw. Content-area viewing might involve listing some of the key ideas, either orally or in writing. Follow this with a summarizing discussion. Finally, students might want to list questions they still have and want to pursue.

Teachers have included film versions of stories as a part of genre studies. Examples of folk tales, adventure stories, historical fiction, and science fiction are easy to find in video versions. These can be included in studies of these genres. Older students can compare their own responses to various media and compare them as art forms.

Students should be encouraged to create their own representations through video. They will soon discover that the planning, filming, editing, and presenting required for this kind of effort are not unlike the writing process.

Teaching as Professional Inquiry and Change

TEACHERS AS LEARNERS IN THE PRIMARY GRADES

Myra Brown has been happily teaching first grade for many years. Her "sixes and sevens," as she calls her students, are at an age when "they blossom right before my very eyes. It's gratifying to watch them grow and to see the effects of my influence as a teacher." However, over her years as a teacher of young children, Myra's approach to teaching has changed dramatically. Myra's change in perspective did not take place overnight, nor was it a linear change, moving smoothly from point A to point B. Like anyone treading new ground, Myra has had her share of faulty starts, misgivings, and downright flops. Myra's search for new direction evolved gradually as she began to re-examine her teaching, seek new ideas, and reflect with others on the learning environment in her classroom. A look at "Myra Yesterday" and "Myra Today" reveals two very different first grade teachers and classrooms and gives insight into the most significant changes in her teaching.

"Myra yesterday." Perhaps the best way to characterize Myra's teaching during her early years is to say that like most teachers during that era, Myra considered the first few months of first grade as the readiness period, a time devoted to getting children ready for the real instruction in reading. During this period, the readiness workbook that accompanied the first grade reading program was the staple for all the children. It focused on the alphabet, sound/symbol relationships, and a few sight words. Progress, or the lack of it, through the readiness workbook was the determining factor for placement in the three reading groups that followed. Small-group instruction in the preprimers and primer reading texts and their accompanying workbooks generally began after the first of the year. Most children stayed in the same ability groups for the remainder of the year.

Myra would begin each day with a discussion of the calendar, the weather, and a brief daily newspaper that she wrote on the chalkboard in very precise manuscript handwriting. This was then copied by the children as part of the seat work to be done during reading group time. In addition to copying the newspaper, children might also complete several reading workbook pages and supplementary phonics worksheets. All this kept children working quietly while Myra worked with small groups for reading instruction. Copying the newspaper was especially useful, because the stress on neatness and good penmanship kept the children busy for an extended time. Because it was generally believed that young children had neither the interest nor ability to compose at this stage of their development, little was done by Myra to encourage her students to write their own stories and messages.

Having a special affinity for children's literature, Myra planned to read aloud to her students every day. However, because read-aloud time was scheduled for the last period of the day, it was frequently canceled due to a shortage of time. Children were taken to the library to select books on a regular basis. The books were kept in the children's desks to be read during reading group time by those who had completed all of their assigned seat work. Because the less capable children tended to work slowly, they rarely got to open these books between library visits.

Myra entered the profession with an awareness of the value of teaching through themes or units. During her preservice training she enjoyed preparing a science unit on the solar system and hoped to create many more units when she started teaching. She soon found it extremely hard to reconcile the teaching of themes with the need to spend specific amounts of time on each subject area during the week. Despite the kudos Myra received for her well-organized and beautifully decorated classroom, her students' successful worksheets, and the personal attachment she obviously enjoyed with her students, Myra began some serious self-questioning about the quality of the learning and teaching in her classroom.

"Myra today." A specific turning point in Myra's thinking came during her participation in a writing workshop put on by a local professional organization. The workshop presenters were two primary-grade teachers from a neighboring school district, and Myra was impressed both with the ideas they shared and with the work samples they showed from their classrooms. It was not until weeks later, however, that Myra read and reflected on what that workshop was all about. Months later, after attending more workshops, engaging in discussions with teachers in her building, and more reading, Myra launched a writing program in her first grade classroom. It was the program that eventually led to the abandonment of most of the workbook and worksheet activity in her classroom. The children simply needed more time to write. Revamping her priorities, Myra reduced her focus on neatness and form, thus granting her students the freedom to express the many good ideas they had to share.

Looking at writing as a process also caused Myra to reconsider her reading program. Perhaps reading could be taught through a process approach also. Myra expanded her students' independent reading time as a major part of the reading instruction. She started holding reading conferences, as well as writing conferences. Recognizing how important literature was for models of good writing, she moved her read-aloud period to prime time. And, she often based read-aloud selections on current topics in the class's science and social studies units. This helped Myra break down the subject-matter barriers that constrained her efforts to implement an integrated curriculum. Gradually she began to notice how the subject matter areas naturally spilled over into one another. Her planning changed dramatically. She began to think in terms of large blocks of time and to combine various areas of study. Textbooks remain important in Myra's classroom, but she now uses them alongside trade books and various other media, and her students view textbooks as one of many resources available.

Probably the most fundamental change took place within Myra herself. She saw her role shift from that of primary source and dispenser of knowledge to that of guide and facilitator of her students' learning. Along with her students, Myra has become a learner too.

Myra's journey is typical of many kindergarten and primary-grade teachers. They use literature more effectively than ever before, introduce writing earlier, and integrate the language arts with all other areas of the curriculum throughout the day. As they expand their vision of a language arts curriculum, they are mindful of the local and state standards set for their students and for themselves. Beginning teachers, who tend to revert to the methods used when they were in school, can learn from the experiences of teachers like Myra and the others highlighted throughout this book.

Establishing routines and a strong underlying structure are key components to success in today's more process-oriented classrooms. Teachers have moved away from the exclusive use of textbooks and an overreliance on worksheets as the focus of their daily planning and activities. Rather than have textbooks govern the curriculum, teachers look first to their overall goals and then to their more immediate objectives as a guide to planning the classroom environment and the learning experiences. The goal is a classroom

Bernice Cullinan

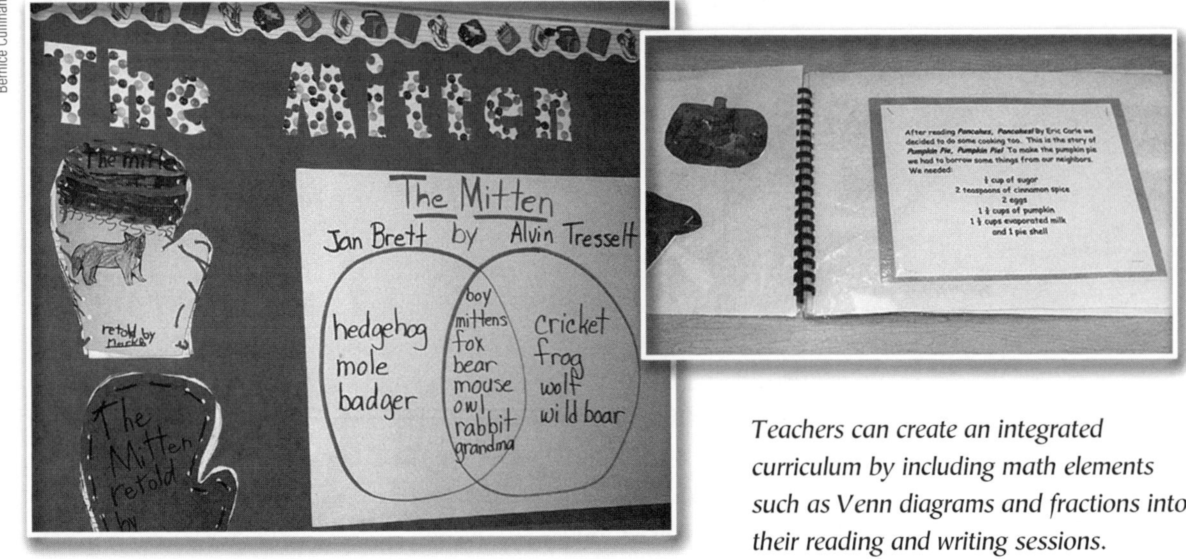

Teachers can create an integrated curriculum by including math elements such as Venn diagrams and fractions into their reading and writing sessions.

in which children share in the responsibility for the care and conduct of materials and activities and in making decisions about their own learning.

Skilled teachers know that putting a program such as this in place takes time, effort, and careful planning throughout the year. Some teachers characterize the process as one of "getting it started, keeping it going, and sailing along." Getting it started requires the gradual establishment of routines and activities. Keeping it going involves the constant monitoring of classroom events with a view toward adding to the complexity of existing learning opportunities and the addition of new ones. Sailing along occurs as routines and organizational structures become so well established that they free the teacher and students to focus their attention on the learning. Paradoxically, by establishing reasonably firm underlying structures, teachers and students actually attain a greater degree of flexibility and freedom from routines. (See Figure 13.3 on page 520, which gives the guidelines that one teacher uses in her classroom to establish classroom routines.)

Outstanding teacher Joanne Lionetti is a great teacher because she has also always been an avid learner. When engaging people and thoughts enter her life, she is always receptive to them, although she tries out new ideas in her classroom very cautiously. Here is what she says about her early days as a teacher.

> I was lucky. When I started teaching, my principal, Dr. Alfred Solomon, encouraged me to use trade books in all areas of the curriculum. He said, 'You have textbooks for every subject, but you can use them as one of many resources. You don't need to follow them blindly. But, you must

address the skills and strategies outlined in our curriculum guide and pay attention to the specific needs of your students.' He also asked me what my interests were and told me that I could start teaching children through these as well. I looked up the topics specified in the curriculum for science and social studies for my grade level, and then I went to the library and collected as many books as I could find on those topics. I began to develop thematic units of inquiry. I approached reading and language arts a bit differently, however.

Our reading specialist at that time insisted that we stick to the basal reader and cover all the skills and read every story in precisely the order they were presented. She came in to check to see if we had attained a certain level by the end of the semester and always had our next set of readers ready to bring in. I remember feeling very daring when I first skipped a few questions in the teacher's manual. Instead, we used response journals in which children wrote responses to prompts based on the selections they read and then discussed them in the way we did literature circles. I encouraged students to read books related to the themes in our core program. Our discussions were rich, and I learned a great deal about how students were comprehending. When my students took the end-of-unit tests, they did just fine. Of course, they were reading a lot, so they got a lot of practice.

Gradually, I moved into a more enriched reading program. I would look at the theme of the next unit in our reading program and then pick out trade books on that theme or books by the same authors. I read them aloud, made them available for independent reading in the classroom, and even sent them along as home reading books. Occasionally, I still used some of the comprehension questions offered in the teacher's guide and used it as a resource for teaching skills and strategies. Only now I was using the materials to make informed decisions rather than mindlessly following them without regard to my students' needs. Perhaps most important, the students seemed to enjoy language arts more, and they definitely read more. However, it wasn't until we got a new reading supervisor, and I had taken a workshop on integrating the language, that I really began to reconcile curriculum objectives with an expanded view of my language arts program.

We did an author study of Tomie de Paola again this year, but we did totally different things. I've learned to follow my students' interests, and this group took off on Tomie's legends. We read all the legends Tomie has written, and then we wrote our own legends. Tomie puts an 'Author's Note' at the back of his books to explain the origin of each legend, so we put an 'Author's Note' at the end of our book. We sent our finished book to Tomie, and he wrote a 'Rave Review' about it. I stapled his review inside the back of the book, and when the children took the book along for home reading, I included review sheets for the parents to comment. Each morning we read the parents' comments aloud—their reviews are thoughtful and very

> rewarding to our authors. I mapped some of the skills and strategies that were to be addressed during the year into the author study.
>
> I guess one of the most important things I've learned is to trust the children, to follow their lead. They work a lot harder, read and write more, and learn more when they're responsible for their own learning. I could never go back to the old ways. I address curriculum goals in a systematic, but flexible manner that gives students some choice of the books they read and the topics they write about. Sometimes, they must choose within the given theme. Often, they must demonstrate specific skills and strategies. Nevertheless, they have options, and this empowers them to take greater responsibility for their learning. This approach is much more exciting for me and valuable for my students; they're really readers and writers now.

Joanne Lionetti has gradually changed her philosophy about teaching reading and language arts. She adheres to certain district standards, but no longer follows teacher's guides rigidly nor does she simply ask three questions to check on students' comprehension after reading. The changes in her philosophy go much deeper than these surface features. Her beliefs about how children learn language and how they learn to read and write have changed dramatically. She has developed confidence in her ability to follow the children's lead; she finds out what they know and need to know, then creates situations for them to discover it. She views reading and writing as part of language learning. Her beliefs cause her to teach differently from the way she used to teach.

Joanne continues to read, attend workshops, and talk with other teachers who are also moving toward a new philosophy of language arts teaching. She is eager to learn, skilled in observing her students, willing to try out new ideas, and patient enough to know that lasting change does not come overnight.

TEACHERS AS LEARNERS IN THE INTERMEDIATE GRADES

Many teachers in the intermediate grades remain uncertain as to their role in teaching in an integrated program. They know that their students are not the same as primary-grade students and that what works in the primary grades does not necessarily work in the intermediate and upper grades. Intermediate-grade students differ from primary-level students in many ways: age, interests, competencies, sophistication, independence, social concerns, reliance on peers, cognitive reach, and willingness to cooperate. Most of them know how to read and write; the dew is off the blossom of learning to master skills that primary-grade children think are magical in and of themselves. Intermediate-grade students rarely read for the sake of showing off a newfound skill—nor will they write solely for the sake of writing. There must be something inherently interesting in what they read to attract them to reading; they must have a goal in writing beyond demonstrating their skill at writing.

In reading, students in the intermediate grades move from unconscious enjoyment of literature toward conscious delight in it. Their progress is similar to that of novices in music appreciation. When they first hear a symphony, they "hear" only the combined sounds and melodies. When they know the added effects of each instrument, they listen differently. They appreciate the oboe talking to the French horn, the blended sounds of the violins and the violas, and the thundering rumble of the drums. So it is in reading literature. Intermediate-grade students are no longer satisfied with just reading or hearing the plot of Beverly Cleary's *Dear Mr. Henshaw;* they want to know why it won the Newbery Award. What qualities does this book have to cause literary critics to choose it as the best of the year? They want to probe more deeply. They have discovered that reading is not merely about "walking on words" but also about grasping the soul of them. They read like writers who savor the way words are put together. They agree with the poet who said, "I write out loud," because they "hear" the sound of the author's voice inside their heads as they read. They appreciate good writing.

In writing, intermediate-grade students also move through developmental stages, from hesitant mastery of one form to fluency in different forms. They have a growing sense of expertise; they want to master the craft of writing by gaining control over subtle word usage, by achieving rhythm in their sentences, and by creating powerful images through words. They become sensitive to word play and delight in their power to manipulate language.

In oral language, primary-grade students may be proud to present a clear message or merely to say something in front of the class. Intermediate-grade students, however, want to master persuasive techniques in language; they want to use language to convince others of their point of view. They become sensitive to the effective use of the speaker's voice in dramatic presentations. They notice that when teachers read aloud they lower their voice at tense moments in a story, or that listeners are kept dangling in suspense through the use of a pregnant pause. When they hear poets read their work, they hear them give different voices to different characters. They, too, want to control their speaking voice to make others hang on every word. Suggestions for the primary-grade teacher are not adequate for the intermediate-grade teacher.

Organizational plans for the intermediate grades often differ from those for the primary grades. Primary grades are typically organized into self-contained classrooms with one teacher responsible for the major portion of instruction. Intermediate grades are organized in a variety of patterns: self-contained, departmentalized, team teaching, core blocks, middle schools, and other arrangements. At a recent writing workshop conference, fifth grade reading teacher Joan Pearlman complained, "I wish they [the conference speakers] would stop telling me to read aloud to my kids three times a day. I only see my students for 40 minutes a day, and I certainly can't use much of that time to read aloud to them." Joan's colleague, fifth grade English teacher Susan Alford, sat across the table and nodded in agreement. She, too, teaches the same students for the same limited amount of time and shares Joan's frustration. After some discussion, both teachers left the conference determined to change their teaching schedule to allow for some reading aloud during longer blocks of time. These teachers did change their schedule. Joan noted, "I feel like a beginning teacher again. I don't know what to do with this big block of time."

Step into a well-functioning classroom, and it seems that everybody knows the rules and knows what to do; students are busily engaged in a variety of activities. That is not the way it is at the beginning of the year, however. The workshop environment is created one step at a time. Teachers introduce a new process they use repeatedly until they feel students are familiar with it. Once students have mastered a process, teachers then add new elements to their routine.

Diana Cohn, a fourth grade teacher, relies on demonstrations and room arrangement to get her program off and running. She models each new element or strategy, some several times, before she expects students to perform effectively. She also arranges her classroom to encourage student independence; everything is organized to empower students to be independent writers. Materials are within student reach, and certain areas are clearly identified for specific activities. For example, students hold peer conferences on the rug

Bernice Cullinan

A good arrangement of the classroom will encourage student independence and empowerment.

area. Diana moved the rug away from the student desks so that quiet conversations would not disrupt other writers.

First week: Groundwork. Diana lays the groundwork for the reading-writing workshop by explaining writing notebooks. She introduces notebooks early because she relies on them heavily throughout the year. She reads aloud from her own notebook and from notebooks she borrows from last year's students. She shows the students that notebooks are a place to record their thoughts and reflections. She shows them that writers keep journals or notebooks. Then she shares samples of student writing that have grown from entries in the notebooks. She is modeling a process: write, read, reflect, ponder, write, reflect, read, ponder. It is a cyclical process that thoughtful people use to make sense of their world.

Diana models beginning workshop routines by reading aloud one chapter of Lynne Reid Banks' *The Indian in the Cupboard*. In the first chapter, Omri discovers that a small plastic Indian figure comes to life when it is placed inside a metal cupboard, but it can freeze movement when Omri's mother comes into the room. Children look at each other quizzically; the murmur of voices shows they are wondering about what is happening. Questions hang in the air. Diana suggests that they write what they are thinking and pondering in their response journals before they discuss it. She is establishing the reading-writing-thinking-reflecting-predicting cycle that she encourages repeatedly.

Diana deliberately arranges the room so that different parts are set up for specific functions. Students write independently at their desks; they meet with peers for conferences on an area rug; they meet in response groups at their cluster of desks; and they move together for whole-class sharing. The ebb and flow of group movement resembles an amoeba constantly changing shape.

Second week: Shortened periods. Diana continues to rely on demonstrations to ease her students into routines, but instead of using a normal amount of time, which she will eventually allot, each segment lasts only about 5 minutes. She goes through each segment and includes group evaluation of their process as a part of each step. For example, she pulls suggestions from students about what they can do if they need help with spelling or cannot read a word, where they can get materials, where they might put completed work, or what to do if someone is annoying them. She demonstrates a "think-aloud" process in which she states orally the questions and comments that pass through her mind as she reads. Diana helps students become independent by modeling the behaviors mature readers and writers use.

Third week: Role-play conferences. Diana uses role-playing as a teaching strategy. She conducts teacher conferences and has students hold peer conferences by role-playing them in front of the group. She points out the value of conferences but cautions that they not be overused; students are encouraged to have conferences among themselves before they go to her. The group evaluates what helps conferences and what bogs them down. They talk about what conferences are supposed to accomplish. Listen to Diana's voice as she confers with Jamal:

> **Diana:** Well, how's it going?
>
> **Jamal:** I'm all done.
>
> **Diana:** I'd love to hear it. Would you like to read it to me?
>
> [Jamal reads.]
>
> **Diana [retells Jamal's story]:** You said you went to the playground with your big sister and that she talked to a boy, and you told your mother about it because your sister is not supposed to talk to boys. Then your mother scolded you and sent you to your room, and you're angry because you don't think that's fair. Right?
>
> **Jamal:** Yes, and my sister is always telling Mom what I do at the playground, and Mom listens to her but she won't listen to me. My sister is not supposed to talk to boys, and she did. Just because I told Mom, she sent me to my room. It's not fair!
>
> **Diana:** I know how you feel. It's hard to have a big sister if your parents listen to her more than they do to you. Do you think people who read your story will know what usually happens at your house?
>
> **Jamal:** Well, they will if they have a big-mouthed sister like mine.
>
> **Diana:** Do you think you could put in any more information so readers will know about your family even if they don't have a big sister? Where do you think you might work that in? Give it a try. Read it to some other people to see if they understand.

Diana is trying to get Jamal to think about writing like a reader. She is also trying to get Jamal to assume responsibility for writing and to make decisions about what he should do with it. In essence, she is trying to teach the writer, not fix the writing.

Fourth week and beyond: Role-playing evaluation, demonstrating evaluation sessions, probing into one genre. Diana starts every evaluation conference by commenting positively on something the child is doing well. She says, for example, "Sam, your stories are getting longer. You're using colorful words so that I can see the picture you're describing. You're using a nice bouncy rhythm that I can hear in my head as I read. Your sentences sound just like you do when you talk."

Diana wants students to internalize the questions writers ask of themselves about their emerging drafts. She is not interested so much in getting Sam to fix this particular piece of writing as she is in making him an independent writer. Near the end of a conference, she moves to a very specific point: She wants to help Sam think about his writing in a new way. "What do you want me to feel about the detective who is trying to solve this mystery?" When she senses that Sam has narrowed his focus, she says, "Well, that might be a good place to start."

Diana uses demonstrations to launch each type of literature she introduces during the year. Her basic plan for studying biography, fantasy, and mystery, for example, is to (1) have students read independently within the genre and to select a book from the genre for read aloud, (2) draw from students lists of words and characters they frequently find in that genre, and (3) have students write in that genre.

For a genre study on mystery stories, Diana reads aloud a mystery set in the school's urban neighborhood, *The Shadow Nose* by Elizabeth Levy. In their response journals, students draw a map of their neighborhood and place symbols for the characters who were present at each scene in which a plot event took place. The maps are used to sequence, track clues, make hypotheses, and check out predictions.

Diana helps students become aware of what they already know about mystery stories. She writes on a chart: "What words come to mind when we think of the word 'mystery'?" Students volunteer the following words:

Murder	Detectives	Action
Suspense	Robbery	Scary
Curiosity	Supernatural things	A maze
Details	Fingerprints	Killing
Clues	Sherlock Holmes's hat	Excitement

Students discover that they know more collectively than they do individually; they share their common knowledge and continue to add to the list as they read more mysteries.

During another session, Diana writes on a chart: "Detectives we have met in mystery books and movies." She is continuing to bring background knowledge to their awareness and to show them what they know collectively. Students list, among others:

Sherlock Holmes and Watson	Nate the Great
Jessica Fletcher	Cam Jansen
Nancy Drew	Pink Panther
Hardy Boys	Encyclopedia Brown
Dick Tracy	Perry Mason
Matlock	Garfield

Students discover what they already know about patterns in the mystery genre. During a minilesson, Diana asks students to talk about things they notice when they think about mysteries they have read or seen. She asks them what usually happens, what mysteries often have in them, or what makes a mystery story a mystery story. She writes on a chart the comments students make:

> Misleading clues.
>
> It is usually solved.
>
> The maid and butler are suspects.
>
> It's like a riddle with clues and solutions.
>
> They make people wonder.
>
> Usually there is a murder.

Students know that they will write a mystery of their own, but instead of making it a large amorphous assignment, Diana works with them, building background knowledge and focusing on the elements that go into a mystery. For example, students write descriptions of a detective they created. Here is part of the description fourth-grader Anna Robertson wrote:

> *Hi! My name is Lisa D. I have shoulder-length blond hair and I am very tall. My favorite sports are baseball and basketball. I am a detective. I wear a Mets jacket and cap. If you saw me walking down the street I'm sure you couldn't miss me. There's always a little bump in my coat. That's my partner. He's a little dog who I always keep in my inside pocket of my Mets jacket . . .*

Diana wants students to realize that setting is a crucial element in a mystery. She asks them to describe the setting of the place they choose as the scene for their mystery. They write descriptions and draw pictures of the setting, and then they write their own mysteries. And their mysteries turn out to be very good. Why? Because the prewriting activities and background building bring to their consciousness information they know, give them new knowledge, and make them aware of elements of the genre in which they are writing.

Diana uses the same basic plan for examining each genre and makes certain that students are knowledgeable about a form of writing before she encourages them to create a piece in that form. For each genre, they read widely, look carefully at the types of words and characters they find in the genre, share their knowledge about patterns and elements in the genre, practice writing segments found in the genre, and draft parts of their story as they build a longer piece.

After the mystery focus, Diana leads students in probing their early memories as they prepare to write their autobiographies. She says, "I don't want them to write the typical thing, such as 'I was born on this date; I live at this address.' So we're reading all kinds of books that deal with authors' early memories."

The books she uses include Beverly Cleary's *A Girl from Yamhill,* Roald Dahl's *Boy,* Jean Fritz's *Homesick: My Own Story,* Eloise Greenfield and Lessie Jones Little's *Childtimes: A Three-Generation Memoir,* Jean Little's *Little by Little* and *Hey World, Here I Am,* Milton Meltzer's *Starting from Home, Bill Peet: An Autobiography,* and Cynthia Rylant's *When I Was Young in the Mountains* and *But I'll Be Back Again: An Album.* Diana is immersing her students in a literary form, demonstrating what writers of that form do, building background knowledge, and making her students aware of what they already know before she asks them to use the form of autobiography.

Figure 13.3 lists some of the guidelines Diana uses to establish the routines in her classroom.

Cultural and linguistic diversity

Diana's students represent numerous ethnicities. Black, Asian, Middle Eastern, Hispanic, and other ethnic groups reflect the diversity of the inner city. When a non-English-speaking or limited-English-proficient child enters the classroom, students quickly volunteer to serve as a buddy to see that the new student knows how to get to physical education class, the library, the lunchroom, and the bathroom. These students have grown up in a community that

FIGURE 13.3

Guidelines for Establishing Classroom Routines

1. Establish an overall framework for the language arts block.
2. Post a chart that shows the major schedule and options for various segments of the workshop.
3. Lead students through instruction routines.
4. Model each routine, such as peer conferences.
5. Role-play activities with students assuming leadership roles.
6. Involve students in evaluating classroom procedures. Make refinements based on their suggestions. They will work to maintain rules they help to establish.

values helpfulness, diversity, and multiethnicity; they respond naturally to newcomers.

Students arrange their desks in clusters to create response groups to talk about learning projects; the new student becomes a natural part of a group. Students write in their learning logs in whatever language they know how to write; Diana responds in English. Children learn language rapidly; when they are surrounded by English speakers, they absorb the language and seem to take it into themselves in huge gulps. In a matter of weeks the new student is using English for basic needs and, with the help of peers, is a fully functioning member of the group.

Diana stresses the value of bilingualism and helps the child who speaks a second language feel like an "expert." One new student from Chile, Joanna, was able to demonstrate her expertise when the class had a guest speaker from Nicaragua. Joanna served as the leader who translated children's questions into Spanish and the speaker's responses into English.

Diana believes that language and literacy can be acquired by deep immersion in using the language; it all depends on meaning. She knows that children learn when they attend to *what* is said to them, not *how* it is said. Numerous students have confirmed her beliefs by becoming fluent readers and writers in a 3- to 4-month period.

Children with special needs

Students in Diana's fourth grade are changing from dependent, immature, primary-grade students into independent, responsible learners. Hilary clings to the teacher to ask approval every step of the way. Rashida is quietly independent but keeps her eye on the teacher to see if she is watching.

One child, Michael, was transferred into Diana's class with a cumulative record containing a string of test scores and an evaluation report that virtually screamed "learning disabled." Diana asked his mother about Michael's background. Here are some excerpts from Michael's mother's comments:

> I read to Michael and his older sister every day when they were young. The children loved to listen to stories they picked out. By age 4, Michael asked me a number of times when he would learn to read. I told him he would learn to read when he got to school. When he was 5, he continued with the same questions, "When will I learn to read?" I gave him the same answer, "When you go to school." I encouraged him to follow the words as I read, and I asked people how I could teach my son to read. One kindergarten teacher said, "Just read to him." This was frustrating to me because Michael wanted to read so badly, and I could not help him.
>
> Michael had a series of unfortunate school experiences. Even though his teachers were kind, they seemed to treat him as unable to learn, especially after tests labeled him learning disabled. He was taken out of class for

> resource room and missed what his classmates were doing. He was excused from regular assignments; he was in the bottom reading group; he was allowed to slide by. Now he says he hates school, and he hates reading. I can't believe I have a school dropout, and he's only 10 years old.

Diana listened attentively to the sincere and frustrated mother. She asked questions about his early years, his eating and sleeping habits, his sports activities, his interests, his friends, his hobbies. She was trying to put together as complete a picture as possible about this personable boy who was turned off to school and reading. When she felt she knew a great deal about Michael, she made the following proposal to his mother:

> Let's make a plan together and talk with each other once a week to see how it's going. First of all, I really believe that Michael knows what he needs and that he'll tell us. He's had a difficult time in school, but the whole philosophy of what goes on in this classroom is very different from what he's experienced in the past. I build on a child's feelings of success and their strengths. Michael has strengths, and we will find them; I want him to take charge of his own learning. I have wonderful books, and in this classroom he will be among kids who enjoy them. They share what they are reading every day. Some of that enthusiasm will be contagious. Michael will choose for himself the books he reads both here at school and at home. Don't worry, we'll find some he wants to read. Let him read himself to sleep.
>
> I will write letters to him and urge him to write to me and to his classmates. We keep response journals, and we share our feelings about what we're reading. We will find out what's important to Michael, and we'll build on that to help him feel successful about learning. Let's just start with these basic ingredients and see how he does. I'll do my part here at school to see that he takes an interest in what we are studying.
>
> Now I want to hear your ideas about what you think Michael needs. I'll bet that we find the secret to Michael's learning. And it won't be based on disabilities—it will be found in his abilities.

The home-school cooperation Diana is forging is a necessary part of effective teaching. Like Joanne Lionetti, Diana Cohn involves the parents in their children's learning. Her belief in a child's strengths is a cornerstone of her approach. Diana will search for areas in which Michael can demonstrate his strengths—she is convinced they are there, and she will find them. She will build on his successes—no matter how small—until she finds ways to get Michael to take pride in his accomplishments.

Diana encourages students to be independent, but she also gives them guidance about constructive things to do when they cannot decide what to do alone. Figure 13.4 shows the chart she put up in her classroom.

FIGURE 13.4

Things I Can Do during Reading–Writing Workshop

1. Read through my writing folder.
2. Add ideas to my topic list.
3. Draft a new writing piece or write in my journal.
4. Read a piece to my writing partner.
5. Underline words I'm not sure are spelled correctly.
6. Look for words that need capital letters.
7. Look for a new book to read.
8. Read. Read. Read.
9. Tell my reading partner about the book I'm reading.
10. Rewrite a story as a script for Readers' Theatre.
11. Draw pictures for a story.
12. Make a semantic map of ideas about a topic.
13. Write a summary of a story I have read.
14. Make a story map to show the parts of a story.
15. Make a character collage to show who is in a story.
16. Make a poster of the books I recommend that others read.

TEACHERS AS LEARNERS IN THE UPPER GRADES

Students in grades 6 through 8 are a complex mixture of sophisticated adolescents and rather immature, dependent youngsters. They are in a period of transition from childhood to adolescence, undergoing rapid biological changes and mercurial mood swings. Fred Savage, the 13-year-old star of the TV series "The Wonder Years," nods sagely as his character Kevin says, "Being self-conscious is a full-time job." Early adolescents believe that everybody is looking at them; they want to blend into the crowd and, therefore, dress and style their hair according to the prevailing code of what's "in." They see the raw edges of life in their neighborhood streets, on television, and in movies. They travel in packs and pairs, somewhat impervious to school or family rules. They are shifting their allegiance away from family values toward those of their peer groups. Peer group influence is powerful. Perhaps because of early adolescents' exposure to so many facets of life, their parents make futile attempts to overprotect them and encourage them to hang onto childhood.

Adolescents and preadolescents are preoccupied with trying to find out who they are. They may work toward self-definition by developing mutually dependent relationships with selected peers; they define who they are by seeing who their friends are. Previous to this age, they believed they were immortal but they now find out that they are not, and they must deal with this unsettling concept. Young adolescents strive for autonomy, grapple with learning how to regulate their own behavior, and work toward making responsible choices. They are quick to question authority. They are frequently volatile and confused by all those active hormones. One teacher likened living with junior high school students to trying to keep popping popcorn in a pot without a lid.

Bonnie Roberts and Barbara James, intensive language arts teachers in a Brooklyn, New York, junior high school, meet the challenge of teaching such lively and volatile students with good cheer. They view the multiethnic backgrounds and active minds of their sixth-graders as fertile resources. These teachers are less likely to have large blocks of time. Instructional periods of 40 minutes to an hour prevail. Bonnie and Barbara use the time for the following activities: whole-class homework review and strategy lesson; small-group projects; ongoing peer conferences and teacher conferences with individual students; and whole-class share time (sharing does not occur every day—usually every third day).

Bonnie and Barbara's city students come from an extremely diverse multiethnic population, and include students from the Caribbean, Russia, and the Middle East, as well as students with African-American, Asian, and Hispanic backgrounds. Administrators assign students "at risk of school failure" to Bonnie and Barbara because they have been so successful with them. The two teachers share 150 students a day in 40-minute blocks of time organized in a traditional "change classes" schedule. Although they do not work with the same students nor do they team-teach within the school's traditional framework, they plan together in order to develop an integrated language arts program.

Bonnie and Barbara begin early to develop their students' self-esteem because they believe it is a vital component in promoting positive change in school achievement. Their students have experienced school failure repeatedly, and these teachers are determined to help them turn school failure into school success. They say, "Self-esteem is not something we give students, it's what we have to stop taking away." Their students have been told in many ways that they are not competent, successful, or worthy through "killer statements" such as "You're not good enough," or "What can I expect from the likes of you?" from both school faculty and peers. Bonnie and Barbara use a multicultural perspective to achieve their goal of enhancing self-esteem; they develop the curriculum around a year-long study of "family roots." The family roots unit has four basic focal points: individual self-esteem, group membership and identity, honoring differences, and celebrating differences.

At the beginning of each fall term, Bonnie and Barbara mount a map of the world on a classroom wall; students connect pieces of yarn from a picture of their school to their country of origin. Right from the beginning, the teachers establish a tone to show that all cultures are honored and celebrated and

Bernice Cullinan

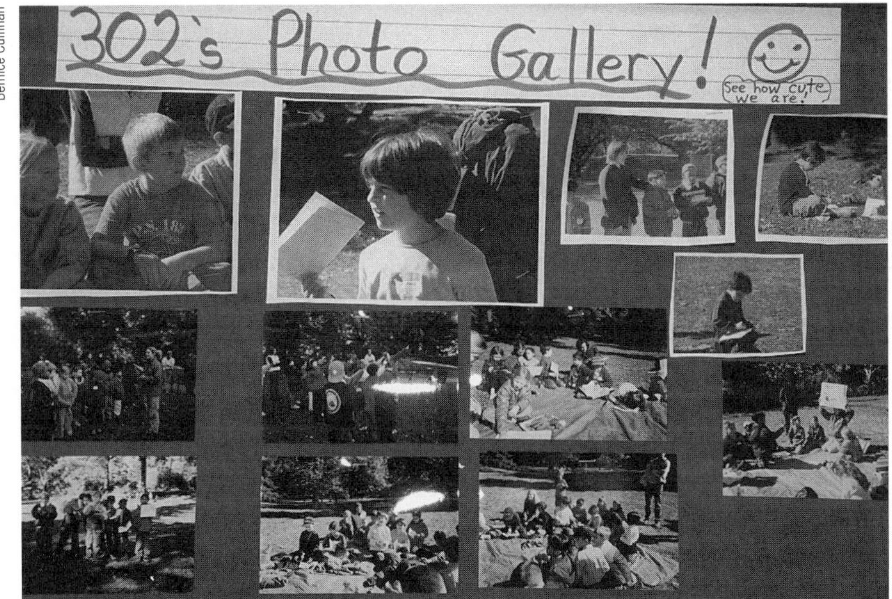

Developing children's self-esteem at an early age is a vital component to their success as students.

that the native culture of each person is appreciated. They do this by asking, for example: "How many of you looked into the mirror this morning and saw a wonderful, unique, talented person? Did you tell that reflection that you are really a good person who tries hard to succeed and that you can do some things no one else can do? How many great artists, musicians, writers, architects, or other talented people can you name that came from the same country you did? Were their contributions due to the fact that they were of Italian, Russian, or Jamaican origin? Were their contributions influenced by the culture from which they came?"

The teachers stress that people from all countries contribute to the good of humankind. They point out that human achievements and individual accomplishments depend most heavily upon the individual alone. They allow that opportunities for learning and educational advantages play a part in success, but they foreshadow the fact that they will probe into the lives of successful people to see how much influence they exerted to gain the opportunities and advantages they had.

Barbara and Bonnie have developed several specific teaching ideas, which we sketch here.

Individual self-esteem

Bonnie and Barbara have one major goal. They want to help each student answer the questions: Who am I? What is unique about me? and What do I do well? This goal guides the first part of their study. They begin by exploring the uniqueness of each person's name. Students examine the importance of naming; they investigate the origins of their first names and trace the history

TEACHING IDEA

Addressing Individual Needs

ALL ABOUT ME: A TRIPTYCH

Materials:

A 12″ × 18″ sheet of stiff poster paper or cardboard. Markers, crayons, or paints. Magazines to cut up for photographs, headlines, labels. Paste.

Fold the poster paper into thirds. It should stand with its sides folded out or lie flat with the sides folded into a tripartite, six-panel (front and back) triptych.

(The example shown here comes from Margarita, one of Barbara James's students.)

Panel 1:

Put your photograph on the cover and cut headlines, slogans, phrases, and adjectives from magazines or newspapers that describe you. Paste the phrases artistically around your picture.

Panel 2:

Tell how you got your name.

Panel 3:

A Portrait Poem

Panel 4:

A Me Map. Put your name or nickname in a circle in the center of the page with spokes leading out from it. At the ends of the spokes, list your favorite things to do, things you dislike, things you have done, or other interesting facts about you. Margarita used her nickname, Margie, for her Me Map.

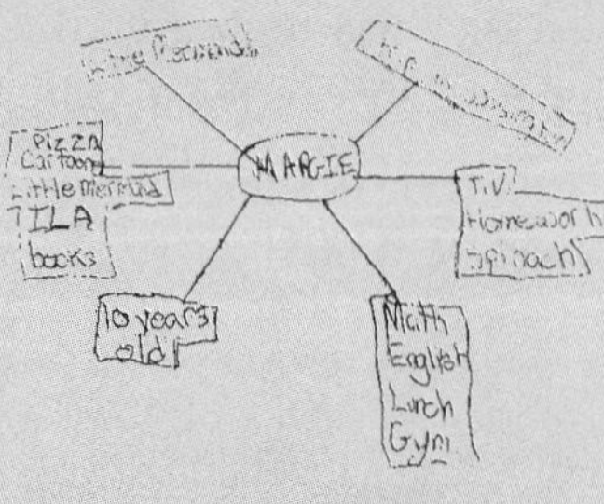

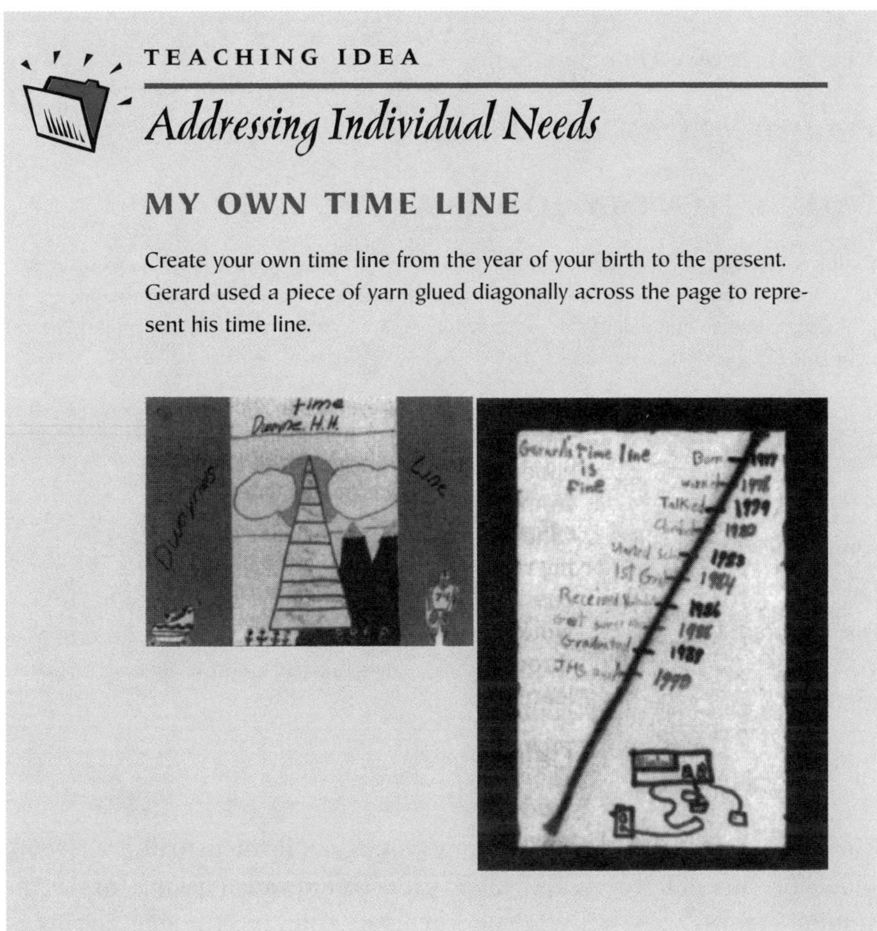

TEACHING IDEA

Addressing Individual Needs

MY OWN TIME LINE

Create your own time line from the year of your birth to the present. Gerard used a piece of yarn glued diagonally across the page to represent his time line.

of their family names. They read *Knots on a Counting Rope* by Bill Martin, Jr., and John Archambault to savor the meaning invested in a Native American child's name. The students make "Me Maps"—semantic webs of likes and dislikes, hobbies, dreams and wishes, family and school experiences, contests they have entered, and awards they have won. They make time lines of significant events in their lives. They write "Portrait Poems" to celebrate their uniqueness. Some of these activities are described in the T*eaching Ideas: All about Me: A Triptych, My Own Time Line,* and *Double-Entry Journals.*

Group membership and identity

Students discover that they are all members of many different groups—from the ones who like pizza to the ones with brown eyes to the ones whose family roots are Russian. People change some of their group memberships from time to time; others are permanent.

Students work in cooperative learning groups of three or four to discover which areas they have in common and which attributes are unique.

TEACHING IDEA

Addressing Individual Needs

DOUBLE-ENTRY JOURNALS

Double-entry journals help students think about their thinking, a process called metacognition. Divide a page with a vertical line down the middle. On the left side, write the fact, problem, or issue. On the right side, write what you are thinking about what you see. The right side is for your thoughts about the process. For example:

Write down the year you were born.	I was born in 1993.
Add 52.	Wonder why 52; maybe 52 weeks in a year?
1993 + 52 = 2045	Answer equals 2045.
Now subtract 1,878.	2045 − 1878 = 167
Multiply by 2, divide by 20.	167 × 2 = 334; 334 ÷ 20 = 16
Finally subtract 9.	That equals 7.*

*Note: The answer is always 7. Discuss this with your students and then ask them to write why they think this happens.

They draw circles to represent the many groups among them to discover commonalities and differences. They find that each individual belongs to several cultural groups: age level, skin color, religion, country of origin, neighborhood, music preference, and people they consider heroes, for example. They read selections from Arnold Adoff's *All the Colors of the Race* and Marlo Thomas's *Free to Be.*

Students engage in numerous activities to explore group membership and individual qualities. They make "Me-biles," mobile hangings strung with symbolic representations of the various groups to which they belong. They create a family coat of arms to depict one important group membership, and they illustrate their unique family values and beliefs.

Honoring differences

Bonnie and Barbara work with students who represent many different ethnic groups; they recognize that their students come to them with a grounding in prejudice and fear about differences. The teachers' goal is to help students see how differences make each of them special; for this reason, they purposely honor differences. Ultimately they hope that knowledge and respect for differences will dispel prejudice and fear.

Bonnie and Barbara heard about a powerful Native American custom that builds tribal and personal strength. Tribal members keep items that are significant to them wrapped in animal skins; they call the collections medicine bundles. The teachers explain the belief and spiritual meaning in the Native American medicine bundles and relate the folklore surrounding them. Many of the objects represent tribal origin myths, which are passed from one generation to the next. Personal bundles contain objects associated with important events in a person's life. When the owners, seated around a campfire, tell the story of each object, their people add their own thoughts. The person is honored for the things that make him or her unique.

Students eagerly accept the teachers' invitation to create their own medicine bundles. They choose items they have saved from important events in their lives, such as a bar mitzvah or confirmation, and ones that symbolize their cultural heritage. The students' collections contain religious symbols, favorite foods, trophies, and tape-recorded songs as well as treasured family stories. Sharing sessions are spirited when students bring Ukrainian Easter bread, a Russian balalaika and a babushka (grandmother) doll, and Chinese moon cakes. Their knowledge of each other's culture grows along with their respect for the differences they honor.

Students are intrigued with another idea, honoring differences in their shoe sizes. They create a shoe museum display, a "shoe-seum," in a hall trophy case and invite viewers to describe what the shoes reveal about the wearers. They research footwear fashions through the ages and around the world. They conduct surveys of shoe sizes and determine the average shoe size in the group. They create art objects from outgrown sneakers with plaster of Paris and paints. They take part in a "Shoe and Tell" oral presentation. The underlying message that there is nothing right or wrong, good or bad about differences in shoe size permeates discussions of other differences that they can accept and honor. Bonnie and Barbara work with other teachers to further integrate the multicultural studies throughout the day.

SUMMARY

Effective teachers create classrooms in which they and their students inquire, reflect, and learn together. Such teachers accept the idea that language is learned best when it is meaningful and functional. Because they constantly seek ways to improve teaching and learning, they are constantly engaged in ongoing professional development. They use what they learn to examine instruction and to bring informed knowledge to the materials and strategies they use. They view themselves as instructional leaders. They are very familiar with the district's expectations for students at their level and consider these as expectations of the parents and community as well. As they work toward those goals, they also work with students to establish routines and goals. They function as coach, facilitator, and creator of situations that put children in charge of their own learning. They encourage students to frame their own questions for inquiry and investigation. They make learning resources available to students and help them master the strategies they need to find out what they want to know. Their goal is to help students become independent learners.

ACTIVITIES

1. **Choose a curriculum-related theme, such as the importance of protecting the environment or keeping a healthy body, appropriate for the intermediate grades.** Locate a variety of sources that will help students explore the theme. Develop a group of inquiry activities of interest to students that require the use of research techniques, such as locating and writing to environmental protection agencies or investigating health-related resources.
2. **Develop questions for an interest survey to use with a specific group of children to help you determine possible themes and topics that might interest them.**
3. **Interview people from different cultural groups (maybe those represented in a class you are taking).** List behaviors they appreciate and ones they don't. Discuss ways you can ensure that you relate well to people from various parts of the world.
4. **Compare the first grade levels of two basal reading programs, one very recent edition and the other published at least 5 or 10 years ago.** Examine the teacher's edition to determine what changes have been made in the way that vocabulary is introduced, the number of skills or objectives covered and how they are covered, and the types of activities and questions suggested.

FURTHER READING

Day, J. P., Spiegel, D., McLellan, J., & Brown, V. (2002). *Moving forward with literature circles: How to plan, manage, and evaluate literature circles that deepen understanding and foster a love of reading.* New York: Scholastic.

McLaughlin, M., & Allen, M. B. (2002). *Guided comprehension: A teaching model for grades 3–8.* Newark, DE: International Reading Association.

Michaels, J. R. (1999). *Dancing with words: Helping students love language through authentic vocabulary instruction.* Champaign-Urbana, IL: National Council of Teachers of English.

Strickland, D. S., Ganske, K., & Monroe, J. K. (2002). *Supporting struggling readers and writers*. Portland, ME: Stenhouse and Newark, DE: International Reading Association.

REFERENCES

Anderson, R. C., Hiebert, E. H., Scott, J. A., & Wilkinson, I. A. (1985). *Becoming a nation of readers: The report of the commission on reading*. Washington, D.C.: National Institute of Education.

Atwell, N. (1998). *In the middle: New understandings about writing, reading, and learning*. Portsmouth, NH: Boynton/Cook, Heinemann.

Britton, J. (1970). *Language and learning*. London: Penguin.

Brown, R. (1973). *A first language*. Cambridge, MA: Harvard University Press.

Calkins, L. M. (1983). *The art of teaching writing*. Portsmouth, NH: Heinemann.

Chomsky, N. (1965). *Aspects of a theory of syntax*. Cambridge, MA: M.I.T. Press.

Fielding, L., Wilson, P. T., & Anderson, R. (1986). A new focus on free reading: The role of trade books in reading instruction. In T. E. Raphael & R. E. Reynolds (Eds.), *The contexts of school-based literacy* (pp. 149–160). New York: Random.

Fox, M. (2001). *Reading magic*. San Diego, CA: Harcourt.

Galda, L., & Cullinan, B. E. (2002). *Literature and the child* (5th ed.). Belmont, CA: Wadsworth/Thomson Learning.

Goodman, S. (2002). *Teaching youth media: A critical guide to literacy, video production, and social change*. Williston, VT: Teachers College Press.

Grabe, M., & Grabe, C. (2000). *Integrating the Internet for meaningful learning*. Boston: Houghton Mifflin.

Graves, D. (1978). *Balance the basics: Let them write*. New York: Ford Foundation.

Greany, V. (1980). *Access to print: Early studies*. Newark, DE: International Reading Association.

Halliday, M. A. K. (1975). *Explorations in the functions of language*. London: Arnold.

______. (1982). Three aspects of children's language development: Learning language, learning through language, and learning about language. In Y. Goodman, M. Haussler, & D. S. Strickland (Eds.), *Oral and written language development research: Impact on the schools* (pp. 7–19). Urbana, IL: National Council of Teachers of English.

Harvey, S., & Goudvis, A. (2000). *Strategies that work: Teaching comprehension to enhance understanding*. Portland, ME: Stenhouse.

Jaggar, A. M., & Smith-Burke, M. T. (1985). *Observing the language learner*. Newark, DE: International Reading Association and Urbana, IL: National Council of Teachers of English.

Janeczko, P. (2001). Poetry: Study and teaching. *Scholastic Instructor, 3*(2), 54 (Sept. 2001).

Juell, P. (1985). The course journal. In A. R. Gere (Ed.), *Roots in the sawdust: Writing to learn across the disciplines* (pp. 187–201). Urbana, IL: National Council of Teachers of English.

Mantione, R. D., & Smead, S. (2003). *Weaving through words: Using the arts to teach reading comprehension strategies*. Newark, DE: International Reading Association.

Ogle, D. (1986). The K-W-L: A teaching model that develops active reading of expository text. *The Reading Teacher, 39*, 564–576.

Pataray-Ching, J., & Roberson, M. (2002). Misconceptions about a curriculum—as inquiry framework. *Language Arts, 79*, 498–505.

Pearlman, J. P. (1998). Teaching and assessing skills in a fifth grade literature-based literacy program. Dissertation, Graduate School of Education, Rutgers University.

Piaget, J., Weaver, H., & Inhelder, B. (1972). *The psychology of the child*. New York: Basic Books.

Reichelderfer, M. (2002). Bringing out the "Super Reader" in everyone. *The Reading Teacher, 55*, 237–238.

Roser, N., & Keehu, S. (2002). Fostering thought, talk, and inquiry: Linking literature and social studies. *The Reading Teacher, 55*, 416–426.

Routman, R. (2000). *Conversations*. Portsmouth, NH: Heinemann.

Smitherman, G. (1977). *Talkin and testifyin: The language of Black America*. Boston: Houghton Mifflin.

______. (1994). The blacker the berry, the sweeter the juice: African American student writers. In A. H. Dyson & C. Genishi (Eds.), *The need for story:*

Cultural diversity in the classroom and community. Urbana, IL: National Council of Teachers of English.

———. (2001). *Talkin the talk;* David Russell Award. Presented at Baltimore, MD. NCTE 2001 by Gordon Pradl. Urbana, IL: National Council of Teachers of English.

Strickland, D. S., Ganske, K., & Monroe, J. K. (2002). *Supporting struggling readers and writers.* Portland, ME: Stenhouse and Newark, DE: International Reading Association.

Trelease, J. (1979, 1982, 1985, 1989, 1990, 2001). *The new read-aloud handbook.* New York: Penguin Books.

Walberg, H. J. and Tsai, S. (1984). Reading achievement and diminishing returns to time. *Journal of Educational Psychology 76*(3): 442–451.

Wells, G. (1981). *Learning through interaction: The study of language development.* Cambridge: Cambridge University Press.

Wells, G. (1976). *The meaning makers: Children learning language and using language to learn.* Portsmouth, NH: Heinemann.

Wooten, D. A. (2000). *Valued voices: An interdisciplinary approach to teaching and learning.* Newark, DE: International Reading Association.

CHILDREN'S LITERATURE REFERENCES

Adoff, A. (1984). *All the colors of the race: Poems.* Illus. J. Steptoe. New York: Morrow.

Banks, L. R. (1980). *The Indian in the cupboard.* New York: Doubleday.

Bunting, E. (2000). *Dreaming of America: An Ellis Island story.* Illus. Ben F. Stahl. Mahwah, NJ: Troll.

Cleary, B. (1988). *A girl from Yamhill.* New York: Morrow/Avon.

———. (1965). *Dear Mr. Henshaw.* New York: Morrow.

Cooper, F. (1996). *Mandela: From the life of the South African statesman.* New York: Philomel.

Creech, S. (2001). *Love that dog.* New York: HarperCollins.

Cummings, P. (1992). *Talking with artists, volume one.* New York: Bradbury.

———. (1995). *Talking with artists, volume two.* New York: Simon & Schuster.

Curtis, C. P. (1999). *Bud, not Buddy.* New York: Delacorte.

Dahl, R. (1984). *Boy: Tales of childhood.* New York: Farrar, Strauss & Giroux.

Deedy, C. A. (2000). *The yellow star: The legend of King Christian X of Denmark.* Illus. H. Sorensen. Atlanta, GA: Peachtree Press.

Fritz, J. (1982). *Homesick: My own story.* New York: Putnam.

Giff, P. R. (2000). *Nory Ryan's song.* New York: Delacorte, Random House.

Greenberg, J., & Jordan, S. (2000). *Frank O. Gehry: Outside in.* New York: DK, Inc.

———. (1999). *Chuck Close, up close.* New York: Dorling Kindersley.

———. (1991). *The painter's eye: Learning to look at contemporary American art.* New York: Delacorte.

———. (1993). *The sculptor's eye: Looking at contemporary American art.* New York: Delacorte.

———. (1995). *The American eye: Eleven artists of the twentieth century.* New York: Delacorte.

Greenfield, E., & Little, L. J. (1979). *Childtimes: A three-generation memoir.* New York: HarperCollins.

Kerley, B. (2001). *The dinosaurs of Waterhouse Hawkins.* Illus. Brian Selznick. New York: Scholastic.

Levy, E. (1983). *The shadow nose.* New York: Scholastic.

Little, J. (1987). *Little by Little: A writer's education.* New York: Viking.

———. (1989). *Hey world, here I am.* New York: HarperCollins.

Lowry, L. (1989). *Number the stars.* Boston: Houghton.

March, M. (1996). *Guide to South Africa.* Columbus, OH: Highlights for Children.

Martin, W., Jr. (1964, 1992). *Brown bear, brown bear, what do you see?* Illus. Eric Carle. New York: Holt.

Martin, W., Jr., and Archambault, J. (1989). *Knots on a counting rope.* New York: Holt.

Melzer, M. (1988). *Starting from home: A writer's beginnings.* New York: Viking.

Nagda, A. W., & Bickel, C. (2000). *Tiger math: Learning to graph from a baby tiger.* New York: Holt.

Naidoo, B. (1988). *Journey to Jo'burg: A South African story.* New York: HarperCollins.

Olaleye, I. (1995). *The distant talking drum: Poems from Nigeria.* Honesdale, PA: Boyds Mills.

Peet, B. (1989). *Bill Peet: An autobiography.* Boston: Houghton.

Polacco, P. (2000). *The butterfly.* New York: Philomel.

Rylant, C. (1982). *When I was young in the mountains.* New York: Dutton.

______. (1989). *But I'll be back again: An album.* New York: Scholastic.

Stein, C. (1998). *Cape Town.* San Francisco: Children's Book Press.

Thomas. M. (1987). *Free to be a family.* New York: Bantam.

Unobagha, U. (2000). *Off to the sweet shores of Africa and other talking drum rhymes.* San Francisco: Chronicle.

Waldman, N. (2001). *They came from the Bronx.* Honesdale, PA: Boyds Mills.

Wilson-Max, K. (1998). *Halala means welcome: A book of Zulu words.* New York: Hyperion.

Zoehfeld. K. W. (2001). *Dinosaur parents, dinosaur young: Uncovering the mystery of dinosaur families.* Illus. Paul Carrick and Bruce Shillinglaw. New York: HarperCollins.

TEACHERS' CHOICES IN CHILDREN'S LITERATURE

Note: (B) indicates a biographical/autobiographical selection, (P) indicates poetry. (Selections from NCTE Notable Books and IRA Choices, 1997–2002.)

PRIMARY SELECTIONS (GRADES K–3)

Families, Friends, and Communities

Amelia and Eleanor Go for a Ride. Ryan, Pam Muñoz. Illus. Brian Selznick. New York: Scholastic, 1999. (B)

Aunt Chip and the Great Triple Creek Dam Affair. Polacco, Patricia. New York: Philomel, 1996.

Boundless Grace. Hoffman, Mary. Illus. Caroline Binch. New York: Dial, 1995.

Bunny Cakes. Wells, Rosemary. New York: Dial, 1997.

Eleanor. Cooney, Barbara. New York: Viking/Penguin, 1996. (B)

Mailing May. Tunnell, Michael O. Illus. Ted Rand. New York: Tambourine/Greenwillow, 1997.

Raising Yoder's Barn. Yolen, Jane. Illus. Bernie Fuchs. Boston: Little, Brown, 1998.

Snow Bear. George, Jean Craighead. Illus. Wendel Minor. New York: Hyperion, 1999.

Wemberly Worried. Henkes, Kevin. New York: Greenwillow, HarperCollins, 2000.

Math and Science

A Desert Scrapbook: Dawn to Dusk in the Sonoran Desert. Author/illustrator: Wright-Frierson, Virginia. New York: Simon & Schuster, 1996.

The Emperor's Egg. Jenkins, Martin. Illus. Jane Chapman. Cambridge, MA: Candlewick, 1999.

In the Swim. Florian, Douglas. San Diego, CA: Harcourt Brace, 1997. (P)

Insectlopedia. Florian, Douglas. San Diego, CA: Harcourt Brace, 1998. (P)

Jelly Beans for Sale. McMillan, Bruce. New York: Scholastic, 1997.

One Grain of Rice. Author/illustrator: Demi. New York: Scholastic, 1997.

Rabbits, Rabbits, and More Rabbits. Gibbons, Gail. New York: Holiday House, 2001.

Raisel's Riddle. Silverman, Erica. Illus. Susan Graber. New York: Farrar, Straus & Giroux, 1999.

Concept Books (ABC, 1-2-3, colors, and so on)

Amazon Alphabet. Jordan, Martin, & Jordan, Tanus. Illus. Martin Jordan. New York: Kingfisher, 1996.

A Beasty Story. Martin, Bill, Jr. Illus. Steven Kellogg. San Diego, CA: Silver Whistle/Harcourt Brace, 1999.

Gathering the Sun: An Alphabet in Spanish and English. Ada, Alma Flor. English translation by Rosa Zubizarreta. Illus. Simon Silva. New York: Lothrop, Lee & Shepard, 1997.

Emerging Literacy (Text awareness and author study)

Author: A True Story. Lester, Helen. Boston: Houghton Mifflin, 1997.

In Enzo's Splendid Gardens. Polacco, Patricia. New York: Philomel, 1997.

Meanwhile. Feiffer, Jules. New York: HarperCollins, 1997.

Miss Alaineous: A Vocabulary Disaster. Frasier, Debra. San Diego, CA: Harcourt, 2000.

A Sign. Lyon, George Ella. Illus. Chris K. Soentpiet. New York: Orchard, 1998.

Tomorrow's Alphabet. Shannon, George. Illus. Donald Crews. New York: Greenwillow, 1996.

Fantasy and Folklore

Dinorella: A Prehistoric Fairy Tale. Edwards, Pamela Duncan. Illus. Henry Cole. New York: Hyperion, 1997.

The Three Sillies. Kellogg, Steven. Cambridge, MA: Candlewick, 1999.

INTERMEDIATE SELECTIONS (GRADES 3–5)

History

At Her Majesty's Request: An African Princess in Victorian England. Myers, Walter Dean. New York: Scholastic, 1999. (B)

The Birchbark House. Erdrich, Louise. New York: Hyperion, 1999.

Christmas in the Big House, Christmas in the Quarters. McKissack, Patricia, & McKissack, Fredrick. Illus. John Thompson. New York: Scholastic, 1994.

I Thought My Soul Would Rise and Fly: The Diary of Patsy, a Freed Girl. Hansen, Joyce. New York: Scholastic, 1997.

Leon's Story. Tillage, Leon Walter. Illus. Susan L. Roth. New York: Farrar, Straus & Giroux, 1997. (B)

Lily's Crossing. Giff, Patricia Reilly. New York: Delacorte/Bantam Doubleday Dell, 1997.

Mary on Horseback: Three Mountain Stories. Wells, Rosemary. Illus. Peter McCarty. New York: Viking, 1999. (B)

Minty: A Story of Young Harriet Tubman. Schroeder, Alan. Illus. Jerry Pinkney. New York: Dial/Penguin, 1996. (B)

Out of Darkness: The Story of Louis Braille. Freedman, Russell. Illus. Kate Kiesler. New York: Clarion, 1997. (B)

Passage to Freedom: The Sugihara Story. Mochizuki, Ken. Illus. Dom Lee. New York: Lee & Low, 1997.

Sees Behind Trees. Dorris, Michael. New York: Hyperion, 1996.

Through My Eyes. Bridges, Ruby. New York: Scholastic, 1999. (B)

Tornado. Byars, Betsy. Illus. Doron Ben-Ami. New York: HarperCollins, 1996.

Math and Science

A Drop of Water: A Book of Science and Wonder. Wick, Walter. New York: Scholastic, 1997.

Echoes for the Eye: Poems to Celebrate Patterns in Nature. Esbensen, Barbara Juster. Illus. Helen K. Davie. New York: HarperCollins, 1996. (P)

An Extraordinary Life: The Story of a Monarch Butterfly. Pringle, Laurence. Illus. Bob Marstall. New York: Orchard, 1997.

Safari. Bateman, Robert, & Archibold, Rick. Illus. Robert Bateman. Boston: Little, Brown, 1998.

One Grain of Rice. Author/illustrator: Demi. New York: Scholastic, 1997.

Water Dance. Locker, Thomas. San Diego, CA: Harcourt Brace, 1997.

Language Study

Book. Lyon, George Ella. Illus. Peter Catalanotto. New York: DK Publishing, 1999. (P)

Miss Alaineous: A Vocabulary Disaster. Frasier, Debra. San Diego, CA: Harcourt, 2000.

Popcorn. Stevenson, James. New York: Greenwillow, Morrow, 1998.

Contemporary Realistic Fiction

Brian's Winter. Paulson, Gary. New York: Bantam, Doubleday Dell, 1996.

Iditarod Dream: Dusty and His Sled Dogs Compete in Alaska's Jr. Iditarod. Wood, Ted. New York: Walker, 1996.

The Landry News. Clements, Andrew. Illus. Savatre Murdocca. New York: Simon & Schuster, 1999.

Sun and Spoon. Henkes, Kevin. New York: Greenwillow, 1997.

Zooman Sam. Lowry, Lois. Illus. Diane DeGroat. Boston: Houghton Mifflin, 1999.

Fantasy and Folklore

Gluskabe and the Four Wishes. Bruchac, Joseph. Illus. Christine Nyburg Schrader. Peterborough, NH: Cobblestone, 1995.

Harry Potter and the Sorcerer's Stone. Rowling, J. K. Illus. Mary Grandpré. New York: Scholastic, 1998.

Midnight Magic. Avi. New York: Scholastic, 1999.

Moaning Bones: African-American Ghost Stories. Haskins, James. Illus. Felicia Marshall. New York: Lothrop, 1998.

Sector 7. Wiesner, David. Boston: Houghton Mifflin, 1999.

ADVANCED SELECTIONS (GRADES 5–8+)

History

The Apprenticeship of Lucas Whitaker. DeFelice, Cynthia. New York: Farrar, Straus & Giroux, 1996.

The Ballad of Lucy Whipple. Cushman, Karen. New York: Clarion, 1996.

Dateline Troy. Fleischman, Paul. Illus. Gwen Frankfeldt and Glen Morrow. Cambridge, MA: Candlewick, 1996.

Fever, 1793. Anderson, Laurie Halse. New York: Simon & Schuster, 2000.

Jip: His Story. Patterson, Katherine. New York: Lodestar, 1996.

The Middle Passage: White Ships, Black Cargo. Feelings, Tom. New York: Dial, 1995.

Out of the Dust. Hesse, Karen. New York: Scholastic, 1997.

Ties That Bind, Ties That Break. Namioka, Lensey. New York: Delacorte, Random House, 1999.

Three Cheers for Catherine the Great. Best, Cari. Illus. Giselle Potter. New York: DK Publishing, 1999.

Witnesses to War: Eight True Life Stories of Nazi Persecution. Leapman, Michael. New York: Viking, Penguin, Putnam, 1998.

Author Study

When I Was Your Age: Original Stories about Growing Up. Ehrlich, Amy. Cambridge, MA: Candlewick, 1996.

Free to Dream—The Making of a Poet: Langston Hughes. Osofsky, Audrey. New York: Lothrop, Lee & Shepard, 1996.

Hang a Thousand Trees with Ribbons: The Story of Phillis Wheatley. Rinaldi, Ann. San Diego, CA: Gulliver/Harcourt Brace, 1996.

Contemporary Realistic Fiction

Belle Prater's Boy. White, Ruth. New York: Farrar, Straus & Giroux, 1996.

Chasing Redbird. Creech, Sharon. New York: Cotler/HarperCollins, 1998.

Dangerous Skies. Staples, Suzanne Fisher. New York: Farrar, Straus & Giroux, 1996.

Holes. Sachar, Louis. New York: Farrar, Straus & Giroux, 1998.

Search for the Shadowman. Nixon, Joan Lowry. New York: Delacorte/Bantam Doubleday Dell, 1996.

Seedfolks. Fleishman, Paul. New York: HarperCollins, 1999.

The Window. Dorris, Michael. New York: Hyperion, 1999.

Wringer. Spinelli, Jerry. New York: HarperCollins, 1997.

Fantasy and Folklore

Ella Enchanted. Levine, Gail Carson. New York: HarperCollins, 1998.

The Islander. Rylant, Cynthia. New York: DK Publishing, 1998.

The King of Shadows. Cooper, Susan. New York: McElderry, 1999.

Zel. Napoli, Donna Jo. New York: Dutton, 1996.

BOOKS FOR CHILDREN OF ALL AGES

Picture Books and Illustrated Text

Black Cat. Myers, Christopher. New York: Scholastic, 1999.

Cuckoo/Cucu. Ehlert, Lois. San Diego, CA: Harcourt Brace, 1997.

Girls Think of Everything: Stories of Ingenious Inventions by Women. Thimmesh, Catherine. Illus. Melissa Sweet. Boston: Houghton Mifflin, 2000.

I Have a Dream. King, Jr., Dr. Martin Luther. New York: Scholastic, 1997.

John Henry. Lester, Julius. Illus. Jerry Pinkney. New York: Penguin, 1999. (B)

Lives of Extraordinary Women: Rulers, Rebels, and What the Neighbors Thought. Krull, Kathleen. Illus. Kathryn Hewitt. San Diego, CA: Harcourt, 2000. (B)

My Name Is Georgia: A Portrait. Winter, Jeanette. New York: Silver Whistle/Harcourt Brace, 1998. (B)

The Old Woman Who Named Things. Rylant, Cynthia. Illus. Kathryn Brown. San Diego, CA: Harcourt, 1996.

Painting the Wind: A Story of Vincent van Gogh. Dionetti, Michelle. Illus. Kevin Hawkes. Boston: Little, Brown, 1996. (B)

Satchmo's Blues. Schroeder, Alan. Illus. Floyd Cooper. New York: Delacorte/Bantam Doubleday Dell, 1996. (B)

Starry Messenger: A Book Depicting the Life of a Famous Scientist, Mathematician, Astronomer, Philosopher, Galileo Galilei. Sis, Peter. New York: Farrar, Straus & Giroux, 1996.

Thank You, Mr. Falker. Polacco, Patricia. New York: Philomel, 1998.

Tomas and the Library Lady. Mora, Pat. Illus. Raul Colon. New York: Knopf/Random House, 1997. (B)

Weslandia. Fleischman, Paul. Illus. Kevin Hawkes. Cambridge, MA: Candlewick, 1999.

William Shakespeare and the Globe. Author/illustrator: Aliki. New York: HarperCollins, 1999. (B)

Poetry Collections

Celebrate America in Poetry and Art. Panzer, Nora. New York: Hyperion, 1995.

Flicker Flash. Graham, Joan Bransfield. Illus. Nancy Davis. Boston: Houghton Mifflin, 1999.

It's Raining Pigs and Noodles. Prelutsky, Jack. Illus. James Stevenson. New York: Greenwillow, HarperCollins, 2000.

Poems Have Roots. Moore, Lilian. Illus. Tad Hills. New York: Atheneum, 1997.

Winter Eyes. Florian, Douglas. New York: Greenwillow, 1999.

MULTICULTURAL POETRY: THE HEART OF LITERACY

Adoff, Arnold.

All the Colors of the Race. Illus. John Steptoe. New York: Harper, 1982.

Black Out Loud. Illus. Alvin Hollingsworth. New York: Macmillan, 1970.

Black Is Brown Is Tan. Illus. Emily McCully. New York: Harper, 1973, 2002.

I Am the Darker Brother: An Anthology of Poems by African Americans. Illus. Benny Andrews. New York: Simon & Schuster, 1971.

Make a Circle Keep Us In: Poems for a Good Day. Illus. Ronald Himler. New York: Delacorte, 1975.

My Black Me: A Beginning Book of Black Poetry. New York: Dutton, 1974.

Brooks, Gwendolyn.

Bronzeville Boys and Girls. New York: Harper, 1967.

Cullinan, Bernice (Ed.).

A Jar of Tiny Stars: Children's Choice of NCTE Poems. Illus. Marc Nadel & Andi Macleod. Honesdale, PA: Boyds Mills/Wordsong, 1996.

Graves, Don.

Baseball, Snakes and Summer Squash. Honesdale, PA: Boyds Mills/Wordsong, 1992.

Greenfield, Eloise.

Honey, I Love and Other Poems. Illus. Leo & Diane Dillon. New York: Harper & Row, 1972.

Nathaniel Talking. Illus. Jan S. Gilchrist. New York: Writers & Readers, 1995.

Night on Neighborhood Street. Illus. Jan S. Gilchrist. New York: Penguin Putnam, 1991.

Under the Sunday Tree. Illus. Amos Ferguson. New York: Harper, 1991.

Grimes, Nikki.

Hopscotch Love: A Family Treasury of Love Poems. Illus. Melodye Rosales. New York: Harpers, 1999.

Meet Danitra Brown. Illus. Floyd Cooper. New York: Lothrop, 1997.

My Man Blue. Illus. Jerome Lagarrigue. New York: Dial Putnam Penguin, 1999.

Gunning, Monica.

Not a Copper Penny in Me House: Poems from the Caribbean. Illus. Frané Lessac. Honesdale, PA: Boyds Mills/Wordsong, 2001.

Under the Breadfruit Tree: Island Poems. Illus. Fabricio Vanden Broeck. Honesdale, PA: Boyds Mills/Wordsong, 1998, 2001.

Holbrook, Sara.

Wham! It's a Poetry Jam: Discovering Performance Poetry. Foreword by Jane Yolen. Honesdale, PA: Boyds Mills/Wordsong, 2002.

Hughes, Langston.

The Block. New York: Viking, 1995.

The Dream Keeper. Illus. Brian Pinkney. New York: Knopf, 1994.

Medina, Jane.

My Name Is Jorge: On Both Sides of the River. Illus. Fabricio Vanden Groeck. Honesdale, PA: Boyds Mills/Wordsong, 2000.

Mora, Pat.

The Desert Is My Mother/El Desierto es Mi Madre. Houston, TX: Arte Publico, 1994.

Listen to the Desert. Illus. Francisco X. Mora. New York: Clarion, 1994.

This Big Sky. New York: Scholastic, 1998.

Newsome, Effie Lee. (Rudine & Bishop Sims, Eds.)

Wonders: The Best Children's Poems of Effie Lee Newsome. Honesdale, PA: Boyds Mills/Wordsong, 2000.

Nye, Naomi Shiab.

This Same Sky: A Collection of Poems from around the World. New York: Simon & Schuster, 1992.

Olaleye, Issac.

The Distant Talking Drum: Poems from Nigeria. Illus. Frané Lessac. Honesdale, PA: Boyds Mills/Wordsong, 1995.

Pomerantz, Charlotte.

If I Had a Paka: Poems in Eleven Languages. New York: Greenwillow, 1992.

Soto, Gary.

Neighborhood Odes. Illus. David Diaz, San Diego, CA: Harcourt, 1992.

Chato's Kitchen. Illus. Susan Guevera, New York: Penguin Putnam, 1997.

Strickland, Dorothy, & Strickland, Michael.

Families: Celebrating the African American Experience. Illus. John Ward. Honesdale, PA: Boyds Mills/Wordsong, 1994.

Weatherford, Carole.

Sidewalk Chalk: Poems of the City. Illus. Dimitrea Tokunbo. Honesdale, PA: Boyds Mills/Wordsong, 1994, 2001.

Whitman, Walt.

Leaves of Grass. New York: Bantam, 1993.

Wong, Janet.

The Rainbow Hand: Poems about Mothers and Children. Illus. Jennifer Hewitson. New York: Simon & Schuster, 1999.

A Suitcase of Seaweed and Other Poems. New York: McElderry, 1996.

Wood, Nancy.

Spirit Walker. Illus. Frank Howell. New York: Doubleday, 1993.

AUTHOR AND TITLE INDEX

Note: Titles in *italic* type indicate professional references; titles in ***bold italic*** type indicate children's literature.

SUBJECT INDEX